Uncertain Multi-Attribute Decision Making

Zeshui Xu

Uncertain Multi-Attribute Decision Making

Methods and Applications

Springer

Zeshui Xu
Business School
Sichuan University
Chengdu
Sichuan
China

ISBN 978-3-662-45639-2 ISBN 978-3-662-45640-8 (eBook)
DOI 10.1007/978-3-662-45640-8

Library of Congress Control Number: 2014958891

Springer Heidelberg New York Dordrecht London

Printed on acid-free paper

Springer is part of Springer Science+Business Media (www.springer.com)

Preface

Multi-attribute decision making (MADM) (or called multi-objective decision making with finite alternatives) is an important component of modern decision science. The theory and methods of MADM have been extensively applied to the fields of engineering project, economy, management and military affairs, such as investment decision making, venture capital project evaluation, facility location, bidding, maintenance services, military system efficiency evaluation, development ranking of industrial sectors, comprehensive evaluation of economic performance, etc. Essentially, MADM is to select the most desirable alternative(s) from a given finite set of alternatives according to a collection of attributes by using a proper means. It mainly consists of two stages: (1) Collect decision information. The decision information generally includes the attribute weights and the attribute values (expressed as real numbers, interval numbers or linguistic labels), especially, how to determine the attribute weights is an important research topic in MADM; (2) Aggregate the decision information through some proper approaches. Currently, four of the most common aggregation techniques are the weighted averaging operator, the weighted geometric operator, the ordered weighted averaging operator, and the ordered weighted geometric operator.

With the increasing complexity and uncertainty of objective things and the fuzziness of human thought, more and more attention has been paid to the investigation on MADM under uncertain environments, and fruitful research results have been achieved over the last decades. This book offers a systematic introduction to the methods for uncertain MADM and their applications to various practical problems. We organize the book as the following four parts, which contain twelve chapters:

Part 1 consists of three chapters (Chaps. 1–3) which introduce the methods for real-valued MADM and their applications. Concretely speaking, Chap. 1 introduces the methods for solving the decision making problems in which the information about attribute weights is completely unknown and the attribute values take the form of real numbers, and applies them to investment decision making in enterprises and information systems, respectively, military spaceflight equipment evaluation, financial assessment in the institutions of higher education, training plane type selection, purchases of fighter planes and artillery weapons, developing new products, and cadre selection. Chapter 2 introduces the methods for MADM in which the information about attribute weights is given in the form of preferences and the attribute values are real numbers, and gives their applications to the efficiency evaluation of equipment maintenance support systems, and the performance evaluation of military administration units. Chapter 3 introduces the methods for decision making with partial attribute weight information and exact attribute values, and applies them to the fire deployment of a defensive battle in Xiaoshan region, the evaluation and ranking of the industrial economic benefits of 16 provinces and municipalities in China, the assessment for the expansion of a coal mine, sorting the order of the enemy's targets to attack, the improvement of old products, and the alternative selection for buying a house.

Part 2 consists of three chapters (Chaps. 4–6) which introduce the methods for interval MADM and their applications. Concretely speaking, Chap. 4 introduces the methods for the decision making problems in which the attribute weights are real numbers and the attribute values are expressed as interval numbers, and gives their applications to the evaluation of schools of a university, the exploitations of leather industry of a region and a new model of cars of an investment company, and the selection of the robots of an advanced manufacturing company. Chapter 5 introduces the methods for the decision making problems in which the information about attribute weights is unknown completely and the attribute values are interval numbers. Also, these methods are applied to the purchase of artillery weapons, cadre selection of a unit, and investment decision making in natural resources. Chapter 6 introduces the methods for interval MADM with the partial attribute weight information, and applies them to determine what kind of air-conditioning system should be installed in the library, evaluate anti-ship missile weapon systems, help select a suitable refrigerator for a family, assess the investment of high technology project of venture capital firms, and purchase college textbooks, respectively.

Part 3 consists of three chapters (Chaps. 7–9) which introduce the methods for linguistic MADM and their applications. Concretely speaking, Chap. 7 introduces the methods for the decision making problems in which the information about attribute weights is unknown completely and the attribute values take the form of linguistic labels, and applies them to investment decision making in enterprises, the fire deployment in a battle, and knowledge management performance evaluation of enterprises. Chapter 8 introduces the methods for the decision making problems in which the attribute weights are real numbers and the attribute values are linguistic labels, and then gives their applications to assess the management information systems of enterprises and evaluate the outstanding dissertation(s). Chapter 9 introduces the MADM methods for the problems where both the attribute weights and the attribute values are expressed in linguistic labels, and applies them to the partner selection of a virtual enterprise, and the quality evaluation of teachers in a middle school.

Part 4 consists of three chapters (Chaps. 10–12) which introduce the methods for uncertain linguistic MADM and their applications. In Chap. 10, we introduce the methods for the decision making problems in which the information about attribute weights is unknown completely and the attribute values are uncertain linguistic variables, and show their applications in the strategic partner selection of an enterprise in the field of supply chain management. Chapter 11 introduces the methods for the decision making problems in which the attribute weights are real numbers and the attribute values are uncertain linguistic variables, and then applies them to appraise and choose investment regions in China, and the maintenance services of manufacturing enterprises. In Chap. 12, we introduce the MADM methods for the problems in which the attribute weights are interval numbers and the attribute values are uncertain linguistic variables, and verify their practicality via the evaluation of the socio-economic systems of cities.

This book can be used as a reference for researchers and practitioners working in the fields of fuzzy mathematics, operations research, information science, management science and engineering, etc. It can also be used as a textbook for postgraduate and senior undergraduate students. This book is a substantial extension of the book "Uncertain Multiple Attribute Decision Making: Methods and Applications" (published by Tsinghua University Press and Springer, Beijing, 2004, in Chinese).

This work was supported by the National Natural Science Foundation of China under Grant 61273209.

Zeshui Xu
Chengdu
October 2014

Contents

Part I
Real-Valued MADM Methods and Their Applications

Chapter 1
Real-Valued MADM with Weight Information Unknown

Multi-attribute decision making (MADM) is to select the most desirable alternative(s) from a given finite set of alternatives according to a collection of attributes by using a proper means. How to make a decision under the situations where the information about attribute weights is unknown completely and the attribute values are real numbers? Aim to this issue, in this chapter, we introduce some common operators for aggregating information, such as the weighted averaging (WA) operator, the weighted geometric (WG) operator, the ordered weighted averaging (OWA) operator, the ordered weighted geometric (OWG) operator, the combined weighted averaging (CWA) operator, and the combined weighted geometric (CWG) operator, etc. Based on these aggregation operators, we introduce some simple and practical approaches to MADM. We also introduce the MADM methods based on maximizing deviations and information entropy, and with preference information on alternatives, respectively. Additionally, we establish a consensus maximization model for determining attribute weights in multi-attribute group decision making (MAGDM). Furthermore, we illustrate these methods in detail with some practical examples.

1.1 MADM Method Based on OWA Operator

1.1.1 OWA Operator

Yager [157] developed a simple nonlinear function for aggregating decision information in MADM, which was defined as below:

Definition 1.1 [157] Let $OWA: \Re^n \to \Re$, if

$$OWA_{\omega}(\alpha_1, \alpha_2, \ldots, \alpha_n) = \sum_{j=1}^{n} \omega_j b_j \tag{1.1}$$

Z.S. Xu, *Uncertain Multi-Attribute Decision Making*,
DOI 10.1007/978-3-662-45640-8_1

then the function OWA is called an ordered weighted averaging (OWA) operator, where b_j is the j th largest of a collection of the arguments $\alpha_i (i = 1, 2, \ldots, n)$, i.e., the arguments $b_j (j = 1, 2, \ldots, n)$ are arranged in descending order: $b_1 \geq b_2 \geq \ldots \geq, b_n$, $\omega = (\omega_1, \omega_2, \ldots, \omega_n)$ is the weighting vector associated with the function OWA, $\omega_j \geq 0, j = 1, 2, \ldots, n, \sum_{j=1}^{n} \omega_j = 1$, and $\Re$ is the set of all real numbers.

The fundamental aspect of the OWA operator is its reordering step. In particular, an argument a_i is not associated with a particular weight ω_i, but rather a weight ω_i is associated with a particular ordered position i of the arguments $\alpha_i (i = 1, 2, \ldots, n)$, and thus, ω_i is the weight of the position i.

Example 1.1 Let $\omega = (0.4, 0.1, 0.2, 0.3)$ be the weighting vector of the OWA operator, and $(7, 18, 6, 2)$ be a collection of arguments, then

$$OWA_\omega(7, 18, 6, 2) = 0.4 \times 18 + 0.1 \times 7 + 0.2 \times 6 + 0.3 \times 2 = 9.70$$

Now we introduce some desirable properties of the OWA operator:

Theorem 1.1 [157] Let $(\alpha_1, \alpha_2, \ldots, \alpha_n)$ be a vector of arguments, and $(\beta_1, \beta_2, \ldots, \beta_n)$ be the vector of the elements in $(\alpha_1, \alpha_2, \ldots, \alpha_n)$, where β_j is the j th largest of $\alpha_i (i = 1, 2, \ldots, n)$, such that $\beta_1 \geq \beta_2 \geq \ldots \geq \beta_n$, then

$$OWA_\omega(\beta_1, \beta_2, \ldots, \beta_n) = OWA_\omega(\alpha_1, \alpha_2, \ldots, \alpha_n)$$

Proof Let

$$OWA_\omega(\beta_1, \beta_2, \ldots, \beta_n) = \sum_{j=1}^{n} \omega_j b_j'$$

$$OWA_\omega(\alpha_1, \alpha_2, \ldots, \alpha_n) = \sum_{j=1}^{n} \omega_j b_j$$

where b_j' is the j th largest of $\beta_i (i = 1, 2, \ldots, n)$, and b_j is the j th largest of $\alpha_i (i = 1, 2, \ldots, n)$. Since $(\beta_1, \beta_2, \ldots, \beta_n)$ is the vector in which $\beta_j (j = 1, 2, \ldots n)$ are arranged in descending order of the elements $\alpha_i (i = 1, 2, \ldots, n)$, then $b_j' = b_j$, $j = 1, 2, \ldots, n$, which completes the proof.

Theorem 1.2 [157] Let $(\alpha_1, \alpha_2, \ldots, \alpha_n)$ and $(\alpha_1', \alpha_2', \ldots, \alpha_n')$ be two vectors of arguments, such that $\alpha_i \geq \alpha_i'$, for any i, where $\alpha_1 \geq \alpha_2 \geq \ldots \geq \alpha_n$ and $\alpha_1' \geq \alpha_2' \geq \ldots \geq \alpha_n'$, then

$$OWA_\omega(\alpha_1, \alpha_2, \ldots, \alpha_n) \geq OWA_\omega(\alpha_1', \alpha_2', \ldots, \alpha_n')$$

Proof Let

$$OWA_\omega(\alpha_1, \alpha_2, \ldots, \alpha_n) = \sum_{j=1}^{n} \omega_j b_j$$

$$OWA_{\omega}(\alpha_1', \alpha_2', \ldots, \alpha_n') = \sum_{j=1}^{n} \omega_j b_j'$$

where b_j is the jth largest of $\alpha_i (i = 1, 2, \ldots, n)$, and b_j' is the jth largest of $\alpha_i' (i = 1, 2, \ldots, n)$. Since $\alpha_1 \geq \alpha_2 \geq \ldots \geq \alpha_n$ and $\alpha_1' \geq \alpha_2' \geq \ldots \geq \alpha_n'$, then $b_j = \alpha_j$, $b_j' = \alpha_j'$, $j = 1, 2, \ldots, n$. Also since $\alpha_i \geq \alpha_i'$, for any i, then $b_j \geq b_j'$, $j = 1, 2, \ldots, n$. Thus, $\sum_{j=1}^{n} \omega_j b_j \geq \sum_{j=1}^{n} \omega_j b_j'$, i.e., $OWA_{\omega}(\alpha_1, \alpha_2, \ldots, \alpha_n) \geq OWA_{\omega}(\alpha_1', \alpha_2', \ldots, \alpha_n')$.

Corollary 1.1 (Monotonicity) [157] Let $(\alpha_1, \alpha_2, \ldots, \alpha_n)$ and $(\beta_1, \beta_2, \ldots, \beta_n)$ be any two vectors of arguments, if $\alpha_i \leq \beta_i$, for any i, then

$$OWA_{\omega}(\alpha_1, \alpha_2, \ldots, \alpha_n) \leq OWA_{\omega}(\beta_1, \beta_2, \ldots, \beta_n)$$

Corollary 1.2 (Commutativity) [157] Let $(\beta_1, \beta_2, \ldots, \beta_n)$ be any permutation of the elements in $(\alpha_1, \alpha_2, \ldots, \alpha_n)$, then

$$OWA_{\omega}(\beta_1, \beta_2, \ldots, \beta_n) = OWA_{\omega}(\alpha_1, \alpha_2, \ldots, \alpha_n)$$

Theorem 1.3 (Idempotency) [157] Let $(\alpha_1, \alpha_2, \ldots, \alpha_n)$ be any vector of arguments, if $\alpha_i = \alpha$, for any i, then

$$OWA_{\omega}(\beta_1, \beta_2, \ldots, \beta_n) = \alpha$$

Proof Since $\sum_{j=1}^{n} \omega_j = 1$, then

$$OWA_{\omega}(\alpha_1, \alpha_2, \ldots, \alpha_n) = \sum_{j=1}^{n} \omega_j b_j = \sum_{j=1}^{n} \omega_j \ \alpha = \alpha \sum_{j=1}^{n} \omega_j = \alpha$$

Theorem 1.4 [157] Let $\omega = \omega^* = (1, 0, \ldots, 0)$, then

$$OWA_{\omega^*}(\alpha_1, \alpha_2, \ldots, \alpha_n) = \max_i \{\alpha_i\}$$

Proof According to Definition 1.1, we have

$$OWA_{\omega^*}(\alpha_1, \alpha_2, \ldots, \alpha_n) = \sum_{j=1}^{n} \omega_j b_j = b_1 = \max_i \{\alpha_i\}$$

Theorem 1.5 [157] Let $\omega = \omega_* = (0, 0, \ldots, 1)$, then

$$OWA_{\omega_*}(\alpha_1, \alpha_2, \ldots, \alpha_n) = \min_i \{\alpha_i\}$$

Proof It follows from Definition 1.1 that

$$OWA_{\omega_*}(\alpha_1,\alpha_2,\ldots,\alpha_n)=\sum_{j=1}^{n}\omega_j b_j=b_n=\min_i\{\alpha_i\}$$

Theorem 1.6 [157] Let $\omega=\omega_{Ave}=\left(\frac{1}{n},\frac{1}{n},\ldots,\frac{1}{n}\right)$, then

$$OWA_{\omega_{Ave}}(\alpha_1,\alpha_2,\ldots,\alpha_n)=\frac{1}{n}\sum_{j=1}^{n}b_j$$

Theorem 1.7 [157] Let $(\alpha_1,\alpha_2,\ldots,\alpha_n)$ be any vector of arguments, then

$$OWA_{\omega^*}(\alpha_1,\alpha_2,\ldots,\alpha_n)\geq OWA_{\omega}(\alpha_1,\alpha_2,\ldots,\alpha_n)\geq OWA_{\omega_*}(\alpha_1,\alpha_2,\ldots,\alpha_n)$$

Proof

$$OWA_{\omega}(\alpha_1,\alpha_2,\ldots,\alpha_n)=\sum_{j=1}^{n}\omega_j b_j\leq\sum_{j=1}^{n}\omega_j b_1=b_1=OWA_{\omega^*}(\alpha_1,\alpha_2,\ldots,\alpha_n)$$

$$OWA_{\omega}(\alpha_1,\alpha_2,\ldots,\alpha_n)=\sum_{j=1}^{n}\omega_j b_j\geq\sum_{j=1}^{n}\omega_j b_n=b_n=OWA_{\omega_*}(\alpha_1,\alpha_2,\ldots,\alpha_n)$$

which completes the proof.

Clearly, the following conclusions also hold:

Theorem 1.8 [157] If $\omega_j=1$, $\omega_i=0$, and $i\neq j$, then

$$OWA_{\omega}(\alpha_1,\alpha_2,\ldots,\alpha_n)=b_j$$

where b_j is the j th largest of a collection of the arguments $(\alpha_1,\alpha_2,\ldots,\alpha_n)$. Especially, if $j=1$, then

$$OWA_{\omega}(\alpha_1,\alpha_2,\ldots,\alpha_n)=OWA_{\omega^*}(\alpha_1,\alpha_2,\ldots,\alpha_n)$$

If $j=n$, then

$$OWA_{\omega}(\alpha_1,\alpha_2,\ldots,\alpha_n)=OWA_{\omega_*}(\alpha_1,\alpha_2,\ldots,\alpha_n)$$

Theorem 1.9 [158] If $\omega_1=\alpha$, $\omega_i=0$, $i=2,\ldots,n-1$, $\omega_n=1-\alpha$, and $\alpha\in[0,1]$, then

$$\alpha\, OWA_{\omega^*}(\alpha_1,\alpha_2,\ldots,\alpha_n)+(1-\alpha)OWA_{\omega_*}(\alpha_1,\alpha_2,\ldots,\alpha_n)$$

$$=OWA_{\omega}(\alpha_1,\alpha_2,\ldots,\alpha_n)$$

Theorem 1.10 [158] (1) If $\omega_1=\frac{1-\alpha}{n}+\alpha$, $\omega_i=\frac{1-\alpha}{n}$, $i\neq 1$, and $\alpha\in[0,1]$, then

$$\alpha\, OWA_{\omega^*}(\alpha_1,\alpha_2,\ldots,\alpha_n)+(1-\alpha)OWA_{\omega_{Ave}}(\alpha_1,\alpha_2,\ldots,\alpha_n)$$

$$=OWA_{\omega}(\alpha_1,\alpha_2,\ldots,\alpha_n)$$

Especially, if $\alpha=0$, then

$$OWA_{\omega_{Ave}}(\alpha_1,\alpha_2,\ldots,\alpha_n)=OWA_{\omega}(\alpha_1,\alpha_2,\ldots,\alpha_n)$$

If $\alpha=1$, then

$$OWA_{\omega^*}(\alpha_1,\alpha_2,\ldots,\alpha_n)=OWA_{\omega}(\alpha_1,\alpha_2,\ldots,\alpha_n)$$

(2) If $\omega_i=\frac{1-\alpha}{n}$, $i\neq n$, $\omega_n=\frac{1-\alpha}{n}+\alpha$, and $\alpha\in[0,1]$, then

$$\alpha\, OWA_{\omega_*}(\alpha_1,\alpha_2,\ldots,\alpha_n)+(1-\alpha)OWA_{\omega_{Ave}}(\alpha_1,\alpha_2,\ldots,\alpha_n)$$

$$=OWA_{\omega}(\alpha_1,\alpha_2,\ldots,\alpha_n)$$

Especially, if $\alpha=0$, then

$$OWA_{\omega_{Ave}}(\alpha_1,\alpha_2,\ldots,\alpha_n)=OWA_{\omega}(\alpha_1,\alpha_2,\ldots,\alpha_n)$$

If $\alpha=1$, then

$$OWA_{\omega_*}(\alpha_1,\alpha_2,\ldots,\alpha_n)=OWA_{\omega}(\alpha_1,\alpha_2,\ldots,\alpha_n)$$

(3) If $\omega_1=\frac{(1-(\alpha+\beta))}{n}+\alpha$, $\omega_i=\frac{(1-(\alpha+\beta))}{n}$, $i=2,\ldots,n-1$,

$\omega_n=\frac{(1-(\alpha+\beta))}{n}+\beta$, $\alpha,\beta\in[0,1]$, and $\alpha+\beta\leq 1$, then

$$\alpha OWA_{\omega^*}(\alpha_1,\alpha_2,\ldots,\alpha_n)+\beta\, OWA_{\omega_*}(\alpha_1,\alpha_2,\ldots,\alpha_n)$$

$$+(1-(\alpha+\beta))\, OWA_{\omega_{Ave}}(\alpha_1,\alpha_2,\ldots,\alpha_n)=OWA_{\omega}(\alpha_1,\alpha_2,\ldots,\alpha_n)$$

Especially, if $\beta=0$, then (3) reduces to (1); If $\alpha=0$, then (3) reduces to (2).

Theorem 1.11 [158]

1. If

$$\omega_i=\begin{cases}0, & i<k,\\ \frac{1}{m}, & k\leq i<k+m,\\ 0, & i\geq k+m,\end{cases}$$

where k and m are integers, and $k+m \le n+1$, then

$$OWA_{\omega}(\alpha_1,\alpha_2,\ldots,\alpha_n)=\frac{1}{m}\sum_{j=k}^{k+m-1} b_j$$

where b_j is the j th largest of a collection of the arguments $\alpha_i (i=1,2,\ldots,n)$.

2. If

$$\omega_i=\begin{cases}0, & i<k-m,\\ \dfrac{1}{2m+1}, & k-m\le i<k+m,\\ 0, & i\ge k+m,\end{cases}$$

where k and m are integers, and $k+m \le n+1$, $k \ge m+1$, then

$$OWA_{\omega}(\alpha_1,\alpha_2,\ldots,\alpha_n)=\frac{1}{2m+1}\sum_{j=k-m}^{k+m-1} b_j$$

where b_j is the j th largest of $\alpha_i (i=1,2,\ldots,n)$.

3. If

$$\omega_i=\begin{cases}\dfrac{1}{k}, & i\le k,\\ 0, & i>k,\end{cases}$$

then

$$OWA_{\omega}(\alpha_1,\alpha_2,\ldots,\alpha_n)=\frac{1}{k}\sum_{j=1}^{k} b_j$$

where b_j is the j th largest of $\alpha_i (i=1,2,\ldots,n)$.

4. If

$$\omega_i=\begin{cases}0, & i<k,\\ \dfrac{1}{(n+1)-k}, & i\ge k,\end{cases}$$

then

$$OWA_{\omega}(\alpha_1,\alpha_2,\ldots,\alpha_n)=\frac{1}{(n+1)-k}\sum_{j=k}^{n} b_j$$

where b_j is the j th largest of $\alpha_i (i=1,2,\ldots,n)$.

Table 1.1 Decision matrix A

	u_1	u_2	$\cdots$	u_m
x_1	a_{11}	a_{12}	$\cdots$	a_{1m}
x_2	a_{21}	a_{22}	$\cdots$	a_{2m}
$\vdots$	$\vdots$	$\vdots$	$\vdots$	$\vdots$
x_n	a_{n1}	a_{n2}	$\cdots$	a_{nm}

1.1.2 Decision Making Method

Based on the OWA operator, in what follows, we introduce a method for MADM:

Step 1 For a MADM problem, let $X = \{x_1, x_2, \ldots, x_n\}$ be a finite set of alternatives, $U = \{u_1, u_2, \ldots, u_m\}$ be a set of attributes, whose weight information is unknown completely. A decision maker (expert) evaluates the alternative x_i with respect to the attribute u_j, and then get the attribute value a_{ij}. All $a_{ij}\,(i=1,2,\ldots,n; j=1,2,\ldots,m)$ are contained in the decision matrix $A=(a_{ij})_{n\times m}$, listed in Table 1.1.

In general, there are six types of attributes in the MADM problems, i.e., (1) benefit type (the bigger the attribute values the better); (2) cost type (the smaller the attribute values the better); (3) fixed type (the closer the attribute value to a fixed value α_j the better); (4) deviation type (the further the attribute value deviates from a fixed value α_j the better); (5) interval type (the closer the attribute value to a fixed interval $\left[q_1^j, q_2^j\right]$ (including the situation where the attribute value lies in the interval) the better); and (6) deviation interval type (the further the attribute value deviates from a fixed interval $\left[q_1^j, q_2^j\right]$ the better). Let $I_i\,(i=1,2,\ldots,6)$ denote the subscript sets of the attributes of benefit type, cost type, fixed type, deviation type, interval type, and deviation interval type, respectively.

In practical applications, the "dimensions" of different attributes may be different. In order to measure all attributes in dimensionless units and facilitate inter-attribute comparisons, here, we normalize each attribute value a_{ij} in the decision matrix $A=(a_{ij})_{n\times m}$ using the following formulas:

$$r_{ij} = \frac{a_{ij}}{\max\limits_i \{a_{ij}\}}, \ i=1,2,\ldots,n; \quad j \in I_1 \tag{1.2}$$

$$r_{ij} = \frac{\min\limits_i \{a_{ij}\}}{a_{ij}}, \ i=1,2,\ldots,n; \quad j \in I_2 \tag{1.3}$$

or

$$r_{ij} = \frac{a_{ij} - \min\limits_i \{a_{ij}\}}{\max\limits_i \{a_{ij}\} - \min\limits_i \{a_{ij}\}}, \ i=1,2,\ldots,n; \quad j \in I_1 \tag{1.2a}$$

$$r_{ij} = \frac{\max_i \{a_{ij}\} - a_{ij}}{\max_i \{a_{ij}\} - \min_i \{a_{ij}\}}, \ i = 1,2,\ldots,n; \qquad j \in I_2 \tag{1.3a}$$

$$r_{ij} = 1 - \frac{a_{ij} - \alpha_j}{\max_i \{|a_{ij} - \alpha_j|\}}, \ i = 1,2,\ldots,n; \qquad j \in I_3 \tag{1.4}$$

$$r_{ij} = |a_{ij} - \alpha_j| - \frac{\min_i \{|a_{ij} - \alpha_j|\}}{\max_i \{|a_{ij} - \alpha_j|\} - \min_i \{|a_{ij} - \alpha_j|\}}, \ i = 1,2,\ldots,n; j \in I_4 \tag{1.5}$$

$$r_{ij} = \begin{cases} 1 - \dfrac{\max_i \{q_1^j - a_{ij}, a_{ij} - q_2^j\}}{\max_i \{q_1^j - \min_i\{a_{ij}\}, \max_i\{a_{ij}\} - q_2^j\}}, & a_{ij} \notin [q_1^j, q_2^j] \\ 1, & a_{ij} \in [q_1^j, q_2^j] \end{cases} \tag{1.6}$$
$$i = 1,2,\ldots,n; \ j \in I_5$$

$$r_{ij} = \begin{cases} \dfrac{\max_i \{q_1^j - a_{ij}, a_{ij} - q_2^j\}}{\max_i \{q_1^j - \min_i\{a_{ij}\}, \max_i\{a_{ij}\} - q_2^j\}}, & a_{ij} \notin [q_1^j, q_2^j] \\ 1, & a_{ij} \in [q_1^j, q_2^j] \end{cases} \tag{1.7}$$
$$i = 1,2,\ldots,n; \ j \in I_6$$

and then construct the normalized decision matrix $R = (r_{ij})_{n \times m}$.

Step 2 Utilize the OWA operator to aggregate all the attribute values r_{ij} ($j = 1,2,\ldots,m$) of the alternative x_i, and get the overall attribute value $z_i(\omega)$:

$$z_i(\omega) = OWA_\omega(r_{i1}, r_{i2}, \ldots, r_{im}) = \sum_{j=1}^m \omega_j b_{ij}$$

where b_{ij} is the j th largest of r_{il} ($l = 1,2,\ldots,m$), $\omega = (\omega_1, \omega_2, \ldots, \omega_m)$ is the weighting vector associated with the OWA operator, $\omega_j \geq 0$, $j = 1,2,\ldots,m$, $\sum_{j=1}^m \omega_j = 1$, which can be obtained by using a proper method presented in Sect. 1.1, or by the normal distribution (Gaussian distribution) based method) [126, 160]:

$$\omega_j = \frac{e^{-\frac{(j-\mu_m)^2}{2\sigma_m^2}}}{\sum_{i=1}^m e^{-\frac{(i-\mu_m)^2}{2\sigma_m^2}}}, \ j = 1,2,\ldots,m$$

where

$$\mu_m = \frac{1}{2}(1+m), \quad \sigma_m = \sqrt{\frac{1}{m}\sum_{i=1}^{m}(i-\mu_m)^2}$$

The prominent characteristic of the method above is that it can relieve the influence of unfair arguments on the decision result by assigning low weights to those "false" or "biased"" ones.

Step 3 Rank all the alternatives $x_i (i = 1,2,\ldots,n)$ according to the values $z_i(\omega)$ $(i = 1,2,\ldots,n)$ in descending order.

1.1.3 Practical Example

Example 1.2 Consider a MADM problem that an investment bank wants to invest a sum of money in the best option of enterprises (alternatives), and there are four enterprises $x_i (i = 1,2,3,4)$ to choose from. The investment bank tries to evaluate the candidate enterprises by using five evaluation indices (attributes) [60]: (1) u_1: output value (10^4\$); (2) u_2: investment cost (10^4\$); (3) u_3: sales volume (10^4\$); (4) u_4: proportion of national income; (5) u_5: level of environmental contamination. The investment bank inspects the performances of last four years of the four companies with respect to the five indices (where the levels of environmental contamination of all these enterprises are given by the related environmental protection departments), and the evaluation values are contained in the decision matrix $A = (a_{ij})_{4\times 5}$, listed in Table 1.2:

Among the five indices $u_j (j = 1,2,3,4,5)$, u_2 and u_5 are of cost type, and the others are of benefit type. The weight information about the indices is also unknown completely.

Considering that the indices have two different types (benefit and cost types), we first transform the attribute values of cost type into the attribute values of benefit type by using Eqs. (1.2) and (1.3), then A is transformed into $R = (r_{ij})_{4\times 5}$, shown in Table 1.3.

Then we utilize the OWA operator (1.1) to aggregate all the attribute values $r_{ij} (j = 1,2,3,4,5)$ of the enterprise x_i, and get the overall attribute value $z_i(\omega)$ (without loss of generality, we use the method given in Theorem 1.10 to determine the weighting vector associated with the OWA operator, and get $\omega = (0.36, 0.16, 0.16, 0.16, 0.16)$, here, we take $\alpha = 0.2$):

$$\begin{aligned} z_1(\omega) &= OWA_\omega(r_{11}, r_{12}, r_{13}, r_{14}, r_{15}) \\ &= 0.36 \times 1.0000 + 0.16 \times 0.9343 + 0.16 \times 0.7647 + 0.16 \\ &\quad \times 0.7591 + 0.16 \times 0.6811 \\ &= 0.8618 \end{aligned}$$

Table 1.2 Decision matrix A

	u_1	u_2	u_3	u_4	u_5
x_1	8350	5300	6135	0.82	0.17
x_2	7455	4952	6527	0.65	0.13
x_3	11,000	8001	9008	0.59	0.15
x_4	9624	5000	8892	0.74	0.28

Table 1.3 Decision matrix R

	u_1	u_2	u_3	u_4	u_5
x_1	0.7591	0.9343	0.6811	1.0000	0.7647
x_2	0.6777	1.0000	0.7246	0.7926	1.0000
x_3	1.0000	0.6189	1.0000	0.7195	0.8667
x_4	0.8749	0.9904	0.9871	0.9024	0.4643

$$\begin{aligned}z_2(\omega) &= OWA_\omega(r_{21}, r_{22}, r_{23}, r_{24}, r_{25}) \\ &= 0.36\times 1.0000 + 0.16\times 1.0000 + 0.16\times 0.7926 \\ &\quad + 0.16\times 0.7246 + 0.16\times 0.6777 \\ &= 0.8712\end{aligned}$$

$$\begin{aligned}z_3(\omega) &= OWA_\omega(r_{31}, r_{32}, r_{33}, r_{34}, r_{35}) \\ &= 0.36\times 1.0000 + 0.16\times 1.0000 + 0.16\times 0.8667 \\ &\quad + 0.16\times 0.7195 + 0.16\times 0.6189 \\ &= 0.8728\end{aligned}$$

$$\begin{aligned}z_4(\omega) &= OWA_\omega(r_{41}, r_{42}, r_{43}, r_{44}, r_{45}) \\ &= 0.36\times 0.9904 + 0.16\times 0.9871 + 0.16\times 0.9024 \\ &\quad + 0.16\times 0.8749 + 0.16\times 0.4643 \\ &= 0.8731\end{aligned}$$

Finally, we rank all the enterprises $x_i (i = 1,2,3,4)$ according to $z_i(\omega)$ $(i = 1,2,3,4)$ in descending order:

$$x_4 \succ x_3 \succ x_2 \succ x_1$$

where "$\succ$" denotes "be superior to", and thus, the best enterprise is x_4.

1.2 MAGDM Method Based on OWA and CWA Operators

1.2.1 CWA Operator

Definition 1.2 [38, 147] Let $WA : \Re^n \to \Re$, if

$$WA_w(\alpha_1, \alpha_2, \ldots, \alpha_n) = \sum_{j=1}^{n} w_j \alpha_j \tag{1.8}$$

where $w = (w_1, w_2, \ldots, w_n)$ is the weight vector of a collection of the arguments $\alpha_i (i = 1, 2, \ldots, n)$, $w_j \geq 0$, $j = 1, 2, \ldots, n$, and $\sum_{j=1}^{n} w_j = 1$, then the function WA is called a weighted averaging (WA) operator.

Clearly, the basic steps of the WA operator are that it first weights all the given arguments by a normalized weight vector, and then aggregates these weighted arguments by addition.

Example 1.3 Let $(7, 18, 6, 2)$ be a collection of arguments, and $w = (0.4, 0.1, 0.2, 0.3)$ be their weight vector, then

$$WA_w(7, 18, 6, 2) = 0.4 \times 7 + 0.1 \times 18 + 0.2 \times 6 + 0.3 \times 2 = 6.4$$

Definition 1.3 [109] Let $CWA : \Re^n \to \Re$, if

$$CWA_{w,\omega}(\alpha_1, \alpha_2, \ldots, \alpha_n) = \sum_{j=1}^{n} \omega_j b_j$$

where $\omega = (\omega_1, \omega_2, \ldots, \omega_n)$ is the weighting vector associated with the CWA operator, $\omega_j \in [0,1], j = 1, 2, \ldots, n$, $\sum_{j=1}^{n} \omega_j = 1$, b_j is the jth largest of a collection of the weighted arguments $n w_i \alpha_i (i = 1, 2, \ldots, n)$; $w = (w_1, w_2, \ldots, w_n)$ is the weight vector of the arguments $\alpha_i (i = 1, 2, \ldots, n)$, $w_i \in [0,1]$, $i = 1, 2, \ldots, n$, $\sum_{i=1}^{n} w_i = 1$, n is the balancing coefficient. Then we call the function CWA a combined weighted averaging (CWA) operator.

Example 1.4 Let $\omega = (0.1, 0.4, 0.4, 0.1)$ be the weighting vector associated with the CWA operator, $(\alpha_1, \alpha_2, \alpha_3, \alpha_4) = (7, 18, 6, 2)$ be a collection of arguments, whose weight vector is $w = (0.2, 0.3, 0.1, 0.4)$, then

$$4w_1 \alpha_1 = 5.6, \quad 4w_2 \alpha_2 = 21.6, \quad 4w_3 \alpha_3 = 2.4, \quad 4w_4 \alpha_4 = 3.2$$

from which we get

$$b_1 = 21.6, \ \ b_2 = 5.6, \ \ b_3 = 3.2, \ \ b_4 = 2.4$$

Therefore,

$$\begin{aligned} CWA_{w,\omega}(\alpha_1, \alpha_2, \ldots, \alpha_4) &= 0.1 \times 21.6 + 0.4 \times 5.6 + 0.4 \times 3.2 + 0.1 \times 2.4 \\ &= 5.92 \end{aligned}$$

Theorem 1.12 [109] The WA operator is a special case of the CWA operator.

Proof Let $\omega = \left(\frac{1}{n}, \frac{1}{n}, \ldots, \frac{1}{n} \right)$, then

$$\begin{aligned} CWA_{w,\omega}(\alpha_1, \alpha_2, \ldots, \alpha_n) &= \sum_{j=1}^{n} \omega_j b_j = \frac{1}{n} \sum_{j=1}^{n} b_j = \sum_{i=1}^{n} w \alpha_j \\ &= WA_w(\alpha_1, \alpha_2, \ldots, \alpha_n) \end{aligned}$$

which completes the proof.

Theorem 1.13 [109] The OWA operator is special case of the CWA operator.

Proof Let $w = \left(\frac{1}{n}, \frac{1}{n}, \ldots, \frac{1}{n} \right)$, then $n w_i \alpha_i = \alpha_i \, (i = 1, 2, \ldots, n)$, thus the weighted version of the arguments, $n w_i \alpha_i \, (i = 1, 2, \ldots, n)$, are also themselves. Therefore,

$$CWA_{w,\omega}(\alpha_1, \alpha_2, \ldots, \alpha_n) = OWA_{\omega}(\alpha_1, \alpha_2, \ldots, \alpha_n)$$

We can see from Theorems 1.12 and 1.13 that the CWA operator generalizes both the WA and OWA operators. It considers not only the importance of each argument itself, but also the importance of its ordered position.

1.2.2 Decision Making Method

For a complicated decision making problem, it usually involves multiple decision makers to participate in the decision making process so as to reach a scientific and rational decision result. In the following, we introduce a MAGDM method based on the OWA and CWAA operators [109]:

Step 1 Let X and U be the sets of alternatives and attributes, respectively, and the information about the attribute weights is unknown. Let $D = \{d_1, d_2, \ldots, d_t\}$ be the set of decision makers (experts), whose weight vector is $\lambda = (\lambda_1, \lambda_2, \ldots, \lambda_t)$, where $\lambda_k \geq 0, \ k = 1, 2, \ldots, t$, and $\sum_{k=1}^{t} \lambda_k = 1$. The decision maker $d_k \in D$ provides his/her preference (or called attribute value) $a_{ij}^{(k)}$ over the alternative $x_i \in X$ with respect to the attribute $u_j \in U$. All the attribute values $a_{ij}^{(k)} (i = 1, 2, \ldots, n; \ j = 1, 2, \ldots, m)$ are contained in the decision matrix A_k. If the "dimensions" of the attributes are different, then we need to normalize each attribute value $a_{ij}^{(k)}$ in the decision matrix A_k using the formulas (1.2)–(1.7) into the normalized decision matrix $R_k = (r_{ij}^{(k)})_{n\times m}$.

Step 2 Utilize the OWA operator (1.1) to aggregate all the attribute values $r_{ij}^{(k)} (j = 1,2,\ldots,m)$ in the i th line of the decision matrix R_k, and then get the overall attribute value $z_i^{(k)}(\omega)$ of the alternative x_i corresponding to the decision maker d_k:

$$z_i^{(k)}(\omega) = OWA_\omega(r_{i1}^{(k)}, r_{i2}^{(k)}, \ldots, r_{im}^{(k)})$$
$$= \sum_{j=1}^{m} \omega_j b_{ij}^{(k)},\ i = 1,2,\ldots,n,\ k = 1,2,\ldots,t$$

where $\omega = (\omega_1, \omega_2, \ldots, \omega_m)$, $\omega_j \geq 0$, $j = 1,2,\ldots,m$, $\sum_{j=1}^{m} \omega_j = 1$, and $b_{ij}^{(k)}$ is the j th largest of $r_{il}^{(k)} (l = 1,2,\ldots,m)$.

Step 3 Aggregate all the overall attribute values $z_i^{(k)}(\omega)(k = 1,2,\ldots,t)$ of the alternative x_i corresponding to the decision makers $d_k (k = 1,2,\ldots,t)$ by using the CWA operator, and then get the collective overall attribute value $z_i(\lambda, \omega')$:

$$z_i(\lambda, \omega') = CWA_{\lambda,\omega'}\left(z_i^{(1)}(\omega), z_i^{(2)}(\omega), \ldots, z_i^{(t)}(\omega)\right)$$
$$= \sum_{k=1}^{t} \omega'_k b_i^{(k)},\ \ i = 1,2,\ldots,n$$

where $\omega' = (\omega'_1, \omega'_2, \ldots, \omega'_t)$ is the weighting vector associated with the CWA operator, $\omega'_k \geq 0, k = 1,2,\ldots,t$, $\sum_{k=1}^{t} \omega'_k = 1$, $b_i^{(k)}$ is the k th largest of a collection of the weighted arguments $t\lambda_l z_i^{(l)}(\omega)(l = 1,2,\ldots,t)$, and t is the balancing coefficient.

Step 4 Rank all the alternatives $x_i (i = 1,2,\ldots,n)$ according to $z_i(\lambda, \omega')(i = 1,2,\ldots,n)$, and then select the most desirable one.

The method above first utilizes the OWA operator to aggregate all the attribute values of an alternative with respect to all the attributes given by a decision maker, and then uses the CWA operator to fuse all the derived overall attribute values corresponding to all the decision makers for an alternative. Considering that in the process of group decision making, some individuals may provide unduly high or unduly low preferences to their preferred or repugnant alternatives. The CWA operator can not only reflect the importance of the decision makers themselves, but also reduce as much as possible the influence of those unduly high or unduly low arguments on the decision result by assigning them lower weights, and thus make the decision results more reasonable and reliable.

1.2.3 Practical Example

Example 1.5 Let's consider a decision making problem of assessing aerospace equipment [10]. The attributes (or indices) which are used here in assessment of four types of aerospace equipments $x_i (i = 1,2,3,4)$ are: (1) u_1: missile early-warning capacities; (2) u_2: imaging detection capability; (3) u_3: communications support capability; (4) u_4: electronic surveillance capacity; (5) u_5: satellite mapping capability; (6) u_6: navigation and positioning capabilities; (7) u_7: marine monitoring capacity; and (8) u_8: weather forecasting capability. The weight information about the attributes is completely unknown, and there are four decision makers $d_k (k = 1,2,3,4)$, whose weight vector is $\lambda = (0.27, 0.23, 0.24, 0.26)$. The decision makers evaluate the aerospace equipments $x_i (i = 1,2,3,4)$ with respect to the attributes $u_j (j = 1,2,\ldots,8)$ by using the hundred-mark system, and then get the attribute values contained in the decision matrices $R_k = (r_{ij}^{(k)})_{4\times8} (k = 1,2,3,4)$, which are listed in Tables 1.4, 1.5, 1.6, and 1.7, respectively.

Since all the attributes $u_j (j = 1,2,\ldots,8)$ are of benefit type, the normalization is not needed.

In what follows, we utilize the method given in Sect. 1.2.2 to solve the problem, which involves the following steps:

Step 1 Utilize the OWA operator (here, we use the method given in Theorem 1.10 (1) to determine the weighting vector associated with the OWA operator, $\omega = (0.3, 0.1, 0.1, 0.1, 0.1, 0.1, 0.1, 0.1)$, when $\alpha = 0.2$) to aggregate all the attribute values in the i th line of the decision matrix R_k, and then get the overall attribute value $z_i^{(k)}(\omega)$ of the decision maker d_k:

$$\begin{aligned} z_1^{(1)}(\omega) &= OWA_\omega(r_{11}^{(1)}, r_{12}^{(1)}, \ldots, r_{18}^{(1)}) \\ &= 0.3\times95 + 0.1\times90 + 0.1\times90 + 0.1\times85 + 0.1\times85 \\ &\quad 0.1\times80 + 0.1\times70 + 0.1\times60 \\ &= 84.50 \end{aligned}$$

Similarly, we have

$$z_2^{(1)}(\omega) = 82,\quad z_3^{(1)}(\omega) = 83,\quad z_4^{(1)}(\omega) = 79,\quad z_1^{(2)}(\omega) = 79,\quad z_2^{(2)}(\omega) = 79$$

$$z_3^{(2)}(\omega) = 82.5,\quad z_4^{(2)}(\omega) = 74.5,\quad z_1^{(3)}(\omega) = 75,\quad z_2^{(3)}(\omega) = 80,\quad z_3^{(3)}(\omega) = 89.5$$

$$z_4^{(3)}(\omega) = 73.5,\quad z_1^{(4)}(\omega) = 80,\quad z_3^{(4)}(\omega) = 87.5,\quad z_4^{(4)}(\omega) = 76$$

Step 2 Aggregate all the overall attribute values $z_i^{(k)}(\omega)(k = 1,2,3,4)$ of the aerospace equipment x_i corresponding to the decision makers $d_k (k = 1,2,3,4)$ by using

Table 1.4 Decision matrix R_1

	u_1	u_2	u_3	u_4	u_5	u_6	u_7	u_8
x_1	85	90	95	60	70	80	90	85
x_2	95	80	60	70	90	85	80	70
x_3	65	75	95	65	90	95	70	85
x_4	75	75	50	65	95	75	85	80

Table 1.5 Decision matrix R_2

	u_1	u_2	u_3	u_4	u_5	u_6	u_7	u_8
x_1	60	75	90	65	70	95	70	75
x_2	85	60	60	65	90	75	95	70
x_3	60	65	75	80	90	95	90	80
x_4	65	60	60	70	90	85	70	65

Table 1.6 Decision matrix R_3

	u_1	u_2	u_3	u_4	u_5	u_6	u_7	u_8
x_1	60	75	85	60	85	80	60	75
x_2	80	75	60	90	85	65	85	80
x_3	95	80	85	85	90	90	85	95
x_4	60	65	50	60	95	80	65	70

Table 1.7 Decision matrix R_4

	u_1	u_2	u_3	u_4	u_5	u_6	u_7	u_8
x_1	70	80	85	65	80	90	70	80
x_2	85	70	70	80	95	70	85	85
x_3	90	85	80	80	95	85	80	90
x_4	65	70	60	65	90	85	70	75

the CWA operator (suppose that its weighting vector $\omega' = \left(\frac{1}{6}, \frac{1}{3}, \frac{1}{3}, \frac{1}{6}\right)$). To do that, we first use λ, t and $z_i^{(k)}(\omega)(i,k=1,2,3,4)$ to derive $t\lambda_k z_i^{(k)}(\omega)$ $(i,k=1,2,3,4)$:

$$4\lambda_1 z_1^{(1)}(\omega) = 91.26, \quad 4\lambda_1 z_2^{(1)}(\omega) = 88.56, \quad 4\lambda_1 z_3^{(1)}(\omega) = 89.64$$

$$4\lambda_1 z_4^{(1)}(\omega) = 85.32, \quad 4\lambda_2 z_1^{(2)}(\omega) = 72.68, \quad 4\lambda_2 z_2^{(2)}(\omega) = 72.68$$

$$4\lambda_2 z_3^{(2)}(\omega) = 75.9, \quad 4\lambda_2 z_4^{(2)}(\omega) = 68.54, \quad 4\lambda_3 z_1^{(3)}(\omega) = 72$$

$$4\lambda_3 z_2^{(3)}(\omega) = 76.8, \quad 4\lambda_3 z_3^{(3)}(\omega) = 85.92, \quad 4\lambda_3 z_4^{(3)}(\omega) = 70.56$$

$$4\lambda_4 z_1^{(4)}(\omega) = 83.20,\ \ 4\lambda_4 z_2^{(4)}(\omega) = 86.32,\ \ 4\lambda_4 z_3^{(4)}(\omega) = 91$$

$$4\lambda_4 z_4^{(4)}(\omega) = 79.56$$

and thus, the collective overall attribute values of the aerospace equipment $x_i (i = 1,2,3,4)$ are

$$z_1(\lambda,\omega') = \frac{1}{6}\times 91.26 + \frac{1}{3}\times 83.20 + \frac{1}{3}\times 72.68 + \frac{1}{6}\times 72 = 79.17$$

$$z_2(\lambda,\omega') = \frac{1}{6}\times 88.56 + \frac{1}{3}\times 86.32 + \frac{1}{3}\times 76.8 + \frac{1}{6}\times 72.68 = 79.87$$

$$z_3(\lambda,\omega') = \frac{1}{6}\times 91 + \frac{1}{3}\times 89.64 + \frac{1}{3}\times 85.92 + \frac{1}{6}\times 75.90 = 86.34$$

$$z_4(\lambda,\omega') = \frac{1}{6}\times 85.32 + \frac{1}{3}\times 79.56 + \frac{1}{3}\times 70.56 + \frac{1}{6}\times 68.54 = 75.68$$

Step 3 Rank the aerospace equipments $x_i (i = 1,2,3,4)$ according to $z_1(\lambda,\omega')$ $(i = 1,2,3,4)$:

$$x_3 \succ x_2 \succ x_1 \succ x_4$$

and then, the best aerospace equipment is x_3.

1.3 MADM Method Based on the OWG Operator

1.3.1 OWG Operator

Definition 1.4 [43, 144] Let $OWG : (\Re^+)^n \rightarrow \Re^+$, if

$$OWG_\omega(\alpha_1,\alpha_2,\ldots,\alpha_n) = \prod_{j=1}^{n} b_j^{\omega_j} \tag{1.9}$$

where $\omega = (\omega_1,\omega_2,\ldots,\omega_n)$ is the exponential weighting vector associated with the OWG operator, $\omega_j \in [0,1]$, $j = 1,2,\ldots,n$, $\sum_{j=1}^{n}\omega_i = 1$, and b_j is the j th largest of a collection of the arguments $\alpha_i (i = 1,2,\ldots,n)$, $\Re^+$ is the set of positive real numbers, then the function OWG is called an ordered weighted geometric (OWG) operator.

The OWG operator has some desirable properties similar to those of the OWA operator, such as monotonicity, commutativity, and idempotency, etc.

Example 1.6 Let $\omega = (0.4, 0.1, 0.2, 0.3)$ be the weighting vector associated with the OWG operator, and $(7, 18, 6, 2)$ be a collection of arguments, then

$$OWG_\omega(7,18,6,2) = 18^{0.4} \times 7^{0.1} \times 6^{0.2} \times 2^{0.3} = 6.8$$

1.3.2 Decision Making Method

Below we introduce a method based on the OWG operator for MADM [109]:

Step 1 For a MADM problem, the weight information is completely unknown, and the decision matrix is $A = (a_{ij})_{n\times m} (a_{ij} > 0)$. Utilize Eqs. (1.2) and (1.3) to normalize the decision matrix A into the matrix $R = (r_{ij})_{n\times m}$.

Step 2 Use the OWG operator to aggregate all the attribute values of the alternative x_i, and get the overall attribute value:

$$z_i(\omega) = OWG_\omega(r_{i1}, r_{i2}, \ldots, r_{im}) = \prod_{j=1}^{m} b_{ij}^{\omega_j}$$

where $\omega = (\omega_1, \omega_2, \ldots, \omega_m)$ is the exponential weighting vector, $\omega_j \in [0,1]$, $j = 1, 2, \ldots, n, \sum_{j=1}^{n} \omega_j = 1$, and b_{ij} is the j th largest of $r_{il} (l = 1, 2, \ldots, m)$.

Step 3 Rank and select the alternatives $x_i (i = 1, 2, \ldots, n)$ according to $z_i(\omega)$ $i = 1, 2, \ldots, n)$.

1.3.3 Practical Example

Example 1.7 The evaluation indices used for information system investment project are mainly as follows [8]:

5. Revenue (u_1) (10^4\$): As with any investment, the primary purpose of information system investment project is to profit, and thus, revenue should be considered as a main factor of investment project evaluation.
6. Risk (u_2): Risk of information system investment is a second factor to be considered, especially, the information investment projects of government department, are impacted by government and the market hugely.
7. Social benefits (u_3): Information construction eventually was to raise the level of social services. Thus, social benefits should be considered as an evaluation index of information project investment. The investment project with remarkable

Table 1.8 Decision matrix A

	u_1	u_2	u_3	u_4	u_5
x_1	300	0.83	0.83	0.83	0.8
x_2	250	0.67	0.67	0.67	0.6
x_3	200	0.5	0.5	0.5	0.2
x_4	100	0.33	0.5	0.5	0.2

social efficiency can not only enhance the enterprise's image, but also are more easily recognized and approved by the government.

8. Market effect (u_4): In the development course of information technology, its market effect is extremely remarkable, which are mainly reflected in two aspects: (i) The speed to occupy market, which is most obvious in the government engineering project. If an enterprise successfully obtains government department's approval most early, then it will be able to quickly occupy the project market with model effect; (ii) Marginal cost reduction. Experience accumulation and scale effect in the technology and project development process may dramatically reduce development costs. Therefore, some investment projects with remarkable market effect can be conducted in a little profit or even loss manner.
9. Technical difficulty (u_5): In the development process of information investment projects, technology is also a key factor. With the development of computer technology, new technologies emerge unceasingly, in order to improve the system's practicality and security, the technical requirements also increase correspondingly.

Among the evaluation indices above, u_2 and u_5 are of cost type, and the others are of benefit type.

In the information management system project of a region, four alternatives $x_i (i = 1,2,3,4)$ are available, i.e., (1) x_1: invested by the company who uses the 8KB CPU card; (2) x_2: invested by the company who uses the 2KB CPU card; (3) x_3: invested by the company who uses the magcard; and (4) x_4: invested by the local government, the company only contracts the system integration. The experts have been organized to evaluate the above four alternatives, and provide their evaluation information, which is listed in Table 1.8.

Assume that the weight information about the indices $u_j (j = 1,2,3,4,5)$ is also unknown completely, and then we utilize the method introduced in Sect. 1.3.2 to derive the optimal alternative:

Step 1 Utilize Eqs. (1.2) and (1.3) to normalize A into the matrix $R = (r_{ij})_{4\times5}$, shown in Table 1.9.

Step 2 Aggregate all the attribute values of the alternative x_i by using the OWG operator, and then get its overall attribute value $z_i(\omega)$ (without loss of generality, let $\omega = (0.1,0.2,0.4,0.2,0.1)$) be the weighting vector associated with the OWG operator):

Table 1.9 Decision matrix R

	u_1	u_2	u_3	u_4	u_5
x_1	1.0000	0.3976	1.0000	1.0000	0.2500
x_2	0.8333	0.4925	0.8072	0.8072	0.3333
x_3	0.6667	0.6600	0.6024	0.6024	1.0000
x_4	0.3333	1.0000	0.6024	0.3976	1.0000

$$\begin{aligned} z_1(\omega) &= OWG_\omega(r_{11}, r_{12}, r_{13}, r_{14}, r_{15}) \\ &= 1.000^{0.10} \times 0.3976^{0.2} \times 1.0000^{0.4} \times 1.0000^{0.2} \times 0.2500^{0.1} \\ &= 0.7239 \end{aligned}$$

$$\begin{aligned} z_2(\omega) &= OWG_\omega(r_{21}, r_{22}, r_{23}, r_{24}, r_{25}) \\ &= 0.8333^{0.10} \times 0.4925^{0.2} \times 0.8072^{0.4} \times 0.8072^{0.2} \times 0.3333^{0.1} \\ &= 0.6715 \end{aligned}$$

$$\begin{aligned} z_3(\omega) &= OWG_\omega(r_{31}, r_{32}, r_{33}, r_{34}, r_{35}) \\ &= 0.6667^{0.10} \times 0.6600^{0.2} \times 0.6024^{0.4} \times 0.6024^{0.2} \times 1.0000^{0.1} \\ &= 0.6520 \end{aligned}$$

$$\begin{aligned} z_4(\omega) &= OWG_\omega(r_{41}, r_{42}, r_{43}, r_{44}, r_{45}) \\ &= 0.3333^{0.10} \times 1.0000^{0.2} \times 0.6024^{0.4} \times 0.3976^{0.2} \times 1.0000^{0.1} \\ &= 0.6083 \end{aligned}$$

Step 3 Rank and select the alternatives $x_i (i = 1, 2, 3, 4)$ according to $z_i(\omega)$ $(i = 1, 2, 3, 4)$:

$$x_1 \succ x_2 \succ x_3 \succ x_4$$

and then, x_1 is the best alternative.

1.4 MADM Method Based on OWG Operator

1.4.1 CWG Operator

Definition 1.5 [1] Let $WG : (\Re^+)^n \to \Re^+$, if

$$WG_w(\alpha_1, \alpha_2, \ldots, \alpha_n) = \prod_{j=1}^{n} \alpha_j^{w_j} \tag{1.10}$$

where $w = (w_1, w_2, \ldots, w_m)$ is the exponential weight vector of the arguments $\alpha_i (i = 1,2,\ldots,n)$, $w_j \in [0,1]$, $j = 1,2,\ldots,n$, and $\sum_{j=1}^{n} w_i = 1$, then the function WG is called a weighted geometric (WG) operator.

Example 1.8 Assume that $(7,18,6,2)$ is a collection of arguments, whose weight vector is $w = (0.4, 0.1, 0.2, 0.3)$, then

$$WG_w(7,18,6,2) = 7^{0.4} \times 18^{0.1} \times 6^{0.2} \times 2^{0.3} = 5.123$$

Definition 1.6 [109] Let $CWG : (\Re^+)^n \to \Re^+$, if

$$CWG_{w,\omega}(\alpha_1, \alpha_2, \ldots, \alpha_n) = \prod_{j=1}^{n} b_j^{\omega_j}$$

where $\omega = (\omega_1, \omega_2, \ldots, \omega_n)$ is the exponential weighting vector associated with the CWG operator, $\omega_j \in [0,1]$, $j = 1,2,\ldots,n$, $\sum_{j=1}^{n} \omega_i = 1$, and b_j is the j th largest of a collection of the exponential weighted arguments $\alpha_i^{nw_i} (i = 1,2,\ldots,n)$, $w = (w_1, w_2, \ldots, w_m)$ is the exponential weight vector of the arguments $\alpha_i (i = 1,2, \ldots,n)$, $w_j \in [0,1]$, $j = 1,2,\ldots,n$, $\sum_{j=1}^{n} w_i = 1$, and n is the balancing coefficient. Then we call the function CWG a combined weighted geometric (CWG) operator.

Example 1.9 Let $\omega = (0.1, 0.4, 0.4, 0.1)$ be the exponential weighting vector associated with the CWG operator, $(\alpha_1, \alpha_2, \alpha_3, \alpha_4)$ be a collection of arguments, whose exponential weight vector is $w = (0.2, 0.3, 0.1, 0.4)$, then

$$\alpha_1^{4w_1} = 4.74, \quad \alpha_2^{4w_2} = 32.09, \quad \alpha_3^{4w_3} = 2.05, \quad \alpha_4^{4w_4} = 3.03$$

and thus,

$$b_1 = 32.09, \quad b_2 = 4.74, \quad b_3 = 3.03, \quad b_4 = 2.05$$

Therefore,

$$CWG_{w,\omega}(\alpha_1, \alpha_2, \alpha_3, \alpha_4) = 32.09^{0.1} \times 4.74^{0.4} \times 3.03^{0.4} \times 2.05^{0.1} = 4.413$$

Theorem 1.14 The WG operator is a special of the CWG operator.

Proof Let $\omega = \left(\frac{1}{n}, \frac{1}{n}, \ldots, \frac{1}{n}\right)$, then

$$\begin{aligned} CWG_{w,\omega}(\alpha_1, \alpha_2, \ldots, \alpha_n) &= \prod_{j=1}^{n} b_j^{\omega_j} = \left(\prod_{j=1}^{n} b_j\right)^{\frac{1}{n}} = \prod_{i=1}^{n} \alpha_i^{w_i} \\ &= WG_w(\alpha_1, \alpha_2, \ldots, \alpha_n) \end{aligned}$$

which completes the proof.

Theorem 1.15 The OWGA operator is a special of the CWG operator.

Proof Let $w = \left(\frac{1}{n}, \frac{1}{n}, \ldots, \frac{1}{n}\right)$, then $\alpha_i^{nw_i} = \alpha_i (i = 1, 2, \ldots, n)$, i.e., the weighted arguments are also the original ones. Therefore,

$$CWG_{w,\omega}(\alpha_1, \alpha_2, \ldots, \alpha_n) = OWG_{\omega}(\alpha_1, \alpha_2, \ldots, \alpha_n)$$

which completes the proof.

From Theorems 1.14 and 1.15, we can see that the CWG operator generalizes both the WG and OWG operators. It not only considers the importance of each argument itself, but also reflects the importance of the ordered position of the argument.

1.4.2 Decision Making Method

Now we introduce a method based on the OWG and CWG operators for MAGDM:

Step 1 For a MAGDM problem, the weight information about attributes is completely unknown, $\lambda = (\lambda_1, \lambda_2, \ldots, \lambda_t)$ is the weight vector of t decision makers, where $\lambda_k \in [0,1]$, $k = 1, 2, \ldots, t$, and $\sum_{k=1}^{t} \lambda_k = 1$. The decision maker $d_k \in D$ evaluates the alternative $x_i \in X$ with respect to the attribute $u_j \in U$, and provides the attribute value $a_{ij}^{(k)} (> 0)$. All these attribute values $a_{ij}^{(k)} (i = 1, 2, \ldots, n, j = 1, 2, \ldots, m)$ are contained in the decision matrix A_k, which is then normalized into the matrix $R_k = (r_{ij}^{(k)})_{n \times m}$.

Step 2 Utilize the OWG operator to aggregate all the attribute values in the i th line of R_k, and get the overall attribute value $z_i^{(k)}(\omega)$:

$$z_i^{(k)}(\omega) = OWG_{\omega}(r_{i1}^{(k)}, r_{i2}^{(k)}, \ldots, r_{im}^{(k)}) = \prod_{j=1}^{m} (b_{ij}^{(k)})^{\omega_j}$$

where $\omega = (\omega_1, \omega_2, \ldots, \omega_m)$ is the exponential weighting vector associated with the OWG operator, $\omega_j \in [0,1]$, $j = 1, 2, \ldots, n$, $\sum_{j=1}^{n} \omega_j = 1$, and $b_{ij}^{(k)}$ is the j th largest of $r_{il}^{(k)} (l = 1, 2, \ldots, m)$.

Step 3 Aggregate $z_i^{(k)}(\omega) (k = 1, 2, \ldots, t)$ corresponding to all the decision makers $d_k (k = 1, 2, \ldots, t)$ by using the CWG operator, and get the collective overall attribute value $z_i(\lambda, \omega')$:

$$z_i(\lambda, \omega') = CWG_{\lambda,\omega'}(z_i^{(1)}(\omega), z_i^{(2)}(\omega), \ldots, z_i^{(t)}(\omega)) = \prod_{k=1}^{t} (b_i^{(k)})^{\omega'_k}$$

where $\omega' = (\omega_1', \omega_2', \ldots, \omega_t')$ is the exponential weighting vector associated with the CWG operator, $\omega_k' \in [0,1]$, $k = 1,2,\ldots,t$, $\sum_{k=1}^{t} \omega_k' = 1$, $b_i^{(k)}$ is the j th largest of the exponential weighted arguments $z_i^{(k)}(\omega)^{t\lambda_k}$ $(k = 1,2,\ldots,t)$, and t is the balancing coefficient.

Step 4 Rank and select the alternatives $x_i (i = 1,2,\ldots,n)$ according to $z_i(\lambda, \omega')$ $(i = 1,2,\ldots,n)$.

1.4.3 Practical Example

Example 1.10 Let's consider a MADM problem concerning the college finance evaluation. Firstly, ten evaluation indices (or attributes) are to be predefined [89], which include (1) u_1: budget revenue performance; (2) budget expenditure performance; (3) u_3: financial and grant from the higher authority; (4) u_4 self-financing; (5) u_5: personnel expenses; (6) u_6: public expenditures; (7) u_7: per capita expenditures; (8) fixed asset utilization; (9) occupancy of current assets; and (10) payment ability. The weight information about indices (or attributes) is completely unknown. There are four experts $d_k (k = 1,2,3,4)$, whose weight vector is $\lambda =$ (0.27,0.23,0.24,0.26). The experts evaluate the financial situations of four colleges (or alternatives) $x_i (i = 1,2,3,4)$ with respect to the indices $u_j (j = 1,2,\ldots,8)$ by using the hundred-mark system, and then get the attribute values contained in the decision matrices $R_k = (r_{ij}^{(k)})_{4\times 10} (k = 1,2,3,4)$, which are listed in Tables 1.10, 1.11, 1.12, and 1.13, respectively, and do not need normalizing them:

In the following, we use the method given in Sect. 1.4.2 to solve this problem:

Step 1 Utilize the OWG operator (let its weighting vector be $\omega = (0.07, 0.08, 0.10, 0.12, 0.13, 0.12, 0.10, 0.08, 0.07)$) to aggregate all the attribute values in the i th line of the matrix R_k, and get the overall attribute value $z_i^{(k)}(\omega)$ of the alternative x_k corresponding to the decision maker d_k:

$$z_1^{(1)}(\omega) = 95^{0.07} \times 95^{0.08} \times 90^{0.10} \times 90^{0.12} \times 90^{0.13} \times 85^{0.13} \times 85^{0.12} \times 70^{0.10} \times 65^{0.08} \times 60^{0.07}$$
$$= 82.606$$

Similarly, we have

$$z_2^{(1)}(\omega) = 81.579, \quad z_3^{(1)}(\omega) = 81.772, \quad z_4^{(1)}(\omega) = 83.807, \quad z_1^{(2)}(\omega) = 80.607$$

$$z_2^{(2)}(\omega) = 81.141, \quad z_3^{(2)}(\omega) = 79.640, \quad z_4^{(2)}(\omega) = 81.992, \quad z_1^{(3)}(\omega) = 80.513$$

$$z_2^{(3)}(\omega) = 80.340, \quad z_3^{(3)}(\omega) = 82.649, \quad z_4^{(3)}(\omega) = 78.949, \quad z_1^{(4)}(\omega) = 81.053$$

$$z_2^{(4)}(\omega) = 78.784, \quad z_3^{(4)}(\omega) = 81.985, \quad z_4^{(4)}(\omega) = 75.418$$

Table 1.10 Decision matrix R_1

	u_1	u_2	u_3	u_4	u_5	u_6	u_7	u_8	u_9	u_{10}
x_1	90	95	60	70	90	85	95	65	85	90
x_2	80	90	75	80	85	90	75	80	70	95
x_3	70	75	90	95	80	90	70	80	85	85
x_4	90	80	85	70	95	85	95	75	75	90

Table 1.11 Decision matrix R_2

	u_1	u_2	u_3	u_4	u_5	u_6	u_7	u_8	u_9	u_{10}
x_1	70	75	95	80	85	60	80	90	80	95
x_2	80	90	70	70	85	95	75	85	75	90
x_3	75	85	80	90	95	70	60	75	80	90
x_4	80	70	90	75	85	95	65	85	85	90

Table 1.12 Decision matrix R_3

	u_1	u_2	u_3	u_4	u_5	u_6	u_7	u_8	u_9	u_{10}
x_1	70	80	85	70	95	85	65	90	75	95
x_2	85	70	65	95	85	90	70	85	75	85
x_3	90	80	80	85	95	95	60	80	85	80
x_4	65	75	95	75	90	85	65	75	90	80

Table 1.13 Decision matrix R_4

	u_1	u_2	u_3	u_4	u_5	u_6	u_7	u_8	u_9	u_{10}
x_1	60	90	95	75	80	95	75	80	85	80
x_2	80	65	60	85	95	90	80	85	70	80
x_3	95	75	85	80	90	85	90	60	75	85
x_4	65	80	65	75	95	85	80	65	60	95

Step 2 Aggregate all the overall attribute values $z_i^{(k)}(\omega)(k=1,2,3,4)$ of the alternative x_i corresponding to the decision makers $d_k(k=1,2,3,4)$ by using the CWG operator (let its weighting vector be $\omega' = \left(\frac{1}{6},\frac{1}{3},\frac{1}{3},\frac{1}{6}\right)$). To do so, we first utilize λ, t and $z_i^{(k)}(\omega)(i,k=1,2,3,4)$ to derive

$$(z_1^{(1)}(\omega))^{4\lambda_1} = 117.591,\quad (z_2^{(1)}(\omega))^{4\lambda_1} = 116.012,\quad (z_3^{(1)}(\omega))^{4\lambda_1} = 116.309$$

$$(z_4^{(1)}(\omega))^{4\lambda_1} = 119.438,\quad (z_1^{(2)}(\omega))^{4\lambda_2} = 56.737,\quad (z_2^{(2)}(\omega))^{4\lambda_2} = 57.082$$

$$(z_3^{(2)}(\omega))^{4\lambda_2} = 56.110,\quad (z_4^{(2)}(\omega))^{4\lambda_2} = 57.633,\quad (z_1^{(3)}(\omega))^{4\lambda_3} = 67.551$$

$$(z_2^{(3)}(\omega))^{4\lambda_3} = 67.412,\ (z_3^{(3)}(\omega))^{4\lambda_3} = 69.270,\ (z_4^{(3)}(\omega))^{4\lambda_3} = 66.291$$

$$(z_1^{(4)}(\omega))^{4\lambda_4} = 96.632,\ (z_2^{(4)}(\omega))^{4\lambda_4} = 93.820,\ (z_3^{(4)}(\omega))^{4\lambda_4} = 97.788$$

$$(z_4^{(4)}(\omega))^{4\lambda_4} = 89.655$$

and then get the collective overall attribute value $z_i(\lambda, \omega')$ of the alternative x_i:

$$z_1(\lambda, \omega') = 117.591^{\frac{1}{6}} \times 96.632^{\frac{1}{3}} \times 67.551^{\frac{1}{3}} \times 56.737^{\frac{1}{6}} = 81.088$$

$$\left(z_i^{(k)}(\omega)\right)^{4\lambda_k}\ (i,k = 1,2,3,4):$$

$$z_2(\lambda, \omega') = 116.012^{\frac{1}{6}} \times 93.820^{\frac{1}{3}} \times 67.412^{\frac{1}{3}} \times 57.082^{\frac{1}{6}} = 80.139$$

$$z_3(\lambda, \omega') = 116.309^{\frac{1}{6}} \times 97.788^{\frac{1}{3}} \times 69.270^{\frac{1}{3}} \times 56.110^{\frac{1}{6}} = 81.794$$

$$z_4(\lambda, \omega') = 119.438^{\frac{1}{6}} \times 89.655^{\frac{1}{3}} \times 66.291^{\frac{1}{3}} \times 57.633^{\frac{1}{6}} = 79.003$$

Step 3 Rank all the alternatives $x_i (i = 1,2,3,4)$ according to $z_i(\lambda, \omega')$ $(i = 1,2,3,4)$:

$$x_3 \succ x_1 \succ x_2 \succ x_4$$

and thus, x_3 is the best alternative.

1.5 MADM Method Based on Maximizing Deviations

1.5.1 Decision Making Method

For a MADM problem, the weight information about attributes is completely unknown. The decision matrix $A = (a_{ij})_{n \times m}$ is normalized into the matrix $R = (r_{ij})_{n \times m}$ by using the formulas given in Sect. 1.1.2.

Let $w = (w_1, w_2, \ldots, w_n)$ be the weight vector of attributes, $w_j \geq 0,\ j = 1,2,\ldots,m$, which satisfies the constrained condition [92]:

$$\sum_{j=1}^{n} w_j^2 = 1 \tag{1.11}$$

Then we can get the overall attribute value of each alternative:

$$z_i(w) = \sum_{j=1}^{m} r_{ij} w_j \tag{1.12}$$

In the process of MADM, we generally need to compare the overall attribute values of the considered alternatives. According to the information theory, if all alternatives have similar attribute values with respect to an attribute, then a small weight should be assigned to the attribute, this is due to that this attribute does not help in differentiating alternatives [167]. As a result, from the viewpoint of ranking the alternatives, the attribute which has bigger deviations among the alternatives should be assigned larger weight. Especially, if there is no indifference among the attribute values of all the alternatives with respect to the attribute u_j, then the attribute u_j will play no role in ranking the alternatives, and thus, its weight can be assigned zero [92]. For the attribute u_j, we use $D_{ij}(w)$ to denote the deviation between the alternative x_i and all the alternatives:

$$D_{ij}(w) = \sum_{k=1}^{n} \left| r_{ij} w_j - r_{kj} w_j \right|$$

Let

$$D_j(w) = \sum_{i=1}^{n} D_{ij}(w) = \sum_{i=1}^{n} \sum_{k=1}^{n} \left| r_{ij} - r_{kj} \right| w_j$$

then $D_j(w)$ denotes the total deviation among all the alternatives with respect to the attribute u_j.

Based on the analysis above, the weight vector w should be obtained so as to maximize the total deviation among all the alternatives with respect to all the attributes. As a result, we construct the objective function:

$$\max D(w) = \sum_{j=1}^{m} D_j(w) = \sum_{j=1}^{m} \sum_{i=1}^{n} \sum_{k=1}^{n} \left| r_{ij} - r_{kj} \right| w_j$$

and thus, Wang [92] used the following optimization model to derive the weight vector w:

$$(\mathbf{M\text{-}1.1}) \quad \begin{cases} \max D(w) = \sum_{j=1}^{m} D_j(w) = \sum_{j=1}^{m} \sum_{i=1}^{n} \sum_{k=1}^{n} \left| r_{ij} - r_{kj} \right| w_j \\ s.t. w_j \geq 0, \ j = 1, 2, \ldots, m, \ \sum_{j=1}^{m} w_j^2 = 1 \end{cases}$$

To solve the model (M-1.1), we construct the Lagrange function:

$$L(w, \zeta) = \sum_{j=1}^{m} \sum_{i=1}^{n} \sum_{k=1}^{n} \left| r_{ij} - r_{kj} \right| w_j + \frac{1}{2} \zeta \left(\sum_{j=1}^{m} w_j^2 - 1 \right)$$

where ζ is the Lagrange multiplier.

Differentiating $L(w,\zeta)$ with respect to $w_j(j=1,2,\ldots,m)$ and ζ, and setting these partial derivatives equal to zero, the following set of equations is obtained:

$$\begin{cases} \dfrac{L(w,\zeta)}{\partial w_j} = \sum_{i=1}^{n}\sum_{k=1}^{n}\left|r_{ij}-r_{kj}\right| + \zeta w_j = 0, \quad j=1,2,\ldots,m \\ \dfrac{L(w,\zeta)}{\partial \zeta} = \sum_{j=1}^{m} w_j^2 - 1 = 0 \end{cases}$$

from which we get the optimal solution:

$$w_j^* = \frac{\sum_{i=1}^{n}\sum_{k=1}^{n}\left|r_{ij}-r_{kj}\right|}{\sqrt{\sum_{j=1}^{m}\left[\sum_{i=1}^{n}\sum_{k=1}^{n}\left|r_{ij}-r_{kj}\right|\right]^2}}, \quad j=1,2,\ldots,m$$

Since the traditional weight vector generally satisfies the normalized constrained condition, then in order to be in accordance to people's habit, we need to normalize w_j^* into the following form:

$$w_j = \frac{w_j^*}{\sum_{j=1}^{m} w_j^*}, \quad j=1,2,\ldots,m$$

from which we have

$$w_j = \frac{\sum_{i=1}^{n}\sum_{k=1}^{n}\left|r_{ij}-r_{kj}\right|}{\sum_{j=1}^{m}\sum_{i=1}^{n}\sum_{k=1}^{n}\left|r_{ij}-r_{kj}\right|}, \quad j=1,2,\ldots,m \tag{1.13}$$

Based on the analysis above, the maximizing deviations-based method for MADM can be summarized as follows:

Step 1 For a MADM problem, a decision matrix $A=(a_{ij})_{n\times m}$ is constructed and then normalized into the matrix $R=(r_{ij})_{n\times m}$.

Step 2 Utilize Eq. (1.13) to calculate the optimal weight vector w.

Step 3 Calculate the overall attribute value $z_i(w)$ of the alternative x_i by using Eq. (1.12).

Step 4 Rank and select the alternatives x_i $(i=1,2,\ldots,n)$ by using $z_i(w)$ $(i=1,2,\ldots,n)$.

Table 1.14 Decision matrix A

	u_1	u_2	u_3	u_4	u_5	u_6
x_1	12	11.5	780	175	22	2.43
x_2	12	14.6	898	165	33.5	2.83
x_3	10.3	13.5	741	181	22.7	3
x_4	12	15.24	1938	204	47.3	4
x_5	11.4	12.19	833.4	180	19	5.9
x_6	9	12.8	667	170	19.8	3.8
x_7	12.2	13.37	991	170	59	3.3
x_8	12	14.3	1048	230	37.2	1.9
x_9	9	6.25	287	105	5	3.6
x_{10}	10.33	15	927	167	52.6	3.14

1.5.2 Practical Example

Example 1.11 Some unit tries to buy a trainer aircraft, there are ten types of trainer aircrafts to choose from [54]: (1) x_1: L-39; (2) x_2: MB339; (3) x_3: T-46; (4) x_4: Hawk; (5) x_5: C101; (6) x_6: S211; (7) x_7: Alpha Jet; (8) x_8: Fighter-teaching; (9) x_9: Early-teaching; and (10) x_{10}: T-4. The attributes (or indices) which are used here in assessment of the trainer aircrafts $x_i (i = 1, 2, \ldots, 10)$ are: (1) u_1: overloaded ranges (g); (2) u_2: maximum height limit (km); (3) u_3: maximum level flight speed (km/h); (4) u_4: landing speed (km/h); (5) u_5: maximum climb rate (m/s); and (6) cruise duration (h). The performances of all candidate trainer aircrafts are listed in Table 1.14.

In the above evaluation indices, u_4 (landing speed) is of cost type, and the others are of benefit type.

In what follows, we utilize the method given in Sect. 1.5.1 to get the decision result:

Step 1 Utilize Eqs. (1.2) and (1.3) to normalize the decision matrix A, and then get the matrix R, listed in Table 1.15.

Step 2 Calculate the optimal weight vector by using Eq. (1.13):

$$w = (0.0950, 0.1464, 0.1956, 0.1114, 0.2849, 0.1667)$$

Step 3 Derive the overall attribute value $z_i(w)$ of the alternative x_i from Eq. (1.12):

$$z_1(w) = 0.5913,\ z_2(w) = 0.7410,\ z_2(w) = 0.7410,\ z_4(w) = 0.8323$$
$$z_5(w) = 0.6847,\ z_6(w) = 0.5894,\ z_7(w) = 0.8553,\ z_8(w) = 0.7107$$
$$z_9(w) = 0.4210,\ z_{10}(w) = 0.8105$$

Table 1.15 Decision matrix R

	u_1	u_2	u_3	u_4	u_5	u_6
x_1	0.984	0.755	0.744	0.600	0.373	0.412
x_2	0.984	0.958	0.857	0.636	0.568	0.480
x_3	0.844	0.886	0.707	0.580	0.385	0.508
x_4	0.984	1	0.990	0.515	0.802	0.678
x_5	0.934	0.800	0.795	0.683	0.322	1
x_6	0.738	0.840	0.636	0.618	0.336	0.644
x_7	1	0.877	0.946	0.618	1	0.559
x_8	0.984	0.938	1	0.457	0.631	0.322
x_9	0.738	0.410	0.274	1	0.085	0.610
x_{10}	0.847	0.984	0.885	0.629	0.892	0.532

Step 4 Rank all the alternatives $x_i (i = 1,2,\ldots,10)$ according to $z_i(w)(i = 1,2,\ldots,10)$:

$$x_{10} \succ x_7 \succ x_4 \succ x_2 \succ x_8 \succ x_5 \succ x_3 \succ x_1 \succ x_6 \succ x_9$$

and thus, the best trainer aircraft is T-4.

1.6 MADM Method Based on Information Entropy

1.6.1 Decision Making Method

The concept of entropy was originated in thermodynamics. At the beginning, it was used to describe the irreversible phenomenon in the moving process. Later, in the information theory, entropy is used to depict the uncertainty that things appear. In what follows, we introduce a MADM method based on information entropy:

Step 1 For a MADM problem, a decision matrix $A = (a_{ij})_{n\times m}$ is first constructed and then normalized into the matrix $R = (r_{ij})_{n\times m}$ using the proper formulas in Sect. 1.1.2.

Step 2 Transform the matrix $R = (r_{ij})_{n\times m}$ into the matrix $\dot{R} = (\dot{r}_{ij})_{n\times m}$ by using the formula:

$$\dot{r}_{ij} = \frac{r_{ij}}{\sum_{i=1}^{n} r_{ij}}, \quad i = 1,2,\ldots,n, j = 1,2,\ldots,m \tag{1.14}$$

Step 3 Calculate the information entropy corresponding to the attribute u_j:

$$E_j = -\frac{1}{\ln n} \sum_{i=1}^{n} \dot{r}_{ij} \ln \dot{r}_{ij}, \quad j = 1,2,\ldots,m \tag{1.15}$$

Table 1.16 Decision matrix A

	u_1	u_2	u_3	u_4	u_5	u_6
x_1	2.0	1.5	2.0	5.5	5	9
x_2	2.5	2.7	1.8	6.5	3	5
x_3	1.8	2.0	2.1	4.5	7	7
x_4	2.2	1.8	2.0	5.0	5	5

Especially, if $\dot{r}_{ij} = 0$, then we stipulate $\dot{r}_{ij} \ln \dot{r}_{ij} = 0$.

Step 4 Derive the weight vector $w = (w_1, w_2, \ldots, w_n)$ of attributes from

$$w_j = \frac{1-E_j}{\sum_{k=1}^{m}(1-E_k)} \tag{1.16}$$

Step 5 Utilize Eq. (1.12) to obtain the overall attribute value $z_i(w)$ of the alternative x_i.

Step 6 Rank and select the alternatives $x_i (i = 1, 2, \ldots, n)$ according to $z_i(w)$ $(i = 1, 2, \ldots, n)$.

1.6.2 Practical Example

Example 1.12 Consider a purchase fighter problem, there are four types of fighters to choose from. According to the performances and costs of fighters, the decision maker considers the following six indices (attributes) [96]: (1) u_1: maximum speed (Ma); (2) u_2: flight range (10^3km); (3) u_3: maximum load (10^4lb, where 1 lb=0.45359237 kg); (4) u_4: purchase expense (10^6\$); (5) u_5: reliability (ten-mark system); (6) u_6: sensitivity (ten-mark system). The performances of all the fighters are listed in Table 1.16.

In the above indices, u_4 is of cost type, and the others are of benefit. Now we use the method of Sect. 1.6.1 to find the desirable fighter, which needs the following steps.

Step 1 Utilize Eqs. (1.2) and (1.3) to normalize A into the matrix R, listed in Table 1.17.

Step 2 Get the following matrix using Eq. (1.14):

$$\dot{R} = \begin{bmatrix} 0.235 & 0.188 & 0.253 & 0.240 & 0.250 & 0.346 \\ 0.294 & 0.337 & 0.228 & 0.203 & 0.150 & 0.192 \\ 0.212 & 0.250 & 0.266 & 0.293 & 0.350 & 0.269 \\ 0.259 & 0.225 & 0.253 & 0.264 & 0.250 & 0.192 \end{bmatrix}$$

Table 1.17 Decision matrix R

	u_1	u_2	u_3	u_4	u_5	u_6
x_1	0.800	0.556	0.952	0.818	0.714	1.000
x_2	1.000	1.000	0.857	0.692	0.429	0.556
x_3	0.720	0.741	1.000	1.000	1.000	0.778
x_4	0.880	0.667	0.952	0.900	0.714	0.556

Step 3 Calculate the information entropy corresponding to the attribute u_j by using Eq. (1.15):

$$E_1 = 0.9947,\ \ E_2 = 0.9832,\ \ E_3 = 0.9989$$

$$E_4 = 0.9936,\ \ E_5 = 0.9703,\ \ E_6 = 0.9768$$

Step 4 Derive the weight vector of attributes from Eq. (1.16):

$$w = (0.0642, 0.2036, 0.0133, 0.0776, 0.3600, 0.2812)$$

Step 5 Obtain the overall attribute value $z_i(w)$ of the alternative x_j from Eq. (1.12):

$$z_1(w) = 0.7789,\ \ z_2(w) = 0.6437,\ \ z_3(w) = 0.8668,\ \ z_4(w) = 0.6882$$

Step 6 Rank and select the alternatives $x_i (i = 1, 2, 3, 4)$ according to $z_i(w)$ $(i = 1, 2, 3, 4)$:

$$x_3 \succ x_1 \succ x_4 \succ x_2$$

and thus, the best alternative is x_3.

1.7 MADM Method with Preference Information on Alternatives

The complexity and uncertainty of objective things and the active participation of decision maker result in the MADM problems with preference information on alternatives, which have been receiving more and more attention from researchers. In this section, we introduce three methods for MADM in which the decision maker has preferences on alternatives.

1.7.1 Preliminaries

Preference relation is one of the most common representation formats of information used in the decision making problems. The most widely used preference relation is called multiplicative preference relation which was first introduced by Saaty [69]:

Definition 1.7 [69] A multiplicative preference relation H on the set X is defined as a reciprocal matrix $H = (h_{ij})_{n\times m} \in X \times X$ under the condition:

$$h_{ij}h_{ji} = 1, \quad h_{ii} = 1, \quad h_{ij} > 0, \quad i, j = 1, 2, \ldots, n$$

where h_{ij} is interpreted as the ratio of the preference intensity of the alternative x_i to that of x_j. In particular, $h_{ij} = 1$ implies indifference between the alternatives x_i and x_j; $h_{ij} > 1$ indicates that the alternative x_i is preferred to the alternative x_j, the greater h_{ij}, the stronger the preference intensity of the alternative x_i over x_j; $h_{ij} < 1$ means that the alternative x_j is preferred to the alternative x_i, the smaller h_{ij}, the greater the preference intensity of the alternative x_j over x_i.

Up to now, fruitful research results have been achieved on the theory and applications about multiplicative preference relations, the interested readers may refer to the documents [25, 35, 43, 69–83, 91, 93, 97–101, 130, 136, 138, 154–166].

Table 1.18 lists four types of reciprocal scales [98]. Since all preference relations constructed by using these four types of reciprocal scales satisfy Definition 1.7, and then they are all multiplicative preference relations.

Table 1.18 Four types of reciprocal scales

1–9 scale	Exponential scale	10/10–18/2 scale	9/9–9/1 scale	Meaning
1	a^0	10/10	9/9	The *i*th and *j*th alternatives contribute equally to the objective
3	a^2	12/8	9/7	Experience and judgment slightly favor the *i*th alternative over the *j*th one
5	a^4	14/6	9/5	Experience and judgment obviously favor the *i*th alternative over the *j*th one
7	a^6	16/4	9/3	The *i*th alternative is strongly favored and its dominance demonstrated in practice
9	a^8	18/2	9/1	The evidence favoring the *i*th alternative over the *j*th one is of the highest possible order of affirmation

Table 1.19 Three types of complementary scales

0–1 scale	0.1–0.9 five scale	0.1–0.9 nine scale	Meaning
0	0.1	0.1	The evidence favoring the *j*th alternative over the *i*th one is of the highest possible order of affirmation
		0.138	The *i*th alternative is strongly favored and its dominance demonstrated in practice
	0.3	0.325	Experience and judgment obviously favor the *j*th alternative over the *i*th one
		0.439	Experience and judgment slightly favor the *j*th alternative over the *i*th one
0.5	0.5	0.5	The *i*th and *j*th alternatives contribute equally to the objective
		0.561	Experience and judgment slightly favor the *i*th alternative over the *j*th one
	0.7	0.675	Experience and judgment obviously favor the *i*th alternative over the *j*th one
		0.862	The *i*th alternative is strongly favored and its dominance demonstrated in practice
1	0.9	0.9	The evidence favoring the -th alternative over the *j*th one is of the highest possible order of affirmation

2, 4, 6, and 8 denote intermediate values between the two adjacent judgments in the 1–9 scale. If the alternative i has one of the above numbers assigned to it when compared with the alternative j, then the jth one has the reciprocal value when compared with the alternative i, i.e., $h_{ji} = 1/h_{ij}$.

Definition 1.8 A fuzzy preference relation B on the set X is represented by a complementary matrix $B = (b_{ij})_{n\times n} \subset X \times X$, with $b_{ij} + b_{ji} = 1$, $b_{ii} = 0.5$, $b_{ij} > 0$, $i = 1, 2, \ldots, n$, where b_{ij} denotes the preference degree of the alternative x_i over x_j. Especially, $b_{ij} = 0.5$ indicates indifference between the alternatives x_i and x_j; $b_{ij} > 0.5$ indicates that the alternative x_i is preferred to x_j, the larger b_{ij}, the greater the preference degree of the alternative x_i over x_j, $b_{ij} < 0.5$ indicates that the alternative x_j is preferred to the alternative x_i, the smaller b_{ij}, the greater the preference degree of the alternative x_j over x_i.

Recently, much more attention has been paid to fuzzy preference relations. The interested readers may refer the related literature [11–13, 30, 32, 44, 50, 58, 62, 63, 67, 68, 88, 94, 98, 117, 118, 121, 135, 137, 140, 142].

Table 1.19 lists three types of complementary scales [98]. Since all preference relations constructed by using these three types of complementary scales satisfy Definition 1.8, and then they are all fuzzy preference relations.

0.2, 0.4, 0.6, and 0.8 denote intermediate values between the two adjacent judgments in the 0.1–0.9 scale. If the alternative *i* has one of the above numbers assigned to it when compared with the alternative j, then the jth one has the complementary value when compared with the alternative i, i.e., $b_{ji}=1-b_{ij}$.

1.7.2 Decision Making Method

1. **The situation where the preference information on alternatives is a multiplicative preference relation** [129]

For a MADM problem, let $A=(a_{ij})_{n\times m}(a_{ij}>0)$. In general, there are benefit attributes and cost attributes. In order to measure all attributes in dimensionless units and to facilitate inter-attribute comparisons, we can utilize Eqs. (1.2) and (1.3) to normalize each expected attribute value a_{ij} in the matrix A into a corresponding element in the matrix $R=(r_{ij})_{n\times m}$. The overall attribute value $z_i(w)$ of the alternative x_i can be derived by using Eq. (1.12).

Suppose that the decision maker uses a reciprocal scale to compare each pair of the alternatives $x_i(i=1,2,\ldots,n)$, and then constructs a multiplicative preference relation $H=(h_{ij})_{n\times n}$. In order to make the decision information uniform, we utilize the following transformation function to transform the overall attribute values $z_i(w)$ $(i=1,2,\ldots,n)$ of all the alternatives $x_i(i=1,2,\ldots,n)$ into the multiplicative preference relation $\bar{H}=(\bar{h}_{ij})_{n\times n}$, where

$$\bar{h}_{ij}=\frac{z_i(w)}{z_j(w)}=\frac{\sum_{k=1}^{m} r_{ik}w_k}{\sum_{k=1}^{m} r_{jk}w_k},\quad i,j=1,2,\ldots,n \tag{1.17}$$

If $H=\bar{H}$, i.e., $h_{ij}=\bar{h}_{ij}$, for all $i,j=1,2,\ldots,n$, then

$$h_{ij}=\frac{z_i(w)}{z_j(w)}=\frac{\sum_{k=1}^{m} r_{ik}w_k}{\sum_{k=1}^{m} r_{jk}w_k},\quad i,j=1,2,\ldots,n \tag{1.18}$$

or

$$h_{ij}\sum_{k=1}^{m} r_{jk}w_k=\sum_{k=1}^{m} r_{ik}w_k,\quad i,j=1,2,\ldots,n \tag{1.19}$$

In this case, we can utilize the priority methods for multiplicative preference relations to derive the priority vector of H, and based on which the alternatives can be ranked and then selected [4, 15, 17, 33, 37, 49, 91, 99, 138, 155].

However, in the general case, there exists a difference between the multiplicative preference relation $H=(h_{ij})_{n\times n}$ and $\bar{H}=(\bar{h}_{ij})_{n\times n}$, i.e., Eq. (1.19) generally does not hold, and thus, we introduce a linear deviation function:

$$f_{ij}(w)=h_{ij}\sum_{k=1}^{m}r_{jk}w_k-\sum_{k=1}^{m}r_{ik}w_k=\sum_{k=1}^{m}(h_{ij}r_{jk}-r_{ik})w_k,\quad i,j=1,2,\ldots,n \tag{1.20}$$

Obviously, to get a reasonable weight vector w of attributes, the above deviation values should be as small as possible. Thus, we establish the following optimization model:

$$(\mathbf{M\text{-}1.2})\begin{cases}\min F(w)=\sum_{i=1}^{n}\sum_{j=1}^{n}f_{ij}^2(w)=\sum_{i=1}^{n}\sum_{j=1}^{n}\left[\sum_{k=1}^{m}(h_{ij}r_{jk}-r_{ik})w_k\right]^2\\ s.t.\ w_j\geq 0,\ j=1,2,\ldots,m,\ \sum_{j=1}^{m}w_j=1\end{cases}$$

To solve the model (M-1.2), we construct the Lagrange function:

$$L(w,\zeta)=F(w)+2\zeta\left(\sum_{j=1}^{m}w_j-1\right)$$

where ζ is the Lagrange multiplier.

Differentiating $L(w,\zeta)$ with respect to $w_l(l=1,2,\ldots,m)$, and setting these partial derivatives equal to zero, i.e., $\frac{\partial L(w,\zeta)}{\partial w_l}=0, l=1,2,\ldots,m$, the following set of equations is obtained:

$$\sum_{i=1}^{n}\sum_{j=1}^{n}\left[\sum_{k=1}^{n}2(h_{ij}r_{jk}-r_{ik})w_k\right](h_{ij}r_{jl}-r_{il})+2\zeta=0,\quad l=1,2,\ldots,m \tag{1.21}$$

i.e.,

$$\sum_{k=1}^{n}\left[\sum_{i=1}^{n}\sum_{j=1}^{n}(h_{ij}r_{jk}-r_{ik})(h_{ij}r_{jl}-r_{il})\right]w_k+\zeta=0,\quad l=1,2,\ldots,m \tag{1.22}$$

If we let $e_m=(1,1,\ldots,1)$ and $Q=(q_{kl})_{m\times m}$, where

$$q_{kl}=\sum_{i=1}^{n}\sum_{j=1}^{n}(h_{ij}r_{jk}-r_{ik})(h_{ij}r_{jl}-r_{il}),\quad l,k=1,2,\ldots,m \tag{1.23}$$

then Eq. (1.22) can be transformed into the following matrix form:

$$Qw^T=-\zeta e_m^T \tag{1.24}$$

Also transforming $\sum_{j=1}^{m}w_j=1$ into the vector form, then

$$e_m w^T = 1 \tag{1.25}$$

where T denotes "transposition".

Combining Eqs. (1.24) and (1.25), we get the optimal solution:

$$w^* = \frac{Q^{-1}e_m^T}{e_m Q^{-1} e_m^T} \tag{1.26}$$

and Q is a positive definite matrix (see Theorem 1.16).

If $w^* \geq 0$, whose elements are greater than or equal to zero, then combining Eqs. (1.26) and (1.12), we obtain the overall attribute values, based on which all the alternatives $x_i (i = 1, 2, \dots, n)$ are ranked and then selected. If $w^* < 0$ (whose elements are less than zero), then we can utilize the quadratic programming method [39] to solve the model (M-1.2) so as to get the overall attribute values, by which the alternatives can be ranked.

Theorem 1.16 If $H \neq \bar{H}$, then Q^{-1} exists, and Q is a positive definite matrix.

Proof

$$\begin{aligned} wQw^T &= \sum_{i=1}^{n}\sum_{j=1}^{n}\sum_{k=1}^{m}(h_{ij}r_{jk} - r_{ik})^2 w_k^2 + \sum_{i=1}^{n}\sum_{j=1}^{n}\sum_{k=1,k\neq l}^{m}(h_{ij}r_{jk} - r_{ik})(h_{ij}r_{jl} - r_{il})w_k w_l \\ &= \sum_{i=1}^{n}\sum_{j=1}^{n}\left[\sum_{k=1}^{m}(h_{ij}r_{jk} - r_{ik})w_k\right]^2 \\ &= \sum_{i=1}^{n}\sum_{j=1}^{n} f_{ij}^2(w) \end{aligned}$$

and $H \neq \bar{H}$, thus when $w \neq 0$ (at least one of its elements is not zero), $wQw^T > 0$ always holds. Also since Q is a symmetric matrix, then according to the definition of quadratic form, we can see that Q is a positive definite matrix. It follows from the property of positive definite matrix that Q is an invertible matrix, and thus, Q^{-1} exists.

Example 1.13 A customer wants to buy a house, and four alternatives $x_i (i = 1, 2, 3, 4)$ are available. The customer evaluates the alternatives by using four indices (attributes) [29]: (1) u_1: house price (10,000$); (2) u_2: residential area (m^2); (3) u_3: the distance between the place of work and house (km); (4) u_4: natural environment, where u_2 and u_4 are of benefit type, while u_1 and u_3 are of cost type. The weight information about attributes is completely unknown, and the corresponding decision matrix is listed in Table 1.20.

Now we utilize the method of Sect. 1.7.2 to derive the best alternatives, which needs the following steps:

Step 1 Utilize Eqs. (1.2) and (1.3) to normalize the decision matrix A into the matrix R (Table 1.21).

Table 1.20 Decision matrix A

	u_1	u_2	u_3	u_4
x_1	3.0	100	10	7
x_2	2.5	80	8	5
x_3	1.8	50	20	11
x_4	2.2	70	12	9

Table 1.21 Decision matrix R

	u_1	u_2	u_3	u_4
x_1	0.600	1.000	0.800	0.636
x_2	0.720	0.800	1.000	0.455
x_3	1.000	0.500	0.400	1.000
x_4	0.818	0.700	0.667	0.818

Step 2 Without loss of generality, assume that the decision maker uses the 1–9 scale to compare each pair of the alternatives $x_i (i = 1,2,3,4)$, and then constructs the multiplicative preference relation:

$$H = (h_{ij})_{4\times4} = \begin{pmatrix} 1 & 2 & \frac{1}{4} & \frac{1}{5} \\ \frac{1}{2} & 1 & \frac{1}{2} & \frac{1}{3} \\ 4 & 2 & 1 & \frac{1}{2} \\ 5 & 3 & 2 & 1 \end{pmatrix}$$

then by using Eq. (1.22), we get the weight vector of attributes:

$$w = (0.1247, 0.1648, 0.3266, 0.3839)$$

Step 3 Derive the overall attribute values $z_i(w)(i = 1,2,3,4)$ of all the alternatives $x_i (i = 1,2,3,4)$:

$$z_1(w) = 0.7451, \quad z_2(w) = 0.7229, \quad z_3(w) = 0.7216, \quad z_4(w) = 0.7492$$

from which we get the ranking of the alternatives:

$$x_4 \succ x_1 \succ x_2 \succ x_3$$

and thus, the best alternative is x_4.

2. **The situation where the preference information on alternatives is a fuzzy preference relation** [112]

Assume that the decision maker compares each pair of the alternatives $x_i (i = 1,2,\ldots,n)$ by using the complementary scales, and then constructs a fuzzy preference relation $B=(b_{ij})_{n\times n}$. To make the decision information uniform, we utilize the following linear transformation function to transform the overall attribute values of all the alternatives $x_i (i=1,2,\dots,n)$ into a fuzzy preference relation $\bar{B}=(\bar{b}_{ij})_{n\times n}$, where

$$\bar{b}_{ij}=\frac{1}{2}[1+z_i(w)-z_j(w)]$$
$$=\frac{1}{2}\left[1+\sum_{k=1}^{m} r_{ik}w_k-\sum_{k=1}^{m} r_{jk}w_k\right]$$
$$=\frac{1}{2}\left[1+\sum_{k=1}^{m}(r_{ik}-r_{jk})w_k\right],\quad i,j=1,2\dots,n \tag{1.27}$$

It is clear that $\bar{b}_{ij}+\bar{b}_{ji}=1$, $\bar{b}_{ii}=0.5$, $\bar{b}_{ij}\ge 0$, $i,j=1,2,\dots,n$.

In the general case, there is an indifference between the fuzzy preference relation $B=(b_{ij})_{n\times n}$ and $\bar{B}=(\bar{b}_{ij})_{n\times n}$, and then here we introduce a linear deviation function:

$$f_{ij}=b_{ij}-\bar{b}_{ij}=b_{ij}-\frac{1}{2}\left[1+\sum_{k=1}^{m}(r_{ik}-r_{jk})w_k\right]$$
$$=\frac{1}{2}\left[\sum_{k=1}^{m}(r_{ik}-r_{jk})w_k-(2b_{ij}-1)\right],\quad i,\ j=1,2,\dots,n \tag{1.28}$$

Clearly, to derive a reasonable vector of attribute weights, $w=(w_1,w_2,\dots,w_m)$, the deviation above should be as small as possible, and as a result, we can establish the following optimization model:

$$(\textbf{M-1.3})\quad \begin{cases} \min F(w)=\sum_{i=1}^{n}\sum_{j=1}^{n} f_{ij}^2=\frac{1}{4}\sum_{i=1}^{n}\sum_{j=1}^{n}\left[\sum_{k=1}^{m}(r_{ik}-r_{jk})w_k+(2b_{ij}-1)\right]^2 \\ s.t.\ \ w_j\ge 0,\ j=1,2,\dots,m,\ \sum_{j=1}^{m} w_j=1. \end{cases}$$

To solve the model (M-1.3), we construct the Lagrange function:

$$L(w,\zeta)=F(w)+2\zeta\left(\sum_{j=1}^{m} w_j-1\right)$$

where ζ is the Lagrange multiplier.

Differentiating $L(w,\zeta)$ with respect to $w_l (l=1,2,\ldots,m)$, and setting these partial derivatives equal to zero, i.e., $\frac{\partial L(w,\zeta)}{\partial w_l}=0, l=1,2,\ldots,m$, the following set of equations is obtained:

$$\frac{1}{2}\sum_{i=1}^{n}\sum_{j=1}^{n}\left[\sum_{k=1}^{m}(r_{ik}-r_{jk})w_k-(2b_{ij}-1)\right](r_{il}-r_{jl})+\frac{1}{2}\zeta=0,\ l=1,2,\ldots,m \tag{1.29}$$

i.e.,

$$\sum_{k=1}^{m}\left[\sum_{i=1}^{n}\sum_{j=1}^{n}(r_{ik}-r_{jk})(r_{il}-r_{jl})\right]w_k=\sum_{i=1}^{n}\sum_{j=1}^{n}(1-2b_{ij})(r_{il}-r_{jl})-\zeta,\ l=1,2,\ldots,m \tag{1.30}$$

If we let $e_m=(1,1,\ldots,1)$, $\overline{g}_m=(g_1,g_2,\ldots,g_m)$, $Q=(q_{lk})_{m\times m}$, where

$$g_l=\sum_{i=1}^{n}\sum_{j=1}^{n}(1-2b_{ij})(r_{il}-r_{jl}),\ l=1,2,\ldots,m$$

and

$$q_{lk}=\sum_{i=1}^{n}\sum_{j=1}^{n}(r_{ik}-r_{jk})(r_{il}-r_{jl}),\ l,k=1,2,\ldots,m \tag{1.31}$$

then Eq. (1.30) can be transformed into the following form:

$$Qw^T=\overline{g}_m^T-\zeta e_m^T \tag{1.32}$$

Changing $\sum_{j=1}^{m}w_j=1$ into the vector form, then we have

$$e_m w^T=1 \tag{1.33}$$

Combining Eqs. (1.32) and (1.33), we get the optimal solution:

$$w^*=Q^{-1}(\overline{g}_m^T-\zeta e_m^T) \tag{1.34}$$

where

$$\zeta=\frac{e_m Q^{-1}\overline{g}_m^T-1}{e_m Q^{-1}\overline{g}_m^T} \tag{1.35}$$

and Q is a positive definite matrix (see Theorem 1.17).

If $w^*\geq 0$, then we bring Eq. (1.34) into Eq. (1.12), and get the overall attribute values, by which we rank and select the given alternatives. Especially, if for any i, j, $\sum_{k=1}^{m} r_{ik} w_k = \sum_{k=1}^{m} r_{jk} w_k$, i.e., the overall attribute values of all the alternatives are the same, then this indicates that all the alternatives have no difference.

If $w^* < 0$, then we can utilize the quadratic programming method [39] to solve the model (M-1.3) so as to get the overall attribute values, by which the alternatives can be ranked.

Theorem 1.17 If the importance degrees of at least one pair of alternatives are different, then Q^{-1} exists, and Q is a positive definite matrix.

Proof Since

$$
\begin{aligned}
wQw^T &= \sum_{i=1}^{n}\sum_{j=1}^{n}\sum_{k=1}^{m}(r_{ik} - r_{jk})^2 w_k^2 + \sum_{i=1}^{n}\sum_{j=1}^{n}\sum_{k=1,k\neq l}^{m}(r_{ik} - r_{jk})(r_{il} - r_{jl}) w_k w_l \\
&= \sum_{i=1}^{n}\sum_{j=1}^{n}\left[\sum_{k=1}^{m}(r_{ik} - r_{jk}) w_k\right]^2 \\
&= \sum_{i=1}^{n}\sum_{j=1}^{n}\left[\sum_{k=1}^{m} r_{ik} w_k - \sum_{k=1}^{m} r_{jk} w_k\right]^2 \\
&= \sum_{i=1}^{n}\sum_{j=1}^{n}\left[z_i(w) - z_j(w)\right]^2
\end{aligned}
$$

If there exists at least a pair (i, j), and when $i \neq j$, $z_i(w) \neq z_j(w)$, i.e., if the importance degrees of at least one pair of alternatives are different (it can be seen from Eq. (1.12)), then $wQw^T > 0$ holds for $w = (w_1, w_2, \ldots, w_m) \neq 0$. Also since Q is symmetrical matrix, then according to the definition of quadratic form, we know that Q is a positive definite matrix. By the property of the positive definite matrix, it can be seen that Q is an invertible matrix, and thus, Q^{-1} exists.

Example 1.14 In order to develop new products, there are five investment projects $x_i (i = 1, 2, 3, 4, 5)$ to choose from. A decision maker is invited to evaluate these projects under the attributes: (1) u_1: investment amount (10^5\$); (2) expected net-profit amount (10^5 \$); (3) u_3: venture profit amount (10^5\$); and (4) u_4: venture loss amount (10^5\$). The evaluated attribute values of all the projects $x_i (i = 1, 2, 3, 4, 5)$ are listed in Table 1.22.

Among the attributes $u_j (j = 1, 2, 3, 4)$, u_2 and u_3 are of benefit type, while u_1 and u_4 are of cost type. The weight information is completely unknown.

In what follows, we utilize the method above to rank and select the investment projects:

Step 1 Utilize Eqs. (1.2) and (1.3) to normalize the decision matrix A into the matrix R, listed in Table 1.23.

Step 2 Suppose that the decision maker uses the 0.1–0.9 scale to compare each pair of the investment projects, and constructs the construct fuzzy preference relation:

Table 1.22 Decision matrix A

	u_1	u_2	u_3	u_4
x_1	5.20	5.20	4.73	0.473
x_2	10.08	6.70	5.71	1.599
x_3	5.25	4.20	3.82	0.473
x_4	9.72	5.25	5.54	1.313
x_5	6.60	3.75	3.30	0.803

Table 1.23 Decision matrix R

	u_1	u_2	u_3	u_4
x_1	1	0.776	0.828	1
x_2	0.516	1	1	0.296
x_3	0.990	0.627	0.669	1
x_4	0.535	0.784	0.970	0.360
x_5	0.788	0.560	0.578	0.589

$$B = \begin{pmatrix} 0.5 & 0.6 & 0.5 & 0.9 & 0.7 \\ 0.4 & 0.5 & 0.4 & 0.7 & 0.5 \\ 0.5 & 0.6 & 0.5 & 0.7 & 0.2 \\ 0.1 & 0.3 & 0.3 & 0.5 & 0.1 \\ 0.3 & 0.5 & 0.8 & 0.9 & 0.5 \end{pmatrix}$$

based on which we utilize Eq. (1.34) to get the vector of attribute weights:

$$w = (0.2014, 0.1973, 0.5893, 0.0120)$$

Step 3 Based on the weight vector w, we use Eq. (1.12) to derive the overall attribute values $z_i(w)$ of all the investment projects $x_i (i = 1,2,3,4,5)$:

$$z_1(w) = 0.8544, \quad z_2(w) = 0.8941, \quad z_3(w) = 0.7293$$
$$z_4(w) = 0.8384, \quad z_5(w) = 0.6169$$

from which we get the ranking of the projects:

$$x_2 \succ x_1 \succ x_4 \succ x_3 \succ x_5$$

then the best project is x_2.

3. The situation where the preferences on alternatives are utility values
Assume that the decision maker provides his/her preference over the alternative x_i by using of the utility value ϑ_i, where $\vartheta_i \in [0,1]$. The closer ϑ_i to the value 1, the more the decision maker prefers the alternative x_i. Here, the attribute value r_{ij} of the normalized matrix $R = (r_{ij})_{n\times m}$ can be regarded as the objective preference value over the alternative x_i under the attribute u_j.

Due to the restrictions of various conditions, there exist some differences between the subjective preferences of the decision maker and the objective preferences. To make the decision result more reasonable, the optimal weight vector w should be determined so as to make the total deviations between the subjective preferences of the decision maker and the objective preferences (attribute values) as small as possible. As a result, we establish the following optimization model:

$$
(\mathbf{M\text{-}1.4})\quad \begin{cases} \min F(w)=\sum_{i=1}^{n}\sum_{j=1}^{m}\left[(r_{ij}-\vartheta_i)w_j\right]^2=\sum_{i=1}^{n}\sum_{j=1}^{m}(r_{ij}-\vartheta_i)^2 w_j^2 \\ s.t.\quad w_j\ge 0,\ j=1,2,\ldots,m,\ \sum_{j=1}^{m}w_j=1 \end{cases}
$$

To solve the model (M-1.4), we construct the Lagrange function:

$$
L(w,\zeta)=\sum_{i=1}^{n}\sum_{j=1}^{m}(r_{ij}-\vartheta_i)^2 w_j^2+2\zeta\left(\sum_{j=1}^{m}w_j-1\right)
$$

where ζ is the Lagrange multiplier.

Differentiating $L(w,\zeta)$ with respect to $w_j\,(j=1,2,\ldots,m)$ and ζ, and setting these partial derivatives equal to zero, i.e.,

$$
\begin{cases} \dfrac{\partial L}{\partial w_j}=2\sum_{i=1}^{n}(r_{ij}-\vartheta_i)^2 w_j+2\zeta=0, \quad j=1,2,\ldots,m \\ \dfrac{\partial L}{\partial \zeta}=\sum_{j=1}^{m}w_j-1=0 \end{cases}
$$

Then

$$
\begin{cases} w_j=-\dfrac{\zeta}{\sum_{i=1}^{n}(r_{ij}-\vartheta_i)^2}, \quad j=1,2,\ldots,m & (1.36) \\ \sum_{j=1}^{m}w_j=1 & (1.37) \end{cases}
$$

based on which we get

$$
\zeta=-\frac{1}{\sum_{j=1}^{m}\dfrac{1}{\sum_{i=1}^{n}(r_{ij}-\vartheta)^2}} \tag{1.38}
$$

Table 1.24 Decision matrix R

	u_1	u_2	u_3	u_4	u_5	u_6
x_1	0.95	0.90	0.93	0.85	0.91	0.95
x_2	0.90	0.88	0.85	0.92	0.93	0.91
x_3	0.92	0.95	0.96	0.84	0.87	0.94
x_4	0.89	0.93	0.88	0.94	0.92	0.90
x_5	0.93	0.91	0.90	0.89	0.92	0.95

and it follows from Eqs. (1.36) and (1.38) that

$$w_j = \frac{1}{\left(\sum_{j=1}^{m} \frac{1}{\sum_{i=1}^{n} (r_{ij} - \vartheta)^2} \right) \left(\sum_{i=1}^{n} (r_{ij} - \vartheta_i \right)^2}, \quad j = 1, 2, \ldots, m \tag{1.39}$$

After deriving the optimal weight vector, we utilize Eq. (1.12) to calculate the overall attribute values $z_i(w)(i = 1, 2, \ldots, n)$, from which the alternatives $x_i (i = 1, 2, \ldots, n)$ can be ranked and then selected.

Example 1.15 A practical use of the developed approach involves the evaluation of cadres for tenure and promotion in a unit. The attributes which are considered here in evaluation of five candidates $x_i (i = 1, 2, 3, 4, 5)$ are: (1) u_1: moral level; (2) u_2: work attitude; (3) u_3: working style; (4) u_4: literacy level and knowledge structure; (5) u_5: leadership ability; and (6) u_6: exploration capacity. The weight information about the attributes $u_j (j = 1, 2, \ldots, 6)$ is completely unknown, and the evaluation information on the candidates $x_i (i = 1, 2, 3, 4, 5)$ with respect to the attributes $u_j (i = 1, 2, \ldots, 6)$ is characterized by membership degrees, which are contained in the normalized decision matrix R, as shown in Table 1.24.

Assume that the decision maker provides his/her subjective preferences over the candidates $x_i (i = 1, 2, 3, 4, 5)$ as follows:

$$\vartheta_1 = 0.82, \quad \vartheta_2 = 0.85, \quad \vartheta_3 = 0.90, \quad \vartheta_4 = 0.75, \quad \vartheta_5 = 0.95$$

Then it follows from Eq. (1.39) that

$$w_1 = 0.1778, \quad w_2 = 0.1615, \quad w_3 = 0.2015$$
$$w_4 = 0.1441, \quad w_5 = 0.1565, \quad w_6 = 0.1586$$

based on which we utilize Eq. (1.12) to calculate the overall attribute values $z_i(w)$ $(i = 1, 2, 3, 4, 5)$:

$$z_1(w) = 0.9172, \quad z_2(w) = 0.8959, \quad z_3(w) = 0.9162,$$
$$z_4(w) = 0.9079, \quad z_5(w) = 0.9166$$

and thus, we can rank the candidates $x_i (i = 1,2,3,4,5)$ in descending order according to $z_i(w)$ (i = 1,2,3,4,5):

$$x_1 \succ x_5 \succ x_3 \succ x_4 \succ x_2$$

then the best candidate is x_1.

1.8 Consensus Maximization Model for Determining Attribute Weights in MAGDM [135]

1.8.1 Consensus Maximization Model

At the beginning, we give a brief introduction to a MAGDM problem. Given a finite set of alternatives, X, and a discrete set of attributes, U (whose weight vector $w = (w_1, w_2, \dots, w_m)$ is to be determined, where $w_i \ge 0$, $i = 1,2,\dots,m$, and $\sum_{i=1}^{m} w_i = 1$), additionally, a group of decision makers $d_k (k = 1,2,\dots,t)$ (whose weight vector is $\lambda = (\lambda_1, \lambda_2, \dots, \lambda_t)$, $\lambda_k \ge 0$, $k = 1,2,\dots,t$, and $\sum_{k=1}^{t} \lambda_k = 1$) is invited to participate in decision making process. There are t decision matrices $A_k = (a_{ij}^{(k)})_{n\times m}$ $(k = 1,2,\dots,t)$, where $a_{ij}^{(k)}$ is a positive attribute value provided by the decision maker d_k over the alternative x_i with respect to the attribute u_j. The formulas in Sect. 1.1.2 can be used to transform the decision matrix $A_k = (a_{ij}^{(k)})_{n\times m}$ into a normalized matrix $R_k = (r_{ij}^{(k)})_{n\times m}$ so as to measure all attributes in dimensionless units [48]:

The WA operator [38, 48] is a common tool used to fuse individual data. In order to get the group opinion, here we utilize the WA operator to aggregate all the individual normalized decision matrices $R_k = (r_{ij}^{(k)})_{n\times m}$ $(k = 1,2,\dots,t)$ into the collective normalized decision matrix $R = (r_{ij})_{n\times m}$, where

$$r_{ij} = \sum_{k=1}^{t} \lambda_k r_{ij}^{(k)}, \quad \text{for all } i = 1,2,\dots,n, \quad j = 1,2,\dots,m \tag{1.40}$$

If the group is of complete consensus, then each individual decision matrix should be equal to the collective decision matrix, i.e., $R_k = R$, for all $k = 1,2,\dots,t$, thus

$$r_{ij}^{(k)} = \sum_{k=1}^{t} \lambda_k r_{ij}^{(k)}, \quad \text{for all } k = 1,2,\dots,t, \quad i = 1,2,\dots,n,\ j = 1,2,\dots,m \tag{1.41}$$

and the weighted form of Eq. (1.41) is expressed as:

$$w_i r_{ij}^{(k)} = \sum_{k=1}^{t} \lambda_k w_i r_{ij}^{(k)}, \text{ for all } k = 1,2,\ldots,t,$$
$$i = 1,2,\ldots,n, \; j = 1,2,\ldots,m \tag{1.42}$$

However, Eq. (1.42) generally does not hold because the decision makers have own experiences, knowledge structures, and so forth. Consequently, we introduce a deviation variable $e_{ij}^{(k)}$ as:

$$e_{ij}^{(k)} = \left(w_i r_{ij}^{(k)} - \sum_{k=1}^{s} \lambda_k w_i r_{ij}^{(k)} \right)^2 = \left(r_{ij}^{(k)} - \sum_{k=1}^{s} \lambda_k r_{ij}^{(k)} \right)^2 w_i^2$$
$$\text{for all } k = 1,2,\ldots,t, \quad i = 1,2,\ldots,n, \quad j = 1, 2,\ldots,m \tag{1.43}$$

and construct the deviation function:

$$f(w) = \sum_{k=1}^{t} \sum_{i=1}^{n} \sum_{j=1}^{m} e_{ij}^{(k)} = \sum_{k=1}^{t} \sum_{i=1}^{n} \sum_{j=1}^{m} \left(r_{ij}^{(k)} - \sum_{k=1}^{t} \lambda_k r_{ij}^{(k)} \right)^2 w_i^2 \tag{1.44}$$

In group decision making, a desirable decision result should be reached with a high group consensus, that is, the difference between each individual opinion and the group opinion should be as small as possible by minimizing the deviation of each individual decision matrix and collective decision matrix. Motivated by this idea and the analysis above, we establish the following quadratic programming model [135]:

(M - 1.5)
$$f(\ ^*) = \min \sum_{k=1}^{t} \sum_{i=1}^{n} \sum_{j=1}^{m} \left(r_{ij}^{(k)} - \sum_{k=1}^{t} \lambda_k r_{ij}^{(k)} \right)^2 w_i^2$$
$$s.t. w_j \geq 0, \; j = 1,2,\ldots,n, \; \sum_{j=1}^{m} w_j = 1$$

To solve this model, we construct the Lagrange function:

$$L(w,\zeta) = \sum_{k=1}^{t} \sum_{i=1}^{n} \sum_{j=1}^{m} \left(r_{ij}^{(k)} - \sum_{k=1}^{t} \lambda_k r_{ij}^{(k)} \right)^2 w_j^2 - 2\zeta \left(\sum_{j=1}^{m} w_j - 1 \right) \tag{1.45}$$

where ζ is the Lagrange multiplier.

Differentiating Eq. (1.45) with respect to $w_j (j = 1,2,\ldots,m)$ and ζ, and setting these partial derivatives equal to zero, the following set of equations is obtained:

$$\frac{\partial L(w,\zeta)}{\partial w_j} = 2\sum_{k=1}^{t}\sum_{i=1}^{n}\left(r_{ij}^{(k)} - \sum_{k=1}^{t}\lambda_k r_{ij}^{(k)}\right)^2 w_j - 2\zeta = 0, \quad j = 1,2,\ldots,m \quad (1.46)$$

$$\frac{\partial L(w,\zeta)}{\partial \zeta} = \sum_{j=1}^{m} w_j - 1 = 0 \quad (1.47)$$

We simplify Eq. (1.46) as:

$$\sum_{k=1}^{t}\sum_{i=1}^{n}\left(r_{ij}^{(k)} - \sum_{k=1}^{t}\lambda_k r_{ij}^{(k)}\right)^2 w_j - \zeta = 0, \quad j = 1,2,\ldots,m \quad (1.48)$$

By Eq. (1.48), it follows that

$$w_j = \frac{\zeta}{\sum_{k=1}^{t}\sum_{i=1}^{n}\left(r_{ij}^{(k)} - \sum_{k=1}^{t}\lambda_k r_{ij}^{(k)}\right)^2}, \quad j = 1,2,\ldots,m \quad (1.49)$$

From Eqs. (1.47) and (1.49), it can be obtained that

$$\zeta = \frac{1}{\sum_{j=1}^{m}\frac{1}{\sum_{k=1}^{t}\sum_{i=1}^{n}\left(r_{ij}^{(k)} - \sum_{k=1}^{t}\lambda_k r_{ij}^{(k)}\right)^2}} \quad (1.50)$$

and thus, by Eqs. (14) and (15), we get

$$w_j^* = \frac{\frac{1}{\sum_{j=1}^{m}\frac{1}{\sum_{k=1}^{t}\sum_{i=1}^{n}\left(r_{ij}^{(k)} - \sum_{k=1}^{t}\lambda_k r_{ij}^{(k)}\right)^2}}}{\sum_{k=1}^{t}\sum_{i=1}^{n}\left(r_{ij}^{(k)} - \sum_{k=1}^{t}\lambda_k r_{ij}^{(k)}\right)^2}, \quad j = 1,2,\ldots,m \quad (1.51)$$

which is the optimal solution to the model (M-1.5). Especially, if the denominator of Eq. (1.51) is zero, then Eq. (1.41) holds, i.e., the group is of complete consensus, and thus each individual decision matrix R_k is equal to the collective decision matrix R. In this case, we stipulate that all the attributes are assigned equal weights.

Then, based on the collective decision matrix $R=(r_{ij})_{n\times m}$ and the optimal attribute weights $w_j^*\ (j=1,2,\ldots,m)$, we get the overall attribute value $z_i(w^*)$ of the alternative x_i by using the WA operator:

$$z_i(w^*)=\sum_{j=1}^{m} w_j^* r_{ij},\quad i=1,2,\ldots,n \tag{1.52}$$

where $w^*=(w_1^*,w_2^*,\ldots,w_n^*)$, and then by Eq. (1.52) we can rank all the alternatives $x_i(i=1,2,\ldots,n)$, and then select the best one.

1.8.2 Practical Example

Example 1.16 [135] A military unit is planning to purchase new artillery weapons and there are four feasible artillery weapons (alternatives) $x_i(i=1,2,3,4)$ to be selected. When making a decision, the attributes considered are as follows: (1) u_1: assault fire capability indices (m); (2) u_2: reaction capability indices (evaluated using 1–5 scale); (3) u_3: mobility indices (m); (4) u_4: survival ability indices (evaluated using 0–1 scale); and (5) u_5: cost ($). Among these five attributes, $u_j(j=1,2,3,4)$ are of benefit type; and u_5 is of cost type. An expert group which consists of three experts $d_k(k=1,2,3)$(whose weight vector is $\lambda=(0.4,0.3,0.3)$) has been set up to provide assessment information on $x_i(i=1,2,3,4)$. These experts evaluate the alternatives $x_i(i=1,2,3,4)$ with respect to the attributes $u_j(j=1,2,3,4,5)$, and construct three decision matrices $A_k=(a_{ij}^{(k)})_{4\times5}$ (see Tables 1.25, 1.26, and 1.27).

Since the attributes $u_j(j=1,2,3,4,5)$ have different dimension units, then we utilize Eqs. (1.2) and (1.3) to transform the decision matrices $A_k=(a_{ij}^{(k)})_{4\times5}$ $(k=1,2,3)$ into the normalized decision matrices $R_k=(r_{ij}^{(k)})_{4\times5}$ (k = 1,2,3) (see Tables 1.28, 1.29, and 1.30):

By Eq. (1.40) and the weight vector $\lambda=(0.4,0.3,0.3)$ of the experts $e_k(k=1,2,3)$, we aggregate all the individual normalized decision matrices $R_k=(r_{ij}^{(k)})_{4\times5}$ (k = 1,2,3) into the collective normalized decision matrix $R=(r_{ij})_{4\times5}$ (see Table 1.31).

Let the weight vector of the attributes $u_j(j=1,2,3,4,5)$ be $w=(w_1,w_2,w_3,w_4,w_5)$, then based on the decision information contained in Tables 1.28,1.29, 1.30, and 1.31 employ Eq. (1.51) to determine the optimal weight vector w^*, and get

$$w^*=(0.06,0.02,0.56,0.08,0.28) \tag{1.53}$$

and the corresponding optimal objective value $f(w^*)=0.004$.

Table 1.25 Decision matrix A_1

	u_1	u_2	u_3	u_4	u_5
x_1	26,000	3	19,000	0.8	15,000
x_2	70,000	4	16,000	0.3	28,000
x_3	50,000	2	17,000	0.7	25,000
x_4	45,000	1	28,000	0.5	16,000

Table 1.26 Decision matrix A_2

	u_1	u_2	u_3	u_4	u_5
x_1	27,000	4	18,000	0.7	16,000
x_2	60,000	3	17,000	0.4	27,000
x_3	55,000	2	15,000	0.8	26,000
x_4	40,000	2	29,000	0.4	15,000

Table 1.27 Decision matrix A_3

	u_1	u_2	u_3	u_4	u_5
x_1	28,000	3	20,000	0.7	17,000
x_2	60,000	4	18,000	0.4	26,000
x_3	60,000	3	16,000	0.7	27,000
x_4	50,000	2	30,000	0.4	18,000

Table 1.28 Normalized decision matrix R_1

	u_1	u_2	u_3	u_4	u_5
x_1	0.37	0.75	0.68	1.00	1.00
x_2	1.00	1.00	0.57	0.38	0.54
x_3	0.71	0.50	0.61	0.88	0.60
x_4	0.64	0.25	1.00	0.63	0.94

Table 1.29 Normalized decision matrix R_2

	u_1	u_2	u_3	u_4	u_5
x_1	0.45	1.00	0.62	0.88	0.94
x_2	1.00	0.75	0.59	0.50	0.56
x_3	0.92	0.50	0.52	1.00	0.58
x_4	0.67	50	1.00	0.50	1.00

Table 1.30 Normalized decision matrix R_3

	u_1	u_2	u_3	u_4	u_5
x_1	0.47	0.75	0.67	1.00	1.00
x_2	1.00	1.00	0.60	0.57	0.65
x_3	1.00	0.75	0.53	1.00	0.63
x_4	0.83	0.50	1.00	0.57	0.94

Table 1.31 Collective normalized decision matrix R

	u_1	u_2	u_3	u_4	u_5
x_1	0.42	0.83	0.66	0.96	0.98
x_2	1.00	0.93	0.59	0.47	0.58
x_3	0.86	0.58	0.56	0.95	0.60
x_4	0.71	0.40	1.00	0.57	0.96

Based on Eqs. (1.52), (1.53) and the collective normalized decision matrix $R = (r_{ij})_{4\times 5}$, we get the overall attribute values $z_i(w^*)\ (i = 1,2,3,4)$:

$$z_1(w^*) = 0.76,\quad z_2(w^*) = 0.60,\quad z_3(w^*) = 0.62,\quad z_4(w^*) = 0.93$$

and the ranking of the alternatives $x_i (i = 1,2,3,4)$:

$$x_4 \succ x_1 \succ x_3 \succ x_2$$

from which we get the best artillery weapon x_4.

Chapter 2
MADM with Preferences on Attribute Weights

For this type of problems, the decision makers cannot provide directly the attribute weights, but utilize a scale to compare each pair of alternatives, and then construct preference relations (in general, there are multiplicative preference relations and fuzzy preference relations). After that, some proper priority methods are used to derive the priority vectors of preference relations, from which the attribute weights can be obtained. The priority theory and methods of multiplicative preference relations have achieved fruitful research results. The investigation on the priority methods of fuzzy preference relations has also been receiving more and more attention recently. Considering the important role of the priority methods of fuzzy preference relations in solving the MADM problems in which the attribute values are interval numbers, in this chapter, we introduce mainly the priority theory and methods of fuzzy preference relations. Based on the WAA, CWA, WG and CWG operators, we also introduce some MADM methods, and illustrate these methods in detail with several practical examples.

2.1 Priority Methods for a Fuzzy Preference Relation

2.1.1 Translation Method for Priority of a Fuzzy Preference Relation

Definition 2.1 [88] Let $B = (b_{ij})_{n \times n}$ be a fuzzy preference relation, if

$$(b_{ik} - 0.5) + (b_{kj} - 0.5) = b_{ij} - 0.5,\ i, j, k = 1, 2, \ldots, n \tag{2.1}$$

i.e., $b_{ij} = b_{ik} - b_{jk} + 0.5,\ i, j, k = 1, 2, \ldots, n$, then B is called an additive consistent fuzzy preference relation.

Let G be the set of all fuzzy preference relations with n order. A n-dimension positive vector $w = (w_1, w_2, \ldots, w_n)$ is called a priority vector, each of the elements

Z.S. Xu, *Uncertain Multi-Attribute Decision Making*,
DOI 10.1007/978-3-662-45640-8_2

of w is the weight of an object (attribute or alternative). Let Λ be the set of all the priority vectors, where

$$\Lambda = \left\{ w = (w_1, w_2, \ldots, w_n) \mid w_j > 0, j = 1, 2, \ldots, n, \sum_{j=1}^{n} w_j = 1 \right\}$$

A priority method can be regarded as a mapping from G to Λ, denoted by $w = \Gamma(B)$, and w is the priority vector of the fuzzy preference relation B.

Definition 2.2 [93] A priority method is called of strong rank preservation, if $b_{ik} \geq b_{jk}$, then $w_i \geq w_j$, for any k, with $w_i = w_j$ if and only if $b_{ik} = b_{jk}$, for any k.

Definition 2.3 [105] A fuzzy preference relation $B = (b_{ij})_{n \times n}$ is called of rank transitivity, if the following two conditions are satisfied:

1. If $b_{ij} \geq 0.5$, then $b_{ij} \geq b_{jk}$, for all k;
2. If $b_{ij} = 0.5$, then $b_{ij} \geq b_{jk}$, for all k, or $b_{ij} \leq b_{jk}$, for all k.

Definition 2.4 [105] Let $\Gamma(\bullet)$ be a priority method, B be any fuzzy preference relation, $w = \Gamma(B)$. If $\Psi w^T = \Gamma(\Psi B \Psi^T)$, for any permutation matrix Ψ, then the priority method $\Gamma(\bullet)$ is called of permutation invariance.

Theorem 2.1 [22] For the fuzzy preference relation $B = (b_{ij})_{n \times n}$, let

$$b_i = \sum_{j=1}^{n} b_{ij}, \quad i = 1, 2, \ldots, n \tag{2.2}$$

which is the sum of all the elements in the i th line of B, and based on Eq. (2.2), we give the following mathematical transformation:

$$\bar{b}_{ij} = \frac{b_i - b_j}{a} + 0.5 \tag{2.3}$$

then the matrix $\bar{B} = (\bar{b}_{ij})_{n \times n}$ is called an additional consistent fuzzy preference relation.

In general, it is suitable to take $a = 2(n-1)$, which can be shown as follows [103]:

1. If we take the 0–1 scale, then the value range of the element $\bar{b}_{ij}$ of the matrix $\bar{B} = (\bar{b}_{ij})_{n \times n}$ is $0 \leq \bar{b}_{ij} \leq 1$, and combining Eq. (2.3), we get

$$a \geq 2(n-1) \tag{2.4}$$

2. If we take the 0.1–0.9 scale, then Eq. (2.4) also holds.

It is clear that the larger the value of a, the smaller the value range of $\bar{b}_{ij}$ derived from Eq. (2.3), and thus, the lower the closeness degree between the constructed additive consistent fuzzy preference relation and the original fuzzy preference relation (i.e., the less judgment information got from the original fuzzy preference relation). Thus, when a takes the smallest value $2(n-1)$, the additive consistent fuzzy preference relation constructed by using Eq. (2.3) can remain as much as possible the judgment information of the original fuzzy preference relation, and the deviations between the elements of these two fuzzy preference relations can also correspondingly reduce to the minimum. Obviously, this type of deviation is caused by the consistency improvement for the original fuzzy preference relation. For fuzzy preference relations with different orders, the value of a will change with the increase of the order n, and thus, it is more compatible with the practical situations. In addition, the additive consistent fuzzy preference relation derived by Eq. (2.3) is in accordance with the consistency of human decision thinking, and has good robustness (i.e., the sub-matrix derived by removing any line and the corresponding column is also an additive consistent fuzzy preference relation) and transitivity.

For the given fuzzy preference relation $B=(b_{ij})_{n\times n}$, we employ the transformation formula (2.3) to get the additive consistent fuzzy preference relation $\bar{B}=(\bar{b}_{ij})_{n\times n}$, after that, we can use the normalizing rank aggregation method to derive its priority vector.

Based on the idea above, in what follows, we introduce a formula for deriving the priority vector of a fuzzy preference relation.

Theorem 2.2 [103] Let $B=(b_{ij})_{n\times n}$ be a fuzzy preference relation, then we utilize Eq. (2.2) and the following mathematical transformation:

$$\bar{b}_{ij}=\frac{b_i-b_j}{2(n-1)}+0.5 \tag{2.5}$$

to get the matrix $\bar{B}=(\bar{b}_{ij})_{n\times n}$, based on which the normalizing rank aggregation method is used to derive the priority vector, which satisfies

$$w_i=\frac{\sum_{j=1}^{n}b_{ij}+\frac{n}{2}-1}{n(n-1)},\quad i=1,2,\ldots,n \tag{2.6}$$

This priority method is called the translation method for priority of a fuzzy preference relation.

Proof By Eqs. (2.1), (2.2) and (2.5), we get

$$w_i=\frac{\sum_{j=1}^{n}\bar{b}_{ij}}{\sum_{i=1}^{n}\sum_{j=1}^{n}\bar{b}_{ij}}=\frac{\sum_{j=1}^{n}\bar{b}_{ij}}{\sum_{1\le i<j\le n}(\bar{b}_{ij}+\bar{b}_{ji})+0.5n}$$

$$= \frac{\sum_{j=1}^{n} \overline{b}_{ij}}{\frac{n(n-1)}{2} + \frac{n}{2}} = \frac{\sum_{j=1}^{n} \overline{b}_{ij}}{\frac{n^2}{2}} = \frac{\sum_{j=1}^{n} \left[\frac{b_i - b_j}{2(n-1)} + 0.5 \right]}{\frac{n^2}{2}} = \frac{\sum_{j=1}^{n} \frac{b_i - b_j}{n-1} + n}{n^2}$$

$$= \frac{b_i + \frac{n}{2} - 1}{n(n-1)} = \frac{\sum_{j=1}^{n} b_{ij} + \frac{n}{2} - 1}{n(n-1)}$$

Theorem 2.3 [103] The translation method is of strong rank preservation.

Proof Let $w = (w_1, w_2, \ldots, w_n)$ be the priority vector of the fuzzy preference relation $B = (b_{ij})_{n \times n}$, then

$$w_i = \frac{\sum_{j=1}^{n} b_{ij} + \frac{n}{2} - 1}{n(n-1)}, \quad w_l = \frac{\sum_{j=1}^{n} b_{lj} + \frac{n}{2} - 1}{n(n-1)}$$

If $b_{ij} \geq b_{lj}$, for any j, then by the two formulas above, we can see $w_i \geq w_l$, with equality if and only $b_{ij} = b_{lj}$, for all j. Thus, the translation method is of strong rank preservation.

By Definition 2.3 and Theorem 2.3, we have

Theorem 2.4 [103] Let the fuzzy preference relation $B = (b_{ij})_{n \times n}$ be rank transitive. If $b_{ij} \geq 0.5$, then $w_i \geq w_l$; If $b_{ij} = 0.5$, then $w_i \geq w_l$ or $w_i \leq w_l$, where $w = (w_1, w_2, \ldots, w_n)$ is a priority vector derived by the translation method for the fuzzy preference relation B.

Theorem 2.5 [103] The translation method has the permutation invariance.

Proof Let $B = (b_{ij})_{n \times n}$ be a fuzzy preference relation, and let Ψ be a permutation matrix, such that $C = (c_{ij})_{n \times n} = \Psi B \Psi^T$, $w = (w_1, w_2, \ldots, w_n)$ and $v = (v_1, v_2, \ldots, v_n)$ be the priority vectors derived by the translation method for B and C, respectively. Then, after the permutation, the i th line of B becomes the l th line of C, the i th column of B becomes the l th column of C, and thus

$$w_i = \frac{\sum_{j=1}^{n} b_{ij} + \frac{n}{2} - 1}{n(n-1)} = \frac{\sum_{j=1}^{n} c_{lj} + \frac{n}{2} - 1}{n(n-1)} = v_l$$

which indicates that the translation method has the permutation invariance.

According to Theorem 2.2, we can know that the translation method has the following characteristics:

1. By using Eq. (2.6), the method can directly derive the priority vector from the original fuzzy preference relation.
2. The method can not only sufficiently utilize the desirable properties and judgment information of the additive consistent fuzzy preference relation, but also needs much less calculation than that of the other existing ones.
3. The method omits many unnecessary intermediate steps, and thus, it is very convenient to be used in practical applications.

However, the translation method also has the disadvantage that the differences among the elements of the derived priority vector are somewhat small, and thus, sometimes, are not easy to differentiate them.

2.1.2 *Least Variation Method for Priority of a Fuzzy Preference Relation*

From the viewpoint of optimization, i.e., from the angle of the additive consistent fuzzy preference relation constructed by the priority weights approaching the original fuzzy preference relation, in what follows, we introduce a least variation method for deriving the priority vector of a fuzzy preference relation.

Let $B=(b_{ij})_{n\times n}$ be a fuzzy preference relation, $w=(w_1,w_2,\ldots,w_n)$ be the priority vector of B, if

$$b_{ij}=w_i-w_j+0.5,\quad i,j=1,2,\ldots,n \tag{2.7}$$

then $b_{ij}=b_{il}-b_{jl}+0.5$, for any $l=1,2,\ldots,n$, and thus, $B=(b_{ij})_{n\times n}$ is an additive consistent fuzzy preference relation. If B is not an additive consistent fuzzy preference relation, then Eq. (2.7) usually does hold. As a result, we introduce a deviation element, i.e.,

$$f_{ij}=b_{ij}-(w_i-w_j+0.5),\quad i,j=1,2,\ldots,n$$

and construct a deviation function:

$$F(w)=\sum_{i=1}^{n}\sum_{j=1}^{n}f_{ij}^2=\sum_{i=1}^{n}\sum_{j=1}^{n}[b_{ij}-(w_i-w_j+0.5)]^2$$

A reasonable priority vector w^* should be determined so as to minimize $F(w)$, i.e.,

$$F(w^*)=\min_{w\in\Lambda}F(w)=\sum_{i=1}^{n}\sum_{j=1}^{n}[b_{ij}-(w_i-w_j+0.5)]^2$$

holds, we term this approach the least variation method for deriving the priority vector of a fuzzy preference relation. The following conclusion can be obtained for $F(w)$:

Theorem 2.6 [105] Let $B=(b_{ij})_{n\times n}$ be a fuzzy preference relation, then the priority vector $w=(w_1,w_2,\ldots,w_n)$ derived by the least variation method satisfies:

$$w_i=\frac{1}{n}\left(\sum_{j=1}^{n}b_{ij}+1-\frac{n}{2}\right),\quad i=1,2,\ldots,n \tag{2.8}$$

Proof We construct the Lagrange function:

$$L(w,\zeta)=F(w)+\zeta\left(\sum_{j=1}^{n}w_j-1\right)$$

where ζ is the Lagrange multiplier.

Differentiating $L(w,\zeta)$ with respect to $w_i(i=1,2,\ldots,n)$ and ζ, and setting these partial derivatives equal to zero, then

$$\sum_{j=1}^{n}2[b_{ij}-(w_i-w_j+0.5)](-1)+\zeta=0,\ i=1,2,\ldots,n$$

and simplifies it as follows:

$$-2\left[\sum_{j=1}^{n}b_{ij}-nw_i+1-\frac{n}{2}\right]+\zeta=0,\ i=1,2,\ldots,n \tag{2.9}$$

Summing both the sides of Eq. (2.9) with respect to $i=1,2,\ldots,n$, we have

$$-2\left[\sum_{i=1}^{n}\sum_{j=1}^{n}b_{ij}-\frac{n^2}{2}\right]+\zeta=0 \tag{2.10}$$

According to the property of fuzzy preference relation, we get

$$\sum_{i=1}^{n}\sum_{j=1}^{n}b_{ij}=\frac{n^2}{2} \tag{2.11}$$

Thus, bringing Eq. (2.10) into Eq. (2.11), it can be obtained that $\zeta=0$. Then we combine $\zeta=0$ with Eq. (2.9) to get Eq. (2.8), which completes the proof.

Similar to Theorems 2.3–2.5, we can derive the following result:

Theorem 2.7 [105] The least variation method is of strong rank preservation.

Theorem 2.8 [105] Let the fuzzy preference relation $B = (b_{ij})_{n \times n}$ be rank transitive. If $b_{ij} \geq 0.5$, then $w_i \geq w_l$; If $b_{ij} = 0.5$, then $w_i \geq w_l$ or $w_i \leq w_l$, where $w = (w_1, w_2, \ldots, w_n)$ is a priority vector derived by the least variation method for the fuzzy preference relation B.

Theorem 2.9 [105] The least variation method has the permutation invariance.

By using Eq. (2.8), we can derive the priority vector of a fuzzy preference relation. In many practical applications, we have found that if the judgments given by the decision maker are not in accordance with the practical situation, i.e., the fuzzy preference relation constructed by the decision maker is seriously inconsistent, then the value of $\sum_{j=1}^{n} b_{ij}$ maybe less than $\frac{n}{2} - 1$, which results in the case that $w_i \leq 0$. In such cases, we need to return the fuzzy preference relation to the decision maker for re-revaluation or we can utilize the consistency improving method to repair the fuzzy preference relation.

2.1.3 Least Deviation Method for Priority of a Fuzzy Preference Relation

From another viewpoint of optimization, i.e., from the angle of the multiplicative consistent fuzzy preference relation constructed by the priority weights approaching the original fuzzy preference relation, in what follows, we introduce a least deviation method for deriving the priority vector of a fuzzy preference relation.

2.1.3.1 Preliminaries

In the process of MADM, the decision maker compares each pair of attributes, and provides his/her judgment (preference):

1. If the decision maker uses the 1–9 scale [98] to express his/her preferences, and constructs the multiplicative preference relation $H = (h_{ij})_{n \times n}$, which has the following properties:

$$h_{ij} \in \left[\frac{1}{9}, 9\right], \quad h_{ji} = \frac{1}{h_{ij}}, \quad h_{ii} = 1, \quad i, j = 1, 2, \ldots, n$$

If $h_{ij} = h_{ik} h_{kj}$, $i, j, k = 1, 2, \ldots, n$, then $H = (h_{ij})_{n \times n}$ is called a consistent multiplicative preference relation [69, 93].

2. If the decision maker uses the 0.1–0.9 scale [98] to express his/her preferences, and constructs the fuzzy preference relation $B = (b_{ij})_{n \times n}$, which has the following properties:

$$b_{ij} \in [0.1, 0.9], \quad b_{ij} + b_{ji} = 1, \quad b_{ii} = 0.5, \quad i, j = 1, 2, \ldots, n$$

If $b_{ik} b_{kj} b_{ji} = b_{ki} b_{jk} b_{ij}$, $i, j, k = 1, 2, \ldots, n$, then $B = (b_{ij})_{n \times n}$ is called a multiplicative consistent fuzzy preference relation [63, 111].

Based on the multiplicative preference relation $H = (h_{ij})_{n \times n}$, we employ the transformation formula [98]:

$$b_{ij} = \frac{h_{ij}}{h_{ij} + 1}, \quad i, j = 1, 2, \ldots, n$$

to get the fuzzy preference relation $B = (b_{ij})_{n \times n}$. Based on the fuzzy preference relation $B = (b_{ij})_{n \times n}$, we employ the transformation formula [98]:

$$h_{ij} = \frac{b_{ij}}{1 - b_{ij}}, \quad i, j = 1, 2, \ldots, n$$

to get the multiplicative preference relation $H = (h_{ij})_{n \times n}$.

The following theorems can be proven easily:

Theorem 2.10 [98] Let $H = (h_{ij})_{n \times n}$ be a multiplicative preference relation, then the corresponding fuzzy preference relation $B = (b_{ij})_{n \times n}$ can be derived by using the following transformation formula:

$$b_{ij} = \frac{1}{1 + h_{ji}}, \quad i, j = 1, 2, \ldots, n \tag{2.12}$$

Theorem 2.11 [109] Let $B = (b_{ij})_{n \times n}$ be a fuzzy preference relation, then the corresponding multiplicative preference relation $H = (h_{ij})_{n \times n}$ can be derived by using the following transformation formula:

$$h_{ij} = \frac{b_{ij}}{b_{ji}}, \quad i, j = 1, 2, \ldots, n \tag{2.13}$$

Theorem 2.12 [109] If $H = (h_{ij})_{n \times n}$ is a consistent multiplicative preference relation, then the fuzzy preference relation $B = (b_{ij})_{n \times n}$ derived by using Eq. (2.12) is a multiplicative fuzzy preference relation.

Theorem 2.13 [109] If $B = (b_{ij})_{n \times n}$ is a multiplicative fuzzy preference relation, then the multiplicative preference relation $H = (h_{ij})_{n \times n}$ derived from Eq. (2.13) is a consistent multiplicative preference relation.

Definition 2.5 [109] Let $B=(b_{ij})_{n\times n}$ be a fuzzy preference relation, then $H=(h_{ij})_{n\times n}$ is called the transformation matrix of B, where $h_{ij}=\frac{b_{ij}}{b_{ji}}$, $i,j=1,2,\ldots,n$.

Since Eqs. (2.12) and (2.13) establish a close relation between two different types of preference information, and thus, they has great theoretical importance and wide application potential.

2.1.3.2 Main Results

Let $\gamma=(\gamma_1,\gamma_2,\ldots,\gamma_n)$ be the priority vector of the multiplicative preference relation $H=(h_{ij})_{n\times n}$, where $\gamma_j>0$, $j=1,2,\ldots,n$, and $\sum_{j=1}^{n}\gamma_j=1$, then when H is a consistent multiplicative preference relation, we have $h_{ij}=\frac{\gamma_i}{\gamma_j}$, $i,j=1,2,\ldots,n$. If we combine $h_{ij}=\frac{\gamma_i}{\gamma_j}$ with Eq. (2.12), then $b_{ij}=\frac{\gamma_i}{\gamma_i+\gamma_j}$, $i,j=1,2,\ldots,n$. If we bring $b_{ij}=\frac{\gamma_i}{\gamma_i+\gamma_j}$ into $b_{ik}b_{kj}b_{ji}=b_{ki}b_{jk}b_{ij}$, $i,j,k=1,2,\ldots,n$, this equality holds, i.e., $B=(b_{ij})_{n\times n}$ is a multiplicative consistent fuzzy preference relation. Therefore, if we let $w=(w_1,w_2,\ldots,w_n)$ be the priority vector of the fuzzy preference relation B, where $w_j>0$, $j=1,2,\ldots,n$, and $\sum_{j=1}^{n}w_j=1$, then when B is a multiplicative consistent fuzzy preference relation, we have $b_{ij}=\frac{w_i}{w_i+w_j}$, $i,j=1,2,\ldots,n$, i.e., $(1-b_{ij})w_i=b_{ij}w_j$, $i,j=1,2,\ldots,n$. Since $b_{ij}+b_{ji}=1$, then

$$b_{ji}w_i=b_{ij}w_j,\quad i,j=1,2,\ldots,n \tag{2.14}$$

i.e.,

$$w_i=\frac{b_{ij}}{b_{ji}}w_j,\quad i,j=1,2,\ldots,n \tag{2.15}$$

or

$$\frac{b_{ij}}{b_{ji}}\frac{w_j}{w_i}=\frac{b_{ji}}{b_{ij}}\frac{w_i}{w_j}=1,\quad i,j=1,2,\ldots,n \tag{2.16}$$

Combining Eq. (2.15) and $\sum_{j=1}^{n}w_j=1$, we get the exact solution to the priority vector of the multiplicative consistent fuzzy preference relation B:

$$w = \left(\frac{1}{\sum_{i=1}^{n} \frac{b_{i1}}{b_{1i}}}, \frac{1}{\sum_{i=1}^{n} \frac{b_{i2}}{b_{2i}}}, \ldots, \frac{1}{\sum_{i=1}^{n} \frac{b_{in}}{b_{ni}}} \right) \tag{2.17}$$

Considering that the fuzzy preference relation provided by the decision maker in the decision making process is usually inconsistent, Eq. (2.16) generally does not hold. As a result, we introduce the deviation factor:

$$f_{ij} = \frac{b_{ij}}{b_{ji}} \frac{w_j}{w_i} + \frac{b_{ji}}{b_{ij}} \frac{w_i}{w_j} - 2, \quad i, j = 1, 2, \ldots, n \tag{2.18}$$

and construct the deviation function:

$$F(w) = \sum_{i=1}^{n} \sum_{j=1}^{n} \left(\frac{b_{ij}}{b_{ji}} \frac{w_j}{w_i} + \frac{b_{ji}}{b_{ij}} \frac{w_i}{w_j} - 2 \right), \quad i, j = 1, 2, \ldots, n \tag{2.19}$$

Obviously, a reasonable priority vector w^* should be determined so as to minimize $F(w)$, i.e.,

$$\begin{cases} \min F(w) = \sum_{i=1}^{n} \sum_{j=1}^{n} \left(\frac{b_{ij}}{b_{ji}} \frac{w_j}{w_i} + \frac{b_{ji}}{b_{ij}} \frac{w_i}{w_j} - 2 \right) \\ s.t. \quad w_j > 0, \quad j = 1, 2, \ldots, n, \quad \sum_{j=1}^{n} w_j = 1 \end{cases} \tag{2.20}$$

We term this approach the least deviation method for deriving the priority vector of a fuzzy preference relation [150]. The following conclusion can be obtained for $F(w)$:

Theorem 2.14 [150] The least deviation function $F(w)$ has a unique minimum point w^*, which is also the unique solution of the following set of equations in Λ:

$$\sum_{j=1}^{n} \frac{b_{ij}}{b_{ji}} \frac{w_j}{w_i} = \sum_{j=1}^{n} \frac{b_{ji}}{b_{ij}} \frac{w_i}{w_j}, \quad i, j = 1, 2, \ldots, n \tag{2.21}$$

where Λ is defined as in Sect. 2.1.1.

Proof (1) **(Existence)** Since Λ is a bounded vector space, $F(w)$ is a continuous function in Λ, for any $w \in \Lambda$, and

$$\frac{b_{ij}}{b_{ji}} \frac{w_j}{w_i} + \frac{b_{ji}}{b_{ij}} \frac{w_i}{w_j} \geq 2 \sqrt{\frac{b_{ij}}{b_{ji}} \frac{b_{ji}}{b_{ij}} \frac{w_j}{w_i} \frac{w_i}{w_j}} = 2, \quad \text{for any } i, j$$

then $F(w) \geq 0$. As $w_i > 0,\ i = 1,2,\ldots,n$, we have

$$\frac{\partial F(w)}{\partial w_i} = \sum_{j=1}^{n}\left(\frac{b_{ij}}{b_{ji}}\left(-\frac{w_j}{w_i^2}\right) + \frac{b_{ji}}{b_{ij}}\left(\frac{1}{w_j}\right)\right)$$

and then $F(w)$ is differentiable for $w_i > 0$, $i = 1,2,\ldots,n$. Also since

$$\frac{\partial^2 F(w)}{\partial w_i^2} = 2\sum_{j=1}^{n}\left(\frac{b_{ij}}{b_{ji}}\frac{w_j}{w_i^3}\right) > 0, \quad i = 1,2,\ldots,n$$

then we have that $F(w)$ is strictly convex for $w_i > 0,\ i = 1,2,\ldots,n$. As a result, $F(w)$ has an infimum, i.e., there exists a constant d such that $d = \inf\{F(w) \mid w \in \Lambda\}$. Hence, there exists $w^* \in \Lambda$ such that $F(w^*) = d$ (because if w goes to the bounds of Λ, i.e., some w_i goes to 0, then $F(w)$ goes to $+\infty$). Thus, w^* is the minimum point w^* of Λ, and correspondingly, $F(w^*)$ reaches the minimum value. As w^* is the solution to the conditional extremum problem:

$$\begin{cases} \min F(w) \\ s.t.\quad w_j > 0, \quad j = 1,2,\ldots,n, \quad \sum_{j=1}^{n} w_j = 1 \end{cases} \tag{2.22}$$

We can construct the Lagrange function:

$$L(w,\zeta) = F(w) + \zeta\left(\sum_{j=1}^{n} w_j - 1\right) \tag{2.23}$$

where ζ is the Lagrange multiplier.

Differentiating $L(w,\zeta)$ with respect to $w_i (i = 1,2,\ldots,n)$ and ζ, and setting these partial derivatives equal to zero, then

$$-\sum_{j=1}^{n}\frac{b_{ij}}{b_{ji}}\frac{w_j}{w_i^2} + \sum_{j=1}^{n}\frac{b_{ji}}{b_{ij}}\frac{1}{w_j} + \zeta = 0, \quad i = 1,2,\ldots,n \tag{2.24}$$

Multiplying Eq. (2.24) by $w_i (i = 1,2,\ldots,n)$, we have

$$-\sum_{j=1}^{n}\frac{b_{ij}}{b_{ji}}\frac{w_j}{w_i} + \sum_{j=1}^{n}\frac{b_{ji}}{b_{ij}}\frac{w_i}{w_j} + \zeta w_i = 0, \quad i = 1,2,\ldots,n \tag{2.25}$$

i.e.,

$$-\sum_{i=1}^{n}\sum_{j=1}^{n}\frac{b_{ij}}{b_{ji}}\frac{w_j}{w_i} + \sum_{i=1}^{n}\sum_{j=1}^{n}\frac{b_{ji}}{b_{ij}}\frac{w_i}{w_j} + \zeta = 0, \quad i = 1,2,\ldots,n \tag{2.26}$$

Since

$$\sum_{i=1}^{n}\sum_{j=1}^{n}\frac{b_{ij}}{b_{ji}}\frac{w_j}{w_i}=\sum_{i=1}^{n}\sum_{j=1}^{n}\frac{b_{ji}}{b_{ij}}\frac{w_i}{w_j} \tag{2.27}$$

then $\zeta=0$. Therefore, Combining $\zeta=0$ with Eq. (2.25), we get

$$\sum_{j=1}^{n}\frac{b_{ij}}{b_{ji}}\frac{w_j}{w_i}=\sum_{j=1}^{n}\frac{b_{ji}}{b_{ij}}\frac{w_i}{w_j},\quad i=1,2,\ldots,n \tag{2.28}$$

and thus, w^* is the solution to the set of Eq. (2.21).

(2) (**Uniqueness**) Assume that $w=(w_1,w_2,\ldots,w_n)\in\Lambda$ and $v=(v_1,v_2,\ldots,v_n)\in\Lambda$ are the solutions to the set of Eq. (2.21). Let $\theta_i=\frac{v_i}{w_i}$, $\delta_l=\mathbf{max}_j\{\delta_j\}$. If there exists j such that $\delta_j<\delta_l$, then

$$\sum_{j=1}^{n}\frac{b_{ij}}{b_{ji}}\frac{w_j}{w_l}>\sum_{j=1}^{n}\frac{b_{ij}}{b_{ji}}\frac{w_j}{w_l}\frac{\delta_j}{\delta_l}=\sum_{j=1}^{n}\frac{b_{ij}}{b_{ji}}\frac{v_j}{v_l} \tag{2.29}$$

and

$$\sum_{j=1}^{n}\frac{b_{ji}}{b_{ij}}\frac{w_l}{w_j}<\sum_{j=1}^{n}\frac{b_{ji}}{b_{ij}}\frac{w_l}{w_j}\frac{\delta_l}{\delta_j}=\sum_{j=1}^{n}\frac{b_{ji}}{b_{ij}}\frac{v_l}{v_j} \tag{2.30}$$

Thus, by Eqs. (2.21), (2.29) and (2.30), we get

$$\sum_{j=1}^{n}\frac{b_{ij}}{b_{ji}}\frac{w_j}{w_l}>\sum_{j=1}^{n}\frac{b_{ji}}{b_{ij}}\frac{w_l}{w_j} \tag{2.31}$$

which contradicts the set of Eq. (2.21). Thus, for any i, we have $\delta_i=\delta_l$, i.e.,

$$\frac{w_1}{v_1}=\frac{w_2}{v_2}=\cdots\frac{w_n}{v_n}$$

Also since $w,v\in\Lambda$, then $w_i=v_i$, $i=1,2,\ldots,n$, i.e., $w=v$, which completes the proof of the theorem.

Theorem 2.15 [150] The least deviation method is of strong rank preservation.

Proof Since the priority vector $w=(w_1,w_2,\ldots,w_n)$ derived by the least deviation method for the fuzzy preference relation B satisfies:

$$\sum_{k=1}^{n}\frac{b_{ik}}{b_{ki}}\frac{w_k}{w_i}=\sum_{k=1}^{n}\frac{b_{ki}}{b_{ik}}\frac{w_i}{w_k} \tag{2.32}$$

i.e.,

$$\sum_{k=1}^{n} \frac{b_{ik}}{b_{ki}} w_k = \sum_{k=1}^{n} \frac{b_{ki}}{b_{ik}} \frac{w_i^2}{w_k} \tag{2.33}$$

Also since

$$\sum_{k=1}^{n} \frac{b_{jk}}{b_{kj}} \frac{w_k}{w_j} = \sum_{k=1}^{n} \frac{b_{kj}}{b_{jk}} \frac{w_j}{w_k} \tag{2.34}$$

then

$$\sum_{k=1}^{n} \frac{b_{jk}}{b_{kj}} w_k = \sum_{k=1}^{n} \frac{b_{kj}}{b_{jk}} \frac{w_j^2}{w_k} \tag{2.35}$$

Since for any k, $b_{ik} \geq b_{jk}$, then $b_{ki} \leq b_{kj}$, i.e., $\frac{1}{b_{ki}} \geq \frac{1}{b_{kj}}$. Therefore, $\frac{b_{ik}}{b_{ki}} \geq \frac{b_{jk}}{b_{kj}}$, and thus,

$$\frac{b_{ik}}{b_{ki}} w_k \geq \frac{b_{jk}}{b_{kj}} w_k \tag{2.36}$$

Therefore,

$$\sum_{k=1}^{n} \frac{b_{ik}}{b_{ki}} w_k \geq \sum_{k=1}^{n} \frac{b_{jk}}{b_{kj}} w_k \tag{2.37}$$

It follows from Eqs. (2.33), (2.35) and (2.37) that

$$\sum_{k=1}^{n} \frac{b_{ki}}{b_{ik}} \frac{w_i^2}{w_k} \geq \sum_{k=1}^{n} \frac{b_{kj}}{b_{jk}} \frac{w_j^2}{w_k} \tag{2.38}$$

Also since $b_{ik} \geq b_{jk}$ (i.e., $b_{ki} \leq b_{kj}$), then for any k, we have $\frac{b_{ki}}{b_{ik}} \geq \frac{b_{kj}}{b_{jk}}$. Therefore,

$$\sum_{k=1}^{n} \frac{w_i^2}{w_k} \geq \sum_{k=1}^{n} \frac{w_j^2}{w_k} \tag{2.39}$$

According to Eq. (2.39), we get $w_i^2 \geq w_j^2$, then $w_i \geq w_j$, which completes the proof.

By Theorem 2.15, the following theorem can be proven easily:

Theorem 2.16 [150] Let the fuzzy preference relation $B = (b_{ij})_{n \times n}$ be rank transitive. If $b_{ij} \geq 0.5$, then $w_i \geq w_j$; If $b_{ij} = 0.5$, then $w_i \geq w_j$ or $w_i \leq w_j$, where $w = (w_1, w_2, \ldots, w_n)$ is a priority vector derived by the least deviation method for the fuzzy preference relation B.

2.1.3.3 Convergent Iterative Algorithm

Let $B=(b_{ij})_{n\times n}$ be a fuzzy preference relation, and let k be the number of iterations. To solve the set of Eq. (2.21), we give a simple convergent iterative algorithm as follows [150]:

Step 1 Given an original weight vector $w(0)=(w_1(0), w_2(0),\ldots, w_n(0))\in\Lambda$, specify the parameter ε ($0\le\varepsilon<1$), and let $k=0$.

Step 2 Calculate

$$\eta_i[w(k)]=\sum_{j=1}^{n}\left(\frac{b_{ij}}{b_{ji}}\frac{w_j(k)}{w_i(k)}-\frac{b_{ji}}{b_{ij}}\frac{w_i(k)}{w_j(k)}\right),\quad i=1,2,\ldots,n \tag{2.40}$$

If $|\eta_i[w(k)]|<\varepsilon$ holds, for any i, then $w=w(k)$, go to Step 5; Otherwise, continue to Step 3.

Step 3 Determine the number l such that $|\eta_l[w(k)]|=\max_i\{|\eta_i[w(k)]|\}$, and compute

$$v(k)=\left(\frac{\sum_{j\neq k}\frac{b_{lj}}{b_{jl}}\frac{w_j(k)}{w_l(k)}}{\sum_{j\neq l}\frac{b_{jl}}{b_{lj}}\frac{w_l(k)}{w_j(k)}}\right)^{\frac{1}{2}} \tag{2.41}$$

$$w_i'(k)=\begin{cases}(k)w_l(k), & i=l,\\ w_i(k), & i\neq l,\end{cases} \tag{2.42}$$

$$w_i(k+1)=\frac{w_i'(k)}{\sum_{j=1}^{n}w_j'(k)},\quad i=1,2,\ldots,n \tag{2.43}$$

Step 4 Let $k=k+1$; Go to Step 2.

Step 5 Output w, which is the priority vector of the fuzzy preference relation B.

Remark 2.1 If $\varepsilon=0$, then the priority vector w of B obtained using the above algorithm is a unique minimum point w^* (defined in Theorem 2.14) of $F(w)$; If $0<\varepsilon<1$, then the priority vector w of B obtained using the above algorithm is an approximation of w^*.

Theorem 2.17 [150] For any $0\le\varepsilon<1$, and the original weight vector $w(0)=(w_1(0), w_2(0),\ldots, w_n(0))\in\Lambda$, the above iterative algorithm is convergent.

Proof Consider a change of $F(w)$, $w \in \Lambda$. Suppose that $\alpha > 0$, and let

$$r(\alpha) = F(\dot{w}(k)) = F(w_1(k), w_2(w), \ldots, w_{l-1}(k), \alpha w_l(k), w_{l+1}(k), \ldots, w_n(k))$$

$$= 2\left(\sum_{j \neq l} \frac{b_{lj}}{b_{jl}} \frac{w_j(k)}{\alpha w_l(k)} + \sum_{j \neq l} \frac{b_{jl}}{b_{lj}} \frac{\alpha w_l(k)}{w_j(k)} + \sum_{i \neq l} \sum_{j \neq l} \frac{b_{ij}}{b_{ji}} \frac{w_j(k)}{w_i(k)} - (n^2 - 1) \right) \quad (2.44)$$

Let

$$h_0 = \sum_{i \neq l} \sum_{j \neq l} \frac{b_{ij}}{b_{ji}} \frac{w_j(k)}{w_i(k)} - (n^2 - 1) \quad (2.45)$$

$$h_1 = \sum_{j \neq l} \frac{b_{lj}}{b_{jl}} \frac{w_j(k)}{w_l(k)} \quad (2.46)$$

$$h_2 = \sum_{j \neq l} \frac{b_{jl}}{b_{lj}} \frac{w_l(k)}{w_j(k)} \quad (2.47)$$

then Eq. (2.44) can be rewritten as $r(\alpha) = 2\left(\frac{h_1}{\alpha} + h_2 \alpha + h_0 \right)$. Differentiating $r(\alpha)$ with respect to α, i.e., Setting $\frac{dr}{d\alpha} = 0$, there exist α^* and $r(\alpha^*)$ such that $r(\alpha^*) = \min r(\alpha)$. Namely,

$$\alpha^* = \left(\frac{\sum_{j \neq k} \frac{b_{lj}}{b_{jl}} \frac{w_j(k)}{w_l(k)}}{\sum_{j \neq l} \frac{b_{jl}}{b_{lj}} \frac{w_l(k)}{w_j(k)}} \right)^{\frac{1}{2}} \quad (2.48)$$

$$r(\alpha^*) = 4\sqrt{h_1 h_2} + 2h_0 \quad (2.49)$$

If $\alpha^* = 1$, then by Eq. (2.48), we have

$$\sum_{j=1}^{n} \frac{b_{lj}}{b_{jl}} \frac{w_j(k)}{w_l(k)} = \sum_{j=1}^{n} \frac{b_{jl}}{b_{lj}} \frac{w_l(k)}{w_j(k)} \quad (2.50)$$

By the definition of l in Step 3 of the iterative algorithm, we have

$$\sum_{j=1}^{n} \frac{b_{ij}}{b_{ji}} \frac{w_j(k)}{w_i(k)} = \sum_{j=1}^{n} \frac{b_{ji}}{b_{ij}} \frac{w_i(k)}{w_j(k)}, \quad i = 1, 2, \ldots, n \quad (2.51)$$

From Theorem 2.14, it follows that the iterative algorithm terminates and $w^* = w(k)$. If $\alpha^* \neq 1$, then

$$F(w(k)) - F(\dot{w}(k)) = r(1) - r(\alpha^*)$$

$$= 2(h_1 + h_2 - 2\sqrt{h_1 h_2})$$

$$= 2(\sqrt{h_1} - \sqrt{h_2})^2 > 0 \tag{2.52}$$

Since $F(w)$ is a homogenous function, $F(\dot{w}(k)) = F(w(k+1))$. Eq. (2.52) shows that $F(w(k+1)) < F(w(k))$ holds, for all k, i.e., $\{F(w(k))\}$ is a monotone decreasing sequence. Also since $F(w)$ is a nonnegative function with an infimum in Λ, by the principle of mathematical analysis, we know that a monotone decreasing bounded sequence must be convergent. This completes the proof.

2.1.4 Eigenvector Method for Priority of a Fuzzy Preference Relation

Saaty [69] developed an eigenvector method for the priority of a multiplicative preference relation. The prominent characteristic of the eigenvector method is that it has cumulative dominance, that is, using the limit of the weighted averaging cumulative dominance vector to reveal the ranking of the attributes' importance degrees. Xu [111] utilized the relationship between the fuzzy preference relation and the multiplicative preference relation to develop the eigenvector method for priority of a fuzzy preference relation.

Let $B = (b_{ij})_{n\times n}$ be a multiplicative consistent fuzzy preference relation. Since the transformation matrix $H = (h_{ij})_{n\times n}$ of B is a consistent multiplicative preference relation, where $h_{ij} = \frac{w_i}{w_j}$, $i, j = 1, 2, \ldots, n$, $w = (w_1, w_2, \ldots, w_n)$ is the priority vector of B, and thus, there exists an eigenvalue problem:

$$Hw^T = nw^T \tag{2.53}$$

However, judgments of people depend on personal psychological aspects, such as experience, learning, situation, state of mind, and so forth [101], hence, in the process of decision making, the judgments (or preferences) given by the decision makers are usually inconsistent. As a result, Eq. (2.53) does not hold in the general case. Thus, we can replace Eq. (2.53) with the following eigenvalue problem approximately:

$$Hw^T = \lambda_{\max} w^T \tag{2.54}$$

where $\lambda_{\max}$ is the maximal eigenvalue of the multiplicative preference relation H, w is the eigenvector corresponding to the maximal eigenvalue $\lambda_{\max}$, After the normalization of w, it becomes the priority vector of the multiplicative preference relation H, clearly, it is also the priority vector of the fuzzy preference relation B. We term this approach the eigenvector method for deriving the priority vector of a fuzzy preference relation [111].

The eigenvector method has the following property:

Theorem 2.18 [111] Let $B=(b_{ij})_{n\times n}$ be a fuzzy preference relation, and $w=(w_1,w_2,\ldots,w_n)$ be the priority vector of B derived by using the eigenvector method. If $b_{ik}\geq b_{jk}(b_{ik}\leq b_{jk})$, for any k, then $w_i\geq w_j(w_i\leq w_j)$, with equality if and only $b_{ik}=b_{jk}$, for any k.

In order to obtain the priority vector $w=(w_1,w_2,\ldots,w_n)$ of the fuzzy preference relation B derived by using the eigenvector method, Xu [111] developed the following iterative algorithm:

Step 1 Utilize the transformation formula $h_{ij}=\dfrac{b_{ij}}{b_{ji}}$ $(i,j=1,2,\ldots,n)$ to transform the given fuzzy preference relation $B=(b_{ij})_{n\times n}$ into the corresponding matrix $H=(h_{ij})_{n\times n}$.

Step 2 Given an original weight vector $w(0)=(w_1(0),w_2(0),\ldots,w_n(0))\in\Lambda$, specify the parameter ε $(0\leq\varepsilon<1)$, and let $k=0$.

Step 3 Calculate

$$q_0=\max_j\{w_j(0)\},\bar{w}(0)=\frac{w(0)}{q_0}$$

Step 4 Calculate iteratively

$$w(k+1)^T=H\bar{w}(k)^T,\quad q_{k+1}=\max_j\{w_j(k+1)\},\quad \bar{w}(k+1)=\frac{w(k+1)}{q_{k+1}}$$

Step 5 If $|q_{k+1}-q_k|<\varepsilon$, then go to Step 6; Otherwise, let $k=k+1$, and return to Step 4.

Step 6 Normalize $\bar{w}(k+1)$, i.e.,

$$w=\frac{\bar{w}(k+1)}{\sum_{j=1}^{n}\bar{w}_j(k+1)}$$

which is the priority vector of the transformation matrix H, and also the priority vector of the fuzzy preference relation B.

2.1.5 Consistency Improving Algorithm for a Fuzzy Preference Relation

An ideal preference relation should satisfy consistency condition, if the fuzzy preference relation B dissatisfies the consistency condition, then B is an inconsistent fuzzy preference relation, its corresponding transformation matrix H is also an inconsistent multiplicative preference relation. To ensure the reliability and accuracy of the priority of a preference relation, it is necessary to check its consistency. Wang [91] gave a consistency index of the multiplicative preference relation H:

$$CI = \frac{1}{n(n-1)} \sum_{1 \le i < j \le n} \left(a_{ij} \frac{w_j}{w_i} + a_{ji} \frac{w_i}{w_j} - 2 \right) \tag{2.55}$$

Saaty [69] put forward a consistency ratio for checking a multiplicative preference relation:

$$CR = \frac{CI}{RI} \tag{2.56}$$

where RI is the mean consistency index of randomly generated preference relations, shown in Table 2.1.

If $CR < 0.1$, then the corresponding multiplicative preference relation is of acceptable consistency.

Combining Eqs. (2.13), (2.55) and (2.56), we can get a general formula for checking the consistency of the fuzzy preference relation B:

$$\begin{cases} CI = \dfrac{1}{n(n-1)} \displaystyle\sum_{1 \le i < j \le n} \left(\dfrac{b_{ij}}{b_{ji}} \dfrac{w_j}{w_i} + \dfrac{b_{ji}}{b_{ij}} \dfrac{w_i}{w_j} - 2 \right), \\ CR = \dfrac{CI}{RI}. \end{cases} \tag{2.57}$$

If $CR < 0.1$, then the fuzzy preference relation B is of acceptable consistency; Otherwise, B is of unacceptable consistency. In this case, the decision maker is asked to re-evaluate the elements of B, or we can improve the consistency of B by using the following three algorithms from different angles:

Table 2.1 Mean consistency index (RI) of randomly generated preference relations

n	1	2	3	4	5	6	7	8
RI	0	0	0.52	0.89	1.12	1.26	1.36	1.41
n	9	10	11	12	13	14	15	
RI	1.46	1.49	1.52	1.54	1.56	1.58	1.59	

(1) Repair all the elements of a fuzzy preference relation at each iteration (Algorithm I)

$$\text{Let } \Re_n^+ = \{v = (v_1, v_2, \dots, v_n) \mid v_i > 0, v_i \in \Re, \quad i = 1, 2, \dots, n\}.$$

Lemma 2.1 (Perron) [2] Let $H = (h_{ij})_{n \times n}$ be a positive matrix (i.e., $h_{ij} > 0, \quad i, j = 1, 2, \dots, n$), and $\lambda_{\max}$ is the maximal eigenvalue of H, then

$$\lambda_{\max} = \min_{v \in \Re_n^+} \max_i \sum_{j=1}^n h_{ij} \frac{v_j}{v_i}$$

Lemma 2.2 [146] Let $x > 0, \ y > 0, \ \alpha > 0, \ \beta > 0, \ \alpha + \beta = 1$, then

$$x^\alpha y^\beta \le \alpha x + \beta y$$

holds if and only if $x = y$.

Lemma 2.3 [146] Let $H = (h_{ij})_{n \times n}$ be a positive multiplicative preference relation (i.e., $h_{ij} > 0, \quad h_{ji} = \frac{1}{h_{ij}}, \quad i, j = 1, 2, \dots, n$), and $\lambda_{\max}$ is the maximal eigenvalue of H, then

$$\lambda_{\max} \ge n$$

with equality if and only if H is consistent.

Theorem 2.19 [146] Let $H = (h_{ij})_{n \times n}$ be a positive multiplicative preference relation, $\lambda_{\max}$ is the maximal eigenvalue of H, and $\gamma = (\gamma_1, \gamma_2, \dots, \gamma_n)$ is the eigenvector of H corresponding to $\lambda_{\max}$. Let $H^* = (h_{ij}^*)_{n \times n}$, where

$$h_{ij}^* = h_{ij}^\alpha \left(\frac{\gamma_i}{\gamma_j} \right)^{1-\alpha}, \quad i, j = 1, 2, \dots, n, \quad 0 < \alpha < 1$$

and let $\mu_{\max}$ be the maximal eigenvalue of H^*, then $\mu_{\max} \le \lambda_{\max}$, with equality if and only if H^* is consistent.

Proof Let $e_{ij} = h_{ij} \left(\frac{\gamma_j}{\gamma_i} \right)$, $i, j = 1, 2, \dots, n$, then $\lambda_{\max} = \sum_{j=1}^n e_{ij}$, and $h_{ij}^* = e_{ij}^\alpha \left(\frac{\gamma_i}{\gamma_j} \right)$. It follows from Lemmas 2.1 to 2.3 that

$$\mu_{\max} = \min_{v \in \Re_n^+} \max_i \sum_{j=1}^n h_{ij}^* \frac{v_j}{v_i} \le \max_i \sum_{j=1}^n h_{ij}^* \frac{\gamma_j}{\gamma_i}$$

$$= \max_i \sum_{j=1}^{n} e_{ij}^{\alpha} \leq \max_i \sum_{j=1}^{n} (\alpha e_{ij} + 1 - \alpha)$$

$$\leq \alpha\lambda_{\max} + (1-\alpha)n \leq \lambda_{\max}$$

with equality if and only if $\lambda_{\max} = n$, i.e., H is a consistent multiplicative preference relation. This completes the proof.

Theorem 2.20 [146] Let $H = (h_{ij})_{n\times n}$ be a positive multiplicative preference relation, $\lambda_{\max}$ is the maximal eigenvalue of H, and $\gamma = (\gamma_1, \gamma_2, \ldots, \gamma_n)$ is the eigenvector of H corresponding to $\lambda_{\max}$. Let $H^* = (h_{ij}^*)_{n\times n}$, where

$$h_{ij}^* = \begin{cases} \alpha h_{ij} + (1-\alpha)\dfrac{\gamma_i}{\gamma_j}, & i = 1,2,\ldots,n,\ j = i, i+1,\ldots,n, \\ \dfrac{1}{\alpha h_{ji} + (1-\alpha)\dfrac{\gamma_j}{\gamma_i}}, & i = 2,3,\ldots,n,\ j = 1,2,\ldots,i-1, \quad 0 < \alpha < 1, \end{cases}$$

and let $\mu_{\max}$ be the maximal eigenvalue, then

$$\mu_{\max} \leq \lambda_{\max}$$

with equality if and only if H^* is consistent.

Proof Let $e_{ij} = a_{ij}\left(\dfrac{w_j}{w_i}\right)$, $i, j = 1,2,\ldots,n$, then $\lambda_{\max} = \sum_{j=1}^{n} e_{ij}$. We first prove

$$\frac{1}{\alpha e_{ji} + (1-\alpha)} \leq \alpha e_{ij} + (1-\alpha) \tag{2.58}$$

i.e.,

$$(\alpha e_{ij} + (1-\alpha))(\alpha e_{ji} + (1-\alpha)) \geq 1 \tag{2.59}$$

which can be simplified as:

$$e_{ij} + \frac{1}{e_{ij}} \geq 2 \tag{2.60}$$

Clearly, Eq. (2.60) must hold, and thus, Eq. (2.58) also holds. This completes the proof.

From Lemma 2.1 and Eq. (2.58), we can get

$$\mu_{\max} = \min_{v\in\Re_n^+} \max_i \sum_{j=1}^{n} h_{ij}^* \frac{v_j}{v_i} \leq \max_i \sum_{j=1}^{n} h_{ij}^* \frac{\gamma_j}{\gamma_i}$$

$$= \max_i \left\{ \sum_{j=1}^{i-1} \frac{1}{\alpha h_{ji} + (1-\alpha)\left(\frac{\gamma_j}{\gamma_i}\right)} + \sum_{j=i}^{n} \left(\alpha h_{ij} + (1-\alpha)\left(\frac{\gamma_i}{\gamma_j}\right)\right) \right\} \left(\frac{\gamma_j}{\gamma_i}\right)$$

$$= \max_i \left\{ \sum_{j=1}^{i-1} \frac{1}{\alpha e_{ji} + (1-\alpha)} + \sum_{j=i}^{n} (\alpha e_{ij} + (1-\alpha)) \right\}$$

$$\leq \max_i \left\{ \sum_{j=1}^{i-1} (\alpha e_{ij} + (1-\alpha)) + \sum_{j=i}^{n} (\alpha e_{ij} + (1-\alpha)) \right\}$$

$$\leq \max_i \sum_{j=1}^{n} (\alpha e_{ij} + (1-\alpha)) = \alpha \max_i \sum_{j=1}^{n} e_{ij} + (1-\alpha)n$$

$$\leq \alpha\lambda_{\max} + (1-\alpha)n \leq \alpha\lambda_{\max} + (1-\alpha)\lambda_{\max} = \lambda_{\max}$$

with equality if and only if $\lambda_{\max} = n$, i.e., H is a consistent multiplicative preference relation. This completes the proof.

In what follows, we give a convergent iterative algorithm for improving fuzzy preference relation, and then introduce two criteria for checking the effectiveness of improvement [146]:

(Algorithm I) Let $B = (b_{ij})_{n\times n}$ be a fuzzy preference relation with unacceptable consistency, k be the number of iterative times and $\alpha \in (0,1)$.

Step 1 Let $B^{(0)} = \left(b_{ij}^{0}\right)_{n\times n} = \left(b_{ij}\right)_{n\times n}$, and $k = 0$.

Step 2 From Eq. (2.13), we get the multiplicative preference relation $H^{(0)} = (h_{ij}^{(0)})_{n\times n}$.

Step 3 Calculate the weight vector $\gamma^{(k)} = \left(\gamma_1^{(k)}, \gamma_2^{(k)}, \ldots, \gamma_n^{(k)}\right)$ of $H^{(k)} = \left(h_{ij}^{(k)}\right)_{n\times n}$.

Step 4 Derive the consistency ratio $CR^{(k)}$ from Eqs. (2.55) and (2.56). If $CR^{(k)} < 0.1$, then turn to Step 7; Otherwise, go to the next step:

Step 5 Let $H^{(k+1)} = \left(h_{ij}^{(k+1)}\right)_{n\times n}$, where $h_{ij}^{(k+1)}$ can be derived by using:

(1) The weighted geometric mean:

$$h_{ij}^{(k+1)} = (h_{ij}^{(k)})^{\alpha} \left(\frac{\gamma_i^{(k)}}{\gamma_j^{(k)}} \right)^{1-\alpha}, \quad i, j = 1, 2, \ldots, n$$

(2) The weighted arithmetic average:

$$h_{ij}^{(k+1)} = \begin{cases} \alpha h_{ij}^{(k)} + (1-\alpha)\left(\dfrac{\gamma_i^{(k)}}{\gamma_j^{(k)}}\right), & i = 1,2,\ldots,n, \quad j = i, i+1, \ldots, n \\ \dfrac{1}{\alpha h_{ji}^{(k)} + (1-\alpha)\left(\dfrac{\gamma_j^{(k)}}{\gamma_i^{(k)}}\right)}, & i = 2,3,\ldots,n, \quad j = 1,2,\ldots,i-1 \end{cases}$$

Step 6 Let $k = k+1$, then turn to Step 3.

Step 7 Derive the corresponding fuzzy preference relation $B^{(k)} = \left(b_{ij}^{(k)}\right)_{n\times n}$.

Step 8 Output k, $B^{(k)}$ and $CR^{(k)}$, then $B^{(k)}$ is an improved fuzzy preference relation with acceptable consistency.

Similar to the proof of Theorem 2 given by Xu and Wei [154], and according to Theorems 2.19 and 2.20, we can get the following result:

Theorem 2.21(The convergence of Algorithm I) [146] For the algorithm above, we have

$$CR^{(k+1)} < CR^{(k)}, \quad \lim_{k\to+\infty} CR^{(k)} = 0$$

It follows from Theorem 2.21 that Algorithm I terminates in a finite number of iterations.

To check the effectiveness of the improvement above, we give the following two checking criteria:

$$\delta^k = \max_{i,j} \left\{\left|b_{ij}^{(k)} - b_{ij}^{(0)}\right|\right\}, \quad i,j = 1,2,\ldots,n$$

$$\sigma^{(k)} = \frac{\sqrt{\sum_{i=1}^{n}\sum_{j=1}^{n}\left(b_{ij}^{(k)} - b_{ij}^{(0)}\right)^2}}{n}$$

The formulas above can be regarded as an index to measure the deviation degree between $B^{(k)}$ and $B^{(0)}$. Obviously, $\delta^{(k)} \ge \sigma^{(k)} \ge 0$.

In general, if $\delta^{(k)} < 0.2$ and $\sigma^{(k)} < 0.1$, then the improvement is considered to be acceptable. In this case, the improved fuzzy preference relation can contain the judgment information of the original fuzzy preference relation as much as possible.

Similarly, we give the following two algorithms:

(2) Algorithm II which only repairs all the elements in one line and its corresponding column in the fuzzy preference relation at each iteration [110]:

Algorithm II only replaces Step 5 of Algorithm I as follows, and the other steps keep unchanged:

Step 5 Normalize all the columns of $H^{(k)} = \left(h_{ij}^{(k)}\right)_{n\times n}$, and then get the corresponding normalized matrix: $\bar{H}^{(k)} = \left(h_1^{(k)}, h_2^{(k)}, \ldots, h_n^{(k)}\right)$, where $h_i^{(k)} (i = 1, 2, \ldots, n)$ is the line vector of $\bar{H}^{(k)}$. After that, we calculate the angle consine of $\gamma^{(k)}$ and $h_i^{(k)}$:

$$\cos\theta_i^{(k)} = \frac{<\gamma^{(k)}, h_i^{(k)}>}{\left|\gamma^{(k)}\right|\left|h_i^{(k)}\right|}$$

where $<\gamma^{(k)}, h_i^{(k)}> = \sum_{j=1}^{n} \gamma_j^{(k)} h_{ij}^{(k)}$, $\left|\gamma^{(k)}\right| = \sqrt{\sum_{j=1}^{n} (\gamma_j^{(k)})^2}$, $\left|h_i^{(k)}\right| = \sqrt{\sum_{j=1}^{n} (h_{ij}^{(k)})^2}$

Then we determine l such that $\cos\theta_l^{(k)} = \min_i \left\{\cos\theta_i^{(k)}\right\}$. Let $H^{(k+1)} = \left(h_{ij}^{(k+1)}\right)_{n\times n}$, where $\left(h_{ij}^{(k+1)}\right)$ can be determined by using one of the following forms:

1. The weighted geometric mean:

$$h_{ij}^{(k+1)} = \begin{cases} (h_{il}^{(k)})^{\alpha} \left(\dfrac{\gamma_i^{(k)}}{\gamma_l^{(k)}}\right)^{(1-\alpha)}, & j = l \\ (h_{lj}^{(k)})^{\alpha} \left(\dfrac{\gamma_l^{(k)}}{\gamma_j^{(k)}}\right)^{(1-\alpha)}, & i = l \\ h_{ij}^{(k)}, & otherwise \end{cases}$$

2. The weighted arithmetic average:

$$h_{ij}^{(k+1)} = \begin{cases} \alpha h_{il}^{(k)} + (1-\alpha)\left(\dfrac{\gamma_i^{(k)}}{\gamma_l^{(k)}}\right), & j = l \\ \dfrac{1}{\alpha h_{jl}^{(k)} + (1-\alpha)\left(\dfrac{\gamma_j^{(k)}}{\gamma_l^{(k)}}\right)}, & i = l \\ h_{ij}^{(k)}, & otherwise \end{cases}$$

(3) Algorithm III which only repairs the pair of elements with the largest deviation in the fuzzy preference relation at each iteration [110]:

Algorithm III keeps Steps 1–4 and 6–8, and only replaces Step 5 of Algorithm I as below:

Step 5 Let $e_{ij}^{(k)} = h_{ij}^{(k)}\left(\frac{\gamma_j^{(k)}}{\gamma_i^{(k)}}\right)$, and determine l, s such that $e_{ls}^{(k)} = \max_{i,j}\left\{e_{ij}^{(k)}\right\}$. Let $H^{(k+1)} = \left(h_{ij}^{(k+1)}\right)_{n\times n}$, where $h_{ij}^{(k+1)}$ can be derived by one of the following form:

1. The weighted geometric mean:

$$h_{ij}^{(k+1)} = \begin{cases} \left(h_{ls}^{(k)}\right)^{\alpha}\left(\frac{\gamma_l^{(k)}}{\gamma_s^{(k)}}\right)^{1-\alpha}, & (i,l) = (l,s) \\ \left(h_{sl}^{(k)}\right)^{\alpha}\left(\frac{\gamma_s^{(k)}}{\gamma_l^{(k)}}\right)^{1-\alpha}, & (i,j) = (s,l) \\ h_{ij}^{(k)}, & (i,j) \neq (l,s),(s,l) \end{cases}$$

2. The weighted arithmetic average:

$$h_{ij}^{(k+1)} = \begin{cases} \alpha h_{ls}^{(k)} + (1-\alpha)\left(\frac{\gamma_l^{(k)}}{\gamma_s^{(k)}}\right), & (i,j) = (l,s) \\ \frac{1}{\alpha h_{ls}^{(k)} + (1-\alpha)\left(\frac{\gamma_l^{(k)}}{\gamma_s^{(k)}}\right)}, & (i,j) = (s,l) \\ h_{ij}^{(k)}, & (i,j) \neq (l,s),(s,l) \end{cases}$$

Example 2.1 Let

$$B = \begin{pmatrix} 0.5 & 0.6 & 0.4 & 0.3 \\ 0.4 & 0.5 & 0.6 & 0.6 \\ 0.6 & 0.4 & 0.5 & 0.7 \\ 0.7 & 0.4 & 0.3 & 0.5 \end{pmatrix}$$

be an original fuzzy preference relation, and its priority vector w and CR are as follows:

$$w = (0.2044, 0.2697, 0.2973, 0.2286)$$

$$CR = 0.1593$$

Then we use the algorithms above to improve the fuzzy preference relation B. The results are listed as in Tables 2.2, 2.3, 2.4, 2.5, 2.6, 2.7:

Table 2.2 Fuzzy preference relations and their corresponding parameters derived by using the weighted geometric mean in Algorithm I

α	k	$H^{(k)}$				$\gamma^{(k)}$	$CR^{(k)}$	$\delta^{(k)}$	$\sigma^{(k)}$
0.1	1	0.500	0.448	0.407	0.454	0.204	0.002	0.154	0.098
		0.552	0.500	0.488	0.547	0.270			
		0.593	0.512	0.500	0.579	0.298			
		0.546	0.453	0.421	0.500	0.228			
0.3	1	0.500	0.482	0.405	0.418	0.203	0.014	0.118	0.076
		0.518	0.500	0.513	0.559	0.271			
		0.595	0.487	0.500	0.608	0.299			
		0.582	0.441	0.392	0.500	0.227			
0.5	1	0.500	0.516	0.404	0.382	0.203	0.039	0.084	0.053
		0.484	0.500	0.538	0.571	0.271			
		0.596	0.462	0.500	0.635	0.299			
		0.618	0.429	0.365	0.500	0.227			
0.7	1	0.500	0.550	0.402	0.349	0.204	0.076	0.050	0.032
		0.450	0.500	0.563	0.582	0.271			
		0.598	0.437	0.500	0.662	0.298			
		0.651	0.418	0.338	0.500	0.227			
0.9	3	0.500	0.555	0.402	0.344	0.204	0.083	0.045	0.028
		0.445	0.500	0.567	0.585	0.271			
		0.598	0.433	0.500	0.666	0.298			
		0.656	0.415	0.334	0.500	0.227			

2.1.6 Example Analysis

Example 2.2 For a MADM problem, there are four attributes $u_i (i = 1,2,3,4)$. To determine their weights, a decision maker utilizes the 0.1–0.9 scale to compare each pair of $u_i (i = 1,2,3,4)$, and then constructs the following fuzzy preference relation:

$$B = \begin{bmatrix} 0.5 & 0.7 & 0.6 & 0.8 \\ 0.3 & 0.5 & 0.4 & 0.6 \\ 0.4 & 0.6 & 0.5 & 0.7 \\ 0.2 & 0.4 & 0.3 & 0.5 \end{bmatrix}$$

1. If we employ the translation method to derive the priority vector of B, then

$$w = (0.3000, 0.2333, 0.2667, 0.2000)$$

Table 2.3 Fuzzy preference relations and their corresponding parameters derived by using the weighted arithmetic average in Algorithm I

α	k	$H^{(k)}$				$\gamma^{(k)}$	$CR^{(k)}$	$\delta^{(k)}$	$\sigma^{(k)}$
0.2	1	0.500	0.475	0.406	0.444	0.208	0.008	0.144	0.085
		0.525	0.500	0.506	0.554	0.269			
		0.594	0.494	0.500	0.601	0.299			
		0.556	0.446	0.399	0.500	0.224			
0.4	1	0.500	0.513	0.404	0.414	0.210	0.028	0.114	0.062
		0.487	0.500	0.534	0.567	0.270			
		0.596	0.466	0.500	0.631	0.300			
		0.586	0.433	0.369	0.500	0.220			
0.6	1	0.500	0.546	0.403	0.381	0.210	0.059	0.081	0.041
		0.454	0.500	0.558	0.578	0.270			
		0.597	0.442	0.500	0.658	0.300			
		0.619	0.422	0.342	0.500	0.220			
0.8	2	0.500	0.553	0.403	0.377	0.211	0.066	0.077	0.037
		0.447	0.500	0.563	0.582	0.271			
		0.597	0.437	0.500	0.666	0.300			
		0.623	0.418	0.337	0.500	0.219			

2. If we employ the least variation method to derive the priority vector of B, then

$$w = (0.4000, 0.2000, 0.3000, 0.1000)$$

3. If we employ the least deviation method to derive the priority vector of B, then

$$w = (0.4302, 0.1799, 0.2749, 0.1150)$$

4. If we employ the eigenvector method to derive the priority vector of B, then

$$w = (0.4303, 0.1799, 0.2748, 0.1150)$$

The consistency ratio is $CR = 0.0091 < 0.1$.

From the results above, we can see that the differences among the results derived by using the translation method is smaller than those of the least variation method, the least deviation method and the eigenvector method, while the results derived from the latter three methods are basically similar. But the rankings of the four attribute weights derived by using these four methods are the same, i.e.,

$$u_1 \succ u_2 \succ u_3 \succ u_4$$

Table 2.4 Fuzzy preference relations and their corresponding parameters derived by using the weighted geometric mean in Algorithm II

α	k	$H^{(k)}$				$\gamma^{(k)}$	$CR^{(k)}$	$\delta^{(k)}$	$\sigma^{(k)}$
0.1	1	0.500	0.448	0.407	0.454	0.198	0.038	0.154	0.077
		0.552	0.500	0.600	0.600	0.314			
		0.593	0.400	0.500	0.700	0.301			
		0.546	0.400	0.300	0.500	0.184			
0.3	1	0.500	0.482	0.405	0.418	0.199	0.028	0.114	0.062
		0.518	0.500	0.600	0.600	0.305			
		0.595	0.400	0.500	0.700	0.302			
		0.582	0.400	0.300	0.500	0.194			
0.5	1	0.500	0.546	0.403	0.381	0.210	0.054	0.118	0.059
		0.454	0.500	0.558	0.578	0.270			
		0.597	0.442	0.500	0.658	0.300			
		0.619	0.422	0.342	0.500	0.220			
0.7	2	0.500	0.509	0.402	0.389	0.200	0.072	0.091	0.045
		0.491	0.500	0.600	0.600	0.297			
		0.598	0.400	0.500	0.700	0.302			
		0.611	0.400	0.300	0.500	0.201			
0.9	4	0.500	0.540	0.402	0.358	0.202	0.095	0.060	0.030
		0.460	0.500	0.600	0.600	0.288			
		0.598	0.400	0.500	0.700	0.301			
		0.642	0.400	0.300	0.500	0.209			

The result of consistency ratio CR shows that the fuzzy preference relation B is of acceptable consistency.

2.2 Incomplete Fuzzy Preference Relation

A decision maker compares each pair of n alternatives with respect to the given criterion, and constructs a complete fuzzy preference relation, which needs $\frac{1}{2}n(n-1)$ judgments in its entire top triangular portion. However, the decision maker sometimes cannot provide his/her judgments over some pairs of alternatives, especially for the fuzzy preference relation with high order, because of time pressure, lack of knowledge, and the decision maker's limited expertise related with the problem domain. The decision maker may develop an incomplete fuzzy preference relation in which some of the elements cannot be provided [118]. In this section, we introduce the incomplete fuzzy preference relation and its special forms, such as the totally incomplete fuzzy preference relation, the additive consistent incomplete fuzzy

Table 2.5 Fuzzy preference relations and their corresponding parameters derived by using the weighted arithmetic average in Algorithm II

α	k	$H^{(k)}$				$\gamma^{(k)}$	$CR^{(k)}$	$\delta^{(k)}$	$\sigma^{(k)}$
0.1	1	0.500	0.444	0.407	0.446	0.196	0.039	0.156	0.076
		0.556	0.500	0.600	0.600	0.315			
		0.593	0.400	0.500	0.700	0.301			
		0.554	0.400	0.300	0.500	0.188			
0.3	1	0.500	0.471	0.405	0.403	0.194	0.056	0.129	0.058
		0.529	0.500	0.600	0.600	0.307			
		0.595	0.400	0.500	0.700	0.302			
		0.597	0.400	0.300	0.500	0.197			
0.5	1	0.500	0.502	0.404	0.367	0.194	0.077	0.098	0.042
		0.498	0.500	0.600	0.600	0.298			
		0.596	0.400	0.500	0.700	0.301			
		0.633	0.400	0.300	0.500	0.207			
0.7	2	0.500	0.490	0.400	0.369	0.191	0.072	0.110	0.046
		0.510	0.500	0.600	0.600	0.301			
		0.600	0.400	0.500	0.700	0.303			
		0.631	0.400	0.300	0.500	0.206			
0.9	4	0.500	0.521	0.400	0.343	0.193	0.095	0.079	0.032
		0.479	0.500	0.600	0.600	0.292			
		0.600	0.400	0.500	0.700	0.302			
		0.657	0.400	0.300	0.500	0.213			

preference relation, the multiplicative consistent incomplete fuzzy preference relation, and the acceptable incomplete fuzzy preference relation. Then we introduce a priority method for an incomplete fuzzy preference relation, and analyze the situations where the judgment information is unknown completely.

Remark 2.2 For the fuzzy preference relation whose elements are known completely, we still call it a fuzzy preference relation.

Definition 2.6 [118] Let $C = (c_{ij})_{n\times n}$ be a fuzzy preference relation, if some of its elements are missing, then C is called an incomplete fuzzy preference relation.

For the unknown element c_{ij}, we denote it as "x", and denote the corresponding unknown element c_{ji} as "$1-x$".

Let Ψ be the set of all the known elements in the incomplete fuzzy preference relation C.

Definition 2.7 [118] Let $C = (c_{ij})_{n\times n}$ be a fuzzy preference relation, if the elements in the main diagonal of C are 0.5, and all the other elements are unknown, then C is called a totally incomplete fuzzy preference relation.

Table 2.6 Fuzzy preference relations and their corresponding parameters derived by using the weighted geometric mean in Algorithm III

α	k	$H^{(k)}$				$\gamma^{(k)}$	$CR^{(k)}$	$\delta^{(k)}$	$\sigma^{(k)}$
0.1	3	0.500	0.469	0.400	0.454	0.204	0.022	0.154	0.079
		0.531	0.500	0.507	0.600	0.278			
		0.600	0.495	0.500	0.700	0.331			
		0.546	0.400	0.300	0.500	0.187			
0.3	3	0.500	0.494	0.400	0.418	0.202	0.038	0.118	0.062
		0.506	0.500	0.524	0.600	0.277			
		0.600	0.476	0.500	0.700	0.326			
		0.582	0.400	0.300	0.500	0.195			
0.5	4	0.500	0.461	0.400	0.382	0.189	0.044	0.139	0.060
		0.539	0.500	0.600	0.600	0.311			
		0.600	0.400	0.500	0.653	0.286			
		0.608	0.400	0.347	0.500	0.213			
0.7	6	0.500	0.475	0.400	0.383	0.191	0.055	0.125	0.054
		0.525	0.500	0.569	0.600	0.294			
		0.600	0.431	0.500	0.700	0.312			
		0.617	0.400	0.300	0.500	0.203			
0.9	12	0.500	0.501	0.400	0.358	0.192	0.077	0.099	0.041
		0.499	0.500	0.600	0.600	0.298			
		0.600	0.400	0.500	0.690	0.299			
		0.642	0.400	0.310	0.500	0.211			

By the definition of incomplete fuzzy preference relation, we can see that the following theorem holds:

Theorem 2.22 [118] Let $C=(c_{ij})_{n\times n}$ be an incomplete fuzzy preference relation, then the sum of all the elements in C is

$$\sum_{i=1}^{n}\sum_{j=1}^{n} c_{ij} = \frac{n^2}{2}$$

Definition 2.8 [118] Let $C=(c_{ij})_{n\times n}$ be an incomplete fuzzy preference relation, then its directed graph $G(C)=(N,E)$ is given as:

$$N=\{1,2,\ldots,n\},\quad E=\{(i,j)\,|\,c_{ij}\in\Psi\}$$

where N is the set of nodes, E is the set of directed arcs, and c_{ij} is the entry of the directed arc (i,j).

Definition 2.9 [118] Let $C=(c_{ij})_{n\times n}$ be an incomplete fuzzy preference relation, the elements c_{ij} and c_{kl} are called adjoining, if $(i,j)\cap(k,l)\neq\phi$, where ϕ is the

Table 2.7 Fuzzy preference relations and their corresponding parameters derived by using the weighted arithmetic average in Algorithm III

α	k	$H^{(k)}$				$\gamma^{(k)}$	$CR^{(k)}$	$\delta^{(k)}$	$\sigma^{(k)}$
0.1	3	0.500	0.473	0.400	0.446	0.203	0.024	0.146	0.076
		0.527	0.500	0.507	0.600	0.277			
		0.600	0.493	0.500	0.700	0.331			
		0.554	0.400	0.300	0.500	0.189			
0.3	3	0.500	0.503	0.400	0.403	0.202	0.046	0.103	0.056
		0.497	0.500	0.528	0.600	0.275			
		0.600	0.472	0.500	0.700	0.324			
		0.597	0.400	0.300	0.500	0.199			
0.5	4	0.500	0.477	0.400	0.367	0.190	0.054	0.123	0.052
		0.523	0.500	0.600	0.600	0.306			
		0.600	0.400	0.500	0.656	0.287			
		0.633	0.400	0.344	0.500	0.217			
0.7	6	0.500	0.496	0.400	0.370	0.194	0.065	0.104	0.045
		0.504	0.500	0.600	0.600	0.301			
		0.600	0.400	0.500	0.675	0.293			
		0.630	0.400	0.325	0.500	0.212			
0.9	16	0.500	0.502	0.400	0.364	0.193	0.075	0.098	0.042
		0.498	0.500	0.600	0.600	0.298			
		0.600	0.400	0.500	0.692	0.299			
		0.636	0.400	0.308	0.500	0.209			

empty set. For the unknown c_{ij}, if there exists the adjoining known elements c_{ij_1}, $c_{j_1 j_2}, \cdots, c_{j_k j}$, then c_{ij} is called available indirectly.

Definition 2.10 [118] Let $C=(c_{ij})_{n\times n}$ be an incomplete fuzzy preference relation, if each unknown element can be obtained by its adjoining known elements, then C is called acceptable; Otherwise, C is called unacceptable.

Definition 2.11 [118] For the directed graph $G(C)=(N,E)$, if each pair nodes are reachable, then $G(C)$ is called strong connected.

Theorem 2.23 [118] The incomplete fuzzy preference relation $C=(c_{ij})_{n\times n}$ is acceptable if and only if the directed graph $G(C)$ is strong connected.

Proof (Sufficiency) If $G(C)$ is strong connected, then for any unknown element c_{ij}, there must exist a connected line between the nodes i and j:

$$i \to j_1 \to j_2 \to \cdots \to j_k \to j$$

and there exist a sequence of known elements: $c_{ij_1}, c_{j_1 j_2}, \cdots, c_{j_k j}$, therefore, C is acceptable.

(**Necessity**) If $C=(c_{ij})_{n\times n}$ is acceptable, then according to Definition 2.11, any unknown element of C can be derived from the known elements, i.e., for any unknown element c_{ij}, there must exist a sequence of known elements: $c_{ij_1}, c_{j_1 j_2}, \cdots, c_{j_k j}$, such that there is a connected line between the nodes i and j: $i\to j_1\to j_2\to\cdots\to j_k\to j$, i.e., the pair nodes i and j are reachable. Therefore, the directed graph of $C=(c_{ij})_{n\times n}$ is strong connected. This completes the proof.

Theorem 2.24 [118] Let $C=(c_{ij})_{n\times n}$ be an incomplete fuzzy preference relation. If we remove the i th row and i th column from C, then the preference relation C' composed by the remainder $(n-1)$ rows and $(n-1)$ columns of C is also a fuzzy preference relation or an incomplete fuzzy preference relation.

Proof (1) If all the unknown elements are contained in the removed line and column, then all the elements in the derived C' are the known ones, and for any $c'_{ij}\in C'$, it holds that $c'_{ij}+c'_{ji}=1$, $c'_{ii}=0.5$, $c'_{ij}\ge 0$, and thus, C' is a fuzzy preference relation.

(2) If some of the unknown elements of C are contained in the removed line and column, and the other known elements are left in the other lines and columns, or all the unknown elements are left in the other lines and columns of C, then the derived C' still contains the unknown elements, and the known elements in C' satisfy the conditions $c'_{ij}+c'_{ji}=1$, $c'_{ii}=0.5$, and $c'_{ij}\ge 0$. Therefore, C' is still an incomplete fuzzy preference relation. This completes the proof.

Definition 2.12 [118] Let $C=(c_{ij})_{n\times n}$ be an incomplete fuzzy preference relation.

1. If $c^T_{ij}=c_{ji}(i,j=1,2,\ldots,n)$, then $C^T=(c^T_{ij})_{n\times n}$ is the transpose matrix of C.
2. If $\bar{c}_{ij}=1-c_{ij}(i,j=1,2,\ldots,n)$, then $\bar{C}=(\bar{c}_{ij})_{n\times n}$ is the supplement matrix of C.

Theorem 2.25 [118] The transpose matrix C^T and the supplement matrix $\bar{C}$ of the incomplete fuzzy preference relation $C=(c_{ij})_{n\times n}$ are the same, and both are incomplete fuzzy preference relation.

Proof (1) Let $C^T=(c^T_{ij})_{n\times n}$ and $\bar{C}=(\bar{c}_{ij})_{n\times n}$. By Definition 2.12, we have

$$c^T_{ij}=c_{ji}=1-c_{ij}=\bar{c}_{ij}$$

i.e., $C^T=\bar{C}$.

(2) Since the transposes of the unknown elements in the incomplete fuzzy preference relation C are also the unknown elements, and the transposes of the known elements of C still satisfy:

$$c^T_{ij}=c_{ji}\ge 0,\quad c^T_{ii}=c_{ii}=0.5,\quad c^T_{ij}=c_{ji}=c_{ji}+c_{ij}=1$$

Therefore, C^T is an incomplete fuzzy preference relation, and by (1), we can know that $\bar{C}$ is also an incomplete fuzzy preference relation. This completes the proof.

Definition 2.13 [118] Let $C = (c_{ij})_{n \times n}$ be an incomplete fuzzy preference relation. If

$$c_{ik} + c_{kj} \geq c_{ij}, \quad \text{for any} \quad c_{ik}, c_{kj}, c_{ij} \in \Psi$$

then we say C satisfies the triangle condition.

Definition 2.14 [118] Let $C = (c_{ij})_{n \times n}$ be an incomplete fuzzy preference relation. If $c_{ik} \geq 0.5$, $c_{kj} \geq 0.5 \Rightarrow c_{ij} \geq 0.5$, for all $c_{ik}, c_{kj}, c_{ij} \in \Psi$, then we say C satisfies the weak transitivity property.

Definition 2.15 [118] Let $C = (c_{ij})_{n \times n}$ be an incomplete fuzzy preference relation. If $c_{ij} \geq \min\{c_{ik}, c_{kj}\}$, for any $c_{ik}, c_{kj}, c_{ij} \in \Psi$, then we say C satisfies the max-min transitivity property.

Definition 2.16 [118] Let $C = (c_{ij})_{n \times n}$ be an incomplete fuzzy preference relation. If $c_{ij} \geq \max\{c_{ik}, c_{kj}\}$, for any $c_{ik}, c_{kj}, c_{ij} \in \Psi$, then we say C satisfies the max-max transitivity property.

Definition 2.17 [118] Let $C = (c_{ij})_{n \times n}$ be an incomplete fuzzy preference relation. If $c_{ik} \geq 0.5$, $c_{kj} \geq 0.5 \Rightarrow c_{ij} \geq \min\{c_{ik}, c_{kj}\}$, then we say C satisfies the restricted max-min transitivity property.

Definition 2.18 [118] Let $C = (c_{ij})_{n \times n}$ be an incomplete fuzzy preference relation. If $c_{ik} \geq 0.5, c_{kj} \geq 0.5 \Rightarrow c_{ij} \geq \max\{c_{ik}, c_{kj}\}$, then we say C satisfies the restricted max-max transitivity property.

Definition 2.19 [118] Let $C = (c_{ij})_{n \times n}$ be an incomplete fuzzy preference relation. If $c_{ik}c_{kj}c_{ji} = c_{ki}c_{ij}c_{jk}$, then C is called a multiplicative consistent incomplete fuzzy preference relation.

Definition 2.20 [118] Let $C = (c_{ij})_{n \times n}$ be an incomplete fuzzy preference relation. If $c_{ij} = c_{ik} - c_{ji} + 0.5$, then C is called an additive consistent incomplete fuzzy preference relation.

Theorem 2.26 [118] Let $C = (c_{ij})_{n \times n}$ be an incomplete fuzzy preference relation.

1. If C satisfies the triangle condition, then the transpose C^T and the supplement matrix $\bar{C}$ of C also satisfy the triangle condition.
2. If C is a multiplicative consistent incomplete fuzzy preference relation, then the transpose C^T and the supplement matrix $\bar{C}$ of C are also the multiplicative consistent incomplete fuzzy preference relations.
3. If C is an additive consistent incomplete fuzzy preference relation, then the transpose C^T and the supplement matrix $\bar{C}$ of C are also the additive consistent incomplete fuzzy preference relations.

Proof (1) Since $C=(c_{ij})_{n\times n}$ satisfies the triangle condition, i.e., $c_{ik}+c_{kj}\geq c_{ij}$, for any $c_{ik},c_{kj},c_{ij}\in\Psi$, then

$$c_{ik}^{T}+c_{kj}^{T}=c_{ki}+c_{jk}=c_{jk}+c_{ki}\geq c_{ji}=c_{ij}^{T},\quad \text{for any}\quad c_{ik}^{T},c_{kj}^{T},c_{ij}^{T}\in\Psi$$

and thus, C^T satisfies the triangle condition. According to the equivalence of C^T and $\overline{C}$, we can see that $\overline{C}$ also satisfies the triangle condition.

(2) Since C is a multiplicative consistent incomplete fuzzy preference relation, i.e., $c_{ik}c_{kj}c_{ji}=c_{ki}c_{ij}c_{jk}$, for any $c_{ik},c_{kj},c_{ij}\in\Psi$, then

$$c_{ik}^{T}c_{kj}^{T}c_{ji}^{T}=c_{ki}c_{jk}c_{ij}=c_{ki}c_{ij}c_{jk}=c_{ik}c_{kj}c_{ji}=c_{kj}^{T}c_{ij}^{T}c_{jk}^{T},\quad \text{for any}\quad c_{ik}^{T},c_{kj}^{T},c_{ij}^{T}\in\Psi$$

and thus, C^T and $\overline{C}$ are also multiplicative consistent incomplete fuzzy preference relation.

(3) Since C is an additive consistent incomplete fuzzy preference relation, i.e., $c_{ij}=c_{ik}-c_{jk}+0.5$, for any $c_{ik},c_{jk},c_{ij}\in\Psi$, then

$$\begin{aligned}c_{ij}^{T}&=c_{ji}=1-c_{ij}=1-(c_{ik}-c_{jk}+0.5)\\&=(1-c_{ik})-(1-c_{jk})+0.5\\&=c_{ki}-c_{kj}+0.5\\&=c_{ik}^{T}-c_{jk}^{T}+0.5\end{aligned}$$

thus, C^T and $\overline{C}$ are also additive consistent incomplete fuzzy preference relation. This completes the proof.

Let $C=(c_{ij})_{n\times n}$ be an incomplete fuzzy preference relation, and $w=(w_1,w_2,\ldots w_n)$ be the priority vector of C, where $w_j\geq 0,\ j=1,2,\ldots,n$, and $\sum_{j=1}^{n}w_j=1$. If

$$c_{ij}=\alpha(w_i-w_j)+0.5, 0<\alpha<1,\quad \text{for any}\quad c_{ij}\in\Psi \tag{2.61}$$

then $c_{ij}=c_{ik}-c_{jk}+0.5$, for any $c_{ij},c_{ik},c_{jk}\in\Psi$. Therefore, C is an additive consistent incomplete fuzzy preference relation. In general, we take $\alpha=0.5$.

In fact, by using $0\leq c_{ij}\leq 1$ and Eq. (2.61), we have

$$-0.5\leq\alpha(w_i-w_j)\leq 0.5 \tag{2.62}$$

Since $w_j \geq 0,\ j = 1, 2, \ldots, n$, and $\sum_{j=1}^{n} w_j = 1$, then

$$-1 \leq w_i - w_j \leq 1 \tag{2.63}$$

Combining Eqs. (2.62) and (2.63), we can know that it is suitable to take $\alpha = 0.5$.

If $\alpha = 0.5$, then Eq. (2.61) reduces to

$$c_{ij} = 0.5(w_i - w_j + 1) \tag{2.64}$$

Now we replace the unknown element c_{ij} with $0.5(w_i - w_j + 1)$ in the incomplete fuzzy preference relation $C = (c_{ij})_{n \times n}$, i.e., we utilize Eq. (2.64) to construct an auxiliary matrix $\dot{C} = (\dot{c}_{ij})_{n \times n}$, where

$$\dot{c}_{ij} = \begin{cases} c_{ij}, & c_{ij} \neq x \\ 0.5(w_i - w_j + 1), & c_{ij} = x \end{cases}$$

Example 2.3 Assume that

$$C = \begin{pmatrix} 0.5 & 0.4 & x \\ 0.6 & 0.5 & 0.7 \\ 1 - x & 0.3 & 0.5 \end{pmatrix}$$

then its auxiliary matrix is

$$\dot{C} = \begin{pmatrix} 0.5 & 0.4 & 0.5(w_1 - w_3 + 1) \\ 0.6 & 0.5 & 0.7 \\ 0.5(w_3 - w_1 + 1) & 0.3 & 0.5 \end{pmatrix}$$

Using the normalization formula:

$$w_i = \frac{\sum_{j=1}^{n} \dot{c}_{ij}}{\sum_{i=1}^{n} \sum_{j=1}^{n} \dot{c}_{ij}} = \frac{\sum_{j=1}^{n} \dot{c}_{ij}}{\frac{n^2}{2}}, \quad i = 1, 2, \ldots, n \tag{2.65}$$

we get the system of linear equations:

$$\begin{cases} w_1 = \dfrac{0.5+0.4+0.5(w_1 - w_3 + 1)}{4.5} \\ w_2 = \dfrac{0.6+0.5+0.7}{4.5} \\ w_2 = \dfrac{0.5(w_3 - w_4 + 1) + 0.3 + 0.5}{4.5} \end{cases}$$

from which we get the weights: $w_1 = 0.31$, $w_2 = 0.40$, and $w_3 = 0.29$. Then the priority vector of C is

$$w = (0.31, 0.40, 0.29)$$

Based on the idea above, we give a simple priority method for an incomplete fuzzy preference relation [118]:

Step 1 For a decision making problem, the decision maker utilizes the 0–1 scale to compare each pairs of objects under a criterion, and then constructs an incomplete fuzzy preference relation $C = (c_{ij})_{n\times n}$. The unknown element c_{ij} in C is denoted by "x", and the corresponding element c_{ji} is denoted by "$1-x$".

Step 2 Construct the auxiliary matrix $\dot{C} = (\dot{c}_{ij})_{n\times n}$ of $C = (c_{ij})_{n\times n}$ where

$$\dot{c}_{ij} = \begin{cases} c_{ij}, & c_{ij} \neq x \\ 0.5(w_i - w_j + 1), & c_{ij} = x \end{cases}$$

Step 3 Utilize Eq. (2.65) to establish a system of linear equations, from which the priority vector $w = (w_1, w_2, \ldots, w_n)$ of C can be derived.

Especially, if the decision maker cannot provide any comparison information, then we can get the following conclusion:

Theorem 2.27 [118] If $C = (c_{ij})_{n\times n}$ is a totally incomplete fuzzy preference relation, then the priority vector of C derived by using the priority method above is

$$w = \left(\frac{1}{n}, \frac{1}{n}, \ldots, \frac{1}{n}\right)$$

Proof Since $C = (c_{ij})_{n\times n}$ is a totally incomplete fuzzy preference relation, then we get its auxiliary matrix $\dot{C} = (\dot{c}_{ij})_{n\times n}$:

$$\dot{c}_{ij} = \begin{cases} 0.5, & i = j \\ 0.5(w_i - w_j + 1), & i \neq j \end{cases}$$

Utilizing Eq. (2.65), we get a system of linear equations:

$$w_i = \frac{0.5 + \sum_{j \neq i} 0.5(w_i - w_j + 1)}{\frac{n^2}{2}}, \quad i = 1, 2, \ldots, n$$

which can be simplified as:

$$n^2 w_i = n + (n-1)w_i - \sum_{j \neq i} w_j = n + (n-1)w_i - (1 - w_i)$$

$$= n + nw_i - 1, \quad i = 1, 2, \ldots, n$$

i.e.,

$$w_i = \frac{1}{n}, \quad i = 1, 2, \ldots, n$$

therefore, the priority vector of C is $w = \left(\frac{1}{n}, \frac{1}{n}, \cdots \frac{1}{n}\right)$. This completes the proof.

Considering that in the cases where there is no any judgment information, people cannot know which object is better, and thus, all the objects can only be assigned the equal weights. Therefore, the result in Theorem 2.27 is in accordance with the practical situations.

2.3 Linear Goal Programming Method for Priority of a Hybrid Preference Relation

For the situations where the decision maker provides different types of preferences, below we introduce the concepts of hybrid preference relation and consistent hybrid preference relation, and then present a linear goal programming method for the priority of a hybrid preference relation:

Definition 2.21 [143] C is called a consistent hybrid preference relation, if the multiplicative preference information in C satisfies $c_{ij} = c_{ik}c_{kj}$, $i, j, k = 1, 2, \ldots, n$ and the fuzzy preference information in C satisfies $c_{ik}c_{kj}c_{ji} = c_{ki}c_{jk}c_{ij}$, $i, j, k = 1, 2, \ldots, n$.

Let $\gamma = (\gamma_1, \gamma_2, \ldots, \gamma_n)$ be a priority vector of multiplicative preference relation $H = (h_{ij})_{n \times n}$, where $\gamma_j > 0$, $j = 1, 2, \ldots, n$, and $\sum_{j=1}^{n} \gamma_j = 1$, then if $H = (h_{ij})_{n \times n}$ is a consistent multiplicative preference relation, i.e., $h_{ij} = h_{ik}h_{kj}$, for any i, j, k, then

$$h_{ij} = \frac{\gamma_i}{\gamma_j}, \quad i, j = 1, 2, \ldots, n$$

Let $w=(w_1,w_2,\ldots,w_n)$ be the priority vector of the fuzzy preference relation $B=(b_{ij})_{n\times n}$, where $w_i>0,\ j=1,2,\ldots,n$, and $\sum_{j=1}^{n} w_j=1$, then if B is a multiplicative consistent fuzzy preference relation, then

$$b_{ij}=\frac{w_i}{w_i+w_j},\quad i,j=1,2,\ldots,n$$

i.e.,

$$b_{ji}w_i=b_{ij}w_j,\quad i,j=1,2,\ldots,n$$

For the hybrid preference relation $C=(c_{ij})_{n\times n}$, let $v=(v_1,v_2,\ldots,v_n)$ be the priority vector of C, where $v_i>0,\ j=1,2,\ldots,n$, and $\sum_{j=1}^{n} v_j=1$. Let I_i be the set of subscripts of the columns that the multiplicative preference information of the i th line of C lies, where $I_i\cup J_i=N$, then if $C=(c_{ij})_{n\times n}$ is a consistent hybrid preference relation, then the multiplicative preference information of C satisfies $c_{ij}=\frac{v_i}{v_j}$, $i=1,2,\ldots,n,\ j\in I_i$, i.e.,

$$v_i=c_{ij}v_j,\ i=1,2,\ldots,n,\ j\in I_i \tag{2.66}$$

and the fuzzy preference information of C satisfies $c_{ij}=\frac{v_i}{v_i+v_j}$, $i=1,2,\ldots,n$, $j\in J_i$, i.e.,

$$c_{ji}v_i=c_{ij}v_j,\quad i=1,2,\ldots,n,\quad j\in J_i \tag{2.67}$$

Considering that the hybrid preference relation provided by the decision maker is generally inconsistent, i.e., Eqs. (2.66) and (2.67) generally do not hold, and thus, we introduce the following deviation functions:

$$f_{ij}=|v_i-c_{ij}v_j|,\quad i=1,2,\ldots,n,\quad j\in I_i$$

$$f_{ij}=|c_{ji}v_i-c_{ij}v_j|,\quad i=1,2,\ldots,n,\quad j\in J_i$$

Obviously, to get a reasonable priority vector $v=(v_1,v_2,\ldots,v_n)$, the values of deviation functions above should be as small as possible. Consequently, we construct the following multi-objective optimization model:

$$(\mathbf{M-2.1})\begin{cases}\min f_{ij}=|c_{ji}v_i-c_{ij}v_j|,\ i=1,2,\ldots,n,\quad j\in I_i\\ \min f_{ij}=|c_{ji}v_i-c_{ij}v_j|,\ i=1,2,\ldots,n,\quad j\in J_i\\ s.t.\ v_j>0, j=1,2,\ldots,n,\ \sum_{j=1}^{n} v_j=1\end{cases}$$

To solve the model (M-2.1), and considering that all the objective functions f_{ij} $(i, j = 1, 2, \ldots, n)$ are fair, we can change the model (M-2.1) into the following linear goal programming model [143]:

$$
(\mathbf{M-2.2}) \quad \begin{cases} \min J = \sum_{i=1}^{n} \sum_{\substack{j=1 \\ j \neq i}}^{n} (s_{ij} d_{ij}^{+} + t_{ij} d_{ij}^{-}) \\ s.t.\ v_i - c_{ij} v_j - d_{ij}^{+} + d_{ij}^{-} = 0, \quad i = 1, 2, \ldots, n,\ j \in I_i, \quad i \neq j \\ \quad c_{ji} v_i - c_{ij} v_j - d_{ij}^{+} + d_{ij}^{-} = 0, \quad i = 1, 2, \ldots, n,\ j \in J_i, \quad i \neq j \\ \quad \sum_{j=1}^{n} v_j = 1, \qquad v_j > 0,\ j = 1, 2, \ldots, n \\ \quad d_{ij}^{+} \geq 0,\ d_{ij}^{-} \geq 0, \qquad i, j = 1, 2, \ldots, n, \quad i \neq j \end{cases}
$$

where d_{ij}^{+} is the positive deviation from the target of the objective function f_{ij}, defined as:

$$d_{ij}^{+} = (v_i - c_{ij} v_j) \vee 0, \quad i = 1, 2, \ldots, n, \quad j \in I_i, \quad i \neq j$$

$$d_{ij}^{+} = (c_{ji} v_i - c_{ij} v_j) \vee 0, \quad i = 1, 2, \ldots, n, \quad j \in J_i, \quad i \neq j$$

d_{ij}^{-} is the negative deviation from the target of the objective function f_{ij}, defined as:

$$d_{ij}^{-} = (c_{ij} v_j - v_i) \vee 0, \quad i = 1, 2, \ldots, n, \quad j \in I_i, \quad i \neq j$$

$$d_{ij}^{-} = (c_{ij} v_j - c_{ji} v_i) \vee 0, \quad i = 1, 2, \ldots, n, \quad j \in J_i, \quad i \neq j$$

s_{ij} is the weighting factor corresponding to the positive deviation d_{ij}^{+}, t_{ij} is the weighting factor corresponding to the negative deviation d_{ij}^{-}. By solving the model (M-2.2), we can get the priority vector v of the hybrid preference relation C.

Example 2.4 For a MADM problem, there are four attributes $u_i (i = 1, 2, 3, 4)$, the decision maker compares each pair of the attributes, uses the 0.1–0.9 scale and the 1–9 scale to express his/her preferences, and gives the following hybrid preference relation:

$$
C = \begin{pmatrix} 1 & 3 & 7 & 0.9 \\ \frac{1}{3} & 1 & 0.7 & 5 \\ \frac{1}{7} & 0.3 & 1 & 3 \\ 0.1 & \frac{1}{5} & \frac{1}{3} & 1 \end{pmatrix}
$$

If we take $s_{ij} = t_{ij} = 1,\ i, j = 1,2,3,4$, then we can derive the priority vector of the hybrid preference relation C from the model (M-2.2):

$$v = (0.6130, 0.2302, 0.1082, 0.0486)$$

2.4 MAGDM Method Based on WA and CWA Operators

In a MADM problem where there is only one decision maker. The decision maker uses the fuzzy preference relation to provide weight information over the predefined attributes. We can utilize the method introduced above to derive the attribute weights, and then employ the WA operator to aggregate the decision information, based on which the considered alternatives can be ranked and selected.

For the group settings, in what follows, we introduce a MAGDM methods based on the WA and CWA operators:

Step 1 Consider a MADM problem, assume that there are t decision makers whose weight vector is $\lambda = (\lambda_1, \lambda_2, \ldots \lambda_t)$, and the decision maker $d_k \in D$ uses the fuzzy preference relation B_k to provide weight information over the predefined attributes. Additionally, the decision maker d_k gives the attribute value $a_{ij}^{(k)}$ over the alternative x_i with respect to the attribute u_j, and thus get a decision matrix $A_k = (a_{ij}^{(k)})_{n\times m}$. If the "dimensions" of the attributes are different, then we need to normalize A into the matrix $R_k = (r_{ij}^{(k)})_{n\times m}$.

Step 2 Utilize the corresponding priority method to derive the priority vector of the fuzzy preference relation given by each decision maker, i.e., to derive the attribute weight vector $w^{(k)} = (w_1^{(k)}, w_2^{(k)}, \ldots, w_m^{(k)})$ from the attribute weight information given by each decision maker.

Step 3 Employ the WA operator to aggregate the attribute values of the i th line of the decision matrix R_k, and get the overall attribute values $z_i(w^{(k)})\ (i = 1,2,\ldots,n)$ of the alternatives x_i ($(i = 1,2,\ldots,n)$ corresponding to the decision maker d_k:

$$z_i(w^{(k)}) = WA_{w^{(k)}}(r_{i1}^{(k)}, r_{i2}^{(k)}, \ldots, r_{im}^{(k)}) = \sum_{j=1}^{m} w_j^{(k)} r_{ij}^{(k)}, \quad i = 1,2,\ldots,n, \quad k = 1,2,\ldots,t$$

Step 4 Use the CWA operator to aggregate the overall attribute values $z_i(w^{(k)})$ ($k = 1,2,\ldots,t$) of the alternative x_i corresponding to t decision makers, and then get the collective overall attribute value of the alternative x_i:

$$z_i(\lambda, \omega) = CWA_{\lambda,w}(z_i(w^{(1)}), z_i(w^{(2)}), \ldots, z_i(w^{(t)})) = \sum_{k=1}^{t} \omega_k b_i^{(k)}, \quad i = 1,2,\ldots,n$$

where $\omega = (\omega_1, \omega_2, \ldots, \omega_t)$ is the weighting vector associated with the CWA operator, $\omega_k \in [0,1]$, $k = 1,2,\ldots,t$, $\sum_{k=1}^{t} \omega_k = 1$, $b_i^{(k)}$ is the k th largest of $(t\lambda_1 z_i(w^{(1)}), t\lambda_2 z_i(w^{(2)}), \ldots, t\lambda_t z_i(w^{(t)}))$, and t is the balancing coefficient.

2.5 Practical Example

Example 2.5 An equipment repair support system is composed of a series of the integrated and optimized repair support factors (i.e., material resources, human sources, information resources, and management tools). System efficiency is used to measure the degree that a system can meet the requirements of a group of specific tasks, and is a function of the system effectiveness, reliability and capacity. The indices (attributes) used to evaluate the efficiency of the equipment repair support systems are listed as follows [61]: (1) u_1: technical efficiency; (2) u_2: management efficiency; (3) u_3: repair equipment efficiency; (4) u_4: the efficiency of repair instrument, equipment, and facilities; (5) u_5: technical information efficiency; (6) u_6: computer software performance; (7) u_7: funds management effectiveness; and (8) u_8: the effectiveness of resource management. There are four decision makers d_k $(k = 1,2,3,4)$, whose weight vector is $\lambda = (0.27, 0.23, 0.24, 0.26)$, they utilize the 0.1–0.9 scale or the 1–9 scale to compare each pair of the attributes above, and then construct the multiplicative preference relation B_1, the fuzzy preference relation B_2, the incomplete fuzzy preference relation B_3, and the hybrid preference relation B_4, respectively:

$$B_1 = \begin{pmatrix} 1 & 3 & 5 & \frac{1}{4} & \frac{1}{7} & 6 & \frac{1}{5} & 4 \\ \frac{1}{3} & 1 & 4 & 2 & 8 & 3 & \frac{1}{7} & \frac{1}{5} \\ \frac{1}{5} & \frac{1}{4} & 1 & 5 & \frac{1}{8} & 6 & 3 & 7 \\ 4 & \frac{1}{2} & \frac{1}{5} & 1 & 9 & 3 & \frac{1}{6} & 7 \\ 7 & \frac{1}{8} & 8 & \frac{1}{9} & 1 & 5 & 3 & \frac{1}{4} \\ \frac{1}{6} & \frac{1}{3} & \frac{1}{6} & \frac{1}{3} & \frac{1}{5} & 1 & 8 & 5 \\ 5 & 7 & \frac{1}{3} & 6 & \frac{1}{3} & \frac{1}{8} & 1 & \frac{1}{4} \\ \frac{1}{4} & 5 & \frac{1}{7} & \frac{1}{7} & 4 & \frac{1}{5} & 4 & 1 \end{pmatrix}$$

$$B_2 = \begin{pmatrix} 0.5 & 0.6 & 0.7 & 0.4 & 0.2 & 0.7 & 0.4 & 0.6 \\ 0.4 & 0.5 & 0.6 & 0.5 & 0.9 & 0.6 & 0.3 & 0.4 \\ 0.3 & 0.4 & 0.5 & 0.7 & 0.2 & 0.7 & 0.6 & 0.8 \\ 0.6 & 0.5 & 0.3 & 0.5 & 0.9 & 0.6 & 0.4 & 0.8 \\ 0.8 & 0.1 & 0.8 & 0.1 & 0.5 & 0.7 & 0.6 & 0.4 \\ 0.3 & 0.4 & 0.3 & 0.4 & 0.3 & 0.5 & 0.9 & 0.6 \\ 0.6 & 0.7 & 0.4 & 0.6 & 0.4 & 0.1 & 0.5 & 0.4 \\ 0.4 & 0.6 & 0.2 & 0.2 & 0.6 & 0.4 & 0.6 & 0.5 \end{pmatrix}$$

$$B_3 = \begin{pmatrix} 0.5 & 0.6 & x & 0.4 & 0.3 & 0.7 & 0.4 & 0.6 \\ 0.4 & 0.5 & 0.6 & 0.5 & 0.9 & 1-x & 0.3 & 0.4 \\ 1-x & 0.4 & 0.5 & 0.7 & 0.3 & 0.7 & 0.6 & 0.9 \\ 0.6 & 0.5 & 0.3 & 0.5 & 0.9 & 0.6 & 0.4 & 0.8 \\ 0.7 & 0.1 & 0.5 & 0.1 & 0.5 & 0.7 & x & 0.4 \\ 0.3 & x & 0.3 & 0.4 & 0.3 & 0.5 & 0.9 & 0.6 \\ 0.6 & 0.7 & 0.4 & 0.6 & 1-x & 0.1 & 0.5 & 0.3 \\ 0.4 & 0.6 & 0.1 & 0.2 & 0.6 & 0.4 & 0.7 & 0.5 \end{pmatrix}$$

$$B_4 = \begin{pmatrix} 0.5 & 2 & 0.7 & 0.4 & 0.2 & 7 & 0.4 & 0.6 \\ \frac{1}{2} & 0.5 & 0.6 & 0.5 & 8 & 0.6 & 0.3 & 0.4 \\ 0.3 & 0.4 & 0.5 & 0.7 & \frac{1}{7} & 0.7 & 0.6 & 9 \\ 0.6 & 0.5 & 0.3 & 0.5 & 0.9 & 0.6 & 0.4 & 0.8 \\ 0.8 & \frac{1}{8} & 7 & 0.1 & 0.5 & 6 & 0.6 & 0.4 \\ \frac{1}{7} & 0.4 & 0.3 & 0.4 & \frac{1}{6} & 0.5 & 8 & 0.6 \\ 0.6 & 0.7 & 0.4 & 0.6 & 0.4 & \frac{1}{8} & 0.5 & 0.4 \\ 0.4 & 0.6 & \frac{1}{9} & 0.2 & 0.6 & 0.4 & 0.6 & 0.5 \end{pmatrix}$$

Additively, they evaluate the repair support systems $x_i (i = 1, 2, 3, 4)$ with respect to the attributes $u_j (j = 1, 2, \ldots, 8)$, and provide the attribute values $r_{ij}^{(k)} (k = 1, 2, 3, 4)$ by using the centesimal system (taking the values from the interval [0, 100]), listed in the decision matrices $R_k (k = 1, 2, 3, 4)$ (see Tables 2.8, 2.9, 2.10, 2.11).

Table 2.8 Decision matrix R_1

	u_1	u_2	u_3	u_4	u_5	u_6	u_7	u_8
x_1	85	90	95	60	70	80	90	85
x_2	95	80	60	70	90	85	80	70
x_3	65	75	95	65	90	95	70	85
x_4	75	75	50	65	95	75	85	80

Table 2.9 Decision matrix R_2

	u_1	u_2	u_3	u_4	u_5	u_6	u_7	u_8
x_1	60	75	90	65	70	95	70	75
x_2	85	60	60	65	90	75	95	70
x_3	60	65	75	80	90	95	90	80
x_4	65	60	60	70	90	85	70	65

Table 2.10 Decision matrix R_3

	u_1	u_2	u_3	u_4	u_5	u_6	u_7	u_8
x_1	60	75	85	60	85	80	60	75
x_2	80	75	60	90	85	65	85	80
x_3	95	80	85	85	90	90	85	95
x_4	60	65	50	60	95	80	65	70

Table 2.11 Decision matrix R_4

	u_1	u_2	u_3	u_4	u_5	u_6	u_7	u_8
x_1	70	80	85	65	80	90	70	80
x_2	85	70	70	80	95	70	85	85
x_3	90	85	80	80	95	85	80	90
x_4	65	70	60	65	90	85	70	75

Remark 2.3 Since all the attributes are benefit-type attributes, and the "dimensions" of the attributes are same, thus, for convenience, we do not need to normalize the decision matrices $R_k\,(k=1,2,3,4)$.

In what follows, we use the method presented in Sect. 2.4 to solve this problem:

Step 1 (1) Derive the priority vector of B_1 by using the eigenvector method:

$$w^{(1)} = (0.1118, 0.1273, 0.1333, 0.1534, 0.1483, 0.0929, 0.1337, 0.0993)$$

(2) Use the least variation priority method of fuzzy preference relation to derive the priority vector of B_2:

$$w^{(2)} = (0.1375, 0.1500, 0.1500, 0.2000, 0.1250, 0.0875, 0.0875, 0.0625)$$

(3) Use the priority method of incomplete fuzzy preference relation to derive the priority vector of B_3:

$$w^{(3)} = (0.1247, 0.1283, 0.1440, 0.1438, 0.1156, 0.1186, 0.1156, 0.1094)$$

(4) Use the linear goal programming priority method of the hybrid preference relation to derive the priority vector of B_4:

$$w^{(4)} = (0.1274, 0.1499, 0.1213, 0.1592, 0.1025, 0.0974, 0.1279, 0.1144)$$

Step 2 Utilize the WA operator to aggregate the attribute values of the i th line of the decision matrix R_k into the overall attribute value $z_i\,(w^{(k)})$ corresponding to the decision maker d_k:

$$\begin{aligned} z_1\,(w^{(1)}) &= WA_{w^{(1)}}(r_{11}^{(1)}, r_{12}^{(1)}, \ldots, r_{18}^{(1)}) \\ &= 0.1118 \times 85 + 0.1273 \times 90 + 0.1333 \times 95 + 0.1534 \times 60 \\ &+ 0.1483 \times 70 + 0.0929 \times 80 + 0.1337 \times 90 + 0.0993 \times 85 \\ &= 81.1140 \end{aligned}$$

Similarly, we have

$$z_2(w^{(1)}) = 78.4315, \quad z_3(w^{(1)}) = 79.4210, \quad z_4(w^{(1)}) = 74.9330$$

$$z_1(w^{(2)}) = 73.8750, \quad z_2(w^{(2)}) = 73.1875, \quad z_3(w^{(2)}) = 77.6875$$

$$z_4(w^{(2)}) = 69.8125, \quad z_1(w^{(3)}) = 72.4275, \quad z_2(w^{(3)}) = 77.2935$$

$$z_3(w^{(3)}) = 87.8705, \quad z_4(w^{(3)}) = 67.2915, \quad z_1(w^{(4)}) = 76.6635$$

$$z_2(w^{(4)}) = 79.7255, \quad z_3(w^{(4)}) = 85.2190 \quad z_4(w^{(4)}) = 71.4595$$

Step 3 Employ the CWA operator (suppose that the weighting vector is $\omega = \left(\frac{1}{6}, \frac{1}{3}, \frac{1}{3}, \frac{1}{6}\right)$) to aggregate the overall attribute values $z_i\,(w^{(k)})(k = 1,2,3,4)$ of the repair support system x_i corresponding to the decision makers $d_k\,(k = 1,2,3,4)$: First, we use λ, t and $z_i\,(w^{(k)})(i,k = 1,2,3,4)$ to get $t\lambda_k z_i\,(w^{(k)})(i,k = 1,2,3,4)$:

$$4\lambda_1 z_1(w^{(1)}) = 87.6031,\ 4\lambda_1 z_2(w^{(1)}) = 84.7060,\ 4\lambda_1 z_3(w^{(1)}) = 85.7747,$$
$$4\lambda_1 z_4(w^{(1)}) = 80.9276,\ 4\lambda_2 z_1(w^{(1)}) = 67.9650,\ 4\lambda_2 z_2(w^{(2)}) = 67.3325$$
$$4\lambda_2 z_3(w^{(2)}) = 71.4725,\ 4\lambda_2 z_4(w^{(2)}) = 64.2275,\ 4\lambda_3 z_1(w^{(3)}) = 69.5304$$
$$4\lambda_3 z_2(w^{(3)}) = 74.2018,\ 4\lambda_3 z_3(w^{(3)}) = 84.3557,\ 4\lambda_3 z_4(w^{(3)}) = 66.5198$$
$$4\lambda_4 z_1(w^{(4)}) = 79.7300,\ 4\lambda_4 z_2(w^{(4)}) = 82.9145,\ 4\lambda_4 z_3(w^{(4)}) = 88.6278$$
$$4\lambda_4 z_4(w^{(4)}) = 74.3179$$

Therefore, the collective overall attribute values of the repair support systems x_i ($i = 1,2,3,4$) are

$$z_1(\lambda,\omega) = 75.6815,\ z_2(\lambda,\omega) = 77.7119$$

$$z_3(\lambda,\omega) = 83.3935,\ z_4(\lambda,\omega) = 71.1384$$

Step 4 Rank the repair support systems $x_i (i = 1,2,3,4)$ according to $z_i(\lambda,\omega)(i = 1,2,3,4): x_3 \succ x_2 \succ x_1 \succ x_4$, and thus, x_3 is the best one.

2.6 MAGDM Method Based on WG and CWG Operators

For the situations where there is only one decision maker, and the elements in the normalized decision matrix are positive, we can utilize the WG operator to aggregate the decision information, and then rank and select the considered alternatives.

For the group decision making problems, in what follows, we present a group decision making method based on the WG and CWG operators [109]:

Step 1 For a MAGDM problem, assume that the weight vector of decision makers is $\lambda = (\lambda_1, \lambda_2, \ldots, \lambda_t)$, and the decision maker $d_k \in D$ uses the fuzzy preference relation B_k to provide the weight information on attributes. Furthermore, the decision maker d_k gives the attribute value $a_{ij}^{(k)}$ of the alternative x_i with respect to u_j, and then constructs the decision matrix $A_k = (a_{ij}^{(k)})_{n\times m}$, where $a_{ij}^{(k)} > 0,\ i = 1,2,\ldots,n$, $j = 1,2,\ldots,m$, and $k = 1,2,\ldots,t$. If the "dimensions" of the attributes are different, then we need to normalize A_k into the matrix $R_k = (r_{ij}^{(k)})_{n\times m}$, where $r_{ij}^{(k)} > 0$, $i = 1,2,\ldots,n,\ j = 1,2,\ldots,m,\ k = 1,2,\ldots,t$.

Step 2 Use the corresponding priority method to derive the priority vector of the preference relation provided by each decision maker, i.e., to derive the corresponding weight vector of attributes, $w^{(k)} = (w_1^{(k)}, w_2^{(k)}, \ldots, w_m^{(k)})$, from the weight information provided by each decision maker.

Step 3 Utilize the WG operator to aggregate the attribute values of the ith line in the decision matrix R_k into the overall attribute value $z_i(w^{(k)})(i = 1,2,\ldots,n,\ k = 1,2,\ldots,t)$:

$$z_i(w^{(k)}) = WG_{w^{(k)}}(r_{i1}^{(k)}, r_{i2}^{(k)}, \ldots, r_{im}^{(k)}) = \prod_{j=1}^{m} (r_{ij}^{(k)})^{w_j^{(k)}}$$

$$k = 1,2,\ldots,t, \quad i = 1,2,\ldots,n$$

Step 4 Employ the CWG operator to aggregate the overall attribute values $z_i(w^{(k)})(k=1,2,\ldots,t)$ of the alternative x_i corresponding to t decision makers into the collective overall attribute value:

$$z_i(\lambda,\omega) = CWG_{\lambda,\omega}(z_i(w^{(1)}), z_i(w^{(2)}), \ldots, z_i(w^{(t)})) = \prod_{k=1}^{t} (b_i^{(k)})^{\omega_k}, i = 1,2,\ldots,n$$

where $\omega = (\omega_1, \omega_2, \ldots, \omega_t)$ is the exponential weighting vector associated with the CWG operator, $\omega_k \in [0,1]$, $k = 1,2,\ldots,t$, $\sum_{k=1}^{t} \omega_k = 1$, $b_i^{(k)}$ is the k th largest of ($z_i(w^{(1)})^{t\lambda_1}, z_i(w^{(2)})^{t\lambda_2}, \ldots, z_i(w^{(t)})^{t\lambda_t}$), and t is the balancing coefficient.

Step 5 Rank and select the alternatives $x_i(i=1,2,\ldots,n)$ according to $z_i(\lambda,\omega)(i=1,2,\ldots,n)$.

2.7 Practical Example

Example 2.6 There are military administrative units $x_i(i=1,2,3,4)$, whose performances are to be evaluated with respect to six indices (or attributes): (1) u_1: political education; (2) military training; (3) conduct and discipline; (4) equipment management; (5) logistics; and (6) safety management. Suppose that there are three decision makers $d_k(k=1,2,3)$, whose weight vector is $\lambda = (0.33, 0.34, 0.33)$, they use the 0.1–0.9 scale and the 1–9 scale to compare each pair of the indices $u_j(j=1,2,\ldots,6)$, and then construct the multiplicative preference relation H, the fuzzy preference relation B, and the incomplete fuzzy preference relation C:

$$H = \begin{pmatrix} 1 & 5 & \frac{1}{6} & 7 & \frac{1}{4} & 8 \\ \frac{1}{5} & 1 & 4 & 5 & \frac{1}{6} & 7 \\ 6 & \frac{1}{4} & 1 & 6 & \frac{1}{5} & 8 \\ \frac{1}{7} & \frac{1}{5} & \frac{1}{6} & 1 & 3 & 4 \\ 4 & 6 & \frac{1}{5} & \frac{1}{3} & 1 & \frac{1}{7} \\ \frac{1}{8} & \frac{1}{7} & \frac{1}{8} & \frac{1}{4} & 7 & 1 \end{pmatrix}$$

$$B = \begin{pmatrix} 0.5 & 0.7 & 0.3 & 0.8 & 0.4 & 0.8 \\ 0.3 & 0.5 & 0.6 & 0.7 & 0.3 & 0.6 \\ 0.7 & 0.4 & 0.5 & 0.6 & 0.3 & 0.8 \\ 0.2 & 0.3 & 0.4 & 0.5 & 0.6 & 0.7 \\ 0.6 & 0.7 & 0.7 & 0.4 & 0.5 & 0.3 \\ 0.2 & 0.4 & 0.2 & 0.3 & 0.7 & 0.5 \end{pmatrix}$$

$$C = \begin{pmatrix} 0.5 & 0.6 & x & 0.7 & 0.5 & 0.7 \\ 0.4 & 0.5 & 0.7 & 0.6 & x & 0.9 \\ 1-x & 0.3 & 0.5 & 0.7 & 0.4 & 0.8 \\ 0.3 & 0.4 & 0.3 & 0.5 & 0.6 & 1-x \\ 0.5 & 1-x & 0.6 & 0.4 & 0.5 & 0.2 \\ 0.3 & 0.1 & 0.2 & x & 0.8 & 0.5 \end{pmatrix}$$

Additively, they evaluate the military administrative units $x_i (i = 1,2,3,4)$ with respect to the indices $u_j (j = 1,2,\ldots,8)$, and provide the attribute values $r_{ij}^{(k)} (k = 1,2,3)$ by using the centesimal system, listed in the decision matrices $R_k (k = 1,2,3)$ (see Tables 2.12, 2.13, 2.14).

Remark 2.4 Since all the indices are the benefit-type indices, and the "dimensions" of the indices are the same, then, for convenience, we do not need to normalize the decision matrices $R_k (k = 1,2,3)$.

In what follows, we use the method introduced in Sect. 2.6 to solve the problem:

Step 1 (1) Utilize the eigenvector method to derive the priority vector of H:

$$w^{(1)} = (0.2167, 0.1833, 0.2316, 0.0880, 0.1715, 0.1088)$$

(2) Utilize the least variation priority method of the fuzzy preference relation to derive the priority vector of B:

Table 2.12 Decision matrix R_1

	u_1	u_2	u_3	u_4	u_5	u_6
x_1	70	80	85	75	90	80
x_2	90	80	70	60	95	70
x_3	65	75	70	85	90	95
x_4	75	70	60	60	95	90

Table 2.13 Decision matrix R_2

	u_1	u_2	u_3	u_4	u_5	u_6
x_1	80	65	95	60	80	90
x_2	65	70	90	95	70	65
x_3	70	75	95	90	70	75
x_4	85	90	65	75	95	75

Table 2.14 Decision matrix R_3

	u_1	u_2	u_3	u_4	u_5	u_6
x_1	75	85	95	75	80	95
x_2	95	80	70	60	95	75
x_3	65	95	85	80	95	90
x_4	85	80	90	60	90	85

$$w^{(2)} = (0.2500, 0.1667, 0.2167, 0.1167, 0.2000, 0.0500)$$

(3) Use the priority method of the incomplete fuzzy preference relation to derive the priority vector of C:

$$w^{(3)} = (0.1949, 0.2015, 0.1773, 0.1448, 0.1485, 0.1330)$$

Step 2 Use the WG operator to aggregate the attribute values of the i th line of the decision matrix R_k, and then get the overall attribute value $z_i(w^{(k)})$ of the alternative x_i corresponding to the decision maker d_k:

$$\begin{aligned} z_1(w^{(1)}) &= WG_{w^{(1)}}(r_{11}^{(1)}, r_{12}^{(1)}, \ldots, r_{16}^{(1)}) \\ &= 70^{0.2167} \times 80^{0.1833} \times 85^{0.2316} \times 75^{0.0880} \times 90^{0.1715} \times 80^{0.1088} \\ &= 79.9350 \end{aligned}$$

Similarly, we have

$$z_2(w^{(1)}) = 78.7135,\ z_3(w^{(1)}) = 77.7927,\ z_4(w^{(1)}) = 73.2201$$

$$z_1(w^{(2)}) = 78.0546,\ z_2(w^{(2)}) = 74.9473,\ z_3(w^{(2)}) = 78.2083$$

$$z_4(w^{(2)}) = 81.1153,\ z_1(w^{(3)}) = 83.5666,\ z_2(w^{(3)}) = 78.8167$$

$$z_3(w^{(3)}) = 83.7737,\ z_4(w^{(3)}) = 81.3388,\ z_2(w^{(3)}) = 78.8167$$

Step 3 Aggregate the overall attribute values $z_i(w^{(k)})(k=1,2,3)$ of the alternative x_i corresponding to three decision makers $d_k(k=1,2,3)$ by using the CWG operator (suppose that its weighting vector is $\omega = \left(\frac{1}{4}, \frac{1}{2}, \frac{1}{4}\right)$): Firstly, we utilize λ, t and $z_i(w^{(k)})(i=1,2,3,4,\ k=1,2,3)$ to derive $z_i(w^{(k)})^{t\lambda_k}\ (i=1,2,3,4,\ k=1,2,3)$:

$$z_1(w^{(1)})^{3\lambda_1} = 76.5085,\ z_2(w^{(1)})^{3\lambda_1} = 75.3509,\ z_3(w^{(1)})^{3\lambda_1} = 74.4782$$
$$z_4(w^{(1)})^{3\lambda_1} = 70.1429,\ z_1(w^{(2)})^{3\lambda_2} = 85.1621,\ z_2(w^{(2)})^{3\lambda_2} = 81.7055$$
$$z_3(w^{(2)})^{3\lambda_2} = 85.3332,\ z_4(w^{(2)})^{3\lambda_2} = 88.5696,\ z_1(w^{(3)})^{3\lambda_3} = 79.9489$$
$$z_2(w^{(3)})^{3\lambda_3} = 75.4488,\ z_3(w^{(3)})^{3\lambda_3} = 80.1450,\ z_4(w^{(3)})^{3\lambda_3} = 77.8386$$

Thus, the collective attribute values of the alternatives $x_i(i=1,2,3,4)$ are

$$z_1(\lambda,\omega) = 80.3332,\ z_2(\lambda,\omega) = 76.9416$$

$$z_3(\lambda,\omega) = 79.9328,\ z_4(\lambda,\omega) = 78.3271$$

Step 4 Rank the alternatives according to $z_i(\lambda,\omega)(i=1,2,3,4)$: $x_1 \succ x_3 \succ x_4 \succ x_2$, from which we get the best alternative x_1.

Chapter 3
MADM with Partial Weight Information

There are lots of research results on the MADM problems where there is only partial weight information and the attribute values are real numbers. In this section, we introduce some main decision making methods for these problems, and give some practical examples.

3.1 MADM Method Based on Ideal Point

3.1.1 Decision Making Method

For a MADM problem, let X and U be the sets of alternatives and attributes, respectively. The weight vector of attributes is $w=(w_1, w_2, \ldots, w_n)$, Φ is the set of attribute weight vectors determined by the known weight information, $w \in \Phi$. $A=(a_{ij})_{n\times m}$ and $R=(r_{ij})_{n\times m}$ are, respectively, the decision matrix and its normalized matrix. The line vector $(r_{i1}, r_{i2}, \ldots, r_{im})$ corresponds to the alternative x_i. According to the matrix R, we let $x^+=(1,1,\ldots,1)$ and $x^-=(0,0,\ldots,0)$ be the positive ideal point (positive ideal alternative) and the negative ideal point (negative ideal alternative), respectively. Obviously, the better the alternative is closer to the positive ideal point, or the better the alternative is further from the negative ideal point. Therefore, we can use the following method to rank and select the alternatives [66]:

1. Let

$$e_i^+(w)=\sum_{j=1}^{m}|r_{ij}-1|\,w_j=\sum_{j=1}^{m}(1-r_{ij})w_j,\quad i=1,2,\ldots,n$$

Z.S. Xu, *Uncertain Multi-Attribute Decision Making*,
DOI 10.1007/978-3-662-45640-8_3

be the weighted deviation between the alternative x_i and the positive ideal point. Since the better the alternative is closer to the positive ideal point, then the smaller $e_i^+(w)$, the better the alternative x_i. As a result, we can establish the following multi-objective optimization model:

$$(\mathbf{M\text{-}3.1})\quad \begin{cases} \min e^+(w) = (e_1^+(w), e_2^+(w), \ldots, e_n^+(w)) \\ s.t.\ w \in \Phi \end{cases}$$

Considering that all the functions $e_i^+(w)(i=1,2,\ldots,n)$ are fair, we can assign them the equal importance, and then transform the model (M-3.1) into the following single-objective optimization model:

$$(\mathbf{M-3.2})\quad \begin{cases} \min e^+(w) = \sum_{i=1}^{n} e_i^+(w) \\ s.t.\ w \in \Phi \end{cases}$$

i.e.,

$$(\mathbf{M\text{-}3.3})\quad \begin{cases} \min e^+(w) = n - \sum_{i=1}^{n}\sum_{j=1}^{n} r_{ij} w_j \\ s.t.\ w \in \Phi \end{cases}$$

Solving the model, we get the optimal solution $w^+ = (w_1^+, w_2^+, \ldots, w_m^+)$. Then we solve $e_i^+(w)(i=1,2,\ldots,n)$ with w^+, and rank the alternatives $x_i(i=1,2,\ldots,n)$ according to $e_i^+(w^+)(i=1,2,\ldots,n)$ in ascending order. The best alternative corresponds to the minimal value of $e_i^+(w^+)(i=1,2,\ldots,n)$.

In particular, if the decision maker cannot offer any weight information, then we can establish a simple single-objective optimization model as below:

$$(\mathbf{M-3.4})\quad \begin{cases} \min F^+(w) = \sum_{i=1}^{n} f_i^+(w) \\ s.t.\ w_j \ge 0,\ j=1,2,\ldots,m,\ \sum_{j=1}^{m} w_j = 1 \end{cases}$$

where $f_i^+(w) = \sum_{j=1}^{m}(1-r_{ij})w_j^2$ denotes the deviation between the alternative x_i and the positive ideal point.

Solving the model, we establish the Lagrange function:

$$L(w,\zeta) = \sum_{i=1}^{n}\sum_{j=1}^{m}(1-r_{ij})w_j^2 + 2\zeta\left(\sum_{j=1}^{m} w_j - 1\right)$$

Differentiating $L(w,\zeta)$ with respect to $w_j (j=1,2,\ldots,m)$ and ζ, and setting these partial derivatives equal to zero, the following set of equations is obtained:

$$\begin{cases} \dfrac{\partial L(w,\zeta)}{\partial \omega_j} = 2\sum_{i=1}^{n}(1-r_{ij})w_j + 2\zeta \\ \dfrac{\partial L(w,\zeta)}{\partial \zeta} = \sum_{j=1}^{m} w_j - 1 = 0 \end{cases}$$

to which the optimal solution is

$$w_j^+ = \frac{\dfrac{1}{n-\sum_{i=1}^{n} r_{ij}}}{\sum_{j=1}^{m}\dfrac{1}{n-\sum_{i=1}^{n} r_{ij}}}, \quad j=1,2,\ldots,m \tag{3.1}$$

Then we solve $f_i^+(w)(i=1,2,\ldots,n)$ with $w^+ = (w_1^+, w_2^+, \ldots, w_m^+)$, and rank the alternatives $x_i (i=1,2,\ldots,n)$ according to $f_i^+(w^+)(i=1,2,\ldots,n)$ in descending order. The best alternative corresponds to the minimal value of $f_i^+(w^+)(i=1,2,\ldots,n)$.

Let

$$e_i^-(w) = \sum_{j=1}^{m} | r_{ij} - 0 | w_j = \sum_{j=1}^{m} r_{ij} w_j, \quad i=1,2,\ldots,n$$

be the weighted deviation between the alternative x_i and the negative ideal point. Since the better the alternative x_i is further from the negative ideal point, then the larger $e_i^-(w)$, the better the alternative x_i. Then similar to the discussion in (1), we can establish the following multi-objective optimization model:

$$(\mathbf{M-3.5}) \quad \begin{cases} \max e^-(w) = \sum_{i=1}^{n} e_i^-(w) \\ s.t.\ w \in \Phi \end{cases}$$

i.e.,

$$(\mathbf{M-3.6}) \quad \begin{cases} \max e^-(w) = \sum_{i=1}^{n}\sum_{j=1}^{m} r_{ij} w_j \\ s.t.\ w \in \Phi \end{cases}$$

Solving the model, we get the optimal solution $w^- = (w_1^-, w_2^-, \ldots, w_m^-)$. Then we solve $e_i^-(w)(i=1,2,\ldots,n)$ with w^-, and rank the alternatives $x_i(i=1,2,\ldots,n)$ according to $e_i^-(w^-)(i=1,2,\ldots,n)$ in descending order. The best alternative corresponds to the maximal value of $e_i^-(w^-)(i=1,2,\ldots,n)$.

3.1.2 Practical Example

In the following, we consider a military problem [56] that concerns MADM:

Example 3.1 Fire system is a dynamic system achieved by collocating and allocating various firearms involved in an appropriate way. The fire system of a tank unit is an essential part when the commander tries to execute fire distribution in a defensive combat. The fire deployment is of great importance in fulfilling a fixed goal, improving the defensive stability, annihilating enemies, and protecting ourselves. The first company of our tank unit is organizing a defensive battle in Xiaoshan region and there are four heights (alternatives) $x_i(i=1,2,3,4)$ available for the commander. The evaluation indices are as follows: (1) u_1—visibility rate; (2) u_2—fire control distance; (3) u_3—the number of the heights being looked down; (4) u_4—slope; and (5) u_5—the difference of elevation. Suppose that $w=(w_1, w_2, \ldots, w_5)$ ($w_j \geq 0, j=1,2,3,4,5$, and $\sum_{j=1}^{5} w_j = 1$) is the weight vector to be derived. The characters of the four heights $x_i(i=1,2,3,4)$ can be described as $A=(a_{ij})_{4\times 5}$. All the data are shown in Table 3.1.

Step 1 Although all $u_j(j=1,2,3,4,5)$ are benefit-type indices, their "dimensions" are different. We utilize Eq. (1.2) to normalize the decision matrix A into the matrix R, listed in Table 3.2.

Table 3.1 Decision matrix A

	u_1	u_2	u_3	u_4	u_5
x_1	0.37	1800	2	19°	90
x_2	0.58	2800	5	28°	105
x_3	0.52	3500	5	32°	130
x_4	0.43	1900	3	27°	98

Table 3.2 Decision matrix R

	u_1	u_2	u_3	u_4	u_5
x_1	0.6379	0.5143	0.4000	0.5938	0.6923
x_2	1.0000	0.8000	1.0000	0.8750	0.8077
x_3	0.8966	1.0000	1.0000	1.0000	1.0000
x_4	0.7414	0.5429	0.6000	0.7538	0.8438

Step 2 Now we consider two cases:

1. If the weight information on attributes is unknown completely, then we use Eq. (3.1) to derive the weight vector of attributes as:

$$w^{+} = (0.2282, 0.1446, 0.1653, 0.2404, 0.2215)$$

and obtain the values of $f_i^{+}(w^{+})(i = 1, 2, 3, 4)$:

$$f_1^{+}(w^{+}) = 0.0840,\ f_2^{+}(w^{+}) = 0.0208,\ f_3^{+}(w^{+}) = 0.0054,\ f_4^{+}(w^{+}) = 0.055$$

from which we get the ranking of the alternatives $x_i (i = 1, 2, 3, 4)$:

$$x_3 \succ x_2 \succ x_4 \succ x_1$$

and thus the best alternative is x_3.

2. If the known weight information is

$$\Phi = \Big\{ w = (w_1, w_2, w_3, w_4, w_5) \mid 0.15 \le w_1 \le 0.25,\ 0.13 \le w_2 \le 0.15$$

$$0.15 \le w_3 \le 0.20,\ 0.20 \le w_4 \le 0.25,\ 0.20 \le w_5 \le 0.23, \sum_{j=1}^{5} w_j = 1 \Big\}$$

then we derive the weight vector of attributes from the models (M-3.3) and (M-3.6) as:

$$w^{+} = w^{-} = (0.22, 0.15, 0.20, 0.20, 0.23)$$

based on which we get $e_i^{+}(w^{+}), e_i^{-}(w^{-})(i = 1, 2, 3, 4)$:

$$e_1^{+}(w^{+}) = 0.4245,\ e_2^{+}(w^{+}) = 0.0992,\ e_3^{+}(w^{+}) = 0.0227$$

$$e_4^{+}(w^{+}) = 0.2933,\ e_1^{-}(w^{-}) = 0.5755,\ e_2^{-}(w^{-}) = 0.9008$$

$$e_3^{-}(w^{-}) = 0.9773,\ e_4^{-}(w^{-}) = 0.7067$$

Therefore, the rankings derived by the methods above are also:

$$x_3 \succ x_2 \succ x_4 \succ x_1$$

and x_3 is the best alternative.

3.2 MADM Method Based on Satisfaction Degrees of Alternatives

3.2.1 Decision Making Method

Consider a MADM problem, let X and U be the sets of alternatives and attributes, respectively, w and Φ be the weight vector of attributes, and the set of the possible weight vectors determined by the known weight information, respectively. Let $A=(a_{ij})_{n\times m}$ and $R=(r_{ij})_{n\times m}$ be the decision matrix and its normalized decision matrix.

Definition 3.1 [152] If $w=(w_1,w_2,\ldots,w_n)$ is the optimal solution to the single-objective optimization model:

$$(\mathbf{M-3.7})\quad \begin{cases} \max z_i(w)=\sum_{j=1}^{m} r_{ij}w_j,\ i=1,2,\ldots,n \\ s.t.\ w\in\Phi \end{cases}$$

then $z_i^{\max}=\sum_{j=1}^{m} r_{ij}w_j$ is the positive ideal overall attribute value of the alternatives $x_i(i=1,2,\ldots,n)$.

Definition 3.2 [152] If $w=(w_1,w_2,\ldots,w_n)$ is the optimal solution to the single-objective optimization model:

$$(\mathbf{M-3.8})\quad \begin{cases} \min z_i(w)=\sum_{j=1}^{m} r_{ij}w_j,\ i=1,2,\ldots,n \\ s.t.\ w\in\Phi \end{cases}$$

then $z_i^{\min}=\sum_{j=1}^{m} r_{ij}w_j$ is the negative ideal overall attribute value of the alternatives $x_i(i=1,2,\ldots,n)$.

Definition 3.3 [152] If

$$\rho_i(w)=\frac{z_i(w)-z_i^{\min}}{z_i^{\max}-z_i^{\min}} \tag{3.2}$$

then $\rho_i(w)$ is called the satisfaction degree of the alternative x_i.

In general, the larger $\rho_i(w)$, the better the alternative x_i, considering that the overall attribute value of each alternative should be derived from one weight vector $w=(w_1,w_2,\ldots,w_n)$, here we establish the following multi-objective optimization model:

$$(\mathbf{M-3.9})\quad \begin{cases} \max\ \rho(w) = (\rho_1(w), \rho_2(w), \ldots, \rho_n(w)) \\ s.t.\ w \in \Phi \end{cases}$$

Since all the functions $\rho_i(w)(i = 1,2,\ldots,n)$ are fair, we can assign them the equal importance, and then transform the model (M-3.9) into the following single-objective optimization model [152]:

$$(\mathbf{M-3.10})\quad \begin{cases} \max\ \rho(w) = \sum_{i=1}^{n} \rho_i(w) \\ s.t.\ w \in \Phi \end{cases}$$

Solving the model (M-3.10), we get $w^+ = (w_1^+, w_2^+, \ldots, w_m^+)$, then the overall attribute value of the alternative x_i:

$$z_i(w^+) = \sum_{j=1}^{m} r_{ij} w_i^+,\ i = 1,2,\ldots,n$$

according to which we can rank and select the best alternative.

3.2.2 Practical Example

Example 3.2 Based on the statistic data of main industrial economic benefit indices provided in China Industrial Economic Statistical Yearbook (2003), below we make an analysis on economic benefits of 16 provinces and the municipalities directly under central government. Given the set of alternatives:

$X = \{x_1, x_2, \ldots, x_{16}\}$ = {Beijing, Tianjin, Shanghai, Jiangsu, Zhejiang, Anhui, Fujian, Guangdong, Liaoning, Shandong, Hubei, Hunan, Henan, Jiangxi, Hebei, Shanxi}

The indices used to evaluate the alternatives $x_i(i = 1,2,\ldots,16)$ are as follows: (1) u_1 : all personnel labor productivity (yuan per person); (2) u_2 : tax rate of capital interest (%); (3) u_3 : profit of per 100 yuan sales income (yuan); (4) u_4 : circulating capital occupied by 100 yuan industrial output value; and (5) u_5 : profit rate of production (%). Among them, u_4 is cost-type index, the others are benefit-type index.

All the data can be shown in Table 3.3.

The weight information of attributes is as follows:

$$\Phi = \{w = (w_1, w_2, \ldots, w_5) \mid 0.22 \le w_1 \le 0.24,\ 0.18 \le w_2 \le 0.20,$$

Table 3.3 Decision matrix A

	u_1	u_2	u_3	u_4	u_5
x_1	47,177	16.61	8.89	31.05	15.77
x_2	43,323	9.08	3.65	29.80	8.44
x_3	59,023	13.84	6.06	26.55	12.87
x_4	46,821	10.59	3.51	22.46	7.41
x_5	41,646	13.24	4.64	24.33	9.33
x_6	26,446	10.16	2.38	26.80	9.85
x_7	38,381	11.97	4.79	26.45	10.64
x_8	57,808	10.29	4.54	23.00	9.23
x_9	28,869	7.68	2.12	31.08	9.05
x_{10}	38,812	8.92	3.38	25.68	8.73
x_{11}	30,721	10.87	4.15	30.36	11.44
x_{12}	24,848	10.77	2.42	30.71	11.37
x_{13}	26,925	9.34	3.06	30.11	10.84
x_{14}	23,269	8.25	2.58	32.57	8.62
x_{15}	28,267	8.13	3.17	29.25	9.17
x_{16}	21,583	7.41	4.66	35.35	11.27

$$0.15 \leq w_3 \leq 0.17,\ 0.23 \leq w_4 \leq 0.26,\ 0.16 \leq w_5 \leq 0.17,\ \sum_{j=1}^{5} w_j = 1 \Bigg\}$$

In the following, we rank the alternatives using the method introduced in Sect. 3.2.1:

Step 1 Utilize Eqs. (1.2) and (1.3) to normalize the decision matrix A into the matrix R, shown in Table 3.4.

Step 2 Utilize the models (M-3.7) and (M-3.8) to derive the positive ideal overall attribute values $z_i^{\max}(i = 1,2,\ldots,16)$ and the negative ideal overall attribute values $z_i^{\min}(i = 1,2,\ldots,16)$ of the alternatives $x_i(i = 1,2,\ldots,16)$, respectively:

$$z_1^{\max} = 0.890,\ z_2^{\max} = 0.623,\ z_3^{\max} = 0.851,\ z_4^{\max} = 0.706$$

$$z_5^{\max} = 0.735,\ z_6^{\max} = 0.585,\ z_7^{\max} = 0.890,\ z_8^{\max} = 0.777$$

$$z_9^{\max} = 0.522,\ z_{10}^{\max} = 0.633,\ z_{11}^{\max} = 0.631,\ z_{12}^{\max} = 0.576$$

$$z_{13}^{\max} = 0.575,\ z_{14}^{\max} = 0.502,\ z_{15}^{\max} = 0.555,\ z_{16}^{\max} = 0.534$$

$$z_1^{\min} = 0.704,\ z_2^{\min} = 0.581,\ z_3^{\min} = 0.797,\ z_4^{\min} = 0.654$$

Table 3.4 Decision matrix R

	u_1	u_2	u_3	u_4	u_5
x_1	0.799	1.000	1.000	0.723	1.000
x_2	0.734	0.547	0.411	0.754	0.535
x_3	1.000	0.833	0.682	0.846	0.816
x_4	0.793	0.638	0.395	1.000	0.470
x_5	0.706	0.797	0.522	0.923	0.592
x_6	0.448	0.612	0.268	0.838	0.625
x_7	0.650	0.721	0.539	0.849	0.675
x_8	0.979	0.620	0.511	0.977	0.585
x_9	0.489	0.462	0.238	0.723	0.574
x_{10}	0.658	0.537	0.380	0.875	0.554
x_{11}	0.520	0.654	0.467	0.740	0.725
x_{12}	0.421	0.648	0.272	0.731	0.721
x_{13}	0.456	0.562	0.344	0.746	0.687
x_{14}	0.394	0.497	0.290	0.690	0.547
x_{15}	0.479	0.489	0.357	0.768	0.581
x_{16}	0.366	0.430	0.524	0.635	0.715

$$z_5^{\min} = 0.684,\ z_6^{\min} = 0.542,\ z_7^{\min} = 0.657,\ z_8^{\min} = 0.722$$

$$z_9^{\min} = 0.485,\ z_{10}^{\min} = 0.588,\ z_{11}^{\min} = 0.588,\ z_{12}^{\min} = 0.534$$

$$z_{13}^{\min} = 0.535,\ z_{14}^{\min} = 0.466,\ z_{15}^{\min} = 0.517,\ z_{16}^{\min} = 0.497$$

Step 3 Utilize the satisfaction degree of each alternative, and then use the model (M-3.10) to establish the following optimal model:

$$\begin{cases} \max\ \rho(w) = 0.464w_1 + 0.466w_2 + 0.339w_3 + 0.584w_4 + 0.473w_5 - 0.477 \\ s.t.\ \ 0.22 \le w_1 \le 0.24,\ 0.18 \le w_2 \le 0.20,\ 0.15 \le w_3 \le 0.17 \\ \quad\ \ 0.23 \le w_4 \le 0.26,\ 0.16 \le w_5 \le 0.17,\ \sum_{j=1}^{5} w_j = 1 \end{cases}$$

Solving this model, we get the optimal solution:

$$w = (0.22, 0.20, 0.15, 0.26, 0.17)$$

from which we derive the overall index value $z_i(w)$ of the alternative x_i:

$$z_1(w) = 0.8838,\ z_2(w) = 0.6195,\ z_3(w) = 0.8476,\ z_4(w) = 0.7012$$

$$z_5(w) = 0.7336,\ z_6(w) = 0.5853,\ z_7(w) = 0.7035,\ z_8(w) = 0.7695$$

$$z_9(w) = 0.5212,\ z_{10}(w) = 0.6308,\ z_{11}(w) = 0.6309,\ z_{12}(w) = 0.5757$$

$$z_{13}(w) = 0.5750,\ z_{14}(w) = 0.5020,\ z_{15}(w) = 0.5552,\ z_{16}(w) = 0.5318$$

Step 4 Rank all the alternatives $x_i (i = 1,2,\ldots,16)$ according to $z_i(w)(i = 1,2,\ldots,16)$:

$$x_1 \succ x_3 \succ x_8 \succ x_5 \succ x_7 \succ x_4 \succ x_{11} \succ x_{10} \succ x_2$$
$$\succ x_6 \succ x_{12} \succ x_{13} \succ x_{15} \succ x_{16} \succ x_9 \succ x_{14}$$

It can be seen from the ranking results above that as the center of politics economics and culture, Beijing's industrial economic benefit level is the best among all the 16 provinces and the municipalities directly under central government. This indicates the strong economic foundation and strength of Beijing. Next comes the industrial economic benefit level of Shanghai; The other provinces ranked three to ten are Guangdong, Zhejiang, Fujian, Jiangsu, Hubei, Shandong, Tianjin and Anhui, most of them are the open and coastal provinces and cities. As the old revolutionary base areas and interior provinces, Jiangxi and Shanxi provinces have weak economic foundations, backward technologies, and low management levels, their industrial economic benefit levels rank 16th and 14th, respectively. Liaoning as China's heavy industrial base has also low industrial economic benefit level which ranks the last second, due to its old aging equipment, the lack of funds, and backward technologies. These results are in accordance with the actual situations at that time.

3.3 MADM Method Based on Maximizing Variation Model

3.3.1 Decision Making Method

For a MADM decision making problem, the deviation between the alternative x_i and any other alternative with respect to the attribute u_j can be defined as:

$$d_{ij}(w) = \sum_{k=1}^{n} (r_{ij} - r_{kj})^2 w_j, \quad i = 1,2,\ldots,n,\ j = 1,2,\ldots,m$$

Let

$$d_j(w) = \sum_{i=1}^{n} d_{ij}(w) = \sum_{i=1}^{n}\sum_{k=1}^{n} (r_{ij} - r_{kj})^2 w_j, \quad j = 1, 2, \ldots, m$$

be the total deviation among all the alternatives and the other alternatives with respect to the attribute u_j. According to the analysis of Sect. 1.5, the selection of the weight vector w should maximize the total deviation of all the alternatives. Consequently, we can construct the following deviation function:

$$d(w) = \sum_{j=1}^{m} d_j(w) = \sum_{j=1}^{m}\sum_{i=1}^{n} d_{ij}(w) = \sum_{j=1}^{m}\sum_{i=1}^{n} (r_{ij} - r_{kj})^2 w_j$$

from which we can construct the linear programming problem:

$$(\mathbf{M-3.11}) \quad \begin{cases} \max d(w) = \sum_{j=1}^{m}\sum_{i=1}^{n}\sum_{k=1}^{n} (r_{ij} - r_{kj})^2 w_j \\ s.t. \ w \in \Phi \end{cases}$$

Solving this simple linear programming model, we get the optimal attribute weight vector w.

Based on the analysis above, we introduce the following algorithm:

Step 1 For a MADM problem, let a_{ij} be the attribute value of the alternative x_i with respect to the attribute u_j, and construct the decision matrix $A = (a_{ij})_{n \times n}$. The corresponding normalized matrix is $R = (r_{ij})_{n \times m}$.

Step 2 The decision maker provides the possible partial weight information Φ.

Step 3 Derive the optimal weight vector w from the single-objective decision model (M-3.11).

Step 4 Calculate the overall attribute values $z_i(w)(i = 1, 2, \ldots, n)$ of the alternatives $x_i(i = 1, 2, \ldots, n)$.

Step 5 Rank the alternatives $x_i(i = 1, 2, \ldots, n)$ according to $z_i(w)(i = 1, 2, \ldots, n)$.

3.3.2 Practical Example

Example 3.3 A mine outside has rich reserves. In order to improve the output of raw coal, three expansion plans $x_i(i = 1, 2, 3)$ are put forward, and three indices (attributes) $u_j(j = 1, 2, 3)$ are used to evaluate the plans [46]: (1) u_1: the total amount of investment ($ 10^3); (2) u_2 : well construction period (year); (3) u_3 : farmland occupation (acreage); (4) u_4 : the annual increase in output (10^4 tons); (5) u_5 : prenatal plan can produce coal quality (10^3 tons); (6) u_6 : safety condition (the centesimal system); (7) u_7 : recoverable period (year); and (8) u_8 : staff productivity (tons per person), where u_1, u_2 and u_3 are the cost-type attributes, and the others are benefit-type attributes. The known attribute weight information is as follows:

$$\Phi = \{w = (w_1, w_2, \ldots w_8) \mid 0.1 \le w_1 \le 0.2, 0.12 \le w_2 \le 0.14$$

$$0.11 \le w_3 \le 0.15, 0.12 \le w_4 \le 0.16, 0.07 \le w_5 \le 0.12$$

$$0.2 \le w_6 \le 0.3, 0.18 \le w_7 \le 0.21, 0.9 \le w_8 \le 0.22, \sum_{j=1}^{8} w_j = 1\}$$

The decision matrix is shown in Table 3.5.

Now we use the method in Sect. 3.3.1 to derive the ranking of the expansion plans $x_i (i = 1, 2, 3)$, which involves the following steps:

Step 1 Utilize Eqs. (1.2) and (1.3) to normalize the decision matrix A, and thus get the matrix R, listed in Table 3.6.

Table 3.5 Decision matrix A

	u_1	u_2	u_3	u_4	u_5	u_6	u_7	u_8
x_1	18,400	3	100	80	300	60	40	1.2
x_2	19,600	4	120	100	400	80	40	1.3
x_3	29,360	6	540	120	150	100	50	1.5

Table 3.6 Decision matrix R

	u_1	u_2	u_3	u_4	u_5	u_6	u_7	u_8
x_1	1.0000	1.0000	1.0000	0.6667	0.7500	0.6000	0.8000	0.8000
x_2	0.9388	0.7500	0.8333	0.8333	1.0000	0.8000	0.8000	0.8000
x_3	0.6267	0.5000	1.0000	1.0000	0.3750	1.0000	1.0000	1.0000

Step 2 Utilize the single-objective decision making model (M-3.11) to establish the following model:

$$\begin{cases} \max d(w) = 0.4860w_1 + 0.7500w_2 + 2.2234w_3 + 0.3333w_4 + 1.1875w_5 \\ \qquad + 0.4800w_6 + 0.1600w_7 + 0.1244w_8 \\ s.t.\ 0.1 \le w_1 \le 0.2,\ 0.12 \le w_2 \le 0.14,\ 0.11 \le w_3 \le 0.15 \\ \quad 0.12 \le w_4 \le 0.16,\ 0.07 \le w_5 \le 0.12,\ 0.2 \le w_6 \le 0.3 \\ \quad 0.18 \le w_7 \le 0.21,\ 0.09 \le w_8 \le 0.22,\ \sum_{j=1}^{8} w_j = 1 \end{cases}$$

from which we get the optimal weight vector:

$$w = (0.10, 0.12, 0.12, 0.12, 0.07, 0.20, 0.18, 0.09)$$

Step 3 By Eq. (1.12), we get the overall attribute values of all expansion plans $x_i (i = 1, 2, 3)$ as follows:

$$z_1(w) = 0.8085,\ z_2(w) = 0.8359,\ z_3(w) = 0.7611$$

Step 4 Rank the expansion plans $x_i (i = 1, 2, 3)$ according to $z_i(w)(i = 1, 2, 3)$:

$$x_2 \succ x_1 \succ x_3$$

and then the optimal plan is x_2.

3.4 Two-Stage-MADM Method Based on Partial Weight Information

3.4.1 Decision Making Method

MADM is generally to rank and select the given alternatives according to their overall attribute values. Clearly, the bigger the overall attribute value $z_i(w)$, the better the alternative x_i.

We first consider the situation where the overall attribute value of each alternative x_i reaches the maximum and the corresponding attribute weights. To do that, we establish the following single-objective decision making model:

$$(\mathbf{M-3.12}) \quad \begin{cases} \max \sum_{j=1}^{m} w_j r_{ij} \\ s.t.\ w \in \Phi \end{cases}$$

Solving this model, we get the optimal attribute weight vector corresponding to the alternative x_i:

$$w^{(i)} = (w_1^{(i)}, w_2^{(i)}, \ldots, w_m^{(i)})$$

In what follows, we utilize the normalized matrix $R = (r_{ij})_{n\times m}$ and the weight vectors $w^{(i)} (i = 1,2,\ldots,n)$ to derive the best compromise weight vector of attributes. Suppose that the matrix composed of the weight vectors $w^{(i)} (i = 1,2,\ldots,n)$ is

$$W = \begin{pmatrix} w_1^{(1)} & w_1^{(2)} & \cdots & w_1^{(n)} \\ w_2^{(1)} & w_2^{(2)} & \cdots & w_2^{(n)} \\ \vdots & \vdots & & \vdots \\ w_m^{(1)} & w_m^{(2)} & \cdots & w_m^{(n)} \end{pmatrix}$$

then we get the combinational weight vector obtained by linearly combining the n weight vectors $w^{(i)} (i = 1,2,\ldots,n)$:

$$w = Wv \tag{3.3}$$

where w is the combination weight vector, v is a n dimensional column vector, which satisfies the condition: $vv^T = 1$. Let $r_i = (r_{i1}, r_{i2}, \ldots, r_{im})(i = 1,2,\ldots,n)$, then $R = (r_1, r_2, \ldots, r_n)$. Thus,

$$z_i(v) = \sum_{j=1}^{m} w_j r_{ij} = r_i W v \tag{3.4}$$

A reasonable weight vector v should make the overall attribute values of all the alternatives as large as possible. As a result, we construct the following multi-objective decision making model:

$$(\mathbf{M-3.13}) \quad \begin{cases} \max(z_1(v), z_2(v), \ldots, z_n(v)) \\ s.t. \ vv^T = 1 \end{cases}$$

Considering that all the overall attribute values $z_i(v)(i = 1,2,\ldots,n)$ are fair, the model (M-3.13) can be transformed into the equally weighted single-objective optimization model:

$$(\mathbf{M-3.14}) \quad \begin{cases} \max z(v) z(v)^T \\ s.t. \ vv^T = 1 \end{cases}$$

where $z(v) = (z_1(v), z_2(v), \ldots, z_n(v)) = RWv$. Let $f(v) = z(v)z(v)^T$, then by Eq. (3.4), we have

$$f(v) = z(v)z(v)^T = v(RW)(RW)^T v^T$$

According to the matrix theory, $f(v)$ exists, whose maximal value is $(RW)(RW)^T$, the maximal eigenvalue is $\lambda_{\max}$, and v is the corresponding eigenvector. Since the matrix $(RW)(RW)^T$ is symmetric nonnegative definite, then it follows from the Perron-Frobenius theory of nonnegative irreducible matrix that $\lambda_{\max}$ is unique, and the corresponding eigenvector $v > 0$. Therefore, by using Eq. (3.3), we can get the combinational weight vector (i.e., the best compromise vector), and use Eq. (1.12) to derive the overall attribute values of all the alternatives, and then rank these alternatives.

Based on the analysis above, we introduce the following algorithm [108]:

Step 1 For a MADM problem, let a_{ij} be the attribute value of the alternative x_i with respect to the attribute u_j, and construct the decision matrix $A = (a_{ij})_{n\times m}$, whose corresponding normalized matrix is $R = (r_{ij})_{n\times m}$.

Step 2 The decision maker provides the attribute weight information Φ.

Step 3 Use the single-objective decision making model (M-3.12) to derive the optimal weight vector of the alternative x_i:

$$w^{(i)} = (w_1^{(i)}, w_2^{(i)}, \ldots, w_m^{(i)})$$

Step 4 Construct the matrix W composed of the n weight vectors $w^{(i)}\ (i = 1,2,\ldots,n)$, and calculate the maximal eigenvalue $\lambda_{\max}$ of the matrix $(RW)(RW)^T$ and the corresponding eigenvector v (which has been normalized).

Step 5 Calculate the combinational weight vector by using Eq. (3.3), and then derive the overall attribute values $z_i(w)(i = 1,2,\ldots,n)$ of the alternatives $x_i (i = 1,2,\ldots,n)$ using Eq. (1.12).

Step 6 Rank the alternatives $x_i (i = 1,2,\ldots,n)$ according to $z_i(w)(i = 1,2,\ldots,n)$.

3.4.2 *Practical Example*

Example 3.4 An artillery group discovers six enemy targets $x_i (i = 1,2,\ldots,6)$ and obtains some other information. The order to attack these targets is needed to be predetermined. According to the actual situations, the operational commander evaluates these targets with respect to six factors (attributes): (1) u_1 : importance of the target; (2) u_2 : urgency of fire mission; (3) u_3 : reliability of the information for the target; (4) u_4 : visibility of the target's location; (5) u_5 : vulnerability of the target;

Table 3.7 Decision matrix A

	u_1	u_2	u_3	u_4	u_5	u_6
x_1	7	9	9	9	7	7
x_2	7	7	7	7	5	9
x_3	8	9	7	7	6	9
x_4	8	6	7	5	2	6
x_5	8	7	7	0	5	9
x_6	5	0	7	1	6	8

and (6) u_6 : consistency of fire mission. Then the following decision matrix A is constructed (see Table 3.7).

Among all the factors, $u_i(i=1,2,3,4)$ are benefit-type attributes, u_5 is cost-type attribute, while u_6 is fixed-type attribute. The weights of the attributes $u_i(i=1,2,\ldots,6)$ cannot be determined completely, and the weight information is given as follows:

$$\Phi=\{w=(w_1,w_2,\ldots,w_6)\,|\,0.4\le w_1\le 0.5,\ 0.2\le w_2\le 0.3,$$

$$0.13\le w_3\le 0.2,\ 0.1\le w_4\le 0.25,\ 0.08\le w_5\le 0.2,$$

$$\left.0\le w_6\le 0.5,\ \sum_{j=1}^{6} w_j=1\right\}$$

We can use the algorithm in Sect. 3.4.1 to rank the targets, which involves the following steps:

Step 1 Utilize Eqs. (1.2a), (1.3a) and (1.4) to normalize the decision matrix A into the matrix R, listed in Table 3.8.

Step 2 For the alternative x_1, we utilize the single-objective decision model (M-3.12) to establish the following model:

$$\begin{cases} \max\,(0.667w_1+w_2+w_3+w_4+w_6) \\ s.t.\ \ 0.4\le w_1\le 0.5,0.2\le w_2\le 0.3,0.13\le w_3\le 0.2 \\ \qquad 0.1\le w_4\le 0.25,0.08\le w_5\le 0.2,0\le w_6\le 0.5,\sum_{j=1}^{6} w_j=1 \end{cases}$$

The optimal solution to this model is the weight vector of attributes, shown as below:

Table 3.8 Decision matrix R

	u_1	u_2	u_3	u_4	u_5	u_6
x_1	$\frac{2}{3}$	1	1	1	0	1
x_2	$\frac{2}{3}$	$\frac{7}{9}$	0	$\frac{7}{9}$	$\frac{2}{5}$	0
x_3	1	1	0	$\frac{7}{9}$	$\frac{1}{5}$	0
x_4	1	$\frac{5}{9}$	0	$\frac{5}{9}$	1	1/2
x_5	1	$\frac{7}{9}$	0	0	$\frac{2}{5}$	0
x_6	0	0	0	$\frac{1}{9}$	$\frac{1}{5}$	$\frac{1}{2}$

$$w^{(1)} = (w_1^{(1)}, w_2^{(1)}, w_3^{(1)}, w_4^{(1)}, w_5^{(1)}, w_6^{(1)}) = (0.4, 0.2, 0.13, 0.1, 0.08, 0.09)$$

Similarly, for the alternatives $x_i (i = 2,3,4,5,6)$, we can establish the single-objective decision models, and then get the corresponding optimal weight vectors:

$$w^{(2)} = (w_1^{(2)}, w_2^{(2)}, w_3^{(2)}, w_4^{(2)}, w_5^{(2)}, w_6^{(2)}) = (0.49, 0.2, 0.13, 0.1, 0.08, 0)$$

$$w^{(3)} = (w_1^{(3)}, w_2^{(3)}, w_3^{(3)}, w_4^{(3)}, w_5^{(3)}, w_6^{(3)}) = (0.49, 0.2, 0.13, 0.1, 0.08, 0)$$

$$w^{(4)} = (w_1^{(4)}, w_2^{(4)}, w_3^{(4)}, w_4^{(4)}, w_5^{(4)}, w_6^{(4)}) = (0.49, 0.2, 0.13, 0.1, 0.08, 0)$$

$$w^{(5)} = (w_1^{(5)}, w_2^{(5)}, w_3^{(5)}, w_4^{(5)}, w_5^{(5)}, w_6^{(5)}) = (0.49, 0.2, 0.2, 0.12, 0.08, 0)$$

$$w^{(6)} = (w_1^{(6)}, w_2^{(6)}, w_3^{(6)}, w_4^{(6)}, w_5^{(6)}, w_6^{(6)}) = (0.49, 0.2, 0.13, 0.1, 0.08, 0)$$

Step 3 Construct the following matrix using the weight vectors $w^{(i)} = (i = 1, 2, \ldots, 6)$:

$$W = \begin{bmatrix} 0.4 & 0.4 & 0.49 & 0.49 & 0.4 & 0.4 \\ 0.2 & 0.29 & 0.2 & 0.2 & 0.2 & 0.2 \\ 0.13 & 0.13 & 0.13 & 0.13 & 0.13 & 0.13 \\ 0.1 & 0.1 & 0.1 & 0.1 & 0.19 & 0.1 \\ 0.08 & 0.08 & 0.08 & 0.08 & 0.08 & 0.08 \\ 0.09 & 0 & 0 & 0 & 0 & 0.09 \end{bmatrix}$$

Calculating the matrix $(RW)(RW)^T$, we get

$$(RW)(RW)^T = \begin{bmatrix} 2.214 & 2.355 & 2.387 & 2.387 & 2.301 & 2.214 \\ 2.355 & 2.516 & 2.549 & 2.549 & 2.454 & 2.355 \\ 2.387 & 2.549 & 2.583 & 2.583 & 2.486 & 2.387 \\ 2.387 & 2.549 & 2.583 & 2.583 & 2.486 & 2.387 \\ 2.301 & 2.454 & 2.566 & 2.566 & 2.398 & 2.301 \\ 2.214 & 2.355 & 2.355 & 2.387 & 2.301 & 2.214 \end{bmatrix}$$

whose maximal eigenvalue $\lambda_{\max}$ and its eigenvector w are

$$\lambda_{\max} = 14.522, \ w = (0.159, 0.170, 0.172, 0.172, 0.168, 0.159)$$

respectively.

Step 4 Use Eq. (3.3) to derive the combinational weight vector (the best compromise weight vector), and normalize it as:

$$w = (0.431, 0.215, 0.130, 0.115, 0.080, 0.029)$$

Then by Eq. (1.12), we get the overall attribute values of the alternatives $x_i (i = 1, 2, \ldots, 6)$:

$$z_1(w) = 0.776, \ z_2(w) = 0.576, \ z_3(w) = 0.751$$

$$z_4(w) = 0.709, \ z_5(w) = 0.630, \ z_6(w) = 0.043$$

Step 5 Rank all the alternatives according to $z_i(w) (i = 1, 2, \ldots, 6)$ in descending order:

$$x_1 \succ x_3 \succ x_4 \succ x_5 \succ x_2 \succ x_6$$

and thus, the optimal alternative is x_1.

3.5 MADM Method Based on Linear Goal Programming Models

Consider that the uncertain MADM problem with incomplete attribute weight information can result in the uncertainty in selecting the optimal decision alternatives. Thus, it is necessary for the decision maker to participate in the process of practical decision making. In this section, we only introduce the methods for the MADM problems in which there is only partial weight information, and the preferences provided by the decision maker over the alternatives take the form of multiplicative preference relation, fuzzy preference relation and utility values, respectively. Based on the above three distinct preference structures, we establish the linear goal programming models, respectively, from which we can get the weight vector of attributes, and then introduce a MADM method based on linear goal programming models.

3.5.1 Models

1. **The situations where the preferences provided by the decision maker over the alternatives take the form of multiplicative preference relation** [120]

For a MADM problem, let $A=(a_{ij})_{n\times m}(a_{ij}>0)$, whose normalized matrix is $R=(r_{ij})_{n\times m}(r_{ij}>0)$. The decision maker uses the ratio scale [98] to compare each pair of alternatives $x_i (i=1,2,\dots,n)$, and then constructs the multiplicative preference relation $H=(h_{ij})_{n\times n}$, where $h_{ij}h_{ji}=1$, $h_{ii}=1$, $h_{ij}>0$, $i,j=1,2,\dots,n$. In order to make all the decision information uniform, by using Eq. (1.2), we can transform the overall attribute values of the alternatives $x_i (i=1,2,\dots,n)$ into the multiplicative preference relation $\overline{H}=(\overline{h}_{ij})_{n\times n}$, where

$$\overline{h}_{ij}=\frac{z_i(w)}{z_j(w)}=\frac{\sum_{k=1}^{m} r_{ik}w_k}{\sum_{k=1}^{m} r_{jk}w_k},\quad i,j=1,2,\dots,n \tag{3.5}$$

i.e.,

$$\overline{h}_{ij}\sum_{k=1}^{m} r_{jk}w_k=\sum_{k=1}^{m} r_{ik}w_k,\quad i,j=1,2,\dots,n \tag{3.6}$$

In general case, there is a difference between the multiplicative preference relations $H=(h_{ij})_{n\times n}$ and $\overline{H}=(\overline{h}_{ij})_{n\times n}$. As a result, we introduce a deviation function:

$$f_{ij}=\left|\sum_{k=1}^{m}(h_{ij}r_{jk}-r_{ik})w_k\right|,\quad i,j=1,2,\dots,n \tag{3.7}$$

Obviously, a reasonable attribute weight vector should minimize the deviation function f_{ij}, and thus, we construct the following multi-objective optimization model:

$$
(\mathbf{M-3.15}) \quad \begin{cases} \min f_{ij} = \left| \sum_{k=1}^{m} \left(h_{ij} r_{jk} - r_{ik} \right) w_k \right|, \; i,j = 1,2,\ldots,n \\ s.t. \;\; w \in \Phi \end{cases}
$$

To solve the model (M-3.15), and considering that all the objective functions are fair, we transform the model (M-3.15) into the following linear goal programming model:

$$
(\mathbf{M-3.16}) \quad \begin{cases} \min J = \sum_{i=1}^{n} \sum_{\substack{j=1 \\ j \neq i}}^{n} \left(s_{ij} d_{ij}^{+} + t_{ij} d_{ij}^{-} \right) \\ s.t. \;\; \sum_{k=1}^{m} \left(h_{ij} r_{jk} - r_{ik} \right) w_k - d_{ij}^{+} + d_{ij}^{-} = 0, \; i,j = 1,2,\ldots,n, \; i \neq j \\ w \in \Phi \\ d_{ij}^{+} \geq 0, \, d_{ij}^{-} \geq 0, \; i,j = 1,2,\ldots,n, \; i \neq j \end{cases}
$$

where d_{ij}^{+} is the positive deviation from the target of the objective $\sum_{k=1}^{m} (h_{ij} r_{jk} - r_{ik}) w_k$, defined as:

$$
d_{ij}^{+} = \left(\sum_{k=1}^{m} \left(h_{ij} r_{jk} - r_{ik} \right) w_k \right) \vee 0
$$

and d_{ij}^{-} is the negative deviation from the target of the objective $\sum_{k=1}^{m} (h_{ij} r_{jk} - r_{ik}) w_k$, defined as:

$$
d_{ij}^{-} = \left(\sum_{k=1}^{m} \left(r_{ik} - h_{ij} r_{jk} \right) w_k \right) \vee 0
$$

s_{ij} is the weighting factor corresponding to the positive deviation d_{ij}^{+}, t_{ij} is the weighting factor corresponding to the negative deviation d_{ij}^{-}. Solving the model (M-3.16), we can get the weight vector w of attributes. From Eq. (1.12), we can derive the overall attribute value of each alternative, by which the considered alternatives can be ranked and selected.

2. **The situations where the preferences provided by the decision maker over the alternatives take the form of fuzzy preference relation** [120]

Suppose that the decision maker utilizes the 0–1 scale [98] to compare each pair of alternatives $x_i (i = 1,2,\ldots,n)$, and then constructs the fuzzy preference relation $B = (b_{ij})_{n \times n}$, where $b_{ij} + b_{ji} = 1$, $b_{ii} = 0.5$, $b_{ij} \geq 0$, $i,j = 1,2,\ldots,n$. In order to make all the decision information uniform, we can transform the overall attribute values of the alternatives $x_i (i = 1,2,\ldots,n)$ into the fuzzy preference relation $\bar{B} = (\bar{b}_{ij})_{n \times n}$, where [29]

$$\bar{b}_{ij} = \frac{z_i(w)}{z_i(w)+z_j(w)} = \frac{\sum_{k=1}^{m} r_{ik} w_k}{\sum_{k=1}^{m} (r_{ik}+r_{jk}) w_k} \tag{3.8}$$

i.e.,

$$\bar{b}_{ij} \sum_{k=1}^{m} (r_{ik}+r_{jk}) w_k = \sum_{k=1}^{m} r_{ik} w_k \tag{3.9}$$

In general case, there exists a difference between the fuzzy preference relations $B=(b_{ij})_{n\times n}$ and $\bar{B}=(\bar{b}_{ij})_{n\times n}$, and then we introduce the following deviation function:

$$h_{ij} = \left| \sum_{k=1}^{m} (\bar{b}_{ij}(r_{ik}+r_{jk}) - r_{ik}) w_k \right|, \quad i,j=1,2,\ldots,n \tag{3.10}$$

Obviously, a reasonable attribute weight vector should minimize the deviation function h_{ij}, thus, we construct the following multi-objective optimization model:

$$(\mathbf{M-3.17}) \quad \begin{cases} \min h_{ij} = \left| \sum_{k=1}^{m} \left(\bar{b}_{ij}(r_{ik}+r_{jk}) - r_{ik}\right) w_k \right|, \quad i,j=1,2,\ldots,n \\ s.t. \quad w \in \Phi \end{cases} \tag{3.11}$$

To solve the model (M-3.17), considering that all the objective functions are fair and similar to the model (M-3.16), we can transform the model (M-3.17) into the following linear goal programming model:

$$(\mathbf{M-3.18}) \quad \begin{cases} \min J = \sum_{i=1}^{n} \sum_{j=1, j\neq i}^{n} \left(s_{ij} d_{ij}^{+} + t_{ij} d_{ij}^{-}\right) \\ s.t. \quad \sum_{k=1}^{m} \left(\bar{b}_{ij}(r_{ik}+r_{jk}) - r_{ik}\right) w_k - d_{ij}^{+} + d_{ij}^{-} = 0, \quad i,j=1,2,\ldots,n, \quad i\neq j \\ w \in \Phi \\ d_{ij}^{+} \geq 0, d_{ij}^{-} \geq 0, \quad i,j=1,2,\ldots,n, \quad i \neq j \end{cases}$$

where d_{ij}^{+} is the positive deviation from the target of the objective $\sum_{k=1}^{m} (\bar{b}_{ij}(r_{ik}+r_{jk}) - r_{ik}) w_k$, defined as:

$$d_{ij}^{+} = \sum_{k=1}^{m} (\bar{b}_{ij}(r_{ik}+r_{jk}) - r_{ik}) w_k \vee 0$$

and d_{ij}^- is the negative deviation from the target of the objective $\left(\sum_{k=1}^{m} \bar{b}_{ij}(r_{ik}+r_{jk})-r_{ik}\right)w_k$, defined as:

$$d_{ij}^- = \sum_{k=1}^{m}(r_{ik}-\bar{b}_{ij}(r_{ik}+r_{jk}))w_k \vee 0$$

s_{ij} and t_{ij} are the weighting factors corresponding to the positive deviation d_{ij}^+ and the negative deviation d_{ij}^-, respectively.

Using the goal simplex method to solve the model (M-3.18), we can get the weight vector w of attributes. From Eq. (1.12), we can derive the overall attribute value of each alternative, by which the considered alternatives can be ranked and selected.

3. **The situations where the preferences provided by the decision maker over the alternatives take the form of utility values**

Suppose that the decision maker has preferences on alternatives, and his/her preference values take the form of utility values $\vartheta_i (i = 1, 2, \ldots, n)$.

Due to the restrictions of subjective and objective conditions in practical decision making, there usually are some differences between the subjective preference values and the objective preference values (the overall attribute values). In order to describe the differences quantitatively, we introduce the positive deviation variable d_i^+ and the negative deviation variable d_i^- for the overall attribute value of each alternative x_i, where d_i^+, $d_i^- \geq 0$, d_i^+ denotes the degree that the i th objective preference value goes beyond the i th subjective preference value, while d_i^- denotes the value that the i th subjective preference value goes beyond the i th objective preference value. Thus, we get the following set of equations:

$$(\mathbf{M-3.19}) \begin{cases} \min J = \sum_{i=1}^{n}\left(t_i^+ d_{ij}^+ + t_i^- d_{ij}^-\right) \\ s.t. \ \sum_{j=1}^{m} r_{ij} w_j + d_i^- - d_i^+ = \vartheta_i \ \ i = 1, 2, \ldots, n \\ w \in \Phi \\ d_i^+ \geq 0, d_i^- \geq 0, \ i = 1, 2, \ldots, n \end{cases}$$

where t_i^+ and t_i^- are the weighting factors corresponding to the positive deviation d_{ij}^+ and the negative deviation d_{ij}^-, respectively. Using the goal simplex method to solve the model (M-3.19), we can get the weight vector w of attributes. From Eq. (1.12), we can derive the overall attribute value of each alternative, by which the considered alternatives can be ranked and selected.

3.5.2 Decision Making Method

In what follows, we introduce a MADM method based on linear goal programming models, which needs the following steps:

Step 1 For a MADM problem, the attribute values of the considered alternatives $x_i(i=1,2,\ldots,n)$ with respect to the attributes $u_j(j=1,2,\ldots,m)$ are contained in the decision matrix $A=(a_{ij})_{n\times m}$. By using Eqs. (1.2) and (1.3), we normalize A into the decision matrix $R=(r_{ij})_{n\times m}$.

Step 2 If the preferences provided by the decision maker over the alternatives take the form of multiplicative preference relation, then we utilize the model (M-3.16) to derive the weight vector w; If the preferences provided by the decision maker over the alternatives take the form of fuzzy preference relation, then we utilize the model (M-3.18) to derive the weight vector w; If the preferences provided by the decision maker over the alternatives take the form of utility values, then we utilize the model (M-3.19) to derive the weight vector w.

Step 3 Utilize Eq. (1.12) to derive the overall attribute values $z_i(w)(i=1,2,\ldots,n)$, based on which we rank and select the alternatives $x_i(i=1,2,\ldots,n)$.

3.5.3 Practical Example

Example 3.5 A unit determines to improve its old product, and five alternatives $x_i(i=1,2,3,4,5)$ are available. To evaluate these alternatives, four indices (attributes) are considered [95]: (1) u_1: cost (yuan); (2) u_2: efficiency (%); (3) u_3: the work time with no failure (hour); and (4) u_4: product life (year). The attribute values of all alternatives are listed in Table 3.9.

Among all the attributes, u_1 is the cost-type attribute, and the others are benefit-type attributes. The attribute weights cannot be determined completely. The known weight information is as follows:

$$\Phi=\{w=(w_1,w_2,\ldots,w_5)\,|\,0.3\le w_1\le 0.45,\ w_2\le 0.15,\ 0.1\le w_3\le 0.35,$$

Table 3.9 Decision matrix A

	u_1	u_2	u_3	u_4
x_1	8500	90	20,000	13
x_2	7500	85	15,000	14
x_3	7000	87	11,000	13
x_4	6500	72	8000	11
x_5	4500	70	7500	12

Table 3.10 Decision matrix R

	u_1	u_2	u_3	u_4
x_1	0.529	1.000	1.000	0.929
x_2	0.600	0.944	0.750	1.000
x_3	0.643	0.967	0.550	0.929
x_4	0.692	0.800	0.400	0.786
x_5	1.000	0.778	0.375	0.857

$$\left. w_4 \geq 0.03, \ \sum_{j=1}^{4} w_j = 1, \ w_j \geq 0, \ j = 1,2,3,4 \right\}$$

Now we utilize the method of Sect. 3.5.2 to solve this problem, which involves the following steps:

Step 1 Using Eqs. (1.2) and (1.3), we normalize A, and thus get the matrix R, listed in Table 3.10.

Step 2 Without loss of generality, suppose that the decision maker uses the 1–9 ratio scale to compare each pair of alternatives $x_i (i = 1,2,3,4,5)$, and constructs the multiplicative preference relation:

$$H = \begin{pmatrix} 1 & 3 & 1 & 7 & 5 \\ 1/3 & 1 & 1/3 & 5 & 1 \\ 1 & 3 & 1 & 5 & 1/3 \\ 1/7 & 1/5 & 1/5 & 1 & 1/7 \\ 1/5 & 1 & 3 & 7 & 1 \end{pmatrix}$$

then we derive the weight vector of attributes from the model (M-3.16):

$$w = (0.45, 0, 0, 0.35, 0.2)$$

and

$$d_{12}^{+} = 1.4237, \ d_{12}^{-} = 0, \ d_{13}^{+} = 0, \ d_{13}^{-} = 0.1062, \ d_{14}^{+} = 3.4864$$

$$d_{14}^{-} = 0, \ d_{15}^{+} = 2.9894, \ d_{15}^{-} = 0, \ d_{21}^{+} = 0, \ d_{21}^{-} = 0.4746$$

$$d_{23}^{+} = 0, \ d_{23}^{-} = 0.5060, \ d_{24}^{+} = 2.3105, \ d_{24}^{-} = 0, \ d_{25}^{+} = 0.0202$$

$$d_{25}^{-} = 0, \ d_{31}^{+} = 0.1062, \ d_{31}^{-} = 0, \ d_{32}^{+} = 1.129, \ d_{32}^{-} = 0$$

$$d_{34}^{+} = 2.3754,\ d_{34}^{-} = 0,\ d_{35}^{+} = 0,\ d_{35}^{-} = 0.4168,\ d_{41}^{+} = 0$$

$$d_{45}^{+} = 0,\ d_{45}^{-} = 0.5011,\ d_{51}^{+} = 0,\ d_{51}^{-} = 0.5979,\ d_{52}^{+} = 0$$

$$d_{52}^{-} = 0.0202,\ d_{53}^{+} = 1.2503,\ d_{53}^{-} = 0,\ d_{54}^{+} = 3.7220,\ d_{54}^{-} = 0$$

Step 3 Derive the overall attribute values by using Eq. (1.12):

$$z_1(w) = 0.7739,\ z_2(w) = 0.7325,\ z_3(w) = 0.6677$$

$$z_4(w) = 0.6086,\ z_5(w) = 0.7527$$

Step 4 Rank the alternatives $x_i (i = 1,2,3,4,5)$ according to $z_i(w)(i = 1,2,3,4,5)$: $x_1 \succ x_5 \succ x_2 \succ x_3 \succ x_4$, and thus, the alternative x_1 is the best one.

3.6 Interactive MADM Method Based on Reduction Strategy for Alternatives

In this section, we introduce the interaction idea of multi-objective decision making into the field of MADM, and provide an approach to uncertain MADM with partially weight information.

3.6.1 Decision Making Method

Definition 3.4 For the alternative $x_p \in X$, if there exists an alternative $x_q \in X$ such that $z_q(w) > z_p(w)$, then the alternative x_p is called the dominated alternative; Otherwise, it is called the non-dominated alternative, where the overall attribute values $z_p(w)$ and $z_q(w)$ of the alternatives x_p and x_q are defined by Eq. (1.12).

It follows from Definition 3.4 that the dominated alternative should be eliminated in the process of optimization, such that the given alternative set will get diminished.

The following theorem will provide an approach to discriminate the dominated alternative:

Theorem 3.1 With the known partial weight information Φ, the alternative $x_p \in X$ is the dominated one if and only if $J_p < 0$, where

$$\begin{cases} J_p = \max\left(\sum_{j=1}^{m} r_{pj} w_j + \theta\right) \\ s.t. \sum_{j=1}^{m} r_{ij} w_i + \theta \le 0,\ i \ne p,\ i = 1,2,\ldots,n \\ w \in \Phi \end{cases}$$

and θ is an unconstrained auxiliary variable, which has no actual meaning.

Proof (Sufficiency) If $J_p < 0$, then by the constraint condition, we have $\sum_{j=1}^{m} r_{ij} w_i \le -\theta$, for any $i = 1,2,\ldots,n,\ i \ne p$. In the case where the optimal solution is reached, there exists at least q, such that when $i = p$, the equality holds, i.e., $\sum_{j=1}^{m} r_{qj} w_j = -\theta$. It follows from $J_p < 0$ that

$$J_p = \max\left(\sum_{j=1}^{m} r_{pj} w_j + \theta\right) = \max_w\left(\sum_{j=1}^{m} r_{pj} w_j - \sum_{j=1}^{m} r_{qj} w_j\right) < 0$$

then $\sum_{j=1}^{m} r_{pj} w_j < \sum_{j=1}^{m} r_{qj} w_j$, i.e., $z_p(w) < z_q(w)$, therefore, x_p is the dominated alternative.

(**Necessity**) Since x_p is the dominated alternative, then there exists $x_q \in X$, such that $\sum_{j=1}^{m} r_{pj} w < \sum_{j=1}^{m} r_{qj} w$. By the constraint condition, we have $\sum_{j=1}^{m} r_{qj} w_j \le -\theta$, and thus,

$$\sum_{j=1}^{m} r_{pj} w_j - (-\theta) \le \sum_{j=1}^{m} r_{pj} w_j - \sum_{j=1}^{m} r_{qj} w_j < 0$$

i.e., $J_p < 0$. This completes the proof.

We only need to identify every alternative in X and understand whether it is a dominated alternative or not. As a result, we can eliminate any dominated alternatives from the alternative set X, and then the set $\bar{X}$ whose elements are the non-dominated alternatives can be obtained. Obviously, $\bar{X}$ is a subset of X, and thus, the alternative set X is diminished.

By Theorem 3.1, below we develop an interactive procedure to find out the most preferred alternative:

Step 1 For a MADM problem, the attribute values of the considered alternatives $x_i (i = 1,2,\ldots,n)$ with respect to the attributes $u_j (j = 1,2,\ldots,m)$ are contained in the decision matrix $A = (a_{ij})_{n\times m}$. By using Eqs. (1.2) and (1.3), we normalize A into the decision matrix $R = (r_{ij})_{n\times m}$.

Step 2 According to the overall attribute values of alternatives and the known partial attribute weight information, and by Theorem 3.1, we identify whether the alternative x_i is a dominated alternative or not, eliminate the dominated alternatives, and then get a set $\overline{X}$, whose elements are the non-dominated alternatives. If most of the decision makers suggest that an alternative x_i be superior to any other alternatives in $\overline{X}$, or the alternative x_i is the only one alternative left in $\overline{X}$, then the most preferred alternative is x_i; Otherwise, go to the next step:

Step 3 Interact with the decision makers, and add the decision information provided by the decision makers as the weight information to the set Φ. If the added information given by a decision maker contradicts the information in Φ, then return it to the decision maker for reassessment, and go to Step 2.

The above interactive procedure is convergent. With the increase of the weight information, the number of alternatives in $\overline{X}$ will be diminished gradually. Ultimately, either most of the decision makers suggest that a certain alternative in $\overline{X}$ be the most preferred one, or there is only one alternative left in the set $\overline{X}$, then this alternative is the most preferred one.

Remark 3.1 The decision making method above can only be used to find the optimal alternative, but is unsuitable for ranking alternatives.

3.6.2 Practical Example

Example 3.6 Let us consider a customer who intends to buy a house. There are six locations (alternatives) $x_i (i = 1, 2, \ldots, 6)$ to be selected. The customer takes into account four indices (attributes) to decide which house to buy: (1) $u_i (i = 1, 2, 3, 4)$ price (10^3\$); (2) u_2 : use area (m^2); (3) distance of the house to the working place (km); and (4) environment (evaluation value). Among the indices, u_1 and u_3 are cost-type attributes, u_2 and u_4 are benefit-type attributes. The evaluation information on the locations $x_i (i = 1, 2, \ldots, 6)$ provided by the customer with respect to these indices is listed in Table 3.11:

Table 3.11 Decision matrix A

	u_1	u_2	u_3	u_4
x_1	3.0	100	10	7
x_2	2.5	80	8	5
x_3	1.8	50	20	11
x_4	2.2	70	12	9
x_5	3.2	120	25	12
x_6	3.3	110	26	10

Table 3.12 Decision matrix R

	u_1	u_2	u_3	u_4
x_1	0.600	0.833	0.800	0.583
x_2	0.720	0.667	1	0.417
x_3	1	0.417	0.400	0.917
x_4	0.818	0.583	0.667	0.750
x_5	0.563	1	0.320	1
x_6	0.545	0.917	0.308	0.833

The known attribute weight information is as follows:

$$\Phi = \Big\{ w = (w_1, w_2, w_3, w_4) \mid 0.1 \le w_1 \le 0.45, w_2 \le 0.2, 0.1 \le w_3 \le 0.4,$$

$$w_4 \ge 0.03, \sum_{j=1}^{4} w_j = 1, \ \ w_j \ge 0, j = 1,2,3,4 \Big\}$$

In what follows, we utilize the method in Sect. 3.6.1 to solve this problem:

We first utilize Eqs. (1.2) and (1.3) to normalize the decision matrix A into the matrix R, listed in Table 3.12.

Clearly, all the normalized attribute values of the alternative x_6 are smaller than the corresponding attribute values of the alternative x_5, thus, $z_6(w) < z_5(w)$, therefore, the alternative x_6 can be omitted firstly. For the other five alternatives, we can utilize Theorem 3.1 to identify:

For the alternative x_1, according to Theorem 3.1, we can get the following linear programming problem:

$$\begin{cases} J_1 = \max(\theta_1 - \theta_2 + 0.600w_1 + 0.833w_2 + 0.800w_3 + 0.583w_4) \\ s.t. \ \ \theta_1 - \theta_2 + 0.720w_1 + 0.677w_2 + w_3 + 0.417w_4 \le 0 \\ \qquad \theta_1 - \theta_2 + w_1 + 0.417w_2 + 0.400w_3 + 0.913w_4 \le 0 \\ \qquad \theta_1 - \theta_2 + 0.818w_1 + 0.583w_2 + 0.667w_3 + 0.750w_4 \le 0 \\ \qquad \theta_1 - \theta_2 + 0.563w_1 + w_2 + 0.320w_3 + w_4 \le 0 \\ \qquad 0.1 \le w_1 \le 0.45, \ w_2 \le 0.2, \ 0.1 \le w_3 \le 0.4, \ w_4 \ge 0.03 \\ \qquad \sum_{j=1}^{4} \omega_j = 1, \ \omega_j \ge 0, \ j = 1,2,3,4 \end{cases}$$

from which we get $J_1 = 0.0381 > 0$, similarly, for the alternatives $x_i (i = 2,3,4,5)$, we have $J_2 = -0.2850 < 0$, $J_3 = -0.0474 < 0$, $J_4 = -0.0225 > 0$, and $J_5 = 0.01147 > 0$. Thus, x_2 and x_3 are the dominated alternatives, which should be deleted, and we get the set of the non-dominated alternatives, $\bar{X} = \{x_1, x_4, x_5\}$. Then we interact with the decision maker, and suppose that the decision maker prefers x_1 and x_4 to x_5, and thus, $z_1(w) > z_5(w)$, $z_4(w) > z_5(w)$, i.e.,

$$0.037w_1 - 0.167w_2 + 0.480w_3 - 0.417w_4 > 0$$

$$0.255w_1 - 0.417w_2 + 0.347w_3 - 0.250w_4 > 0$$

Now we add these two inequalities as the known attribute weight information to the set Φ, and for the diminished alternative set $\bar{X} = \{x_1, x_2\}$, we use Theorem 3.1 again to establish the linear programming models:

For the alternative x_1, we have

$$\begin{cases} J_1 = \max(\theta_1 - \theta_2 + 0.600w_1 + 0.833w_2 + 0.800w_3 + 0.583w_4) \\ s.t.\ \ \theta_1 - \theta_2 + 0.720w_1 + 0.667w_2 + w_3 + 0.417w_4 \le 0 \\ \quad \theta_1 - \theta_2 + w_1 + 0.417w_2 + 0.400w_3 + 0.917w_4 \le 0 \\ \quad \theta_1 - \theta_2 + 0.818w_1 + 0.583w_2 + 0.667w_3 + 0.750w_4 \le 0 \\ \quad \theta_1 - \theta_2 + 0.563w_1 + w_2 + 0.320w_3 + w_4 \le 0 \\ \quad 0.037w_1 - 0.167w_2 + 0.480w_3 - 0.417w_4 > 0 \\ \quad 0.255\omega_1 - 0.417\omega_2 + 0.347\omega_3 - 0.250\omega_4 > 0 \\ \quad 0.1 \le \omega_1 \le 0.45,\ \omega_2 \le 0.2,\ 0.1 \le \omega_3 \le 0.4 \\ \quad \omega_4 \ge 0.03,\ \sum_{j=1}^{4} \omega_j = 1,\ \omega_j \ge 0,\ j = 1,2,3,4 \end{cases}$$

For the alternative x_4, we have

$$\begin{cases} J_4 = \max(\theta_1 - \theta_2 + 0.818w_1 + 0.583w_2 + 0.667w_3 + 0.750w_4) \\ s.t.\ \ \theta_1 - \theta_2 + 0.600w_1 + 0.833w_2 + 0.800w_3 + 0.583w_4 \le 0 \\ \quad \theta_1 - \theta_2 + 0.720w_1 + 0.667w_2 + w_3 + 0.417w_4 \le 0 \\ \quad \theta_1 - \theta_2 + w_1 + 0.417w_2 + 0.400w_3 + 0.917w_4 \le 0 \\ \quad \theta_1 - \theta_2 + 0.563w_1 + w_2 + 0.320w_3 + w_4 \le 0 \\ \quad 0.037w_1 - 0.167w_2 + 0.480w_3 - 0.417w_4 > 0 \\ \quad 0.255\omega_1 - 0.417\omega_2 + 0.347\omega_3 - 0.250\omega_4 > 0 \\ \quad 0.1 \le \omega_1 \le 0.45,\ \omega_2 \le 0.2,\ 0.1 \le \omega_3 \le 0.4 \\ \quad \omega_4 \ge 0.03,\ \sum_{j=1}^{4} \omega_j = 1,\ \omega_j \ge 0,\ j = 1,2,3,4 \end{cases}$$

Solving the model, we get $J_4 = 0$. Thus, x_1 is the dominated alternative, which should be deleted, and we get the non-dominated alternative set $\bar{X} = \{x_4\}$. Therefore, x_4 is the optimal alternative.

3.7 Interactive MADM Method Based on Achievement Degrees and Complex Degrees of Alternatives

In this section, we introduce an interactive MADM method based on achievement degrees and complex degrees of alternatives in the situations where the weight information on attributes is not known completely. The interactive method can not only employ sufficiently the known objective information, but also consider as much as possible the decision makers' interaction requirements and exert their subjective initiatives. The decision makers can provide and modify the achievement degrees and complex degrees of alternatives gradually in the process of decision making, and thus make the decision result more reasonable.

3.7.1 Definitions and Theorems

MADM generally needs to compare and rank the overall attribute values of alternatives, and the uncertainty of the attribute weights may result in the uncertainty of the overall attribute values of alternatives, that is, the different values of attribute weights may produce different rankings of alternatives. In this case, the decision makers' active participations and exert their subjective initiatives in the process of decision making will play an important role in making reasonable decisions.

For the given attribute weight vector $w \in \Phi$, the greater the overall attribute values $z_i(w)(i = 1, 2, \ldots, n)$ the better. As a result, we establish the following multi-objective decision making model:

$$(\mathbf{M-3.20}) \quad \begin{cases} \max z(w) = (z_1(w), z_2(w), \ldots, z_n(w)) \\ s.t. \ \ w \in \Phi \end{cases}$$

Definition 3.5 [106] If there is no $w \in \Phi$, such that $z_i(w) \geq z_i(w^0)$, $i = 1, 2, \ldots, n$, $w^{(0)} \in \Phi$, and at least an inequality $z_{i_0}(w) > z_{i_0}(w^0)$ holds, then w^0 is an efficient solution to the model (M-3.20).

Definition 3.6 [106] The level value $\bar{z}_i$ of the overall attribute value $z_i(w)$ of the alternative x_i that the decision maker desires to reach is called the expectation level of the alternative x_i.

Definition 3.7 [106] If

$$\varphi(z_i(w)) = \frac{z_i(w) - z_i^{\min}}{z_i - z_i^{\min}}, \quad i = 1, 2, \ldots, n \tag{3.12}$$

then $\varphi(z_i(w))$ is called the achievement degree of the alternative x_i.

The function $\varphi(z_i(w))$ has the following characteristics:

1. The achievement degree of the alternative x_i is the percentage of the overall attribute values and the expectation level on the premise of taking the minimum of the overall attribute values of alternatives as a reference point. The farther the overall attribute value $z_i(w)$ from the negative ideal overall attribute value, the larger the achievement degree of the alternative x_i.
2. For $w^1, w^2 \in \Phi$, if $z_i(w^1) > z_i(w^2)$, then $\varphi(z_i(w^1)) > \varphi(z_i(w^2))$, i.e., $\varphi(z_i(w))$ is a strictly monotone increasing function of $z_i(w)$.

Definition 3.8 [106] If $c(w) = \sum_{i=1}^{n} (z_i(w) - z_i^{\min})$, then $c(w)$ is called the complex degree of the alternative x_i.

Clearly, the complex degree $c(w)$ is a strictly monotone increasing function of $z_i(w)$, based on which we establish the following single-objective optimal model:

$$(\mathbf{M-3.21}) \quad \begin{cases} \max c(w) \\ s.t. \ \ w \in \Phi \end{cases}$$

Solving this model, we get the optimal solution w, the overall attribute value $z_i(w)$, the complex degree $c(w)$, and the achievement degree $\varphi(z_i(w))$ of the alternative x_i, based on which the decision maker predefines the original achievement degree φ_i^0 and the lower limit value c_0 of the complex degree $c(w)$.

Theorem 3.2 [106] The optimal solution of the single-objective optimization model (M-3.21) is the efficient solution of the multi-objective optimization model (M-3.20).

Proof Here we prove by contradiction. If $w^{(0)}$ is not the efficient solution of the multi-objective optimization model (M-3.20), then there exists $w' \in \Phi$, such that for any i, we have $z_i(w^0) \leq z_i(w')$, and there exists i_0, such that $z_{i_0}(w^0) < z_{i_0}(w')$. Since $c(w)$ is the strictly monotone increasing function of $z_i(w) (i = 1, 2, \ldots, n)$, then $c(w^0) < c(w')$, thus, w^0 is not the optimal solution of the single-objective optimization model (M-3.21), which contradicts the condition. Therefore, the optimal solution of the single-objective optimization model (M-3.21) is the efficient solution of the multi-objective optimization model (M-3.20). This completes the proof.

Obviously, the larger the complex degrees $c(w)$, the better the alternatives on the whole can meet the requirements of the decision makers, but this may make the achievement degrees of some alternatives take smaller values, which depart from their good states; On the other hand, if we only employ the achievement degrees as the measure, then it cannot efficiently achieve the balances among the alternatives. Consequently, we establish the following single-objective decision making model:

$$(\mathbf{M-3.22})\quad \begin{cases} \max J = \sum_{i=1}^{n} \varphi_i \\ s.t.\ c(w) \geq c_0 \\ \qquad \varphi(z_i(w)) \geq \varphi_i \geq \varphi_i^0,\ i = 1,2,\ldots,n \\ \qquad w \in \Phi \end{cases}$$

Solving the model (M-3.22), if there is no solution, then the decision maker needs to redefine the original achievement degrees $\varphi_i^0 (i = 1,2,\ldots,n)$ and the lower limit value c_0 of the complex degree $c(w)$; Otherwise, the following theorem holds:

Theorem 3.3 [106] The optimal solution of the single-objective optimization model (M-3.22) is the efficient solution of the multi-objective optimization model (M-3.20).

Proof Here we prove by contradiction. If $w^{(0)}$ is not the efficient solution of the multi-objective optimization model (M.3.20), then there exists $w' \in \Phi$, such that for any i, we have $z_i(w^0) \leq z_i(w')$, and there exists i_0, such that $z_{i_0}(w^0) < z_{i_0}(w')$. Since $c(w)$ and $\varphi(z_i(w))$ are the strictly monotone increasing functions of $z_i(w)(i = 1,2,\ldots,n)$, then $c(w^0) < c(w')$, and for any i, we have $\varphi(z_i(w^0)) \leq \varphi(z_i(w'))$, and $\varphi(z_{i_0}(w^0)) < \varphi(z_{i_0}(w'))$. Therefore, $c(w') \geq c_0$, and for any i, we have $\varphi(z_i(w') \geq \varphi_i \geq \varphi_i^0$, and there exists $\lambda_{i_0'}$, such that $\varphi(z_{i_0}(w') \geq \varphi_{i_0'} > \varphi_{i_0} \geq \varphi_i^0$, thus, we get

$$\sum_{i=1, i \neq i_0}^{n} \varphi_i + \varphi_{i_0'} > \sum_{i=1}^{n} \varphi_i$$

which contradicts the condition. Thus, the optimal solution of the single-objective optimization model (M-3.22) is the efficient solution of the multi-objective optimization model (M-3.20). This completes the proof.

Theorems 3.2 and 3.3 guarantee that the optimal solutions of the single-objective decision making models (M-3.21) and (M-3.22) are the efficient solutions of the original multi-objective optimization model (M-3.20). If the decision maker is satisfied with the result derived from the model (M-3.22), then we can calculate the overall attribute values of all the alternatives and rank these alternatives according the overall attribute values in descending order, and thus get the satisfied alternatives; Otherwise, the decision maker can properly raise the lower limit values of achievement degrees of some alternatives and at the same time, reduce the lower limit values of achievement degrees of some other alternatives. If necessary, we can also adjust properly the lower limit values of the complex degrees of alternatives. Then we resolve the model (M-3.21) until the decision maker is satisfied with the derived result.

3.7.2 Decision Making Method

Based on the theorems and models above, in what follows, we introduce an interactive MADM method based on achievement degrees and complex degrees of alternatives [106]:

Step 1 For a MADM problem, the attribute values of the considered alternatives $x_i (i = 1, 2, \ldots, n)$ with respect to the attributes $u_j (j = 1, 2, \ldots, m)$ are contained in the decision matrix $A = (a_{ij})_{n \times m}$. By using Eqs. (1.2) and (1.3), we normalize A into the decision matrix $R = (r_{ij})_{n \times m}$.

Step 2 Utilize the model (M-3.8) to derive the negative ideal overall attribute value $z_i^{\min}$, and the decision maker gives the expectation level values $\bar{z}_i \ (i = 1, 2, \ldots, n)$ of the alternatives $x_i \ (i = 1, 2, \ldots, n)$.

Step 3 Solve the single-objective optimal model (M-3.21), get the optimal solution w^0, the overall attribute values $z_i(w^0)(i = 1, 2, \ldots, n)$, the complex degree $c(w^0)$, and then derive the achievement degrees $\varphi(z_i(w^0))(i = 1, 2, \ldots, n)$ of the alternatives $x_i \ (i = 1, 2, \ldots, n)$, based on which the decision maker gives the original achievement degrees $\varphi_i^0 (i = 1, 2, \ldots, n)$ and the lower limit value c_0 of the complex degree of the alternatives. Let $k = 1$.

Step 4 Solve the single-objective decision model (M-3.22), get the optimal solution w^k, the complex degree $c(w^k)$, the achievement degrees $\varphi(z_i(w^i))(i = 1, 2, \ldots, n)$, and the corresponding vector $z(w^k)$ of the overall attribute values of alternatives.

Step 5 If the decision maker thinks that the above result has met his/her requirements, and does not give any suggestion, then go to Step 6; Otherwise, the decision maker can properly raise the lower limit values of achievement degrees of some alternatives and at the same time, reduce the lower limit values of achievement degrees of some other alternatives. If necessary, we can also adjust properly the lower limit values of the complex degrees of alternatives. Let $k = k + 1$, and go to Step 4.

Step 6 Rank all the alternatives according to their overall attribute values in descending order, and then get the satisfied alternative.

3.7.3 Practical Example

Example 3.7 Now we utilize Example 3.5 to illustrate the method above, which involves the following steps:

Step 1 See Step 1 of Sect. 3.5.3.

Step 2 Utilize the model (M-3.8) to derive the negative ideal overall attribute values $z_i^{\min}(i=1,2,3,4,5)$ of the alternatives $x_i(i=1,2,3,4,5)$:

$$z_1^{\min}=0.906,\ z_2^{\min}=0.432,\ z_3^{\min}=0.824,\ z_4^{\min}=0.474,\ z_5^{\min}=0.640$$

The decision maker gives the expectation level values $\overline{z}_i\ (i=1,2,3,4,5)$:

$$\overline{z}_1=0.97,\ \overline{z}_2=0.65,\ \overline{z}_3=0.90,\ \overline{z}_4=0.55,\ \overline{z}_5=0.75$$

Step 3 Solve the single-objective optimization model (M-3.21), and thus get

$$w^0=(0.45,0.15,0.35,0.05)$$

and the overall attribute values $z_i(w^0)(i=1,2,3,4,5)$:

$$z_1(w^0)=0.906,\ z_2(w^0)=0.747,\ z_3(w^0)=0.824$$

$$z_4(w^0)=0.716,\ z_5(w^0)=0.670$$

the complex degree $c(w^0)=0.586$, and the achievement degrees $\varphi(z_i(w^0))$ $(i=1,2,3,4,5)$:

$$\varphi(z_1(w^0))=0,\ \varphi(z_2(w^0))=1.445,\ \varphi(z_3(w^0))=0$$

$$\varphi(z_4(w^0))=3.184,\ \varphi(z_5(w^0))=0.266$$

based on which the decision maker gives the original achievement degrees $\varphi_i^0\ (i=1,2,3,4,5)$:

$$\varphi_1^0=0.50,\ \varphi_2^0=0.90,\ \varphi_3^0=0.50,\ \varphi_4^0=2.00,\ \varphi_5^0=0.30$$

and the lower limit value $c_0=0.50$ of the complex degree of the alternatives.

Step 4 Solve the single-objective decision making model (M-3.22), and thus get the optimal solution:

$$w^1=(0.45,0,0.35,0.20)$$

and the overall attribute values $z_i(w^1)(i = 1,2,3,4,5)$ of the alternatives:

$$z_1(w^1) = 0.940,\ z_2(w^1) = 0.641,\ z_3(w^1) = 0.880$$

$$z_4(w^1) = 0.652,\ z_5(w^1) = 0.675$$

the complex degree $c(w^1) = 0.51$, and the achievement degrees $\varphi(z_i(w^1))(i = 1,2,3,4,5)$:

$$\varphi(z_1(w^1)) = 0.530,\ \varphi(z_2(w^1)) = 0.959,\ \varphi(z_3(w^1)) = 0.737$$

$$\varphi(z_4(w^1)) = 2.342,\ \varphi(z_5(w^1)) = 0.312$$

which the decision maker is satisfied with, and thus, the ranking of the alternatives $x_i(i = 1,2,3,4,5)$ according to $z_i(w^1)(i = 1,2,3,4,5)$ in descending order is

$$x_1 \succ x_3 \succ x_5 \succ x_4 \succ x_2$$

and then x_1 is the best alternative.

Part II
Interval MADM Methods and Their Applications

Chapter 4
Interval MADM with Real-Valued Weight Information

With the development of society and economics, the complexity and uncertainty of the considered problems and the fuzziness of the human's thinking have been increasing constantly. In the process of practical decision making, the decision information is sometimes expressed in the form of interval numbers. Some researchers have paid their attention on this issue. In this chapter, we introduce the concepts of interval-valued positive ideal point and interval-valued negative ideal point, the relations among the possibility degree formulas for comparing interval numbers, and then introduce the MADM methods based on possibility degrees, projection model, interval TOPSIS, and the UBM operators. Moreover, we establish the minimizing group discordance optimization models for deriving expert weights. We also illustrate these methods and models in detail with some practical examples.

4.1 MADM Method Based on Possibility Degrees

4.1.1 Possibility Degree Formulas for Comparing Interval Numbers

Let $\tilde{a} = [a^L, a^U] = \{x \mid 0 \le a^L \le x \le a^U, a^L, a^U \in \Re\}$, then $\tilde{a}$ is called an interval number. Especially, if $a^L = a^U$, then $\tilde{a}$ reduces to a real number.

We first introduce the operational laws of interval numbers [156]:

Let $\tilde{a} = [a^L, a^U]$ and $\tilde{b} = [b^L, b^U]$, and $\beta \ge 0$, then

1. $\tilde{a} = \tilde{b}$ if and only if $a^L = b^L$ and $a^U = b^U$.
2. $\tilde{a} + \tilde{b} = [a^L + b^L, a^U + b^U]$.
3. $\beta\tilde{a} = [\beta a^L, \beta b^L]$, where $\beta \ge 0$. Especially, if $\beta = 0$, then $\beta\tilde{a} = 0$.
4. $\tilde{a}\tilde{b} = [a^L, a^U] \cdot [b^L, b^U] = [a^L b^L, a^U b^U]$.
5. $\tilde{a}^\beta = [a^L, a^U]^\beta = [(a^L)^\beta, (a^U)^\beta]$.

Z.S. Xu, *Uncertain Multi-Attribute Decision Making*,
DOI 10.1007/978-3-662-45640-8_4

Definition 4.1 [107] If $\tilde{a}$ and $\tilde{b}$ are real numbers, then we call

$$p(\tilde{a} > \tilde{b}) = \begin{cases} 1, & \text{if } \tilde{a} > \tilde{b}, \\ \frac{1}{2}, & \text{if } \tilde{a} = \tilde{b}, \\ 0, & \text{if } \tilde{a} < \tilde{b} \end{cases} \tag{4.1}$$

a possibility degree of $\tilde{a} > \tilde{b}$.

Definition 4.2 [149] Let both $\tilde{a}$ and $\tilde{b}$ be interval numbers or one of them is an interval number, where $\tilde{a} = [a^L, a^U]$, $\tilde{b} = [b^L, b^U]$, and let $l_{\tilde{a}} = a^U - a^L$, and $l_{\tilde{b}} = b^U - b^L$, then

$$p(\tilde{a} \geq \tilde{b}) = \frac{\min\left\{l_{\tilde{a}} + l_{\tilde{b}}, \max\left\{a^U - b^L, 0\right\}\right\}}{l_{\tilde{a}} + l_{\tilde{b}}} \tag{4.2}$$

is called the possibility degree of $\tilde{a} \geq \tilde{b}$, and let the order relation between $\tilde{a}$ and $\tilde{b}$ be $\tilde{a} \underset{p}{\geq} \tilde{b}$.

Da and Liu [18], and Facchinetti et al. [26] gave two possibility degree formulas for comparing interval numbers:

Definition 4.3 [26] Let

$$p(\tilde{a} \geq \tilde{b}) = \min\left\{\max\left\{\frac{a^U - b^L}{l_{\tilde{a}} + l_{\tilde{b}}}, 0\right\}, 1\right\} \tag{4.3}$$

then $p(\tilde{a} \geq \tilde{b})$ is called a possibility degree of $\tilde{a} \geq \tilde{b}$.

Definition 4.4 [18] Let

$$p(\tilde{a} \geq \tilde{b}) = \frac{\max\left\{0, l_{\tilde{a}} + l_{\tilde{b}} - \max\left\{b^U - a^L, 0\right\}\right\}}{l_{\tilde{a}} + l_{\tilde{b}}} \tag{4.4}$$

then $p(\tilde{a} \geq \tilde{b})$ is called a possibility degree of $\tilde{a} \geq \tilde{b}$.

According to the definitions above, we can prove the following conclusions:

Theorem 4.1 [149] Let $\tilde{a}=[a^L,a^U]$ and $\tilde{b}=[b^L,b^U]$, then

1. $0\le p(\tilde{a}\ge\tilde{b})\le 1$.
2. $p(\tilde{a}\ge\tilde{b})=1$ if and only if $b^U\le a^L$.
3. $p(\tilde{a}\ge\tilde{b})=0$ if and only if $a^U\le b^L$.
4. $p(\tilde{a}\ge\tilde{b})+p(\tilde{b}\ge\tilde{a})=1$. Especially, $p(\tilde{a}\ge\tilde{a})=\dfrac{1}{2}$.
5. $p(\tilde{a}\ge\tilde{b})\ge\dfrac{1}{2}$ if and only if $a^U+a^L\ge b^U+b^L$. Especially, $p(\tilde{a}\ge\tilde{b})=\dfrac{1}{2}$ if and only if $a^U+a^L=b^U+b^L$.
6. For three interval numbers $\tilde{a},\tilde{b}$ and $\tilde{c}$, if $p(\tilde{a}\ge\tilde{b})\ge\dfrac{1}{2}$ and $p(\tilde{b}\ge\tilde{c})\ge\dfrac{1}{2}$, then $p(\tilde{a}\ge\tilde{c})\ge\dfrac{1}{2}$.

In the following, we investigate the relations among Definitions 4.2–4.4:

Theorem 4.2 [149] Definitions 4.2–4.4 are equivalent, i.e., Eq. (4.2) ⇔Eq. (4.3)⇔ Eq. (4.4).

Proof We first prove Eq. (4.2)⇔ Eq. (4.3). By Eq. (4.2), we have

$$\begin{aligned}
p(\tilde{a}\ge\tilde{b}) &= \frac{\min\left\{l_{\tilde{a}}+l_{\tilde{b}},\ \max\left\{a^U-b^L,0\right\}\right\}}{l_{\tilde{a}}+l_{\tilde{b}}}\\
&= \min\left\{\frac{l_{\tilde{a}}+l_{\tilde{b}}}{l_{\tilde{a}}+l_{\tilde{b}}},\ \frac{\max\left\{a^U-b^L,0\right\}}{l_{\tilde{a}}+l_{\tilde{b}}}\right\}\\
&= \min\left\{1,\ \max\left\{\frac{a^U-b^L}{l_{\tilde{a}}+l_{\tilde{b}}},0\right\}\right\}
\end{aligned}$$

i.e.,

$$p(\tilde{a}\ge\tilde{b})=\min\left\{\max\left\{\frac{a^U-b^L}{l_{\tilde{a}}+l_{\tilde{b}}},0\right\},1\right\}$$

and thus, Eq. (4.2)⇔Eq. (4.3).

Now we prove Eq. (4.3)⇔Eq. (4.4). By Eqs. (4.3), (4.2)⇔Eq. (4.3), and the complementarity of possibility degrees, we get

$$\begin{aligned}
p(\tilde{b} \geq \tilde{a}) &= 1 - p(\tilde{a} \geq \tilde{b}) \\
&= 1 - \min\left\{ \max\left(\frac{a^U - b^L}{l_{\tilde{a}} + l_{\tilde{b}}}, 0 \right), 1 \right\} \\
&= 1 - \frac{\min\left\{ l_{\tilde{a}} + l_{\tilde{b}}, \max\left\{ a^U - b^L, 0 \right\} \right\}}{l_{\tilde{a}} + l_{\tilde{b}}} \\
&= \frac{\max\left\{ 0, l_{\tilde{a}} + l_{\tilde{b}} - \max\left\{ a^U - b^L, 0 \right\} \right\}}{l_{\tilde{a}} + l_{\tilde{b}}}
\end{aligned}$$

i.e.,

$$p(\tilde{b} \geq \tilde{a}) = \frac{\max\left\{ 0, l_{\tilde{a}} + l_{\tilde{b}} - \max\left\{ a^U - b^L, 0 \right\} \right\}}{l_{\tilde{a}} + l_{\tilde{b}}}$$

and thus, Eq. (4.3)⇔Eq. (4.4). This completes the proof.

Similarly, we give the following definition, and can also prove that it is equivalent to Definitions 4.2–4.4.

Definition 4.5 [18] Let

$$p(\tilde{a} \geq \tilde{b}) = \max\left\{ 1 - \max\left\{ \frac{b^U - a^L}{l_{\tilde{a}} + l_{\tilde{b}}}, 0 \right\}, 0 \right\} \tag{4.5}$$

then $p(\tilde{a} \geq \tilde{b})$ is called a possibility degree of $\tilde{a} \geq \tilde{b}$.

4.1.2 Ranking of Interval Numbers

For a collection of interval numbers $\tilde{a}_i = [a_i^L, a_i^U] (i = 1, 2, \ldots, n)$, we compare each pair of these interval numbers, and utilize one of the formulas (4.2)–(4.5) to derive the possibility degree $p(\tilde{a}_i \geq \tilde{a}_j)$, denoted by $p_{ij} (i, j = 1, 2, \ldots, n)$ for brevity, and construct the possibility degree matrix $P = (p_{ij})_{n \times n}$. The matrix contains all the possibility degree information derived from comparing all pairs of alternatives. Thus, the ranking problem of interval numbers can be transformed into the problem for deriving the priority vector of a possibility degree matrix. It follows from Theorem 4.1 that the matrix P is a fuzzy preference relation. In Chap. 2, we have introduced in detail the priority theory of fuzzy preference relations. Here, we utilize the simple priority formula (2.6) given in Sect. 2.1.1 to derive the priority vector of P, i.e.,

$$v_i = \frac{1}{n(n-1)}\left(\sum_{j=1}^{n} p_{ij} + \frac{n}{2} - 1\right), \quad i = 1, 2, \ldots, n \tag{4.6}$$

from which we get the priority vector $v = (v_1, v_2, \ldots, v_n)$ of the possibility degree matrix P, and then rank the interval numbers $\tilde{a}_i (i = 1, 2, \ldots, n)$ according to v_i $(i = 1, 2, \ldots, n)$.

4.1.3 Decision Making Method

Based on the concept the possibility degree of comparing interval numbers, now we introduce a MADM method, which has the following steps [149]:

Step 1 For a MADM problem, the information on attribute weights is known completely and expressed in real numbers. For the alternative x_i, the attribute value $\tilde{a}_{ij} = [a_{ij}^L, a_{ij}^U]$ is given with respect to the attribute u_j, and all $\tilde{a}_{ij} (i = 1, 2, \ldots, n,$ $j = 1, 2, \ldots, m)$ are contained in the uncertain decision matrix $\tilde{A} = (\tilde{a}_{ij})_{n \times m}$. The most widely used attribute types are benefit type and cost type. Let $I_i (i = 1, 2)$ denote the subscript sets of the attributes of benefit type and cost type, respectively.

In order to measure all attributes in dimensionless units and to facilitate inter-attribute comparisons, here, we normalize the uncertain decision matrix $\tilde{A} = (\tilde{a}_{ij})_{n \times m}$ into the matrix $\tilde{R} = (\tilde{r}_{ij})_{n \times m}$ using the following formulas:

$$\tilde{r}_{ij} = \frac{\tilde{a}_{ij}}{\|\tilde{a}_j\|}, \quad i = 1, 2, \ldots, n, \quad j \in I_1 \tag{4.7}$$

$$\tilde{r}_{ij} = \frac{1/\tilde{a}_{ij}}{\|1/\tilde{a}_j\|}, \quad i = 1, 2, \ldots, n, \quad j \in I_2 \tag{4.8}$$

$$\|\tilde{a}_j\| = \sqrt{\sum_{i=1}^{n} \tilde{a}_{ij}^2}, \; j \in I_1, \quad \|1/\tilde{a}_j\| = \sqrt{\sum_{i=1}^{n} (1/\tilde{a}_{ij})^2}, \quad j \in I_2$$

According to the operational laws of interval numbers, we transform Eqs. (4.7) and (4.8) into the following formulas:

$$\begin{cases} r_{ij}^L = \dfrac{a_{ij}^L}{\sqrt{\sum_{i=1}^{n}(a_{ij}^U)^2}}, \\ r_{ij}^U = \dfrac{a_{ij}^U}{\sqrt{\sum_{i=1}^{n}(a_{ij}^L)^2}}, \end{cases} \quad i=1,2,\ldots,n, \ \ j \in I_1 \tag{4.9}$$

$$\begin{cases} r_{ij}^L = \dfrac{1/a_{ij}^U}{\sqrt{\sum_{i=1}^{n}(1/a_{ij}^L)^2}}, \\ r_{ij}^U = \dfrac{1/a_{ij}^L}{\sqrt{\sum_{i=1}^{n}(1/a_{ij}^U)^2}}, \end{cases} \quad i=1,2,\ldots,n, \ \ j \in I_2 \tag{4.10}$$

or [28]

$$\tilde{r}_{ij} = \frac{\tilde{a}_{ij}}{\sum_{i=1}^{n}\tilde{a}_{ij}}, \ i=1,2,\ldots,n, \ \ j \in I_1 \tag{4.11}$$

$$\tilde{r}_{ij} = \frac{1/\tilde{a}_{ij}}{\sum_{i=1}^{n}(1/\tilde{a}_{ij})}, \ i=1,2,\ldots,n, \ \ j \in I_2 \tag{4.12}$$

According to the operational laws of interval numbers, we transform Eqs. (4.11) and (4.12) into the following forms:

$$\begin{cases} r_{ij}^L = \dfrac{a_{ij}^L}{\sum_{i=1}^{n}(a_{ij}^U)}, \\ r_{ij}^U = \dfrac{a_{ij}^U}{\sum_{i=1}^{n}(a_{ij}^L)}, \end{cases} \quad i=1,2,\ldots,n, \ \ j \in I_1 \tag{4.13}$$

$$\begin{cases} r_{ij}^L = \dfrac{1/a_{ij}^U}{\sum_{i=1}^{n}(1/a_{ij}^L)}, \\ r_{ij}^U = \dfrac{1/a_{ij}^L}{\sum_{i=1}^{n}(1/a_{ij}^U)}, \end{cases} \quad i=1,2,\ldots,n, \; j \in I_2 \tag{4.14}$$

Step 2 Utilize the uncertain weighted averaging (UWA) operator to aggregate the attribute values of the alternatives $x_i(i=1,2,\ldots,n)$, and get the overall attribute values $\tilde{z}_i(w)(i=1,2,\ldots,n)$:

$$\tilde{z}_i(w) = \sum_{j=1}^{m} w_j \tilde{r}_{ij}, \; i=1,2,\ldots,n \tag{4.15}$$

Step 3 Use the possibility degree formula (4.2) to compare the overall attribute values $\tilde{z}_i(w)(i=1,2,\ldots,n)$, and construct the possibility degree matrix $P=(p_{ij})_{n\times n}$, where $p_{ij}=p(\tilde{z}_i(w)\geq \tilde{z}_j(w)),\; i,j=1,2,\ldots,n$.

Step 4 Employ Eq. (4.6) to derive the priority vector $v=(v_1,v_2,\ldots,v_n)$ of the possibility degree matrix P and rank the alternatives $x_i(i=1,2,\ldots,n)$ according to $v_i(i=1,2,\ldots,n)$ in descending order, and then get the best alternative.

4.1.4 Practical Example

In this section, a MADM problem of evaluating university faculty for tenure and promotion is used to illustrate the developed procedure.

A practical use of the developed procedure involves the evaluation of university faculty for tenure and promotion. The criteria (attributes) used at some universities are: (1) u_1: teaching; (2) u_2: research; and (3) u_3: service, whose weight vector is $w=(0.4,0.4,0.2)$. Five faculty candidates (alternatives) $x_i(i=1,2,3,4,5)$ are to be evaluated using interval numbers. The normalized uncertain decision matrix $\tilde{R}=(\tilde{r}_{ij})_{5\times 3}$ is listed in Table 4.1.

Table 4.1 Uncertain decision matrix $\tilde{R}$

	u_1	u_2	u_3
x_1	[0.214, 0.220]	[0.166, 0.178]	[0.184, 0.190]
x_2	[0.206, 0.225]	[0.220, 0.229]	[0.182, 0.191]
x_3	[0.195, 0.204]	[0.192, 0.198]	[0.220, 0.231]
x_4	[0.181, 0.190]	[0.195, 0.205]	[0.185, 0.195]
x_5	[0.175, 0.184]	[0.193, 0.201]	[0.201, 0.211]

By using the formula $\tilde{z}_i(w)=\sum_{j=1}^{3} w_j \tilde{r}_{ij}$, we get the overall attribute values of all the faculties $x_i (i=1,2,3,4,5)$ as the interval values:

$$\tilde{z}_1(w)=[0.1888,0.1972],\ \tilde{z}_2(w)=[0.2068,0.2198]$$
$$\tilde{z}_3(w)=[0.1988,0.2070],\ \tilde{z}_4(w)=[0.1874,0.1970]$$
$$\tilde{z}_5(w)=[0.1874,0.1962]$$

In order to rank all the alternatives, we first utilize Eq. (4.2) to compare each pair of $\tilde{z}_i(w)(i=1,2,3,4,5)$, and then derive the possibility degree matrix:

$$P=\begin{pmatrix} 0.5 & 0 & 0 & 0.5444 & 0.5698 \\ 1 & 0.5 & 0.9906 & 1 & 1 \\ 1 & 0.0094 & 0.5 & 1 & 1 \\ 0.4556 & 0 & 0 & 0.5 & 0.5217 \\ 0.4302 & 0 & 0 & 0.4783 & 0.5 \end{pmatrix}$$

and then we utilize Eq. (4.6) to obtain the priority vector of the possibility degree matrix P:

$$v=(0.1557,0.2995,0.2505,0.1489,0.1454)$$

Based on the priority vector and the possibility degrees in the matrix P, we get the ranking of the interval numbers $\tilde{z}_i(w)(i=1,2,3,4,5)$:

$$\tilde{z}_2(w)\underset{0.9906}{\geq}\tilde{z}_3(w)\underset{1}{\geq}\tilde{z}_1(w)\underset{0.5444}{\geq}\tilde{z}_4(w)\underset{0.5217}{\geq}\tilde{z}_5(w)$$

If we use the symbol "$\underset{p}{\succ}$" to denote the priority relations among the alternatives with the possibility degrees, then the corresponding ranking of the five faculties $x_i (i=1,2,3,4,5)$ is

$$x_2 \underset{0.9906}{\succ} x_3 \underset{1}{\succ} x_1 \underset{0.5444}{\succ} x_4 \underset{0.5217}{\succ} x_5$$

and thus, the faculty x_2 has the best overall evaluation value.

4.2 MADM Method Based on Projection Model

4.2.1 Decision Making Method

We first construct the weighted normalized decision matrix $\tilde{Y} = (\tilde{y}_{ij})_{n \times m}$, where $\tilde{y}_{ij} = [y_{ij}^L, y_{ij}^U]$, and $\tilde{y}_{ij} = w_j \tilde{r}_{ij}$, $i = 1,2,\ldots,n$, $j = 1,2,\ldots,m$.

Definition 4.6 [148] $\tilde{y}^+ = (\tilde{y}_1^+, \tilde{y}_2^+, \ldots, \tilde{y}_m^+)$ is called the interval-valued positive ideal point, where

$$\tilde{y}_j^+ = [y_j^{+L}, y_j^{+U}] = [\max_i(y_{ij}^L), \max_i(y_{ij}^U)], \quad j = 1,2,\ldots,m \tag{4.16}$$

Definition 4.7 [148] Let $\alpha = (\alpha_1, \alpha_2, \ldots, \alpha_m)$ and $\beta = (\beta_1, \beta_2, \ldots, \beta_m)$ be two vectors, then

$$\cos(\alpha, \beta) = \frac{\sum_{j=1}^{m} \alpha_j \beta_j}{\sqrt{\sum_{j=1}^{m} \alpha_j^2} \cdot \sqrt{\sum_{j=1}^{m} \beta_j^2}} \tag{4.17}$$

Definition 4.8 Let $\alpha = (\alpha_1, \alpha_2, \ldots, \alpha_m)$, then $|\alpha| = \sqrt{\sum_{j=1}^{m} \alpha_j^2}$ is called the module of the vector α.

As it is well known that a vector is composed of direction and modular size, $\cos(\alpha, \beta)$, however, only reflects the similarity measure between the directions of the vectors α and β. In order to measure the similarity degree between the vectors α and β from the global point of view, in the following, we introduce the formula of projection of the vector α on β as follows:

Definition 4.9 [148] Let $\alpha = (\alpha_1, \alpha_2, \ldots, \alpha_m)$ and $\beta = (\beta_1, \beta_2, \ldots, \beta_m)$ be two vectors, then

$$\Pr j_\beta(\alpha) = \frac{\sum_{j=1}^{m} \alpha_j \beta_j}{\sqrt{\sum_{j=1}^{m} \alpha_j^2} \sqrt{\sum_{j=1}^{m} \beta_j^2}} \sqrt{\sum_{j=1}^{m} \alpha_j^2} = \frac{\sum_{j=1}^{m} \alpha_j \beta_j}{\sqrt{\sum_{j=1}^{m} \beta_j^2}} \tag{4.18}$$

is the projection of the vector α on β. In general, the larger $\Pr j_\beta(\alpha)$, the closer the vector α to β. Let

$$\Pr j_{\tilde{y}^+}(\tilde{y}_i) = \frac{\sum_{j=1}^{m}[\tilde{y}_{ij}^L y_j^{+L} + \tilde{y}_{ij}^U y_j^{+U}]}{\sqrt{\sum_{j=1}^{m}[(\tilde{y}_j^L)^2 + (\tilde{y}_{ij}^{+U})^2]}} \tag{4.19}$$

where $\tilde{y}_i = (\tilde{y}_{i1}, \tilde{y}_{i2}, \ldots, \tilde{y}_{im})$, $i = 1, 2, \ldots, n$.

Obviously, the larger $\Pr j_{\tilde{y}^+}(\tilde{y}_i)$, the closer the alternative x_i to the interval-valued positive ideal point $\tilde{y}^+$, and thus, the better the alternative x_i.

According to the definition above, in the following, we introduce a MADM method based on projection model [148]:

Step 1 For a MADM problem, the weight information on attributes is unknown completely. The decision maker evaluates all the alternatives $x_i (i = 1, 2, \ldots, n)$ with respect to the attributes $u_j (j = 1, 2, \ldots, m)$, and constructs the uncertain decision matrix $\tilde{A} = (\tilde{a}_{ij})_{n \times m}$. Then, by using Eqs. (4.9) and (4.10), we transform the matrix $\tilde{A}$ into the normalized uncertain decision matrix $\tilde{R} = (\tilde{r}_{ij})_{n \times m}$.

Step 2 Use the attribute weight vector w and the normalized uncertain decision matrix $\tilde{R}$ to construct the weighted normalized uncertain decision matrix $\tilde{Y} = (\tilde{y}_{ij})_{n \times m}$.

Step 3 Utilize Eq. (4.16) to calculate the interval-valued positive ideal point $\tilde{y}^+$.

Step 4 Utilize Eq. (4.19) to derive the projection $\Pr j_{\tilde{y}^+}(\tilde{y}_i)$ of the alternative x_i on the interval-valued positive ideal point $\tilde{y}^+$.

Step 5 Rank and select the alternatives $x_i (i = 1, 2, \ldots, n)$ according to $\Pr j_{\tilde{y}^+}(\tilde{y}_i)$ $(i = 1, 2, \ldots, n)$.

4.2.2 Practical Example

Example 4.2 The maintainability design is that, in the process of product development, the researcher should give full consideration to some important factors, including the overall structure of the system, the preparation and connection of all parts of the system, standardization and modularization, so that the users can restore its function in the case of product failure. Now there are three maintainability design schemes to choose from, the criteria (attributes) used to evaluate these schemes [23] are: (1) u_1 : life cycle cost (10^3\$); (2) u_2 : average life span (hour); (3) u_3 : average repair time (hour); (4) u_4 : availability; (5) u_5 : comprehensive performance. The uncertain decision matrix $\tilde{A}$ is listed as Table 4.2.

The known attribute weight vector is

$$w = (0.2189, 0.2182, 0.1725, 0.2143, 0.1761)$$

Table 4.2 Uncertain decision matrix $\tilde{A}$

	u_1	u_2	u_3	u_4	u_5
x_1	[58.9, 59.0]	[200, 250]	[1.9, 2.1]	[0.990, 0.991]	[0.907, 0.909]
x_2	[58.5, 58.7]	[340, 350]	[3.4, 3.5]	[0.990, 0.992]	[0.910, 0.912]
x_3	[58.0, 58.5]	[290, 310]	[2.0, 2.2]	[0.992, 0.993]	[0.914, 0.917]

Table 4.3 Normalized uncertain decision matrix $\tilde{R}$

	u_1	u_2	u_3	u_4	u_5
x_1	[0.5721, 0.5757]	[0.3772, 0.5106]	[0.6080, 0.1265]	[0.5762, 0.5775]	[0.5738, 0.5765]
x_2	[0.5750, 0.5796]	[0.6413, 0.7149]	[0.3648, 0.4098]	[0.5762, 0.5781]	[0.5757, 0.5784]
x_3	[0.5770, 0.5846]	[0.5470, 0.6332]	[0.5803, 0.6967]	[0.5774, 0.5787]	[0.5782, 0.5816]

Table 4.4 Weighted normalized decision matrix $\tilde{Y}$

	u_1	u_2	u_3	u_4	u_5
x_1	[0.1252, 0.1260]	[0.0823, 0.1114]	[0.1049, 0.1265]	[0.1235, 0.1238]	[0.1010, 0.1015]
x_2	[0.1259, 0.1269]	[0.1399, 0.1560]	[0.0629, 0.0707]	[0.1235, 0.1239]	[0.1014, 0.1019]
x_3	[0.1263, 0.1280]	[0.1194, 0.1382]	[0.1001, 0.1202]	[0.1237, 0.1240]	[0.1018, 0.1024]

Among all the attributes $u_j (j = 1,2,3,4,5)$, u_1 and u_3 are cost-type attributes, the others are benefit-type attributes.

Now we use the method of Sect. 4.2.1 to select the schemes. The decision making steps are as follows:

Step 1 Utilize Eqs. (4.9) and (4.10) to transform the uncertain decision matrix $\tilde{A}$ into the normalized uncertain decision matrix $\tilde{R}$, listed in Table 4.3.

Step 2 Construct the weighted normalized uncertain decision matrix $\tilde{Y}$ (see Table 4.4) using the attribute weight vector w and the normalized uncertain decision matrix $\tilde{R}$:

Step 3 Calculate the interval-valued positive ideal point utilizing Eq. (4.16):

$$\tilde{y}^+ = ([0.1263, 0.1280], [0.1399, 0.1560], [0.1049, 0.1265], \\ [0.1237, 0.1240], [0.1018, 0.1024])$$

Step 4 Derive the projections $\Pr j_{\tilde{y}^+}(\tilde{y}_i)\ (i=1,2,3)$ using Eq. (4.19):

$$\Pr j_{\tilde{y}^+}(\tilde{y}_1)=0.3537,\quad \Pr j_{\tilde{y}^+}(\tilde{y}_2)=0.2717,\quad \Pr j_{\tilde{y}^+}(\tilde{y}_3)=0.3758$$

Step 5 Rank the schemes $x_i(i=1,2,3)$ according to $\Pr j_{\tilde{y}^+}(\tilde{y}_i)\ (i=1,2,3)$:

$$x_3 \succ x_1 \succ x_2$$

and thus, the scheme x_3 is the best one.

4.3 MADM Method Based on Interval TOPSIS

4.3.1 Decision Making Method

Definition 4.10 $\tilde{y}^- = (\tilde{y}_1^-, \tilde{y}_2^-, \ldots, \tilde{y}_m^-)$ is called interval-valued negative ideal point, where

$$\tilde{y}_j^- = [y_j^{-L}, y_j^{-U}] = [\min_i(y_{ij}^L), \min_i(y_{ij}^U)],\quad j=1,2,\ldots,n \tag{4.20}$$

Now we introduce a MADM method based on interval TOPSIS (the technique for order performance by similarity to ideal solution [48]), whose steps are as below:

Step 1 For a MADM problem, the weight information on attributes is known completely. $\tilde{A}=(\tilde{a}_{ij})_{n\times m}$ and $\tilde{R}=(\tilde{r}_{ij})_{n\times m}$ are the uncertain decision matrix and the normalized uncertain decision matrix, respectively.

Step 2 Construct the weighted normalized uncertain decision matrix $\tilde{Y}=(\tilde{y}_{ij})_{n\times m}$ using the attribute weight vector w and the normalized uncertain decision matrix $\tilde{R}$.

Step 3 Utilize Eqs. (4.16) and (4.20) to calculate the interval-valued positive ideal point $\tilde{y}^+$ and the interval-valued negative ideal point $\tilde{y}^-$, respectively.

Step 4 Calculate the distances of each alternative to the interval-valued positive ideal point $\tilde{y}^+$ and the interval-valued negative ideal point $\tilde{y}^-$, respectively:

$$D_i^+ = \sum_{j=1}^m \left\|\tilde{y}_{ij} - \tilde{y}_j^+\right\| = \sum_{j=1}^m \left[\left|y_{ij}^L - y_j^{+L}\right| + \left|y_{ij}^U - y_j^{+U}\right|\right],\quad i=1,2,\ldots,n \tag{4.21}$$

$$D_i^- = \sum_{j=1}^{m} \left\| \tilde{y}_{ij} - \tilde{y}_j^+ \right\| = \sum_{j=1}^{m} \left[\left| y_{ij}^L - y_j^{-L} \right| + \left| y_{ij}^U - y_j^{-U} \right| \right], \quad i = 1, 2, \ldots, n \tag{4.22}$$

Step 5 Obtain the closeness degree of each alternative to the interval-valued positive ideal point:

$$c_i = \frac{D_i^-}{D_i^+ + D_i^-}, \quad i = 1, 2, \ldots, n \tag{4.23}$$

Step 6 Rank the alternatives $x_i (i = 1, 2, \ldots, n)$ according to $c_i (i = 1, 2, \ldots, n)$. The larger c_i, the better x_i.

4.3.2 Practical Example

Example 4.3 One area is rich in rawhide. In order to develop the leather industry of this area, the relevant departments put forward five alternatives $x_i (i = 1, 2, 3, 4, 5)$ to choose from. Taking into account the distribution of production resources and other factors closely related to the leather industry, the following eight attributes are used to evaluate the considered alternatives: (1) u_1 : energy demand (10^2kw. h/d); (2) u_2 : the demand of water ($1*10^5$ gallons per day); (3) u_3 : waste water discharge mode (ten mark system); (4) u_4 : the cost of plant and equipment ($1*10^6$ dollars); (5) u_5 : the cost of operation ($1*10^4$ dollars per year); (6) u_6 : the relevant region's economic development (ten mark system); (7) u_7 : research and development opportunities (ten mark system); and (8) u_8 : return on investment (1 as the base). The attribute weight vector is given as:

$$w = (0.10, 0.12, 0.15, 0.13, 0.17, 0.11, 0.12, 0.10)$$

and the attribute values of the alternatives $x_i (i = 1, 2, 3, 4, 5)$ with respect to the attributes $u_j (j = 1, 2, \ldots, 8)$ are listed in Table 4.5.

Among the attributes $u_j (j = 1, 2, \ldots, 8)$, u_1, u_2, u_4 and u_5 are cost-type attributes, and the others are benefit-type attributes.

In the following, we use the method of Sect. 4.3.1 to solve the problem:

Step 1 Transform the uncertain decision matrix $\tilde{A}$ into the normalized uncertain decision matrix $\tilde{R}$ utilizing Eqs. (4.9) and (4.10), listed in Table 4.6.

Step 2 Use the attribute weight vector w and the normalized uncertain decision matrix $\tilde{R}$ to construct the weighted normalized uncertain decision matrix $\tilde{Y}$, listed in Table 4.7.

Table 4.5 Uncertain decision matrix $\tilde{A}$

	u_1	u_2	u_3	u_4	u_5	u_6	u_7	u_8
x_1	[1.5, 1.9]	[9, 9.5]	[8, 9]	[10, 12]	[12, 13]	[8, 9]	[2, 3]	[1.2, 1.3]
x_2	[2.7, 3.1]	[5, 6]	[9, 9.5]	[4, 5]	[4, 5]	[7, 8]	[9, 10]	[1.1, 1.2]
x_3	[1.8, 2]	[8.5, 9.1]	[7, 8]	[8, 9]	[9, 10]	[8.5, 9]	[5, 6]	[1, 1.3]
x_4	[2.5, 2.8]	[5, 6]	[9, 10]	[6, 7]	[6, 8]	[7, 7.5]	[8, 9]	[0.8, 0.9]
x_5	[2, 2.5]	[4, 5]	[8, 9]	[5, 6]	[5, 7]	[8, 9]	[5, 6]	[0.6, 0.7]

Table 4.6 Normalized uncertain decision matrix $\tilde{R}$

	u_1	u_2	u_3	u_4
x_1	[0.46, 0.71]	[0.26, 0.32]	[0.18, 0.22]	[0.21, 0.31]
x_2	[0.28, 0.39]	[0.41, 0.58]	[0.20, 0.23]	[0.51, 0.76]
x_3	[0.44, 0.59]	[0.27, 0.34]	[0.15, 0.20]	[0.28, 0.38]
x_4	[0.31, 0.42]	[0.41, 0.58]	[0.20, 0.24]	[0.36, 0.51]
x_5	[0.35, 0.53]	[0.49, 0.73]	[0.18, 0.22]	[0.42, 0.61]
	u_5	u_6	u_7	u_8
x_1	[0.20, 0.27]	[0.19, 0.23]	[0.06, 0.10]	[0.22, 0.24]
x_2	[0.52, 0.82]	[0.16, 0.21]	[0.26, 0.34]	[0.20, 0.22]
x_3	[0.26, 0.37]	[0.20, 0.23]	[0.15, 0.22]	[0.19, 0.24]
x_4	[0.32, 0.55]	[0.16, 0.19]	[0.24, 0.31]	[0.15, 0.17]
x_5	[0.37, 0.66]	[0.19, 0.23]	[0.15, 0.21]	[0.11, 0.13]

Table 4.7 Weighted normalized uncertain decision matrix $\tilde{Y}$

	u_1	u_2	u_3	u_4
x_1	[0.046, 0.071]	[0.026, 0.032]	[0.018, 0.022]	[0.021, 0.031]
x_2	[0.028, 0.039]	[0.041, 0.058]	[0.020, 0.023]	[0.051, 0.076]
x_3	[0.044, 0.059]	[0.027, 0.034]	[0.015, 0.020]	[0.028, 0.038]
x_4	[0.031, 0.042]	[0.041, 0.058]	[0.020, 0.024]	[0.036, 0.051]
x_5	[0.035, 0.053]	[0.049, 0.073]	[0.018, 0.022]	[0.042, 0.061]
	u_5	u_6	u_7	u_8
x_1	[0.020, 0.027]	[0.019, 0.023]	[0.006, 0.010]	[0.022, 0.024]
x_2	[0.052, 0.082]	[0.016, 0.021]	[0.026, 0.034]	[0.020, 0.022]
x_3	[0.026, 0.037]	[0.020, 0.023]	[0.015, 0.022]	[0.019, 0.024]
x_4	[0.032, 0.055]	[0.016, 0.019]	[0.024, 0.031]	[0.015, 0.017]
x_5	[0.037, 0.066]	[0.019, 0.023]	[0.015, 0.021]	[0.011, 0.013]

Step 3 Calculate the interval-valued positive ideal point $\tilde{y}^+$ and the interval-valued negative ideal point $\tilde{y}^-$, respectively, utilizing Eqs. (4.16) and (4.20):

$$\tilde{y}^+ = ([0.046, 0.071], [0.059, 0.088], [0.030, 0.036], [0.066, 0.099], [0.088, 0.139], [0.022, 0.025], [0.031, 0.041], [0.022, 0.024])$$

$$\tilde{y}^- = ([0.021, 0.039], [0.031, 0.038], [0.023, 0.030], [0.027, 0.040], [0.034, 0.046], [0.018, 0.021], [0.007, 0.021], [0.011, 0.013])$$

Step 4 Get the distances of each alternative to $\tilde{y}^+$ and $\tilde{y}^-$, respectively:

$$D_1^+ = 0.383,\ D_2^+ = 0.089,\ D_3^+ = 0.333,\ D_4^+ = 0.230,\ D_5^+ = 0.170$$

$$D_1^- = 0.093,\ D_2^- = 0.387,\ D_3^- = 0.143,\ D_4^- = 0.246,\ D_5^- = 0.306$$

Step 5 Obtain the closeness degree of each alternative to the interval-valued positive ideal point:

$$c_1 = 0.195,\ c_2 = 0.813,\ c_3 = 0.300,\ c_4 = 0.517,\ c_5 = 0.643$$

Step 6 Rank the alternatives $x_i (i = 1, 2, 3, 4, 5)$ according to $c_i (i = 1, 2, 3, 4, 5)$:

$$x_2 \succ x_5 \succ x_4 \succ x_3 \succ x_1$$

and then we get the best alternative x_2.

4.4 MADM Methods Based on UBM Operators

The Bonferroni mean (BM), originally introduced by Bonferroni [5], is a traditional mean type aggregation operator, which is suitable to aggregate the crisp data and can capture the expressed interrelationship between the individual data. Recently, Yager [161] generalized the BM by replacing the simple average by other mean type operators such as the OWA operator [157] and Choquet integral [14] as well as associating differing importance with the data. Considering the desirable property of the BM, and the need of extending its potential applications to more extensive areas, such as decision making under uncertainty, fuzzy clustering analysis, and uncertain programming, etc., Xu [134] extended the BM to aggregate uncertain data, developed some uncertain BM operators, uncertain ordered weighted BM operator, and uncertain Bonferroni Choquet operator, etc., and studied their properties. He also gave their applications to MADM under uncertainty.

4.4.1 The UBM Operators and Their Application in MADM

Given a collect of crisp data $a_i (i = 1, 2, \ldots, n)$, where $a_i \geq 0$, for all i, and $p, q \geq 0$. Bonferroni [5] originally introduced an aggregation operator, denoted as $B^{p,q}$ such that

$$B^{p,q}(a_1, a_2, \ldots, a_n) = \left(\frac{1}{n(n-1)} \sum_{\substack{i,j=1 \\ i \neq j}}^{n} a_i^p a_j^q \right)^{\frac{1}{p+q}} \tag{4.24}$$

Recently, the operator $B^{p,q}$ has been discussed by Yager [161], Beliakov et al. [3] and Bullen [6], and called Bonferroni mean (BM). For the special case where $p = q = 1$, the BM reduces to the following [161]:

$$B(a_1, a_2, \ldots, a_n) = \left(\frac{1}{n(n-1)} \sum_{\substack{i,j=1 \\ i \neq j}}^{n} a_i a_j \right)^{\frac{1}{2}} = \left(\frac{1}{n} \sum_{i=1}^{n} \varsigma_i a_i \right)^{\frac{1}{2}} \tag{4.25}$$

where $\varsigma_i = \frac{1}{n-1} \sum_{\substack{j=1 \\ j \neq i}}^{n} a_j$.

Yager [161] replaced the simple average used to obtain ς_i by an OWA aggregation of all $a_j (j \neq i)$:

$$BON-OWA(a_1, a_2, \ldots, a_n) = \left(\frac{1}{n} \sum_{i=1}^{n} a_i OWA_\omega(\beta^i) \right)^{\frac{1}{2}} \tag{4.26}$$

where β^i is the $n-1$ tuple $(a_1, \ldots, a_{i-1}, a_{i+1}, \ldots, a_n)$, ω is an OWA weighting vector of dimension $n-1$, with the components $\omega_j \geq 0$, $\sum_j \omega_j = 1$, and

$$OWA_\omega(\beta^i) = \sum_{j=1}^{n-1} \omega_j a_{\sigma_i(j)} \tag{4.27}$$

where $a_{\sigma_i(j)}$ is the jth largest element in the tuple β^i.

If each a_i has its personal importance, denoted by w_i, then Eq. (4.26) can be further generalized as:

$$BON-OWA_{\omega}(a_1,a_2,\ldots,a_n)=\left(\sum_{i=1}^{n} w_i a_i OWA_{\omega}(\beta^i)\right)^{\frac{1}{2}} \tag{4.28}$$

where $w_i \in [0,1]$, $i=1,2,\ldots,n$, and $\sum_{i=1}^{n} w_i = 1$.

In MADM, let $U=\{u_1,u_2,\ldots,u_m\}$ be a set of attributes, and let $U^i = \Omega - \{u_i\}$ be the set of all attributes except u_i, then a monotonic set measure m_i over U^i is $m_i: 2^{U^i} \to [0,1]$, which has the properties: (1) $m_i(\phi)=0$; (2) $m_i(U^i)=1$; and (3) $m_i(F_1) \geq m_i(F_2)$, if $F_1 \subseteq F_2$. Using the measure m_i, Yager [161] further defined a Bonferroni Choquet operator as:

$$BON-CHOQ(a_1,a_2,\ldots,a_n)=\left(\sum_{i=1}^{n} w_i a_i C_{m_i}(\beta^i)\right)^{\frac{1}{2}} \tag{4.29}$$

where

$$C_{m_i}(\beta^i)=\sum_{j=1}^{n-1} v_{ij}\left(m_i(H_j^i)-m_i(H_{j-1}^i)\right) \tag{4.30}$$

and H_j^i is the subset of U^i consisting the j criteria with the largest satisfactions, and $H_0^i=\phi$. $v_{i1},v_{i2},\ldots,v_{in-1}$ are the elements in β^i, and these elements have been ordered so that $v_{ij_1} \geq v_{ij_2}$ if $j_1 < j_2$.

Xu [134] extended the above results to uncertain environments in which the input data are interval numbers.

Given two interval numbers $\tilde{a}_i=[a_i^L,a_i^U]\,(i=1,2)$, to compare them, we first calculate their expected values:

$$E(\tilde{a}_i)=\eta a_i^L+(1-\eta)a_i^U,\ i=1,2,\ \eta\in[0,1] \tag{4.31}$$

The bigger the value $E(\tilde{a}_i)$, the greater the interval number $\tilde{a}_i$. In particular, if both $E(\tilde{a}_i)\,(i=1,2)$ are equal, then we calculate the uncertainty indices of $\tilde{a}_i\,(i=1,2)$:

$$l_{\tilde{a}_i}=a_i^U-a_i^L,\quad i=1,2 \tag{4.32}$$

The smaller the value $l_{\tilde{a}_i}$, the less the uncertainty degree of $\tilde{a}_i$ is, and thus in this case, it is reasonable to stipulate that the greater the interval number $\tilde{a}_i$.

Based on both Eqs. (4.31) and (4.32), we can compare any two interval numbers. Especially, if $E(\tilde{a}_1) = E(\tilde{a}_2)$ and $l_{\tilde{a}_1} = l_{\tilde{a}_2}$, then by Eqs. (4.31) and (4.32), we have

$$\begin{cases} \eta a_1^L + (1-\eta) a_1^U = \eta a_2^L + (1-\eta) a_2^U \\ a_1^U - a_1^L = a_2^U - a_2^L \end{cases} \tag{4.33}$$

by which we get $a_1^L = a_2^L$ and $a_1^U = a_2^U$, i.e., $\tilde{a}_1 = \tilde{a}_2$.

Let $\tilde{a}_i = [a_i^L, a_i^U]$ $(i = 1, 2, \ldots, n)$ be a collection of interval numbers, and $p, q \geq 0$, then we call

$$UB^{p,q}(\tilde{a}_1, \tilde{a}_2, \ldots, \tilde{a}_n) = \left(\frac{1}{n(n-1)} \sum_{\substack{i,j=1 \\ i \neq j}}^{n} \tilde{a}_i^p \tilde{a}_j^q \right)^{\frac{1}{p+q}} \tag{4.34}$$

an uncertain Bonferroni mean (UBM) operator [134].

Based on the operations above, the UBM operator can be transformed into the following form:

$$UB^{p,q}(\tilde{a}_1, \tilde{a}_2, \ldots, \tilde{a}_n) = \left[\left(\frac{1}{n(n-1)} \sum_{\substack{i,j=1 \\ i \neq j}}^{n} \left(a_i^L\right)^p \left(a_j^L\right)^q \right)^{\frac{1}{p+q}}, \left(\frac{1}{n(n-1)} \sum_{\substack{i,j=1 \\ i \neq j}}^{n} \left(a_i^U\right)^p \left(a_j^U\right)^q \right)^{\frac{1}{p+q}} \right] \tag{4.35}$$

Example 4.4 Given three interval numbers: $\tilde{a}_1 = [10, 15]$, $\tilde{a}_2 = [8, 10]$, and $\tilde{a}_3 = [20, 30]$. Without loss of generality, let $p = q = 1$, then by Eq. (4.35), we have

$$\begin{aligned} UB^{1,1}(\tilde{a}_1, \tilde{a}_2, \tilde{a}_3) &= \left[\left(\frac{1}{6} (10 \times 8 + 10 \times 20 + 8 \times 20 + 8 \times 10 + 20 \times 10 + 20 \times 8) \right)^{\frac{1}{2}}, \right. \\ &\quad \left. \left(\frac{1}{6} (15 \times 10 + 15 \times 30 + 10 \times 30 + 10 \times 15 + 30 \times 15 + 30 \times 10) \right)^{\frac{1}{2}} \right] \\ &= [12.1, 17.3] \end{aligned}$$

In the following, Let us discuss some special cases of the UBM operator [134]:

1. If $q = 0$, then Eq. (4.35) reduces to

$$UB^{p,0}(\tilde{a}_1, \tilde{a}_2, \ldots, \tilde{a}_n) = \left[\left(\frac{1}{n} \sum_{i=1}^{n} \left(a_i^L\right)^p \right)^{\frac{1}{p}}, \left(\frac{1}{n} \sum_{i=1}^{n} \left(a_i^U\right)^p \right)^{\frac{1}{p}} \right] = \left(\frac{1}{n} \sum_{i=1}^{n} \tilde{a}_i^p \right)^{\frac{1}{p}} \tag{4.36}$$

which we call a generalized uncertain averaging operator.

2. If $p \to +\infty$ and $q = 0$, then Eq. (4.35) reduces to

$$\lim_{p \to +\infty} UB^{p,0}(\tilde{a}_1, \tilde{a}_2, \ldots, \tilde{a}_n) = \left[\lim_{p \to +\infty} \left(\frac{1}{n} \sum_{i=1}^{n} \left(a_i^L\right)^p \right)^{\frac{1}{p}}, \lim_{p \to +\infty} \left(\frac{1}{n} \sum_{i=1}^{n} \left(a_i^U\right)^p \right)^{\frac{1}{p}} \right]$$
$$= \left[\max_i \{a_i^L\}, \max_i \{a_i^U\} \right] \tag{4.37}$$

3. If $p = 1$ and $q = 0$, then Eq. (4.35) reduces to

$$UB^{1,0}(\tilde{a}_1, \tilde{a}_2, \ldots, \tilde{a}_n) = \left[\frac{1}{n} \sum_{i}^{n} a_i^L, \frac{1}{n} \sum_{i}^{n} a_i^U \right] = \frac{1}{n} \sum_{i=1}^{n} \tilde{a}_i \tag{4.38}$$

which is the uncertain averaging operator.

4. If $p \to 0$ and $q = 0$, then Eq. (4.35) reduces to

$$\lim_{p \to 0} UB^{p,0}(\tilde{a}_1, \tilde{a}_2, \ldots, \tilde{a}_n) = \left[\lim_{p \to 0} \left(\frac{1}{n} \sum_{i=1}^{n} \left(a_i^L\right)^p \right)^{\frac{1}{p}}, \lim_{p \to 0} \left(\frac{1}{n} \sum_{i=1}^{n} \left(a_i^U\right)^p \right)^{\frac{1}{p}} \right]$$
$$= \left[\prod_{i=1}^{n} \left(a_i^L\right)^{\frac{1}{n}}, \prod_{i=1}^{n} \left(a_i^U\right)^{\frac{1}{n}} \right]$$
$$= \left[\prod_{i=1}^{n} \left(a_i^L\right), \prod_{i=1}^{n} \left(a_i^U\right) \right]^{\frac{1}{n}} = \left(\prod_{i=1}^{n} \tilde{a}_i \right)^{\frac{1}{n}} \tag{4.39}$$

which is the uncertain geometric mean operator.

5. If $p=q=1$, then Eq. (4.35) reduces to

$$UB^{1,1}(\tilde{a}_1,\tilde{a}_2,\ldots,\tilde{a}_n)=\left[\left(\frac{1}{n(n-1)}\sum_{\substack{i,j=1\\ i\neq j}}^{n}\left(a_i^L a_j^L\right)^2\right)^{\frac{1}{2}},\left(\frac{1}{n(n-1)}\sum_{\substack{i,j=1\\ i\neq j}}^{n}\left(a_i^U a_j^U\right)^2\right)^{\frac{1}{2}}\right]$$

$$=\left(\frac{1}{n(n-1)}\sum_{\substack{i,j=1\\ i\neq j}}^{n}\left(\tilde{a}_i\tilde{a}_j\right)^2\right)^{\frac{1}{2}} \tag{4.40}$$

which we call an interrelated uncertain square mean operator.

The UBM operator has the following properties:

Theorem 4.3 [134] Let $\tilde{a}_i=[a_i^L,a_i^U]\,(i=1,2,\ldots,n)$ be a collection of interval numbers, and $p,q\geq 0$, then

1. (**Idempotency**) $UB^{p,q}(\tilde{a},\tilde{a},\ldots,\tilde{a})=\tilde{a}$, if $\tilde{a}_i=\tilde{a}$, for all i.
2. (**Monotonicity**) Let $\tilde{d}_i=[d_i^L,d_i^U]\,(i=1,2,\ldots,n)$ be a collection of interval numbers, if $a_i^L\geq d_i^L$ and $a_i^U\geq d_i^U$, for all i, then

$$UB^{p,q}(\tilde{a}_1,\tilde{a}_2,\ldots,\tilde{a}_n)\geq B^{p,q}(\tilde{d}_1,\tilde{d}_2,\ldots,\tilde{d}_n)$$

3. (**Commutativity**) $UB^{p,q}(\tilde{a}_1,\tilde{a}_2,\ldots,\tilde{a}_n)=UB^{p,q}(\dot{\tilde{a}}_1,\dot{\tilde{a}}_2,\ldots,\dot{\tilde{a}}_n)$, for any permutation $(\dot{\tilde{a}}_1,\dot{\tilde{a}}_2,\ldots,\dot{\tilde{a}}_n)$ of $(\tilde{a}_1,\tilde{a}_2,\ldots,\tilde{a}_n)$.
4. (**Boundedness**)

$$\left[\min_i\{a_i^L\},\min_i\{a_i^U\}\right]\leq UB^{p,q}(\tilde{a}_1,\tilde{a}_2,\ldots,\tilde{a}_n)\leq\left[\max_i\{a_i^L\},\max_i\{a_i^U\}\right]$$

Proof

1. Let $\tilde{a}=[a^L,a^U]$, then by Eq. (4.35), we have

$$UB^{p,q}(\tilde{a},\tilde{a},\ldots,\tilde{a})$$

$$=\left[\left(\frac{1}{n(n-1)}\sum_{\substack{i,j=1\\i\neq j}}^{n}\left(a^L\right)^p\left(a^L\right)^q\right)^{\frac{1}{p+q}},\left(\frac{1}{n(n-1)}\sum_{\substack{i,j=1\\i\neq j}}^{n}\left(a^U\right)^p\left(a^U\right)^q\right)^{\frac{1}{p+q}}\right]$$

$$=\left[\left(\frac{1}{n(n-1)}\sum_{\substack{i,j=1\\i\neq j}}^{n}\left(a^L\right)^{p+q}\right)^{\frac{1}{p+q}},\left(\frac{1}{n(n-1)}\sum_{\substack{i,j=1\\i\neq j}}^{n}\left(a^U\right)^{p+q}\right)^{\frac{1}{p+q}}\right]$$

$$=\left[\left(\left(a^L\right)^{p+q}\right)^{\frac{1}{p+q}},\left(\left(a^U\right)^{p+q}\right)^{\frac{1}{p+q}}\right]=[a^L,a^U]=\tilde{a} \tag{4.41}$$

2. Since $a_i^L \geq d_i^L$ and $a_i^U \geq d_i^U$, for all i, then

$$UB^{p,q}(\tilde{a}_1,\tilde{a}_2,\ldots,\tilde{a}_n)$$

$$=\left[\left(\frac{1}{n(n-1)}\sum_{\substack{i,j=1\\i\neq j}}^{n}\left(a_i^L\right)^p\left(a_j^L\right)^q\right)^{\frac{1}{p+q}},\left(\frac{1}{n(n-1)}\sum_{\substack{i,j=1\\i\neq j}}^{n}\left(a_i^U\right)^p\left(a_j^U\right)^q\right)^{\frac{1}{p+q}}\right]$$

$$\geq\left[\left(\frac{1}{n(n-1)}\sum_{\substack{i,j=1\\i\neq j}}^{n}\left(d_i^L\right)^p\left(d_j^L\right)^q\right)^{\frac{1}{p+q}},\left(\frac{1}{n(n-1)}\sum_{\substack{i,j=1\\i\neq j}}^{n}\left(d_i^U\right)^p\left(d_j^U\right)^q\right)^{\frac{1}{p+q}}\right]$$

$$=UB^{p,q}(\tilde{d}_1,\tilde{d}_2,\ldots,\tilde{d}_n) \tag{4.42}$$

3. Let $\dot{\tilde{a}}_i=[\dot{a}_i^L,\dot{a}_i^U]$ $(i=1,2,\ldots,n)$, then

$$UB^{p,q}(\dot{\tilde{a}}_1,\dot{\tilde{a}}_2,\ldots,\dot{\tilde{a}}_n)$$

$$=\left[\left(\frac{1}{n(n-1)}\sum_{\substack{i,j=1\\i\neq j}}^{n}\left(\dot{a}_i^L\right)^p\left(\dot{a}_j^L\right)^q\right)^{\frac{1}{p+q}},\left(\frac{1}{n(n-1)}\sum_{\substack{i,j=1\\i\neq j}}^{n}\left(\dot{a}_i^U\right)^p\left(\dot{a}_j^U\right)^q\right)^{\frac{1}{p+q}}\right]$$

$$=\left[\left(\frac{1}{n(n-1)}\sum_{\substack{i,j=1\\i\neq j}}^{n}\left(\dot{a}_i^L\right)^p\left(\dot{a}_j^L\right)^q\right)^{\frac{1}{p+q}},\left(\frac{1}{n(n-1)}\sum_{\substack{i,j=1\\i\neq j}}^{n}\left(\dot{a}_i^U\right)^p\left(\dot{a}_j^U\right)^q\right)^{\frac{1}{p+q}}\right] \tag{4.43}$$

Since $(\dot{\tilde{a}}_1, \dot{\tilde{a}}_2, \ldots, \dot{\tilde{a}}_n)$ is a permutation of $(\tilde{a}_1, \tilde{a}_2, \ldots, \tilde{a}_n)$, then by Eqs. (4.35) and (4.43), we know that

$$\left[\left(\frac{1}{n(n-1)}\sum_{\substack{i,j=1\\ i\neq j}}^{n}\left(\dot{a}_i^L\right)^p\left(\dot{a}_j^L\right)^q\right)^{\frac{1}{p+q}}, \left(\frac{1}{n(n-1)}\sum_{\substack{i,j=1\\ i\neq j}}^{n}\left(\dot{a}_i^U\right)^p\left(\dot{a}_j^U\right)^q\right)^{\frac{1}{p+q}}\right]$$
$$=\left[\left(\frac{1}{n(n-1)}\sum_{\substack{i,j=1\\ i\neq j}}^{n}\left(a_i^L\right)^p\left(a_j^L\right)^q\right)^{\frac{1}{p+q}}, \left(\frac{1}{n(n-1)}\sum_{\substack{i,j=1\\ i\neq j}}^{n}\left(a_i^U\right)^p\left(a_j^U\right)^q\right)^{\frac{1}{p+q}}\right] \tag{4.44}$$

i.e., $UB^{p,q}(\tilde{a}_1, \tilde{a}_2, \ldots, \tilde{a}_n) = UB^{p,q}(\dot{\tilde{a}}_1, \dot{\tilde{a}}_2, \ldots, \dot{\tilde{a}}_n)$.

4. $UB^{p,q}(\tilde{a}_1, \tilde{a}_2, \ldots, \tilde{a}_n)$

$$=\left[\left(\frac{1}{n(n-1)}\sum_{\substack{i,j=1\\ i\neq j}}^{n}\left(a_i^L\right)^p\left(a_j^L\right)^q\right)^{\frac{1}{p+q}}, \left(\frac{1}{n(n-1)}\sum_{\substack{i,j=1\\ i\neq j}}^{n}\left(a_i^U\right)^p\left(a_j^U\right)^q\right)^{\frac{1}{p+q}}\right]$$
$$=\left[\left(\frac{1}{n(n-1)}\sum_{\substack{i,j=1\\ i\neq j}}^{n}\left(\max_i\{a_i^L\}\right)^{p+q}\right)^{\frac{1}{p+q}}, \left(\frac{1}{n(n-1)}\sum_{\substack{i,j=1\\ i\neq j}}^{n}\left(\max_i\{a_i^U\}\right)^{p+q}\right)^{\frac{1}{p+q}}\right]$$
$$\leq\left[\left(\frac{1}{n(n-1)}\sum_{\substack{i,j=1\\ i\neq j}}^{n}\left(\max_i\{a_i^L\}\right)^{p}\left(\max_i\{a_i^L\}\right)^{q}\right)^{\frac{1}{p+q}},\right.$$
$$\left.\left(\frac{1}{n(n-1)}\sum_{\substack{i,j=1\\ i\neq j}}^{n}\left(\max_i\{a_i^U\}\right)^{p}\left(\max_i\{a_i^U\}\right)^{q}\right)^{\frac{1}{p+q}}\right]$$
$$=\left[\max_i\{a_i^L\}, \max_i\{a_i^U\}\right] \tag{4.45}$$

Similarly, we can prove $UB^{p,q}(\tilde{a}_1,\tilde{a}_2,\ldots,\tilde{a}_n) \geq \left[\min_i\{a_i^L\},\min_i\{a_i^U\}\right]$.

As the input data usually come from different sources, and each datum has own importance, thus each datum should be assigned a weight. In this case, we should consider the weighted form of the UBM operator.

Let $\tilde{a}_i = [a_i^L, a_i^U]\,(i=1,2,\ldots,n)$ be a collection of interval numbers, each $\tilde{a}_i$ has the weight w_i, satisfying $w_i \geq 0$, $i=1,2,\ldots,n$, and $\sum_{i=1}^{n} w_i = 1$. Then we call

$$UB_w^{p,q}(\tilde{a}_1,\tilde{a}_2,\ldots,\tilde{a}_n) = \left(\frac{1}{\Delta}\sum_{\substack{i,j=1\\ i\neq j}}^{n}(w_i\tilde{a}_i)^p(w_j\tilde{a}_j)^q\right)^{\frac{1}{p+q}} \tag{4.46}$$

a weighted uncertain Bonferroni mean (WUBM) operator [134], where

$$\Delta = \sum_{\substack{i,j=1\\ i\neq j}}^{n}(w_i)^p(w_j)^q \tag{4.47}$$

Based on the operations of interval numbers, the WUBM operator Eq. (4.46) can be further written as:

$$UB_w^{p,q}(\tilde{a}_1,\tilde{a}_2,\ldots,\tilde{a}_n) = \left[\left(\frac{1}{\Delta}\sum_{\substack{i,j=1\\ i\neq j}}^{n}\left(w_i a_i^L\right)^p\left(w_j a_j^L\right)^q\right)^{\frac{1}{p+q}}, \left(\frac{1}{\Delta}\sum_{\substack{i,j=1\\ i\neq j}}^{n}\left(w_i a_i^U\right)^p\left(w_j a_j^U\right)^q\right)^{\frac{1}{p+q}}\right] \tag{4.48}$$

In the case where $w = \left(\frac{1}{n},\frac{1}{n},\ldots,\frac{1}{n}\right)$, then

$$\Delta = \sum_{\substack{i,j=1\\ i\neq j}}^{n}(w_i)^p(w_j)^q = n(n-1)\left(\frac{1}{n}\right)^{p+q} \tag{4.49}$$

and then Eq. (4.48) can be transformed into

$$
\begin{aligned}
& UB_w^{p,q}(\tilde{a}_1,\tilde{a}_2,\ldots,\tilde{a}_n) \\
&= \left[\left(\frac{1}{\Delta} \sum_{\substack{i,j=1 \\ i\neq j}}^{n} \left(\frac{1}{n} a_i^L\right)^p \left(\frac{1}{n} a_j^L\right)^q \right)^{\frac{1}{p+q}}, \left(\frac{1}{\Delta} \sum_{\substack{i,j=1 \\ i\neq j}}^{n} \left(\frac{1}{n} a_i^U\right)^p \left(\frac{1}{n} a_j^U\right)^q \right)^{\frac{1}{p+q}} \right] \\
&= \left[\left(\frac{1}{\Delta} \left(\frac{1}{n}\right)^{p+q} \sum_{\substack{i,j=1 \\ i\neq j}}^{n} \left(a_i^L\right)^p \left(a_j^L\right)^q \right)^{\frac{1}{p+q}}, \left(\frac{1}{\Delta} \left(\frac{1}{n}\right)^{p+q} \sum_{\substack{i,j=1 \\ i\neq j}}^{n} \left(a_i^U\right)^p \left(a_j^U\right)^q \right)^{\frac{1}{p+q}} \right] \\
&= \left[\left(\frac{1}{n(n-1)} \sum_{\substack{i,j=1 \\ i\neq j}}^{n} \left(a_i^L\right)^p \left(a_j^L\right)^q \right)^{\frac{1}{p+q}}, \left(\frac{1}{n(n-1)} \sum_{\substack{i,j=1 \\ i\neq j}}^{n} \left(a_i^U\right)^p \left(a_j^U\right)^q \right)^{\frac{1}{p+q}} \right] \\
&= UB^{p,q}(\tilde{a}_1,\tilde{a}_2,\ldots,\tilde{a}_n) \qquad (4.50)
\end{aligned}
$$

which reduces to the UBM operator.

With the WUBM operator, Xu [134] gave a simple approach to MADM under uncertainty:

Step 1 Let X and U be the sets of alternatives and attribute, respectively. Each attribute has a weight w_i, with $w_i \geq 0$, $i = 1,2,\ldots,m$, and $\sum_{i=1}^{m} w_i = 1$. The performance of the alternative $x_i \in X$ with respect to the attribute $u_j \in U$ is described by a value range $\tilde{a}_{ij} = [a_{ij}^L, a_{ij}^U]$, which is listed in the uncertain decision matrix $\tilde{A} = (\tilde{a}_{ij})_{n\times m}$. In general, there are two types of attributes, i.e., benefit-type attributes and cost-type attributes. We may normalize the matrix $\tilde{A} = (\tilde{a}_{ij})_{n\times m}$ into the matrix $\tilde{R} = (\tilde{r}_{ij})_{n\times m}$ by the formulas (4.9) and (4.10), where $\tilde{r}_{ij} = [r_{ij}^L, r_{ij}^U]$, $i = 1,2,\ldots,n$, $j = 1,2,\ldots,m$.

Step 2 Utilize the WUBM operator Eq. (4.46) (for the sake of intuitiveness and simplicity, in general, we take $p = q = 1$):

$$
\tilde{z}_i(w) = [z_i^L(w), z_i^U(w)] = UB_w^{p,q}(\tilde{r}_{i1}, \tilde{r}_{i2}, \ldots, \tilde{r}_{im}) \qquad (4.51)
$$

to aggregate all the performance values $\tilde{r}_{ij}\, (j = 1,2,\ldots,m)$ of the j th line of $\tilde{R}$, and get the overall performance value $\tilde{z}_i(w)$ corresponding to the alternative x_i.

Step 3 Utilize Eqs. (4.31) and (4.32) to rank the overall performance values $\tilde{z}_i(w)$ (i=1,2,...,n), and by which we rank and select the alternatives $x_i\, (i = 1,2,\ldots,n)$ following the principle that the greater the value $\tilde{z}_i(w)$, the better the alternative x_i.

The prominent characteristic of the above approach is that it utilizes the WUBM operator to fuse the performance values of the alternatives, which can capture the interrelationship of the individual criteria.

Now we provide a numerical example to illustrate the application of the above approach:

Example 4.5 [134] Robots are used extensively by many advanced manufacturing companies to perform dangerous and/or menial tasks [34, 131]. The selection of a robot is an important function for these companies because improper selection of the robots may adversely affect their profitability. A manufacturing company intends to select a robot from five robots $x_i (i = 1, 2, 3, 4, 5)$. The following four attributes $u_j (j = 1, 2, 3, 4)$ (whose weight vector is $w = (0.2, 0.3, 0.4, 0.1)$) have to be considered: (1) u_1 : velocity (m/s) which is the maximum speed the arm can achieve; (2) u_2 : load capacity (kg) which is the maximum weight a robot can lift; (3) u_3 : purchase, installation and training costs (10^3\$); (4) u_4 : repeatability (mm) which is a robot's ability to repeatedly return to a fixed position. The mean deviation from that position is a measure of a robot's repeatability.

Among these attributes, u_1 and u_2 are of benefit type, u_3 and u_4 are of cost type. The decision information about robots is listed in Table 4.8, and the normalized uncertain decision information by using Eqs. (4.13) and (4.14) is listed in Table 4.9 (adopted from Xu [131]).

Here we employ the WUBM operator Eq. (4.48) (let $p = q = 1$) to aggregate $\tilde{r}_{ij} (i = 1, 2, 3, 4)$, and get the overall performance value $\tilde{z}_i(w)$ of the robot x_i. Since

Table 4.8 Uncertain decision matrix $\tilde{A}$

	u_1	u_2	u_3	u_4
x_1	[1.8, 2.0]	[90, 95]	[9.0, 9.5]	[0.45, 0.50]
x_2	[1.4, 1.6]	[80, 85]	[5.5, 6.0]	[0.30, 0.40]
x_3	[0.8, 1.0]	[65, 70]	[4.0, 4.5]	[0.20, 0.25]
x_4	[1.0, 1.2]	[85, 90]	[9.5, 10]	[0.25, 0.30]
x_5	[0.9, 1.1]	[70, 80]	[9.0, 10]	[0.35, 0.40]

Table 4.9 Normalized uncertain decision matrix $\tilde{R}$

	u_1	u_2	u_3	u_4
x_1	[0.26, 0.34]	[0.21, 0.24]	[0.14, 0.16]	[0.11, 0.16]
x_2	[0.20, 0.27]	[0.19, 0.22]	[0.22, 0.26]	[0.14, 0.23]
x_3	[0.12, 0.17]	[0.15, 0.18]	[0.29, 0.36]	[0.23, 0.35]
x_4	[0.14, 0.20]	[0.20, 0.23]	[0.13, 0.15]	[0.19, 0.28]
x_5	[0.13, 0.19]	[0.17, 0.21]	[0.13, 0.16]	[0.14, 0.20]

$$\Delta = \sum_{\substack{i,j=1 \\ i \neq j}}^{4} \left(w_i w_j \right) = (0.2 \times 0.3 + 0.2 \times 0.4 + 0.2 \times 0.1 + 0.3 \times 0.4$$
$$+0.3 \times 0.1 + 0.4 \times 0.1) \times 2 = 0.70$$

then

$$\tilde{z}_1(w) = UB_w^{1,1}(\tilde{r}_{11}, \tilde{r}_{21}, \tilde{r}_{31}, \tilde{r}_{41})$$
$$= \Bigg[\Bigg(\frac{1}{0.7} ((0.2 \times 0.26) \times (0.3 \times 0.21) + (0.2 \times 0.26) \times (0.4 \times 0.14)$$
$$+(0.2 \times 0.26) \times (0.1 \times 0.11) + (0.3 \times 0.21) \times (0.4 \times 0.14) + (0.3 \times 0.21) \times (0.1 \times 0.11)$$
$$+(0.4 \times 0.14) \times (0.1 \times 0.11)) \times 2 \Bigg)^{\frac{1}{2}},$$
$$\frac{1}{0.7} ((0.2 \times 0.34) \times (0.3 \times 0.24) + (0.2 \times 0.34) \times (0.4 \times 0.16) + (0.2 \text{ x } 0.34) \times (0.1 \text{ x } 0.16)$$
$$+(0.3 \times 0.24) \times (0.4 \times 0.16) + (0.3 \times 0.24) \times (0.1 \times 0.16) + (0.4 \times 0.16) \times (0.1 \times 0.16)) \times 2 \Bigg)^{\frac{1}{2}} \Bigg]$$
$$= [0.182, 0.221]$$

Similarly,

$$\tilde{z}_2(w) = [0.196, 0.246], \ \tilde{z}_3(w) = [0.195, 0.254]$$
$$\tilde{z}_4(w) = [0.160, 0.200], \ \tilde{z}_5(w) = [0.143, 0.186]$$

Using Eq. (4.31), we calculate the expected values of $\tilde{z}_i(w) (i = 1, 2, 3, 4, 5)$:

$$E(\tilde{z}_1(w)) = 0.221 - 0.039\eta, \ E(\tilde{z}_2(w)) = 0.246 - 0.050\eta$$
$$E(\tilde{z}_3(w)) = 0.254 - 0.059\eta, \ E(\tilde{z}_4(w)) = 0.200 - 0.040\eta$$
$$E(\tilde{z}_5(w)) = 0.186 - 0.043\eta$$

Then by analyzing the parameter η, we have

1. If $0 \leq \eta < \frac{8}{9}$, then

$$E(\tilde{z}_3(w)) > E(\tilde{z}_2(w)) > E(\tilde{z}_1(w)) > E(\tilde{z}_4(w)) > E(\tilde{z}_5(w))$$

Thus, $\tilde{z}_3(w) > \tilde{z}_2(w) > \tilde{z}_1(w) > \tilde{z}_4(w) > \tilde{z}_5(w)$, by which we get the ranking of the robots:

$$x_3 \succ x_2 \succ x_1 \succ x_4 \succ x_5$$

2. If $\frac{8}{9} < \eta \le 1$, then

$$E(\tilde{z}_2(w)) > E(\tilde{z}_3(w)) > E(\tilde{z}_1(w)) > E(\tilde{z}_4(w)) > E(\tilde{z}_5(w))$$

Thus, $\tilde{z}_2(w) > \tilde{z}_3(w) > \tilde{z}_1(w) > \tilde{z}_4(w) > \tilde{z}_5(w)$, by which we get the ranking of the robots:

$$x_2 \succ x_3 \succ x_1 \succ x_4 \succ x_5$$

3. If $\eta = \frac{8}{9}$, then

$$E(\tilde{z}_2(w)) = E(\tilde{z}_3(w)) > E(\tilde{z}_1(w)) > E(\tilde{z}_4(w)) > E(\tilde{z}_5(w))$$

In this case, we utilize Eq. (4.32) to calculate the uncertainty indices of $\tilde{r}_2$ and $\tilde{r}_3$:

$$l_{\tilde{r}_2} = 0.246 - 0.196 = 0.050,\ l_{\tilde{r}_3} = 0.254 - 0.195 = 0.059$$

Since $l_{\tilde{r}_2} < l_{\tilde{r}_3}$, then $\tilde{r}_2 > \tilde{r}_3$. In this case, $\tilde{z}_2(w) > \tilde{z}_3(w) > \tilde{z}_1(w) > \tilde{z}_4(w) > \tilde{z}_5(w)$, therefore, the ranking of the robots is

$$x_2 \succ x_3 \succ x_1 \succ x_4 \succ x_5$$

From the analysis above, it is clear that the ranking of the robots maybe different as we change the parameter η. When $\frac{8}{9} \le \eta \le 1$, the robot x_2 is the best choice, while the robot x_3 is the second best one. But as $0 \le \eta < \frac{8}{9}$, the ranking of x_2 and x_3 is reversed, i.e., the robot x_3 ranks first, while the robot x_2 ranks second. However, the ranking of the other robots $x_i (i = 1,4,5)$ keeps unchanged, i.e., $x_1 \succ x_4 \succ x_5$, for any $\eta \in [0,1]$.

4.4.2 UBM Operators Combined with OWA Operator and Choquet Integral and Their Application in MADM

Xu [134] extended Yager's [161] results to the uncertain situations by only considering the case where the parameters $p = q = 1$ in the UBM operator.

Let $\tilde{a}_i = [a_i^L, a_i^U]\ (i = 1,2,\ldots,n)$ be a collection of interval numbers, then from Eq. (4.34), it yields

$$UB^{1,1}(\tilde{a}_1,\tilde{a}_2,...,\tilde{a}_n)=\left(\frac{1}{n(n-1)}\sum_{\substack{i,j=1\\ i\neq j}}^{n}\tilde{a}_i\tilde{a}_j\right)^{\frac{1}{2}}$$

$$=\left(\frac{1}{n}\sum_{i=1}^{n}\tilde{a}_i\left(\frac{1}{n-1}\sum_{\substack{j=1\\ j\neq i}}^{n}\tilde{a}_j\right)\right)^{\frac{1}{2}} \quad (4.52)$$

For convenience, we denote $UB^{1,1}(\tilde{a}_1, \tilde{a}_2, \ldots, \tilde{a}_n)$ as $UB(\tilde{a}_1, \tilde{a}_2, \ldots, \tilde{a}_n)$, and let $\tilde{\varsigma}_i = \frac{1}{n-1}\sum_{\substack{j=1\\ j\neq i}}^{n}\tilde{a}_j$, which is the uncertain average of all the interval numbers $\tilde{a}_j\ (j\neq i)$. Then Eq. (4.52) can be denoted as:

$$UB(\tilde{a}_1,\tilde{a}_2,\ldots,\tilde{a}_n)=\left(\frac{1}{n}\sum_{i=1}^{n}\tilde{a}_i\tilde{\varsigma}_i\right)^{\frac{1}{2}} \quad (4.53)$$

Suppose that $\tilde{\beta}^i$ is the $n-1$ tuple $(\tilde{a}_1,\ldots,\tilde{a}_{i-1},\tilde{a}_{i+1},\ldots,\tilde{a}_n)$. An uncertain ordered weighted averaging (UOWA) operator of dimension $n-1$ can be defined as:

$$UOWA_{\omega}(\tilde{\beta}^i)=\sum_{j=1}^{n-1}\omega_j\tilde{a}_{\sigma_i(j)}=\left[\sum_{j=1}^{n-1}\omega_j\tilde{a}^L_{\sigma_i(j)},\sum_{j=1}^{n-1}\omega_j\tilde{a}^U_{\sigma_i(j)}\right] \quad (4.54)$$

where $\tilde{a}_{\sigma(j)}=[a^L_{\sigma_i(j)},a^U_{\sigma_i(j)}]$ is the jth largest interval number in the tuple $\tilde{\beta}^i$, $\omega=(\omega_1,\omega_2,\ldots,\omega_{n-1})$ is the weighting vector associated with the UOWA operator, $\omega_j\geq 0,\ j=1,2,\ldots,n-1$, and $\sum_{j=1}^{n-1}\omega_j=1$.

If we replace the uncertain average $\tilde{\varsigma}_i$ in Eq. (4.53) with the UOWA aggregation of all $\tilde{a}_j\ (j\neq i)$, then from Eq. (4.54), it follows that

$$UB-OWA(\tilde{a}_1,\tilde{a}_2,\ldots,\tilde{a}_n)=\left(\frac{1}{n}\sum_{i=1}^{n}\tilde{a}_i\,UOWA_{\omega}(\tilde{\beta}^i)\right)^{\frac{1}{2}} \quad (4.55)$$

which we call an UBM-OWA operator. Especially, if $\omega=\left(\frac{1}{n-1},\frac{1}{n-1},\ldots,\frac{1}{n-1}\right)$, then Eq. (4.55) reduces to the UBM operator.

If we take the weights of the data into account, and let $w = (w_1, w_2, \ldots, w_n)$ be the weight vector of $\tilde{a}_i$ $(i = 1, 2, \ldots, n)$, with $w_i \geq 0$, $i = 1, 2, \ldots, n$, and $\sum_{i=1}^{n} w_i = 1$. Then Eq. (4.55) can be generalized as:

$$UB-OWA(\tilde{a}_1, \tilde{a}_2, \ldots, \tilde{a}_n) = \left(\sum_{i=1}^{n} w_i \tilde{a}_i UOWA_\omega(\tilde{\beta}^i) \right)^{\frac{1}{2}} \tag{4.56}$$

In particular, if $w = \left(\frac{1}{n}, \frac{1}{n}, \ldots, \frac{1}{n} \right)$, then Eq. (4.56) reduces to Eq. (4.55).

Example 4.6 [134] Let $\tilde{a}_1 = [3,5]$, $\tilde{a}_2 = [1,2]$, and $\tilde{a}_3 = [7,9]$ be three interval numbers, $w = (0.3, 0.4, 0.3)$ be the weight vector of $\tilde{a}_i (i = 1, 2, 3)$, and $\omega = (0.6, 0.4)$ be the weighting vector associated with the UOWA operator of dimension 2.

Since $\tilde{a}_3 > \tilde{a}_1 > \tilde{a}_3$, then we first calculate the values of the $UOWA_\omega(\tilde{\beta}^i)$ $(i = 1, 2, 3)$:

$$UOWA_\omega(\tilde{\beta}^1) = UOWA_\omega(\tilde{a}_2, \tilde{a}_3) = \omega_1 \tilde{a}_3 + \omega_2 \tilde{a}_2 = 0.6 \times [7,9] + 0.4 \times [1,2] = [4.6, 6.2]$$

$$UOWA_\omega(\tilde{\beta}^2) = UOWA_\omega(\tilde{a}_1, \tilde{a}_3) = \omega_1 \tilde{a}_3 + \omega_1 \tilde{a}_1 = 0.6 \times [7,9] + 0.4 \times [3,5] = [5.4, 7.4]$$

$$UOWA_\omega(\tilde{\beta}^3) = UOWA_\omega(\tilde{a}_1, \tilde{a}_2) = \omega_1 \tilde{a}_1 + \omega_2 \tilde{a}_2 = 0.6 \times [3,5] + 0.4 \times [1,2] = [2.2, 3.8]$$

and then by Eq. (4.56), we have

$$\begin{aligned}
UB-OWA(\tilde{a}_1, \tilde{a}_2, \tilde{a}_3) &= \left(\sum_{i=1}^{3} w_i \tilde{a}_i UOWA_\omega(\tilde{\beta}^i) \right)^{\frac{1}{2}} \\
&= (w_1 \tilde{a}_1 UOWA_\omega(\tilde{\beta}^1) + w_2 \tilde{a}_2 UOWA_\omega(\tilde{\beta}^2) + w_3 \tilde{a}_3 UOWA_\omega(\tilde{\beta}^3))^{\frac{1}{2}} \\
&= (0.3 \times [3,5] \times [4.6, 6.2] + 0.4 \times [1,2] \times [5.4, 7.4] + 0.3 \times [7,9] \times [2.2, 3.8])^{\frac{1}{2}} \\
&= ([4.14, 9.30] + [2.16, 5.92] + [5.67, 8.36])^{\frac{1}{2}} \\
&= ([4.14, 9.30] + [2.16, 5.92] + [5.67, 8.36])^{\frac{1}{2}} \\
&= [11.97, 23.58]^{\frac{1}{2}} \\
&= [3.46, 4.86]
\end{aligned}$$

Xu [134] further considered how to combine the UBM operator with the well-known Choquet integral:

Let the attribute sets U, U^i and the monotonic set measure m_i over U^i be defined previously. In addition, let $\tilde{a}_{\sigma_i(1)}, \tilde{a}_{\sigma_i(2)}, \ldots, \tilde{a}_{\sigma_i(n-1)}$ be the ordered interval numbers in $\tilde{\beta}^i$, such that $\tilde{a}_{\sigma_i(k-1)} \geq \tilde{a}_{\sigma_i(k)}$, $k = 2,3,\ldots,n-1$, and let $\tilde{B}_{\sigma_i(j)} = \{\tilde{a}_{\sigma_i(k)} \mid k \leq j\}$, when $j \geq 1$ and $\tilde{B}_{\sigma_i(0)} = \phi$. Then the Choquet integral of $\tilde{\beta}^i$ with respect to m_i can be defined as:

$$C_{m_i}(\tilde{\beta}^i) = \sum_{j=1}^{n-1} \tilde{a}_{\sigma_i(j)} (m_i(\tilde{B}_{\sigma_i(j)}) - m_i(\tilde{B}_{\sigma_i(j-1)})) \tag{4.57}$$

by which we define

$$UB - CHOQ(\tilde{a}_1, \tilde{a}_2, \ldots, \tilde{a}_n) = \left(\frac{1}{n} \sum_{i=1}^{n} \tilde{a}_i C_{m_i}(\tilde{\beta}^i) \right)^{\frac{1}{2}} \tag{4.58}$$

as an uncertain Bonferroni Choquet (UBM-CHOQ) operator [134].

If we take the weight w_i of each $\tilde{a}_i$ into account, then by Eq. (4.58), we have

$$UB - CHOQ(\tilde{a}_1, \tilde{a}_2, \ldots, \tilde{a}_n) = \left(\sum_{i=1}^{n} w_i \tilde{a}_i C_{m_i}(\tilde{\beta}^i) \right)^{\frac{1}{2}} \tag{4.59}$$

In the special case where $w = \left(\frac{1}{n}, \frac{1}{n}, \ldots, \frac{1}{n} \right)$, Eq. (4.59) reduces to Eq. (4.58).

To illustrate the UB-CHOQ operator, we give the following example:

Example 4.7 [134] Assume that we have three attributes $u_j (j = 1,2,3)$, whose weight vector is $w = (0.5, 0.3, 0.2)$, the performances of an alternative x with respect to the attributes $u_j (j = 1,2,3)$ are described by the interval numbers: $\tilde{a}_1 = [3,4]$, $\tilde{a}_2 = [5,7]$, and $\tilde{a}_3 = [4,6]$. Let

$$m_1(\phi) = m_2(\phi) = m_3(\phi) = 0,\ m_1(\{\tilde{a}_2\}) = m_3(\{\tilde{a}_2\}) = 0.3$$
$$m_1(\{\tilde{a}_3\}) = m_2(\{\tilde{a}_3\}) = 0.5,\ m_2(\{\tilde{a}_1\}) = m_3(\{\tilde{a}_1\}) = 0.6$$
$$m_1(\{\tilde{a}_2, \tilde{a}_3\}) = m_2(\{\tilde{a}_3, \tilde{a}_1\}) = m_3(\{\tilde{a}_2, \tilde{a}_1\}) = 1$$

Then by Eq. (4.57), we have

$$\begin{aligned} C_{m_1}(\tilde{\beta}^1) &= \sum_{j=1}^{2} \tilde{a}_{\sigma_1(j)}(m_1(\tilde{B}_{\sigma_1(j)}) - m_1(\tilde{B}_{\sigma_1(j-1)})) \\ &= \tilde{a}_2 \times (m_1(\{\tilde{a}_2\}) - m_1(\phi)) + \tilde{a}_3 \times (m_1(\{\tilde{a}_2, \tilde{a}_3\}) - m_1(\{\tilde{a}_2\})) \\ &= [5,7] \times (0.3 - 0) + [4,6] \times (1 - 0.3) \\ &= [4.3, 6.3] \end{aligned}$$

$$\begin{aligned} C_{m_2}(\tilde{\beta}^2) &= \sum_{j=1}^{2} \tilde{a}_{\sigma_2(j)}(m_2(\tilde{B}_{\sigma_2(j)}) - m_2(\tilde{B}_{\sigma_2(j-1)})) \\ &= \tilde{a}_3 \times (m_2(\{\tilde{a}_3\}) - m_2(\phi)) + \tilde{a}_1 \times (m_2(\{\tilde{a}_3, \tilde{a}_1\}) - m_2(\{\tilde{a}_3\})) \\ &= [4,6] \times (0.5 - 0) + [3,4] \times (1 - 0.5) \\ &= [3.5, 5.0] \end{aligned}$$

$$\begin{aligned} C_{m_3}(\tilde{\beta}^3) &= \sum_{j=1}^{2} \tilde{a}_{\sigma_3(j)}(m_3(\tilde{B}_{\sigma_3(j)}) - m_3(\tilde{B}_{\sigma_3(j-1)})) \\ &= \tilde{a}_2 \times (m_3(\{\tilde{a}_2\}) - m_3(\phi)) + \tilde{a}_1 \times (m_3(\{\tilde{a}_2, \tilde{a}_1\}) - m_1(\{\tilde{a}_2\})) \\ &= [5,7] \times (0.3 - 0) + [3,4] \times (1 - 0.3) \\ &= [3.6, 4.9] \end{aligned}$$

and then from Eq. (4.59), it yields

$$\begin{aligned} UB-CHOQ(\tilde{a}_1, \tilde{a}_2, \tilde{a}_3) &= \left(\sum_{i=1}^{3} w_i \tilde{a}_i C_{m_i}(\tilde{\beta}^i) \right)^{\frac{1}{2}} \\ &= (0.5 \times [3,4] \times [4.3, 6.3] + 0.3 \times [5,7] \times [3.5, 5.0] + 0.2 \times [4,6] \times [3.6, 4.9])^{\frac{1}{2}} \\ &= ([6.45, 12.60] + [5.25, 10.50] + [2.88, 5.88])^{\frac{1}{2}} \\ &= [14.58, 28.98]^{\frac{1}{2}} \\ &= [3.82, 5.38] \end{aligned}$$

4.5 Minimizing Group Discordance Optimization Models for Deriving Expert Weights

4.5.1 Decision Making Method

Consider an uncertain MAGDM problem. Let X, U, w, D, and λ be as defined previously. The experts $d_k (k = 1,2,\ldots,t)$ provide their preferences over the alternatives $x_i (i = 1,2,\ldots,n)$ with respect to each attribute u_j, and construct the uncertain decision matrices $\tilde{A}_k = (\tilde{a}_{ij}^{(k)})_{n\times m}$ $(k = 1,2,\ldots,t)$, where $\tilde{a}_{ij}^{(k)} = [a_{ij}^{L(k)}, a_{ij}^{U(k)}]$ $(i = 1,2,\ldots,n,\ j = 1,2,\ldots,m,\ k = 1,2,\ldots,t)$ are interval numbers. In order to measure all attributes in dimensionless units, we normalize each attribute value $\tilde{a}_{ij}^{(k)}$ in the matrix $\tilde{A}_k = (\tilde{a}_{ij}^{(k)})_{n\times m}$ into a corresponding element in the matrix $\tilde{R}_k = (\tilde{r}_{ij}^{(k)})_{n\times m}$ by using Eqs. (4.13) and (4.14), where $\tilde{r}_{ij}^{(k)} = [r_{ij}^{L(k)}, r_{ij}^{U(k)}] (i = 1,2,\ldots,n,\ j = 1,2,\ldots,m,$ $k = 1,2,\ldots t)$.

By the operational laws of interval numbers [156], we employ the UWA operator (4.15) to aggregate all the normalized individual uncertain decision matrices $\tilde{R}_k = (\tilde{r}_{ij}^{(k)})_{n\times m}$ into the collective uncertain decision matrix $\tilde{R} = (\tilde{r}_{ij})_{n\times m}$.

If each individual opinion is consistent with the group opinion, i.e., $\tilde{R}_k = \tilde{R}$, for all $k = 1,2,\ldots,t$, then

$$\tilde{r}_{ij}^{(k)} = \sum_{k=1}^{t} \lambda_k \tilde{r}_{ij}^{(k)}, \text{ for all } i = 1,2,\ldots,n,\ j = 1,2,\ldots,m,\ k = 1,2,\ldots,t \tag{4.60}$$

i.e.,

$$r_{ij}^{L(k)} = \sum_{k=1}^{t} \lambda_k r_{ij}^{L(k)},\ r_{ij}^{U(k)} = \sum_{k=1}^{t} \lambda_k r_{ij}^{U(k)}$$
$$\text{for all } i = 1,2,\ldots,n,\ j = 1,2,\ldots,m,\ k = 1,2,\ldots,t \tag{4.61}$$

However, Eq. (4.61) does not generally hold in practical applications, i.e., there is always a difference between $\tilde{R}_k$ and $\tilde{R}$. Consequently, we introduce a general deviation variable $\tilde{e}_{ij}^{(k)}$ with a positive parameter ρ:

$$\tilde{e}_{ij}^{(k)} = \left| r_{ij}^{L(k)} - \sum_{k=1}^{t} \lambda_k r_{ij}^{L(k)} \right|^{\rho} + \left| r_{ij}^{U(k)} - \sum_{k=1}^{t} \lambda_k r_{ij}^{U(k)} \right|^{\rho} \ (\rho > 0)$$
$$\text{for all } i = 1,2,\ldots,n,\ j = 1,2,\ldots,m,\ k = 1,2,\ldots,t \tag{4.62}$$

and construct the following deviation function:

$$\tilde{F}_\rho(\lambda) = \left(\sum_{k=1}^{t} \sum_{i=1}^{n} \sum_{j=1}^{m} w_j \tilde{e}_{ij}^{(k)} \right)^{1/\rho}$$

$$= \left(\sum_{k=1}^{t} \sum_{i=1}^{n} \sum_{j=1}^{m} w_j \left(\left| r_{ij}^{L(k)} - \sum_{k=1}^{t} \lambda_k r_{ij}^{L(k)} \right|^\rho + \left| r_{ij}^{U(k)} - \sum_{k=1}^{t} \lambda_k r_{ij}^{U(k)} \right|^\rho \right) \right)^{1/\rho} \quad (\rho > 0) \tag{4.63}$$

where $w = (w_1, w_2, \ldots, w_m)$ is the weight vector of the attributes $u_j\,(j = 1, 2, \ldots, m)$, with $w_j \geq 0,\ j = 1, 2, \ldots, m$, and $\sum_{j=1}^{m} w_j = 1$, which is predefined by all the experts.

To determine the weight vector $\lambda = (\lambda_1, \lambda_2, \ldots, \lambda_t)$ of the experts $d_k\,(k = 1, 2, \ldots, t)$, Xu and Cai [139] established the following general nonlinear optimization model:

(M-4.1) $\tilde{F}_\rho(\lambda^*) = \min \tilde{F}_\rho(\lambda)$

$$= \min \left(\sum_{k=1}^{t} \sum_{i=1}^{n} \sum_{j=1}^{m} w_j \left(\left| r_{ij}^{L(k)} - \sum_{k=1}^{t} \lambda_k r_{ij}^{L(k)} \right|^\rho + \left| r_{ij}^{U(k)} - \sum_{k=1}^{t} \lambda_k r_{ij}^{U(k)} \right|^\rho \right) \right)^{1/\rho} \quad (\rho > 0)$$

$$s.t.\quad \lambda_k \geq 0,\quad k = 1, 2, \ldots, t,\ \sum_{k=1}^{t} \lambda_k = 1$$

To solve the model (M-4.1), Xu and Cai [139] adopted the following procedure:

Step 1 Fix the parameter ρ and predefine the maximum iteration number s^*, and randomly generate an initial population $\Theta^{(s)} = \{\lambda^{(1)}, \lambda^{(2)}, \ldots, \lambda^{(p)}\}$, where $s = 0$, and $\lambda^{(l)} = \{\lambda_1^{(l)}, \lambda_2^{(l)}, \ldots, \lambda_t^{(l)}\}$ $(l = 1, 2, \ldots, p)$ are the weight vectors of the experts (or chromosomes). Then we input the attribute weights $w_j\,(j = 1, 2, \ldots, m)$ and all the normalized individual uncertain decision matrices $\tilde{R}_k = (\tilde{r}_{ij}^{(k)})_{n \times m}$ $(k = 1, 2, \ldots, t)$.

Step 2 By the general nonlinear optimization model (M-4.1), we define the fitness function as:

$$\tilde{F}_\rho(\lambda^{(l)}) = \left(\sum_{k=1}^{t} \sum_{i=1}^{n} \sum_{j=1}^{m} w_j \left(\left| r_{ij}^{L(k)} - \sum_{k=1}^{t} \lambda_k^{(l)} r_{ij}^{L(k)} \right|^\rho + \left| r_{ij}^{U(k)} - \sum_{k=1}^{t} \lambda_k^{(l)} r_{ij}^{U(k)} \right|^\rho \right) \right)^{1/\rho} \tag{4.64}$$

and then compute the fitness value $\tilde{F}_\rho(\lambda^{(l)})$ of each $\lambda^{(l)}$ in the current population $\Theta^{(s)}$, where $\lambda_k^{(l)} \geq 0$, $k = 1,2,\ldots,t$, and $\sum_{k=1}^{t} \lambda_k^{(l)} = 1$.

Step 3 Create new weight vectors (or chromosomes) by mating the current weight vectors, and apply mutation and recombination as the parent chromosomes mate.

Step 4 Delete members of the current population $\Theta^{(s)}$ to make room for the new weight vectors.

Step 5 Utilize Eq. (4.64) to compute the fitness values of the new weight vectors, and insert these vectors into the current population $\Theta^{(s)}$.

Step 6 If there is no further decrease of the minimum fitness value, or $s = s^*$, then go to Step 7; Otherwise, let $s = s+1$, and go to Step 3.

Step 7 Output the minimum fitness value $\tilde{F}_\rho(\lambda^*)$ and the corresponding weight vector λ^*.

Based on the optimal weight vector λ^* and Eq. (4.15), we get the collective uncertain decision matrix $\tilde{R} = (\tilde{r}_{ij})_{n \times m}$, and then utilize the UWA operator:

$$\tilde{z}_i(w) = \sum_{j=1}^{m} w_j \tilde{r}_{ij}, \text{ for all } \quad i = 1,2,\ldots,n \tag{4.65}$$

to aggregate all the attribute values in the ith line of $\tilde{R}$, and get the overall attribute value $\tilde{r}_i$ corresponding to the alternative x_i, where $\tilde{z}_i(w) = [z_i^L(w), z_i^U(w)]$.

To rank these overall attribute values $\tilde{z}_i(w)\,(i = 1,2,\ldots,n)$, we calculate their expected values:

$$E(\tilde{z}_i(w)) = \eta z_i^L(w) + (1-\eta) z_i^U(w), \quad \eta \in [0,1], \quad i = 1,2,\ldots,n \tag{4.66}$$

and then rank all the alternatives $x_i\ (i = 1,2,\ldots,n)$ and select the best one according to $E(\tilde{z}_i(w))(i = 1,2,\ldots,n)$.

In practical applications, we generally take $\rho = 1$, and then the model (M-4.1) reduces to a goal programming model as follows:

$$\textbf{(M-4.2)} \quad \tilde{F}(\lambda^*) = \min \tilde{F}(\lambda)$$

$$= \min \sum_{k=1}^{t} \sum_{i=1}^{n} \sum_{j=1}^{m} w_j \left(\left| r_{ij}^{L(k)} - \sum_{k=1}^{t} \lambda_k r_{ij}^{L(k)} \right| + \left| r_{ij}^{U(k)} - \sum_{k=1}^{t} \lambda_k r_{ij}^{U(k)} \right| \right)$$

$$s.t.\ \lambda_k \geq 0,\ k = 1,2,\ldots,t,\ \sum_{k=1}^{t} \lambda_k = 1$$

The solution to the model (M-4.2) can also be derived from the procedure above or by using a simplex method [21].

4.5.2 Practical Example

Example 4.8 Here we adapt Example 1.14 to illustrate the method in Sect. 4.5.2. Suppose that the weight vector of the attributes $u_j\,(j=1,2,3,4)$ is $w=(0.2,\ 0.3,0.4,0.1)$. An expert group is formed which consists of three experts $d_k\,(k=1,2,3)$. These experts are invited to evaluate the investment projects $x_i\,(i=1,2,3,\ 4,5)$ with respect to the attributes $u_j\,(j=1,2,3,4)$, and construct the following three uncertain decision matrices (see Tables 4.10, 4.11, 4.12).

By Eqs. (4.13) and (4.14), we first normalize the uncertain decision matrices $\tilde{A}_k\,(k=1,2,3)$ into the normalized uncertain decision matrices $\tilde{R}_k\,(k=1,2,3)$ (see Tables 4.13, 4.14, 4.15).

Based on the normalized decision matrices $\tilde{R}_k\,(k=1,2,3)$, we utilize the procedure (let $\rho=1$) of Sect. 4.5.1 to solve the model (M-4.2), and get the weight vector of the experts and the corresponding optimal objective value, respectively:

$$\lambda^* = (0.5455, 0.2727, 0.1818), \quad F(\lambda^*) = 0.3157$$

Based on the derived optimal weight vector λ^* and Eq. (4.15), we get the collective uncertain decision matrix $\tilde{R}=(\tilde{r}_{ij})_{5\times 4}$ (see Table 4.16).

Table 4.10 Uncertain decision matrix $\tilde{A}_1$

	u_1	u_2	u_3	u_4
x_1	[5.5, 6.0]	[5.0, 6.0]	[4.5, 5.0]	[0.4, 0.6]
x_2	[9.0, 10.5]	[6.5, 7.0]	[5.0, 6.0]	[1.5, 2.0]
x_3	[5.0, 5.5]	[4.0, 4.5]	[3.5, 4.0]	[0.4, 0.5]
x_4	[9.5, 10.0]	[5.0, 5.5]	[5.0, 7.0]	[1.3, 1.5]
x_5	[6.5, 7.0]	[3.5, 4.5]	[3.0, 4.0]	[0.8, 1.0]

Table 4.11 Uncertain decision matrix $\tilde{A}_2$

	u_1	u_2	u_3	u_4
x_1	[5.0, 5.5]	[5.0, 5.5]	[4.5, 5.5]	[0.4, 0.5]
x_2	[10.0, 11.0]	[6.0, 7.0]	[5.5, 6.0]	[1.5, 2.5]
x_3	[5.0, 6.0]	[4.0, 5.0]	[3.0, 4.5]	[0.4, 0.6]
x_4	[9.0, 10.0]	[5.0, 6.0]	[5.5, 6.0]	[1.0, 2.0]
x_5	[6.0, 7.0]	[3.0, 4.0]	[3.0, 3.5]	[0.8, 0.9]

Table 4.12 Uncertain decision matrix $\tilde{A}_3$

	u_1	u_2	u_3	u_4
x_1	[5.2, 5.5]	[5.2, 5.4]	[4.7, 5.0]	[0.3, 0.5]
x_2	[10.0, 10.5]	[6.5, 7.5]	[5.5, 6.0]	[1.6, 1.8]
x_3	[5.0, 5.5]	[3.0, 4.0]	[3.0, 4.0]	[0.3, 0.5]
x_4	[9.5, 10.0]	[4.5, 5.5]	[5.0, 6.0]	[1.2, 1.4]
x_5	[6.5, 7.0]	[3.5, 5.0]	[3.0, 5.0]	[0.7, 0.9]

Table 4.13 Normalized uncertain decision matrix $\tilde{R}_1$

	u_1	u_2	u_3	u_4
x_1	[0.22, 0.26]	[0.18, 0.25]	[0.17, 0.24]	[0.22, 0.43]
x_2	[0.13, 0.16]	[0.24, 0.29]	[0.19, 0.29]	[0.07, 0.11]
x_3	[0.24, 0.29]	[0.15, 019]	[0.13, 0.19]	[0.26, 0.43]
x_4	[0.13, 0.15]	[0.18, 0.23]	[0.19, 0.33]	[0.09, 0.13]
x_5	[0.19, 0.22]	[0.13, 0.19]	[0.12, 0.19]	[0.13, 0.21]

Table 4.14 Normalized uncertain decision matrix $\tilde{R}_2$

	u_1	u_2	u_3	u_4
x_1	[0.23, 0.29]	[0.18, 0.24]	[0.18, 0.26]	[0.25, 0.44]
x_2	[0.12, 0.15]	[0.22, 0.30]	[0.22, 0.28]	[0.05, 0.12]
x_3	[0.21, 0.29]	[0.15, 0.22]	[0.12, 0.21]	[0.21, 0.44]
x_4	[0.13, 0.16]	[0.18, 0.26]	[0.22, 0.28]	[0.06, 0.18]
x_5	[0.18, 0.24]	[0.11, 0.17]	[0.12, 0.16]	[0.14, 0.22]

Table 4.15 Normalized uncertain decision matrix $\tilde{R}_3$

	u_1	u_2	u_3	u_4
x_1	[0.24, 0.27]	[0.19, 0.24]	[0.18, 0.24]	[0.21, 0.52]
x_2	[0.13, 0.14]	[0.24, 0.33]	[0.21, 0.28]	[0.06, 0.10]
x_3	[0.24, 0.29]	[0.11, 0.18]	[0.12, 0.19]	[0.21, 0.52]
x_4	[0.13, 0.15]	[0.16, 0.24]	[0.19, 0.28]	[0.07, 0.13]
x_5	[0.19, 0.22]	[0.13, 0.22]	[0.12, 0.24]	[0.12, 0.22]

and then based on Table 4.16, we utilize the UWA operator Eq. (4.65) to get the overall attribute values $\tilde{z}_i(w)\,(i=1,2,3,4,5)$ corresponding to the alternatives $x_i(i=1,2,3,4,5)$:

$$\tilde{z}_1(w)=[0.192,0.270],\ \tilde{z}_2(w)=[0.183,0.246],\ \tilde{z}_3(w)=[0.163,0.240]$$
$$\tilde{z}_4(w)=[0.166,0.240],\ \tilde{z}_5(w)=[0.136,0.200]$$

Table 4.16 Collective uncertain decision matrix $\tilde{R}$ with λ^*

	u_1	u_2	u_3	u_4
x_1	[0.226, 0.270]	[0.182, 0.245]	[0.175, 0.245]	[0.226, 0.449]
x_2	[0.127, 0.154]	[0.235, 0.300]	[0.202, 0.285]	[0.063, 0.111]
x_3	[0.232, 0.290]	[0.143, 0.196]	[0.125, 0.195]	[0.237, 0.449]
x_4	[0.130, 0.153]	[0.176, 0.240]	[0.198, 0.307]	[0.078, 0.144]
x_5	[0.187, 0.225]	[0.125, 0.190]	[0.120, 0.191]	[0.131, 0.215]

To rank these overall attribute values $\tilde{z}_i(w)(i=1,2,3,4,5)$, we calculate their expected values by using Eq. (4.66) (without loss of generality, here we let $\eta=0.5$):

$$E(\tilde{z}_1(w))=0.231,\quad E(\tilde{z}_2(w))=0.214,\quad E(\tilde{z}_3(w))=0.202$$
$$E(\tilde{z}_4(w))=0.203,\quad E(\tilde{z}_5(w))=0.168$$

and then rank all the alternatives $x_i(i=1,2,3,4,5)$ according to $E(\tilde{z}_i(w))$ $(i=1,2,3,4,5)$: $x_1 \succ x_2 \succ x_4 \succ x_3 \succ x_5$, from which we get the best investment project x_1.

If all experts $d_k(k=1,2,3)$ have identical weights, i.e., $\lambda_1^*=\lambda_2^*=\lambda_3^*=\frac{1}{3}$, then we can employ the uncertain averaging operator:

$$\tilde{r}_{ij}=\frac{1}{3}\sum_{k=1}^{3}\tilde{r}_{ij}^{(k)}=\left[\frac{1}{3}\sum_{k=1}^{3}r_{ij}^{L(k)},\frac{1}{3}\sum_{k=1}^{3}r_{ij}^{U(k)}\right],$$
$$\text{for all } i=1,2,3,4,5,\ j=1,2,3,4 \tag{4.67}$$

to aggregate all the normalized individual uncertain decision matrices $\tilde{R}_k=(\tilde{r}_{ij}^{(k)})_{5\times4}$ $(k=1,2,3)$ into the collective uncertain decision matrix $\tilde{R}=(\tilde{r}_{ij})_{5\times4}$ (see Table 4.17).

Then from Eq. (4.65), we get the overall attribute value of each alternative:

$$\tilde{z}_1(w)=[0.194,0.250],\quad \tilde{z}_2(w)=[0.180,0.243]$$
$$\tilde{z}_3(w)=[0.157,0.268],\quad \tilde{z}_4(w)=[0.169,0.232]$$
$$\tilde{z}_5(w)=[0.135,0.204]$$

Table 4.17 Collective uncertain decision matrix $\tilde{R}$ with λ^*

	u_1	u_2	u_3	u_4
x_1	[0.230, 0.273]	[0.183, 0.243]	[0.177, 0.247]	[0.227, 0.463]
x_2	[0.127, 0.150]	[0.233, 0.307]	[0.207, 0.283]	[0.060, 0.110]
x_3	[0.230, 0.290]	[0.137, 0.197]	[0.123, 0.243]	[0.227, 0.463]
x_4	[0.130, 0.153]	[0.173, 0.243]	[0.200, 0.273]	[0.073, 0.147]
x_5	[0.187, 0.227]	[0.123, 0.193]	[0.120, 0.197]	[0.130, 0.217]

whose expected values calculated by using Eq. (4.66) (let $\eta = 0.5$) are

$$E(\tilde{z}_1(w)) = 0.222, \quad E(\tilde{z}_2(w)) = 0.211, \quad E(\tilde{z}_3(w)) = 0.213$$
$$E(\tilde{z}_4(w)) = 0.201, \quad E(\tilde{z}_5(w)) = 0.169$$

and then rank all the alternatives x_i ($i = 1,2,3,4,5$):

$$x_1 \succ x_3 \succ x_2 \succ x_4 \succ x_5$$

and thus, the best investment project is also x_1. The objective value with respect to the parameter value $\rho = 1$ is $F(\lambda^*) = 0.3635$.

From the numerical results above, we know that the overall attribute values of the alternatives (investment projects), obtained by using the identical weights and the uncertain averaging operator (4.67), are different from those derived from the model (M-4.2) and the UWA operator (4.65), and the ranking of the alternatives $x_i (i = 1,2,3,4)$ has also a slightly difference with the previous one, due to that we have taken different expert weights. Additionally, the objective value corresponding to the identical weights under the parameter value $\rho = 1$ is greater than the corresponding optimal objective value derived from the model (M-4.2). Analogous analysis can be given by considering more sets of discrepant data provided by the experts. This indicates that the result derived by Xu and Cai's [139] method can reach group decision with higher level of agreement among the experts than the result obtained by the other method. In fact, this useful conclusion can be guaranteed theoretically by the following theorem:

Theorem 4.4 Let $\lambda^* = (\lambda_1^*, \lambda_2^*, \ldots, \lambda_t^*)$ be the weight vector of the experts obtained by using the model (M-4.2) and $\lambda^- = (\lambda_1^-, \lambda_2^-, \ldots, \lambda_t^-)$ be the weight vector of the experts derived from any other method, $\tilde{F}(\lambda^*)$ and $\tilde{F}(\lambda^-)$ be the corresponding objective values respectively, then $\tilde{F}(\lambda^*) \le \tilde{F}(\lambda^-)$.

Proof By the model (M-4.2), we have

$$\tilde{F}(\lambda^-) = \sum_{k=1}^{t}\sum_{i=1}^{n}\sum_{j=1}^{m} w_j \left(\left| r_{ij}^{L(k)} - \sum_{k=1}^{t} \lambda_k^- r_{ij}^{L(k)} \right| + \left| r_{ij}^{U(k)} - \sum_{k=1}^{t} \lambda_k^- r_{ij}^{U(k)} \right| \right)$$

$$F(\lambda^*) = \sum_{k=1}^{t}\sum_{i=1}^{n}\sum_{j=1}^{m} w_j \left(\left| r_{ij}^{L(k)} - \sum_{k=1}^{t} \lambda_k^* r_{ij}^{L(k)} \right| + \left| r_{ij}^{U(k)} - \sum_{k=1}^{t} \lambda_k^* r_{ij}^{U(k)} \right| \right)$$
$$= \min \sum_{k=1}^{t}\sum_{i=1}^{n}\sum_{j=1}^{m} w_j \left(\left| r_{ij}^{L(k)} - \sum_{k=1}^{t} \lambda_k r_{ij}^{L(k)} \right| + \left| r_{ij}^{U(k)} - \sum_{k=1}^{t} \lambda_k r_{ij}^{U(k)} \right| \right)$$

Since

$$\min \sum_{k=1}^{t}\sum_{i=1}^{n}\sum_{j=1}^{m} w_j \left(\left| r_{ij}^{L(k)} - \sum_{k=1}^{t} \lambda_k r_{ij}^{L(k)} \right| + \left| r_{ij}^{U(k)} - \sum_{k=1}^{t} \lambda_k r_{ij}^{U(k)} \right| \right)$$
$$\leq \sum_{k=1}^{t}\sum_{i=1}^{n}\sum_{j=1}^{m} w_j \left(\left| r_{ij}^{L(k)} - \sum_{k=1}^{t} \lambda_k^{-} r_{ij}^{L(k)} \right| + \left| r_{ij}^{U(k)} - \sum_{k=1}^{t} \lambda_k^{-} r_{ij}^{U(k)} \right| \right)$$

then $\tilde{F}(\lambda^{*}) \leq \tilde{F}(\lambda^{-})$, which completes the proof.

Chapter 5
Interval MADM with Unknown Weight Information

There has been little research on interval MADM with unknown weight information up to now. Based on the deviation degrees of interval numbers and the idea of maximizing deviations of attributes, in this chapter, we first introduce a simple and straightforward formula, and in the situations where the decision maker has no preferences on alternatives, we introduce a MADM method based on possibility degrees and deviation degrees of interval numbers. Then for the situations where the decision maker has preferences on alternatives, we introduce a MADM method which can not only sufficiently consider the priori fuzzy information of normalization evaluations, but also meet the decision maker's subjective requirements as much as possible. Finally, we introduce a ranking method for alternatives based on the UOWA operator, and establish a consensus maximization model for determining attribute weights in uncertain MAGDM. In order to make the readers easy to understand and master the methods, we illustrate them with some practical examples.

5.1 MADM Method Without Preferences on Alternatives

5.1.1 Formulas and Concepts

For a MADM problem, whose attribute weight vector is $w=(w_1,w_2,\dots w_m)$, and satisfies the unitization constraint condition:

$$w_j \geq 0,\ \ j=1,2,\dots,m,\ \ \sum_{j=1}^{m} w_j^2 = 1 \tag{5.1}$$

and let the uncertain decision matrix be $\tilde{A}=(\tilde{a}_{ij})_{n\times m}$, where $\tilde{a}_{ij}=[a_{ij}^L, a_{ij}^U]$, $i=1,2,\dots,n,\ \ j=1,2,\dots,m$, the normalized uncertain decision matrix of $\tilde{A}$ is $\tilde{R}=(\tilde{r}_{ij})_{n\times m}$.

Z.S. Xu, *Uncertain Multi-Attribute Decision Making*,
DOI 10.1007/978-3-662-45640-8_5

In order to measure the similarity degree of two interval numbers, we first introduce the concept of deviation degree of interval numbers:

Definition 5.1 Let $\tilde{a} = [a^L, a^U]$ and $\tilde{b} = [b^L, b^U]$, if

$$\left\|\tilde{a} - \tilde{b}\right\| = \left|b^L - a^L\right| + \left|b^U - a^U\right|$$

then $d(\tilde{a}, \tilde{b}) = \left\|\tilde{a} - \tilde{b}\right\|$ is called the deviation degree of the interval numbers $\tilde{a}$ and $\tilde{b}$. Obviously, the larger $d(\tilde{a}, \tilde{b})$, the greater the deviation degree of $\tilde{a}$ and $\tilde{b}$. Especially, if $d(\tilde{a}, \tilde{b}) = 0$, then $\tilde{a} = \tilde{b}$.

5.1.2 Decision Making Method

Consider a MADM problem, in general, it needs to obtain the overall attribute values of the given alternatives, and can be achieved by using the UWA operator (4.15) based on the normalized uncertain decision matrix $\tilde{R} = (\tilde{r}_{ij})_{n \times m}$ and the attribute weight vector $w = (w_1, w_2, \ldots, w_n)$.

In the case where the attribute weights $w_j (j = 1, 2, \ldots, m)$ are the known real numbers, the ranking of the alternatives $x_i (i = 1, 2, \ldots, n)$ can be got using the overall attribute values $\tilde{z}_i(w)(i = 1, 2, \ldots, n)$; Otherwise, we can not derive the overall attribute values from Eq. (4.15).

In what follows, we consider the situations where the attribute weights are unknown completely, the attribute values are interval numbers, and the decision maker has no preferences on alternatives.

Since the elements in the normalized uncertain decision matrix $\tilde{R} = (\tilde{r}_{ij})_{n \times m}$ take the form of interval numbers, and cannot be compared directly, then based on the analysis in Sect. 1.5 and Definition 5.1, we let $d(\tilde{r}_{ij}, \tilde{r}_{kj}) = \left\|\tilde{r}_{ij} - \tilde{r}_{kj}\right\|$ denote the deviation degree of the elements $\tilde{r}_{ij}$ and $\tilde{r}_{kj}$ in $\tilde{R} = (\tilde{r}_{ij})_{n \times m}$, where

$$\left\|\tilde{r}_{ij} - \tilde{r}_{kj}\right\| = \left|r_{ij}^L - r_{kj}^L\right| + \left|r_{ij}^U - r_{kj}^U\right|$$

For the attribute u_j, if we denote $D_{ij}(w)$ as the deviation between the alternative x_i and the other alternatives, then

$$D_{ij}(w) = \sum_{l=1}^{n} \left\|\tilde{r}_{ij} - \tilde{r}_{lj}\right\| w_j = \sum_{l=1}^{n} d(\tilde{r}_{ij}, \tilde{r}_{lj}) w_j, \ i = 1, 2, \ldots, n, \ j = 1, 2, \ldots, m \tag{5.2}$$

and let

$$D_j(w) = \sum_{i=1}^{n} D_{ij}(w) = \sum_{i=1}^{n} \sum_{l=1}^{n} d(\tilde{r}_{ij}, \tilde{r}_{lj}) w_j, \ j = 1, 2, \ldots, n \tag{5.3}$$

For the attribute u_j, $D_j(w)$ denotes the deviation sum of each alternative and the other alternatives. A reasonable weight vector w should make the total deviation of all the alternatives with respect to all the attributes as much as possible. In order to do so, we can construct the following deviation function:

$$\max D(w)=\sum_{j=1}^{n} D_j(w)=\sum_{i=1}^{n}\sum_{j=1}^{m}\sum_{l=1}^{n} d(\tilde{r}_{ij},\tilde{r}_{lj})w_j \tag{5.4}$$

Thus, solving the attribute weight vector w is equivalent to solving the following single-objective optimization model [153]:

$$\begin{cases} \max D(w)=\sum_{i=1}^{n}\sum_{j=1}^{m}\sum_{l=1}^{n} d(\tilde{r}_{ij},\tilde{r}_{lj})w_j & (5.5)\\ s.t. \sum_{j=1}^{m} w_j^2=1,\ w_j\geq 0,\ j=1,2,\ldots,m & (5.6)\end{cases}$$

Solving this model, we get

$$w_j=\frac{\sum_{i=1}^{n}\sum_{l=1}^{n} d(\tilde{r}_{ij},\tilde{r}_{lj})}{\sqrt{\sum_{j=1}^{m}\left(\sum_{i=1}^{n}\sum_{l=1}^{n} d(\tilde{r}_{ij},\tilde{r}_{lj})\right)^2}},\quad j=1,2,\ldots,n \tag{5.7}$$

Normalizing the weights derived from Eq. (5.7), we get

$$w_j=\frac{\sum_{i=1}^{n}\sum_{l=1}^{n} d(\tilde{r}_{ij},\tilde{r}_{lj})}{\sum_{j=1}^{m}\left(\sum_{i=1}^{n}\sum_{l=1}^{n} d(\tilde{r}_{ij},\tilde{r}_{lj})\right)},\quad j=1,2,\ldots,n \tag{5.8}$$

The characteristic of Eq. (5.8) is that it employs the deviation degrees of interval numbers to unify all the known objective decision information into a simple formula, and it is easy to implement on a computer or a calculator.

After obtaining the optimal weight vector w of attributes, we still need to calculate the overall attribute values $\tilde{z}_i(w)(i=1,2,\ldots,n)$ of alternatives by using Eq. (4.15). Since $\tilde{z}_i(w)(i=1,2,\ldots,n)$ are also interval numbers, it is inconvenient to rank the alternatives directly. Therefore, we can utilize Eq. (4.2) to calculate the possibility degrees of comparing the interval numbers $\tilde{z}_i(w)(i=1,2,\ldots,n)$, and then construct the possibility degree matrix $P=(p_{ij})_{n\times n}$, where $p_{ij}=p(\tilde{z}_i(w)\geq \tilde{z}_j(w))\ (i,j=1,2,\ldots,n)$.

After that, we use Eq. (4.6) to derive the priority vector $v = (v_1, v_2, \ldots, v_n)$ of P, and rank the alternatives according to the elements of v in descending order, and thus get the optimal alternative.

Based on the analysis above, we give the following algorithm [153]:

Step 1 For a MADM problem, the decision maker evaluates the alternative x_i with respect to the attribute u_j, and the evaluated value is expressed in an interval number $\tilde{a}_{ij} = [a_{ij}^L, a_{ij}^U]$. All $\tilde{a}_{ij} (i = 1, 2, \ldots, n, j = 1, 2, \ldots, m)$ are contained in the uncertain decision matrix $\tilde{A} = (\tilde{a}_{ij})_{n \times m}$, whose the normalized uncertain decision matrix is $\tilde{R} = (\tilde{r}_{ij})_{n \times m}$.

Step 2 Utilize Eq. (5.7) to obtain the weight vector $w = (w_1, w_2, \ldots, w_m)$ of the attributes $u_j (j = 1, 2, \ldots, m)$.

Step 3 Use Eq. (4.15) to calculate the overall attribute values $\tilde{z}_i(w) (i = 1, 2, \ldots, n)$ of the alternatives $x_i (i = 1, 2, \ldots, n)$.

Step 4 Employ Eq. (4.2) to calculate the possibility degrees of comparing interval numbers $\tilde{z}_i(w) (i = 1, 2, \ldots, n)$, and construct the possibility degree matrix $P = (p_{ij})_{n \times n}$.

Step 5 Derive the priority vector $v = (v_1, v_2, \ldots, v_n)$ of P.

Step 6 Rank the alternatives $x_i (i = 1, 2, \ldots, n)$ according to the elements of v in descending order, and then get the optimal alternative.

5.1.3 Practical Example

Example 5.1 Consider a problem that a force plans to purchase some guns. Now there are four series of candidate guns $x_i (i = 1, 2, 3, 4)$, which are to be evaluated using the following five indices (attributes): (1) u_1: fire attack ability; (2) u_2: reaction ability; (3) u_3: maneuverability; (4) u_4: survival ability; and (5) u_5: cost. The evaluation values over the guns $x_i (i = 1, 2, 3, 4)$ with respect to the indices $u_j (j = 1, 2, 3, 4)$ are listed in Table 5.1.

All the indices, u_5 is cost-type attribute, and the others are benefit-type attributes. Now we use the method of Sect. 5.1.2 to rank the alternatives:

Step 1 By using Eqs. (4.9) and (4.10), we transform the uncertain decision matrix $\tilde{A}$ into the normalized uncertain decision matrix $\tilde{R}$, listed in Table 5.2.

Step 2 According to Eq. (5.7), we get the attribute weight vector w as:

$$w = (0.2189, 0.2182, 0.1725, 0.2143, 0.1761)$$

Step 3 Utilize Eq. (4.15) to derive the overall attribute values of all the alternatives as the interval numbers:

Table 5.1 Uncertain decision matrix $\tilde{A}$

	u_1	u_2	u_3	u_4	u_5
x_1	[26,000, 27,000]	[2, 4]	[18,000, 19,000]	[0.7, 0.8]	[15,000, 16,000]
x_2	[60,000, 70,000]	[3, 4]	[16,000, 17,000]	[0.3, 0.4]	[27,000, 28,000]
x_3	[50,000, 60,000]	[2, 3]	[15,000, 16,000]	[0.7, 0.8]	[24,000, 26,000]
x_4	[40,000, 50,000]	[1, 2]	[28,000, 29,000]	[0.4, 0.5]	[15,000, 17,000]

Table 5.2 Normalized decision matrix $\tilde{R}$

	u_1	u_2	u_3	u_4	u_5
x_1	[0.240, 0.295]	[0.298, 0.943]	[0.431, 0.477]	[0.538, 0.721]	[0.571, 0.663]
x_2	[0.554, 0.765]	[0.447, 0.943]	[0.383, 0.426]	[0.231, 0.361]	[0.326, 0.368]
x_3	[0.462, 0.656]	[0.298, 0.707]	[0.359, 0.401]	[0.538, 0.721]	[0.351, 0.414]
x_4	[0.369, 0.546]	[0.149, 0.471]	[0.670, 0.728]	[0.308, 0.451]	[0.537, 0.663]

$$\tilde{z}_1(w) = [0.4077, 0.6239], \ \tilde{z}_2(w) = [0.3918, 0.5888]$$

$$\tilde{z}_3(w) = [0.40527, 0.5945], \ \tilde{z}_4(w) = [0.3994, 0.5613]$$

Step 4 Compare each pair of $\tilde{z}_i(w)(i = 1,2,3,4)$, and then construct the possibility degree matrix:

$$P = \begin{pmatrix} 0.5 & 0.5617 & 0.5393 & 0.6042 \\ 0.4383 & 0.5 & 0.4753 & 0.5405 \\ 0.4607 & 0.5247 & 0.5 & 0.5678 \\ 0.3958 & 0.4595 & 0.4322 & 0.5 \end{pmatrix}$$

and utilizes Eq. (4.6) to derive the priority vector of the possibility degree matrix P:

$$v = (0.2671, 0.2462, 0.2544, 0.2323)$$

Step 5 Use the priority vector v and the possibility degrees of P to derive the ranking of the interval numbers $\tilde{z}_i(w)(i = 1,2,3,4)$:

$$\tilde{z}_1(w) \underset{0.5393}{\geq} \tilde{z}_3(w) \underset{0.5247}{\geq} \tilde{z}_2(w) \underset{0.5405}{\geq} \tilde{z}_4(w)$$

Step 6 Rank the alternatives $x_i (i=1,2,3,4)$ according to $\tilde{z}_i(w)(i=1,2,3,4)$ in descending order:

$$x_1 \underset{0.5393}{\succ} x_3 \underset{0.5247}{\succ} x_2 \underset{0.5405}{\succ} x_4$$

which indicates that x_1 is the best one.

5.2 MADM Method with Preferences on Alternatives

5.2.1 Decision Making Method

For the MADM problem where the attribute weights are unknown completely and the attribute values take the form of interval numbers. If the decision maker has a preference over the alternative x_i, then let the subjective preference value be $\tilde{\vartheta}_i$ (where $\tilde{\vartheta}_i = [\vartheta_i^L, \vartheta_i^U]$, $0 \le \vartheta_i^L \le \vartheta_i^U \le 1$. The subjective preferences can be provided by the decision maker or the other methods). Here, we regard the attribute values $\tilde{r}_{ij} = [r_{ij}^L, r_{ij}^U]$ in the normalized uncertain decision matrix $\tilde{R} = (\tilde{r}_{ij})_{n\times m}$ as the objective preference values of the alternative x_i under the attribute u_j.

Due to the restrictions of some conditions, there is a difference between the subjective preferences of the decision maker and the objective preferences. In order to make a reasonable decision, the attribute weight vector w should be chosen so as to make the total differences of the subjective preferences and the objective preferences (attributes) as small as possible.

Considering that the elements in the normalized uncertain decision matrix $\tilde{R} = (\tilde{r}_{ij})_{n\times m}$ and the subjective preference values provided by the decision maker take the form of interval numbers, according to Definition 5.1, we can establish the following single-objective optimization models [107]:

$$\textbf{(M-5.2)} \quad \begin{cases} \min F(w) = \sum_{i=1}^{n}\sum_{j=1}^{m}\left(d(\tilde{r}_{ij},\tilde{\vartheta}_i)w_j\right)^2 = \sum_{i=1}^{n}\sum_{j=1}^{m} d^2(\tilde{r}_{ij},\tilde{\vartheta}_i)w_j^2 \\ s.t. \sum_{j=1}^{m} w_j = 1,\ w_j \ge 0,\ j=1,2,\ldots,m \end{cases}$$

where

$$d(\tilde{r}_{ij},\tilde{\vartheta}_i) = \left\|\tilde{r}_{ij} - \tilde{\vartheta}_i\right\| = \left|r_{ij}^L - \vartheta_i^L\right| + \left|r_{ij}^U - \vartheta_i^U\right|$$

denotes the deviation between the subjective preference value $\tilde{\vartheta}_i$ of the decision maker over the alternative x_i and the corresponding objective preference value (attribute value) $\tilde{r}_{ij}$ with respect to the attribute u_j, w_j is the weight of the attribute u_j, the single-objective function $F(w)$ denotes the total deviation among the subjective preference values of the decision maker over all the alternatives and the corresponding objective preference values with respect to all the attributes. To solve this model, we construct the Lagrange function:

$$L(w,\zeta)=\sum_{i=1}^{n}\sum_{j=1}^{m}d^2(\tilde{r}_{ij},\tilde{\vartheta}_i)w_j^2+2\zeta\left(\sum_{j=1}^{m}w_j-1\right)$$

Differentiating the function $L(w,\zeta)$ with respect to w_j and ζ, and setting these partial derivatives equal to zero, the following set of equations is obtained:

$$\begin{cases}\dfrac{L(w,\zeta)}{\partial w_j}=2\sum_{i=1}^{n}d^2(\tilde{r}_{ij},\tilde{\vartheta}_i)^2w_j+2\zeta=0, \quad j=1,2,\ldots,m\\ \dfrac{L(w,\zeta)}{\partial\zeta}=\sum_{j=1}^{m}w_j=1\end{cases}$$

then

$$w_j=-\frac{\zeta}{\sum_{i=1}^{n}d^2(\tilde{r}_{ij},\tilde{\vartheta}_i)}, \quad j=1,2,\ldots,m \tag{5.9}$$

$$\sum_{j=1}^{m}w_j=1 \tag{5.10}$$

By Eqs. (5.9) and (5.10), we get

$$\zeta=-\frac{1}{\sum_{j=1}^{m}\frac{1}{\left(\sum_{i=1}^{n}d^2(\tilde{r}_{ij},\tilde{\vartheta}_i)\right)}} \tag{5.11}$$

Also using Eqs. (5.9) and (5.11), we have

$$w_j=\frac{\frac{1}{\sum_{i=1}^{n}d^2(\tilde{r}_{ij},\tilde{\vartheta}_i)}}{\sum_{j=1}^{m}\frac{1}{\sum_{i=1}^{n}d^2(\tilde{r}_{ij},\tilde{\vartheta}_i)}}, \quad j=1,2,\ldots,m \tag{5.12}$$

The characteristic of Eq. (5.12) is that it employs the deviation degrees of interval numbers to unify all the known objective decision information (attribute values) into a simple formula, and it is easy to implement on a computer or a calculator.

After obtaining the optimal weight vector w of attributes, we still need to calculate the overall attribute values $\tilde{z}_i(w)(i=1,2,\ldots,n)$ of alternatives by using Eq. (4.15). Since $\tilde{z}_i(w)(i=1,2,\ldots,n)$ are also interval numbers, it is inconvenient to rank the alternatives directly. Therefore, we can utilize Eq. (4.2) to calculate the possibility degrees of comparing the interval numbers $\tilde{z}_i(w)(i=1,2,\ldots,n)$, and then construct the possibility degree matrix $P=(p_{ij})_{n\times n}$, where $p_{ij}=p(\tilde{z}_i(w)\geq \tilde{z}_j(w))$ $(i,j=1,2,\ldots,n)$. After that, we use Eq. (4.6) to derive the priority vector $v=(v_1,v_2,\ldots,v_n)$ of P, and rank the alternatives according to the elements of v in descending order, and thus get the optimal alternative.

Based on the analysis above, we give the following algorithm [107]:

Step 1 For a MADM problem, the decision maker evaluates the alternative x_i with respect to the attribute u_j, and the evaluated value is expressed in an interval number $\tilde{a}_{ij}=[a_{ij}^L,a_{ij}^U]$. All $\tilde{a}_{ij}(i=1,2,\ldots,n,j=1,2,\ldots,m)$ are contained in the uncertain decision matrix $\tilde{A}=(\tilde{a}_{ij})_{n\times m}$, whose the normalized uncertain decision matrix is $\tilde{R}=(\tilde{r}_{ij})_{n\times m}$.

Step 2 The decision maker provides his/her subjective preferences $\tilde{\vartheta}_i(i=1,2,\ldots,n)$ over the alternatives $x_i(i=1,2,\ldots,n)$.

Step 3 Utilize Eq. (5.12) to obtain the weight vector $w=(w_1,w_2,\ldots,w_m)$ of the attributes $u_j(j=1,2,\ldots,n)$.

Step 4 Use Eq. (4.15) to calculate the overall attribute values $\tilde{z}_i(w)(i=1,2,\ldots,n)$ of the alternatives $x_i(i=1,2,\ldots,n)$.

Step 5 Employ Eq. (4.2) to calculate the possibility degrees of comparing interval numbers $\tilde{z}_i(w)(i=1,2,\ldots,n)$, and construct the possibility degree matrix $P=(p_{ij})_{n\times n}$.

Step 6 Derive the priority vector $v=(v_1,v_2,\ldots,v_n)$ of P using Eq. (4.6).

Step 7 Rank the alternatives $x_i(i=1,2,\ldots,n)$ according to the elements of v, and then get the optimal alternative.

5.2.2 Practical Example

Example 5.2 Assessment and selection of cadres is a MADM problem. On the one hand, the decision maker should select talented people to leadership positions; On the other hand, in the case of the same condition, the decision maker also hopes to appoint the preferred candidate [31]. The attributes which are considered by a certain unit in selection of cadre candidates are: (1) u_1: thought & morality; (2) u_2 : working attitude; (3) u_3: working; (4) G_4: literacy and knowledge structure; (5) G_5 : leadership ability; and (6) G_6: develop capacity. First, the masses are asked to recommend and evaluate the initial candidates with respect to the attribute above

Table 5.3 Uncertain decision matrix $\tilde{A}$

	u_1	u_2	u_3	u_4	u_5	u_6
x_1	[85, 90]	[90, 92]	[91, 94]	[93, 96]	[90, 91]	[95, 97]
x_2	[90, 95]	[89, 91]	[90, 92]	[90, 92]	[94, 97]	[90, 93]
x_3	[88, 91]	[84, 86]	[91, 94]	[91, 94]	[86, 89]	[91, 92]
x_4	[93, 96]	[91, 93]	[85, 88]	[86, 89]	[87, 90]	[92, 93]
x_5	[86, 89]	[90, 92]	[90, 95]	[91, 93]	[90, 92]	[85, 87]

by using the hundred mark system. Then, after the statistical processing, five candidates $x_i (i = 1,2,3,4,5)$ have been identified. The decision information on each candidate with respect to the attributes $u_j (j = 1,2,\ldots,6)$ takes the form of interval numbers, and is described in the uncertain decision matrix $\tilde{A}$ (see Table 5.3).

Now we utilize the method of Sect. 5.2.1 to rank the five candidates, whose steps are given as follows:

Step 1 Since all the attributes are benefit type attributes, then we can transform the uncertain decision matrix $\tilde{A}$ into the normalized uncertain decision matrix $\tilde{R}$ using Eq. (4.9), shown in Table 5.4.

Step 2 Suppose that the decision maker's preferences over the five candidates $x_i (i = 1,2,3,4,5)$ are

$$\tilde{\vartheta}_1 = [0.3, 0.5],\ \tilde{\vartheta}_2 = [0.5, 0.6],\ \tilde{\vartheta}_3 = [0.3, 0.4]$$

$$\tilde{\vartheta}_4 = [0.4, 0.6],\ \tilde{\vartheta}_5 = [0.4, 0.5]$$

then we utilize the formula $d(\tilde{r}_{ij}, \tilde{\vartheta}_i) = \left| r_{ij}^L - \tilde{\vartheta}_i^L \right| + \left| r_{ij}^U - \tilde{\vartheta}_i^U \right|$, $i = 1,2,3,4,5$, $j = 1,2,\ldots,6$ to calculate the deviation degrees of the objective preference values (attribute values) and the subjective preference values, listed in Table 5.5.

Table 5.4 Normalized uncertain decision matrix $\tilde{R}$

	u_1	u_2	u_3	u_4	u_5	u_6
x_2	[0.436, 0.480]	[0.438, 0.458]	[0.434, 0.460]	[0.434, 0.456]	[0.458, 0.485]	[0.438, 0.459]
x_1	[0.412, 0.455]	[0.443, 0.463]	[0.439, 0.470]	[0.448, 0.476]	[0.438, 0.455]	[0.460, 0.478]
x_3	[0.427, 0.460]	[0.414, 0.433]	[0.439, 0.470]	[0.438, 0.466]	[0.419, 0.445]	[0.440, 0.454]
x_4	[0.451, 0.485]	[0.448, 0.468]	[0.410, 0.440]	[0.414, 0.441]	[0.424, 0.450]	[0.445, 0.459]
x_5	[0.417, 0.450]	[0.443, 0.463]	[0.434, 0.475]	[0.438, 0.461]	[0.438, 0.460]	[0.411, 0.429]

Table 5.5 Deviation degrees of the objective preference values and the subjective preference values

	u_1	u_2	u_3	u_4	u_5	u_6
$d(\tilde{r}_{1j},\tilde{\vartheta}_1)$	0.157	0.180	0.109	0.172	0.183	0.182
$d(\tilde{r}_{2j},\tilde{\vartheta}_2)$	0.184	0.204	0.206	0.210	0.157	0.206
$d(\tilde{r}_{3j},\tilde{\vartheta}_3)$	0.187	0.147	0.209	0.204	0.164	0.194
$d(\tilde{r}_{4j},\tilde{\vartheta}_4)$	0.166	0.180	0.170	0.173	0.174	0.186
$d(\tilde{r}_{5j},\tilde{\vartheta}_5)$	0.067	0.080	0.059	0.077	0.078	0.082

Step 3 Since the weights of all attributes are unknown, then we utilize Eq. (5.12) to derive the attribute weight vector:

$$w = (0.1794, 0.1675, 0.1727, 0.1490, 0.1855, 0.1458)$$

Step 4 Use Eq. (4.15) to derive the overall attribute weights of the five candidates:

$$\tilde{z}_1(w) = [0.4390, 0.4654],\ \tilde{z}_2(w) = [0.4396, 0.4671],\ \tilde{z}_3(w) = [0.4289, 0.4544]$$
$$\tilde{z}_4(w) = [0.4320, 0.4575],\ \tilde{z}_5(w) = [0.4348, 0.4569]$$

Step 5 Employ Eq. (4.2) to construct the possibility degree matrix P by comparing each pair of $\tilde{z}_i(w)(i = 1,2,3,4,5)$:

$$P = \begin{bmatrix} 0.5000 & 0.4787 & 0.7033 & 0.6435 & 0.6309 \\ 0.5213 & 0.5000 & 0.7208 & 0.6623 & 0.6512 \\ 0.2967 & 0.2792 & 0.5000 & 0.4392 & 0.4118 \\ 0.3565 & 0.3377 & 0.5608 & 0.5000 & 0.4769 \\ 0.3691 & 0.3488 & 0.5882 & 0.5231 & 0.5000 \end{bmatrix}$$

Step 6 Derive the priority vector of P using Eq. (4.6):

$$v = (0.2228, 0.2278, 0.1713, 0.1866, 0.1915)$$

and then based on the priority vector v and the possibility degrees of P, we get the ranking of the interval numbers $\tilde{z}_i(w)(i = 1,2,3,4,5)$:

$$\tilde{z}_2(w) \underset{0.5213}{\geq} \tilde{z}_1(w) \underset{0.6309}{\geq} \tilde{z}_5(w) \underset{0.5231}{\geq} \tilde{z}_4(w) \underset{0.5608}{\geq} \tilde{z}_3(w)$$

Step 7 Rank all the candidates $x_i (i = 1,2,3,4,5)$ according to $\tilde{z}_i(w)(i = 1,2,3,4,5)$ in descending order:

$$x_2 \underset{0.5213}{\succ} x_1 \underset{0.6309}{\succ} x_5 \underset{0.5231}{\succ} x_4 \underset{0.5608}{\succ} x_3$$

from which we get the best candidate x_2.

5.3 UOWA Operator

Let Ω be the set of all interval numbers.

Definition 5.2 Let $UOWA : \Omega^n \to \Omega$, if

$$UOWA_\omega(\tilde{\alpha}_1, \tilde{\alpha}_2, \ldots, \tilde{\alpha}_n) = \sum_{j=1}^{n} \omega_j \tilde{b}_j$$

where $\omega = (\omega_1, \omega_2, \ldots, \omega_n)$ is the weighting vector associated with the UOWA operator, $\omega_j \in [0,1]$, $j = 1,2,\ldots,n$, $\sum_{j=1}^{n} \omega_j = 1$, $\tilde{a}_i \in \Omega$, and $\tilde{b}_j$ is the jth largest of a collection of arguments $(\tilde{a}_1, \tilde{a}_2, \ldots, \tilde{a}_n)$, then the function UOWA is called an uncertain OWA (UOWA) operator.

We can utilize the method for determining the OWA operator in Chap. 1 or the following formula to derive the weighted vector $\omega = (\omega_1, \omega_2, \ldots, \omega_n)$, where

$$\omega_k = f\left(\frac{k}{n}\right) - f\left(\frac{k-1}{n}\right), \; k = 1,2,\ldots,n \tag{5.13}$$

where f is a fuzzy linguistic quantifier:

$$f(r) = \begin{cases} 0, & r < a \\ \dfrac{r-a}{b-a}, & a \le r \le b \\ 1, & r > b \end{cases} \tag{5.14}$$

and $a, b, r \in [0,1]$. Some examples of non-decreasing proportional fuzzy linguistic quantifiers are [43]: "most" ((a,b) =(0.3, 0.8)), "at least half" ((a,b) = (0, 0.5)), and "as many as possible" ((a,b) =(0.5, 1)).

Example 5.3 Given a collection of interval numbers:

$$\tilde{\alpha}_1 = [3,5], \; \tilde{\alpha}_2 = [4,6], \; \tilde{\alpha}_3 = [4,7], \; \tilde{\alpha}_4 = [3,6]$$

We utilize Eq. (4.2) to compare each pair of four interval numbers $\tilde{\alpha}_i (i=1,2,3,4)$, and then construct the possibility degree matrix:

$$P=\begin{bmatrix} 0.50 & 0.25 & 0.20 & 0.40 \\ 0.75 & 0.50 & 0.40 & 0.60 \\ 0.80 & 0.60 & 0.50 & 0.80 \\ 0.60 & 0.40 & 0.20 & 0.50 \end{bmatrix}$$

whose priority vector can be derived from Eq. (4.6):

$$v=(0.196, 0.271, 0.308, 0.225)$$

based on which we rank the interval numbers $\tilde{\alpha}_i (i=1,2,3,4)$ as:

$$\tilde{b}_1=\tilde{\alpha}_3,\ \tilde{b}_2=\tilde{\alpha}_2,\ \tilde{b}_3=\tilde{\alpha}_4,\ \tilde{b}_4=\tilde{\alpha}_1$$

If we suppose that the weighting vector associated with the UOWA operator is

$$\omega=(0.3, 0.2, 0.4, 0.1)$$

then utilize the UOWA operator to aggregate the interval numbers $\tilde{\alpha}_i (i=1,2,3,4)$, and get

$$\begin{aligned} UOWA_{\omega}(\tilde{\alpha}_1,\tilde{\alpha}_2,\tilde{\alpha}_3,\tilde{\alpha}_4) &= \sum_{j=1}^{4} \omega_j \tilde{b}_j \\ &= 0.3\times[4,7]+0.2\times[4,6]+0.4\times[3,6]+0.1\times[3,5] \\ &= [3.5, 6.2] \end{aligned}$$

Below we consider the situations where there is partial weight information and the decision maker has subjective preference over the arguments, and introduce a linear goal programming model to determine the weighting vector associated with the UOWA operator:

Given m samples, and each sample comprises of a collection of n arguments $(\tilde{a}_{k1},\tilde{a}_{k2},\ldots,\tilde{a}_{kn})(k=1,2,\ldots,m)$, and a subjective preference value $\tilde{\vartheta}_k$ is given corresponding to each collection of arguments, where

$$\tilde{a}_{kj}=[a_{kj}^L, a_{kj}^U],\ \tilde{\vartheta}_k=[\vartheta_k^L, \vartheta_k^U],\ j=1,2,\ldots,n,\ k=1,2,\ldots,m$$

and let Φ' be the set of the known partial weight information.

Its weighting vector $\omega=(\omega_1,\omega_2,\ldots,\omega_n)$ needs to be determined, such that

$$g(\tilde{a}_{k1},\tilde{a}_{k2},\ldots,\tilde{a}_{kn})=\tilde{\vartheta}_k,\ k=1,2,\ldots,m \tag{5.15}$$

We can use the possibility degree formula to compare the kth collection of sample arguments and construct the possibility degree matrix, whose priority vector can be derived by using the priority formula given previously. Then according to the elements of the derived priority vector to rank the kth collection of sample data $(\tilde{a}_{k1}, \tilde{a}_{k2}, \ldots, \tilde{a}_{kn})$ in descending order, and get $\tilde{b}_{k1}, \tilde{b}_{k2}, \ldots, \tilde{b}_{kn}$, $k = 1, 2, \ldots, m$. Thus, Eq. (5.15) can be rewritten as:

$$\sum_{j=1}^{n} \omega_j \tilde{b}_{kj} = \tilde{\vartheta}_k,\ k = 1, 2, \ldots, m \tag{5.16}$$

i.e.,

$$\sum_{j=1}^{n} \omega_j b_{kj}^L = \vartheta_k^L,\ \sum_{j=1}^{n} \omega_j b_{kj}^U = \vartheta_k^U,\ k = 1, 2, \ldots, m \tag{5.17}$$

In actual decision making problems, Eq. (5.17) generally does not hold, and so, we introduce the deviation factors e_{1k} and e_{2k}, where

$$e_{1k} = \left| \sum_{j=1}^{n} \omega_j b_{kj}^L - \vartheta_k^L \right|,\ e_{2k} = \left| \sum_{j=1}^{n} \omega_j b_{kj}^U - \vartheta_k^U \right|,\ k = 1, 2, \ldots, m$$

A reasonable weighting vector should make the deviation factors e_{1k} and e_{2k} as small as possible, and thus, we establish the following multi-objective programming model:

$$\begin{cases} \min e_{1k} = \left| \sum_{j=1}^{n} \omega_j b_{kj}^L - \vartheta_k^L \right|,\ k = 1, 2, \ldots, m \\ \min e_{2k} = \left| \sum_{j=1}^{n} \omega_j b_{kj}^U - \vartheta_k^U \right|,\ k = 1, 2, \ldots, m \\ s.t.\ \omega \in \Phi' \end{cases}$$

To solve the model (M-5.3), and considering that all the deviation factors are fair, we transform the model (M-5.3) into the following linear goal programming model:

$$\begin{cases} \min J = \sum_{k=1}^{m} [(e_{1k}^+ + e_{1k}^-) + (e_{2k}^+ + e_{2k}^-)] \\ s.t.\ \sum_{j=1}^{n} b_{kj}^L \omega_j - \vartheta_k^L - e_{1k}^+ + e_{1k}^- = 0,\quad k = 1, 2, \ldots, m \\ \sum_{j=1}^{n} b_{kj}^U \omega_j - \vartheta_k^U - e_{2k}^+ + e_{2k}^- = 0,\quad k = 1, 2, \ldots, m \\ \omega \in \Phi',\ e_{1k}^+ \geq 0,\ e_{1k}^- \geq 0, e_{2k}^+ \geq 0,\ e_{2k}^- \geq 0,\ k = 1, 2, \ldots, m \end{cases}$$

Table 5.6 Sample data

Samples	Collections of arguments	Subjective preference values
1	[0.4, 0.7] [0.2, 0.5] [0.7, 0.8]	[0.3, 0.7]
2	[0.3, 0.4] [0.6, 0.8] [0.3, 0.5]	[0.4, 0.5]
3	[0.2, 0.6] [0.3, 0.4] [0.5, 0.8]	[0.3, 0.6]
4	[0.5, 0.8] [0.3, 0.5] [0.3, 0.4]	[0.4, 0.6]

where e_{1k}^{+} is the positive deviation from the target of the objective $\sum_{j=1}^{n} b_{kj}^{L}\omega_j - \vartheta_k^{L}$ over the expected value zero; e_{1k}^{-} is the negative deviation from the target of the objective $\sum_{j=1}^{n} b_{kj}^{L}\omega_j - \vartheta_k^{L}$ below the expected value zero; e_{2k}^{+} is the positive deviation from the target of the objective $\sum_{j=1}^{n} b_{kj}^{U}\omega_j - \vartheta_k^{U}$ over the expected value zero; e_{2k}^{-} is the negative deviation from the target of the objective $\sum_{j=1}^{n} b_{kj}^{U}\omega_j - \vartheta_k^{U}$ below the expected value zero. Solving the model (M-5.4), we can get the weighting vector ω associated with the UOWA operator.

Example 5.4 Given four samples, and each sample comprises of a collection of three arguments $(\tilde{a}_{k1}, \tilde{a}_{k2}, \tilde{a}_{k3})(k = 1,2,3)$, and a subjective preference value $\tilde{\vartheta}_k$ expressed as an interval number is given corresponding to each collection of arguments, listed in Table 5.6.

We first use the possibility degree formula to compare each pair of the kth sample of arguments and construct the possibility degree matrices $P^{(k)}(k = 1,2,3,4)$, and then derive the priority vectors $v^{(k)}(k = 1,2,3,4)$ using the priority formula for the possibility degree matrices:

$$P^{(1)} = \begin{pmatrix} 0.5 & 0.833 & 0 \\ 0.167 & 0.5 & 0 \\ 1 & 1 & 0.5 \end{pmatrix}, \quad P^{(2)} = \begin{pmatrix} 0.5 & 0 & 0.333 \\ 1 & 0.5 & 1 \\ 0.667 & 0 & 0.5 \end{pmatrix}$$

$$P^{(3)} = \begin{pmatrix} 0.5 & 0.6 & 0.143 \\ 0.4 & 0.5 & 0 \\ 0.857 & 1 & 0.5 \end{pmatrix}, \quad P^{(4)} = \begin{pmatrix} 0.5 & 1 & 1 \\ 0 & 0.5 & 0.667 \\ 0 & 0.333 & 0.5 \end{pmatrix}$$

$$v^{(1)} = (0.305, 0.195, 0.500), \quad v^{(2)} = (0.222, 0.5, 0.278)$$

$$v^{(3)} = (0.291, 0.233, 0.476), \quad v^{(4)} = (0.5, 0.278, 0.222)$$

based on which we rank the k th sample of arguments $\tilde{a}_{k1}, \tilde{a}_{k2}, \tilde{a}_{k3}$ in descending order, and get $\tilde{b}_{k1}, \tilde{b}_{k2}, \tilde{b}_{k3}$:

$$\tilde{b}_{11} = [0.7, 0.8],\ \tilde{b}_{12} = [0.4, 0.7],\ \tilde{b}_{13} = [0.2, 0.5]$$

$$\tilde{b}_{21} = [0.6, 0.8],\ \tilde{b}_{22} = [0.3, 0.5],\ \tilde{b}_{23} = [0.3, 0.4]$$

$$\tilde{b}_{31} = [0.5, 0.8],\ \tilde{b}_{32} = [0.2, 0.6],\ \tilde{b}_{33} = [0.3, 0.4]$$

$$\tilde{b}_{41} = [0.5, 0.8],\ \tilde{b}_{42} = [0.3, 0.5],\ \tilde{b}_{43} = [0.3, 0.4]$$

By using the model (M-5.4), we get the weighting vector $\omega = (0.3, 0.3, 0.4)$ associated with the UOWA operator. Then

$$UOWA_{\omega}(\tilde{a}_{11}, \tilde{a}_{12}, \tilde{a}_{13}) = 0.3 \times \tilde{b}_{11} + 0.3 \times \tilde{b}_{12} + 0.4 \times \tilde{b}_{13} = [0.41, 0.65]$$

$$UOWA_{\omega}(\tilde{a}_{21}, \tilde{a}_{22}, \tilde{a}_{23}) = 0.3 \times \tilde{b}_{21} + 0.3 \times \tilde{b}_{22} + 0.4 \times \tilde{b}_{23} = [0.39, 0.55]$$

$$UOWA_{\omega}(\tilde{a}_{31}, \tilde{a}_{32}, \tilde{a}_{33}) = 0.3 \times \tilde{b}_{31} + 0.3 \times \tilde{b}_{32} + 0.4 \times \tilde{b}_{33} = [0.32, 0.60]$$

$$UOWA_{\omega}(\tilde{a}_{41}, \tilde{a}_{42}, \tilde{a}_{43}) = 0.3 \times \tilde{b}_{41} + 0.3 \times \tilde{b}_{42} + 0.4 \times \tilde{b}_{43} = [0.36, 0.57]$$

5.4 MADM Method Based on UOWA Operator

5.4.1 MADM Method Without Preferences on Alternatives

Now we introduce a method for solving the MADM problems where the decision maker has no preference on alternatives. The method needs the following steps:

Step 1 For a MADM problem, the uncertain decision matrix and its corresponding normalized uncertain decision matrix are $\tilde{A} = (\tilde{a}_{ij})_{n \times m}$ and $\tilde{R} = (\tilde{r}_{ij})_{n \times m}$, respectively, where $\tilde{a}_{ij} = [a_{ij}^L, a_{ij}^U]$ and $\tilde{r}_{ij} = [r_{ij}^L, r_{ij}^U]$, $i = 1, 2, \ldots, n$, $j = 1, 2, \ldots, n$.

Step 2 Compare each pair of the attribute values $\tilde{r}_{ij}\,(i = 1, 2, \ldots, n, j = 1, 2, \ldots, n)$ by using Eq. (4.2), and construct the possibility degree matrix $P^{(i)}$, employ Eq. (4.6) to derive the priority vector $v^{(i)} = (v_1^{(i)}, v_2^{(i)}, \ldots, v_m^{(i)})$, then rank the attribute values $\tilde{r}_{ij}\,(j = 1, 2, \ldots, n)$ of the alternative x_i according to the weights $v_j^{(i)}\,(j = 1, 2, \ldots, m)$, and get the ordered arguments $\tilde{b}_{i1}, \tilde{b}_{i2}, \ldots, \tilde{b}_{im}$.

Step 3 Utilize the UOWA operator to aggregate the ordered attribute values of the alternative x_i, and get the overall attribute value:

$$\tilde{z}_i(\omega) = UOWA_\omega(\tilde{r}_{i1}, \tilde{r}_{i2}, \ldots, \tilde{r}_{im}) = \sum_{j=1}^{m} \omega_j \tilde{b}_{ij},\ i = 1, 2, \ldots, n$$

whose weighting vector $\omega = (\omega_1, \omega_2, \ldots, \omega_m)$ can be determined by using Eqs. (5.13) and (5.14) or the method introduced in Sect. 1.1.

Step 4 Calculate the possibility degrees $p_{ij} = p(\tilde{z}_i(\omega) \geq \tilde{z}_j(\omega))(i, j = 1, 2, \ldots, n)$ of comparing the overall attribute values of each alternative by using Eq. (4.2), and construct the possibility degree matrix $P = (p_{ij})_{n \times n}$.

Step 5 Drive the priority vector $v = (v_1, v_2, \ldots, v_n)$ from $P = (p_{ij})_{n \times n}$ by using Eq. (4.6), and rank and select the alternatives according to the elements of v.

5.4.2 *Practical Example*

Example 5.5 According to the local natural resources, a county invested several projects a few years ago. After several years of operation, it plans to reinvest a new project, which are chosen from the following five candidate alternatives [59]: (1) x_1: chestnut juice factory; (2) x_2: poultry processing plant; (3) x_3: flowers planting base; (4) x_4: brewery; and (5) x_5: tea factory. These alternatives are evaluated using four indices (attributes): (1) u_1: investment amount; (2) u_2: expected net profit amount; (3) u_3: venture profit amount; and (4) u_4: venture loss amount. All the decision information (attribute values (10^3\$)) are contained in the uncertain decision matrix $\tilde{A}$, shown in Table 5.7.

Among the attributes $u_j(j = 1, 2, 3, 4)$, u_2 and u_3 are benefit-type attributes, u_1 and u_4 are cost-type attributes, and the attribute weight information is unknown completely.

Now we utilize the method of Sect. 5.4.1 to solve the problem, which involves the following steps:

Step 1 Using Eqs. (4.9) and (4.10), we normalize the uncertain decision matrix $\tilde{A}$ into the matrix $\tilde{R}$, shown as Table 5.8.

Table 5.7 Uncertain decision matrix $\tilde{A}$

	u_1	u_2	u_3	u_4
x_1	[5, 7]	[4, 5]	[4, 6]	[0.4, 0.6]
x_2	[10, 11]	[6, 7]	[5, 6]	[1.5, 2]
x_3	[5, 6]	[4, 5]	[3, 4]	[0.4, 0.7]
x_4	[9, 11]	[5, 6]	[5, 7]	[1.3, 1.5]
x_5	[6, 8]	[3, 5]	[3, 4]	[0.8, 1]

Table 5.8 Uncertain normalized decision matrix $\tilde{B}$

	u_1	u_2	u_3	u_4
x_1	[0.40, 0.71]	[0.32, 0.50]	[0.32, 0.65]	[0.43, 0.98]
x_2	[0.25, 0.35]	[0.47, 0.69]	[0.40, 0.65]	[0.13, 0.26]
x_3	[0.46, 0.71]	[0.32, 0.50]	[0.24, 0.44]	[0.37, 0.98]
x_4	[0.25, 0.39]	[0.40, 0.59]	[0.40, 0.76]	[0.17, 0.30]
x_5	[0.35, 0.59]	[0.24, 0.50]	[0.24, 0.44]	[0.26, 0.49]

Step 2 Utilize Eq. (4.2) to compare each pair of the attribute values $\tilde{r}_{ij}\,(j=1,2,3,4)$ of the alternative x_i, and construct the possibility degree matrix $P^{(i)}\,(i=1,2,3,4,5)$:

$$P^{(1)}=\begin{pmatrix}0.50 & 0.76 & 0.61 & 0.33\\ 0.24 & 0.50 & 0.35 & 0.10\\ 0.39 & 0.65 & 0.50 & 0.25\\ 0.67 & 0.90 & 0.75 & 0.50\end{pmatrix},\quad P^{(2)}=\begin{pmatrix}0.5 & 0 & 0 & 0.96\\ 1 & 0.50 & 0.62 & 1\\ 1 & 0.38 & 0.50 & 1\\ 0.04 & 0 & 0 & 0.50\end{pmatrix}$$

$$P^{(2)}=\begin{pmatrix}0.50 & 0.91 & 1 & 0.40\\ 0.09 & 0.50 & 0.68 & 0.16\\ 0 & 0.32 & 0.50 & 0.09\\ 0.60 & 0.84 & 0.91 & 0.50\end{pmatrix},\quad P^{(4)}=\begin{pmatrix}0.50 & 0 & 0 & 0.81\\ 1 & 0.50 & 0.35 & 1\\ 1 & 0.65 & 0.50 & 1\\ 0.19 & 0 & 0 & 0.50\end{pmatrix}$$

$$P^{(5)}=\begin{pmatrix}0.50 & 0.70 & 0.80 & 0.70\\ 0.30 & 0.50 & 0.57 & 0.49\\ 0.20 & 0.43 & 0.50 & 0.42\\ 0.30 & 0.51 & 0.58 & 0.50\end{pmatrix}$$

Employ Eq. (4.6) to derive the priority vector $v^{(i)}=(v_1^{(i)},v_2^{(i)},v_3^{(i)},v_4^{(i)})\ (i=1,2,3,4,5)$ from the possibility degree matrix $P^{(i)}$:

$$v^{(1)}=(0.267,0.182,0.233,0.318),\ v^{(2)}=(0.205,0.343,0.323,0.128)$$

$$v^{(3)}=(0.318,0.202,0.159,0.321),\ v^{(4)}=(0.193,0.321,0.346,0.141)$$

$$v^{(5)}=(0.308,0.238,0.212,0.241)$$

Step 3 Rank the attribute values of the alternative x_i according to the elements of $v^{(i)}=(v_1^{(i)},v_2^{(i)},v_3^{(i)},v_4^{(i)})$ in descending order, and get $\tilde{b}_{i1},\tilde{b}_{i2},\tilde{b}_{i3},\tilde{b}_{i4}\,(i=1,2,3,4,5)$:

$$\tilde{b}_{11}=[0.43,0.98],\ \tilde{b}_{12}=[0.40,0.71],\ \tilde{b}_{13}=[0.32,0.65],\ \tilde{b}_{14}=[0.32,0.50]$$

$$\tilde{b}_{21}=[0.47,0.69],\ \tilde{b}_{22}=[0.40,0.65],\ \tilde{b}_{23}=[0.25,0.35],\ \tilde{b}_{24}=[0.13,0.26]$$

$$\tilde{b}_{31}=[0.37,0.98],\ \tilde{b}_{32}=[0.46,0.71],\ \tilde{b}_{33}=[0.32,0.50],\ \tilde{b}_{34}=[0.24,0.44]$$

$$\tilde{b}_{41}=[0.40,0.76],\ \tilde{b}_{42}=[0.40,0.59],\ \tilde{b}_{43}=[0.25,0.39],\ \tilde{b}_{44}=[0.17,0.30]$$

$$\tilde{b}_{51}=[0.35,0.596],\ \tilde{b}_{52}=[0.29,0.49],\ \tilde{b}_{53}=[0.24,0.50],\ \tilde{b}_{54}=[0.24,0.44]$$

Step 4 Determine the weighting vector by using the method (taking $\alpha=0.2$) in Theorem 1.10:

$$\omega=(0.4,0.2,0.2,0.2)$$

and use the UOWA operator to aggregate the attribute values of the alternatives $x_i(i=1,2,3,4,5)$, and get the overall attribute values $\tilde{z}_i(\omega)(i=1,2,3,4,5)$:

$$\tilde{z}_1(\omega)=UOWA_\omega(\tilde{r}_{11},\tilde{r}_{12},\tilde{r}_{13},\tilde{r}_{14})=\sum_{j=1}^{4}\omega_j\tilde{b}_{1j}=[0.380,0.764]$$

$$\tilde{z}_2(\omega)=UOWA_\omega(\tilde{r}_{21},\tilde{r}_{22},\tilde{r}_{23},\tilde{r}_{24})=\sum_{j=1}^{4}\omega_j\tilde{b}_{2j}=[0.344,0.528]$$

$$\tilde{z}_3(\omega)=UOWA_\omega(\tilde{r}_{31},\tilde{r}_{32},\tilde{r}_{33},\tilde{r}_{34})=\sum_{j=1}^{4}\omega_j\tilde{b}_{3j}=[0.352,0.722]$$

$$\tilde{z}_4(\omega)=UOWA_\omega(\tilde{r}_{41},\tilde{r}_{42},\tilde{r}_{43},\tilde{r}_{44})=\sum_{j=1}^{4}\omega_j\tilde{b}_{4j}=[0.324,0.560]$$

$$\tilde{z}_5(\omega)=UOWA_\omega(\tilde{r}_{51},\tilde{r}_{52},\tilde{r}_{53},\tilde{r}_{54})=\sum_{j=1}^{4}\omega_j\tilde{b}_{5j}=[0.288,0.522]$$

Step 5 Utilize Eq. (4.2) to compare each pair of $\tilde{z}_i(\omega)(i=1,2,3,4,5)$, and construct the possibility degree matrix:

$$P=\begin{pmatrix} 0.5 & 0.739 & 0.546 & 0.710 & 0.770 \\ 0.261 & 0.5 & 0.318 & 0.486 & 0.574 \\ 0.454 & 0.680 & 0.5 & 0.657 & 0.719 \\ 0.290 & 0.514 & 0.343 & 0.5 & 0.579 \\ 0.230 & 0.426 & 0.281 & 0.421 & 0.5 \end{pmatrix}$$

Step 6 Derive the priority vector of P by using Eq. (4.6):

$$v = (0.238, 0.182, 0.226, 0.186, 0.168)$$

Based on the priority vector v and the possibility degree matrix P, we get the ranking of the interval numbers $\tilde{z}_i(\omega)(i = 1,2,3,4,5)$:

$$\tilde{z}_1(\omega) \underset{0.546}{\geq} \tilde{z}_3(\omega) \underset{0.657}{\geq} \tilde{z}_4(\omega) \underset{0.514}{\geq} \tilde{z}_2(\omega) \underset{0.574}{\geq} \tilde{z}_5(\omega)$$

Step 7 Rank the alternatives $x_i(i = 1,2,3,4,5)$ according to $\tilde{z}_i(\omega)(i = 1,2,3,4,5)$ in descending order:

$$x_1 \underset{0.546}{\succ} x_3 \underset{0.657}{\succ} x_4 \underset{0.514}{\succ} x_2 \underset{0.574}{\succ} x_5$$

from which we get the best alternative x_1.

5.4.3 MADM Method with Preference Information on Alternatives

In what follows, we introduce a method for MADM in which the decision maker has preferences on alternatives:

Step 1 For a MADM problem, the uncertain decision matrix and its normalized uncertain decision matrix are $\tilde{A} = (\tilde{a}_{ij})_{n\times m}$ and $\tilde{R} = (\tilde{r}_{ij})_{n\times m}$, respectively. Suppose that the decision maker has preferences over the considered alternatives $x_i(i = 1,2,\ldots,n)$, and the preference values take the form of interval numbers $\tilde{\vartheta}_i = [\tilde{\vartheta}_i^L, \tilde{\vartheta}_i^U]$, where $0 \leq \tilde{\vartheta}_i^L \leq \tilde{\vartheta}_i^U \leq 1,\ i = 1,2,\ldots,n$.

Step 2 Use Eq. (4.2) to compare each pair of the attribute values $\tilde{r}_{ij}(j = 1,2,\ldots,n)$ of the alternative x_i and construct the possibility degree matrix $P^{(i)}$. Then we use Eq. (4.6) to derive the priority vector $v^{(i)} = (v_1^{(i)}, v_2^{(i)}, v_3^{(i)}, v_4^{(i)})$ of $P^{(i)}$ and rank the attribute values of the alternative x_i according to the elements of $v^{(i)}$ in descending order, and thus get $\tilde{b}_{i1}, \tilde{b}_{i2},\ldots,\tilde{b}_{im}$.

Step 3 Use the UOWA operator to aggregate the ordered attribute values of the alternative x_i, and obtain the overall attribute value $\tilde{z}_i(\omega)$:

$$\tilde{z}_i(\omega) = UOWA_\omega(\tilde{r}_{i1}, \tilde{r}_{i2},\ldots,\tilde{r}_{im}) = \sum_{j=1}^{n} \omega_j \tilde{b}_{ij},\quad i = 1,2,\ldots,n$$

where the weighting vector $\omega = (\omega_1, \omega_2, \ldots, \omega_n)$ can be determined by the model (M-5.4).

Step 4 Employ Eq. (4.2) to calculate the possibility degrees $p_{ij} = p(\tilde{z}_i(\omega) \geq \tilde{z}_j(\omega))$ $(i, j = 1, 2, \ldots, n)$, and construct the possibility degree matrix $P = (p_{ij})_{n \times n}$.

Step 5 Utilize Eq. (4.6) to derive the priority vector $v = (v_1, v_2, \ldots, v_n)$ of $P = (p_{ij})_{n \times n}$ and rank the alternatives $x_i (i = 1, 2, \ldots, n)$ according to the elements of v in descending order, and then get the optimal alternative.

5.4.4 Practical Example

Example 5.6 Now we illustrate the method of Sect. 5.4.3 with Example 5.2:

Step 1 See Step 1 of Sect. 5.2.2.

Step 2 Compare each pair of the attributes $\tilde{r}_{ij} (j = 1, 2, \ldots, 6)$ of each alternative x_i by using Eq. (4.2), and construct the possibility degree matrix $P^{(i)}$:

$$P^{(1)} = \begin{pmatrix} 0.5 & 0.208 & 0.121 & 0 & 0.224 & 0 \\ 0.792 & 0.5 & 0.356 & 0.156 & 0.556 & 0.023 \\ 0.879 & 0.644 & 0.5 & 0.320 & 0.707 & 0.204 \\ 1 & 0.844 & 0.680 & 0.5 & 0.927 & 0.388 \\ 0.776 & 0.444 & 0.293 & 0.073 & 0.5 & 0 \\ 1 & 0.977 & 0.796 & 0.612 & 1 & 0.5 \end{pmatrix}$$

$$P^{(2)} = \begin{pmatrix} 0.5 & 0.714 & 0.625 & 0.625 & 0.290 & 0.583 \\ 0.286 & 0.5 & 0.381 & 0.381 & 0 & 0.348 \\ 0.375 & 0.619 & 0.5 & 0.5 & 0.083 & 0.457 \\ 0.375 & 0.619 & 0.5 & 0.5 & 0.083 & 0.457 \\ 0.710 & 1 & 0.917 & 0.917 & 0.5 & 0.846 \\ 0.417 & 0.652 & 0.543 & 0.543 & 0.154 & 0.5 \end{pmatrix}$$

$$P^{(3)} = \begin{pmatrix} 0.5 & 0.977 & 0.240 & 0.240 & 0.694 & 0.293 \\ 0.023 & 0.5 & 0 & 0 & 0.233 & 0 \\ 0.760 & 1 & 0.5 & 0.5 & 0.959 & 0.610 \\ 0.760 & 1 & 0.5 & 0.5 & 0.959 & 0.610 \\ 0.306 & 0.767 & 0.041 & 0.041 & 0.5 & 0.050 \\ 0.707 & 1 & 0.390 & 0.390 & 0.950 & 0.5 \end{pmatrix}$$

$$P^{(4)}=\begin{pmatrix} 0.5 & 0 & 0.444 & 0.341 & 0.227 & 0 \\ 1 & 0.5 & 1 & 0.977 & 0.864 & 0.444 \\ 0.556 & 0 & 0.5 & 0.408 & 0.306 & 0 \\ 0.659 & 0.023 & 0.592 & 0.5 & 0.396 & 0 \\ 0.773 & 0.136 & 0.694 & 0.604 & 0.5 & 0.050 \\ 1 & 0.556 & 1 & 1 & 0.950 & 0.5 \end{pmatrix}$$

$$P^{(5)}=\begin{pmatrix} 0.5 & 0.211 & 0.211 & 0.079 & 0.211 & 0.811 \\ 0.789 & 0.5 & 0.5 & 0.292 & 0.5 & 1 \\ 0.789 & 0.5 & 0.5 & 0.292 & 0.5 & 1 \\ 0.921 & 0.708 & 0.708 & 0.5 & 0.708 & 1 \\ 0.789 & 0.5 & 0.5 & 0.292 & 0.5 & 1 \\ 0.189 & 0 & 0 & 0 & 0 & 0.5 \end{pmatrix}$$

Step 3 Utilize Eq. (4.6) to derive the priority vector $v^{(i)}=(v_1^{(i)},v_2^{(i)},v_3^{(i)},v_4^{(i)})$ $(i=1,2,3,4,5)$ from the possibility degree matrix $P^{(i)}$:

$$v^{(1)}=(0.128,0.194,0.238,0.292,0.179,0.319)$$

$$v^{(2)}=(0.242,0.170,0.202,0.202,0.320,0.215)$$

$$v^{(3)}=(0.222,0.113,0.291,0.291,0.160,0.272)$$

$$v^{(4)}=(0.151,0.314,0.164,0.183,0.213,0.325)$$

$$v^{(5)}=(0.176,0.254,0.254,0.302,0.254,0.109)$$

and then rank all the attribute values of the alternative x_i according to the elements of $v^{(i)}$ in descending order, and thus get $\tilde{b}_{i1},\tilde{b}_{i2},\ldots,\tilde{b}_{i6}(i=1,2,3,4,5)$:

$$\tilde{b}_{11}=[0.415,0.437],\ \tilde{b}_{12}=[0.407,0.432],\ \tilde{b}_{13}=[0.398,0.423]$$

$$\tilde{b}_{14}=[0.394,0.414],\ \tilde{b}_{15}=[0.394,0.410],\ \tilde{b}_{16}=[0.372,0.405]$$

$$\tilde{b}_{21}=[0.411,0.438],\ \tilde{b}_{22}=[0.394,0.429],\ \tilde{b}_{23}=[0.394,0.419]$$

$$\tilde{b}_{24}=\tilde{b}_{25}=[0.394,0.415],\ \tilde{b}_{26}=[0.389,0.410]$$

$$\tilde{b}_{31} = \tilde{b}_{32} = [0.408, 0.433],\ \tilde{b}_{33} = [0.408, 0.424]$$

$$\tilde{b}_{34} = [0.395, 0.420],\ \tilde{b}_{35} = [0.386, 0.410],\ \tilde{b}_{36} = [0.377, 0.396]$$

$$\tilde{b}_{41} = [0.417, 0.433],\ \tilde{b}_{42} = [0.413, 0.433],\ \tilde{b}_{43} = [0.395, 0.419]$$

$$\tilde{b}_{44} = [0.390, 0.414],\ \tilde{b}_{45} = [0.385, 0.410],\ \tilde{b}_{46} = [0.385, 0.405]$$

$$\tilde{b}_{51} = [0.407, 0.419],\ \tilde{b}_{52} = \tilde{b}_{53} = \tilde{b}_{54} = [0.402, 0.414]$$

$$\tilde{b}_{55} = [0.384, 0.410],\ \tilde{b}_{56} = [0.380, 0.391]$$

Step 4 If the known partial weighting information associated with the UOWA operator is

$$\Phi' = \Big\{ \omega = (\omega_1, \omega_2, \ldots, \omega_6) \ \Big|\ 0.1 \le \omega_1 \le 0.2,\ 0.5 \le \omega_2 \le 0.3,\ 0.15 \le \omega_3 \le 0.2,$$
$$0.2 \le \omega_4 \le 0.25,\ 0.1 \le \omega_5 \le 0.3,\ 0.2 \le \omega_6 \le 0.4,\ \sum_{j=1}^{6} \omega_j = 1 \Big\}$$

and the decision maker has preferences over the five candidates $x_i (i = 1, 2, 3, 4, 5)$, which are expressed in interval numbers:

$$\tilde{\vartheta}_1 = [0.3, 0.5],\ \tilde{\vartheta}_2 = [0.5, 0.6],\ \tilde{\vartheta}_3 = [0.3, 0.4],\ \tilde{\vartheta}_4 = [0.4, 0.6],\ \tilde{\vartheta}_5 = [0.4, 0.5]$$

Then we utilize the model (M-5.4) to derive the weighting vector associated with the UOWA operator:

$$\omega = (0.2, 0.15, 0.15, 0.2, 0.1, 0.2)$$

Step 5 Aggregate the attribute values of the alternative x_i using the UOWA operator and get

$$\tilde{z}_1(\omega) = UOWA_\omega(\tilde{r}_{11}, \tilde{r}_{12}, \tilde{r}_{13}, \tilde{r}_{14}, \tilde{r}_{15}, \tilde{r}_{16}) = \sum_{j=1}^{6} \omega_j \tilde{b}_{1j} = [0.3964, 0.4205]$$

$$\tilde{z}_2(\omega) = UOWA_\omega(\tilde{r}_{21}, \tilde{r}_{22}, \tilde{r}_{23}, \tilde{r}_{24}, \tilde{r}_{25}, \tilde{r}_{26}) = \sum_{j=1}^{6} \omega_j \tilde{b}_{2j} = [0.3964, 0.4213]$$

$$\tilde{z}_3(\omega) = UOWA_\omega(\tilde{r}_{31}, \tilde{r}_{32}, \tilde{r}_{33}, \tilde{r}_{34}, \tilde{r}_{35}, \tilde{r}_{36}) = \sum_{j=1}^{6} \omega_j \tilde{b}_{3j} = [0.3970, 0.4194]$$

$$\tilde{z}_4(\omega) = UOWA_\omega(\tilde{r}_{41}, \tilde{r}_{42}, \tilde{r}_{43}, \tilde{r}_{44}, \tilde{r}_{45}, \tilde{r}_{46}) = \sum_{j=1}^{6} \omega_j \tilde{b}_{4j} = [0.3981, 0.4192]$$

$$\tilde{z}_5(\omega) = UOWA_\omega(\tilde{r}_{51}, \tilde{r}_{52}, \tilde{r}_{53}, \tilde{r}_{54}, \tilde{r}_{55}, \tilde{r}_{56}) = \sum_{j=1}^{6} \omega_j \tilde{b}_{5j} = [0.3968, 0.4100]$$

Step 6 Utilize Eq. (4.2) to compare each pair of $\tilde{z}_j(\omega)(j = 1, 2, 3, 4, 5)$, and then construct the possibility degree matrix:

$$P = \begin{pmatrix} 0.5 & 0.4918 & 0.5054 & 0.4956 & 0.6354 \\ 0.5082 & 0.5 & 0.5137 & 0.5043 & 0.6430 \\ 0.4946 & 0.4863 & 0.5 & 0.4897 & 0.6348 \\ 0.5044 & 0.4957 & 0.5103 & 0.5 & 0.6531 \\ 0.3646 & 0.3570 & 0.3652 & 0.3469 & 0.5 \end{pmatrix}$$

Step 7 Derive the priority vector of P using Eq. (4.6):

$$v = (0.2064, 0.2085, 02.53, 0.2082, 0.1717)$$

based on which and the possibility degrees in P, we get the ranking the interval numbers $\tilde{z}_i(\omega)(i = 1, 2, 3, 4, 5)$:

$$\tilde{z}_2(\omega) \underset{0.5043}{\geq} \tilde{z}_4(\omega) \underset{0.5044}{\geq} \tilde{z}_1(\omega) \underset{0.5054}{\geq} \tilde{z}_3(\omega) \underset{0.6348}{\geq} \tilde{z}_5(\omega)$$

Step 8 Rank the five candidates $x_i(i = 1, 2, 3, 4, 5)$ according to $\tilde{z}_i(w)(i = 1, 2, 3, 4, 5)$:

$$x_2 \underset{0.5043}{\succ} x_4 \underset{0.5044}{\succ} x_1 \underset{0.5054}{\succ} x_3 \underset{0.6348}{\succ} x_5$$

and thus, x_2 is the best candidate.

5.5 Consensus Maximization Model for Determining Attribute Weights in Uncertain MAGDM [135]

5.5.1 Consensus Maximization Model under Uncertainty

In an uncertain MAGDM problem, the decision makers $d_k(k = 1, 2, \ldots, t)$ evaluate all the alternatives $x_i(i = 1, 2, \ldots, n)$ with respect to the attributes $u_j(j = 1, 2, \ldots, m)$, and construct the uncertain decision matrices $\tilde{A}_k = (\tilde{a}_{ij}^{(k)})_{n\times m}$ $k = 1, 2, ..., t$, where $\tilde{a}_{ij}^{(k)} = [a_{ij}^{L(k)}, a_{ij}^{U(k)}]$ $(i = 1, 2, \ldots, n, j = 1, 2, \ldots, m, k = 1, 2, \ldots, t)$ are interval numbers.

In order to measure all attributes in dimensionless units, we employ the following formulas to transform the uncertain decision matrix $\tilde{A}_k = (\tilde{a}_{ij}^{(k)})_{n\times m}$ into the normalized uncertain decision matrix $\tilde{R}_k = (\tilde{r}_{ij}^{(k)})_{n\times m}$:

$$\tilde{r}_{ij}^{(k)} = [r_{ij}^{L(k)}, r_{ij}^{U(k)}] = \frac{\tilde{a}_{ij}^{(k)}}{\max_i \{a_{ij}^{U(k)}\}} = \left[\frac{a_{ij}^{L(k)}}{\max_i \{a_{ij}^{U(k)}\}}, \frac{a_{ij}^{U(k)}}{\max_i \{a_{ij}^{U(k)}\}}\right], \quad \text{for benefit-type attribute } u_j \tag{5.18}$$

$$\tilde{r}_{ij}^{(k)} = [r_{ij}^{L(k)}, r_{ij}^{U(k)}] = \frac{\min_i \{a_{ij}^{L(k)}\}}{\tilde{a}_{ij}^{(k)}} = \left[\frac{\min_i \{a_{ij}^{L(k)}\}}{a_{ij}^{U(k)}}, \frac{\min_i \{a_{ij}^{L(k)}\}}{a_{ij}^{L(k)}}\right], \quad \text{for cost-type attribute } u_j \tag{5.19}$$

Based on all the individual normalized uncertain decision matrices $\tilde{R}_k = (\tilde{r}_{ij}^{(k)})_{n\times m} (k = 1, 2, \ldots, t)$ and the operational laws of interval numbers, we get the collective normalized uncertain decision matrix $\tilde{R} = (\tilde{r}_{ij})_{n\times m}$ by using the UWA operator (4.15).

Now we discuss the relationship between each individual opinion and the group opinion. If $R_k = R$, for all $k = 1, 2, \ldots, t$, then the group is of complete consensus, i.e.,

$$\tilde{r}_{ij}^{(k)} = \sum_{k=1}^{t} \lambda_k \tilde{r}_{ij}^{(k)}, \text{ for all } k = 1, 2, \ldots, t, \quad i = 1, 2, \ldots, n, j = 1, 2, \ldots, m \tag{5.20}$$

whose weighted form is:

$$w_j \tilde{r}_{ij}^{(k)} = \sum_{k=1}^{t} \lambda_k w_j \tilde{r}_{ij}^{(k)}, \text{ for all } k = 1, 2, \ldots, t, \quad i = 1, 2, \ldots, m, j = 1, 2, \ldots, n \tag{5.21}$$

which can be concretely expressed as:

$$w_j r_{ij}^{L(k)} = \sum_{k=1}^{t} \lambda_k w_j r_{ij}^{L(k)}, \quad w_j r_{ij}^{U(k)} = \sum_{k=1}^{t} \lambda_k w_j r_{ij}^{U(k)}, \quad \text{for all } k = 1, 2, \ldots, t, \ i = 1, 2, \ldots, m, j = 1, 2, \ldots, n \tag{5.22}$$

Equation (5.22) is a very strict condition, and in practical circumstances this is not satisfied in the general case. As a result, here we introduce a deviation variable:

$$\tilde{e}_{ij}^{(k)} = \left(w_j r_{ij}^{L(k)} - \sum_{k=1}^{t} \lambda_k w_j r_{ij}^{L(k)} \right)^2 + \left(w_j r_{ij}^{U(k)} - \sum_{k=1}^{t} \lambda_k w_j r_{ij}^{U(k)} \right)^2$$

$$= \left(\left(r_{ij}^{L(k)} - \sum_{k=1}^{t} \lambda_k r_{ij}^{L(k)} \right)^2 + \left(r_{ij}^{U(k)} - \sum_{k=1}^{t} \lambda_k r_{ij}^{U(k)} \right)^2 \right) w_j^2 \tag{5.23}$$

for all $k = 1, 2, \ldots, t, \quad i = 1, 2, \ldots, m, \quad j = 1, 2, \ldots, n$

and construct the deviation function:

$$\tilde{f}(w) = \sum_{k=1}^{t} \sum_{i=1}^{n} \sum_{j=1}^{m} \tilde{e}_{ij}^{(k)}$$

$$= \sum_{k=1}^{t} \sum_{i=1}^{n} \sum_{j=1}^{m} \left(\left(r_{ij}^{L(k)} - \sum_{k=1}^{t} \lambda_k r_{ij}^{L(k)} \right)^2 + \left(r_{ij}^{U(k)} - \sum_{k=1}^{t} \lambda_k r_{ij}^{U(k)} \right)^2 \right) w_j^2 \tag{5.24}$$

To maximize the group consensus, on the basis of Eq. (5.24), we establish the following quadratic programming model [135]:

$$(\mathbf{M\text{-}5.5}) \quad \tilde{f}(w^*) = \min \sum_{k=1}^{t} \sum_{i=1}^{n} \sum_{j=1}^{m}$$

$$\left(\left(r_{ij}^{L(k)} - \sum_{k=1}^{t} \lambda_k r_{ij}^{L(k)} \right)^2 + \left(r_{ij}^{U(k)} - \sum_{k=1}^{t} \lambda_k r_{ij}^{U(k)} \right)^2 \right) w_j^2$$

$$s.t. \quad w_j \geq 0, \ j = 1, 2, \ldots, m, \ \sum_{j=1}^{m} w_j = 1$$

The solution to this model can be exactly expressed as:

$$w_j^* = \frac{\dfrac{1}{\sum_{j=1}^{m} \dfrac{1}{\sum_{k=1}^{t} \sum_{i=1}^{n} \left(\left(r_{ij}^{L(k)} - \sum_{k=1}^{t} \lambda_k r_{ij}^{L(k)} \right)^2 + \left(r_{ij}^{U(k)} - \sum_{k=1}^{t} \lambda_k r_{ij}^{U(k)} \right)^2 \right)}}}{\sum_{k=1}^{t} \sum_{i=1}^{n} \left(\left(r_{ij}^{L(k)} - \sum_{k=1}^{t} \lambda_k r_{ij}^{L(k)} \right)^2 + \left(r_{ij}^{U(k)} - \sum_{k=1}^{t} \lambda_k r_{ij}^{U(k)} \right)^2 \right)}, \ j = 1, 2, \ldots, m \tag{5.25}$$

Especially, if the denominator of Eq. (5.25) is zero, then Eq. (5.20) holds, i.e., the group is of complete consensus. In this case, we stipulate that all the attributes are assigned equal weights.

If the decision makers can provide some information about attribute weights described in Sect. 3.1, then, we generalize the model (M-5.5) to the following form [135]:

$$\textbf{(M-5.6)}\quad \bar{\bar{f}}(w^*) = \min \sum_{k=1}^{t}\sum_{i=1}^{n}\sum_{j=1}^{m}\left(\left|r_{ij}^{L(k)} - \sum_{k=1}^{t}\lambda_k r_{ij}^{L(k)}\right|^{\rho} + \left|r_{ij}^{U(k)} - \sum_{k=1}^{t}\lambda_k r_{ij}^{U(k)}\right|^{\rho}\right) w_j^{\rho} \ (\rho > 0)$$

$$s.t.\quad w = (w_1, w_2, \ldots, w_m)^T \in \Phi$$

$$w_j \geq 0,\ j = 1,2,\ldots,m,\ \sum_{j=1}^{m} w_j = 1$$

By using the mathematical software MATLAB 7.4.0, we can solve the model (M-5.6) so as to derive the optimal weight vector $w^* = (w_1^*, w_2^*, \ldots, w_m^*)$ with respect to the parameter ρ.

Based on the collective uncertain decision matrix $\tilde{R} = (\tilde{r}_{ij})_{n\times m}$ and the optimal attribute weights $w_j^*(j = 1,2,\ldots,m)$, we get the overall attribute value $\tilde{z}_i(w^*)$ of the alternative x_i by the UWA operator (4.15).

Considering that $\tilde{z}_i(w^*)(i = 1,2,\ldots,n)$ are a collection of interval numbers, in order to get their ranking, we compare each pair of $\tilde{z}_i(w^*)(i = 1,2,\ldots,n)$ by using a possibility degree formula (4.2), and construct a fuzzy preference relation $P = (p_{ij})_{n\times n}$, where $p_{ij} = p(\tilde{z}_i(w^*) \geq \tilde{z}_j(w^*))$, $p_{ij} \geq 0$, $p_{ij} + p_{ji} = 1$, $p_{ii} = 0.5$, $i, j = 1,2,\ldots,n$.

Summing all elements in each line of P, we get [145]:

$$p_i = \sum_{j=1}^{n} p_{ij},\ i = 1,2,\ldots,n \tag{5.26}$$

and rank all the alternatives $x_i(i = 1,2,\ldots,n)$ according to $p_i(i = 1,2,\ldots,n)$, and then select the best one. We can also use the formula (4.6) to extract the priority weights $v_i(i = 1,2,\ldots,n)$ from the fuzzy preference relation P, where $v_i \geq 0$, $j = 1,2,\ldots,n$, and $\sum_{j=1}^{n} v_j = 1$. Additionally, using the OWA operator (1.1) and the concept of fuzzy majority, Chiclana et al. [12] applied two choice degrees (i.e., the quantifier-guided dominance degree and the quantifier-guided non-dominance degree) of alternatives over the fuzzy preference relation P, so as to quantify the dominance that one alternative has over all the others in a fuzzy majority sense.

Obviously, the ranking orders derived by Eqs. (4.6) and (5.26) for the alternatives $x_i(i = 1,2,\ldots,n)$ are always the same. However, the former is simpler and more straightforward, the latter can not only rank the alternatives but also determine their importance weights, while the quantifier-guided choice degrees given by Chiclana et al. [12] can consider the ordered positions of the arguments, and utilize the majority (but not all) of the arguments to derive the ranking order of the alternatives, which may lead to the loss of decision information in the process of information aggregation. With the above analysis, we can see that Eq. (5.26) may be the most convenient tool for ranking the alternatives, which will be used in the following numerical example.

5.5.2 Practical Example

Example 5.7 [135] Take the example in Sect. 1.8.2, we consider the cases where the experts provide their preferences by means of interval numbers, we can employ the optimization models developed in Sect. 5.5.1 to derive the attribute weights, and then select the most desirable alternative. Assume that the experts evaluate the alternatives $x_i (i = 1,2,3,4)$ with respect to the attributes $u_j (j = 1,2,3,4,5)$, and construct three uncertain decision matrices (see Tables 5.9, 5.10, and 5.11).

Then we utilize Eqs. (5.18) and (5.19) to transform the uncertain decision matrices $\tilde{A}_k = (\tilde{a}_{ij}^{(k)})_{4\times5} (k = 1,2,3))$ into the normalized uncertain decision matrices $\tilde{R}_k = (\tilde{r}_{ij}^{(k)})_{4\times5} (k = 1,2,3)$ (see Tables 5.12, 5.13, and 5.14).

Table 5.9 Uncertain decision matrix $\tilde{A}_1$

	u_1	u_2	u_3	u_4	u_5
x_1	[26,000, 26,500]	[2, 3]	[19,000, 20,000]	[0.7, 0.8]	[14,000, 15,000]
x_2	[65,000, 70,000]	[3, 4]	[15,000, 16,000]	[0.2, 0.3]	[26,000, 28,000]
x_3	[50,000, 55,000]	[2, 4]	[16,000, 17,000]	[0.7, 0.9]	[24,000, 25,000]
x_4	[40,000, 45,000]	[1, 2]	[26,000, 28,000]	[0.5, 0.6]	[14,000, 16,000]

Table 5.10 Uncertain decision matrix $\tilde{A}_2$

	u_1	u_2	u_3	u_4	u_5
x_1	[27,000, 28,000]	[4, 5]	[18,000, 20,000]	[0.7, 0.9]	[16,000, 17,000]
x_2	[60,000, 70,000]	[2, 4]	[16,000, 18,000]	[0.3, 0.5]	[26,000, 27,000]
x_3	[55,000, 60,000]	[1, 3]	[14,000, 16,000]	[0.7, 1.0]	[24,000, 26,000]
x_4	[40,000, 45,000]	[2, 3]	[28,000, 30,000]	[0.4, 0.5]	[15,000, 17,000]

Table 5.11 Uncertain decision matrix $\tilde{A}_3$

	u_1	u_2	u_3	u_4	u_5
x_1	[27,000, 29,000]	[3, 4]	[20,000, 22,000]	[0.6, 0.8]	[17,000, 18,000]
x_2	[60,000, 80,000]	[4, 5]	[17,000, 18,000]	[0.4, 0.5]	[26,000, 26,500]
x_3	[40,000, 60,000]	[2, 5]	[15,000, 17,000]	[0.8, 0.9]	[26,000, 27,000]
x_4	[50,000, 55,000]	[2, 3]	[29,000, 30,000]	[0.4, 0.7]	[17,000, 19,000]

Table 5.12 Normalized uncertain decision matrix $\tilde{R}_1$

	u_1	u_2	u_3	u_4	u_5
x_1	[0.37, 0.38]	[0.50, 0.75]	[0.68, 0.71]	[0.78, 0.89]	[0.93, 1.00]
x_2	[0.93, 1.00]	[0.75, 1.00]	[0.54, 0.57]	[0.22, 0.33]	[0.50, 0.54]
x_3	[0.71, 0.79]	[0.50, 1.00]	[0.57, 0.61]	[0.78, 1.00]	[0.56, 0.58]
x_4	[0.57, 0.64]	[0.25, 0.50]	[0.93, 1.00]	[0.56, 0.67]	[0.88, 1.00]

Table 5.13 Normalized uncertain decision matrix $\tilde{R}_2$

	u_1	u_2	u_3	u_4	u_5
x_1	[0.39, 0.40]	[0.80, 1.00]	[0.60, 0.67]	[0.70, 0.90]	[0.88, 0.94]
x_2	[0.86, 1.00]	[0.40, 0.80]	[0.53, 0.60]	[0.30, 0.50]	[0.56, 0.58]
x_3	[0.79, 0.86]	[0.20, 0.60]	[0.47, 0.53]	[0.70, 1.00]	[0.58, 0.63]
x_4	[0.57, 0.64]	[0.40, 0.60]	[0.93, 1.00]	[0.40, 0.50]	[0.88, 1.00]

Table 5.14 Normalized uncertain decision matrix $\tilde{R}_3$

	u_1	u_2	u_3	u_4	u_5
x_1	[0.34, 0.36]	[0.60, 0.80]	[0.67, 0.73]	[0.60, 0.80]	[0.94, 1.00]
x_2	[0.75, 1.00]	[0.80, 1.00]	[0.57, 0.60]	[0.40, 0.50]	[0.64, 0.65]
x_3	[0.50, 0.75]	[0.40, 1.00]	[0.50, 0.57]	[0.80, 0.90]	[0.63, 0.65]
x_4	[0.63, 0.69]	[0.40, 0.60]	[0.97, 1.00]	[0.40, 0.70]	[0.90, 1.00]

By Eq. (4.15) and the weight vector $\lambda = (0.4, 0.3, 0.3)$ of the experts $d_k (k = 1, 2, 3)$, we aggregate all the individual normalized uncertain decision matrices $\tilde{R}_k = (\tilde{r}_{ij}^{(k)})_{4\times5}$ into the collective normalized uncertain decision matrix $\tilde{R} = (\tilde{r}_{ij})_{4\times5}$ (see Table 5.15).

Table 5.15 Collective normalized uncertain decision matrix $\tilde{R}$

	u_1	u_2	u_3	u_4	u_5
x_1	[0.37, 0.38]	[0.62, 0.84]	[0.65, 0.70]	[0.70, 0.87]	[0.92, 0.98]
x_2	[0.86, 1.00]	[0.66, 0.94]	[0.55, 0.59]	[0.30, 0.43]	[0.56, 0.59]
x_3	[0.67, 0.80]	[0.38, 0.88]	[0.52, 0.57]	[0.76, 0.97]	[0.59, 0.62]
x_4	[0.59, 0.66]	[0.34, 0.56]	[0.94, 1.00]	[0.46, 0.63]	[0.89, 1.00]

Based on the decision information contained in Tables 5.12, 5.13, 5.14, and 5.15, we employ Eq. (5.25) to determine the optimal weight vector w^*, and get

$$w^* = (0.11, 0.02, 0.49, 0.08, 0.30) \tag{5.27}$$

and the corresponding optimal objective value $\tilde{f}(w^*) = 0.008$.

Based on Eqs. (4.15) and (5.27) and the collective normalized uncertain decision matrix $\tilde{R} = (\tilde{r}_{ij})_{4\times 5}$, we get the overall uncertain attribute values $\tilde{z}_i(w^*)(i = 1,2,3,4)$:

$$\tilde{z}_1(w^*) = [0.70, 0.77], \tilde{z}_2(w^*) = [0.57, 0.63]$$

$$\tilde{z}_3(w^*) = [0.57, 0.65], \tilde{z}_4(w^*) = [0.84, 0.92]$$

Comparing each pair of $\tilde{z}_i(w)(i = 1,2,3,4)$ by using Eq. (4.2), we can construct a fuzzy preference relation:

$$P = \begin{pmatrix} 0.5 & 1 & 1 & 0 \\ 0 & 0.5 & 0.4286 & 0 \\ 0 & 0.5714 & 0.5 & 0 \\ 1 & 1 & 1 & 0.5 \end{pmatrix}$$

Summing all elements in each line of P, we get

$$p_1 = 2.5,\ p_2 = 0.9286,\ p_3 = 1.0714,\ p_4 = 3.5$$

and by which we rank all the alternatives: $x_4 \succ x_1 \succ x_3 \succ x_2$, and thus the best one is x_4.

Chapter 6
Interval MADM with Partial Weight Information

Some scholars have investigated the interval MADM with partial weight information. For example, Fan and Hu [27] gave a goal programming model for determining the attribute weights, but did not give the approach to ranking alternatives. Yoon [163] put forward some linear programming models that deal with each alternative separately. Based on the linear programming model in Yoon [163], Xu [102] proposed a ranking method for alternatives. However, the intervals that the overall attribute values derived from this model lie in generally do not use the same weight vector of attributes, which makes the evaluations over the alternatives not to be comparable. Fan and Zhang [28] presented an improved model of Yoon [163], but this model still needs to derive the different weight vectors under normal circumstances, and cannot guarantee the existence of intervals that the overall evaluation values belong to. To overcome these drawbacks, Da and Xu [19] established a single-objective optimization model and based on which they developed a MADM method. Motivated by the idea of the deviation degrees and maximizing the deviations of the attribute values of alternatives, Xu [104] proposed a maximizing deviation method for ranking alternatives in the decision making problems where the decision maker has no preferences on alternatives. Xu and Gu [151] developed a minimizing deviation method for the MADM problems where the decision maker has preferences on alternatives. Based on the projection model, Xu [124] put forward a method for MADM with preference information on alternatives. We also illustrate these methods in detail with the practical examples.

6.1 MADM Based on Single-Objective Optimization Model

6.1.1 Model

Consider a MADM problem in which all the attribute weights and the attribute values are interval numbers. Let the uncertain decision matrix and its normalized

Z.S. Xu, *Uncertain Multi-Attribute Decision Making*,
DOI 10.1007/978-3-662-45640-8_6

uncertain decision matrix be $\tilde{A}=(\tilde{a}_{ij})_{n\times m}$ and $\tilde{R}=(\tilde{r}_{ij})_{n\times m}$, respectively, where $\tilde{a}_{ij}=[a_{ij}^L,a_{ij}^U]$ and $\tilde{b}_{ij}=[b_{ij}^L,b_{ij}^U]$, $i=1,2,\ldots,n$, $j=1,2,\ldots,m$, and Φ is the set of possible weights determined by the known partial weight information.

To obtain the overall attribute value of each alternative, Yoon [163] established two linear programming models:

$$(\textbf{M-6.1})\quad \begin{cases} \min z_i^{'}(w)=\sum_{j=1}^{m} r_{ij}^L w_j, \quad i=1,2,\ldots,n \\ s.t. \quad w\in\Phi \end{cases}$$

$$(\textbf{M-6.2})\quad \begin{cases} \min z_i^{'}(w)=\sum_{j=1}^{m} r_{ij}^U w_j, \quad i=1,2,\ldots,n \\ s.t. \quad w\in\Phi \end{cases}$$

Let

$$w_i^{'}=(w_{i1}^{'},w_{i2}^{'},\ldots,w_{im}^{'}),\quad w_i^{''}=(w_{i1}^{''},w_{i2}^{''},\ldots,w_{im}^{''}),\quad i=1,2,\ldots,n$$

be the optimal solutions derived from the models (M-6.1) and (M-6.2), respectively, then the overall attribute values of the alternatives $x_i(i=1,2,\ldots,n)$ are $\tilde{z}_i=[z_i^L(w_i^{'}),z_i^U(w_i^{''})](i=1,2,\ldots,n)$, where

$$z_i^L(w_i^{'})=\sum_{j=1}^{m} r_{ij}^L w_{ij}^{'},\quad z_i^U(w_i^{''})=\sum_{j=1}^{m} r_{ij}^U w_{ij}^{''},\quad i=1,2,\ldots,n \tag{6.1}$$

Solving the $2n$ linear programming models above, we can get the overall attribute values of all the alternatives $x_i(i=1,2,\ldots,n)$.

In the general case, the overall attribute values of all alternatives derived from the models (M-6.1) and (Model 6.2) do not use the same weight vector of attributes, which makes the evaluations over the alternatives not to be comparable, and thus have no actual meaning.

Considering that all the alternatives are fair, Fan and Zhang [28] improved the models (M-6.1) and (M-6.2), and adopted the linear equally weighted summation method to establish the following models:

$$(\textbf{M-6.3})\quad \begin{cases} \min z_0^{'}(w)=\sum_{i=1}^{n}\sum_{j=1}^{m} r_{ij}^L w_j \\ s.t. \quad w\in\Phi \end{cases}$$

$$(\textbf{M-6.4})\quad \begin{cases} \min z_0''(w) = \sum_{i=1}^{n}\sum_{j=1}^{m} r_{ij}^U w_j \\ s.t.\ \ w \in \Phi \end{cases}$$

Let

$$w' = (w_1', w_2', \ldots, w_m'),\ \ w'' = (w_1'', w_2'', \ldots, w_m'')$$

be the optimal solutions of the models, then the overall attribute values of the alternatives are the interval numbers $\tilde{z}_i = [z_i^L(w'), z_i^U(w'')](i = 1, 2, ..., n)$, where

$$z_i^L(w') = \sum_{j=1}^{m} r_{ij}^L w_j', z_i^U(w'') = \sum_{j=1}^{m} r_{ij}^U w_j'',\ i = 1, 2, \ldots, n \tag{6.2}$$

Although $z_i^L(w')(i = 1, 2, ..., n)$ and $z_i^U(w'')(i = 1, 2, \ldots, n)$ adopt the same weight vector, separately, and also need less calculation, in the general case, the two weight vectors w' and w'' are still different. Thus, by the models (M-6.3) and (M-6.4) and the formula (6.2), we can know that sometimes it may have the situations that $z_i^L(w')$ and $z_i^U(w'')$, i.e., the interval numbers $\tilde{z}_i = [z_i^L(w'), z_i^U(w'')]$ may not exist. To solve this problem, and consider that the model (M-6.3) is equivalent to the following model:

$$(\textbf{M-6.5})\quad \begin{cases} \max z_0'(w) = -\sum_{i=1}^{n}\sum_{j=1}^{m} r_{ij}^L w_j \\ s.t.\ \ w \in \Phi \end{cases}$$

and also since the models (M-6.4) and (M-6.5) have the same constraint condition, then by synthesizing the models (M-6.4) and (M-6.5), we can establish the following single optimization model [19]:

$$(\textbf{M-6.6})\quad \begin{cases} \max z(w) = \sum_{i=1}^{n}\sum_{j=1}^{m} (r_{ij}^U - r_{ij}^L) w_j \\ s.t.\ \ w \in \Phi \end{cases}$$

Suppose that $w = (w_1, w_2, \ldots, w_m)$ is the optimal solution of the model (M-6.6), then the overall attribute value of the alternative is the interval number $\tilde{z}_i(w) = [z_i^L(w), z_i^U(w)]$, where

$$z_i^L(w) = \sum_{j=1}^{m} r_{ij}^L,\ \ z_i^U(w) = \sum_{j=1}^{m} r_{ij}^U w_j,\ i = 1, 2, \ldots, n \tag{6.3}$$

Since $z_i^L(w)(i=1,2,\ldots,n)$ and $z_i^U(w)(i=1,2,\ldots,n)$ only adopt the single weight vector, then all the alternatives are comparable, and for any i, we have $z_i^L(w)\le z_i^U(w)$, it can be seen from the models (M-6.1)~(M-6.6) that, on the whole, the models introduced in this section are simple and straightforward, and need much less calculation effort than the existing other models, and thus have much more practicality in actual applications. By using the models (M-6.1), (M-6.2) and (M-6.3), we can derive the following theorem:

Theorem 6.1 [19] Let $\tilde{y}_i(w)=[y_i^L(w),y_i^U(w)]$ and $\tilde{z}_i(w)=[z_i^L(w),z_i^U(w)]$ be the interval numbers that the overall attribute value of the alternative x_i belong to, which are derived by using the models (M-6.1), (M-6.2) and (M-6.6), then

$$[y_i^L(w),y_i^U(w)]\supseteq[z_i^L(w),z_i^U(w)]$$

Since all the overall attribute values $\tilde{z}_i(w)(i=1,2,\ldots,n)$ are the interval numbers, and are inconvenient to be ranked directly, then we can utilize Eq. (4.2) to calculate the possibility degrees $p_{ij}=p(\tilde{z}_i(w)\ge\tilde{z}_j(w))(i,j=1,2,\ldots,n)$ of comparing each pair of the overall attribute values of all the alternatives $x_i(i=1,2,\ldots,n)$, and construct the possibility degree matrix $P=(p_{ij})_{n\times n}$. After that, we utilize Eq. (4.6) to derive the priority vector $v=(v_1,v_2,\ldots,v_n)$, based on which we rank and select the alternatives $x_i(i=1,2,\ldots,n)$.

6.1.2 Practical Example

In this section, a MADM problem of determining what kind of air-conditioning system should be installed in the library (adapted from Yoon [163]) is used to illustrate the developed models above.

Example 6.1 A city is planning to build a municipal library. One of the problems facing the city development commissioner is to determine what kind of air-conditioning system should be installed in the library. The contractor offered five feasible plans, which might be adapted to the physical structure of the library. The alternatives $x_i(i=1,2,3,4,5)$ are to be evaluated under three major impacts: economic, functional and operational. Two monetary attributes and six non-monetary attributes (that is, (1) u_1: owning cost ($/ft²); (2) u_2: operating cost ($/ft²), (3) u_3: performance (*); (4) u_4: comfort (noise level, Db); (5) u_5: maintainability (*); (6) u_6: reliability (%); (7) u_7: flexibility (*); (8) u_8: safety, where * unit from 10-point scale, from 1 (worst) to 10 (best), three attributes u_1, u_2 and u_4 are cost-type attributes, and the other five attributes are benefit-type attributes) emerged from three impacts in Table 6.1.

The value ranges of attribute weights are as follows:

Table 6.1 Decision matrix $\tilde{A}$

	u_1	u_2	u_3	u_4
x_1	[3.7, 4.7]	[5.9, 6.9]	[8, 10]	[30, 40]
x_2	[1.5, 2.5]	[4.7, 5.7]	[4, 6]	[65, 75]
x_3	[3, 4]	[4.2, 5.2]	[4, 6]	[60, 70]
x_4	[3.5, 4.5]	[4.5, 5.5]	[7, 9]	[35, 45]
x_5	[2.5, 3.5]	[5, 6]	[6, 8]	[50, 60]
	u_5	u_6	u_7	u_8
x_1	[3, 5]	[90, 100]	[3, 5]	[6, 8]
x_2	[3, 5]	[70, 80]	[7, 9]	[4, 6]
x_3	[7, 9]	[80, 90]	[7, 9]	[5, 7]
x_4	[8, 10]	[85, 95]	[6, 8]	[7, 9]
x_5	[5, 7]	[85, 95]	[4, 6]	[8, 10]

$$\Phi = \{w = (w_1, w_2, \ldots, w_8) \mid 0.0419 \leq w_1 \leq 0.0491, 0.0840 \leq w_2 \leq 0.0982,$$
$$0.1211 \leq w_3 \leq 0.1373, 0.1211 \leq w_4 \leq 0.1373, 0.1680 \leq w_5 \leq 0.1818,$$
$$0.2138 \leq w_6 \leq 0.2294, 0.0395 \leq w_7 \leq 0.0457, 0.1588 \leq w_8 \leq 0.1706,$$
$$\left.\sum_{j=1}^{8} w_j = 1\right\}$$

then how to find the best alternative?

In what follows, we utilize the method of Sect. 6.1.1 to solve this issue:

Step 1 Utilize Eqs. (4.9) and (4.10) to normalize the decision matrix $\tilde{A}$ into the matrix $\tilde{R}$, shown as in Table 6.2.

Step 2 Solve the models (M-6.1) and (M-6.2) to derive the optimal solution corresponding to the alternative x_i:

$$w_i' = (w_{i1}', w_{i2}', \ldots, w_{im}'), \ w_i'' = (w_{i1}'', w_{i2}'', \ldots, w_{im}''), \ i = 1, 2, 3, 4, 5$$

and the intervals $\tilde{z}_i = [z_i^L(w_i'), z_i^U(w_i'')] (i = 1, 2, 3, 4, 5)$ that the overall attribute values of the alternatives $x_i (i = 1, 2, 3, 4, 5)$ belong to, which are listed in Table 6.3:

Step 3 The optimal solution derived from the models (M-6.3) and (M-6.4) for the alternative x_i:

$$w' = (w_1', w_2', \ldots, w_8'), \ w'' = (w_1'', w_2'', \ldots, w_8'')$$

and the intervals $\tilde{z}_i = [z_i^L(w_i'), z_i^U(w_i'')] (i = 1, 2, 3, 4, 5)$ that the overall attribute values of the alternatives $x_i (i = 1, 2, 3, 4, 5)$ belong to:

Table 6.2 Normalized decision matrix $\tilde{R}$

	u_1	u_2	u_3	u_4
x_1	[0.2281, 0.4281]	[0.3089, 0.4382]	[0.4493, 0.7433]	[0.4690, 0.7904]
x_2	[0.4288, 0.7146]	[0.3740, 0.5501]	[0.2247, 0.4460]	[0.2501, 0.3648]
x_3	[0.2680, 0.3573]	[0.4099, 0.5075]	[0.2247, 0.4460]	[0.2680, 0.3952]
x_4	[0.2382, 0.3063]	[0.3876, 0.4737]	[0.3932, 0.6690]	[0.4169, 0.6775]
x_5	[0.3063, 0.4288]	[0.3553, 0.4263]	[0.3370, 0.5946]	[0.3126, 0.4743]
	u_5	u_6	u_7	u_8
x_1	[0.1793, 0.4003]	[0.4363, 0.5435]	[0.1771, 0.3965]	[0.3303, 0.5804]
x_2	[0.1793, 0.4003]	[0.3394, 0.4348]	[0.4132, 0.7139]	[0.2202, 0.4353]
x_3	[0.4183, 0.7206]	[0.3878, 0.4892]	[0.4132, 0.7139]	[0.2752, 0.5078]
x_4	[0.4781, 0.8008]	[0.4121, 0.5164]	[0.3542, 0.6344]	[0.3853, 0.6529]
x_5	[0.2988, 0.5604]	[0.4121, 0.5164]	[0.2361, 0.4758]	[0.4404, 0.7255]

Table 6.3 Results derived from the models (M-6.1) and (M-6.2)

	w'_{i1}	w'_{i2}	w'_{i3}	w'_{i4}	w'_{i5}	w'_{i6}	w'_{i7}	w'_{i8}
x_1	0.0491	0.0982	0.1211	0.1211	0.1818	0.2138	0.0457	0.1692
x_2	0.0419	0.0840	0.1373	0.1311	0.1818	0.2138	0.0395	0.1706
x_3	0.0491	0.0840	0.1373	0.1373	0.1680	0.2142	0.0395	0.1706
x_4	0.0491	0.0982	0.1335	0.1211	0.1680	0.2138	0.0457	0.1706
x_5	0.0491	0.0840	0.1295	0.1373	0.1818	0.2138	0.0457	0.1588
	w''_{i1}	w''_{i2}	w''_{i3}	w''_{i4}	w''_{i5}	w''_{i6}	w''_{i7}	w''_{i8}
x_1	0.0419	0.0840	0.1373	0.1373	0.1680	0.2214	0.0395	0.1706
x_2	0.0491	0.0982	0.1373	0.1211	0.1680	0.2138	0.0457	0.1668
x_3	0.0419	0.0982	0.1211	0.1211	0.1818	0.2196	0.0457	0.1706
x_4	0.0419	0.0840	0.1373	0.1373	0.1818	0.2138	0.0395	0.1644
x_5	0.0419	0.0840	0.1373	0.1211	0.1818	0.2238	0.0395	0.1706

$$w' = (0.0491, 0.0840, 0.1373, 0.1211, 0.1818, 0.2138, 0.0457, 0.1672)$$

$$w'' = (0.0419, 0.0840, 0.1373, 0.1249, 0.1818, 0.2138, 0.0457, 0.1706)$$

$$\tilde{z}_1 = [0.3448, 0.5616],\ \tilde{z}_2 = [0.2745, 0.4556],\ \tilde{z}_3 = [0.3348, 0.5230]$$
$$\tilde{z}_4 = [0.4044, 0.6255],\ \tilde{z}_5 = [0.3559, 0.5525]$$

Step 4 Derive the optimal solution $w = (w_1, w_2, \ldots, w_m)$ corresponding to the alternative x_i from the model (M-6.6), and the intervals $\tilde{z}_i(w) = [z_i^L(w_i), z_i^U(w_i)] (i = 1,2,3,4,5)$ that the overall attribute values of the alternatives $x_i (i = 1,2,3,4,5)$ belong to:

$$w = (0.0419, 0.0840, 0.1373, 0.1249, 0.1818, 0.2138, 0.0457, 0.1706)$$

$$\tilde{z}_1(w) = [0.3461, 0.5616],\ \tilde{z}_2(w) = [0.2731, 0.4556]$$
$$\tilde{z}_3(w) = [0.3348, 0.5230],\ \tilde{z}_4(w) = [0.4055, 0.6255]$$
$$\tilde{z}_5(w) = [0.3563, 0.5525]$$

From the results above, we can see that, in general, compared to the existing models, the intervals of the overall attributes of all the alternatives derived from the model (M-6.6) have the least range.

In order to rank the alternatives, we first use Eq. (4.2) to compare each pair of the overall attribute values of the alternatives derived from the three models above, and construct the possibility degree matrix, then we utilize Eq. (4.6) to rank the alternatives, the results are shown as below:

(1)

$$P^{(1)} = \begin{pmatrix} 0.5 & 0.7157 & 0.5647 & 0.3674 & 0.5032 \\ 0.2843 & 0.5 & 0.3369 & 0.1385 & 0.2729 \\ 0.4353 & 0.6631 & 0.5 & 0.2920 & 0.4344 \\ 0.6326 & 0.8615 & 0.7080 & 0.5 & 0.6443 \\ 0.4968 & 0.7271 & 0.5656 & 0.3557 & 0.5 \end{pmatrix}$$

$$v = (0.2076, 0.1516, 0.1912, 0.2423, 0.2073)$$

based on which and the possibility degrees of P, we derive the ranking of the interval numbers $\tilde{z}_i(w)(i = 1, 2, 3, 4, 5)$:

$$\tilde{z}_4(w) \underset{0.6326}{\geq} \tilde{z}_1(w) \underset{0.5032}{\geq} \tilde{z}_5(w) \underset{0.5656}{\geq} \tilde{z}_3(w) \underset{0.6631}{\geq} \tilde{z}_2(w)$$

from which we get the ranking of the alternatives $x_i(i = 1, 2, 3, 4, 5)$:

$$x_4 \underset{0.6326}{\succ} x_1 \underset{0.5032}{\succ} x_5 \underset{0.5656}{\succ} x_3 \underset{0.6631}{\succ} x_2$$

Similarly, we can get (2) and (3) as follows:

(2)

$$P^{(2)} = \begin{pmatrix} 0.5 & 0.7157 & 0.5647 & 0.3674 & 0.5032 \\ 0.2843 & 0.5 & 0.3369 & 0.1385 & 0.2729 \\ 0.4353 & 0.6631 & 0.5 & 0.2920 & 0.4344 \\ 0.6326 & 0.8615 & 0.7080 & 0.5 & 0.6443 \\ 0.4968 & 0.7271 & 0.5656 & 0.3557 & 0.5 \end{pmatrix}$$

$$v = (0.2069, 0.1498, 0.1919, 0.2435, 0.2079)$$

$$x_4 \underset{0.6454}{\succ} x_5 \underset{0.5024}{\succ} x_1 \underset{0.5600}{\succ} x_3 \underset{0.6729}{\succ} x_2$$

(3)

$$P^{(3)} = \begin{pmatrix} 0.5 & 0.7249 & 0.5618 & 0.3584 & 0.4987 \\ 0.2751 & 0.5 & 0.3259 & 0.1245 & 0.2622 \\ 0.4382 & 0.6741 & 0.5 & 0.2898 & 0.4337 \\ 0.6416 & 0.8755 & 0.7122 & 0.5 & 0.6468 \\ 0.5013 & 0.7378 & 0.5663 & 0.3532 & 0.5 \end{pmatrix}$$

$$v = (0.2072, 0.1494, 0.1917, 0.2435, 0.2079)$$

$$x_4 \underset{0.6468}{\succ} x_5 \underset{0.5013}{\succ} x_1 \underset{0.5618}{\succ} x_3 \underset{0.6741}{\succ} x_2$$

Therefore, the rankings of the alternatives are the same in (2) and (3), and compared to (1), the ranking of the alternatives x_1 and x_5 is reversed. But all derive the best alternative x_4.

6.2 MADM Method Based on Deviation Degree and Possibility Degree

6.2.1 *Algorithm*

In the following, we introduce a maximizing deviation algorithm based on the deviation degrees and possibility degrees for solving the MADM problems. The steps are as follows:

Step 1 For a MADM problem, let X, U, $\tilde{A}$, $\tilde{R}$ and Φ be the set of alternatives, the set of attributes, the decision matrix, the normalized decision matrix and the set of possible weights of attributes determined by the known partial weight information respectively.

Step 2 Utilize the deviation degrees of interval numbers (Definition 5.1) and the idea of maximizing the attribute values of alternatives, and establish the single-objective optimization model:

$$\text{(M- 6.7)} \begin{cases} \max D(w) = \sum_{i=1}^{n}\sum_{j=1}^{m}\sum_{l=1}^{n} \left\| \tilde{r}_{ij} - \tilde{r}_{lj} \right\| w_j \\ \qquad = \sum_{i=1}^{n}\sum_{j=1}^{m}\sum_{l=1}^{n} (| r_{ij}^{L} - r_{lj}^{L} | + | r_{ij}^{U} - r_{lj}^{U} |)\omega_j \\ s.t. \ w \in \Phi \end{cases}$$

Solving this model, we get the optimal weight vector w.

Step 3 Derive the overall attribute values $\tilde{z}_i(w)(i = 1,2,\dots,n)$ of the alternatives $x_i (i = 1,2,\dots,n)$ by using Eq. (4.15).

Step 4 Calculate the possibility degrees $p_{ij} = p(\tilde{z}_i(w) \geq \tilde{z}_j(w))(i, j = 1,2,\dots,n)$ of comparing each pair of the overall attribute values of the alternatives by using Eq. (4.2), and construct the possibility degree matrix $P = (p_{ij})_{n\times n}$.

Step 5 Obtain the priority vector $v = (v_1, v_2, \dots, v_n)$ of the possibility degree matrix P using Eq. (4.6), and then rank and select the alternatives according to v.

6.2.2 *Practical Example*

Example 6.2 Consider a MADM problem that a manufacturer intends to develop some kind of anti-ship missile weapon system. There are five alternatives $x_i (i = 1,2,3,4,5)$ for the manufacturer to choose. The six main indices (attributes) used to evaluate the performances of the anti-ship missile weapon systems are as follows Zhang et al. [168]: (1) u_1: missile hit and damage capability; (2) u_2: fire control systems combat ability; (3) u_3: anti jamming ability; (4) u_4: missile flight control ability; (5) u_5: missile guidance ability; (6) u_6: carrier mobility. All these indices are of benefit type, and the decision maker evaluates the alternatives $x_i (i = 1,2,3,4,5)$ under the indices $u_j (j = 1,2,\dots,6)$ by using the 10-point scale, from 1 (worst) to 10 (best). The evaluation information is contained in the uncertain decision matrix $\tilde{A}$, shown as Table 6.4.

The known attribute weight information is

$$\Phi = \Big\{ w = (w_1, w_2, \dots, w_6) \,|\, 0.16 \leq w_1 \leq 0.20, 0.14 \leq w_2 \leq 0.16,$$
$$0.15 \leq w_3 \leq 0.18, 0.13 \leq w_4 \leq 0.17, 0.14 \leq w_5 \leq 0.18, 0.11 \leq w_6 \leq 0.19,$$
$$\sum_{j=1}^{6} w_j = 1 \Big\}$$

Table 6.4 Uncertain decision matrix $\tilde{A}$

	u_1	u_2	u_3	u_4	u_5	u_6
x_1	[5, 6]	[6, 8]	[6, 7]	[4, 6]	[7, 8]	[8, 10]
x_2	[6, 8]	[5, 7]	[8, 9]	[7, 8]	[4, 7]	[7, 8]
x_3	[5, 7]	[6, 7]	[8, 10]	[7, 9]	[5, 7]	[6, 7]
x_4	[8, 10]	[5, 6]	[4, 7]	[5, 7]	[6, 8]	[4, 7]
x_5	[8, 10]	[6, 8]	[5, 6]	[6, 9]	[7, 9]	[5, 8]

Now we utilize the method of Sect. 6.2.1 to rank the five alternatives. The following steps are involved:

Step 1 Normalize the uncertain decision matrix $\tilde{A}$ by using Eq. (4.9) into the matrix $\tilde{R}$ (see Table 6.5).

Step 2 Use the model of the algorithm to establish the following single-objective optimization model:

$$\begin{cases} \max D(w) = 4.932w_1 + 2.336w_2 + 5.276w_3 + 4.224w_4 + 3.348w_5 + 4.236w_6 \\ s.t. 0.16 \le w_1 \le 0.20, 0.14 \le w_2 \le 0.16, 0.15 \le w_3 \le 0.18, \\ 0.13 \le w_4 \le 0.17, 0.14 \le w_5 \le 0.18, 0.11 \le w_6 \le 0.19, \sum_{j=1}^{6} w_j = 1 \end{cases}$$

Table 6.5 Normalized uncertain decision matrix $\tilde{R}$

	u_1	u_2	u_3
x_1	[0.268, 0.410]	[0.371, 0.636]	[0.338, 0.489]
x_2	[0.321, 0.547]	[0.309, 0.557]	[0.451, 0.629]
x_3	[0.268, 0.479]	[0.371, 0.557]	[0.451, 0.698]
x_4	[0.428, 0.684]	[0.309, 0.477]	[0.225, 0.489]
x_5	[0.428, 0.684]	[0.371, 0.636]	[0.282, 0.419]
	u_4	u_5	u_6
x_1	[0.227, 0.454]	[0.400, 0.605]	[0.443, 0.725]
x_2	[0.397, 0.605]	[0.228, 0.529]	[0.338, 0.580]
x_3	[0.397, 0.680]	[0.285, 0.529]	[0.332, 0.508]
x_4	[0.284, 0.529]	[0.342, 0.605]	[0.222, 0.508]
x_5	[0.340, 0.680]	[0.400, 0.680]	[0.277, 0.580]

Solving this model, we get the optimal weight vector:

$$w = (0.20, 0.14, 0.18, 0.15, 0.14, 0.19)$$

Step 3 Derive the overall attribute values $\tilde{z}_i(w)(i = 1,2,3,4,5)$ by using Eq. (4.2):

$$\tilde{z}_1(w) = [0.3406, 0.5496], \tilde{z}_2(w) = [0.3538, 0.5756]$$
$$\tilde{z}_3(w) = [0.3493, 0.5720], \tilde{z}_4(w) = [0.3020, 0.5522]$$
$$\tilde{z}_5(w) = [0.3479, 0.6087]$$

Step 4 Utilize Eq. (4.2) to calculate the possibility degrees of comparing each pair of the overall attribute values of the alternatives, and establish the possibility degree matrix:

$$P = \begin{pmatrix} 0.5 & 0.4545 & 0.4640 & 0.5392 & 0.4293 \\ 0.5455 & 0.5 & 0.5091 & 0.5797 & 0.4718 \\ 0.5360 & 0.4909 & 0.5 & 0.5709 & 0.4635 \\ 0.4608 & 0.4203 & 0.4291 & 0.5 & 0.3998 \\ 0.5707 & 0.5282 & 0.5365 & 0.6002 & 0.5 \end{pmatrix}$$

Step 5 Derive the priority vector of P by using Eq. (4.6):

$$v = (0.1943, 0.2053, 0.2031, 0.1855, 0.2118)$$

based on which and the possibility degrees of P, we derive the ranking of the interval numbers $\tilde{z}_i(w)(i = 1,2,3,4,5)$:

$$\tilde{z}_5(w) \underset{0.5282}{\geq} \tilde{z}_2(w) \underset{0.5091}{\geq} \tilde{z}_3(w) \underset{0.5360}{\geq} \tilde{z}_1(w) \underset{0.5392}{\geq} \tilde{z}_4(w)$$

from which we get the ranking of the alternatives $x_i(i = 1,2,3,4,5)$:

$$x_5 \underset{0.5282}{\succ} x_2 \underset{0.5091}{\succ} x_3 \underset{0.5360}{\succ} x_1 \underset{0.5392}{\succ} x_4$$

and thus, x_5 is the best alternative.

6.3 Goal Programming Method for Interval MADM

6.3.1 Decision Making Method

Let $w=(w_1, w_2, \ldots, w_m)$ be the weight vector of attributes, where

$$w_j \in [w_j^L, w_j^U],\ w_j \geq 0,\ j=1,2,\ldots,m,\ \sum_{j=1}^{m} w_j = 1$$

and let the normalized decision matrix be $\tilde{R}=(\tilde{r}_{ij})_{n\times m}$, where $\tilde{r}_{ij}=[r_{ij}^L, r_{ij}^U]$, $i=1,2,\ldots,n, j=1,2,\ldots,m$.

The overall attribute value of the alternative x_i is given as the interval number $\tilde{z}_i(w)=[z_i^L(w), z_i^U(w)]$, according to Eq. (4.15), we have

$$z_i^L(w)=\sum_{j=1}^{m} r_{ij}^L w_j,\ i=1,2,\ldots,n \tag{6.4}$$

$$z_i^U(w)=\sum_{j=1}^{m} r_{ij}^U w_j,\ i=1,2,\ldots,n \tag{6.5}$$

where w is the solution of the multi-objective optimization model:

$$(\mathbf{M\text{-}6.8})\quad \begin{cases} \min z_i^{'}(w)=\sum_{j=1}^{m} r_{ij}^L w_j, \quad i=1,2,\ldots,n \\ \max z_i^{''}(w)=\sum_{j=1}^{m} r_{ij}^U w_j, \quad i=1,2,\ldots,n \\ s.t. w_j \in [w_j^L, w_j^U], w_j \geq 0, j=1,2,\ldots,n, \sum_{j=1}^{m} w_j = 1 \end{cases}$$

This model needs to determine the intervals that the overall attribute value of each alternative and only uses the single weight vector, and thus all the alternatives are comparable. It follows from the model (M-6.8) that the value that the objective function $z_i^{'}(w)$ expects to reach is $\sum_{j=1}^{m} r_{ij}^L w_j^L$, while the value that the objective function $z_i^{''}(w)$ expects to reach is $\sum_{j=1}^{m} r_{ij}^U w_j^U$. In such a case, in order to solve the model (M-6.8), we can transform it into the following linear goal programming model:

$$
\text{(M-6.9)} \quad \begin{cases} \min J = P_1 \sum_{i=1}^{n} (\alpha_{1i} d_i^- + \beta_{1i} e_i^+) + P_2 \sum_{i=1}^{n} (\alpha_{2i} d_i^+ + \beta_{2i} e_i^-) \\ s.t. \sum_{j=1}^{m} r_{ij}^L w_j + d_i^- - d_i^+ = \sum_{j=1}^{m} r_{ij}^L w_j^L, \ i = 1, 2, \ldots, n \\ \sum_{j=1}^{m} r_{ij}^U w_j + e_i^- - e_i^+ = \sum_{j=1}^{m} r_{ij}^U w_j^U, \ i = 1, 2, \ldots, n \\ w_j \in [w_j^L, w_j^U], w_j \geq 0, \ j = 1, 2, \ldots, n, \ \sum_{j=1}^{m} w_j = 1 \\ d_i^-, d_i^+, e_i^-, e_i^+ \geq 0, \ i = 1, 2, \ldots, n \end{cases}
$$

where $P_i (i = 1, 2)$ are the priority factors, which denote the importance degrees of the objectives $\sum_{i=1}^{n} (\alpha_{1i} d_i^- + \beta_{1i} e_i^+)$ and $\sum_{i=1}^{n} (\alpha_{2i} d_i^+ + \beta_{2i} e_i^-)$, d_i^- is the negative deviation variable of the objective function $z_i'(w)$ below the expected value $\sum_{j=1}^{m} r_{ij}^L w_j^L$; d_i^+ is the positive deviation variable of the objective function $z_i'(w)$ over the expected value $\sum_{j=1}^{m} r_{ij}^L w_j^L$; e_i^- is the negative deviation variable of the objective function $z_i''(w)$ below the expected value $\sum_{j=1}^{m} r_{ij}^U w_j^U$; e_i^+ is the positive deviation variable of the objective function $z_i''(w)$ over the expected value $\sum_{j=1}^{m} r_{ij}^U w_j^U$; α_{1i} and β_{1i} are the weight coefficients of d_i^- and e_i^+, respectively; α_{2i} and β_{2i} are the weight coefficients of d_i^+ and e_i^-, respectively. Here we can consider that all the objective functions are fair, and thus can take $\alpha_{1i} = \beta_{1i} = \alpha_{2i} = \beta_{2i} = 1, \ i = 1, 2, \ldots, n$.

Solving the model (M-6.9), we can get the optimal attribute weight vector $w = (w_1, w_2, \ldots, w_m)$. Combining the vector w with Eqs. (6.4) and (6.5), we get the overall attribute values $\tilde{z}_i(w)(i = 1, 2, \ldots, n)$ of all the alternatives $x_i (i = 1, 2, \ldots, n)$. After doing so, we can utilize Steps 4 and 5 of the algorithm in Sect. 6.2.1 to derive the ranking of all the alternatives $x_i (i = 1, 2, \ldots, n)$, and then choose the best one.

6.3.2 *Practical Example*

Example 6.3 Here we take Example 6.2 to illustrate the method of Sect. 6.3.1: Suppose that the known attribute weight information is

$$
\Phi = \{ w = (w_1, w_2, \ldots, w_m) \mid 0.3350 \leq w_1 \leq 0.3755, \ 0.3009 \leq w_2 \leq 0.3138, \\ 0.3194 \leq w_3 \leq 0.3363, \ w_1 + w_2 + w_3 = 1 \}
$$

In the following, we use the method of Sect. 6.3.1 to solve this problem, which needs the following procedure:

Step 1 Based on the model (M-6.9), we establish the goal programming model:

$$\begin{cases} \min J = P_1 \sum_{i=1}^{5} (d_i^- + e_i^+) + P_2 \sum_{i=1}^{5} (d_i^- + e_i^-) \\ s.t.\ 0.214w_1 + 0.166w_2 + 0.184w_3 + d_1^- - d_1^+ = 0.1804 \\ \quad 0.206w_1 + 0.220w_2 + 0.182w_3 + d_2^- - d_2^+ = 0.1938 \\ \quad 0.195w_1 + 0.192w_2 + 0.220w_3 + d_3^- - d_3^+ = 0.1934 \\ \quad 0.181w_1 + 0.195w_2 + 0.185w_3 + d_4^- - d_4^+ = 0.1784 \\ \quad 0.175w_1 + 0.193w_2 + 0.201w_3 + d_5^- - d_5^+ = 0.1809 \\ \quad 0.220w_1 + 0.178w_2 + 0.190w_3 + e_1^- - e_1^+ = 0.2024 \\ \quad 0.225w_1 + 0.229w_2 + 0.191w_3 + e_2^- - e_2^+ = 0.2206 \\ \quad 0.204w_1 + 0.198w_2 + 0.231w_3 + e_3^- - e_3^+ = 0.2164 \\ \quad 0.190w_1 + 0.205w_2 + 0.195w_3 + e_4^- - e_4^+ = 0.2012 \\ \quad 0.184w_1 + 0.201w_2 + 0.211w_3 + e_5^- - e_5^+ = 0.2031 \\ \quad 0.3350 \le w_1 \le 0.3755,\ 0.3009 \le w_2 \le 0.3138 \\ \quad 0.3194 \le w_3 \le 0.3363,\ w_1 + w_2 + w_3 = 1 \\ \quad d_i^-, d_i^+, e_i^-, e_i^+ \ge 0,\ i = 1,2,3,4,5 \end{cases}$$

Solving this model by adopting the multi-stage goal programming method, and then get the optimal attribute weight vector:

$$w = (0.3755, 0.3009, 0.3236)$$

Step 2 Derive the overall attribute values $\tilde{z}_i(w)(i = 1,2,3,4,5)$ of the alternatives $x_i (i = 1,2,3,4,5)$ by using Eqs. (6.4) and (6.5):

$$\tilde{z}_1(w) = [0.1898, 0.1977],\ \tilde{z}_2(w) = [0.2020, 0.2152]$$
$$\tilde{z}_3(w) = [0.2022, 0.2109],\ \tilde{z}_4(w) = [0.1865, 0.1961]$$
$$\tilde{z}_5(w) = [0.1888, 0.1979]$$

Step 3 Use Eq. (4.2) to calculate the possibility degrees by comparing each pair of the overall attribute values $\tilde{z}_i(w)(i = 1,2,3,4,5)$, and establish the possibility degree matrix:

$$P = \begin{pmatrix} 0.5 & 0 & 0 & 0.6400 & 0.5235 \\ 1 & 0.5 & 0.6047 & 1 & 1 \\ 1 & 0.3953 & 0.5 & 0 & 0 \\ 0.3600 & 0 & 1 & 0.5 & 0.3904 \\ 0.4765 & 0 & 1 & 0.6096 & 0.5 \end{pmatrix}$$

whose priority vector can by derived by using Eq. (4.6):

$$v = (0.1582, 0.2802, 0.1698, 0.1875, 0.2043)$$

based on which and the possibility degrees of P, we derive the ranking of the interval numbers $\tilde{z}_i(w)(i = 1, 2, 3, 4, 5)$:

$$\tilde{z}_2(w) \underset{1}{\geq} \tilde{z}_5(w) \underset{0.6096}{\geq} \tilde{z}_4(w) \underset{1}{\geq} \tilde{z}_3(w) \underset{1}{\geq} \tilde{z}_1(w)$$

Step 4 Rank the alternatives $x_i (i = 1, 2, 3, 4, 5)$ according to $\tilde{z}_i(w)(i = 1, 2, 3, 4, 5)$ in descending order:

$$x_2 \underset{1}{\succ} x_5 \underset{0.6096}{\succ} x_4 \underset{1}{\succ} x_3 \underset{1}{\succ} x_1$$

and thus, the alternative x_2 is the best one.

6.4 Minimizing Deviations Based Method for MADM with Preferences on Alternatives

6.4.1 Decision Making Method

Below we introduce a minimizing deviation method for solving the MADM problems in which the decision maker has preferences on alternatives:

Step 1 For the MADM problems where there is only partial attribute weight information, and the attribute values are interval numbers, if the decision maker has subjective preference over the alternative x_i, and let the preference value be the interval number $\tilde{\vartheta}_i = [\vartheta_i^L, \vartheta_i^U]$, where $0 \leq \vartheta_i^L \leq \vartheta_i^U \leq 1$. Here, we regard the attribute value $\tilde{r}_{ij} = [r_{ij}^L, r_{ij}^U]$ in the normalized uncertain decision matrix $\tilde{R} = (\tilde{r}_{ij})_{n \times m}$ as the objective preference value of the decision maker for the alternative x_i with respect to the attribute u_j.

Due to the restrictions of some conditions, there is a difference between the subjective preferences of the decision maker and the objective preferences. In order to make a reasonable decision, the attribute weight vector w should be chosen so as to make the total differences of the subjective preferences and the objective preferences (attributes) as small as possible. As a result, based on the concept of deviation degree of comparing interval numbers given by Definition 5.1, we establish the following single-objective optimization model:

$$
\textbf{(M-6.10)} \quad \begin{cases} \max D(w) = \sum_{i=1}^{n} \sum_{j=1}^{m} \left\| \tilde{r}_{ij} - \tilde{s}_j \right\| w_j \\ \qquad\qquad = \sum_{i=1}^{n} \sum_{j=1}^{m} \left(| r_{ij}^L - s_j^L | + | r_{ij}^U - s_j^U | \right) w_j \\ s.t. \ \ w \in \Phi \end{cases}
$$

Solving the model above, we get the optimal weight vector w.

Step 2 Use Eq. (5.6) to calculate the overall attribute values $\tilde{z}_i(w)(i = 1, 2, \ldots, n)$ of the alternatives $x_i (i = 1, 2, \ldots, n)$.

Step 3 Employ Eq. (4.2) to calculate the possibility degrees of comparing interval numbers $\tilde{z}_i(w)(i = 1, 2, \ldots, n)$, and construct the possibility degree matrix $P = (p_{ij})_{n \times n}$.

Step 4 Derive the priority vector $v = (v_1, v_2, \ldots, v_n)$ of P using Eq. (4.6), rank the alternatives $x_i (i = 1, 2, \ldots, n)$ according to the elements of v in descending order, and then get the optimal alternative.

6.4.2 *Practical Example*

Example 6.4 Let us consider a customer who intends to buy a refrigerator. Five types of refrigerators (alternatives) $x_i (i = 1, 2, 3, 4, 5)$ are available. The customer takes into account six attributes to decide which car to refrigerator: (1) u_1: safety; (2) u_2: refrigeration performance; (3) u_3: design; (4) u_4: reliability; (5) u_5: economic; and (6) u_6: aesthetics. All these attributes are benefit-type attributes, and the decision maker evaluates the refrigerators $x_i (i = 1, 2, 3, 4, 5)$ under the attributes $u_j (j = 1, 2, \ldots, 6)$ by using the 10-point scale, from 1 (worst) to 10 (best), and construct the uncertain decision matrix $\tilde{A}$ (see Table 6.6).

The known attribute weight information is:

$$
\Phi = \Big\{ w = (w_1, w_2, \ldots, w_6) \,|\, 0.25 \le w_1 \le 0.30, 0.15 \le w_2 \le 0.20, 0.10 \le w_3 \le 0.20,
$$

$$
0.12 \le w_4 \le 0.24, 0.11 \le w_5 \le 0.18, 0.15 \le w_6 \le 0.22, \sum_{j=1}^{6} w_j = 1 \Big\}
$$

Table 6.6 Uncertain decision matrix $\tilde{A}$

	u_1	u_2	u_3	u_4	u_5	u_6
x_1	[6, 8]	[8, 9]	[7, 8]	[5, 6]	[6, 7]	[8, 9]
x_2	[7, 9]	[5, 7]	[6, 7]	[7, 8]	[6, 8]	[7, 9]
x_3	[5, 7]	[6, 8]	[7, 9]	[6, 7]	[7, 8]	[8, 9]
x_4	[6, 7]	[7, 8]	[7, 9]	[5, 6]	[8, 9]	[7, 8]
x_5	[7, 8]	[6, 7]	[6, 8]	[4, 6]	[5, 7]	[9, 10]

Below we solve this problem using the method of Sect. 6.4.1:

Step 1 Normalize the uncertain decision matrix $\tilde{A}$ into the matrix $\tilde{R}$ (see Table 6.7) by using Eq. (4.13).

Step 2 Suppose that the decision maker has subjective preference values (after normalized) over the five types of refrigerators $x_i (i = 1, 2, 3, 4, 5)$:

$$\tilde{\vartheta}_1 = [0.16, 0.18], \ \tilde{\vartheta}_2 = [0.17, 0.19], \ \tilde{\vartheta}_3 = [0.23, 0.25]$$
$$\tilde{\vartheta}_4 = [0.15, 0.20], \ \tilde{\vartheta}_5 = [0.18, 0.22]$$

and utilizes $d(\tilde{r}_{ij}, \tilde{\vartheta}_i) = | r_{ij}^L - \vartheta_i^L | + | r_{ij}^U - \vartheta_i^U | \ (i = 1, 2, 3, 4, 5, j = 1, 2, \ldots, 6)$ to calculate the deviation degrees of the objective preference values (attribute values) and the subjective preference values, listed in Table 6.8.

Using the model (M-6.10), we establish the following single-objective optimization model:

Table 6.7 Normalized uncertain decision matrix $\tilde{R}$

	u_1	u_2	u_3
x_1	[0.154, 0.258]	[0.205, 0.281]	[0.171, 0.242]
x_2	[0.179, 0.290]	[0.128, 0.219]	[0.146, 0.212]
x_3	[0.128, 0.226]	[0.154, 0.250]	[0.171, 0.273]
x_4	[0.154, 0.226]	[0.179, 0.250]	[0.171, 0.273]
x_5	[0.179, 0.258]	[0.154, 0.219]	[0.146, 0.242]
	u_4	u_5	u_6
x_1	[0.152, 0.222]	[0.154, 0.219]	[0.178, 0.231]
x_2	[0.212, 0.296]	[0.154, 0.250]	[0.156, 0.231]
x_3	[0.182, 0.259]	[0.179, 0.250]	[0.178, 0.231]
x_4	[0.152, 0.222]	[0.205, 0.281]	[0.156, 0.205]
x_5	[0.121, 0.222]	[0.128, 0.219]	[0.200, 0.256]

Table 6.8 Deviation degrees of the objective preference values and the subjective preference values

	u_1	u_2	u_3	u_4	u_5	u_6
$d(\tilde{r}_{1j}, \tilde{\vartheta}_1)$	0.084	0.146	0.073	0.050	0.045	0.069
$d(\tilde{r}_{2j}, \tilde{\vartheta}_2)$	0.109	0.071	0.046	0.148	0.076	0.055
$d(\tilde{r}_{3j}, \tilde{\vartheta}_3)$	0.126	0.076	0.082	0.057	0.051	0.071
$d(\tilde{r}_{4j}, \tilde{\vartheta}_4)$	0.030	0.079	0.094	0.024	0.136	0.011
$d(\tilde{r}_{5j}, \tilde{\vartheta}_5)$	0.039	0.027	0.056	0.061	0.055	0.056

$$\begin{cases} \min D(w) = 0.388w_1 + 0.399w_2 + 0.351w_3 + 0.340w_4 + 0.363w_5 + 0.262w_6 \\ s.t.\ 0.25 \le w_1 \le 0.30, 0.15 \le w_2 \le 0.20, 0.10 \le w_3 \le 0.20, \\ 0.12 \le w_4 \le 0.24, 0.11 \le w_5 \le 0.18, 0.15 \le w_6 \le 0.22, \sum_{j=1}^{6} w_j = 1 \end{cases}$$

Solving this model, we get the optimal weight vector:

$$w = (0.25, 0.15, 0.10, 0.17, 0.11, 0.22)$$

Step 3 Utilize Eq. (4.5) to derive the overall attribute values $\tilde{z}_i(w)(i = 1,2,3,4,5)$:

$$\begin{aligned} &\tilde{z}_1(w) = [0.1683, 0.2435],\ \tilde{z}_2(w) = [0.1659, 0.2552] \\ &\tilde{z}_3(w) = [0.1620, 0.2437],\ \tilde{z}_4(w) = [0.1652, 0.2351] \\ &\tilde{z}_5(w) = [0.1611, 0.2397] \end{aligned}$$

Step 4 Calculate the possibility degrees of the overall attribute values of all the refrigerators $x_i (i = 1,2,3,4,5)$ by using Eq. (4.2), and establish the possibility degree matrix:

$$P = \begin{pmatrix} 0.5 & 0.4717 & 0.5194 & 0.5396 & 0.5358 \\ 0.5283 & 0.5 & 0.5450 & 0.5653 & 0.5605 \\ 0.4806 & 0.4550 & 0.5 & 0.5178 & 0.5153 \\ 0.4604 & 0.4347 & 0.4822 & 0.5 & 0.4983 \\ 0.4642 & 0.4395 & 0.4847 & 0.5017 & 0.5 \end{pmatrix}$$

Step 5 Derive the priority vector of P using Eq. (4.6):

$$v = (0.2033, 0.2100, 0.1984, 0.1938, 0.1945)$$

based on which and the possibility degrees of P, we derive the ranking of the interval numbers $\tilde{z}_i(w)(i = 1,2,3,4,5)$:

$$\tilde{z}_2(w) \underset{0.5283}{\geq} \tilde{z}_1(w) \underset{0.5194}{\geq} \tilde{z}_3(w) \underset{0.5153}{\geq} \tilde{z}_5(w) \underset{0.5017}{\geq} \tilde{z}_4(w)$$

Step 6 Rank the alternatives $x_i(i = 1,2,3,4,5)$ according to $\tilde{z}_i(w)(i = 1,2,3,4,5)$ in descending order:

$$x_2 \underset{0.5283}{\succ} x_1 \underset{0.5194}{\succ} x_3 \underset{0.5153}{\succ} x_5 \underset{0.5017}{\succ} x_4$$

and thus, the refrigerator x_2 is the best one.

6.5 Interval MADM Method Based on Projection Model

6.5.1 Model and Method

Let $\tilde{z}(w) = (\tilde{z}_1(w), \tilde{z}_2(w), \dots, \tilde{z}_n(w))$ be the vector of overall attribute values, where

$$\tilde{z}_i(w) = [z_i^L(w), z_i^U(w)] = \sum_{j=1}^{m} w_j \tilde{r}_{ij} = \left[\sum_{j=1}^{m} w_j r_{ij}^L, \sum_{j=1}^{m} w_j r_{ij}^U\right]$$

and let

$$z^L(w) = (z_1^L(w), z_2^L(w), \dots, z_n^L(w))$$

$$z^U(w) = (z_1^U(w), z_2^U(w), \dots, z_n^U(w))$$

then $\tilde{z}(w) = [z^L(w), z^U(w)]$.

Suppose that the decision maker has subjective preferences over the alternatives, i.e., $\tilde{\vartheta} = (\tilde{\vartheta}_1, \tilde{\vartheta}_2, \dots, \tilde{\vartheta}_n)$, and let

$$\vartheta^L = (\vartheta_1^L, \vartheta_2^L, \dots, \vartheta_n^L), \ \ \vartheta^U = (\vartheta_1^U, \vartheta_2^U, \dots, \vartheta_n^U)$$

then $\tilde{\vartheta} = [\vartheta^L, \vartheta^U]$.

For a MADM problem, we generally use the overall attribute values to rank and select the considered alternatives. If the vector $\tilde{z}(w)$ of the overall attribute values of the alternatives is completely consistent with the vector $\tilde{\vartheta}$ of the subjective preference values, then we can use the vector $\tilde{\vartheta}$ to rank and select the alternatives. However, due to the restrictions of some conditions, there is a difference between the vectors $\tilde{z}(w)$ and $\tilde{\vartheta}$. In order to make a reasonable decision, the determination of the attribute weight vector w should make the deviation between these two vectors as soon as possible, and thus, we let

$$\cos\theta_1 = \cos(z^L(w),\ \vartheta^L) = \frac{\sum_{i=1}^{n} z_i^L(w)\vartheta_i^L}{\sqrt{\sum_{i=1}^{n}\left(z_i^L(w)\right)^2}\sqrt{\sum_{i=1}^{n}\left(\vartheta_i^L\right)^2}} \tag{6.6}$$

$$\cos\theta_2 = \cos(z^U(w),\ \vartheta^U) = \frac{\sum_{i=1}^{n} z_i^U(w)\vartheta_i^U}{\sqrt{\sum_{i=1}^{n}\left(z_i^U(w)\right)^2}\sqrt{\sum_{i=1}^{n}\left(\vartheta_i^U\right)^2}} \tag{6.7}$$

Clearly, the smaller the values of $\cos\theta_1$ and $\cos\theta_2$, the closer the directions of $z^L(w)$ and ϑ^L, $z^U(w)$ and ϑ^U. However, as it is well known that a vector is composed of direction and modular size, $\cos\theta_1$ and $\cos\theta_2$, however, only reflect the similarity measures between the directions of the vectors $z^L(w)$ and ϑ^L, $z^U(w)$ and ϑ^U, and the modular sizes of $z^L(w)$ and $z^U(w)$ should also be taken into account. In order to measure similarity degree between the vectors α and β from the global point of view, in the following, we introduce the formulas of projections of the vector $z^L(w)$ on the vector ϑ^L, and of the vector $z^U(w)$ on ϑ^U, respectively, as follows:

$$\begin{aligned}
\Pr j_{\vartheta^L}(z^L(w)) &= \left|z^L(w)\right|\cos\theta_1 \\
&= \sqrt{\sum_{i=1}^{n}(z_i^L(w))^2}\,\frac{\sum_{i=1}^{n} z_i^L(w)\vartheta_i^L}{\sqrt{\sum_{i=1}^{n}(z_i^L(w))^2}\sqrt{\sum_{i=1}^{n}(\vartheta_i^L)^2}} \\
&= \frac{\sum_{i=1}^{n} z_i^L(w)\vartheta_i^L}{\sqrt{\sum_{i=1}^{n}(\vartheta_i^L)^2}} = \sum_{i=1}^{n} z_i^L(w)\overline{\vartheta}_i^L
\end{aligned} \tag{6.8}$$

Similarly, we have

$$\Pr j_{\vartheta^U}(z^U(w)) = \left|z^U(w)\right| \cos\theta_2 = \sum_{i=1}^{n} z_i^U(w)\bar{\vartheta}_i^U \tag{6.9}$$

where

$$\left|z^L(w)\right| = \sqrt{\sum_{i=1}^{n}(z_i^L(w))^2}, \quad \left|z^U(w)\right| = \sqrt{\sum_{i=1}^{n}(z_i^U(w))^2}$$

are the modules of $z^L(w)$ and $z^U(w)$ respectively, and

$$\bar{\vartheta}_i^L = \frac{\vartheta_i^L}{\sqrt{\sum_{i=1}^{n}(\vartheta_i^L)^2}}, \quad \bar{\vartheta}_i^U = \frac{\vartheta_i^U}{\sqrt{\sum_{i=1}^{n}(\vartheta_i^U)^2}}$$

Clearly, the larger the values of $\Pr j_{\vartheta^L}(z^L(w))$ and $\Pr j_{\vartheta^U}(z^U(w))$, the closer $z^L(w)$ to ϑ^L, and $z^U(w)$ to ϑ^U, that is, the closer $\tilde{z}(w)$ to $\tilde{\vartheta}$. Thus, we can construct the lower limit projection model (M-6.11) and the upper limit projection model (M-6.12) respectively:

$$\textbf{(M-6.11)} \begin{cases} \max \Pr j_{\vartheta^L}(z^L(w)) = \sum_{i=1}^{n} z_i^L(w)\bar{\vartheta}_i^L \\ s.t. \ \ w \in \Phi \end{cases}$$

$$\textbf{(M-6.12)} \begin{cases} \max \Pr j_{\vartheta^U}(z^U(w)) = \sum_{i=1}^{n} z_i^U(w)\bar{\vartheta}_i^U \\ s.t. \ \ w \in \Phi \end{cases}$$

To make the rankings of all the alternatives to be comparable, in the process of calculating the overall attribute values of alternatives, we should use the same attribute weight vector.

Considering that the models (M-6.11) and (M-6.12) have the same constraint conditions, we can adopt the equally weighted summation method to synthesize the models (M-6.11) and (M-6.12), and get the following fused projection model:

$$\textbf{(M-6.13)} \begin{cases} \max \Pr j_{\tilde{\vartheta}}(z(w)) = \sum_{i=1}^{n}(z_i^L(w)\bar{\vartheta}_i^L + z_i^U(w)\bar{\vartheta}_i^U) \\ s.t. \ \ w \in \Phi \end{cases}$$

Solving this model, we can get the optimal solution $w=(w_1, w_2, \ldots, w_m)$, and then utilize Eq. (4.15) to calculate the overall attribute values $\tilde{z}_i(w)(i=1,2,\ldots,n)$ of the alternatives x_i $(i=1,2,\ldots,n)$.

In order to rank the alternatives, we use Eq. (4.2) to calculate the possibility degrees by comparing the interval numbers $\tilde{z}_i(w)(i=1,2,\ldots,n)$, construct the possibility degree matrix, and then adopt Eq. (4.6) to get its priority vector, based on which we rank and select the considered alternatives.

Based on the analysis above, below we introduce a method for interval MADM based on the projection model, which needs the following steps [124]:

Step 1 For a MADM problem, the decision maker measures all the considered alternatives x_i $(i=1,2,\ldots,n)$ with respect to the attributes $u_j(j=1,2,\ldots,n)$ and constructs the uncertain decision matrix $\tilde{A}=(\tilde{a}_{ij})_{n\times m}$, and then normalizes it into the matrix $\tilde{R}=(\tilde{r}_{ij})_{n\times m}$. Suppose that the decision maker has also the preferences $\tilde{\vartheta}_i(i=1,2,\ldots,n)$ over the alternatives x_i $(i=1,2,\ldots,n)$.

Step 2 Derive the weight vector $w=(w_1, w_2, \ldots, w_m)$ from the model (M-6.13), and then use Eq. (4.15) to obtain the overall attribute values $\tilde{z}_i(w)(i=1,2,\ldots,n)$ of the alternatives x_i $(i=1,2,\ldots,n)$.

Step 3 Utilize Eq. (4.2) to calculate the possibility degrees $p_{ij}=p(\tilde{z}_i(w)\geq\tilde{z}_j(w))(i,j=1,2,\ldots,n)$ and construct the possibility degree matrix $P=(p_{ij})_{n\times n}$, whose priority vector $v=(v_1,v_2,\ldots,v_n)$ can be derived from Eq. (4.6), and then rank and select the alternatives according to v.

6.5.2 Practical Example

Example 6.5 Consider a MADM problem that a risk investment company plans to invest a project. There are five projects (alternatives) $x_i(i=1,2,3,4,5)$ to choose from. The decision maker now evaluates these projects from the angle of risk factors. The considered risk factors can be divided into six indices (attributes) [29]: (1) u_1: market risk; (2) u_2: technology risk; (3) u_3: management risk; (4) u_4: environment risk; (5) u_5: production risk; and u_6: financial risk. These six indices are of cost type, and the decision maker evaluates the projects $x_i(i=1,2,3,4,5)$ under the indices $u_j(j=1,2,\ldots,6)$ by using the 5-point scale, from 1 (the lowest risk) to 5 (the highest risk). The evaluation values are expressed in interval numbers $\tilde{a}_{ij}(i=1,2,3,4,5, j=1,2,\ldots,6)$, which are contained in the uncertain decision matrix $\tilde{A}$, shown as Table 6.9.

The known attribute weight information is:

$$\Phi=\Big\{w=(w_1,w_2,\ldots,w_6)\,|\,0.15\leq w_1\leq 0.18, 0.16\leq w_2\leq 0.17,, 0.17\leq w_3\leq 0.18,$$

$$0.14\leq w_4\leq 0.19, 0.13\leq w_5\leq 0.16, 0.16\leq w_6\leq 0.20, \sum_{j=1}^{6} w_j=1\Big\}$$

Table 6.9 Uncertain decision matrix $\tilde{A}$

	u_1	u_2	u_3	u_4	u_5	u_6
x_1	[2, 4]	[3, 4]	[2, 3]	[3, 4]	[2, 3]	[4, 5]
x_2	[3, 4]	[2, 3]	[4, 5]	[3, 4]	[2, 4]	[2, 3]
x_3	[2, 3]	[2, 3]	[4, 5]	[3, 4]	[2, 4]	[3, 5]
x_4	[3, 5]	[2, 4]	[2, 3]	[2, 5]	[3, 4]	[2, 3]
x_5	[4, 5]	[3, 4]	[2, 4]	[2, 5]	[3, 5]	[2, 4]

Now we utilize the method of Sect. 6.5.1 to rank the five projects. The steps are involved as below:

Step 1 Normalize the uncertain decision matrix $\tilde{A}$ by using Eq. (4.14), shown as Table 6.10.

Step 2 Suppose that the decision maker has subjective preferences over the projects $x_i (i = 1,2,3,4,5)$, which are expressed in the interval numbers:

$$\tilde{\vartheta}_1 = [0.3, 0.5],\ \tilde{\vartheta}_2 = [0.5, 0.6],\ \tilde{\vartheta}_3 = [0.3, 0.4]$$
$$\tilde{\vartheta}_4 = [0.4, 0.6],\ \tilde{\vartheta}_5 = [0.4, 0.5]$$

Based on the model (M-6.13), we can establish the following single-objective optimization model:

Table 6.10 Normalized uncertain decision matrix $\tilde{R}$

	u_1	u_2	u_3
x_1	[0.1304, 0.4054]	[0.1154, 0.2353]	[0.1667, 0.3797]
x_2	[0.1304, 0.2703]	[0.1538, 0.3529]	[0.1000, 0.1899]
x_3	[0.1739, 0.4054]	[0.1538, 0.3529]	[0.1000, 0.1899]
x_4	[0.1043, 0.2703]	[0.1154, 0.3529]	[0.1667, 0.3797]
x_5	[0.1043, 0.2027]	[0.1154, 0.2353]	[0.1250, 0.3797]
	u_4	u_5	u_6
x_1	[0.1250, 0.2899]	[0.1538, 0.3896]	[0.0960, 0.1899]
x_2	[0.1250, 0.2899]	[0.1154, 0.3896]	[0.1600, 0.3797]
x_3	[0.1250, 0.2899]	[0.1154, 0.3896]	[0.0960, 0.2532]
x_4	[0.1000, 0.4348]	[0.1154, 0.2597]	[0.1600, 0.3797]
x_5	[0.1000, 0.4348]	[0.0923, 0.2597]	[0.1200, 0.3797]

$$\begin{cases} \max \Pr j_{\tilde{\vartheta}}(\tilde{z}(w)) = 1.03050w_1 + 1.04992w_2 + 1.04411w_3 + 1.13063w_4 \\ \qquad\qquad + 1.09161w_5 + 1.09132w_6 \\ s.t.\ \ 0.15 \le w_1 \le 0.18, 0.16 \le w_2 \le 0.17, 0.17 \le w_3 \le 0.18, \\ \quad 0.14 \le w_4 \le 0.19, 0.13 \le w_5 \le 0.16, 0.16 \le w_6 \le 0.20, \sum_{j=1}^{6} w_j = 1 \end{cases}$$

Solving this model, we get the attribute weight vector:

$$w = (0.15, 0.16, 0.17, 0.19, 0.16, 0.17)$$

Step 3 Calculate the overall attribute values $\tilde{z}_i\,(w)(i = 1,2,3,4,5)$ of all the projects $x_i\,(i = 1,2,3,4,5)$ using Eq. (4.15):

$$\tilde{z}_1\,(w) = [0.1310, 0.3127], \tilde{z}_2\,(w) = [0.1306, 0.3113]$$
$$\tilde{z}_3\,(w) = [0.1262, 0.3100], \tilde{z}_4\,(w) = [0.1271, 0.3503]$$
$$\tilde{z}_5\,(w) = [0.1095, 0.3213]$$

Step 4 Derive the possibility degrees $p_{ij} = p(\tilde{z}_i\,(w) \ge \tilde{z}_j\,(w))(i, j = 1,2,3,4,5)$ by using Eq. (4.2), and construct the possibility degree matrix:

$$P = \begin{pmatrix} 0.5 & 0.5025 & 0.5103 & 0.4584 & 0.5164 \\ 0.4975 & 0.5 & 0.5092 & 0.4574 & 0.5154 \\ 0.4897 & 0.4908 & 0.5 & 0.4494 & 0.5068 \\ 0.5416 & 0.5426 & 0.5506 & 0.5 & 0.5536 \\ 0.4836 & 0.4846 & 0.4932 & 0.4464 & 0.5 \end{pmatrix}$$

whose priority vector can be obtained from Eq. (4.6) as:

$$v = (0.1994, 0.1990, 0.1968, 0.2094, 0.1954)$$

Step 5 Using the priority vector v and the possibility degree matrix P, we rank the interval numbers $\tilde{z}_i\,(w)(i = 1,2,3,4,5)$:

$$\tilde{z}_4(w) \underset{0.5416}{\ge} \tilde{z}_1(w) \underset{0.5025}{\ge} \tilde{z}_2(w) \underset{0.5092}{\ge} \tilde{z}_3(w) \underset{0.5068}{\ge} \tilde{z}_5(w)$$

based on which we rank the projects $x_i (i = 1,2,3,4,5)$:

$$x_4 \underset{0.5416}{\succ} x_1 \underset{0.5025}{\succ} x_2 \underset{0.5092}{\succ} x_3 \underset{0.5068}{\succ} x_5$$

which indicates that x_4 is the best project.

6.6 Interactive Interval MADM Method Based on Optimization Level

6.6.1 Decision Making Method

Definition 6.1 Let $\tilde{a} = [a^L, a^U]$ and $\tilde{b} = [b^L, b^U]$ be two interval numbers, $p(\tilde{a} \geq \tilde{b})$ be the possibility degree of $\tilde{a} \geq \tilde{b}$ (defined as in Sect. 4.1), then $p(\tilde{a} \geq \tilde{b}) \geq \beta$ is called the optimization level of $\tilde{a} \geq \tilde{b}$.

Theorem 6.2 With the optimization level β, $\tilde{a} \geq \tilde{b}$ can be transformed into

$$(1-\beta)a^L + \beta a^U \geq \beta b^L + (1-\beta)b^U \tag{6.10}$$

where $\beta \in [0,1]$.

Proof If Eq. (6.10) holds, then by $l_{\tilde{a}} = a^U - a^L$ and $l_{\tilde{b}} = b^U - b^L$, we have

$$\frac{l_{\tilde{a}} + l_{\tilde{b}} - (b^U - a^L)}{l_{\tilde{a}} + l_{\tilde{b}}} \geq \beta$$

It follows from Definition 6.1 that if $b^U - a^L \geq 0$, then $p(\tilde{a} \geq \tilde{b}) \geq \beta$; if $b^U - a^L < 0$, then $p(\tilde{a} \geq \tilde{b}) = 1 \geq \beta$; Otherwise, if $p(\tilde{a} \geq \tilde{b}) \geq \beta$, then we can prove similarly Eq. (6.10) holds. This completes the proof.

We can see that the larger the overall attribute value $\tilde{z}_i(w)$ derived by Eq. (4.15), the better the alternative x_i corresponding to $\tilde{z}_i(w)$.

In order to obtain the optimal alternative, we first introduce the concept of β-dominated alternative.

Definition 6.2 For the alternative $x_p \in X$, if there exist $x_q \in X$ and an optimization level β, such that $z_q^{(\beta)}(w) > z_p^{(\beta)}(w)$, then x_p is called β-dominated alternative; Otherwise, x_p is called β-non-dominated alternative, where

$$z_p^{(\beta)}(w) = \sum_{j=1}^{m} [(1-\beta) r_{pj}^L + \beta r_{pj}^U] w_j$$

and

$$z_q^{(\beta)}(w) = \sum_{j=1}^{m} [(1-\beta) r_{qj}^L + \beta r_{qj}^U] w_j$$

are called the β-overall attribute values of the alternatives x_p and x_q respectively.

From Definition 6.2, we can know that, in the process of optimization, the β-dominated alternative should be eliminated, which makes the set of alternatives get diminished.

By Theorem 6.2 and similar to the proof of Theorem 3.1, we can prove the following theorem easily:

Theorem 6.3 For the known partial weight information Φ and the predefined optimization level β, the alternative $x_p \in X$ is $\beta-$dominated if and only if $J_p < 0$, where

$$\begin{cases} J_p = \max\left(\sum_{j=1}^{m} \left[(1-\beta) r_{qj}^L + \beta r_{qj}^U \right] w_j + \theta \right) \\ s.t. \sum_{j=1}^{m} \left[(1-\beta) r_{qj}^L + \beta r_{qj}^U \right] w_j + \theta \le 0, i \ne p, i = 1, 2, \ldots, n, w \in \Phi \end{cases}$$

and θ is an unconstrained auxiliary variable, which has no actual meaning.

Therefore, we only need to identify in turn each alternative by Theorem 6.3, and ultimately get the set $\bar{X}$ of $\beta-$non-dominated alternatives, where $\bar{X}$ is the subset of X.

Based on the above theoretical analysis, we can develop an interactive interval MADM method as follows:

Step 1 For a MADM problem, the attribute values of the considered alternatives $x_i (i = 1, 2, \ldots, n)$ with respect to the attributes $u_j (j = 1, 2, \ldots, m)$ are contained in the uncertain decision matrix $\tilde{A} = (\tilde{a}_{ij})_{n \times m}$. By using Eqs. (4.9), (4.10), or Eqs. (4.13), (4.14), we normalize $\tilde{A}$ into the decision matrix $\tilde{R} = (\tilde{r}_{ij})_{n \times m}$.

Step 2 According to the predefined optimization level β, the β-overall attribute values of the considered alternatives and the known partial attribute weight information, and by Theorem 6.3, we identify whether the alternative x_i is a β-dominated alternative or not, eliminate the β-dominated alternatives, and then get a set $\bar{X}$, whose elements are the β-non-dominated alternatives. If most of the decision makers suggest that an alternative x_i be superior to any other alternatives in $\bar{X}$, or the alternative x_i is the only one alternative left in $\bar{X}$, then the most preferred alternative is x_i; Otherwise, go to the next step:

Step 3 Interact with the decision makers, and add the decision information provided by the decision maker as the weight information to the set Φ. If the added information given by a decision maker contradicts the information in Φ, then return it to the decision maker for reassessment, and go to Step 2.

The above interactive procedure is convergent. With the increase of the weight information, the number of β-non-dominated alternatives in $\bar{X}$ will be diminished gradually. Ultimately, either most of the decision makers suggest that a certain β-non-dominated alternative in $\bar{X}$ be the most preferred one, or there is only one β-non-dominated alternative left in the set $\bar{X}$, then this alternative is the most preferred one.

Remark 6.1 The decision making method above can only be used to find the optimal alternative, but is unsuitable for ranking alternatives.

Remark 6.2 The investigation on the interactive group decision methods for MADM problems in which the attribute weights and attribute values are incompletely known have received more and more attention from researchers recently. Considering the complexity of computations, here we do not introduce the results on this topic. Interested readers please refer to the literature [51–53, 64, 65, 84, 85, 141].

6.6.2 *Practical Example*

Example 6.6 A university plans to buy textbooks "*Mathematical Analysis*", and now five kinds of the textbooks are available. To choose one from them, four evaluation indices (attributes) are taken into account: (1) u_1: applicability; (2) u_2: the novelty of content; (3) u_3: quality of editing and printing; and (4) u_4: price. Among these indices, u_4 is the cost-type attribute, and the others are benefit-type attributes. The attribute values are provided by using the 10-point scale, from 1 (worst) to 10 (best), and are contained in the decision matrix $\tilde{A}$ (see Table 6.11).

The known attribute weight information is:

$$\Phi = \{ w = (w_1, w_2, w_3, w_4) \mid 0.1 \le w_1 \le 0.45, w_2 \le 0.2, 0.1 \le w_3 \le 0.4,$$
$$w_4 \ge 0.03, \sum_{j=1}^{4} w_j = 1, w_j \ge 0, \ j = 1,2,3,4 \}$$

Below we solve this problem using the method of Sect. 6.6.1:

Step 1 Normalize the uncertain decision matrix $\tilde{A}$ into the matrix $\tilde{R}$ (see Table 6.12) using Eqs. (4.13) and (4.14).

Step 2 Utilize Theorem 6.3 to identify the alternatives: If the optimization level $\beta = 0.7$, then for the alternative x_1, according to Theorem 6.3, we can solve the following linear programming problem:

Table 6.11 Uncertain decision matrix $\tilde{A}$

	u_1	u_2	u_3	u_4
x_1	[8, 9]	[6, 7]	[8, 9]	[7, 8]
x_2	[5, 6]	[8, 10]	[6, 8]	[4, 5]
x_3	[7, 9]	[7, 8]	[5, 6]	[6, 7]
x_4	[5, 7]	[8, 9]	[9, 10]	[7, 8]
x_5	[7, 8]	[6, 8]	[7, 8]	[5, 7]

Table 6.12 Normalized uncertain decision matrix $\tilde{R}$

	u_1	u_2	u_3	u_4
x_1	[0.205, 0.281]	[0.143, 0.200]	[0.195, 0.257]	[0.144, 0.194]
x_2	[0.128, 0.188]	[0.190, 0.286]	[0.146, 0.229]	[0.230, 0.340]
x_3	[0.179, 0.281]	[0.167, 0.229]	[0.122, 0.171]	[0.164, 0.227]
x_4	[0.128, 0.219]	[0.190, 0.257]	[0.220, 0.286]	[0.144, 0.194]
x_5	[0.179, 0.250]	[0.143, 0.229]	[0.171, 0.229]	[0.164, 0.272]

$$\begin{cases} J_1 = \max(\theta_1 - \theta_2 + 0.2582w_1 + 0.1829w_2 + 0.2384w_3 + 0.1790w_4) \\ s.t.\ \theta_1 - \theta_2 + 0.1700w_1 + 0.2572w_2 + 0.2041w_3 + 0.3070w_4 \le 0 \\ \quad \theta_1 - \theta_2 + 0.2504w_1 + 0.2104w_2 + 0.1563w_3 + 0.2081w_4 \le 0 \\ \quad \theta_1 - \theta_2 + 0.1917w_1 + 0.2369w_2 + 0.2662w_3 + 0.1790w_4 \le 0 \\ \quad \theta_1 - \theta_2 + 0.2287w_1 + 0.2032w_2 + 0.2116w_3 + 0.2396w_4 \le 0 \\ \quad 0.1 \le w_1 \le 0.45, 0.1 \le w_2 \le 0.3, 0.05 \le w_3 \le 1 \\ \quad 0.1 \le \omega_4 \le 0.5, \sum_{j=1}^{4} \omega_j = 1,\ \omega_j \ge 0,\ j = 1,2,3,4 \end{cases}$$

Solving this model, we get $J_1 = 0.0284 > 0$. Similarly, for the alternatives $x_i (i = 2,3,4,5)$, we have

$$J_2 = 0.0638 > 0,\ J_3 = 0.0112 > 0,\ J_4 = -0.0234 < 0,\ J_5 = -0.0208 < 0$$

thus, x_4 and x_5 are the β-dominated alternatives, which should be eliminated, and get the set $\overline{X} = \{x_1, x_2, x_3\}$ with three β-non-dominated alternatives. Interacting with the decision maker, and without loss of generality, suppose that the decision maker prefers x_2 to x_1 and x_3, then x_2 is the optimal textbook.

Part III
Linguistic MADM Methods and Their Applications

Chapter 7
Linguistic MADM with Unknown Weight Information

The complexity and uncertainty of objective things and the fuzziness of human thought result in decision making with linguistic information in many real life situations. For example, when evaluating the "comfort" or "design" of a car, linguistic labels like "good", "fair", "poor" are usually used, and evaluating a car's speed, linguistic labels like "very fast", "fast", "slow" can be used. Therefore, the investigation on the MADM problems in which the evaluation information on alternatives is expressed in linguistic labels is an interesting and important research topic, which has achieved fruitful research results in recent years. In this chapter, we introduce some linguistic information aggregation operators, such as the generalized induced ordered weighted averaging (GIOWA) operator, the extended ordered weighted averaging (EOWA) operator, the extended weighted averaging (EWA) operator, and linguistic hybrid aggregation (LHA) operator, etc. Based on these aggregation operators, we also introduce some methods for solving the MADM problems in which the weight information on attributes is unknown completely, and the attribute values are expressed in linguistic labels, and illustrate them with some practical examples.

7.1 MADM Method Based on GIOWA Operator

7.1.1 GIOWA Operator

Definition 7.1 [90] Let $\hat{a} = [a^L, a^M, a^U]$, where $0 < a^L \le a^M \le a^U$, then $\hat{a}$ is called a triangular fuzzy number, whose characteristic (msembership function) can be denoted as:

Z.S. Xu, *Uncertain Multi-Attribute Decision Making*,
DOI 10.1007/978-3-662-45640-8_7

$$\mu_{\hat{a}}(x)=\begin{cases}\dfrac{x-a^L}{a^M-a^L}, & a^L\le x\le a^M\\[2mm] \dfrac{x-a^U}{a^M-a^U}, & a^M\le x\le a^U\\[2mm] 0, & otherwise\end{cases}$$

For the sake of convenience, we first give two operational laws of triangular fuzzy numbers:

1. $\hat{a}+\hat{b}=[a^L,a^M,a^U]+[b^L,b^M,b^U]=[a^L+b^L,a^M+b^M,a^U+b^U]$.
2. $\beta\hat{a}=\left[\beta a^L,\beta a^M,\beta a^U\right]$, where $\beta\ge 0$.

Definition 7.2 [159] The function IOWA operator is called an induced ordered weighted averaging (IOWA) operator, if

$$IOWA_\omega(<\pi_1,a_1>,<\pi_2,a_2>,\ldots,<\pi_n,a_n>)=\sum_{j=1}^{n}\omega_j b_j$$

where $\omega=(\omega_1,\omega_2,\ldots,\omega_n)$ is the weighting vector associated with the IOWA operator, $\omega_j\in[0,1]$, $j=1,2,\ldots,n$, and $\sum_{j=1}^{n}\omega_j=1$. $<\pi_1,a_1>$ is the OWA pair, b_j is the a_i value of the pair $<\pi_i,a_i>$ having the jth largest π_i value. The term π_i is referred as the order inducing variable and a_i is referred as the argument variable.

In the following, we introduce a generalized IOWA operator:

Definition 7.3 [119] If

$$GIOWA_\omega(<\xi_1,\pi_1,a_1>,<\xi_2,\pi_2,a_2>,\ldots,<\xi_n,\pi_n,a_n>)=\sum_{j=1}^{n}\omega_j b_j$$

where $\omega=(\omega_1,\omega_2,\ldots,\omega_n)$ is the associated weighting vector with $\omega_j\in[0,1]$ $j=1,2,\ldots,n$, and $\sum_{j=1}^{n}\omega_j=1$; The object $<\xi_i,\pi_i,a_i>$ consists of three components, where the first component ξ_i represents the importance degree or character of the second component π_i, and the second component π_i is used to induce an ordering through the first component ξ_i over the third components a_i, which are then aggregated. Here, b_j is the a_i value of the object having the jth largest ξ_i $(j=1,2,\ldots,n)$. Then the function *GIOWA* is called a generalized induced ordered weighted averaging (GIOWA) operator. In discussing these objects $<\xi_i,\pi_i,a_i>$ $(i=1,2,\ldots,n)$, because of its role we shall refer to the ξ_i as the direct order inducing variable, the π_i as the indirect order inducing variable, and the a_i as the argument variable.

Especially, if $\xi_i = \text{No}.i$, for all $i = 1,2,\ldots,n$, where No.i is the ordered position of the a_i, then the GIOWA operator is reduced to the WA operator.

Example 7.1 Consider the collection of the objects $<\xi_i, \pi_i, a_i>(i = 1,2,3)$:

$$< No.2, Johnson, 160 >, < No.1, Brown, 70 >$$
$$< No.4, Smith, 20 >, < No.3, Anderson, 100 >$$

By the first component, we get the ordered objects:

$$< No.1, Brown, 70 >, < No.2, Johnson, 160 >$$
$$< No.3, Anderson, 100 >, < No.4, Smith, 20 >$$

The ordering induces the ordered arguments:

$$b_1 = 70, b_2 = 160, b_3 = 100, b_4 = 20$$

If the weighting vector for this aggregation is $\omega = (0.1, 0.2, 0.3, 0.4)$, then we get

$$\begin{aligned}
&GIOWA_\omega(<\xi_1,\pi_1,a_1>,<\xi_2,\pi_2,a_2>,<\xi_3,\pi_3,a_3>,<\xi_4,\pi_4,a_4>)\\
&= GIOWA_\omega(< No.2, Johnson, 160 >,< No.1, Brown, 70 >,\\
&< No.4, Smith, 20 >,< No.3, Anderson, 100 >)\\
&= 0.1\times 70 + 0.2\times 160 + 0.3\times 100 + 0.4\times 20 = 77
\end{aligned}$$

Especially, if there exists two objects $<\xi_i,\pi_i,a_i>$ and $<\xi_j,\pi_j,a_j>$ such that $\xi_i = \xi_j$, then we can follow the policy presented by Yager and Filev (1999), i.e., to replace the arguments of the tied objects by the average of the arguments of the tied. Objects, $<\xi_i,\pi_i,\frac{a_i+a_j}{2}>$ and $<\xi_j,\pi_j,\frac{a_i+a_j}{2}>$. If k items are tied, we replace these by k replica's of their average.

In the following, let us first look at some desirable properties associated with the GIOWA operator [119]:

Theorem 7.1(Commutativity) Let $(<\xi_1,\pi_1,a_1>,<\xi_2,\pi_2,a_2>,\ldots,<\xi_n,\pi_n,a_n>)$ be any vector of arguments, $(<\xi_1',\pi_1',a_1'>,<\xi_2',\pi_2',a_2'>,\ldots,<\xi_n',\pi_n',a_n'>)$ be any permutation of $(<\xi_1,\pi_1,a_1>,<\xi_2,\pi_2,a_2>,\ldots,<\xi_n,\pi_n,a_n>)$, then

$$\begin{aligned}
&GIOWA_\omega(<\xi_1,\pi_1,a_1>,<\xi_2,\pi_2,a_2>,\ldots,<\xi_n,\pi_n,a_n>)\\
&\quad= GIOWA_\omega(<\xi_1',\pi_1',a_1'>,<\xi_2',\pi_2',a_2'>,\ldots,<\xi_n',\pi_n',a_n'>)
\end{aligned}$$

Theorem 7.2 (Idempotency) Let $(<\xi_1,\pi_1,a_1>,<\xi_2,\pi_2,a_2>,\ldots,<\xi_n,\pi_n,a_n>)$ be any vector of arguments, if for any i, $a_i = a$, then

$$GIOWA_{\omega}(<\xi_1,\pi_1,a_1>,<\xi_2,\pi_2,a_2>,\ldots,<\xi_n,\pi_n,a_n>) = a$$

Theorem 7.3 (Monotonicity) Let $(<\xi_1,\pi_1,a_1>,<\xi_2,\pi_2,a_2>,\ldots,<\xi_n,\pi_n,a_n>)$ and $(<\xi_1,\pi_1,\overline{a}_1>,<\xi_2,\pi_2,\overline{a}_2>,\ldots,<\xi_n,\pi_n,\overline{a}_n>)$ be two vectors of arguments, if for any i, $a_i \le \overline{a}_i$, then

$$\begin{aligned} &GIOWA_{\omega}(<\xi_1,\pi_1,a_1>,<\xi_2,\pi_2,a_2>,\ldots,<\xi_n,\pi_n,a_n>) \\ &\quad \le GIOWA_{\omega}(<\xi_1,\pi_1,\overline{a}_1>,<\xi_2,\pi_2,\overline{a}_2>,\ldots,<\xi_n,\pi_n,\overline{a}_n>) \end{aligned}$$

Theorem 7.4 (Bounded) The GIOWA operator lies between the min operator and the max operator, i.e.,

$$\min_i \{a_i\} \le GIOWA_{\omega}(<\xi_1,\pi_1,a_1>,<\xi_2,\pi_2,a_2>,\ldots,<\xi_n,\pi_n,a_n>) \le \max_i \{a_i\}$$

Theorem 7.5 If $\omega = \left(\frac{1}{n},\frac{1}{n},\ldots,\frac{1}{n}\right)$, then the corresponding GIOWA operator is the averaging operator, i.e.,

$$GIOWA_{\omega}(<\xi_1,\pi_1,a_1>,<\xi_2,\pi_2,a_2>,\ldots,<\xi_n,\pi_n,a_n>) = \frac{1}{n}\sum_{i=1}^{n} a_i$$

Theorem 7.6 If for any i, $\xi_i = a_i$, then the GIOWA operator reduces to the OWA operator, i.e., the OWA operator is the special case of the GIOWA operator.

Theorem 7.7 For any i, $\pi_i = \xi_i$, then the GIOWA operator reduces to the IOWA operator, i.e., the IOWA operator is the special case of the GIOWA operator.

7.1.2 Decision Making Method

7.1.2.1 For the Cases where There is Only One Decision Maker

Step 1 For a MADM problem, let X and U be respectively the set of alternatives and the set of attributes. The decision maker provides the evaluation value r_{ij} over the alternative $x_i \in X$ with respect to the attribute $u_j \in U$, and constructs the linguistic decision matrix $R = (r_{ij})_{n\times m}$, where $r_{ij} \in S$, and

$$S = \{extremely\ poor, very\ poor, poor, slightly\ poor, fair, slightly\ good, \\ good, very\ good, extremely\ good\}$$

is the set of linguistic labels, whose corresponding expressions of triangular fuzzy numbers are as follows:

$$extremely\ poor = [0, 0.1, 0.2],\ very\ poor = [0.1, 0.2, 0.3]$$
$$poor = [0.2, 0.3, 0.4],\ slightly\ poor = [0.3, 0.4, 0.5]$$
$$fair = [0.4, 0.5, 0.6],\ slightly\ good = [0.5, 0.6, 0.7]$$
$$good = [0.6, 0.7, 0.8],\ very\ good = [0.7, 0.8, 0.9]$$
$$extremely\ good = [0.8, 0.9, 1]$$

where

$$extremely\ good > very\ good > good > slightly\ good > fair \\ > slightly\ poor > poor > very\ poor > extremely\ poor$$

Step 2 Use the GIOWA operator to aggregate the linguistic evaluation information of the i th line in the matrix $R = (r_{ij})_{n\times m}$, and then get the overall attribute values $z_i(\omega)(i = 1, 2, \ldots, n)$ of the alternatives $x_i(i = 1, 2, \ldots, n)$:

$$z_i(\omega) = GIOWA_\omega(< r_{i1}, u_1, \hat{a}_{i1} >, < r_{i2}, u_2, \hat{a}_{i2} >, \ldots, < r_{im}, u_m, \hat{a}_{im} >) \\ = \sum_{j=1}^{m} \omega_j b_{ij}$$

where $r_{ij} \in S, u_j \in U, \hat{a}_{ij}$ is the corresponding triangular fuzzy number of r_{ij}, $\omega = (\omega_1, \omega_2, \ldots, \omega_m)$ is the weighting vector associated with the GIOWA operator, $\omega_j \in [0,1], j = 1, 2, \ldots, m, \sum_{j=1}^{m} \omega_j = 1$, and $\hat{b}_{ij}$ is the $\hat{a}_{il}$ value of the object $< r_{il}, \pi_l, \hat{a}_{il} >$ having the j th largest $r_{il}(l = 1, 2, \ldots, m)$.

Step 3 Use $z_i(\omega)(i = 1, 2, \ldots, n)$ to rank and select the alternatives.

7.1.2.2 For the Cases where There are Multiple Decision Makers

Step 1 For a MADM problem, let X, U and D be respectively the set of alternatives, the set of attributes, and the set of decision makers. The decision maker

$d_k \in D$ provides the evaluation value $r_{ij}^{(k)}$ over the alternative $x_i \in X$ with respect to the attribute $u_j \in U$, and constructs the linguistic decision matrix $R_k = (r_{ij}^{(k)})_{n\times m}$, where $r_{ij}^{(k)} \in S, i = 1,2,\ldots,n, j = 1,2,\ldots,m, k = 1,2,\ldots,t$.

Step 2 Utilize the GIOWA operator to aggregate the linguistic evaluation information of the i th line in the matrix $R_k = (r_{ij}^{(k)})_{n\times m}$, and then get the overall attribute value $z_i^{(k)}(\omega)$ of the alternative x_i corresponding to the decision maker d_k:

$$z_i^{(k)}(\omega) = GIOWA_{\omega}(< r_{i1}^{(k)}, u_1, \hat{a}_{i1}^{(k)} >, < r_{i2}^{(k)}, u_2, \hat{a}_{i2}^{(k)} >, \ldots, < r_{im}^{(k)}, \pi_m, \hat{a}_{im}^{(k)} >)$$
$$= \sum_{j=1}^{m} \omega_j \hat{b}_{ij}^{(k)}$$

where $r_{ij}^{(k)} \in S$, $u_j \in U$, $\hat{a}_{ij}^{(k)}$ is the corresponding triangular fuzzy number of $r_{ij}^{(k)}$, $\omega = (\omega_1, \omega_2, \ldots, \omega_m)$ is the weighting vector associated with the GIOWA operator, $\omega_j \in [0,1]$, $j = 1,2,\ldots,m$, $\sum_{j=1}^{m} \omega_j = 1$, and $\hat{b}_{ij}^{(k)}$ is the $\hat{a}_{il}^{(k)}$ value of the object $< r_{il}^{(k)}, u_l, \hat{a}_{il}^{(k)} >$ having the j th largest of $r_{il}^{(k)} (l = 1,2,\ldots,m)$.

Step 3 Employ the GIOWA operator to aggregate the overall attribute values $z_i^{(k)}(\omega)(k = 1,2,\ldots,t)$ of the alternative x_i given by the decision makers $d_k (k = 1,2,\ldots,t)$:

$$z_i(\omega') = GIOWA_{\omega'}(< z_i^{(1)}(\omega), d_1, \hat{a}_i^{(1)} >, < z_i^{(2)}(\omega), d_2, \hat{a}_i^{(2)} >, \ldots < z_i^{(t)}(\omega), d_t, \hat{a}_i^{(t)} >)$$
$$= \sum_{k=1}^{t} \omega'_k \hat{b}_i^{(k)}$$

where $z_i^{(k)}(\omega) \in S, d_k \in D, \hat{a}_i^{(k)}$ is the triangular fuzzy number corresponding to $z_i^{(k)}(\omega)$, $\omega' = (\omega'_1, \omega'_2, \ldots, \omega'_t)$ is the weighting vector associated with the GIOWA operator, $\omega'_k \in [0,1], k = 1,2,\ldots,t, \sum_{k=1}^{t} \omega'_k = 1$, and $\hat{b}_i^{(k)}$ is the $\hat{a}_i^{(l)}$ value of the object $< z_i^{(l)}(\omega), d_l, \hat{a}_i^{(l)} >$ having the k th largest of $z_i^{(l)}(\omega)(l = 1,2,\ldots,n)$.

Step 4 Use $z_i(\omega')(i = 1,2,\ldots,n)$ to rank and select the alternatives.

7.1.3 Practical Example

Example 7.2 Consider a MADM problem that a risk investment company plans to invest a high-tech project in an enterprise. Four candidate enterprises (alternatives) $x_i (i = 1,2,3,4)$ are available. To evaluate these enterprises from the angle of

Table 7.1 Linguistic decision matrix R_1

	u_1	u_2	u_3	u_4	u_5	u_6	u_7
x_1	Slightly good	Very good	Very good	Fair	Slightly good	Good	Good
x_2	Very good	Good	Fair	Good	Very good	Good	Slightly poor
x_3	Good	Good	Very good	Slightly good	Extremely good	Very good	Good
x_4	Good	Good	Slightly poor	Slightly good	Very good	Slightly good	Slightly good

Table 7.2 Linguistic decision matrix R_2

	u_1	u_2	u_3	u_4	u_5	u_6	u_7
x_1	Slightly good	Good	Very good	Fair	Good	Good	Extremely good
x_2	Fair	Slightly good	Fair	Slightly good	Good	Good	Slightly good
x_3	Very good	Slightly good	Good	Good	Extremely good	Extremely good	Slightly good
x_4	Fair	Slightly good	Fair	Slightly good	Fair	Slightly good	Slightly poor

Table 7.3 Linguistic decision matrix R_3

	u_1	u_2	u_3	u_4	u_5	u_6	u_7
x_1	Fair	Good	Good	Slightly good	Very good	Good	Very good
x_2	Good	Slightly good	Slightly good	Good	Fair	Good	Slightly poor
x_3	Good	Slightly good	Good	Good	Good	Very good	Good
x_4	Fair	Slightly good	Slightly poor	Slightly good	Fair	Fair	Slightly good

their capabilities, the company puts forward several evaluation indices (attributes) [87] as follows: (1) u_1: sales ability; (2) u_2: management ability; (3) u_3: production capacity; (4) u_4: technical competence; (5) u_5: financial capacity; (6) u_6: risk bearing ability; and (7) u_7: enterprise strategic consistency. Three decision makers $d_k (k = 1,2,3)$ evaluate each enterprise according to these seven indices, and construct three linguistic decision matrices (see Tables 7.1, 7.2, 7.3).

Now we utilize the method of Sect. 7.1.2 to solve this problem, which has the following steps:

Step 1 Let $\omega = (0.2, 0.1, 0.15, 0.2, 0.1, 0.15, 0.1)$, then we utilize the GIOWA operator to aggregate the linguistic evaluation information in the i th line of the matrix R_k, and get the overall attribute evaluation value $z_i^{(k)}(\omega)$ of the enterprise x_i provided by the decision maker d_k. We first calculate the overall attribute evaluation information of each enterprise provided by the decision maker d_1. Since

$$r_{11}^{(1)} = \textit{slightly good}, r_{12}^{(1)} = \textit{very good}, r_{13}^{(1)} = \textit{very good}, r_{14}^{(1)} = \textit{fair},$$
$$r_{15}^{(1)} = \textit{slightly good}, r_{16}^{(1)} = \textit{good}, r_{17}^{(1)} = \textit{good}$$

thus,

$$r_{12}^{(1)} = r_{13}^{(1)} > r_{16}^{(1)} = r_{17}^{(1)} > r_{11}^{(1)} = r_{15}^{(1)} > r_{14}^{(1)}$$

By the linguistic scale given in Sect. 7.1.2, we can see that the triangular fuzzy numbers corresponding to $r_{1j}^{(1)} (j = 1, 2, \ldots, 7)$ are

$$\hat{a}_{11}^{(1)} = [0.5, 0.6, 0.7], \hat{a}_{12}^{(1)} = [0.7, 0.8, 0.9], \hat{a}_{13}^{(1)} = [0.7, 0.8, 0.9]$$
$$\hat{a}_{14}^{(1)} = [0.4, 0.5, 0.6], \hat{a}_{15}^{(1)} = [0.5, 0.6, 0.7], \hat{a}_{16}^{(1)} = [0.6, 0.7, 0.8]$$
$$\hat{a}_{17}^{(1)} = [0.6, 0.7, 0.8]$$

then

$$\hat{b}_{11}^{(1)} = \hat{b}_{12}^{(1)} = \hat{a}_{12}^{(1)} = \hat{a}_{13}^{(1)} = [0.7, 0.8, 0.9]$$
$$\hat{b}_{13}^{(1)} = \hat{b}_{14}^{(1)} = \hat{a}_{16}^{(1)} = \hat{a}_{17}^{(1)} = [0.6, 0.7, 0.8]$$
$$\hat{b}_{15}^{(1)} = \hat{b}_{16}^{(1)} = \hat{a}_{11}^{(1)} = \hat{a}_{15}^{(1)} = [0.5, 0.6, 0.7]$$
$$\hat{b}_{17}^{(1)} = \hat{a}_{14}^{(1)} = [0.4, 0.5, 0.6]$$

thus, by using the GIOWA operator and the operational laws of triangular fuzzy numbers, we have

$$\begin{aligned} z_1^{(1)}(\omega) &= GIOWA_\omega(< r_{11}^{(1)}, u_1, \hat{a}_{11}^{(1)} >, < r_{12}^{(1)}, u_2, \hat{a}_{12}^{(1)} >, \ldots, < r_{17}^{(1)}, u_7, \hat{a}_{17}^{(1)} >) \\ &= \sum_{j=1}^{7} \omega_j \hat{b}_{1j}^{(1)} = [0.6, 0.7, 0.8] = \textit{good} \end{aligned}$$

Similarly, we can get $z_2^{(1)}(\omega) = \textit{good}, z_3^{(1)}(\omega) = \textit{very good}, z_4^{(1)}(\omega) = \textit{slightly good}$.

For d_2 and d_3, we have

$$z_1^{(2)}(\omega) = \textit{good}, z_2^{(2)}(\omega) = \textit{slightly good}, z_3^{(2)}(\omega) = \textit{very good}, z_4^{(2)}(\omega) = \textit{fair}$$
$$z_1^{(3)}(\omega) = \textit{good}, z_2^{(3)}(\omega) = \textit{slightly good}, z_3^{(3)}(\omega) = \textit{good}, z_4^{(3)}(\omega) = \textit{fair}$$

Step 2 Suppose that $\omega' = (0.3, 0.5, 0.2)$, then we utilize the GIOWA operator to aggregate the overall attribute evaluation values $z_i^{(k)}(\omega)(k = 1,2,3,4)$ of the enterprise x_i provided by three decision makers $d_k (k = 1,2,3)$, and get the group's overall attribute evaluation value $z_i(\omega')$ of the enterprise x_i:

$$z_1(\omega') = GIOWA_{\omega'}(< z_1^{(1)}(\omega), d_1, \widehat{a}_1^{(1)} >, < z_1^{(2)}(\omega), d_2, \widehat{a}_1^{(2)} >, < z_1^{(3)}(\omega), d_3, \widehat{a}_1^{(3)} >)$$
$$= good$$
$$z_2(\omega') = GIOWA_{\omega'}(< z_2^{(1)}(\omega), d_2, \widehat{a}_2^{(1)} >, < z_2^{(2)}(\omega), d_2, \widehat{a}_2^{(2)} >, < z_2^{(3)}(\omega), d_3, \widehat{a}_2^{(3)} >)$$
$$= slightly\ good$$

$$z_3(\omega') = GIOWA_{\omega'}(< z_3^{(1)}(\omega), d_1, \widehat{a}_3^{(1)} >, < z_3^{(2)}(\omega), d_2, \widehat{a}_3^{(2)} >, < z_3^{(3)}(\omega), d_3, \widehat{a}_3^{(3)} >)$$
$$= very\ good$$

$$z_4(\omega') = GIOWA_{\omega'}(< z_4^{(1)}(\omega), d_4, \widehat{a}_4^{(1)} >, < z_4^{(2)}(\omega), d_4, \widehat{a}_4^{(2)} >, < z_4^{(3)}(\omega), d_4, \widehat{a}_4^{(3)} >)$$
$$= fair$$

Step 3 Utilize $z_i(\omega')(i = 1,2,3,4)$ to rank the enterprises $x_i (i = 1,2,3,4)$:

$$x_3 \succ x_1 \succ x_2 \succ x_4$$

and then we get the best enterprise x_3.

7.2 MADM Method Based on LOWA Operator

7.2.1 Decision Making Method

Definition 7.4 [109] Let $LOWA : S^n \rightarrow S$, if

$$LOWA_\omega(a_1, a_2, \ldots, a_n) = \max_j \min\{\omega_j, b_j\}$$

where $\omega = (\omega_1, \omega_2, \ldots, \omega_n)$ is the weighting vector associated with the function $LOWA$, $\omega_j \in S$, $j = 1,2,\ldots,n$, and b_j is the j th largest of a collection of arguments $a_i (i = 1,2,\ldots,n)$, then the function $LOWA$ is called a linguistic OWA (LOWA) operator, where S is a linguistic scale, for example,

$$S = \{extremely\ poor, very\ poor, poor, slightly\ poor, fair, slightly\ good, good, very\ good, extremely\ good\}$$

or the other forms, for example,

$$S = \{very\ low, low, medium, high, very\ high\}$$

In Chap. 9, we will introduce the properties of the LOWA operator in detail.

In what follows, we introduce a MADM method based on the LOWA operator [109]:

7.2.1.1 For the Cases where There is Only One Decision Maker

Step 1 For a MADM problem, the decision maker provides the linguistic evaluation value r_{ij} of the alternative $x_i \in X$ with respect to the attribute $u_j \in U$, and construct the evaluation matrix $R = (r_{ij})_{n \times m}$, and $r_{ij} \in S$.

Step 2 Utilize the LOWA operator to aggregate the linguistic evaluation information of the i th line of the evaluation matrix $R = (r_{ij})_{n \times m}$, and get the overall attribute evaluation value $z_i(\omega)$ of the alternative x_i, where

$$z_i(\omega) = \max_j \min\{\omega_j, b_{ij}\},\ i = 1, 2, \ldots, n$$

where $\omega = (\omega_1, \omega_2, \ldots, \omega_m)$ is the weighting vector associated with the LOWA operator, $\omega_j \in S$, $j = 1, 2, \ldots, m$, b_{ij} is the j th largest of $r_{ij}\,(j = 1, 2, \ldots, m)$.

Step 3 Utilize $z_i(\omega)(i = 1, 2, \ldots, n)$ to rank and select the alternatives.

7.2.1.2 For the Cases where There are Multiple Decision Makers

Step 1 For a MADM problem, the decision maker $d_k \in D$ provides the linguistic evaluation value $r_{ij}^{(k)}$ over the alternative x_i with respect to the attribute $u_j \in U$, and constructs the linguistic decision matrix $R_k = (r_{ij}^{(k)})_{n \times m}$, and $r_{ij}^{(k)} \in S$.

Step 2 Utilize the LOWA operator to aggregate the evaluation information of the i th line in the matrix $R_k = (r_{ij}^{(k)})_{n \times m}$, and get the overall attribute evaluation values $z_i^{(k)}(\omega)$ of the alternative x_i with respect to the attribute provided by the decision maker d_k:

$$z_i^{(k)}(\omega) = LOWA_\omega(r_{i1}^{(k)}, r_{i2}^{(k)}, \ldots, r_{im}^{(k)}) = \max_j \min\{\omega_j, b_{ij}^{(k)}\}$$

where $\omega = (\omega_1, \omega_2, \ldots, \omega_m)$ is the weighting vector associated with the LOWA operator, $\omega_j \in S$, $j = 1, 2, \ldots, m$, $b_{ij}^{(k)}$ is the j th largest of $r_{ij}^{(k)}\,(j = 1, 2, \ldots, m)$.

Step 3 Utilize the LOWA operator to aggregate the overall attribute evaluation values $z_i^{(k)}(\omega)(k=1,2,\ldots,t)$ of the alternative x_i provided by the decision makers $d_k(k=1,2,\ldots,t)$ into the group's overall attribute evaluation value $z_i(\omega')$:

$$z_i(\omega') = LOWA_{\omega'}(z_i^{(1)}(\omega), z_i^{(2)}(\omega), \ldots, z_i^{(t)}(\omega)) = \max_k \min\{\omega_k', b_i^{(k)}\}$$

where $\omega' = (\omega_1', \omega_2', \ldots, \omega_t')$ is the weighting vector associated with the LOWA operator, $\omega_k' \in S$, $k=1,2,\ldots,t$, and $b_i^{(k)}$ is the j th largest of $z_i^{(l)}(\omega)(l=1,2,\ldots,t)$.

Step 4 Utilize $z_i(\omega')(i=1,2,\ldots,n)$ to rank and select the alternatives.

7.2.2 Practical Example

In the following, we consider a military problem [55] that concerns MAGDM:

Example 7.3 Fire system is a dynamic system achieved by collocating and allocating various firearms involved in an appropriate way. The fire system of a tank unit is an essential part when the commander tries to execute fire distribution in a defensive combat. The fire deployment is of great importance in fulfilling a fixed goal, improving the defensive stability, annihilating enemies, and protecting ourselves. The third company of our tank unit is organizing a defensive battle in Xiaoshan region and there are four proposals $x_i(i=1,2,3,4)$ available for the commander. The evaluation indices are as follows: (1) u_1: concealment by making use of the landforms; (2) u_2: reduction of the mobility of enemy airplanes; (3) u_3: combination with obstacles; (4) u_4: cooperation with mutual firepower; (5) u_5: air-defense capacity; (6) u_6: the approximation to primary contravallation; (7) u_7: capacity that approaches enemy action; and (8) capacity that reduces the enemy equipment advantage. The evaluation values provided by three decision makers over the four proposals $x_i(i=1,2,3,4)$ with respect to the attributes $u_j(j=1,2,\ldots,8)$ are described in the linguistic decision matrices $R_k=(r_{ij}^{(k)})_{4\times 8}(k=1,2,3)$ (see Tables 7.4, 7.5, 7.6).

Now we utilize the method of Sect. 7.2.1 to solve the problem, which involves the following Steps:

Step 1 Let

$$w = (medium, medium, very high, high, very high, high, high, medium)$$

then we utilize the formula:

$$\begin{aligned} z_i^{(k)}(\omega) &= LOWA_{\omega}(r_{i1}^{(k)}, r_{i2}^{(k)}, \ldots, r_{i8}^{(k)}) \\ &= \max_j \min\{\omega_j, b_{ij}^{(k)}\}(i=1,2,3,4,\ k=1,2,3) \end{aligned}$$

Table 7.4 Linguistic decision matrix R_1

	u_1	u_2	u_3	u_4
x_1	High	Very high	Very high	Medium
x_2	Very high	High	Medium	High
x_3	High	High	Very high	Medium
x_4	High	High	Low	Medium
	u_5	u_6	u_7	u_8
x_1	High	High	Very high	High
x_2	Very high	High	High	High
x_3	Very high	Very high	High	Very high
x_4	Very high	Medium	High	High

Table 7.5 Linguistic decision matrix R_2

	u_1	u_2	u_3	u_4
x_1	Medium	High	Very high	Medium
x_2	High	Medium	Medium	Medium
x_3	Medium	Medium	High	High
x_4	Medium	Medium	Medium	Medium
	u_5	u_6	u_7	u_8
x_1	High	Very high	Medium	High
x_2	Very high	High	Very high	Medium
x_3	Very high	Very high	Very high	High
x_4	Very high	High	Medium	Medium

Table 7.6 Linguistic decision matrix R_3

	u_1	u_2	u_3	u_4
x_1	Medium	High	High	Medium
x_2	High	Medium	Medium	Very high
x_3	Very high	High	High	High
x_4	Medium	Medium	Low	Medium
	u_5	u_6	u_7	u_8
x_1	Very high	High	Medium	High
x_2	High	Medium	Very high	High
x_3	Very high	Very high	High	Very high
x_4	Very high	High	Medium	Medium

to aggregate the attribute values of the i th line in the linguistic decision matrix R_k, and get the overall attribute evaluation value $z_i^{(k)}(\omega)$ of the alternative x_i:

$$z_1^{(1)}(\omega) = very high,\ z_2^{(1)}(\omega) = high,\ z_3^{(1)}(\omega) = very high$$

$$z_4^{(1)}(\omega) = high,\ z_1^{(2)}(\omega) = high,\ z_2^{(2)}(\omega) = high,\ z_3^{(2)}(\omega) = very\,high$$

$$z_4^{(2)}(\omega) = medium,\ z_1^{(3)}(\omega) = high,\ z_2^{(3)}(\omega) = high$$

$$z_3^{(3)}(\omega) = very\,high,\ z_4^{(3)}(\omega) = medium$$

Step 2 Let $\omega' = (medium, very\,high, high)$, then we utilize the LOWA operator:

$$z_i(\omega') = LOWA_{\omega'}(z_i^{(1)}(\omega), z_i^{(2)}(\omega), z_i^{(3)}(\omega)),\ i = 1,2,3,4$$

to aggregate the overall attribute evaluation values $z_i^{(k)}(\omega)(k = 1,2,3)$ of the alternative x_i provided by the decision makers $d_k(k = 1,2,3)$ in Tables 7.4, 7.5, 7.6 into the group's overall attribute evaluation value $z_i(\omega')$:

$$z_1(\omega') = high,\ z_2(\omega') = high,\ z_3(\omega') = very\,high,\ z_4(\omega') = medium$$

Step 3 Rank the alternatives $x_i(i = 1,2,3,4)$ according to $z_i(\omega')(i = 1,2,3,4)$:

$$x_3 \succ x_1 \sim x_2 \succ x_4$$

which indicates that x_3 is the optimal proposal.

The two methods above are simple and straightforward, and easy to be used in actual applications, but they are somewhat rough, and may produce the loss of decision information in the process of aggregation.

In what follows, we shall introduce two practical decision making methods which are simple and does not lose any decision information, i.e., the MADM method based on the EOWA operator, and the MADM method based on the EOWA and LHA operators.

7.3 MADM Method Based on EOWA Operator

7.3.1 EOWA Operator

In a MADM problem, when the decision maker evaluates an alternative with linguistic labels, he/she generally needs a proper linguistic label set to be predefined. Therefore, here we introduce a linguistic label set [125]:

$$S = \{s_\alpha \mid \alpha = -L, \ldots, -1, 0, 1, \ldots, L\}$$

where the cardinality of S is usually odd, for example, we can take a linguistic label set as:

$$S = \{s_{-1}, s_0, s_1\} = \{low, medium, high\}$$

$$S = \{s_{-2}, s_{-1}, s_0, s_1, s_2\} = \{very\,poor, poor, fair, good, very\,good\}$$

$$S = \{s_{-4}, \ldots, s_0, \ldots, s_4\} = \{extremely\,poor, very\,poor, poor, slightly\,poor, \\ fair, slightly\,good, good, very\,good, extremely\,good\}$$

Usually, in these cases, it is required that there exist the following:

1. The set is ordered: $s_\alpha > s_\beta$ if and only if $\alpha > \beta$;
2. There is the negation operator: neg $((s_\alpha) = s_{-\alpha})$.

To preserve all the given information, Xu [125] extended the discrete linguistic label set $S = \{s_\alpha \mid \alpha = -L, \ldots, -1, 0, 1, \ldots, L\}$ to a continuous linguistic set $\overline{S} = \{s_\alpha \mid \alpha \in [-q, q]\}$, where $q(q > L)$ is a sufficiently large positive integer. If $\alpha \in \{-L, \ldots, -1, 0, 1, \ldots, L\}$, then we call s_α the original linguistic label; Otherwise, we call s_α the virtual linguistic label. The continuous linguistic set $\overline{S}$ also satisfies the conditions (1) and (2) above.

Remark 7.1 In general, the decision maker uses the original linguistic labels to evaluate the alternatives, and the virtual linguistic labels can only appear in operations.

In the following, we gave the operational laws of the linguistic labels:

Definition 7.5 [125] Let $s_\alpha, s_\beta \in \overline{S}$, $y, y_1, y_2 \in [0,1]$, then

1. $s_\alpha \oplus s_\beta = s_{\alpha+\beta}$.
2. $s_\alpha \oplus s_\beta = s_\beta \oplus s_\alpha$.
3. $y s_\alpha = s_{y\alpha}$.
4. $y(s_\alpha \oplus s_\beta) = y s_\alpha \oplus y s_\beta$.
5. $(y_1 + y_2) s_\alpha = y_1 s_\alpha \oplus y_2 s_\alpha$.

Definition 7.6 [113] Let $EOWA: \overline{S}^n \to \overline{S}$, if

$$EOWA_\omega(s_{\alpha_1}, s_{\alpha_2}, \ldots, s_{\alpha_n}) = \omega_1 s_{\beta_1} \oplus \omega_2 s_{\beta_2} \oplus \cdots \oplus \omega_n s_{\beta_n} = s_{\overline{\beta}} \tag{7.1}$$

where $\overline{\beta} = \sum_{j=1}^{n} \omega_j \beta_j$, $\omega = (\omega_1, \omega_2, \ldots, \omega_n)$ is the weighting vector associated with the EOWA operator, $\omega_j \in [0,1]$, $j = 1, 2, \ldots, n$, $\sum_{j=1}^{n} \omega_j = 1$, and s_{β_j} is the j th largest of a collection of arguments s_{α_i} $(i=1,2,\ldots,n)$, then the function $EOWA$ is called an extended ordered weighted averaging (EOWA) operator.

Example 7.4 Suppose that $\omega=(0.2,0.3,0.1,0.4)$, then

$$EOWA_{\omega}(s_2,s_3,s_1,s_{-1})=0.2\times s_3\oplus 0.3\times s_2\oplus 0.1\times s_1\oplus 0.4\times s_{-1}=s_{0.9}$$

The EOWA operator has the following properties:

Theorem 7.8 [113] (Commutativity)

$$EOWA_{\omega}(s_{\alpha_1},s_{\alpha_2},\ldots,s_{\alpha_n})=EOWA_{\omega}(\dot{s}_{\alpha_1},\dot{s}_{\alpha_2},\ldots,\dot{s}_{\alpha_n})$$

where $(\dot{s}_{\alpha_1},\dot{s}_{\alpha_2},\ldots,\dot{s}_{\alpha_n})$ is any permutation of a collection of the linguistic arguments $(s_{\alpha_1},s_{\alpha_2},\ldots,s_{\alpha_n})$.

Proof Let

$$EOWA_{\omega}(s_{\alpha_1},s_{\alpha_2},\ldots,s_{\alpha_n})=\omega_1 s_{\beta_1}\oplus\omega_2 s_{\beta_2}\oplus\cdots\oplus\omega_n s_{\beta_n}$$

$$EOWA_{\omega}(\dot{s}_{\alpha_1},\dot{s}_{\alpha_2},\ldots,\dot{s}_{\alpha_n})=\omega_1\dot{s}_{\beta_1}\oplus\omega_2\dot{s}_{\beta_2}\oplus\cdots\oplus\omega_n\dot{s}_{\beta_n}$$

Since $(\dot{s}_{\alpha_1},\dot{s}_{\alpha_2},\ldots,\dot{s}_{\alpha_n})$ is any permutation of $(s_{\alpha_1},s_{\alpha_2},\ldots,s_{\alpha_n})$, then $s_{\beta_j}=\dot{s}_{\beta_j}$ $(j=1,2,\ldots,n)$. Thus, $WA_{\omega}(s_{\alpha_1},s_{\alpha_2},\ldots,s_{\alpha_n})=EOWA_{\omega}(\dot{s}_{\alpha_1},\dot{s}_{\alpha_2},\ldots,\dot{s}_{\alpha_n})$. This completes the proof.

Theorem 7.9 [113] (Idempotency) If $s_{\alpha_j}=s_{\alpha}$, for any j, then

$$\begin{aligned}EOWA_{\omega}(s_{\alpha_1},s_{\alpha_2},\ldots,s_{\alpha_n})&=\omega_1 s_{\beta_1}\oplus\omega_2 s_{\beta_2}\oplus\cdots\oplus\omega_n s_{\beta_n}\\&\le\omega_1 s_{\beta}\oplus\omega_2 s_{\beta}\oplus\cdots\oplus\omega_n s_{\beta}\\&=(\omega_1+\omega_2+\cdots+\omega_n)s_{\beta}\\&=s_{\beta}\end{aligned}$$

which completes the proof.

Theorem 7.10 [113] (Monotonicity) If $s_{\alpha_i}\le s'_{\alpha_i}$, for any i, then

$$EOWA_{\omega}(s_{\alpha_1},s_{\alpha_2},\ldots,s_{\alpha_n})\le EOWA_{\omega}(s'_{\alpha_1},s'_{\alpha_2},\ldots,s'_{\alpha_n})$$

Proof Let

$$EOWA_{\omega}(s_{\alpha_1},s_{\alpha_2},\ldots,s_{\alpha_n})=\omega_1 s_{\beta_1}\oplus\omega_2 s_{\beta_2}\oplus\cdots\oplus\omega_n s_{\beta_n}$$

$$EOWA_{\omega}(s'_{\alpha_1}, s'_{\alpha_2}, \ldots, s'_{\alpha_n}) = \omega_1 s'_{\beta_1} \oplus \omega_2 s'_{\beta_2} \oplus \cdots \oplus \omega_n s'_{\beta_n}$$

Since $s_{\alpha_i} \le s'_{\alpha_i}$, for any i, then $s_{\beta_i} \le s'_{\beta_i}$. Thus,

$$EOWA_{\omega}(s_{\alpha_1}, s_{\alpha_2}, \ldots, s_{\alpha_n}) \le EOWA_{\omega}(s'_{\alpha_1}, s'_{\alpha_2}, \ldots, s'_{\alpha_n})$$

which completes the proof.

Theorem 7.11 [113] (Bounded)

$$\min_i \{s_{\alpha_i}\} \le EOWA_{\omega}(s_{\alpha_1}, s_{\alpha_2}, \ldots, s_{\alpha_n}) \le \max_i \{s_{\alpha_i}\}$$

Proof Let $\max_i \{s_{\alpha_i}\} = s_{\beta}$ and $\min_i \{s_{\alpha_i}\} = s_{\alpha}$, then

$$\begin{aligned} EOWA_{\omega}(s_{\alpha_1}, s_{\alpha_2}, \ldots, s_{\alpha_n}) &= \omega_1 s_{\beta_1} \oplus \omega_2 s_{\beta_2} \oplus \cdots \oplus \omega_n s_{\beta_n} \\ &\le \omega_1 s_{\beta} \oplus \omega_2 s_{\beta} \oplus \cdots \oplus \omega_n s_{\beta} \\ &= (\omega_1 + \omega_2 + \cdots + \omega_n) s_{\beta} \\ &= s_{\beta} \end{aligned}$$

$$\begin{aligned} EOWA_{\omega}(s_{\alpha_1}, s_{\alpha_2}, \ldots, s_{\alpha_n}) &= \omega_1 s_{\beta_1} \oplus \omega_2 s_{\beta_2} \oplus \cdots \oplus \omega_n s_{\beta_n} \\ &\ge \omega_1 s_{\alpha} \oplus \omega_2 s_{\alpha} \oplus \cdots \oplus \omega_n s_{\alpha} \\ &= (\omega_1 + \omega_2 + \cdots + \omega_n) s_{\alpha} \\ &= s_{\alpha} \end{aligned}$$

and thus, $\min_i \{s_{\alpha_i}\} \le EOWA_{\omega}(s_{\alpha_1}, s_{\alpha_2}, \ldots, s_{\alpha_n}) \le \max_i \{s_{\alpha_i}\}$. This completes the proof.

Theorem 7.12 [113] If $\omega = \left(\frac{1}{n}, \frac{1}{n}, \ldots, \frac{1}{n}\right)$, then the EOWA operator reduces to the EA operator, i.e.,

$$EOWA_{\omega}(s_{\alpha_1}, s_{\alpha_2}, \ldots, s_{\alpha_n}) = s_{\bar{\alpha}}$$

where $\bar{\alpha} = \frac{1}{n} \sum_{j=1}^{n} \alpha_j$.

Proof Since $\omega = \left(\frac{1}{n}, \frac{1}{n}, \ldots, \frac{1}{n}\right)$, then

$$\begin{aligned} EOWA_{\omega}(s_{\alpha_1}, s_{\alpha_2}, \ldots, s_{\alpha_n}) &= \omega_1 s_{\beta_1} \oplus \omega_2 s_{\beta_2} \oplus \cdots \oplus \omega_n s_{\beta_n} \\ &= \frac{1}{n}(s_{\beta_1} \oplus s_{\beta_2} \oplus \cdots \oplus s_{\beta_n}) \\ &= \frac{1}{n}(s_{\alpha_1} \oplus s_{\alpha_2} \oplus \cdots \oplus s_{\alpha_n}) \\ &= s_{\overline{\alpha}} \end{aligned}$$

which completes the proof.

Theorem 7.13 [113] If $\omega = (1, 0, \ldots, 0)$, then the EOWA operator is reduced to the max operator, i.e.,

$$EOWA_{\omega}(s_{\alpha_1}, s_{\alpha_2}, \ldots, s_{\alpha_n}) = \max_i \{s_{\alpha_i}\}$$

Proof Since $\omega = (1, 0, \ldots, 0)$, then

$$\begin{aligned} EOWA_{\omega}(s_{\alpha_1}, s_{\alpha_2}, \ldots, s_{\alpha_n}) &= \omega_1 s_{\beta_1} \oplus \omega_2 s_{\beta_2} \oplus \cdots \oplus \omega_n s_{\beta_n} \\ &= s_{\beta_1} = \max_i \{s_{\alpha_i}\} \end{aligned}$$

which completes the proof.

Theorem 7.14 [113] If $\omega = (0, 0, \ldots, 1)$, then the EOWA operator is reduced to the min operator, i.e.,

$$EOWA_{\omega}(s_{\alpha_1}, s_{\alpha_2}, \ldots, s_{\alpha_n}) = \min_i \{s_{\alpha_i}\}$$

Proof Since $\omega = (0, 0, \ldots, 1)$, then

$$\begin{aligned} EOWA_{\omega}(s_{\alpha_1}, s_{\alpha_2}, \ldots, s_{\alpha_n}) &= \omega_1 s_{\beta_1} \oplus \omega_2 s_{\beta_2} \oplus \cdots \oplus \omega_n s_{\beta_n} \\ &= s_{\beta_n} = \min_i \{s_{\alpha_i}\} \end{aligned}$$

which completes the proof.

More generally, if $\omega_j = 1$, $\omega_i = 0$, and $i \neq j$, then

$$EOWA_{\omega}(s_{\alpha_1}, s_{\alpha_2}, \ldots, s_{\alpha_n}) = s_{\beta_j}$$

where s_{β_j} is the j th largest of a collection of the arguments s_{α_i} $(i = 1, 2, \ldots, n)$.

7.3.2 Decision Making Method

In what follows, we introduce a MADM method based on the EOWA operator, which has the following steps [113]:

Step 1 For a MADM problem, the decision maker provides the linguistic evaluation value r_{ij} for the alternative $x_i \in X$ with respect to the attribute $u_j \in U$, and construct the linguistic decision matrix $R = (r_{ij})_{n\times m}$, and $r_{ij} \in S$.

Step 2 Utilize the EOWA operator to aggregate the linguistic evaluation information of the i th line in the matrix $R = (r_{ij})_{n\times m}$, and get the overall attribute evaluation value $z_i(\omega)$, where

$$z_i(\omega) = EOWA_\omega(r_{i1}, r_{i2}, \ldots, r_{im})$$

Step 3 Rank and select the alternatives $x_i(i = 1,2,\ldots,n)$ according to $z_i(\omega)(i = 1,2,\ldots,n)$.

7.3.3 Practical Example

Example 7.5 In order to evaluate the knowledge management performances of four enterprises $x_i(i = 1,2,3,4)$ in a special economic zone, 15 indices (attributes) are taken into account [47]: (1) u_1: customers' profitability; (2) u_2: customers' satisfaction degrees; (3) u_3: the proportion of big customers; (4) u_4: each customer's sales; (5) u_5: the proportion ratio of repeat orders and the proportion ratio of loyal customers; (6) u_6: the investment of internal structures; (7) u_7: the investment amount for information technology; (8) u_8: the proportion ratio of support staff; (9) u_9: the turnover rate of staff; (10) u_{10}: the qualifications of support staff; (11) u_{11}: service length of knowledge employees; (12) u_{12}: the education level of staff; (13) u_{13}: the ratio of knowledge staff; (14) u_{14}: per capita profit of knowledge staff; and (15) u_{15}: the qualifications of knowledge staff. The linguistic label set used to evaluate the enterprises $x_i(i = 1,2,3,4)$ with respect to the 15 indices $u_j(j = 1,2,..,15)$ is

$$S = \{s_{-4},\ldots,s_0,\ldots,s_4\} = \{extremely\,poor, very\,poor, poor, slightly\,poor, \\ fair, slightly\,good, good, very\,good, extremely\,good\}$$

and the evaluation data are contained in the decision matrix R, shown in Table 7.7.

Here we utilize the EOWA operator (suppose that $\omega = (0.03, 0.04, 0.05, 0.06, 0.07, 0.08, 0.09, 0.16, 0.09, 0.08, 0.07, 0.06, 0.05, 0.04, 0.03)$ to aggregate the linguistic evaluation information of the i th line of the linguistic decision matrix R, and get the overall attribute value $z_i(\omega)$ of the enterprise x_i:

$$z_1(\omega) = 0.03\times s_4 \oplus 0.04\times s_3 \oplus 0.05\times s_3 \oplus 0.06\times s_2 \oplus 0.07\times s_2 \oplus 0.08\times s_2 \\ \oplus 0.09\times s_2 \oplus 0.16\times s_2 \oplus 0.09\times s_0 \oplus 0.08\times s_0 \oplus 0.07\times s_0 \\ \oplus 0.06\times s_0 \oplus 0.05\times s_0 \oplus 0.04\times s_0 \oplus 0.03\times s_{-1} = s_{1.28}$$

Table 7.7 Linguistic decision matrix R

	u_1	u_2	u_3	u_4	u_5	u_6	u_7	u_8
x_1	s_2	s_2	s_0	s_0	s_0	s_3	s_3	s_4
x_2	s_3	s_0	s_{-2}	s_0	s_3	s_4	s_3	s_2
x_3	s_2	s_3	s_4	s_4	s_2	s_2	s_2	s_3
x_4	s_4	s_3	s_3	s_0	s_3	s_0	s_3	s_3
	u_9	u_{10}	u_{11}	u_{12}	u_{13}	u_{14}	u_{15}	
x_1	s_2	s_0	s_0	s_2	s_2	s_0	s_{-1}	
x_2	s_{-1}	s_0	s_0	s_{-1}	s_{-1}	s_0	s_0	
x_3	s_2	s_0	s_{-1}	s_3	s_2	s_2	s_2	
x_4	s_0	s_3	s_0	s_2	s_0	s_3	s_2	

$$\begin{aligned} z_2(\omega) = {} & 0.03\times s_4 \oplus 0.04\times s_3 \oplus 0.05\times s_3 \oplus 0.06\times s_3 \oplus 0.07\times s_2 \oplus 0.08\times s_0 \\ & \oplus 0.09\times s_0 \oplus 0.16\times s_0 \oplus 0.09\times s_0 \oplus 0.08\times s_0 \oplus 0.07\times s_0 \\ & \oplus 0.06\times s_{-1} \oplus 0.05\times s_{-1} \oplus 0.04\times s_{-1} \oplus 0.03\times s_{-2} = s_{0.62} \end{aligned}$$

$$\begin{aligned} z_3(\omega) = {} & 0.03\times s_4 \oplus 0.04\times s_3 \oplus 0.05\times s_3 \oplus 0.06\times s_3 \oplus 0.07\times s_3 \oplus 0.08\times s_2 \\ & \oplus 0.09\times s_2 \oplus 0.16\times s_2 \oplus 0.09\times s_2 \oplus 0.08\times s_2 \oplus 0.07\times s_2 \\ & \oplus 0.06\times s_2 \oplus 0.05\times s_2 \oplus 0.04\times s_0 \oplus 0.03\times s_{-1} = s_{2.05} \end{aligned}$$

$$\begin{aligned} z_4(\omega) = {} & 0.03\times s_4 \oplus 0.04\times s_3 \oplus 0.05\times s_3 \oplus 0.06\times s_3 \oplus 0.07\times s_3 \oplus 0.08\times s_3 \\ & \oplus 0.09\times s_3 \oplus 0.16\times s_3 \oplus 0.09\times s_2 \oplus 0.08\times s_2 \oplus 0.07\times s_0 \\ & \oplus 0.06\times s_0 \oplus 0.05\times s_0 \oplus 0.04\times s_0 \oplus 0.03\times s_0 = s_{2.11} \end{aligned}$$

then we use $z_i(\omega)(i=1,2,3,4)$ to rank the alternatives $x_i(i=1,2,3,4)$ in descending order:

$$x_4 \succ x_3 \succ x_1 \succ x_2$$

and thus, the enterprise x_4 is the best one.

7.4 MADM Method Based on EOWA and LHA Operators

7.4.1 EWA Operator

Definition 7.7 [113] Let $EWA: \overline{S}^n \to \overline{S}$, if

$$EWA_w(s_{\alpha_1}, s_{\alpha_2}, \ldots, s_{\alpha_n}) = w_1 s_{\alpha_1} \oplus w_2 s_{\alpha_2} \oplus \cdots \oplus w_n s_{\alpha_n} = s_{\bar{\alpha}} \tag{7.2}$$

where $\bar{\alpha} = \sum_{j=1}^{n} w_j \alpha_j$, $w = (w_1, w_2, \ldots, w_n)$ is the weighting vector of the linguistic arguments s_{α_j} $(j = 1, 2, \ldots, n)$, and $s_{\alpha_j} \in \bar{S}$, $w_j \in [0,1]$, $j = 1, 2, \ldots, n$, and $\sum_{j=1}^{n} w_j = 1$, then the function EWA is called the extended weighted averaging (EWA) operator.

Especially, if $w = \left(\frac{1}{n}, \frac{1}{n}, \ldots, \frac{1}{n}\right)$, then the function EWA is called the extended averaging (EA) operator.

Example 7.6 Suppose that $w = (0.2, 0.3, 0.1, 0.4)$, then

$$EWA_w(s_2, s_3, s_1, s_{-1}) = 0.2 \times s_2 \oplus 0.3 \times s_3 \oplus 0.1 \times s_1 \oplus 0.4 \times s_{-1} = s_1$$

The EWA operator has the following properties:

Theorem 7.15 [113] (Bounded)

$$\min_i \{s_{\alpha_i}\} \le EWA_w(s_{\alpha_1}, s_{\alpha_2}, \ldots, s_{\alpha_n}) \le \max_i \{s_{\alpha_i}\}$$

Proof Let $\max_i \{s_{\alpha_i}\} = s_\beta$, $\min_i \{s_{\alpha_i}\} = s_\alpha$, then

$$\begin{aligned} EWA_w(s_{\alpha_1}, s_{\alpha_2}, \ldots, s_{\alpha_n}) &= w_1 s_{\alpha_1} \oplus w_2 s_{\alpha_2} \oplus \cdots \oplus w_n s_{\alpha_n} \\ &= w_1 s_\beta \oplus w_2 s_\beta \oplus \cdots \oplus w_n s_\beta \\ &= s_\beta \end{aligned}$$

$$\begin{aligned} EWA_w(s_{\alpha_1}, s_{\alpha_2}, \ldots, s_{\alpha_n}) &= w_1 s_{\alpha_1} \oplus w_2 s_{\alpha_2} \oplus \cdots \oplus w_n s_{\alpha_n} \\ &\ge w_1 s_\alpha \oplus w_2 s_\alpha \oplus \cdots \oplus w_n s_\alpha \\ &= s_\alpha \end{aligned}$$

Thus, $\min_i \{s_{\alpha_i}\} \le EWA_w(s_{\alpha_1}, s_{\alpha_2}, \ldots, s_{\alpha_n}) \le \max_i \{s_{\alpha_i}\}$, which completes the proof.

Theorem 7.16 [113] (Idempotency) If $s_{\alpha_j} = s_\alpha$, for any j, then

$$EWA_w(s_{\alpha_1}, s_{\alpha_2}, \ldots, s_{\alpha_n}) = s_\alpha$$

Proof Since $s_{\alpha_j} = s_\alpha$, for any j, then

$$\begin{aligned} EWA_w(s_{\alpha_1}, s_{\alpha_2}, \ldots, s_{\alpha_n}) &= w_1 s_{\alpha_1} \oplus w_2 s_{\alpha_2} \oplus \cdots \oplus w_n s_{\alpha_n} \\ &= w_1 s_\alpha \oplus w_2 s_\alpha \oplus \cdots \oplus w_n s_\alpha \\ &= (w_1 + w_2 + \cdots + w_n) s_\alpha \\ &= s_\alpha \end{aligned}$$

which completes the proof.

Theorem 7.17 [113] (Monotonicity) If $s_{\alpha_i} \le s'_{\alpha_i}$, for any i, then

$$EWA_w(s_{\alpha_1}, s_{\alpha_2}, \ldots, s_{\alpha_n}) \le EWA_w(s'_{\alpha_1}, s'_{\alpha_2}, \ldots, s'_{\alpha_n})$$

Proof Let

$$EWA_w(s_{\alpha_1}, s_{\alpha_2}, \ldots, s_{\alpha_n}) = w_1 s_{\alpha_1} \oplus w_2 s_{\alpha_2} \oplus \cdots \oplus w_n s_{\alpha_n}$$

$$EWA_w(s'_{\alpha_1}, s'_{\alpha_2}, \ldots, s'_{\alpha_n}) = w_1 s'_{\alpha_1} \oplus w_2 s'_{\alpha_2} \oplus \cdots \oplus w_n s'_{\alpha_n}$$

Since $s_{\alpha_i} \le s'_{\alpha_i}$, for any i, then

$$EWA_w(s_{\alpha_1}, s_{\alpha_2}, \ldots, s_{\alpha_n}) \le EWA_w(s'_{\alpha_1}, s'_{\alpha_2}, \ldots, s'_{\alpha_n})$$

which completes the proof.

It can be seen from Definitions 7.5 and 7.6 that the EWA operator weights only the linguistic labels, while the EOWA operator weights only the ordered positions of the linguistic labels instead of weighting the linguistic labels themselves. Thus, both the EWA and EOWA operators have one sidedness. To overcome this limitation, in what follows, we introduce a linguistic hybrid aggregation (LHA) operator.

7.4.2 LHA Operator

Definition 7.8 [113] Let $LHA: \bar{S}^n \to \bar{S}$, if

$$LHA_{w,\omega}(s_{\alpha_1}, s_{\alpha_2}, \ldots, s_{\alpha_n}) = \omega_1 s_{\beta_1} \oplus \omega_2 s_{\beta_2} \oplus \cdots \oplus \omega_n s_{\beta_n}$$

where $\omega = (\omega_1, \omega_2, \cdots, \omega_n)$ is the weighting vector (position vector) associated with the LHA operator, $w_j \in [0,1]$, $j = 1, 2, \ldots, n$, $\sum_{j=1}^n w_j = 1$ and s_{β_j} is the j th largest of a collection of the weighted arguments $(\bar{s}_{\alpha_1}, \bar{s}_{\alpha_2}, \ldots, \bar{s}_{\alpha_n})$, here, $\bar{s}_{\alpha_i} = n w_i s_{\alpha_i}$ $(i = 1, 2, \ldots, n)$, $w = (w_1, w_2, \ldots, w_n)$ is the weight vector of the linguistic labels $s_{\alpha_i}\ (i=1,2,\ldots,n)$, $w_j \in [0,1]$, $j=1,2,\ldots,n$, $\sum_{j=1}^{n} w_j = 1$, and n is the balancing coefficient.

Example 7.7 Let $s_{\alpha_1}=s_2$, $s_{\alpha_2}=s_3$, $s_{\alpha_3}=s_1$, and $s_{\alpha_4}=s_{-1}$ be a collection of linguistic labels, $w=(0.2,0.3,0.1,0.4)$ be their weight vector, $\omega=(0.2,0.2,0.3,0.3)$ be the weighting vector associated with the LHA operator. According to Definition 7.7, we have

$$\bar{s}_{\alpha_1}=4\times 0.2\times s_2=s_{1.6},\ \bar{s}_{\alpha_2}=4\times 0.3\times s_3=s_{3.6}$$
$$\bar{s}_{\alpha_3}=4\times 0.1\times s_1=s_{0.4},\ \bar{s}_{\alpha_4}=4\times 0.4\times s_{-1}=s_{-1.6}$$

then,

$$s_{\beta_1}=s_{3.6},\ s_{\beta_2}=s_{1.6},\ s_{\beta_3}=s_{0.4},\ s_{\beta_4}=s_{-1.6}$$

and thus,

$$\begin{aligned} LHA_{w,\omega}(s_2,s_3,s_1,s_{-1}) &= 0.2\times s_{3.6}\oplus 0.2\times s_{1.6}\oplus 0.3\times s_{0.4}\oplus 0.3\times s_{-1.6} \\ &= s_{6.8} \end{aligned}$$

Theorem 7.18 [113] The EWA operator is a special case of the LHA operator.

Proof Let $\omega=\left(\frac{1}{n},\frac{1}{n},\ldots,\frac{1}{n}\right)$, then

$$\begin{aligned} LHA_{w,\omega}(s_{\alpha_1},s_{\alpha_2},\ldots,s_{\alpha_n}) &= \omega_1 s_{\beta_1}\oplus\omega_2 s_{\beta_2}\oplus\cdots\oplus\omega_n s_{\beta_n} \\ &= \frac{1}{n}(s_{\beta_1}\oplus s_{\beta_2}\oplus\cdots\oplus s_{\beta_n}) \\ &= w_1 s_{\alpha_1}\oplus w_2 s_{\alpha_2}\oplus\cdots\oplus w_n s_{\alpha_n} \\ &= s_{\bar{\alpha}} \end{aligned}$$

where $\bar{\alpha}=\sum_{j=1}^{n} w_j\alpha_j$, which completes the proof.

Theorem 7.19 [113] The EOWA operator is a special case of the LHA operator.

Proof Let $w=\left(\frac{1}{n},\frac{1}{n},\ldots,\frac{1}{n}\right)$, then $\bar{s}_{\alpha_i}=s_{\alpha_i}\ (i=1,2,\ldots,n)$. This completes the proof.

From Theorems 7.18 and 7.19, we can know that the LHA operator extends both the EWA and EOWA operators, it reflects not only the importance degrees of the linguistic labels themselves, but also the importance degrees of the positions of these linguistic labels.

7.4.3 Decision Making Method

In the following, we introduce a MADM method based on the EOWA and LHA operators, whose steps are as follows:

Step 1 For a MADM problem, the attribute weight information is unknown completely, there are t decision makers $d_k (k = 1, 2, \ldots, t)$, whose weight vector is $\lambda = (\lambda_1, \lambda_2, \ldots, \lambda_t)$, $\lambda_k \geq 0$, $k = 1, 2, \ldots, t$, and $\sum_{k=1}^{t} \lambda_k = 1$. The decision maker $d_k \in D$ provides the linguistic evaluation value $r_{ij}^{(k)}$ over the alternative $x_i \in X$ with respect to the attribute $u_j \in U$, and constructs the linguistic decision matrix $R_k = (r_{ij}^{(k)})_{n \times m}$, and $r_{ij}^{(k)} \in S$.

Step 2 Aggregate the linguistic evaluation information of the i th line in $R_k = (r_{ij}^{(k)})_{n \times m}$ by using the EOWA operator, and get the overall attribute value $z_i^{(k)}(\omega)$ of the alternative x_i corresponding to the decision maker d_k:

$$z_i^{(k)}(\omega) = EOWA_\omega(r_{i1}^{(k)}, r_{i2}^{(k)}, \ldots, r_{im}^{(k)}),\ i = 1, 2, \ldots, n,\ k = 1, 2, \ldots, t$$

Step 3 Utilize the LHA operator to aggregate the overall attribute values $z_i^{(k)}(\omega)(k = 1, 2, \ldots, t)$ provided by t decision makers $d_k (k = 1, 2, \ldots, t)$ for the alternative x_i, and get the group's overall attribute value $z_i(\omega')$ of the alternative x_i, where

$$\begin{aligned} z_i(\lambda, \omega') &= LHA_{\lambda, \omega'}(z_i^{(1)}(\omega), z_i^{(2)}(\omega), \ldots, z_i^{(t)}(\omega)) \\ &= \omega_1' b_i^{(1)} \oplus \omega_2' b_i^{(2)} \oplus \cdots \oplus \omega_t' b_i^{(t)}, \quad i = 1, 2, \ldots, n \end{aligned}$$

where $\omega' = (\omega_1', \omega_2', \ldots, \omega_t')$ is the weighting vector associated with the LHA operator, $\omega_k' \in [0, 1]$, $k = 1, 2, \ldots, t$, and $\sum_{k=1}^{t} \omega_k' = 1$, $b_i^{(k)}$ is the k th largest of a collection of the weighted linguistic arguments $(t\lambda_1 z_i^{(1)}(\omega), t\lambda_2 z_i^{(2)}(\omega), \ldots, t\lambda_t z_i^{(t)}(\omega))$, and t is the balancing coefficient.

Step 4 Rank and select the alternatives $x_i (i = 1, 2, \ldots, n)$ according to $z_i(\lambda, \omega')$ $(i = 1, 2, \ldots, n)$.

7.4.4 Practical Example

Example 7.8 Here we take Example 7.5 to illustrate the method of Sect. 7.4.3. Suppose that the linguistic evaluation data in the linguistic decision matrices

Table 7.8 Linguistic decision matrix R_1

	u_1	u_2	u_3	u_4	u_5	u_6	u_7	u_8
x_1	s_1	s_2	s_{-1}	s_0	s_0	s_4	s_3	s_4
x_2	s_3	s_0	s_{-2}	s_1	s_3	s_4	s_4	s_0
x_3	s_2	s_3	s_4	s_3	s_2	s_2	s_4	s_3
x_4	s_4	s_3	s_4	s_0	s_3	s_0	s_2	s_3
	u_9	u_{10}	u_{11}	u_{12}	u_{13}	u_{14}	u_{15}	
x_1	s_2	s_1	s_0	s_2	s_3	s_0	s_{-1}	
x_2	s_{-1}	s_0	s_0	s_{-1}	s_{-1}	s_0	s_1	
x_3	s_2	s_1	s_0	s_3	s_2	s_3	s_2	
x_4	s_0	s_4	s_0	s_2	s_{-1}	s_3	s_2	

Table 7.9 Linguistic decision matrix R_2

	u_1	u_2	u_3	u_4	u_5	u_6	u_7	u_8
x_1	s_3	s_1	s_{-1}	s_0	s_1	s_3	s_2	s_3
x_2	s_4	s_0	s_{-2}	s_1	s_3	s_4	s_3	s_3
x_3	s_2	s_3	s_4	s_3	s_2	s_4	s_2	s_3
x_4	s_4	s_2	s_3	s_0	s_2	s_0	s_3	s_4
	u_9	u_{10}	u_{11}	u_{12}	u_{13}	u_{14}	u_{15}	
x_1	s_2	s_0	s_1	s_2	s_3	s_0	s_{-2}	
x_2	s_{-1}	s_0	s_{-1}	s_{-1}	s_0	s_0	s_1	
x_3	s_3	s_0	s_{-1}	s_3	s_4	s_2	s_3	
x_4	s_0	s_3	s_1	s_2	s_0	s_4	s_0	

$R_k\,(k=1,2,3)$ (see Tables 7.8, 7.9, 7.10) are given by three decision makers $d_k\,(k=1,2,3)$, whose weight vector is $\lambda=(0.3,0.4,0.3)$.

Below we give the detailed decision making steps:

Step 1 Utilize the EOWA operator (suppose that $\omega=(0.03,0.04,0.05,0.06,0.07,0.08,0.09,0.16,0.09,0.08,0.07,0.06,0.05,0.04,0.03)$ to aggregate the linguistic evaluation information of the i th line of the linguistic decision matrix R, and get the overall attribute evaluation value $z_i^{(k)}(\omega)$ provided by the decision maker d_k for the alternative x_i:

$$\begin{aligned}z_1^{(1)}(\omega)&=0.03\times s_4\oplus 0.04\times s_4\oplus 0.05\times s_3\oplus 0.06\times s_3\oplus 0.07\times s_2\oplus 0.08\times s_2\\&\oplus 0.09\times s_2\oplus 0.16\times s_1\oplus 0.09\times s_1\oplus 0.08\times s_0\oplus 0.07\times s_0\\&\oplus 0.06\times s_0\oplus 0.05\times s_0\oplus 0.04\times s_{-1}\oplus 0.03\times s_{-1}=s_{1.27}\end{aligned}$$

Table 7.10 Linguistic decision matrix R_3

	u_1	u_2	u_3	u_4	u_5	u_6	u_7	u_8
x_1	s_2	s_4	s_0	s_0	s_2	s_3	s_2	s_4
x_2	s_3	s_0	s_0	s_0	s_3	s_4	s_3	s_4
x_3	s_2	s_2	s_4	s_3	s_2	s_1	s_2	s_3
x_4	s_4	s_3	s_4	s_0	s_3	s_1	s_3	s_3
	u_9	u_{10}	u_{11}	u_{12}	u_{13}	u_{14}	u_{15}	
x_1	s_2	s_0	s_0	s_3	s_2	s_0	s_{-2}	
x_2	s_{-1}	s_0	s_1	s_{-1}	s_0	s_0	s_0	
x_3	s_3	s_0	s_{-1}	s_3	s_1	s_2	s_4	
x_4	s_{-2}	s_3	s_2	s_2	s_2	s_3	s_2	

Similarly, we have

$$z_2^{(1)}(\omega) = s_{0.55},\ z_3^{(1)}(\omega) = s_{2.39},\ z_4^{(1)}(\omega) = s_{2.01},\ z_1^{(2)}(\omega) = s_{1.25}$$

$$z_2^{(2)}(\omega) = s_{0.78},\ z_3^{(2)}(\omega) = s_{2.62},\ z_4^{(2)}(\omega) = s_{1.87},\ z_1^{(3)}(\omega) = s_{1.53}$$

$$z_2^{(3)}(\omega) = s_{0.83},\ z_3^{(3)}(\omega) = s_{2.12},\ z_4^{(3)}(\omega) = s_{2.40}$$

Step 2 Use the LHA operator (suppose that $\omega' = (0.2, 0.6, 0.2)$) to aggregate the overall attribute evaluation values $z_i^{(k)}(\omega)(k = 1,2,3)$ given by the decision makers $d_k\,(k = 1,2,3)$ for the alternative x_i: we first employ λ, t and $z_i^{(k)}(\omega)(k = 1,2,3)$ to calculate $t\lambda_k z_i^{(k)}(\omega)(k = 1,2,3)$:

$$3\lambda_1 z_1^{(1)}(\omega) = s_{1.143},\ 3\lambda_1 z_2^{(1)}(\omega) = s_{0.495},\ 3\lambda_1 z_3^{(1)}(\omega) = s_{2.151}$$
$$3\lambda_1 z_4^{(1)}(\omega) = s_{1.809},\ 3\lambda_2 z_1^{(2)}(\omega) = s_{1.500},\ 3\lambda_1 z_2^{(2)}(\omega) = s_{0.936}$$
$$3\lambda_2 z_3^{(2)}(\omega) = s_{3.144},\ 3\lambda_2 z_4^{(2)}(\omega) = s_{2.244},\ 3\lambda_3 z_1^{3)}(\omega) = s_{1.377}$$
$$3\lambda_3 z_2^{(3)}(\omega) = s_{0.747},\ 3\lambda_3 z_3^{(3)}(\omega) = s_{1.908},\ 3\lambda_3 z_4^{3)}(\omega) = s_{2.160}$$

and thus, we can get the group's overall attribute values $z_i(\lambda, \omega')(i = 1,2,3,4)$:

$$z_1(\lambda, \omega') = 0.2 \times s_{1.500} \oplus 0.6 \times s_{1.143} \oplus 0.2 \times s_{1.377} = s_{1.4040}$$

$$z_2(\lambda, \omega') = 0.2 \times s_{0.936} \oplus 0.6 \times s_{0.747} \oplus 0.2 \times s_{0.495} = s_{0.7344}$$

$$z_3(\lambda, \omega') = 0.2 \times s_{3.144} \oplus 0.6 \times s_{2.151} \oplus 0.2 \times s_{1.908} = s_{2.300}$$

$$z_4(\lambda, \omega') = 0.2 \times s_{2.244} \oplus 0.6 \times s_{2.160} \oplus 0.2 \times s_{1.809} = s_{2.1066}$$

Step 3 Rank the alternatives $x_i (i = 1, 2, 3, 4)$ according to $z_i(\lambda, \omega')(i = 1, 2, 3, 4)$:

$$x_3 \succ x_4 \succ x_1 \succ x_2$$

and thus, x_3 is the best enterprise.

Chapter 8
Linguistic MADM Method with Real-Valued or Unknown Weight Information

For the MADM problems where the attribute weights are known completely, and the attribute values take the form of linguistic labels, we introduce the MADM method based on the EWA operator and the MADM method based on the EWA and LHA operators, and apply them to solve the problem that evaluates management information systems of an enterprise. In MAGDM with linguistic information, the granularities of linguistic label sets are usually different due to the differences of thinking modes and habits among decision makers. In order to deal with this inconvenience, we introduce the transformation relationships among multigranular linguistic labels (TRMLLs), which are applied to unify linguistic labels with different granularities into a certain linguistic label set with fixed granularity. The TRMLLs are illustrated through an application example involves the evaluation of technical post of teachers. We introduce the concept of two-dimension linguistic labels so as to avoid the biased results and achieve high accuracy in linguistic MADM. We analyze the relationship between a two-dimension linguistic label and a common linguistic label, and then quantify a certain two-dimension linguistic label by using a generalized triangular fuzzy number (TFN). On the basis of the mapping function from two-dimension linguistic labels to the corresponding generalized TFNs and its inverse function, we also introduce a two-dimension linguistic weighted averaging (2DLWA) operator and a two-dimension linguistic ordered weighted averaging (2DLOWA) operator. An example of selecting the outstanding postgraduate dissertation(s) is used to illustrate these two two-dimension linguistic aggregation techniques.

8.1 MADM Method Based on EWA Operator

8.1.1 Decision Making Method

In what follows, we introduce a MADM method based on the EWA operator, whose steps are as below:

Z.S. Xu, *Uncertain Multi-Attribute Decision Making*,
DOI 10.1007/978-3-662-45640-8_8

Step 1 For a MADM problem, let X and U be the set of alternatives and the set of attributes. The decision maker provides the evaluation value $r_{ij}(i=.1,2,\ldots,n,\ j=1,2,\ldots,m)$ for the alternatives $x_i(i=1,2,\ldots,n)$ with respect to the attributes $u_j(j=1,2,\ldots,m)$, and constructs the linguistic decision matrix $R=(r_{ij})_{n\times m}$, and $r_{ij}\in S$.

Step 2 Utilize the EWA operator to aggregate the linguistic evaluation information of the i th line in the matrix $R=(r_{ij})_{n\times m}$ to get the overall attribute evaluation values $z_i(w)(i=1,2,\ldots,n)$:

$$\begin{aligned} z_i(w) &= EWA_w(r_{i1},r_{i2},\ldots,r_{im}) \\ &= w_1 r_{i1}\oplus w_2 r_{i2},\oplus\cdots\oplus w_m r_{im},\quad i=1,2,\ldots,n \end{aligned}$$

where $w=(w_1,w_2,\ldots,w_m)$ is the weight vector of attributes.

Step 3 Utilize $z_i(w)$ $(i=1,2,\ldots,n)$ to rank and select the alternatives $x_i(i=1,2,...,n)$.

8.1.2 *Practical Example*

Example 8.1 The indices used to evaluate the management information systems mainly include the following [36]: (1) u_1: leadership support; (2) u_2: progressiveness; (3) u_3: maintainability; (4) u_4: resource utilization; (5) u_5: safety and reliability; (6) u_6: economy; (7) u_7: timeliness; (8) u_8: man-machine interface's friendliness; (9) u_9: practicability; (10) u_{10}: service level; (11) u_{11}: sharing degree; (12) u_{12}: leading role; (13) u_{13}: importance; (14) u_{14}: benefit; and (15) u_{15}: amount of information.

In the following, we apply the above indices (attributes) to evaluate the management information systems (alternatives) of four enterprises $x_i(i=1,2,3,4)$. Suppose that the set of linguistic labels is

$$\begin{aligned} S=\{s_{-4},\ldots,s_0,\ldots,s_4\}=\{&\textit{extremely poor},\textit{very poor},\textit{poor},\textit{slightly poor},\\ &\textit{fair},\textit{slightly good},\textit{good},\textit{very good},\textit{extremely good}\} \end{aligned}$$

the evaluation data are contained in the linguistic decision matrix R (see Table 8.1), and the weight vector of attributes is given as:

$$w=(0.07,0.08,0.06,0.05,0.09,0.07,0.04,0.06,0.05,0.08,0.09,0.06,0.04,0.09,0.07)$$

Now we use the EWA operator to aggregate the linguistic evaluation information of the ith line in the linguistic decision matrix R, and get the overall attribute value $z_i(w)$ of the alternative x_i:

$$\begin{aligned} z_1(w) = {} & 0.07\times s_3\oplus 0.08\times s_1\oplus 0.06\times s_0\oplus 0.05\times s_2\oplus 0.09\times s_0\oplus 0.07\times s_3 \\ & \oplus 0.04\times s_4\oplus 0.06\times s_4\oplus 0.05\times s_3\oplus 0.08\times s_0\oplus 0.09\times s_0 \\ & \oplus 0.06\times s_3\oplus 0.04\times s_2\oplus 0.09\times s_0\oplus 0.07\times s_1 = s_{1.48} \end{aligned}$$

Table 8.1 Linguistic decision matrix R

	u_1	u_2	u_3	u_4	u_5	u_6	u_7	u_8
x_1	s_3	s_1	s_0	s_2	s_0	s_4	s_4	s_4
x_2	s_3	s_2	s_1	s_1	s_3	s_2	s_3	s_2
x_3	s_2	s_3	s_4	s_3	s_2	s_2	s_4	s_3
x_4	s_2	s_3	s_4	s_0	s_3	s_1	s_3	s_4
	u_9	u_{10}	u_{11}	u_{12}	u_{13}	u_{14}	u_{15}	
x_1	s_3	s_0	s_0	s_3	s_2	s_0	s_1	
x_2	s_1	s_0	s_0	s_{-1}	s_{-1}	s_1	s_1	
x_3	s_2	s_0	s_0	s_3	s_4	s_2	s_0	
x_4	s_0	s_3	s_1	s_2	s_1	s_3	s_2	

$$
\begin{aligned}
z_2(w) = {} & 0.07\times s_3 \oplus 0.08\times s_2 \oplus 0.06\times s_1 \oplus 0.05\times s_1 \oplus 0.09\times s_3 \oplus 0.07\times s_2 \\
& \oplus 0.04\times s_3 \oplus 0.06\times s_2 \oplus 0.05\times s_1 \oplus 0.08\times s_0 \oplus 0.09\times s_0 \\
& \oplus 0.06\times s_{-1} \oplus 0.04\times s_{-1} \oplus 0.09\times s_1 \oplus 0.07\times s_1 = s_{1.24}
\end{aligned}
$$

$$
\begin{aligned}
z_3(w) = {} & 0.07\times s_2 \oplus 0.08\times s_3 \oplus 0.06\times s_4 \oplus 0.05\times s_3 \oplus 0.09\times s_2 \oplus 0.07\times s_2 \\
& \oplus 0.04\times s_4 \oplus 0.06\times s_3 \oplus 0.05\times s_2 \oplus 0.08\times s_0 \oplus 0.09\times s_0 \\
& \oplus 0.06\times s_3 \oplus 0.04\times s_4 \oplus 0.09\times s_2 \oplus 0.07\times s_0 = s_{2.05}
\end{aligned}
$$

$$
\begin{aligned}
z_4(w) = {} & 0.07\times s_2 \oplus 0.08\times s_3 \oplus 0.06\times s_4 \oplus 0.05\times s_0 \oplus 0.09\times s_3 \oplus 0.07\times s_1 \\
& \oplus 0.04\times s_3 \oplus 0.06\times s_4 \oplus 0.05\times s_0 \oplus 0.08\times s_3 \oplus 0.09\times s_1 \\
& \oplus 0.06\times s_2 \oplus 0.04\times s_1 \oplus 0.09\times s_3 \oplus 0.07\times s_2 = s_{2.22}
\end{aligned}
$$

based on which we rank the alternatives $x_i (i = 1, 2, 3, 4)$ in descending order:

$$x_4 \succ x_3 \succ x_1 \succ x_2$$

which indicates that x_4 is the best one.

8.2 MAGDM Method Based on EWA and LHA Operators

8.2.1 Decision Making Method

In what follows, we introduce the MADM method based on the EWA and LHA operators, whose steps are as follows:

Step 1 For a MADM problem, the attribute weight vector is $w=(w_1,w_2,\dots,w_m)$, $w_j \geq 0$, $j=1,2,\dots,n$, and $\sum_{j=1}^{m} w_j = 1$. The weight vector of the decision makers $d_k(k=1,2,\dots,t)$ is $\lambda=(\lambda_1,\lambda_2,\dots,\lambda_t)$, $\lambda_k \geq 0$, $k=1,2,\dots,t$, and $\sum_{k=1}^{t} \lambda_k = 1$. The decision maker $d_k \in D$ gives the linguistic evaluation value $r_{ij}^{(k)}$ for the alternative $x_i \in X$ with respect to $u_j \in U$, and get the linguistic decision matrix $R_k = (r_{ij}^{(k)})_{n\times m}$.

Step 2 Utilize the EWA operator to aggregate the linguistic evaluation information of the i th line in the matrix R_k, and get the overall attribute value $z_i^{(k)}(w)(i=1,2,\dots,n,\ k=1,2,\dots,t)$:

$$
\begin{aligned}
z_i^{(k)}(w) &= EWA_w(r_{i1}^{(k)}, r_{i2}^{(k)}, \dots, r_{im}^{(k)}) \\
&= w_1 r_{i1}^{(k)} \oplus w_2 r_{i2}^{(k)} \oplus \cdots \oplus w_m r_{im}^{(k)},\quad i=1,2,\dots,n,\ k=1,2,\dots,t
\end{aligned}
$$

Step 3 Employ the LHA operator to aggregate the overall attribute value $z_i^{(k)}(w)(k=1,2,\dots,t)$ provided by the decision makers $d_k(k=1,2,\dots,t)$ for the alternative x_i, and then get the group's overall attribute values $z_i(\lambda,\omega)(i=1,2,\dots,n)$:

$$
\begin{aligned}
z_i(\lambda,\omega) &= LHA_{\lambda,\omega}(z_i^{(1)}(w), z_i^{(2)}(w), \dots, z_i^{(t)}(w)) \\
&= \omega_1 b_i^{(1)} \oplus \omega_2 b_i^{(2)} \oplus \cdots \oplus \omega_t b_i^{(t)},\quad i=1,2,\dots,n
\end{aligned}
$$

where $\omega=(\omega_1,\omega_2,\dots,\omega_t)$ is the weighting vector associated with the LHA operator, $\omega_k \in [0,1]$, $k=1,2,\dots,t$, $\sum_{k=1}^{t} \omega_k = 1$, $b_i^{(k)}$ is the k th largest of a collection of the weighted linguistic arguments $(t\lambda_1 z_i^{(1)}(w), t\lambda_2 z_i^{(2)}(w), \dots, t\lambda_t z_i^{(t)}(w))$, and t is the balancing coefficient.

Step 4 Rank and select the alternatives $x_i(i=1,2,\dots,n)$ according to $z_i(\lambda,\omega)$ $(i=1,2,\dots,n)$ in descending order.

8.2.2 *Practical Example*

Example 8.2 Let's illustrate the method of Sect. 8.3 using Example 8.1. Suppose that there are three decision makers $d_k(t=1,2,3)$, whose weight vector is $\lambda=(0.3,0.4,0.3)$. They provide their evaluation information over the management information systems $x_i(i=1,2,3,4)$ with respect to the indices $u_j(j=1,2,\dots,15)$, and construct the linguistic decision matrices $R_k(k=1,2,3)$, shown as in Tables 8.2, 8.3, and 8.4.

The weight vector of attributes is given as:

Table 8.2 Linguistic decision matrix R_1

	u_1	u_2	u_3	u_4	u_5	u_6	u_7	u_8
x_1	s_2	s_3	s_{-1}	s_0	s_2	s_3	s_4	s_4
x_2	s_4	s_0	s_{-1}	s_1	s_4	s_4	s_4	s_0
x_3	s_3	s_4	s_4	s_3	s_2	s_3	s_4	s_4
x_4	s_4	s_3	s_3	s_1	s_3	s_0	s_3	s_3
	u_9	u_{10}	u_{11}	u_{12}	u_{13}	u_{14}	u_{15}	
x_1	s_2	s_1	s_2	s_1	s_3	s_1	s_0	
x_2	s_2	s_0	s_1	s_{-1}	s_1	s_0	s_2	
x_3	s_2	s_1	s_0	s_4	s_2	s_3	s_1	
x_4	s_2	s_4	s_1	s_2	s_0	s_3	s_3	

Table 8.3 Linguistic decision matrix R_2

	u_1	u_2	u_3	u_4	u_5	u_6	u_7	u_8
x_1	s_3	s_2	s_1	s_1	s_2	s_3	s_2	s_1
x_2	s_3	s_1	s_0	s_1	s_3	s_4	s_3	s_3
x_3	s_3	s_4	s_2	s_3	s_2	s_4	s_1	s_3
x_4	s_3	s_2	s_3	s_1	s_2	s_0	s_3	s_4
	u_9	u_{10}	u_{11}	u_{12}	u_{13}	u_{14}	u_{15}	
x_1	s_2	s_2	s_1	s_2	s_2	s_1	s_{-1}	
x_2	s_{-1}	s_0	s_{-1}	s_0	s_0	s_1	s_2	
x_3	s_2	s_0	s_0	s_2	s_4	s_3	s_2	
x_4	s_1	s_3	s_1	s_2	s_0	s_2	s_4	

Table 8.4 Linguistic decision matrix R_3

	u_1	u_2	u_3	u_4	u_5	u_6	u_7	u_8
x_1	s_2	s_4	s_0	s_0	s_2	s_3	s_1	s_4
x_2	s_2	s_0	s_1	s_0	s_2	s_4	s_3	s_4
x_3	s_2	s_3	s_3	s_3	s_2	s_1	s_2	s_4
x_4	s_3	s_3	s_4	s_0	s_3	s_2	s_3	s_3
	u_9	u_{10}	u_{11}	u_{12}	u_{13}	u_{14}	u_{15}	
x_1	s_2	s_1	s_0	s_3	s_3	s_0	s_{-1}	
x_2	s_0	s_0	s_2	s_{-1}	s_0	s_2	s_0	
x_3	s_3	s_1	s_{-1}	s_3	s_3	s_2	s_3	
x_4	s_0	s_3	s_2	s_3	s_2	s_4	s_3	

$$w = (0.07, 0.08, 0.06, 0.05, 0.05, 0.09, 0.07, 0.04, 0.06, 0.05, 0.08, 0.09, 0.06, 0.04, 0.09, 0.07)$$

In what follows, we solve this problem using the method introduced in Sect. 8.2.1:

Step 1 Utilize the EWA operator to aggregate the linguistic evaluation information of the i th line in the matrix R_k, and get the overall attribute values $z_i^{(k)}(w)$ of the management information system x_i corresponding to the decision maker d_k:

$$\begin{aligned} z_1^{(1)}(w) = & 0.07\times s_2 \oplus 0.08\times s_3 \oplus 0.06\times s_{-1} \oplus 0.05\times s_0 \oplus 0.09\times s_2 \oplus 0.07\times s_3 \\ & \oplus 0.04\times s_4 \oplus 0.06\times s_4 \oplus 0.05\times s_2 \oplus 0.08\times s_1 \oplus 0.09\times s_2 \\ & \oplus 0.06\times s_1 \oplus 0.04\times s_3 \oplus 0.09\times s_1 \oplus 0.07\times s_0 = s_{1.74} \end{aligned}$$

Similarly, we get

$$z_2^{(1)}(w) = s_{1.38},\ z_3^{(1)}(w) = s_{2.55},\ z_4^{(1)}(w) = s_{2.43}$$

$$z_1^{(2)}(w) = s_{1.58},\ z_2^{(2)}(w) = s_{1.28},\ z_3^{(2)}(w) = s_{2.18},\ z_4^{(2)}(w) = s_{2.01}$$

$$z_1^{(3)}(w) = s_{1.54},\ z_2^{(3)}(w) = s_{1.32},\ z_3^{(3)}(w) = s_{2.11},\ z_4^{(3)}(w) = s_{2.65}$$

Step 2 Utilize the LHA operator (suppose that its weighting vector is $\omega = (0.2,\ 0.6, 0.2)$) to aggregate the overall attribute evaluation values $z_i^{(k)}(w)$ $(k = 1,2,3)$ of the management information system x_i corresponding to the decision makers $d_k\,(k = 1,2,3)$, i.e., we first utilize λ, t and $z_i^{(k)}(w)(i = 1,2,3,4,\ k = 1,2,3)$ to solve $t\lambda_k z_i^{(k)}(w)(i = 1,2,3,4,\ k = 1,2,3)$:

$$3\lambda_1 z_1^{(1)}(w) = s_{1.566},\ 3\lambda_1 z_2^{(1)}(w) = s_{1.242},\ 3\lambda_1 z_3^{(1)}(w) = s_{2.295}$$

$$3\lambda_1 z_4^{(1)}(w) = s_{2.187},\ 3\lambda_2 z_1^{(2)}(w) = s_{1.896},\ 3\lambda_1 z_2^{(2)}(w) = s_{1.536}$$

$$3\lambda_2 z_3^{(2)}(w) = s_{2.616},\ 3\lambda_2 z_4^{(2)}(w) = s_{2.412},\ 3\lambda_3 z_1^{(3)}(w) = s_{1.386}$$

$$3\lambda_3 z_2^{(3)}(w) = s_{1.188},\ 3\lambda_3 z_3^{(3)}(w) = s_{1.899},\ 3\lambda_3 z_4^{(3)}(w) = s_{2.385}$$

Thus, the group's overall attribute values $z_i(\lambda,\omega)$ of the management information system x_i:

$$z_1(\lambda,\omega) = 0.2\times s_{1.896} \oplus 0.6\times s_{1.566} \oplus 0.2\times s_{1.386} = s_{1.5960}$$

$$z_2(\lambda,\omega) = 0.2\times s_{1.536} \oplus 0.6\times s_{1.242} \oplus 0.2\times s_{1.188} = s_{1.2900}$$

$$z_3(\lambda,\omega) = 0.2 \times s_{2.616} \oplus 0.6 \times s_{2.295} \oplus 0.2 \times s_{1.899} = s_{2.2800}$$

$$z_4(\lambda,\omega) = 0.2 \times s_{2.412} \oplus 0.6 \times s_{2.385} \oplus 0.2 \times s_{2.187} = s_{2.3508}$$

Step 3 Rank all the management information systems $x_i (i = 1,2,3,4)$ according to $z_i(\lambda,\omega)(i = 1,2,3,4)$ in descending order:

$$x_4 \succ x_3 \succ x_1 \succ x_2$$

from which we know that x_4 is the best one.

8.3 MAGDM with Multigranular Linguistic Labels [164]

8.3.1 Transformation Relationships Among TRMLLs

Xu [125] improved the additive linguistic label set $S_1 = \{s_\alpha \mid \alpha = 0,1,2,\ldots,L\}$ [41, 114], and put forward the another additive linguistic label set $S_2 = \{s_\alpha \mid \alpha = -L,\ldots,-1,0,1,\ldots,L\}$ which has been used in Chap. 7 (here for convenience of description, we denote S_1 and S_2 as $S_1^{(L)}$ and $S_2^{(L)}$, respectively), where the mid linguistic label s_0 represents an assessment of "indifference", with the rest of the linguistic labels being placed symmetrically around it, s_{-L} and s_L indicate the lower and upper limits of the linguistic labels of $S_2^{(L)}$, respectively.

Apparently, the above additive linguistic label sets $S_1^{(L)}$ and $S_2^{(L)}$ are balanced since all the absolute values of the deviation between the subscripts of any two adjoining linguistic labels are the same, which sometimes is not accordance with actual applications. Dai et al. [20] thereby presented an unbalanced additive linguistic label set as follows:

$$S_3^{(L)} = \left\{ s_\alpha \middle| \alpha = -\frac{2(L-1)}{L+2-L}, -\frac{2(L-1-1)}{L+2-(L-1)}, \ldots, 0, \ldots, \frac{2(L-1-1)}{L+2-(L-1)}, \frac{2(L-1)}{L+2-L} \right\} \tag{8.1}$$

which can be simplified as:

$$S_3^{(L)} = \left\{ s_\alpha \middle| \alpha = 1-L, \frac{2}{3}(2-L), \ldots, 0, \ldots, \frac{2}{3}(L-2), L-1 \right\} \tag{8.2}$$

where L is a positive integer, the mid linguistic label s_0 represents an assessment of "indifference", with the rest of the linguistic labels being placed symmetrically, but unevenly, around it, s_{1-L} and s_{L-1} indicate the lower and upper limits of the linguistic labels of $S_3^{(L)}$. The linguistic label set $S_3^{(L)}$ satisfies the following conditions: (1) $s_\alpha \geq s_\beta$ iff $\alpha \geq \beta$; and (2) the negation operator is defined: $\text{neg}(s_\alpha) = s_{-\alpha}$, especially $\text{neg}(s_0) = s_{-0}$. We consider the right part of $S_3^{(L)}$ as:

$$S_3^{+(L)} = \left\{ s_\alpha \middle| \alpha = \frac{2(i-1)}{L+2-i}, i = 1,2,\ldots,L \right\} \tag{8.3}$$

while the left part of $S_3^{(L)}$ is

$$S_3^{-(L)} = \left\{ s_\alpha \middle| \alpha = -\frac{2(i-1)}{L+2-i}, i = 1,2,\ldots,L \right\} \tag{8.4}$$

In the following, to explain their relationships, we consider three additive linguistic labels sets $S_1^{(L_1)}$, $S_2^{(L_2)}$ and $S_3^{(L_3)}$. From the definitions of these three additive linguistic label sets, we can find that:

Firstly, there exists discrimination between $L_i (i = 1,2,3)$ and granularities (or cardinalities) of the above three additive linguistic label sets, since the granularities of $S_i^{(L_i)} (i = 1,2,3)$ are $L_1 + 1$, $2L_2 + 1$ and $2L_3 - 1$, respectively.

Secondly, the linguistic labels, which represent assessments of "indifference", are different in the above three additive linguistic label sets, i.e., the linguistic label $s_{L_1/2}$ in $S_1^{(L_1)}$, while s_0 in $S_2^{(L_2)}$ and $S_3^{(L_3)}$.

Finally, the linguistic labels are balanced in the additive linguistic label sets $S_1^{(L_1)}$ and $S_2^{(L_2)}$, i.e., the deviation between the subscripts of any two adjoining linguistic labels are the same, while it is unbalanced for linguistic labels in $S_3^{(L_3)}$.

In this way, we should decide which linguistic label set will be used to deal with a MAGDM problem based on linguistic information by means of relationships of aforementioned three additive linguistic labels sets $S_1^{(L_1)}$, $S_2^{(L_2)}$ and $S_3^{(L_3)}$.

According to Dai et al. [20], the above three additive linguistic label sets $S_1^{(t_1)}$, $S_2^{(t_2)}$ and $S_3^{(t_3)}$ can be extended to the continuous label sets $\overline{S}_1^{(L_1)} = \{ s_\alpha | \alpha \in [0, L_1] \}$, $\overline{S}_2^{(L_2)} = \{ s_\alpha | \alpha \in [-L_2, L_2] \}$ and $\overline{S}_3^{(L_3)} = \{ s_\alpha | \alpha \in [1-L_3, L_3 - 1] \}$, where $L_i (i = 1,2,3)$ are three proper positive integers, $s_\beta (\in S_1^{(L_1)}$, $S_2^{(L_2)}$ or $S_3^{(L_3)})$ is termed an original linguistic label (otherwise, we called it a virtual linguistic label). Generally speaking, the virtual linguistic labels can only appear in calculations, and there are two operational laws with respect to $s_\alpha, s_\beta (\in \overline{S}_2^{(L_2)}$ or $\overline{S}_3^{(L_3)})$ as follows: (1) $s_\alpha \oplus s_\beta = s_{\alpha+\beta}$; and (2) $\lambda s_\alpha = s_{\lambda\alpha}$. These two operational laws are also usable for the multiplicative linguistic label sets to be introduced below:

Multiplicative linguistic label sets [116] further advance the theory of linguistic information so that we can choose a more proper linguistic label set for a certain MADM problem based linguistic information. Multiplicative linguistic label sets have their own characteristics, which can be defined as follows:

Xu [116] introduced the multiplicative linguistic label set $S_4^{(L)} = \left\{ s_\alpha \middle| \alpha = \frac{1}{L}, \ldots, \frac{1}{2}, 1, 2, \ldots, L \right\}$, where L is a positive integer, s_1 represents an assessment of "indifference", $s_{1/L}$ and s_L indicate the lower and upper limits of linguistic labels of $S_4^{(L)}$, respectively. $s_\alpha \in S_4^{(L)}$ has the following characteristics: (1) $s_\alpha \geq s_\beta$, iff $\alpha \geq \beta$; and (2) the reciprocal operator is defined: $\text{rec}(s_\alpha) = s_\beta$, such that $\alpha\beta = 1$, especially, $\text{rec}(s_1) = s_1$. Another multiplicative linguistic label set [133] was defined as $S_5^{(L)} = \left\{ s_\alpha \middle| \alpha = \frac{1}{L}, \frac{2}{L}, \ldots, \frac{L-1}{L}, 1, \frac{L}{L-1}, \ldots, \frac{L}{2}, L \right\}$, where L is a positive integer, s_1 represents an assessment of "indifference", $s_{1/L}$ and s_L indicate the lower and upper limits of linguistic labels of $S_5^{(L)}$, and $s_\alpha \in S_5^{(L)}$ satisfies the following conditions: (1) $s_\alpha \geq s_\beta$, iff $\alpha \geq \beta$; and (2) the reciprocal operator is defined: $\text{rec}(s_\alpha) = s_\beta$, such that $\alpha\beta = 1$, especially, $\text{rec}(s_1) = s_1$. The linguistic label s_1 represents an assessment of "indifference" both in the multiplicative linguistic label sets $S_4^{(L)}$ and $S_5^{(L)}$.

From the definitions of aforementioned multiplicative linguistic label sets $S_4^{(L)}$ and $S_5^{(L)}$, we can characterize them clearly so as to choose the better in an applicative problem, as follows:

Firstly, both these two linguistic label sets' granularities are $2L-1$.

Secondly, the linguistic labels are placed unevenly and asymmetrically in $S_4^{(L)}$ and $S_5^{(L)}$. However, the right part of linguistic labels in $S_4^{(L)}$ and the left part linguistic labels in $S_5^{(L)}$ are well-proportioned, which can be illustrated by the sets of seven multiplicative linguistic labels $S_4^{(4)}$ and $S_5^{(4)}$ graphically (see Fig. 8.1), where

$$S_4^{(4)} = \{ s_{1/4} = \textit{extremely poor},\ s_{1/3} = \textit{very poor},\ s_{1/2} = \textit{poor},\ s_1 = \textit{fair},\ s_2 = \textit{good},\ s_3 = \textit{very good},\ s_4 = \textit{extremely good} \} \tag{8.5}$$

$$S_5^{(4)} = \{ s_{1/4} = \textit{extremely poor},\ s_{1/2} = \textit{very poor},\ s_{3/4} = \textit{poor},\ s_1 = \textit{fair},\ s_{4/3} = \textit{good},\ s_2 = \textit{very good},\ s_4 = \textit{extremely good} \} \tag{8.6}$$

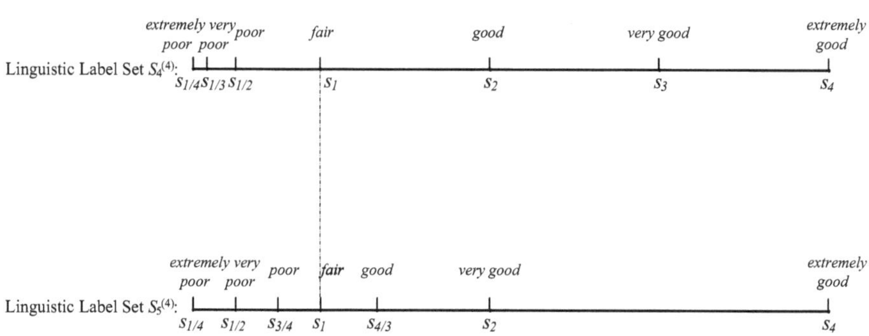

Fig. 8.1 Sets of seven multiplicative linguistic labels $S_4^{(4)}$ and $S_5^{(4)}$

Similarly, for the sake of convenience, and to preserve all the given decision information, the multiplicative linguistic label sets $S_4^{(L)}$ and $S_5^{(L)}$ can be extended to the continuous forms:

$$\overline{S}_4^{(L)} = \left\{ s_\alpha \middle| \alpha \in \left[\frac{1}{L}, L \right] \right\},\ \overline{S}_5^{(L)} = \left\{ s_\beta \middle| \beta \in \left[\frac{1}{L}, L \right] \right\}$$

where the right parts are

$$\overline{S}_4^{+(L)} = \left\{ s_\alpha \middle| \alpha = i, i \in [1, L] \right\},\ \overline{S}_5^{+(L)} = \left\{ s_\beta \middle| \beta = \frac{L}{L-(i-1)}, i \in [1, L] \right\}$$

and the left parts are

$$\overline{S}_4^{-(t)} = \left\{ s_\alpha \middle| \alpha = \frac{1}{i}, i \in (1, L] \right\},\ \overline{S}_5^{-(t)} = \left\{ s_\beta \middle| \beta = \frac{i}{t}, i \in [1, L) \right\}$$

respectively.

In what follows, the continuous forms of linguistic label sets are important, and almost all calculations are based on them. However, in some practical group decision making problems, because of different habits and favors of decision makers, the domain of linguistic labels, used by decision makers, may be different, so the multigranular linguistic MAGDM problems should be introduced in detail.

Multigranular linguistic decision making problems have been mentioned in lots of papers [16, 40, 42, 45, 132]. It is a conception which is correlative with real life, when we consider that the decision makers who may have different backgrounds and levels of knowledge to solve a particular problem. Therefore, in a group decision making problem with linguistic information, it is possible for the decision makers to provide their preferences over alternatives in certain linguistic label sets with different granularities. We now deal with multigranular linguistic MAGDM problems, which may be described as follows:

There are a finite set of alternatives $X = \{x_1, x_2, \ldots, x_n\}$ and a group of decision makers $D = \{d_1, d_2, \ldots, d_t\}$. The decision makers provide their linguistic preferences respectively over the alternatives of X with respect to a set of attributes $U = \{u_1, u_2, \ldots, u_m\}$ by using different linguistic label sets with different granularities (or cardinalities) and/or semantics. How to carry out the decision making by aggregating above preference information is the multigranular linguistic MAGDM problem we care. For convenience, here we suppose that $S_i^{(L_k)} (k = 1, 2, \ldots, t,\ i = 1, 2, 3, 4, 5)$ are the linguistic label sets (which have been mentioned previously) with different granularities provided by the decision makers $d_k (k = 1, 2, \ldots, t)$.

In the real world, the aforementioned multigranular linguistic MAGDM problems usually occur due to the decision makers' different backgrounds and levels of knowledge. To solve the problems, below we define some transformation relationships among multigranular linguistic labels (TRMLLs):

We firstly make a review of transformation functions among multigranular linguistic labels (TFMLLs) presented by Xu [132], and then we will discuss the TRMLLs based on the linguistic label sets $S_i^{(L)}(i=1,2,3,4,5)$, and show the characteristics and merits of the TRMLLs.

According to Xu [132] and the additive linguistic label set $S_3^{(L)}$, let

$$S_3^{(L_1)}=\left\{s_\alpha \left| \alpha=1-L_1,\frac{2}{3}(2-L_1),\frac{2}{4}(3-L_1),\ldots,0,\ldots,\frac{2}{4}(L_1-3),\frac{2}{3}(L_1-2),L_1-1\right.\right\} \tag{8.7}$$

and

$$S_3^{(L_2)}=\left\{s_\beta \left| \beta=1-L_2,\frac{2}{3}(2-L_2),\frac{2}{4}(3-L_2),\ldots,0,\ldots,\frac{2}{4}(L_2-3),\frac{2}{3}(L_2-2),L_2-1\right.\right\} \tag{8.8}$$

be two additive linguistic label sets with different granularities, where $L_i(i=1,2)$ are the positive integers, and $L_1 \neq L_2$. We extend $S_3^{(L_1)}$ and $S_3^{(L_2)}$ to the continuous label sets:

$$\overline{S}_3^{(L_1)}(L_1)=\left\{s_\alpha \,|\, \alpha\in[1-L_1,L_1-1]\right\},\ \overline{S}_3^{(L_2)}(L_2)=\left\{s_\beta \,|\, \beta\in[1-L_2,L_2-1]\right\}$$

respectively, for a feasible numerical calculation among the virtual linguistic labels. Then, the transformation functions among the multigranular linguistic labels in $\overline{S}_3^{(L_1)}$ and $\overline{S}_3^{(L_2)}$ can be defined as follows:

$$F:\overline{S}_3^{(L_1)}\to\overline{S}_3^{(L_2)} \tag{8.9}$$

$$\beta=F(\alpha)=\alpha\frac{L_2-1}{L_1-1} \tag{8.10}$$

$$F^{-1}:\overline{S}_3^{(L_2)}\to\overline{S}_3^{(L_1)} \tag{8.11}$$

$$\alpha=F^{-1}(\beta)=\beta\frac{L_1-1}{L_2-1} \tag{8.12}$$

By Eqs. (8.10) and (8.12), we have

$$\frac{\alpha}{L_1-1}=\frac{\beta}{L_2-1} \tag{8.13}$$

By Eq. (8.13), we can make the linguistic labels in $\overline{S}_3^{(L_1)}$ and $\overline{S}_3^{(L_2)}$ uniform, but the unified labels are not usually in accordance with the normal human being's thinking, which can be shown in the following example:

Example 8.3 Suppose that $D=\{d_1,d_2\}$ is a set of two decision makers d_1 and d_2, and their linguistic label sets are respectively $S_3^{(L_1)}$ and $S_3^{(L_2)}$ with different granularities, where

$$S_3^{(L_1)}=S_3^{(3)}=\{s_{-2}=extreme\ poor,\ s_{-2/3}=poor,\ s_0=fair,\ s_{2/3}=good,\ s_{-2}=extreme\ good\}$$

$$S_3^{(L_2)}=S_3^{(5)}=\{s_{-4}=extreme\ poor,\ s_{-2}=very\ poor,\ s_{-1}=poor, s_{-0.4}=slight\ poor,\ s_0=fair,\ s_{0.4}=slight\ good,\ s_1=good,\ s_2=very\ good,\ s_4=extreme\ good\}$$

We extend $S_3^{(L_k)}(k=1,2)$ to the continuous linguistic label sets $\overline{S}_3^{(L_k)}=\{s_\alpha\,|\alpha\in[1-L_k,L_k-1],\ i=1,2\}$. Then by Eq. (8.13), we can establish a mapping between linguistic labels of additive continuous linguistic label sets $\overline{S}_3^{(L_1)}$ and $\overline{S}_3^{(L_2)}$:

$$\begin{array}{lccccccccccc}
\overline{S}_3^{(L_1)}: & s_{-2} & s_{-1} & s_{-2/3} & s_{-1/2} & s_{-1/5} & s_0 & s_{1/5} & s_{1/2} & s_{2/3} & s_1 & s_2\\
 & \downarrow & \downarrow & \downarrow & \downarrow & \downarrow & \downarrow & \downarrow & \downarrow & \downarrow & \downarrow & \downarrow\\
\overline{S}_3^{(L_2)}: & s_{-4} & s_{-2} & s_{-4/3} & s_{-1} & s_{-2/5} & s_0 & s_{2/5} & s_1 & s_{4/3} & s_2 & s_4
\end{array}$$

From the above mapping between $\overline{S}_3^{(L_1)}$ and $\overline{S}_3^{(L_2)}$, the TFMLLs are very complicated and not accordant with human being's thinking. If three-level assessment indexes have already been given, such as $\{extremely\ poor,\ fair,\ extremely\ good\}$, we just should add two indexes, like *poor* and *good*, and then insert them to three-level assessment indices symmetrically in order to get five-level assessment indexes for simplicity and convenience. Analogically, in the process of extending the additive continuous linguistic label set $\overline{S}_3^{(L_1)}(L_1=3)$ to $\overline{S}_3^{(L_2)}(L_2=5)$, if we straightly insert the linguistic labels "$s_{\alpha_1}=slight\ poor$" and "$s_{\alpha_2}=very\ poor$" into $\overline{S}_3^{(L_1)}$ round linguistic label "$s_{-2/3}=poor$" and insert "$s_{\alpha_3}=slight\ good$" and "$s_{\alpha_4}=very\ good$" into $\overline{S}_3^{(L_1)}$ round "$s_{2/3}=good$", in which $\alpha_i\in[1-L_1,L_1-1](i=1,2,3,4)$, then the TFMLLs are accordant with the normal human being's thinking and the mappings among linguistic labels will be simpler:

$$\begin{array}{lccccccccc}
\overline{S}_3^{(L_1)}: & s_{-2} & s_{\alpha_1} & s_{-2/3} & s_{\alpha_2} & s_0 & s_{\alpha_3} & s_{2/3} & s_{\alpha_4} & s_2\\
 & \downarrow & \downarrow & \downarrow & \downarrow & \downarrow & \downarrow & \downarrow & \downarrow & \downarrow\\
\overline{S}_3^{(L_2)}: & s_{-4} & s_{-2} & s_{-1} & s_{-2/5} & s_0 & s_{2/5} & s_1 & s_2 & s_4
\end{array}$$

and then we can try to present some TRMLLs according to the above analyses.

Based on the additive linguistic label set $S_3^{(L)}$, let

$$S_3^{(L_1)}=\left\{s_\alpha\left|\alpha=1-L_1,\frac{2}{3}(2-L_1),\frac{2}{4}(3-L_1),\ldots,0,\ldots,\frac{2}{4}(L_1-3),\frac{2}{3}(L_1-2),L_1-1\right.\right\} \tag{8.14}$$

and

$$S_3^{(L_2)} = \left\{ s_\beta \middle| \beta = 1 - L_2, \frac{2}{3}(2 - L_2), \frac{2}{4}(3 - L_2), \ldots, 0, \ldots, \frac{2}{4}(L_2 - 3), \frac{2}{3}(L_2 - 2), L_2 - 1 \right\} \tag{8.15}$$

be two additive linguistic label sets with different granularities, where $L_i (i = 1, 2)$ are the positive integers, and $L_1 \neq L_2$. We extend $S_3^{(L_1)}$ and $S_3^{(L_2)}$ to the continuous linguistic label sets $\overline{S}_3^{(L_1)} = \{ s_\alpha | \alpha \in [1 - L_1, L_1 - 1] \}$ and $\overline{S}_3^{(L_2)} = \{ s_\beta | \beta \in [1 - L_2, L_2 - 1] \}$, respectively.

Firstly, we consider the right parts of $\overline{S}_3^{(L_1)}$ and $\overline{S}_3^{(L_2)}$ just like Eq. (8.3), then

$$\alpha = \frac{2(i_1 - 1)}{L_1 + 2 - i_1},\ i_1 \in [1, L_1],\ \beta = \frac{2(i_2 - 1)}{L_2 + 2 - i_2},\ i_2 \in [1, L_2]$$

Here, we can define the TRMLLs in the right parts of $\overline{S}_3^{(L_1)}$ and $\overline{S}_3^{(L_2)}$ as follows:

$$\frac{L_1 - 1}{L_1 + 1} \cdot \left(\frac{1}{2} + \frac{1}{\alpha} \right) = \frac{L_2 - 1}{L_2 + 1} \cdot \left(\frac{1}{2} + \frac{1}{\beta} \right) \tag{8.16}$$

Similarly, for the left parts of $\overline{S}_3^{(L_1)}$ and $\overline{S}_3^{(L_2)}$, where

$$\alpha = -\frac{2(i_1 - 1)}{L_1 + 2 - i_1},\ i_1 \in [1, L_1],\ \beta = -\frac{2(i_2 - 1)}{L_2 + 2 - i_2},\ i_2 \in [1, L_2]$$

and the TRMLLs can be defined as follows:

$$\frac{t_1 - 1}{t_1 + 1} \cdot \left(\frac{1}{2} - \frac{1}{\alpha} \right) = \frac{t_2 - 1}{t_2 + 1} \cdot \left(\frac{1}{2} - \frac{1}{\beta} \right) \tag{8.17}$$

By Eqs. (8.16) and (8.17), we have

$$\frac{L_1 - 1}{L_1 + 1} \cdot \left(\frac{1}{2} + \frac{1}{|\alpha|} \right) = \frac{L_2 - 1}{L_2 + 1} \cdot \left(\frac{1}{2} + \frac{1}{\beta} \right) \tag{8.18}$$

which we call as the TRMLLs based on the additive linguistic label set $S_3^{(L)}$, where $\alpha \cdot \beta \geq 0$.

In order to understand the above two TRMLLs clearly, in what follows, we make two sketch maps of them respectively. Let

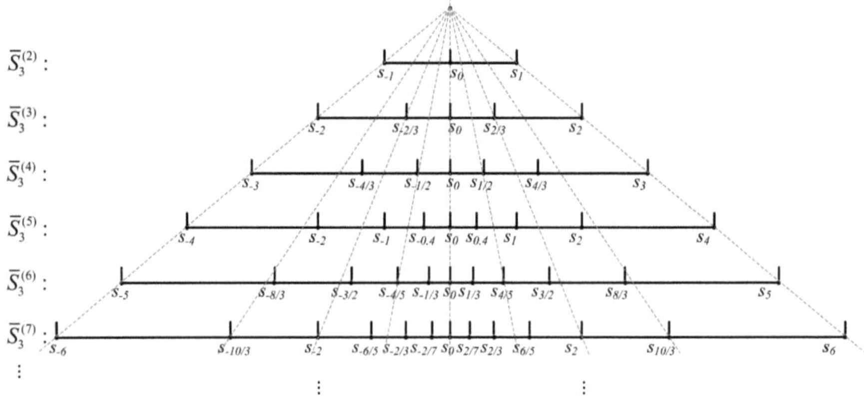

Fig. 8.2 Sketch map according to TFMLLs

$$S_3^{(L)} = \left\{ s_\alpha \,\middle|\, \alpha = 1-L, \frac{2}{3}(2-L), \ldots, 0, \ldots, \frac{2}{3}(L-2), L-1 \right\},\ t = 1,2,\ldots$$

be the additive linguistic label sets, and extend $S_3^{(L)}(L=1,2,\ldots)$ to the continuous linguistic label set $\bar{S}_3^{(L)} = \{ s_\alpha \,|\, \alpha = [1-L, L-1] \}(L=1,2,\ldots)$. By Eqs. (8.13) and (8.18), we can get two sketch maps (see Figs. 8.2 and 8.3), where the segments with different lengths represent the continuous linguistic label sets $\bar{S}_3^{(L)}(L=1,2,\ldots)$ with different granularities, and the broken lines obtained by calculating Eqs. (8.13) and (8.18) show the mapping relationships among the virtual linguistic labels. As we can see, in Fig. 8.2, all the mapping broken lines are straight which imply that the TFMLLs in $\bar{S}_3^{(L)}(L=1,2,\ldots)$ are established by evenly changing the lengths of concerned segments which represent the certain continuous linguistic label sets, while the curving mapping broken lines in Fig. 8.3 denote that we

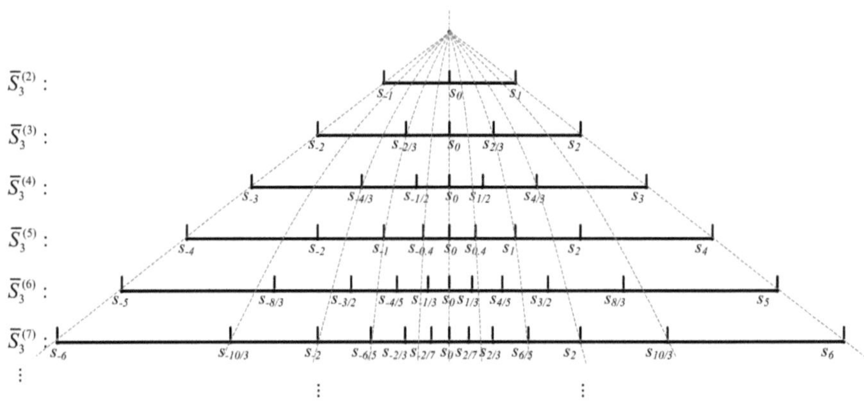

Fig. 8.3 Sketch map according to TRMLLs

transform the multigranular linguistic labels unevenly. According to the TFMLLs in Xu [132], we can see that there exists difference between the transformed linguistic label and the expected linguistic label, i.e., a transformed linguistic label $s_i' \in \bar{S}_3^{(L_2)} = \{s_\beta \,|\, \beta \in [1-L_2, L_2-1]\}$, obtained by the virtual linguistic label $s_i \in \bar{S}_3^{(L_1)} = \{s_\alpha \,|\, \alpha \in [1-L_1, L_1-1]\}$ which represents the linguistic assessment of "*good*", may be close to the virtual linguistic label $s_j \in \bar{S}_3^{(L_2)}$ which represents the linguistic assessment of "*slight good*" when $L_1 >> L_2$, $L_1, L_2 \in N^*$, where N^* is the set of all positive integers. The improved TRMLLs can resolve the above discaccord by using the uneven transformation relationships. However, the calculations of the improved TRMLL based on $S_3^{(L)}$ are more complicated than those in Xu [132], so it is essential to give a simple and straightforward calculation method.

Similarly, based on the linguistic label sets $S_i^{(L)} (i = 1,2,4,5)$, all the MAGDM problems with multigranular linguistic labels can be well solved in actual applications.

Based on the additive linguistic label set $S_1^{(L)}$, we let the linguistic label sets $S_1^{(L_k)} = \{s_\alpha \,|\, \alpha = 0,1,\ldots,L_k\} (k = 1,2,\ldots,t)$ with different granularities, and extend $S_1^{(L_k)} (k = 1,2,\ldots,t)$ to the continuous label sets $\bar{S}_1^{(L_k)} = \{s_\alpha \,|\, \alpha \in [1, L_k]\}$. Then we define some TRMLLs based on $S_1^{(L)}$ as follows:

$$\frac{\alpha_i - 1}{L_i - 1} = \frac{\alpha_j - 1}{L_j - 1}, \quad i, j = 1,2,\ldots,t \tag{8.19}$$

With respect to the symmetrical additive linguistic label set $S_2^{(L)}$, the TRMLLs are also very simple, which can be defined as:

$$\frac{\alpha_i}{L_i} = \frac{\alpha_j}{L_j}, \quad i, j = 1,2,\ldots,t \tag{8.20}$$

in which the linguistic label sets $S_2^{(L_i)} = \{s_\alpha \,|\, \alpha = -L_i,\ldots,-1,0,1,\ldots,L_i\} (i = 1,2,\ldots,t)$ are of different granularities.

However, the TRMLLs based on the multiplicative linguistic label sets $S_4^{(L)}$ and $S_5^{(L)}$ are complicated correspondingly because $S_4^{(L)}$ and $S_5^{(L)}$ are asymmetrical. Let the linguistic label set $S_4^{(L_i)} = \left\{ s_\alpha \,\middle|\, \alpha = \frac{1}{L_i},\ldots,\frac{1}{2},1,2,\ldots,L_i \right\}$, and extend $S_4^{(L_i)} (i = 1,2,\ldots,t)$ to the continuous linguistic label sets $\bar{S}_4^{(L_i)} = \left\{ s_\alpha \,\middle|\, \alpha \in \left[\frac{1}{L_i}, L_i\right] \right\} (i = 1,2,\ldots,t)$. Then the TRMLLs based on $S_4^{(L)}$ can be defined as:

$$\frac{[\alpha_i] - 1}{L_i - 1} = \frac{[\alpha_j] - 1}{L_j - 1}, \quad i, j = 1,2,\ldots,t \tag{8.21}$$

where

$$[\alpha_i] = \begin{cases} \alpha_i, \ \alpha_i \geq 0 \\ \dfrac{1}{\alpha_i}, \ \alpha_i < 0 \end{cases}, \quad i = 1, 2, \ldots, t \tag{8.22}$$

and $\alpha_i \cdot \alpha_j \geq 0 \ (i, j = 1, 2, \ldots, n)$, since it is unpractical to transform a linguistic label which represents *good* to a *poor* and vice versa.

Analogically, let

$$S_5^{(L_i)} = \left\{ s_\alpha \middle| \alpha = \frac{1}{L_i}, \frac{2}{L_i}, \ldots, \frac{L_i - 1}{L_i}, 1, \frac{L_i}{L_i - 1}, \ldots, \frac{L_i}{2}, L_i \right\}$$

be the linguistic label set and extend $S_5^{(L_i)} (i = 1, 2, \ldots, t)$ to the continuous label set $\bar{S}_5^{(L_i)} = \left\{ s_\alpha \middle| \alpha \in \left[\frac{1}{L_i}, L_i \right] \right\}$, then the TRMLLs based on the multiplicative linguistic label set $S_5^{(L)}$ can be defined as:

$$\frac{L_i}{L_i - 1} \left(\frac{1}{[\alpha_i]} - 1 \right) = \frac{L_j}{L_j - 1} \left(\frac{1}{[\alpha_j]} - 1 \right), \quad i, j = 1, 2, \ldots, t \tag{8.23}$$

where $\ln^{\alpha_i} \cdot \ln^{\alpha_j} \geq 0 \ (i, j = 1, 2, \ldots, t)$.

The MAGDM problems with multigranular linguistic labels based on all linguistic label sets can be resolved successfully by Eqs. (8.18)–(8.21) and (8.23).

8.3.2 *Decision Making Method*

Considering that the number of linguistic labels in a linguistic label set, used by the decision makers, is not very big, in the practical applications, the maximum granularity of linguistic label set is not generally greater than 20. In the following, we establish five reference tables based on the above five linguistic label sets with the maximum granularity being 20. Each table is divided into three parts (denoted by τ, α and c), in which the cardinality values of linguistic label sets with different granularities are shown in τ, the values in α are the indexes of linguistic labels, and in c, column values indicate that similar linguistic labels in the linguistic label sets with different granularities are placed in same column, while the larger the column value is, the better the linguistic label is. For example, suppose that three decision makers $d_k (k = 1, 2, 3)$ provide their assessment information, represented by the linguistic labels $s_{0.5}$, $s_{1.1}$ and $s_{1.2}$, based on the linguistic label sets $S_3^{(3)}$, $S_3^{(5)}$ and $S_3^{(7)}$, respectively. From Tables 8.5, 8.6, and 8.7, the column value $c_1 = 14$ since the index of $s_{0.5}$ belongs to the interval $[0.49, 0.67)$, while $c_2 = 15$ due to that the index of $s_{1.1}$

Table 8.5 TRMLL based on the linguistic label set S_1

τ \ c (α: *extremely poor* ← *fair*)	1	2	3	4	5	6	7	8	9	10
3	1	1.06	1.17	1.28	1.39	1.50	1.61	1.72	1.83	1.94
5	1	1.11	1.33	1.56	1.78	2.00	2.22	2.44	2.67	2.89
7	1	1.17	1.50	1.83	2.17	2.50	2.83	3.17	3.50	3.83
9	1	1.22	1.67	2.11	2.56	3.00	3.44	3.89	4.33	4.78
11	1	1.28	1.83	2.39	2.94	3.50	4.06	4.61	5.17	5.72
13	1	1.33	2.00	2.67	3.33	4.00	4.67	5.33	6.00	6.67
15	1	1.39	2.17	2.94	3.72	4.50	5.28	6.06	6.83	7.61
17	1	1.44	2.33	3.22	4.11	5.00	5.89	6.78	7.67	8.56
19	1	1.5	2.5	3.5	4.5	5.5	6.5	7.5	8.5	9.5

τ \ c (α: *fair* → *extremely good*)	10	11	12	13	14	15	16	17	18	19
3	2.06	2.17	2.28	2.39	2.50	2.61	2.72	2.83	2.94	3
5	3.11	3.33	3.56	3.78	4.00	4.22	4.44	4.67	4.89	5
7	4.17	4.50	4.83	5.17	5.50	5.83	6.17	6.50	6.83	7
9	5.22	5.67	6.11	6.56	7.00	7.44	7.89	8.33	8.78	9
11	6.28	6.83	7.39	7.94	8.50	9.06	9.61	10.17	10.72	11
13	7.33	8.00	8.67	9.33	10.00	10.67	11.33	12.00	12.67	13
15	8.39	9.17	9.94	10.72	11.50	12.28	13.06	13.83	14.61	15
17	9.44	10.33	11.22	12.11	13.00	13.89	14.78	15.67	16.56	17
19	10.5	11.5	12.5	13.5	14.5	15.5	16.5	17.5	18.5	19

Table 8.6 TRMLL based on the linguistic label set S_2

α \ c	*extremely poor* ←								*fair*
	1	2	3	4	5	6	7	8	9	10
1	-1	-0.94	-0.83	-0.72	-0.61	-0.50	-0.39	-0.28	-0.17	-0.06
2	-2	-1.89	-1.67	-1.44	-1.22	-1.00	-0.78	-0.56	-0.33	-0.11
3	-3	-2.83	-2.50	-2.17	-1.83	-1.50	-1.17	-0.83	-0.50	-0.17
4	-4	-3.78	-3.33	-2.89	-2.44	-2.00	-1.56	-1.11	-0.67	-0.22
5	-5	-4.72	-4.17	-3.61	-3.06	-2.50	-1.94	-1.39	-0.83	-0.28
6	-6	-5.67	-5.00	-4.33	-3.67	-3.00	-2.33	-1.67	-1.00	-0.33
7	-7	-6.61	-5.83	-5.06	-4.28	-3.50	-2.72	-1.94	-1.17	-0.39
8	-8	-7.56	-6.67	-5.78	-4.89	-4.00	-3.11	-2.22	-1.33	-0.44
9	-9	-8.5	-7.5	-6.5	-5.5	-4.5	-3.5	-2.5	-1.5	-0.5

α \ c	*fair* →								*extremely good*
	10	11	12	13	14	15	16	17	18	19
1	0.06	0.17	0.28	0.39	0.50	0.61	0.72	0.83	0.94	1
2	0.11	0.33	0.56	0.78	1.00	1.22	1.44	1.67	1.89	2
3	0.17	0.50	0.83	1.17	1.50	1.83	2.17	2.50	2.83	3
4	0.22	0.67	1.11	1.56	2.00	2.44	2.89	3.33	3.78	4
5	0.28	0.83	1.39	1.94	2.50	3.06	3.61	4.17	4.72	5
6	0.33	1.00	1.67	2.33	3.00	3.67	4.33	5.00	5.67	6
7	0.39	1.17	1.94	2.72	3.50	4.28	5.06	5.83	6.61	7
8	0.44	1.33	2.22	3.11	4.00	4.89	5.78	6.67	7.56	8
9	0.5	1.5	2.5	3.5	4.5	5.5	6.5	7.5	8.5	9

Table 8.7 TRMLL based on the linguistic label set S_3

α	*extremely poor* ←									*fair*
τ \ c	1	2	3	4	5	6	7	8	9	10
2	-1	-0.93	-0.78	-0.64	-0.52	-0.40	-0.30	-0.21	-0.12	-0.04
3	-2	-1.83	-1.45	-1.15	-0.89	-0.67	-0.49	-0.33	-0.19	-0.06
4	-3	-2.69	-2.04	-1.55	-1.17	-0.87	-0.62	-0.41	-0.23	-0.07
5	-4	-3.51	-2.55	-1.89	-1.39	-1.01	-0.71	-0.46	-0.25	-0.08
6	-5	-4.30	-3.01	-2.17	-1.57	-1.13	-0.78	-0.50	-0.28	-0.09
7	-6	-5.06	-3.42	-2.41	-1.72	-1.22	-0.83	-0.53	-0.29	-0.09
8	-7	-5.79	-3.79	-2.61	-1.84	-1.29	-0.88	-0.56	-0.30	-0.09
9	-8	-6.49	-4.12	-2.79	-1.94	-1.35	-0.92	-0.58	-0.31	-0.10
10	-9	-7.17	-4.42	-2.95	-2.03	-1.40	-0.95	-0.60	-0.32	-0.10

α	*fair* →								*extremely good*	
τ \ c	10	11	12	13	14	15	16	17	18	19
2	0.04	0.12	0.21	0.30	0.40	0.52	0.64	0.78	0.93	1
3	0.06	0.19	0.33	0.49	0.67	0.89	1.15	1.45	1.83	2
4	0.07	0.23	0.41	0.62	0.87	1.17	1.55	2.04	2.69	3
5	0.08	0.25	0.46	0.71	1.01	1.39	1.89	2.55	3.51	4
6	0.09	0.28	0.50	0.78	1.13	1.57	2.17	3.01	4.30	5
7	0.09	0.29	0.53	0.83	1.22	1.72	2.41	3.42	5.06	6
8	0.09	0.30	0.56	0.88	1.29	1.84	2.61	3.79	5.79	7
9	0.10	0.31	0.58	0.92	1.35	1.94	2.79	4.12	6.49	8
10	0.10	0.32	0.60	0.95	1.40	2.03	2.95	4.42	7.17	9

belongs to $[1.1, 1.39)$ and $c_3 = 14$ due to that the index of $s_{1.2}$ belongs to $[0.83, 1.22)$, thus it can be taken for granted that $s_{0.5} \sim s_{1.2} \prec s_{1.1}$ due to $c_1 = c_3 < c_2$, where the notation "~" indicates indifference between two linguistic labels. Therefore, the assessment of the decision maker d_1 is indifferent to d_2, but inferior to d_3.

Referring to the given five reference tables, all linguistic labels are unified to a fixed linguistic label set with 20 granularity denoted by column value, and the calculation complexity in practical applications of TRMLLs can be reduced largely (Tables 8.8 and 8.9).

Now we apply the TRMLLs to MAGDM, which involves the following steps:

Step1 For a MAGDM problem, let $X = \{x_1, x_2, \ldots, x_n\}$ be a set of alternatives, $U = \{u_1, u_2, \ldots, u_m\}$ be a set of attributes, and $D = \{d_1, d_2, \ldots, d_t\}$ be the set of decision makers. The decision makers $d_k (k = 1, 2, \ldots, t)$ provide linguistic preference information over the alternatives $x_i (i = 1, 2, \ldots, n)$ with respect to the given attributes $u_j (j = 1, 2, \ldots, m)$ by using the linguistic label sets $S^{(L_i)} (i = 1, 2, \ldots, t)$, respectively, and the preferences provided by the decision makers $d_k (k = 1, 2, \ldots, t)$ are assembled into the linguistic decision matrices $R_k = (r_{ij}^{(k)})_{n \times m}$ $(k = 1, 2, \ldots, t)$. In addition, let $w = (w_1, w_2, \ldots, w_m)$ be the weight vector of attributes, and $\lambda = (\lambda_1, \lambda_2, \ldots, \lambda_t)$ be the weight vector of decision makers, where $w_j, \lambda_k \geq 0$, $j = 1, 2, \ldots, m$, $k = 1, 2, \ldots, t$, $\sum_{j=1}^{m} w_j = 1$, and $\sum_{k=1}^{t} \lambda_k = 1$.

Step 2 Aggregate the preference information in the i th line of $R_k (k = 1, 2, \ldots, t)$ by using the EWA operator:

$$z_i^{(k)}(w) = EWA_w(r_{i1}^{(k)}, r_{i2}^{(k)}, \ldots, r_{im}^{(k)}) = w_1 r_{i1}^{(k)} \oplus w_2 r_{i2}^{(k)} \oplus \cdots \oplus w_m r_{im}^{(k)}, \quad i = 1, 2, \ldots, n, \; k = 1, 2, \ldots, t \tag{8.24}$$

Then, we transform $z_i^{(k)}(w)$ into the column value $c_i^{(k)}$ according to one of the above five reference tables, where $c_i^{(k)}$ is a column value corresponding to the alternative x_i with respect to the decision maker d_k.

Step 3 Utilize the EWA operator:

$$c_i = EWA_\lambda(c_i^{(1)}, c_i^{(2)}, \ldots, c_i^{(t)}) = \lambda_1 c_i^{(1)} \oplus \lambda_2 c_i^{(2)} \oplus \cdots \oplus \lambda_t c_i^{(t)}, \; i = 1, 2, \ldots, n \tag{8.25}$$

to aggregate $c_i^{(k)} (k = 1, 2, \ldots, t)$, where c_i is called an overall column value corresponding to the alternative x_i.

Step 4 Rank all the alternatives $x_i (i = 1, 2, \ldots, n)$ and select the optimal one(s) in accordance with the overall column values $c_i (i = 1, 2, \ldots, n)$.

Table 8.8 TRMLL based on the linguistic label set S_4

α \ c	*extremely poor* ←									*fair*
	1	2	3	4	5	6	7	8	9	10
2	1/2	0.52	0.55	0.58	0.62	0.67	0.72	0.79	0.87	0.96
3	1/3	0.35	0.38	0.41	0.45	0.50	0.57	0.65	0.76	0.93
4	1/4	0.26	0.29	0.32	0.35	0.40	0.47	0.55	0.68	0.90
5	1/5	0.21	0.23	0.26	0.29	0.34	0.40	0.48	0.62	0.87
6	1/6	0.18	0.19	0.22	0.25	0.29	0.34	0.43	0.56	0.84
7	1/7	0.15	0.17	0.19	0.22	0.25	0.30	0.38	0.52	0.82
8	1/8	0.13	0.15	0.17	0.19	0.22	0.27	0.35	0.48	0.79
9	1/9	0.12	0.13	0.15	0.17	0.20	0.25	0.32	0.45	0.77
10	1/10	0.11	0.12	0.13	0.15	0.18	0.23	0.29	0.42	0.75

α	*fair* →									*extremely good*
	10	11	12	13	14	15	16	17	18	19
2	1.06	1.17	1.28	1.39	1.50	1.61	1.72	1.83	1.94	2
3	1.11	1.33	1.56	1.78	2.00	2.22	2.44	2.67	2.89	3
4	1.17	1.50	1.83	2.17	2.50	2.83	3.17	3.50	3.83	4
5	1.22	1.67	2.11	2.56	3.00	3.44	3.89	4.33	4.78	5
6	1.28	1.83	2.39	2.94	3.50	4.06	4.61	5.17	5.72	6
7	1.33	2.00	2.67	3.33	4.00	4.67	5.33	6.00	6.67	7
8	1.39	2.17	2.94	3.72	4.50	5.28	6.06	6.83	7.61	8
9	1.44	2.33	3.22	4.11	5.00	5.89	6.78	7.67	8.56	9
10	1.50	2.50	3.50	4.50	5.50	6.50	7.50	8.50	9.50	10

Table 8.9 TRMLL based on the linguistic label set S_5

α	*extremely poor* ←									*fair*
c	1	2	3	4	5	6	7	8	9	10
2	1/2	0.53	0.58	0.64	0.69	0.75	0.81	0.86	0.92	0.97
3	1/3	0.37	0.44	0.52	0.59	0.67	0.74	0.81	0.89	0.96
4	1/4	0.29	0.38	0.46	0.54	0.63	0.71	0.79	0.88	0.96
5	1/5	0.24	0.33	0.42	0.51	0.60	0.69	0.78	0.87	0.96
6	1/6	0.21	0.31	0.40	0.49	0.58	0.68	0.77	0.86	0.95
7	1/7	0.19	0.29	0.38	0.48	0.57	0.67	0.76	0.86	0.95
8	1/8	0.17	0.27	0.37	0.47	0.56	0.66	0.76	0.85	0.95
9	1/9	0.16	0.26	0.36	0.46	0.56	0.65	0.75	0.85	0.95
10	1/10	0.15	0.25	0.35	0.45	0.55	0.65	0.75	0.85	0.95

α	*fair* →									*extremely poor*
c	10	11	12	13	14	15	16	17	18	19
2	1.03	1.09	1.16	1.24	1.34	1.45	1.58	1.73	1.93	2
3	1.04	1.13	1.23	1.36	1.51	1.70	1.95	2.29	2.79	3
4	1.05	1.15	1.27	1.42	1.61	1.86	2.21	2.73	3.60	4
5	1.05	1.16	1.29	1.46	1.68	1.98	2.40	3.08	4.35	5
6	1.05	1.16	1.31	1.49	1.73	2.06	2.55	3.38	5.06	6
7	1.05	1.17	1.32	1.51	1.76	2.12	2.67	3.62	5.73	7
8	1.05	1.17	1.33	1.52	1.79	2.17	2.77	3.83	6.35	8
9	1.05	1.18	1.33	1.54	1.81	2.22	2.85	4.01	6.94	9
10	1.06	1.18	1.34	1.55	1.83	2.25	2.92	4.17	7.50	10

8.3.3 Practical Example

Example 8.4 Consider a practical MAGDM problem involves the evaluation of technical post of five teachers $x_i(i=1,2,3,4,5)$. Three main attributes, which may be influential to promotion, are confirmed as abilities of teaching (u_1), scientific research (u_2) and service (u_3), and the attribute weight vector is $w=(0.3,\ 0.5,\ 0.2)$. Three decision makers $d_k(k=1,2,3)$, whose weight vector is $\lambda=(0.3,\ 0.4,\ 0.3)$, compare these five teachers concerning about attributes based on the different granular linguistic label sets $S_3^{(3)}$, $S_3^{(4)}$ and $S_3^{(6)}$, where

$$S_3^{(3)}=\{s_{-2}=\textit{extremely poor},\ s_{-2/3}=\textit{poor},\ s_0=\textit{fair},\\ s_{2/3}=\textit{good},\ s_2=\textit{extremely good}\}$$

$$S_3^{(4)}=\{s_{-3}=\textit{extremely poor},\ s_{-4/3}=\textit{very poor},\ s_{-1/2}=\textit{poor},\ s_0=\textit{fair},\\ s_{1/2}=\textit{good},\ s_{4/3}=\textit{very good},\ s_3=\textit{extremely good}\}$$

$$S_3^{(6)}=\{s_{-5}=\textit{extremely poor},\ s_{-8/3}=\textit{very poor},\ s_{-3/2}=\textit{quite poor},\ s_{-4/5}=\textit{poor},\\ s_{-1/3}=\textit{slightly poor},\ s_0=\textit{fair}, s_{1/3}=\textit{slightly good},\ s_{4/5}=\textit{good},\\ s_{3/2}=\textit{quite good},\ s_{8/3}=\textit{very good},\ s_5=\textit{extremely good}\}$$

and the linguistic decision matrices $R_k(k=1,2,3)$ are listed in Tables 8.10, 8.11, and 8.12.

To get the best alternative, the following steps are involved:

Step 1 By using the EWA operator (8.24), we aggregate the preference information in the i th line of the $R_k(k=1,2,3)$ in order to calculate the values of $z_i^{(k)}(w)$ $(i=1,2,3,4,5,\ k=1,2,3)$:

$$z_1^{(1)}(w)=s_{-0.067},\ z_2^{(1)}(w)=s_{0.533},\ z_3^{(1)}(w)=s_{-1.067},\ z_4^{(1)}(w)=s_{0.467},\ z_5^{(1)}(w)=s_{1.133}$$

Table 8.10 Linguistic decision matrix R_1

	u_1	u_2	u_3
x_1	$s_{-2/3}$	s_0	$s_{2/3}$
x_2	$s_{-2/3}$	$s_{2/3}$	s_2
x_3	$s_{-2/3}$	s_{-2}	$s_{2/3}$
x_4	s_2	s_0	$s_{-2/3}$
x_5	s_0	s_2	$s_{2/3}$

Table 8.11 Linguistic decision matrix R_2

	u_1	u_2	u_3
x_1	$s_{-1/2}$	$s_{4/3}$	$s_{-1/2}$
x_2	$s_{-1/2}$	$s_{4/3}$	$s_{1/2}$
x_3	$s_{-4/3}$	$s_{-4/3}$	s_0
x_4	s_3	$s_{1/2}$	s_0
x_5	$s_{-4/3}$	$s_{4/3}$	s_{-3}

Table 8.12 Linguistic decision matrix R_3

	u_1	u_2	u_3
x_1	$s_{1/3}$	s_2	$s_{3/2}$
x_2	$s_{4/5}$	s_0	s_2
x_3	s_5	$s_{4/5}$	$s_{3/2}$
x_4	s_{-2}	s_2	s_0
x_5	$s_{-3/2}$	$s_{4/5}$	s_2

$$z_1^{(2)}(w) = s_{0.417},\ z_2^{(2)}(w) = s_{0.617},\ z_3^{(2)}(w) = s_{-1.067},\ z_4^{(2)}(w) = s_{1.15},\ z_5^{(2)}(w) = s_{-0.333}$$

$$z_1^{(3)}(w) = s_{1.4},\ z_2^{(3)}(w) = s_{0.64},\ z_3^{(3)}(w) = s_{2.2},\ z_4^{(3)}(w) = s_{0.4},\ z_5^{(3)}(w) = s_{0.35}$$

Step 2 As consulting reference table (see Table 8.7), we can transform $z_i^{(k)}(w)$ into the column value $c_i^{(k)}$ as follows:

$$c_1^{(1)} = 6,\ c_2^{(1)} = 14,\ c_3^{(1)} = 4,\ c_4^{(1)} = 13,\ c_5^{(1)} = 16$$

$$c_1^{(2)} = 13,\ c_2^{(2)} = 13,\ c_3^{(2)} = 5,\ c_4^{(2)} = 15,\ c_5^{(2)} = 8$$

$$c_1^{(3)} = 15,\ c_2^{(3)} = 13,\ c_3^{(3)} = 17,\ c_4^{(3)} = 12,\ c_5^{(3)} = 12$$

Step 3 Utilize the EWA operator (8.25) to aggregate the column values corresponding to the teachers $x_i (i = 1,2,3,4,5)$, and then the overall column values $c_i (i = 1,2,3,4,5)$ can be obtained:

$$c_1 = 11.5,\ c_2 = 13.3,\ c_3 = 8.3,\ c_4 = 13.5,\ c_5 = 11.6$$

Step 4 Utilize the values of $c_i (i = 1,2,3,4,5)$ to rank the teachers:

$$x_4 \succ x_2 \succ x_5 \succ x_1 \succ x_3$$

and thus, the best teacher is x_4.

8.4 MADM with Two-Dimension Linguistic Aggregation Techniques [165]

8.4.1 Two-Dimension Linguistic Labels

In this section, we introduce some basic concepts, such as the 2-tuple linguistic representation, two-dimension linguistic label, and some common aggregation operators.

Generally, a linguistic label can be quantified by a triangular membership function, for instance, a label s_α of the set $S = \{s_\alpha | \alpha = 0, 1, \ldots, L\}$ can be quantified as:

$$f(x) = \begin{cases} x - \alpha + 1, & \alpha - 1 \le x < \alpha \\ -x + \alpha + 1, & \alpha \le x \le \alpha + 1 \\ 0, & otherwise \end{cases}$$

which is the triangular membership function representation model of linguistic labels (see Fig. 8.4). For convenience of computation, we suppose that it is possible that $x < 0$ and $x > L$.

With respect to fuzzy linguistic information, there are mainly four classifications about the computational models: (1) linguistic computational models making use of the extension principle from fuzzy arithmetic average; (2) linguistic symbolic computational models based on ordinal scales; (3) 2-tuple linguistic computational models based on the combination of linguistic term and numeric value; and (4) direct linguistic computational models based on virtual linguistic labels. In what follows, we briefly introduce the third and fourth computational models:

For a continuous linguistic label set $\bar{S} = \{s_\alpha \mid \alpha \in [0, L]\}$ on the basis of the linguistic label set S. If the linguistic label set S has five elements, we can define its continuous set $\bar{S} = \{s_\alpha \mid \alpha \in [0, 4]\}$. In this case, s_α is a virtual linguistic label for $\alpha \in [0, 4] \setminus \{0, 1, 2, 3, 4\}$ or an original linguistic label for $\alpha = 0, 1, 2, 3, 4$ (see Fig. 8.5):

As we know, each original linguistic label is used to represent linguistic information like "*poor*", "*fair*" and "*extremely good*", and so on, but a virtual linguistic label has no actual meaning but a computational symbol. On the basis of the virtual linguistic labels and the original linguistic labels, we can compute with words just using the indices of linguistic labels. The above is the main idea of the fourth com-

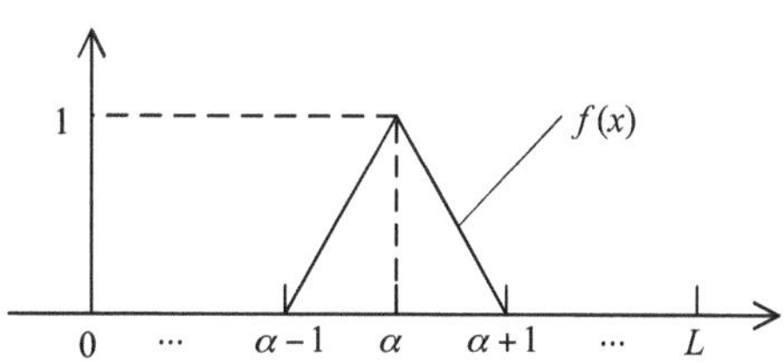

Fig. 8.4 Triangular membership function associated with the linguistic label s_α

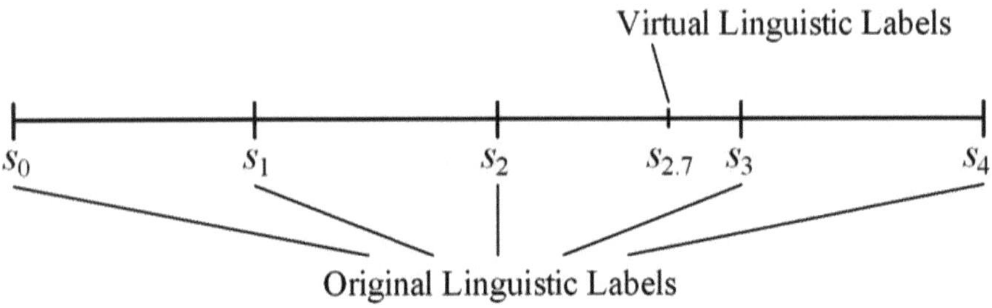

Fig. 8.5 Continuous linguistic label set $\overline{S} = \{s_\alpha \mid \alpha \in [0,4]\}$

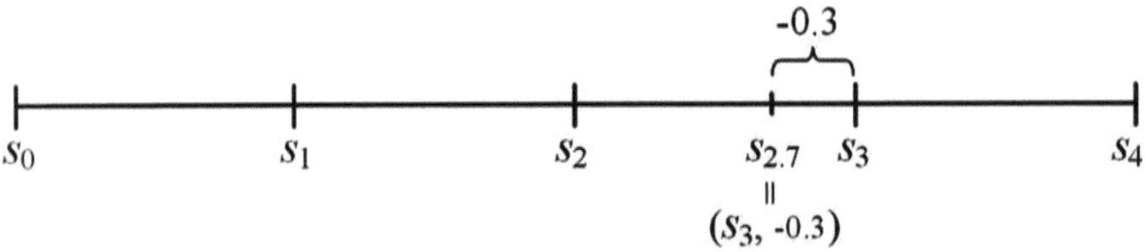

Fig. 8.6 Relationship between virtual linguistic label and 2-tuple linguistic information

putational model. Moreover, there is a relationship between a virtual linguistic label and the corresponding linguistic 2-tuple.

According to Herrera and Martínez [40], a linguistic 2-tuple (s_i, β) $(i = 0,1,2\ldots,L)$ is used to represent linguistic information involved in a linguistic label set $S = \{s_\alpha \mid \alpha = 0,1,\ldots,L\}$, where s_i is a linguistic label and β is a numeric value representing a symbolic translation. A 2-tuple (s_i, β) is equivalent to a virtual linguistic label $s_\alpha \in \overline{S} = \{s_\alpha \mid \alpha \in [0,L]\}$, if let $i = round(\alpha)$ and $\beta = \alpha - i$. In this case, we can establish relationship between the virtual linguistic label and the 2-tuple linguistic information (See Fig. 8.6).

As mentioned by Zhu et al. [169], traditional fuzzy linguistic approaches "can not make effective use of the linguistic assessment information concerning the dependability of a decision maker's subjective judgment", so they introduced new two-dimension linguistic information, which consists of two parts: (1) *principal assessment information*: to assess alternatives or objects; and (2) *self-assessment information*: to depict the dependability of principal assessment information. Firstly, they expressed the two-dimension linguistic assessment information by the frame of subjective evidential reasoning, and then proposed a conflict analysis method to improve the combination rule in order to aggregate two-dimension linguistic assessment information reasonably with intricate debate. Furthermore, a specific comparing rule was devised to rank decision alternatives. As we know that the linguistic information is fuzzy and the common linguistic information is figured as z fuzzy subset(just like the triangular fuzzy number in Fig. 8.4), thus we will analyze the fuzziness of the two-dimension linguistic information to tell the distinction between the two-dimension linguistic information and the common linguistic information, which has not been done by Zhu et al. [169]. Similar to other fuzzy information, we can devise some relevant aggregation operators for applying the two-dimension linguistic information into MADM, which is different from the idea of Zhu et al. [169].

In what follows, we first give a definition of two-dimension linguistic label to represent the two-dimension linguistic information:

Definition 8.1 [165] Suppose that there are two linguistic label sets:

$$S = \{s_\alpha \mid \alpha = 0,1,\ldots,L\},\ S' = \{s'_\beta \mid \beta = 0,1,\ldots,L'\}$$

where both τ and τ' are even positive integers, and we extend them to the continuous linguistic label sets $\overline{S} = \{s_\alpha \mid \alpha \in [0,L]\}$ and $\overline{S}' = \{s'_\beta \mid \beta \in [0,L']\}$. Then a two-dimension linguistic label (2DLL) or called an original 2DLL, is formularized as $< s'_\beta, s_\alpha >$, in which the principal assessment label $s_\alpha \in S$ represents principal assessment information, and the self-assessment label $s'_\beta \in S'$ represents self-assessment information. If $s'_\beta \in \overline{S}'$ and $s_\alpha \in \overline{S}$, then $< s'_\beta, s_\alpha >$ is called a continuous 2DLL. Especially, $< s'_\beta, s_\alpha >$ is called a virtual 2DLL, if $< s'_\beta, s_\alpha >$ is a continuous 2DLL but not an original 2DLL.

Remark 8.1 If there is no ambiguity, 2DLLs can denote either the original 2DLLs or the continuous 2DLLs.

According to the above definition, the assessment information can be divided into two parts: one is the principal assessment label over an object represented by s_α and the other is the dependability of the principal assessment represented by s'_β. When an expert assesses some objects based on 2DLLs during the process of decision making, we should take it into account that there are both the uncertainty of the decision making problem and the subjective uncertainty of decision makers involved in order to improve the reasonability of the evaluation results.

Similar to the common linguistic labels (see Fig. 8.4), any 2DLL can also be quantified by a triangular membership function. Suppose that there are two linguistic label sets $S = \{s_\alpha \mid \alpha = 0,1,\ldots,L\}$ and $S' = \{s'_\beta \mid \beta = 0,1,\ldots,L'\}$ whose continuous forms are $\overline{S} = \{s_\alpha \mid \alpha = [0,L]\}$ and $\overline{S}' = \{s'_\beta \mid \beta = [0,L']\}$, respectively, then according to Definition 8.1, we define a set of 2DLLs as $E = \{\delta =< s'_\beta, s_\alpha >\mid s'_\beta \in S' \wedge s_\alpha \in S\}$ and its continuous form as $\overline{E} = \{\delta =< s'_\beta, s_\alpha >\mid s'_\beta \in \overline{S}' \wedge s_\alpha \in \overline{S}\}$. In this case, each element of the set E or $\overline{E}$ can be quantified by a triangular membership function. For example, a 2DLL $\delta =< s'_\beta, s_\alpha >$ can be quantified as (see Fig. 8.4).

$$f(x) = \begin{cases} \dfrac{x-a+b}{b^2}, & a-b \le x < a \\ \dfrac{-x+a+b}{b^2}, & a \le x \le a+b \\ 0, & otherwise \end{cases}$$

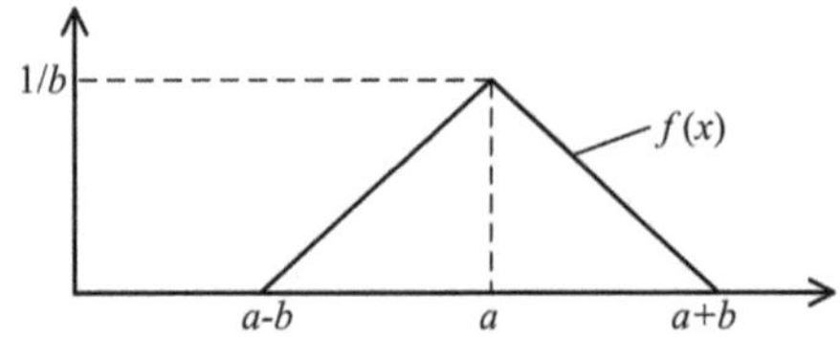

Fig. 8.7 Generalized TFN associated with a 2DLL

where $a = \alpha$ and $b = \sqrt{1 + \frac{3L^2}{2 \cdot 4^i}}$ $(i = \frac{\beta}{L' - \beta})$. That's to say, any 2DLL can be represented by a generalized triangular fuzzy number [7] (generalized TFN), such as $\delta = < s'_\beta, s_\alpha >$ can be represented as a generalized TFN $\tilde{t} = \left(a - b, a, a + b; \frac{1}{b}\right)$.

According to the idea of Chen [7], the TFNs are special cases of the generalized TFNs, because the maximal membership value of the former is 1 but that of the latter belongs to $[0, 1]$, i.e., if the maximal membership value of a generalized TFN equals to 1, then the generalized TFN must be a TFN (Fig. 8.7).

In this case, the common linguistic labels are the special cases of 2DLLs. As mentioned above, a common linguistic label can be represented by a triangular membership function, i.e., a TFN, just like a linguistic label s_α can be represented by TFN $(\alpha - 1, \alpha, \alpha + 1)$. If $\beta = L'$ in $\delta = < s'_\beta, s_\alpha >$, then $a = \alpha$ and $b = \sqrt{1 + \frac{3L^2}{2 \cdot 4^{L'/(L'-L')}}} = 1$, i.e., the 2DLL $< s'_{L'}, s_\alpha >$ can be represented as $(\alpha - 1, \alpha, \alpha + 1; 1)$ which has the same representation form as the common linguistic label s_α. Thus, any one-dimension linguistic label (i.e., a common linguistic label) s_α equals to a 2DLL $< s'_{L'}, s_\alpha >$. So the common linguistic labels are the special cases of 2DLLs, and the aggregation techniques for 2DLLs will be effective when being used to aggregate the common linguistic labels. Meanwhile, we notice that the larger $\beta \in [0, L']$, the smaller $b = \sqrt{1 + \frac{3L^2}{2 \cdot 4^{\beta/(L'-\beta)}}}$, and then the more certain the corresponding generalized TFN is, which is consistent with the fuzziness of 2DLLs.

Two-dimension linguistic information has been used extensively. For example, when an expert is invited to review some postgraduates' dissertations, he will grade these dissertations by means of several words like "*excellent, good, moderate, poor, and extremely poor*". Furthermore, it also should be clear whether or not he is familiar about the main content of each dissertation. Thus we can depict the assessment information of the expert to each dissertation by using the 2DLL, in which the principal assessment information indicates the grade of each dissertation and the self-assessment information indicates the mastery degree of the expert to each dissertation. In this case, the assessment information will be more comprehensive.

Moreover, exactly speaking, the aggregation result of several linguistic labels should be a 2DLL.

Example 8.5 Suppose that there is a set of five labels:

$$S = \{s_0 = extremely\ poor,\ s_1 = poor,\ s_2 = fair,\ s_3 = good,\\ s_4 = extremely\ good\}$$

and two experts (d_1 and d_2) evaluate two alternatives (x_1 and x_2) by using the linguistic labels in the set S. The alternative x_1 is "*good*" in the expert d_1's opinion but "*poor*" in the expert d_2's opinion, however, both the experts regard the alternative x_2 as "*fair*". If the two experts are of the same importance, then the alternative x_1 should be as good as x_2 based on the third or fourth computational models mentioned previously. In fact, the aggregation result of the alternative x_2 should be "*certainly fair*", but that of the alternative x_1 may be "*probably fair*". As a result, they are not the same, but the difference between them cannot be distinguished in traditional computational models. If we have another set of three labels:

$$S' = \{s'_0 = improbably,\ s'_1 = probably,\ s'_2 = certainly\}$$

then according to the above analysis, the common linguistic labels are the special cases of 2DLLs, and the assessment information of x_1 and x_2 can also be represented as: "*certainly good*" ($< s'_2, s_3 >$) and "*certainly fair*" ($< s'_2, s_2 >$), respectively, in the expert d_1's opinion, and "*certainly poor*" ($< s'_2, s_1 >$) and "*certainly fair*" ($< s'_2, s_2 >$), respectively, in the expert d_2's opinion. We aggregate the above 2DLLs for x_1 and x_2 respectively, and shall obtain the aggregation results: $< s'_1, s_2 >$ ("*possibly fair*") for x_1 and $< s'_2, s_2 >$ ("*certainly fair*") for x_2, which can be represented by triangular membership functions as figured illustrations (see Fig. 8.8). According to Fig. 8.8 and the characteristics of fuzzy subsets, it is clear that $< s'_1, s_2 >$ is more uncertain than $< s'_2, s_2 >$ because the triangular membership function associated with the former has a larger value range. In this case, using 2DLLs as the aggregation results is more coincident with the human thinking mode.

From the above descriptions, we can draw a conclusion that the two-dimension linguistic assessment information and its aggregation techniques are worth to be investigated.

In what follows, we first develop a method for the comparison between two two-dimension linguistic labels (2DLLs):

Definition 8.2 [165] Let $\delta_1 =< s'_{\beta_1}, s_{\alpha_1} >$ and $\delta_2 =< s'_{\beta_2}, s_{\alpha_2} >$ be two 2DLLs, then

1. If $\alpha_1 < \alpha_2$, then δ_1 is less than δ_2, denoted by $\delta_1 < \delta_2$;

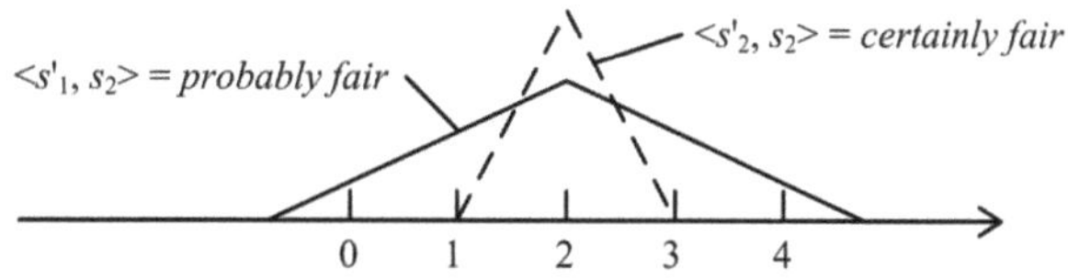

Fig. 8.8 Two-dimension linguistic labels

2. If $\alpha_1 = \alpha_2$, then

   i. If $\beta_1 = \beta_2$, then δ_1 is equal to δ_2, denoted by $\delta_1 = \delta_2$;
   ii. If $\beta_1 < \beta_2$, then δ_1 is less than δ_2, denoted by $\delta_1 < \delta_2$;
   iii. If $\beta_1 > \beta_2$, then δ_1 is greater than δ_2, denoted by $\delta_1 > \delta_2$.

Remark 8.2 In this chapter, if δ_1 is not greater than δ_2, we denote as $\delta_1 \le \delta_2$, but if δ_1 is not less than δ_2, we denote as $\delta_1 \ge \delta_2$.

We then construct a pair of functions to reflect the relationship between a 2DLL $\delta = < s'_\beta, s_\alpha >$ and its corresponding generalized triangular fuzzy number (TFN) $\tilde{t} = \left(a-b, a, a+b; \frac{1}{b}\right)$ as mentioned previously, i.e., $a = \alpha$ and $b = \sqrt{1+\frac{3L^2}{2\cdot 4^i}}$ $(i = \frac{\beta}{L'-\beta})$. Let ψ be a mapping from a 2DLL δ to a generalized TFN $\tilde{t}$, if $\tilde{t} = \psi(\delta)$ and $\delta = \psi^{-1}(\tilde{t})$, then we call ψ the mapping function between a 2DLL and its corresponding generalized TFN. Especially, in accordance with the analyses of the relations between 2DLLs and the generalized TFNs, we can construct a mapping function ψ and its inverse function as follows:

$$\tilde{t} = \psi(\delta) = \psi(< s'_\beta, s_\alpha >)$$
$$= \left(\alpha - \sqrt{1+\frac{3L^2}{2\cdot 4^i}}, \alpha, \alpha + \sqrt{1+\frac{3L^2}{2\cdot 4^i}}; 1 \Big/ \sqrt{1+\frac{3L^2}{2\cdot 4^i}}\right), \; i = \frac{\beta}{L'-\beta} \tag{8.26}$$

and

$$\delta = \psi^{-1}(\tilde{t}) = \psi^{-1}\left[\left(a-b, a, a+b; \frac{1}{b}\right)\right] = < s'_\beta, s_a > \tag{8.27}$$

where $\beta = \dfrac{L' \cdot \log_4^{3L^2/2(b^2-1)}}{1+\log_4^{3L^2/2(b^2-1)}}$.

In this special case, the larger $\alpha \in [0, L]$, the larger a of the corresponding generalized TFN, and vice versa. However, the larger $\beta \in [0, L']$, the smaller $b \in [1, +\infty)$, and vice versa. That is because if we have a function f satisfying $b = f(\beta) = \sqrt{1+\frac{3L^2}{2\cdot 4^{\beta/(L-\beta)}}}$, then we can calculate the corresponding derived function:

$$f'(\beta) = \frac{-3 \cdot \ln 4 \cdot L^2 \cdot L' \cdot 4^{\beta/(L'-\beta)}}{4 \cdot (L'-\beta)^2 \cdot \sqrt{1+\frac{3L^2}{2\cdot 4^{\beta/(L'-\beta)}}}}$$

and then $f'(\beta) < 0$, if $\beta \in [0, L']$. Therefore, f is strictly monotone decreasing in the domain of arguments. Similarly, the inverse function of f is as follows:

$$\beta = f^{-1}(b) = \frac{L' \cdot \log_4^{3L^2/2(b^2-1)}}{1 + \log_4^{3L^2/2(b^2-1)}}$$

which is also strictly monotone decreasing in the domain of arguments, $b \in [1, +\infty)$. Thus, the larger β, the smaller b in their respective feasible regions, and vice versa. In this case, the mapping relationships can be reasonable. The larger a 2DLL is, the larger its corresponding generalized TFN is. Meanwhile, the fuzzier a 2DLL is, the fuzzier its corresponding generalized TFN is.

8.4.2 MADM with 2DLWA Operator

According to the relationship function and its inverse function, we can easily transform a 2DLL to a generalized TFN and vice versa. Thus if there is a method to aggregate several generalized TFNs, we can also use it to aggregate 2DLLs. Yu et al. [165] developed two functions to aggregate the generalized TFNs:

Definition 8.3 [165] Let $\tilde{t}_i = \left(a_i - b_i, a_i, a_i + b_i; \frac{1}{b_i} \right) (i = 1, 2, \ldots, \mathrm{n})$ be a collection of generalized TFNs, and if

$$a = f_s^{(w)}(\tilde{t}_1, \tilde{t}_2, \ldots, \tilde{t}_n) = \sum_{i=1}^{n} w_i a_i \tag{8.28}$$

and

$$b = f_h^{(w)}(\tilde{t}_1, \tilde{t}_2, \ldots, \tilde{t}_n) = \sqrt{\sum_{i=1}^{n} w_i \left[6(a_i - a)^2 + b_i^2 \right]} \tag{8.29}$$

where $w = (w_1, w_2, \ldots, w_n)$ is the weight vector of $\tilde{t}_i$, and $w_i \in [0,1]$, $i = 1, 2, \ldots, n$, and $\sum_{i=1}^{n} w_i = 1$, then we call f_s a score aggregation function and f_h a hesitant aggregation function. If $\tilde{t} = \left(a - b, a, a + b; \frac{1}{b} \right)$, then we call it an overall generalized TFN of $\tilde{t}_i (i = 1, 2, \ldots, 3)$.

For convenience, let $\bar{\nabla}$ be the universe of discourse of all the continuous 2DLLs.

Definition 8.4 [165] Let $\delta_i = < s'_{\beta_i}, s_{\alpha_i} > (i = 1, 2, \ldots, n)$ be a collection of 2DLLs, and let $2DLWA : \bar{\nabla}^n \to \bar{\nabla}$, if

$$2DLWA_w(\delta_1, \delta_2, \ldots, \delta_n) = \psi^{-1}\left[(a - b, a, a + b; \frac{1}{b}) \right] \tag{8.30}$$

where $a = f_s^{(w)}(\psi(\delta_1), \psi(\delta_2), \ldots, \psi(\delta_n))$ and $b = f_h^{(w)}(\psi(\delta_1), \psi(\delta_2), \ldots, \psi(\delta_n))$, and $w = (w_1, w_2, \ldots, w_n)$ is the weight vector of $\delta_i (i = 1, 2, \ldots, n)$, $w_i > 0$, $i = 1, 2, \ldots, n$, and $\sum_{i=1}^{n} w_i = 1$, then the 2DLWA function is called a two-dimension linguistic weighted averaging (2DLWA) operator.

We can understand the 2DLWA operator more clearly from the following examples:

Example 8.6 Suppose that

$$\bar{\nabla} = \left\{ \delta = < s'_\beta, s_\alpha > | \, s_\alpha \in \{ s_i \mid i \in [0,4] \} \wedge s'_\beta \in \{ s_j \mid j \in [0,2] \} \right\} (L = 4, \ L' = 2)$$

is a 2DLL set, three 2DLLs $\delta_1 = < s'_1, s_1 >$, $\delta_2 = < s'_0, s_3 >$ and $\delta_3 = < s'_2, s_4 >$ belong to $\bar{\nabla}$, and $w = (0.3, 0.3, 0.4)$ is a weight vector of the 2DLLs $\delta_i (i = 1, 2, 3)$. By means of the mapping function ψ aforementioned, we first transform the 2DLLs to their corresponding generalized TFNs:

$$\tilde{t}_1 = \psi(\delta_1) = (-1.65, 1, 3.65; 0.38), \ \tilde{t}_2 = \psi(\delta_2) = (-2, 3, 8; 0.2),$$
$$\tilde{t}_3 = \psi(\delta_3) = (3, 4, 5; 1)$$

By using the score aggregation function and the hesitant aggregation function in Definition 8.3, we calculate the overall generalized TFN $\tilde{t} = (-1.49, 2.8, 7.09; 0.233)$. According to the inverse function ψ^{-1}, we can obtain the weighted averaging value of the above three 2DLLs:

$$\delta = 2DLWA_w(\delta_1, \delta_2, \delta_3) = \psi^{-1}(\tilde{t}) = < s'_{0.377}, s_{2.8} >$$

Then the final aggregation result of δ_1, δ_2 and δ_3 is $< s'_{0.377}, s_{2.8} >$.

Example 8.7 Considering the common linguistic labels in Example 8.5, d_1 evaluates x_1 as s_3 and x_2 as s_2, and d_2 evaluates x_1 as s_1 and x_2 as s_2. If the two decision makers are of the same importance $(\lambda = (0.5, 0.5))$, then we can calculate their overall assessment values by using the EWA operator. In this case, we have

$$z_1(\lambda) = s_{0.5 \times 3 + 0.5 \times 1} = s_2, \ z_2(\lambda) = s_{0.5 \times 2 + 0.5 \times 2} = s_2$$

thus $z_1(\lambda) = z_2(\lambda)$, i.e., we have no idea to choose the best one from x_1 and x_2. But if we transform the above common linguistic labels to the corresponding 2DLLs by introducing another linguistic label set $S' = \{ s'_0, \ s'_1, \ s'_2 \}$ mentioned in Example 8.5 (i.e., d_1 evaluates x_1 as $< s'_2, s_3 >$ and x_2 as $< s'_2, s_2 >$, and d_2 evaluates x_1 as $< s'_2, s_1 >$ and x_2 as $< s'_2, s_2 >$), then we can calculate their overall assessment values by means of the 2DLWA operator aforementioned. In this case, we have

$$z_1(\lambda) = < s_1', s_2 >, \quad z_2(\lambda) = < s_2', s_2 >$$

thus $z_1(\lambda) < z_2(\lambda)$, which is in consistence with the analysis in Example 8.5.

The 2DLWA operator has following properties [165]:

Theorem 8.1 (Idempotency) Let $\delta_i = < s'_{\beta_i}, s_{\alpha_i} > (i = 1, 2, \ldots, n)$ be a collection of 2DLLs, and $w = (w_1, w_2, \ldots, w_n)$ be the weight vector of $\delta_i (i = 1, 2, \ldots, n)$, with $w_i > 0$, $i = 1, 2, \ldots, n$, and $\sum_{j=1}^{n} w_j = 1$. If all $\delta_i (i = 1, 2, \ldots, n)$ are equal, i.e., $\delta_i = \delta$, for all i, then

$$2DLWA_w(\delta_1, \delta_2, \ldots, \delta_n) = \delta \tag{8.31}$$

Proof Let $\tilde{t}_i = \psi(\delta_i)(i = 1, 2, \ldots, n)$ and $\tilde{t} = \psi(\delta)$, then $\delta_i = \psi^{-1}(\tilde{t}_i)$ and $\delta = \psi^{-1}(\tilde{t})$. Because $\delta_i = \delta$, for all i, thus $\tilde{t}_i = \tilde{t}$, for all i. Suppose that $\tilde{t}_1 = \tilde{t}_2 = \cdots = \tilde{t}_n = \tilde{t} = \left(a - b, a, a + b; \frac{1}{b} \right)$, then

$$f_s^{(w)}(\psi(\delta_1), \psi(\delta_2), \ldots, \psi(\delta_n)) = f_s^{(w)}(\tilde{t}_1, \tilde{t}_2, \ldots, \tilde{t}_n) = \sum_{i=1}^{n} w_i a = a$$

and

$$f_h^{(w)}(\psi(\delta_1), \psi(\delta_2), \ldots, \psi(\delta_n)) = f_h^{(w)}(\tilde{t}_1, \tilde{t}_2, \ldots, \tilde{t}_n) = \sqrt{\sum_{i=1}^{n} w_i [6(a-a)^2 + b^2]} = b$$

Thus

$$2DLWA_w(\delta_1, \delta_2, \ldots, \delta_n) = \psi^{-1}\left[\left(a - b, a, a + b; \frac{1}{b} \right) \right] = \psi^{-1}(\tilde{t}) = \delta$$

Theorem 8.2 (Boundedness) Let $\overline{\nabla} = \{ \delta_i \mid \delta_i = < s'_{\beta_i}, s_{\alpha_i} >, i = 1, 2, \ldots, n \}$ be a collection of 2DLLs, and let $\delta^- = \min_i \{\delta_i\} = < s'_{\beta^-}, s_{\alpha^-} >$ and $\delta^+ = \max_i \{\delta_i\} = < s'_{\beta^+}, s_{\alpha^+} >$, i.e., δ^-, $\delta^+ \in \overline{\nabla}$ and $\delta^- \le \delta_i$, $\delta^+ \ge \delta_i$, for all i, then

$$\delta^- \le 2DLWA_w(\delta_1, \delta_2, \ldots, \delta_n) \le \delta^+ \tag{8.32}$$

Proof Let

$$\tilde{t}^- = \psi(\delta^-) = \left(a^- - b^-, a^-, a^- + b^-; \frac{1}{b^-} \right)$$

$$\tilde{t}^+ = \psi(\delta^+) = \left(a^+ - b^+, a^+, a^+ + b^+; \frac{1}{b^+} \right)$$

$$\tilde{t}_i = \psi(\delta_i) = \left(a_i - b_i, a_i, a_i + b_i; \frac{1}{b_i} \right), \ i = 1, 2, \ldots, n$$

We first prove the left part of Eq. (8.32):

If $\alpha^- = \alpha_1 = \alpha_2 \ldots = \alpha_n$ and $\beta^- \le \beta_i$, for all i, then by the property of the mapping function ψ aforementioned, we have $a^- = a_1 = a_2 \ldots = a_n$ and $b^- \ge b_i$, for all i. According to Definition 8.3, we can calculate

$$a = f_s^{(w)}(\tilde{t}_1, \tilde{t}_2, \ldots, \tilde{t}_n) = \sum_{i=1}^{n} w_i a_i = a^-$$

$$b = f_h^{(w)}(\tilde{t}_1, \tilde{t}_2, \ldots, \tilde{t}_n) = \sqrt{\sum_{i=1}^{n} w_i \left[6(a_i - a)^2 + b_i^2 \right]}$$

$$= \sqrt{\sum_{i=1}^{n} w_i b_i^2} \le \sqrt{\sum_{i=1}^{n} w_i (b^-)^2} = b^-$$

and then by Eq. (8.27), we have $\alpha = \alpha^-$ and $\beta^- \le \beta$. Thus

$$2DLWA_w(\delta_1, \delta_2, \ldots, \delta_n) = \psi^{-1}\left[\left(a - b, a, a + b; \frac{1}{b} \right) \right] = \langle s'_\beta, s_\alpha \rangle \ge \delta^-$$

(2) If $\alpha^- \le \alpha_i$, for all i and there exists $\alpha_k > \alpha^- (k \in \{1, 2, \ldots, n\})$, then by Eq. (8.26), we have $a^- \le a_i$, and thus

$$a = f_s^{(w)}(\tilde{t}_1, \tilde{t}_2, \ldots, \tilde{t}_n) = \sum_{i=1}^{n} w_i a_i > \sum_{i=1}^{n} w_i a^- = a^-$$

Also by Eq. (8.27), we have $\alpha > \alpha^-$, and thus

$$2DLWA_w(\delta_1, \delta_2, \ldots, \delta_n) = \psi^{-1}\left[\left(a - b, a, a + b; \frac{1}{b} \right) \right] = \langle s'_\beta, s_\alpha \rangle > \delta^-$$

From the analysis above, we know that $2DLWA_w(\delta_1, \delta_2, \ldots, \delta_n) \ge \delta^-$ always holds. Similarly, the right part of Eq. (8.32) can be proven. As a result, we can prove the boundedness property:

$$\delta^- \le 2DLWA_w(\delta_1, \delta_2, \ldots, \delta_n) \le \delta^+$$

Theorem8.3(Monotonicity) Let $\delta_i =< s'_{\beta_i}, s_{\alpha_i} > (i=1,2,\ldots,n)$ and $\delta_i^* =< s'_{\beta_i^*}, s_{\alpha_i^*} >$ $(i=1,2,\ldots,n)$ be two collections of 2DLLs, if $\delta_i \le \delta_i^*$, for all i, then

$$2DLWA_w(\delta_1,\delta_2,\ldots,\delta_n) \le 2DLWA_w(\delta_1^*,\delta_2^*,\ldots,\delta_n^*) \tag{8.33}$$

Proof Let

$$\tilde{t}_i = \psi(\delta_i) = \left(a_i - b_i, a_i, a_i + b_i; \frac{1}{b_i} \right), \ i=1,2,\ldots,n$$

$$\tilde{t}_i^* = \psi(\sigma_i^*) = \left(a_i^* - b_i^*, a_i^*, a_i^* + b_i^*; \frac{1}{b_i^*} \right), \ i=1,2,\ldots,n$$

(1) If $\alpha_i = \alpha_i^*$ and $\beta_i \le \beta_i^*$, for all i, then by Eq. (8.26), we have $a_i = a_i^*$ and $b_i \ge b_i^*$. In this case, we can calculate

$$a = f_s^{(w)}(\tilde{t}_1,\tilde{t}_2,\ldots,\tilde{t}_n) = \sum_{i=1}^n w_i a_i = \sum_{i=1}^n w_i a_i^* = f_s^{(w)}(\tilde{t}_1^*,\tilde{t}_2^*,\ldots,\tilde{t}_n^*) = a^*$$

$$b = f_h^{(w)}(\tilde{t}_1,\tilde{t}_2,\ldots,\tilde{t}_n) = \sqrt{\sum_{i=1}^n w_i \left[6(a_i - a)^2 + b_i^2 \right]}$$
$$\ge \sqrt{\sum_{i=1}^n w_i [6(a_i^* - a^*)^2 + b_i^{*2}]} = f_h^{(w)}(\tilde{t}_1^*,\tilde{t}_2^*,\ldots,\tilde{t}_n^*) = b^*$$

and by Eq. (8.27), we have $\alpha = \alpha^*$ and $\beta \le \beta^*$. Thus

$$2DLWA_w(\delta_1,\delta_2,\ldots,\delta_n) = \psi^{-1}\left[\left(a-b, a, a+b; \frac{1}{b} \right)\right] =< s'_\beta, s_\alpha >$$

$$\le \left\langle s'_{\beta^*}, s_{\alpha^*} \right\rangle = 2DLWA_w(\delta_1^*,\delta_2^*,\ldots,\delta_n^*) = \psi^{-1}\left[\left(a^* - b^*, a^*, a^* + b^*; \frac{1}{b^*} \right)\right] \tag{8.34}$$

(2) If $\alpha_i \le \alpha_i^*$, for all i and there exists $\alpha_k < \alpha_k^*$, then we have

$$a = f_s^{(w)}(\tilde{t}_1,\tilde{t}_2,\ldots,\tilde{t}_n) = \sum_{i=1}^n w_i a_i < \sum_{i=1}^n w_i a_i^* = f_s^{(w)}(\tilde{t}_1^*,\tilde{t}_2^*,\ldots,\tilde{t}_n^*) = a^*$$

Let $2DLWA_w(\delta_1,\delta_2,\ldots,\delta_n)=<s'_\beta,s_\alpha>$ and $2DLWA_w(\delta_1^*,\delta_2^*,\ldots,\delta_n^*)=<s'_{\beta^*},s_{\alpha^*}>$, then $\alpha_i<\alpha_i^*$. Hence

$$2DLWA_w(\delta_1,\delta_2,\ldots,\delta_n)<2DLWA_w(\delta_1^*,\delta_2^*,\ldots,\delta_n^*) \tag{8.35}$$

From the analysis above, we can see that if $\delta_i \le \delta_i^*$, for all i, then Eq. (8.33) always holds.

The 2DLWA operator can be applied to solve the MADM problems with linguistic information represented by linguistic labels or two-dimension linguistic labels. Yu et al. [165] developed a method for MADM under linguistic assessments:

Step 1 For a MADM problem, let X and U be the sets of alternatives and attributes respectively, and assume that there are two linguistic label sets: $S=\{s_\alpha \mid \alpha=0,1,\ldots,L\}$ and $S'=\{s'_\beta \mid \beta=0,1,\ldots,L'\}$. The evaluation information given by the decision maker(s) for the alternatives over the criteria is expressed in the form of either the common linguistic labels of the set of S, or the 2DLLs, in which the principal assessment information is represented by linguistic labels in S and the self-assessment information is represented by linguistic labels in S'.

Step 2 Transform all the common linguistic labels into 2DLLs by denoting their missing self-assessment information as $s'_{L'}$, i.e., any common linguistic label s_α can be transformed into a 2DLL $<s'_{L'},s_\alpha>$. In this case, we can contain all evaluation information into a matrix of 2DLLs, denoted as $\Upsilon=(\delta_{ij})_{m\times n}$, in which any element δ_{ij} is a 2DLL, indicating an evaluation value over the alternative $x_i(i=1,2,\ldots,n)$ with respect to the criteria $u_j(j=1,2,\ldots,m)$.

Step 3 Use the mapping function (8.26) to transform Υ into a matrix of generalized TFNs, $T=(\tilde{t}_{ij})_{n\times m}$.

Step 4 According to the given weights of the attributes, $w=(w_1,w_2,\ldots,w_m)$, and Definition 8.3, we calculate

$$a_i=f_s^{(w)}(\tilde{t}_{i1},\tilde{t}_{i2},\ldots,\tilde{t}_{im})=\sum_{j=1}^{m} w_j a_{ij},\ i=1,2,\ldots,n$$

and

$$b_i=f_h^{(w)}(\tilde{t}_{i1},\tilde{t}_{i2},\ldots,\tilde{t}_{im})=\sqrt{\sum_{j=1}^{m} w_j\left[6(a_{ij}-a_i)^2+b_{ij}^2\right]},\ i=1,2,\ldots,n$$

Step 5 Calculate the overall evaluation values corresponding to the alternatives $x_i(i=1,2,\ldots,n)$:

$$\delta_i=2DLWA_w(\delta_{i1},\delta_{i2},\ldots,\delta_{in})=\psi^{-1}\left[\left(a_i-b_i,a_i,a_i+b_i;\frac{1}{b_i}\right)\right],\ i=1,2,\ldots,m$$

Step 6 Rank all the alternatives according to the overall evaluation values $\delta_i (i=1,2,\ldots,n)$, and then get the most desirable one(s).

8.4.3 MADM with 2DLOWA Operator

Motivated by the idea of ordered aggregation [157], Yu et al. [165] defined a two-dimension linguistic ordered weighted averaging (2DLOWA) operator:

Definition 8.5 [165] A 2DLOWA operator of dimension n is a mapping $2DLOWA: \bar{\nabla}^n \to \bar{\nabla}$ that has an associated vector $\omega = (\omega_1, \omega_2, \ldots, \omega_n)$ with $\omega_i \in [0, 1]$, $i = 1,2,\ldots,n$, and $\sum_{i=1}^{n} \omega_i = 1$. Furthermore

$$2DLOWA_\omega(\delta_1, \delta_2, \ldots, \delta_n) = \psi^{-1}\left[\left(a-b, a, a+b; \frac{1}{b}\right)\right] \tag{8.36}$$

where

$$a = f_s^{(\omega)}(\psi(\delta_{\sigma(1)}), \psi(\delta_{\sigma(2)}), \ldots, \psi(\delta_{\sigma(n)}))$$

$$b = f_h^{(\omega)}(\psi(\delta_{\sigma(1)}), \psi(\delta_{\sigma(2)}), \ldots, \psi(\delta_{\sigma(n)}))$$

and $(\sigma(1), \sigma(2), \ldots, \sigma(n))$ is a permutation of $(1,2,\ldots,n)$ such that $\delta_{\sigma(i-1)} \geq \delta_{\sigma(i)}$, for $i = 2,3,\ldots,n$.

Similar to the 2DLWA operator, the 2DLOWA operator has following properties [165]:

Theorem 8.4 (Idempotency) Let $\delta_i =< s'_{\beta_i}, s_{\alpha_i} > (i=1,2,\ldots,n)$ be a collection of 2DLLs, and $\omega = (\omega_1, \omega_2, \ldots, \omega_n)$ be the weighting vector associated with the 2DLOWA operator, with $\omega_i \in [0, 1]$, $i=1,2,\ldots,n$, and $\sum_{i=1}^{n} \omega_i = 1$. If all $\delta_i (i=1,2,\ldots,n)$ are equal, i.e., $\delta_i = \delta$, for all i, then

$$2DLOWA_w(\delta_1, \delta_2, \ldots, \delta_n) = \delta \tag{8.37}$$

Theorem 8.5 (Boundedness) Let $\bar{D} = \{\delta_i \mid \delta_i =< s'_{\beta_i}, s_{\alpha_i} >, i=1,2,\ldots,n\}$ be a collection of 2DLLs, and let $\delta^- = \min_i\{\delta_i\} =< s'_{\beta^-}, s_{\alpha^-} >$ and $\delta^+ = \max_i\{\delta_i\} =< s'_{\beta^+}, s_{\alpha^+} >$, i.e., δ^-, $\delta^+ \in \bar{\nabla}$ and $\delta^- \leq \delta_i$, $\delta^+ \geq \delta_i$, for all i, then

$$\delta^- \leq 2DLOWA_\omega(\delta_1, \delta_2, \ldots, \delta_n) \leq \delta^+ \tag{8.38}$$

Theorem 8.6 (Monotonicity) Let $\delta_i =< s'_{\beta_i}, s_{\alpha_i} > (i = 1,2,\ldots,n)$ and $\delta_i^* = < s'_{\beta_i^*}, s_{\alpha_i^*} > (i = 1,2,\ldots,n)$ be two collections of 2DLLs, if $\delta_i \le \delta_i^*$, for all i, then

$$2DLOWA_{\omega}(\delta_1, \delta_2, \ldots, \delta_n) \le 2DLOWA_{\omega}(\delta_1^*, \delta_2^*, \ldots, \delta_n^*) \tag{8.39}$$

Theorem 8.7 (Commutativity) Let $\delta_i =< s'_{\beta_i}, s_{\alpha_i} > (i = 1,2,\ldots,n)$ and $\hat{\delta}_i = < s'_{\hat{\beta}_i}, s_{\hat{\alpha}_i} > (i = 1,2,\ldots,n)$ be two collections of 2DLLs, then

$$2DLOWA_{w}(\delta_1, \delta_2, \ldots, \delta_n) = 2DLOWA_{w}(\hat{\delta}_1, \hat{\delta}_2, \ldots, \hat{\delta}_n) \tag{8.40}$$

where $(\hat{\delta}_1, \hat{\delta}_2, \ldots, \hat{\delta}_n)$ is any permutation of $(\delta_1, \delta_2, \ldots, \delta_n)$.

Proof Let

$$2DLOWA_{\omega}(\delta_1, \delta_2, \ldots, \delta_n) = \psi^{-1}\left[\left(a-b, a, a+b; \frac{1}{b}\right)\right]$$

$$2DLOWA_{\omega}(\hat{\delta}_1, \hat{\delta}_2, \ldots, \hat{\delta}_n) = \psi^{-1}\left[\left(\hat{a}-\hat{b}, \hat{a}, \hat{a}+\hat{b}; \frac{1}{\hat{b}}\right)\right]$$

where

$$a = f_s^{(\omega)}(\psi(\delta_{\sigma(1)}), \psi(\delta_{\sigma(2)}), \ldots, \psi(\delta_{\sigma(n)}))$$
$$b = f_h^{(\omega)}(\psi(\delta_{\sigma(1)}), \psi(\delta_{\sigma(2)}), \ldots, \psi(\delta_{\sigma(n)}))$$
$$\hat{a} = f_s^{(\omega)}(\psi(\hat{\delta}_{\sigma(1)}), \psi(\hat{\delta}_{\sigma(2)}), \ldots, \psi(\hat{\delta}_{\sigma(n)}))$$
$$\hat{b} = f_h^{(\omega)}(\psi(\hat{\delta}_{\sigma(1)}), \psi(\hat{\delta}_{\sigma(2)}), \ldots, \psi(\hat{\delta}_{\sigma(n)}))$$

Since $(\hat{\delta}_1, \hat{\delta}_2, \ldots, \hat{\delta}_n)$ is any permutation of $(\delta_1, \delta_2, \ldots, \delta_n)$, then we have $\hat{\delta}_{\sigma(i)} = \delta_{\sigma(i)}$, $i = 1,2,\ldots,n$. Thus, Eq. (8.40) always holds.

Theorem 8.8 Let $\delta_i =< s'_{\beta_i}, s_{\alpha_i} > (i = 1,2,\ldots,n)$ be a collection of 2DLLs, and $\omega = (\omega_1, \omega_2, \ldots, \omega_n)$ be the weighting vector associated with the 2DLOWA operator, with $\omega_i \in [0,1]$, $i = 1,2,\ldots,n$, and $\sum_{i=1}^{n} \omega_i = 1$, then

1. If $\omega_1 \to 1$, then $2DLOWA_{\omega}(\delta_1, \delta_2, \ldots, \delta_n) \to \max_i \{\delta_i\}$;
2. If $\omega_n \to 1$, then $2DLOWA_{\omega}(\delta_1, \delta_2, \ldots, \delta_n) \to \min_i \{\delta_i\}$;
3. If $\omega_i \to 1$, then $2DLOWA_{\omega}(\delta_1, \delta_2, \ldots, \delta_n) \to \delta_{\sigma(i)}^i$, where $\delta_{\sigma(i)}$ is the ith largest of $\delta_i (i = 1,2,\ldots,n)$.

From Definitions 8.4 and 8.5, we know that the 2DLWA operator weights the 2DLLs, while the 2DLOWA operator weights the ordered positions of the 2DLLs instead of weighting the 2DLLs. Similar to the method in Sect. 8.4.2, Yu et al. [165] gave the application of the 2DLOWA operator to MADM:

Step1 See the method of Sect. 8.4.2.

Step 2 See the method of Sect. 8.4.2.

Step 3 Reorder all the elements in each line of Υ in descending order according to the ranking method of 2DLLs, and then get a new matrix $\hat{\Upsilon} = (\delta_{i,\sigma(j)})_{n\times m}$, where $\delta_{i,\sigma(j)} \geq \delta_{i,\sigma(j+1)}$ $(j = 1,2,\ldots,n-1)$.

Step 4 Use the mapping function (8.26) to transform $\hat{\Upsilon}$ into a matrix of generalized TFNs $\hat{T} = (\tilde{t}_{i,\sigma(j)})_{n\times m}$.

Step 5 According to Definition 8.3 and the weights of the 2DLOWA operator $\omega = (\omega_1, \omega_2, \ldots, \omega_m)$ (given or calculated by some existed methods [126, 157], we calculate

$$a_i = f_s^{(w)}(\tilde{t}_{i,\sigma(1)}, \tilde{t}_{i,\sigma(2)}, \ldots, \tilde{t}_{i,\sigma(m)}) = \sum_{j=1}^{m} w_j a_{i,\sigma(j)},\ i = 1,2,\ldots,n$$

and

$$b_i = f_h^{(w)}\left(\tilde{t}_{i,\sigma(1)}, \tilde{t}_{i,\sigma(2)}, \ldots, \tilde{t}_{i,\sigma(m)}\right) = \sqrt{\sum_{j=1}^{m} w_j \left[6(a_{i,\sigma(j)} - a_i)^2 + b_{i,\sigma(j)}^2\right]},\ i = 1,2,\ldots,n$$

Step 6 Calculate the overall evaluation values corresponding to the alternatives $x_i (i = 1,2,\ldots,n)$:

$$\delta_i = 2DLOWA_w(\delta_{i1}, \delta_{i2}, \ldots, \delta_{im}) = \psi^{-1}\left[\left(a_i - b_i, a_i, a_i + b_i; \frac{1}{b_i}\right)\right],\ i = 1,2,\ldots,n$$

Step 7 Rank all the alternatives $x_i (i = 1,2,\ldots,n)$ according to the overall evaluation values $\delta_j (i = 1,2,\ldots,n)$, and then get the most desirable one(s).

8.4.4 Practical Example

In this section, a MADM problem of evaluating the outstanding dissertation(s) is used to illustrate the application of the developed methods.

A decision maker wants to pick out the outstanding dissertation(s) from four postgraduates' dissertations $x_i (i = 1,2,3,4)$ by evaluating five aspects of each dissertation: innovativeness (u_1); contribution (u_2); accurate outcomes (u_3); proper

Table 8.13 Linguistic decision matrix Υ

	u_1	u_2	u_3	u_4	u_5
x_1	$<s_2', s_1>$	$<s_1', s_4>$	$<s_0', s_3>$	$<s_2', s_2>$	$<s_1', s_1>$
x_2	$<s_1', s_4>$	$<s_2', s_4>$	$<s_2', s_3>$	$<s_0', s_0>$	$<s_1', s_3>$
x_3	$<s_0', s_3>$	$<s_2', s_3>$	$<s_1', s_1>$	$<s_0', s_3>$	$<s_2', s_2>$
x_4	$<s_2', s_3>$	$<s_1', s_2>$	$<s_0', s_3>$	$<s_1', s_4>$	$<s_2', s_2>$

structure (u_4); and writing (u_5). The decision maker assesses the four dissertations by using the linguistic label set:

$$S = \{s_0 = \textit{extremely poor},\ s_1 = \textit{poor},\ s_2 = \textit{moderate},\ s_3 = \textit{good},\ s_4 = \textit{excellent}\}$$

Meanwhile, considering that the different contents of the dissertations and the knowledge structures of the decision maker, he/she needs to evaluate the mastery degree to each aspect of dissertations by using the following linguistic label set:

$$S' = \{s_0' = \textit{unfamiliar},\ s_1' = \textit{moderate},\ s_2' = \textit{versed}\}$$

Thus, the 2DLLs are more proper to represent the assessment information, and all the evaluation values are contained in a linguistic decision matrix $\Upsilon = (\delta_{ij})_{4\times 5}$ as listed in Table 8.13.

In what follows, we first use the method of Sect. 8.4.2 to obtain the most outstanding dissertation(s):

Step 1 By means of the mapping function (8.26), we transform the decision matrix above into a matrix of generalized TFNs, $T = (\tilde{t}_{ij})_{4\times 5}$ (see Table 8.14).

Step 2 Calculate the overall generalized TFNs $\tilde{t}_i = \left(a_i - b_i, a_i, a_i + b_i; \frac{1}{b_i}\right)$ of all the $(i = 1,2,3,4)$ generalized TFNs in each line of T by means of the score aggregation

Table 8.14 Decision matrix T

	u_1	u_2	u_3	u_4	u_5
x_1	(0, 1, 2; 1)	(1.35, 4, 6.65; 0.378)	(−2, 3, 8; 0.2)	(1, 2, 3; 1)	(−1.65, 1, 3.65; 0.378)
x_2	(1.35, 4, 6.65; 0.378)	(3, 4, 5; 1)	(2, 3, 4; 1)	(−5, 0, 5; 0.2)	(0.354, 3, 5.65; 0.378)
x_3	(−2, 3, 8; 0.2)	(2, 3, 4; 1)	(−1.65, 1, 3.65; 0.378)	(−2, 3, 8; 0.2)	(1, 2, 3; 1)
x_4	(2, 3, 4; 1)	(−0.646, 2, 4.65; 0.378)	(−2, 3, 8; 0.2)	(1.35, 4, 6.65; 0.378)	(1, 2, 3; 1)

function and the hesitant aggregation function in Definition 8.3 by simply considering the five aspects are equally important (i.e., the weight vector of the five aspects are $w = (0.2, 0.2, 0.2, 0.2, 0.2)$:

$$\tilde{t}_1 = \left(a_1 - b_1, a_1, a_1 + b_1; \frac{1}{b_1} \right) = (-1.84, 2.2, 6.24; 0.247)$$

$$\tilde{t}_2 = \left(a_2 - b_2, a_2, a_2 + b_2; \frac{1}{b_2} \right) = (-1.8, 2.8, 7.4; 0.217)$$

$$\tilde{t}_3 = \left(a_3 - b_3, a_3, a_3 + b_3; \frac{1}{b_3} \right) = (-1.55, 2.4, 6.35; 0.253)$$

$$\tilde{t}_4 = \left(a_4 - b_4, a_4, a_4 + b_4; \frac{1}{b_4} \right) = (-0.6, 2.8, 6.2; 0.294)$$

Step 3 Calculate the overall evaluation values corresponding to the alternatives $x_i (i = 1, 2, 3, 4)$:

$$\delta_1 =< s'_{0.487}, s_{2.2} >, \ \delta_2 =< s'_{0.223}, s_{2.8} >, \ \delta_3 =< s'_{0.526}, s_{2.4} >, \ \delta_4 =< s'_{0.744}, s_{2.8} >$$

Step 4 Rank the overall evaluation values in accordance with Definition 8.2:

$$\delta_4 > \delta_2 > \delta_3 > \delta_1$$

from which we can know that the fourth postgraduates' dissertation is the best one.

However, if the weights of decision makers are not given, we cannot use the method of Sect. 8.4.2 to solve the problem of selecting the outstanding dissertation(s) any longer. In this case, we can use the method of Sect. 8.4.3 to solve the problem:

Step 1 We reorder all the elements in each line of Y in descending order according to the ranking method of 2DLLs in Definition 8.2, and then we can get a new matrix $\hat{Y} = (\delta_{i,\sigma(j)})_{4\times5}$ (see Table 8.15).

Step 2 By means of the mapping function (8.26), we transform the decision matrix above into a matrix of generalized TFNs, $\hat{T} = (\tilde{t}_{ij})_{4\times5}$ (see Table 8.16).

Table 8.15 Ordered decision matrix $\hat{T}$

x_1	$< s'_1, s_4 >$	$< s'_0, s_3 >$	$< s'_2, s_2 >$	$< s'_2, s_1 >$	$< s'_1, s_1 >$
x_2	$< s'_2, s_4 >$	$< s'_1, s_4 >$	$< s'_2, s_3 >$	$< s'_1, s_3 >$	$< s'_0, s_0 >$
x_3	$< s'_2, s_3 >$	$< s'_0, s_3 >$	$< s'_0, s_3 >$	$< s'_2, s_2 >$	$< s'_1, s_1 >$
x_4	$< s'_1, s_4 >$	$< s'_2, s_3 >$	$< s'_0, s_3 >$	$< s'_2, s_2 >$	$< s'_1, s_2 >$

Table 8.16 Decision matrix $\hat{T}$

x_1	(1.35, 4, 6.65; 0.378)	(−2, 3, 8; 0.2)	(1, 2, 3; 1)	(0, 1, 2; 1)	(−1.65, 1, 3.65; 0.378)
x_2	(3, 4, 5; 1)	(1.35, 4, 6.65; 0.378)	(2, 3, 4; 1)	(0.354, 3, 5.65; 0.378)	(−5, 0, 5; 0.2)
x_3	(2, 3, 4; 1)	(−2, 3, 8; 0.2)	(−2, 3, 8; 0.2)	(1, 2, 3; 1)	(−1.65, 1, 3.65; 0.378)
x_4	(1.35, 4, 6.65; 0.378)	(2, 3, 4; 1)	(−2, 3, 8; 0.2)	(1, 2, 3; 1)	(−0.646, 2, 4.65; 0.378)

Step 3 Determine the weights of the 2DLOWA operator. As pointed out by Xu [126] that in real world, a collection of n aggregated arguments $a_1, a_2, \ldots, a_n$ usually takes the form of a collection of n preference values provided by n different individuals. Some individuals may assign unduly high or unduly low preference values to their preferred or repugnant objects. In such a case, we shall assign very low weights to these "false" or "biased" opinions, that is to say, the closer a preference value (argument) is to the mid one(s), the more the weight; Conversely, the further a preference value is apart from the mid one(s), the less the weight, we can determine the weights of the 2DLOWA operator as $\omega = (0.1, 0.2, 0.4, 0.2, 0.1)$ according to Xu's [126] idea.

Step 4 Calculate the overall generalized TFNs $\tilde{t}_i = \left(a_i - b_i, a_i, a_i + b_i; \frac{1}{b_i}\right)$ $(i = 1,2,3,4)$ of all the generalized TFNs in each line of $\hat{T}$ by using the score aggregation function and the hesitant aggregation function in Definition 8.3:

$$\tilde{t}_1 = \left(a_1 - b_1, a_1, a_1 + b_1; \frac{1}{b_1}\right) = (-1.41, 2.1, 5.61; 0.285)$$

$$\tilde{t}_2 = \left(a_2 - b_2, a_2, a_2 + b_2; \frac{1}{b_2}\right) = (-0.61, 3, 6.61; 0.277)$$

$$\tilde{t}_3 = \left(a_3 - b_3, a_3, a_3 + b_3; \frac{1}{b_3}\right) = (-1.71, 2.6, 6.92; 0.232)$$

$$\tilde{t}_4 = \left(a_4 - b_4, a_4, a_4 + b_4; \frac{1}{b_4}\right) = (-0.94, 2.8, 6.54; 0.268)$$

Step 5 Calculate the overall evaluation values corresponding to the alternatives $x_i (i = 1,2,3,4)$:

$$\delta_1 = < s'_{0.702}, s_{2.1} >,\ \delta_2 = < s'_{0.667}, s_3 >,\ \delta_3 = < s'_{0.363}, s_{2.6} >,\ \delta_4 = < s'_{0.615}, s_{2.8} >$$

Step 6 Rank the overall evaluation values in accordance with Definition 8.2:

$$\delta_2 > \delta_4 > \delta_3 > \delta_1$$

from which we can know that the second postgraduates' dissertation is the best one.

In this example, we cope with the selection of the outstanding dissertation(s) in two cases: the weights of the experts are given or not. When the weights of the experts are given, we obtain the best dissertation x_4 by means of the method of Sect. 8.4.2 aforementioned. However, if the weights of the experts are unknown, we cannot resort to this method any longer. In order to solve the problem, we can first calculate the weights of the ordered positions of the parameters by assuming that the further a parameter is apart from the mid one(s) the less the weight according to Xu's [126] idea. Then we determine the outstanding dissertation x_2 rather than x_4 by using the method of Sect. 8.4.3. The reason of the two results' difference is whether or not the initial conditions are sufficient. In our opinion, if the weights and evaluation information are given and complete, we can obtain a reasonable and reliable result; Otherwise, the result, which has some deviation from accurate one, is just for reference but meaningful to a certain extent.

Chapter 9
MADM Method Based on Pure Linguistic Information

In this chapter, we introduce the concepts of linguistic weighted max (LWM) operator and the hybrid linguistic weighted averaging (HLWA) operator. For the MADM problems where the attribute weights and the attribute values take the form of linguistic labels, we introduce the MADM method based on the LWM operator and the MAGDM method based on the LWM and HLWA operators, and then apply them to solve the practical problems such as the partner selection of a virtual enterprise and the quality evaluation of teachers.

9.1 MADM Method Based on LWM Operator

9.1.1 LWM Operator

Definition 9.1 [127] Let $(a_1, a_2, \dots, a_n)$ be a collection of linguistic arguments, if

$$LWM_w(a_1, a_2, \dots, a_n) = \max_i \min\{w_i, a_i\}$$

where $w = (w_1, w_2, \dots, w_n)$ is the weight vector of the linguistic arguments $a_i (i = 1, 2, \dots, n)$, and $a_i, w_i \in S$, $i = 1, 2, \dots, n$, then the function LWM is the linguistic weighted max (LWM) operator, which is the extension of the usual weighted max (WM) operator [24].

Example 9.1 Suppose that $w = (s_{-2}, s_3, s_4, s_1)$, then

$$\begin{aligned} LWM_w(s_{-3}, s_4, s_2, s_0) &= \max\{\min\{s_{-2}, s_{-3}\}, \min\{s_3, s_4\}, \min\{s_4, s_2\}, \min\{s_1, s_0\}\} \\ &= s_3 \end{aligned}$$

Theorem 9.1 The LWM operator is monotonically increasing on the linguistic arguments $a_i (i = 1, 2, \dots, n)$.

Z.S. Xu, *Uncertain Multi-Attribute Decision Making*,
DOI 10.1007/978-3-662-45640-8_9

Proof Suppose that $a_i < a_i^{'}$, $a_j = a_j^{'}\ (j \neq i)$, then

$$\min\{w_i, a_i\} \le \min\left\{w_i, a_i^{'}\right\}, \min\{w_j, a_j\} \le \min\left\{w_j, a_j^{'}\right\}, j \neq i$$

Thus, for any j, we have

$$\max_j \min\{w_j, a_j\} \le \max_j \min\left\{w_j, a_j^{'}\right\}$$

i.e.,

$$LWM_W(a_1, a_2, \ldots, a_n\} \le LWM_w\left(a_1^{'}, a_2^{'}, \ldots, a_n^{'}\right)$$

which completes the proof.

Theorem 9.2 [127] Let $(a_1, a_2, \ldots, a_n)$ be a collection of linguistic arguments, whose weight vector is $w = (w_1, w_2, \ldots, w_n)$. If for any i, we have $w_i \geq a_i$, then

$$LWM_w(a_1, a_2, \ldots, a_n\} = \max_i\{a_i\}$$

Proof Since $w_i \geq a_i$, for any i, then $\min\{w_i, a_i\} = a_i$, thus,

$$LWM_w(a_1, a_2, \ldots, a_n\} = \max_i \min\{w_i, a_i\} = \max_i\{a_i\}$$

which completes the proof.

It follows from Theorem 9.2 that the linguistic max operator is a special case of the LWM operator.

Theorem 9.3 [127] Let $(a_1, a_2, \ldots, a_n)$ be a collection of linguistic arguments, whose weight vector is $w = (w_1, w_2, \ldots, w_n)$. Then

$$\begin{aligned} s_{-L} &\le \min\left\{\min_i\{w_i\}, \min_i\{a_i\}\right\} \\ &\le LWM_W(a_1, a_2, \ldots, a_n) \\ &\le \max\left\{\max_i\{w_i\}, \max_i\{a_i\}\right\} \le s_L \end{aligned}$$

Especially, if there exists i, such that $\min\{w_i, a_i\} = s_L$, then LWM_W $\{a_1, a_2, \ldots, a_n\} = s_L$. If for any i, we have $\min\{w_i, a_i\} = s_{-L}$, then $LWM_w(a_1, a_2, \ldots, a_n) = s_L$.

Proof

$$LWM_W(a_1,a_2,\ldots,a_n)=\max_i \min\{w_i,a_i\}\le \max_i \max\{w_i,a_i\}$$
$$=\max_i\left\{\max\{w_i\},\ \min_i\{a_i\}\right\}\le \max_i\{s_L,s_L\}=s_L$$

$$LWM_W(a_1,a_2,\ldots,a_n)=\max_i \min\{w_i,a_i\}\ge \min_i \min\{w_i,a_i\}$$
$$=\min_i\left\{\min\{w_i\},\min_i\{a_i\}\right\}\ge \max_i\{s_{-L},s_{-L}\}=s_{-L}$$

Thus,

$$s_{-L}\le \min\left\{\min_i\{w_i\},\min_i\{a_i\}\right\}\le LWA_w(a_1,a_2,\ldots,a_n)$$
$$\le \max\left\{\max_i\{w_i\},\max_i\{a_i\}\right\}\le s_L$$

Especially, if there exists i, such that $\min\{w_i,a_i\}=s_L$, then

$$LWM_w(a_1,a_2,\ldots,a_n)=\max_i \min\{w_i,a_i\}=s_L$$

If for any i, we have $\min\{w_i,a_i\}=s_{-L}$, then

$$LWM_w(a_1,a_2,\ldots,a_n)=\max_i \min\{w_i,a_i\}=s_{-L}$$

which completes the proof.

9.1.2 Decision Making Method

In the following, we introduce a MADM method based on the LWM operator, whose steps are as follows:

Step 1 For a MADM problem, let X and U be the set of alternatives and the set of attributes. The decision maker expresses his/her preferences with the linguistic evaluation value r_{ij} over the alternative $x_i \in X$ with respect to the attribute $u_j \in U$, and constructs the evaluation matrix $R=(r_{ij})_{n\times m}$, and $r_{ij}\in S$. The weight vector $w=(w_1,w_2,\ldots,w_m)$, $w_j\in S$, $j=1,2,\ldots,m$.

Step 2 Utilize the LWM operator to aggregate the linguistic evaluation information of the i th line in the matrix $R=(r_{ij})_{n\times m}$, and get the overall attribute evaluation value $z_i(w)$ of the alternative x_i:

$$z_i(w) = \max_i \min\left\{w_j, r_{ij}\right\}, \quad i = 1, 2, \ldots, n$$

Step 3 Rank and select the alternatives $x_i (i = 1, 2, \ldots, n)$ according to $z_i(w)$ $(i = 1, 2, \ldots, n)$.

9.2 Practical Example

Example 9.2 Let us consider a problem concerning the selection of the potential partners of a company. Supply chain management focuses on strategic relationships between companies involved in a supply chain. By effective coordination, companies benefit from lower cost, lower inventory levels, information sharing and thus stronger competitive edge. Many factors may impact the coordination of companies. Among them, the following is the list of four critical factors [9]: (1) u_1: response time and supply capacity; (2) u_2: quality and technical skills; (3) u_3: price and cost; (4) u_4: service level; (5) u_5: the ability of innovation agility; (6) u_6: management level and culture; (7) u_7: logistics and information flow; and (8) u_8: environments. Now there are four potential partners $x_i (i = 1, 2, 3, 4)$. In order to select the best one from them, a company invites a decision maker to assess them with respect to the factors $u_j (j = 1, 2, \ldots, 8)$ (whose weight vector is $w = (s_{-2}, s_0, s_2, s_3, s_4, s_{-1}, s_2, s_4)$), and constructs the evaluation matrix $R = (r_{ij})_{8\times 8}$ (see Table 9.1).

We utilize the LWM operator to aggregate the linguistic evaluation information of the i th line in the matrix R, and get the overall attribute evaluation value $z_i(w)$ of the alternative x_i:

$$\begin{aligned} z_1(w) &= \max_j \min\{w_j, r_{1j}\} \\ &= \max\{\min\{s_{-2}, s_1\}, \min\{s_0, s_2\}, \min\{s_2, s_0\}, \min\{s_3, s_4\}\} \\ &\quad \min\{s_4, s_2\}, \min\{s_{-1}, s_3\}, \min\{s_2, s_{-2}\}, \min\{s_4, s_0\}\} \\ &= \max\{s_{-2}, s_0, s_0, s_3, s_2, s_{-1}, s_{-2}, s_0\} \\ &= s_3 \end{aligned}$$

$$\begin{aligned} z_2(w) &= \max_j \min\{w_j, r_{2j}\} \\ &= \max\{\min\{s_{-2}, s_0\}, \min\{s_0, s_2\}, \min\{s_2, s_3\}, \min\{s_3, s_2\}\} \\ &\quad \min\{s_4, s_{-1}\}, \min\{s_{-1}, s_{-2}\}, \min\{s_2, s_4\}, \min\{s_4, s_1\}\} \\ &= \max\{s_{-2}, s_0, s_2, s_2, s_{-1}, s_{-2}, s_2, s_1\} \\ &= s_2 \end{aligned}$$

Table 9.1 Decision matrix R

	u_1	u_2	u_3	u_4	u_5	u_6	u_7	u_8
x_1	s_1	s_2	s_0	s_4	s_2	s_3	s_{-2}	s_0
x_2	s_0	s_2	s_4	s_2	s_{-1}	s_{-2}	s_4	s_1
x_3	s_2	s_1	s_2	s_4	s_4	s_{-1}	s_2	s_5
x_4	s_2	s_4	s_2	s_{-1}	s_1	s_4	s_4	s_2

$$
\begin{aligned}
z_3(w) &= \max_j \min\{w_j, r_{3j}\} \\
&= \max\{\min\{s_{-2}, s_2\}, \min\{s_0, s_1\}, \min\{s_2, s_2\}, \min\{s_3, s_4\}\} \\
&\quad \min\{s_4, s_3\}, \min\{s_{-1}, s_{-1}\}, \min\{s_2, s_2\}, \min\{s_4, s_5\}\} \\
&= \max\{s_{-2}, s_0, s_2, s_3, s_3, s_{-1}, s_2, s_4\} \\
&= s_4
\end{aligned}
$$

$$
\begin{aligned}
z_4(w) &= \max_j \min\{w_j, r_{4j}\} \\
&= \max\{\min\{s_{-2}, s_2\}, \min\{s_0, s_4\}, \min\{s_2, s_1\}, \min\{s_3, s_{-1}\}\} \\
&\quad \min\{s_4, s_1\}, \min\{s_{-1}, s_1\}, \min\{s_2, s_4\}, \min\{s_4, s_2\}\} \\
&= \max\{s_{-2}, s_0, s_1, s_{-1}, s_1, s_{-1}, s_2, s_2\} \\
&= s_2
\end{aligned}
$$

Then we rank all the alternatives $x_i (i = 1,2,3,4)$ according to $z_i(w)(i = 1,2,3,4)$:

$$x_3 \succ x_1 \succ x_2 \sim x_4$$

and thus the best potential partner is x_3.

9.3 MAGDM Method Based on LWM and HLWA Operators

9.3.1 HLWA Operator

In Sect. 7.2, we introduce the concept of LOWA operator, i.e.,

$$LOWA_\omega(a_1, a_2, \ldots, a_n) = \max_j \min\left\{\omega_j, b_j\right\}$$

where $\omega = (\omega_1, \omega_2, \ldots, \omega_n)$ is the weighting vector associated with the LOWA operator, $a_i \in S, i = 1, 2, \ldots, n$, $\omega_j \in S, j = 1, 2, \ldots, m$, and b_j is the jth largest of the linguistic arguments $(a_1, a_2, \ldots, a_n)$.

Example 9.3 Suppose that $\omega = (s_{-2}, s_{-3}, s_{-1}, s_{-4})$, and

$$a_1 = s_0, \quad a_2 = s_1, \quad a_3 = s_{-1}, \quad a_4 = s_{-2}$$

then by the LOWA operator, we get

$$b_1 = s_1, \quad b_2 = s_0, \quad b_3 = s_{-1}, \quad b_4 = s_{-2}$$

and thus,

$$LOWA_\omega(s_0, s_1, s_{-1}, s_{-2}) = \max\{\min\{s_{-2}, s_1\}, \min\{s_{-3}, s_0\}, \min\{s_{-1}, s_{-1}\}, \min\{s_{-4}, s_{-2}\}\}$$

Below we investigate some desirable properties of the LOWA operator:

Theorem 9.4 [127] (Commutativity) Let $(a_1, a_2, \ldots, a_n)$ be a collection of linguistic arguments, then

$$LOWA_\omega(a_1, a_2, \ldots, a_n) = LOWA_\omega(\dot{a}_1, \dot{a}_2, \ldots, \dot{a}_n)$$

where $(\dot{a}_1, \dot{a}_2, \ldots, \dot{a}_n)$ is any permutation of $(a_1, a_2, \ldots, a_n)$.

Proof Let

$$LOWA_\omega(a_1, a_2, \ldots, a_n) = \max_i \min\left\{\omega_j, b_j\right\}$$

and

$$LOWA_\omega(\dot{a}_1, \dot{a}_2, \ldots, \dot{a}_n) = \max_i \min\left\{\omega_j, \dot{b}_j\right\}$$

Since $(\dot{a}_1, \dot{a}_2, \ldots, \dot{a}_n)$ is any permutation of $(a_1, a_2, \ldots, a_n)$, then $b_j = \dot{b}_j (j = 1, 2, \ldots, n)$, thus, $LOWA_\omega(a_1, a_2, \ldots, a_n) = LOWA_\omega(\dot{a}_1, \dot{a}_2, \ldots, \dot{a}_n)$, which completes the proof.

Theorem 9.5 [127] (Monotonicity) Let $(a_1, a_2, \ldots, a_n)$ and $\left(a_1^{'}, a_2^{'}, \ldots, a_n^{'}\right)$ be two collections of linguistic arguments, if for all i, we have $a_i \le a_i^{'}$, then

$$LOWA_\omega\left(a_1, a_2, \ldots, a_n\right) \le LOWA_\omega\left(a_1^{'}, a_2^{'}, \ldots, a_n\right)$$

Proof Let

$$LOWA_{\omega}(a_1, a_2, \ldots, a_n) = \max_j \min\{\omega_j, b_j\}$$

and

$$LOWA_{\omega}\left(a_1', a_2', \ldots, a_n'\right) = \max_j \min\{\omega_j, b_j'\}$$

Since for all i, we have $a_i \leq a_i'$, then $b_j \leq b_j'$, and thus,

$$LOWA_{\omega}\left(a_1, a_2, \ldots, a_n\right) \leq LOWA_{\omega}\left(a_1', a_2', \ldots, a_n'\right)$$

which completes the proof.

Theorem 9.6 [127] Let $(a_1, a_2, \ldots, a_n)$ be a collection of linguistic arguments, and $\omega = (\omega_1, \omega_2, \ldots, \omega_n)$ be the weighting vector associated with the LOWA operator.

1. If for any j, we have $\omega_j \geq b_j$, then

$$LOWA_{\omega}(a_1, a_2, \ldots, a_n) = \max_i\{a_i\}$$

and thus, the linguistic max operator is a special case of the LOWA operator.

2. If for any $j \neq n$, we have $\omega_n \geq b_n$, and $\omega_n \leq \omega_j$, then

$$LOWA_{\omega}(a_1, a_2, \ldots, a_n) = \min_i\{a_i\}$$

and thus, the linguistic min operator is also the special case of the LOWA operator.

Proof

1. Since for any j, $\omega_j \geq b_j$, then

$$LOWA_{\omega}(a_1, a_2, \ldots, a_n) = \max_i \min\{\omega_j, b_j\} = \max_j\{b_j\} = \max_i\{a_i\}$$

2. Since for any $j \neq n$, $\omega_n \geq b_n$, and $\omega_n \leq \omega_j$, then

$$LOWA_{\omega}(a_1, a_2, \ldots, a_n) = \min\{\omega_n, b_n\} = b_n = \min_i\{a_i\}$$

which completes the proof.

Theorem 9.7 [127] (Bounded) Let $(a_1, a_2, \ldots, a_n)$ be a collection of linguistic arguments, then

$$s_{-L} \leq \min\{\min_j\{\omega_n\}, \min_i\{a_i\}\} \leq LOWA_\omega(a_1, a_2, \ldots, a_n)$$
$$\leq \max\{\max_j\{\omega_j\}, \max_i\{a_i\}\} \leq s_L$$

Especially, if there exists j, such that $\min\{\omega_j, b_j\} = s_L$, then

$$LOWA_\omega(a_1, a_2, \ldots, a_n) = s_{-L}$$

Proof

$$\begin{aligned} LOWA_\omega(a_1, a_2, \ldots, a_n) &= \max_j \min\{\omega_j, b_j\} \leq \max_j \max\{\omega_j, b_j\} \\ &= \max\{\max_j\{\omega_j\}, \max_j\{b_j\}\} \\ &= \max\{\max_j\{\omega_j\}, \max_i\{a_i\}\} \\ &\leq s_L \end{aligned}$$

$$\begin{aligned} LOWA_\omega(a_1, a_2, \ldots, a_n) &= \max_j \min\{\omega_j, b_j\} \geq \max\{\min_j\{\omega_j\}, \min_j\{b_j\}\} \\ &\geq \min\{\min_j\{\omega_j\}, \min_j\{b_j\}\} \\ &= \min\{\min_j\{\omega_j\}, \min_i\{a_i\}\} \\ &\geq s_{-L} \end{aligned}$$

Especially, if there exists j, such that $\min\left\{\omega_j, b_j\right\} = s_L$, then

$$LOWA_\omega(a_1, a_2, \ldots, a_n) = \max_j \min\left\{\omega_j, b_j\right\} = s_L$$

If for any j, we have $\min\left\{\omega_j, b_j\right\} = s_{-L}$, then

$$LOWA_\omega(a_1, a_2, \ldots, a_n) = \max_j \min\left\{\omega_j, b_j\right\} = s_{-L}$$

which completes the proof.

It can be seen from the definitions of the LWM and LOWA operators that the LWM operator weights only the linguistic labels, while the LOWA operator weights only the ordered positions of the linguistic labels instead of weighting the linguistic labels themselves. Thus, both the LWM and LOWA operators have one sidedness. To overcome this limitation, in what follows, we introduce a hybrid linguistic weighted aggregation (HLWA) operator:

Definition 9.2 [127] A hybrid linguistic weighted averaging (HLWA) operator is a mapping $HLWA: S^n \to S$, $\omega = (\omega_1, \omega_2, \ldots, \omega_n)$ is the weighting vector associated with the HLWA operator, and $\omega_j \in S, j = 1, 2, \ldots, n$, such that

$$HLWA_{w,\omega}(a_1, a_2, \ldots, a_n) = \max_j \min\{\omega_j, b_j\}$$

where b_j is the j th largest of a collection of weighted linguistic arguments $\bar{a}_i$ ($\bar{a}_i = \min\{\omega_i, a_i\}, i = 1, 2, \ldots, n$), $w = (w_1, w_2, \ldots, w_n)$ is the weight vector of a collection of linguistic arguments $(a_1, a_2, \ldots, a_n)$, and $w_i \in S$, $i = 1, 2, \ldots, n$.

Example 9.4 Suppose that $a_1 = s_0$, $a_2 = s_1$, $a_3 = s_{-1}$, and $a_4 = s_{-2}$ are a collection of linguistic arguments, whose weight vector is $w = (s_0, s_{-2}, s_{-2}, s_{-3})$, $\omega = (s_{-2}, s_{-3}, s_{-1}, s_{-4})$ is the weighting vector of the HLWA operator. Then by Definition 9.2, we have

$$\bar{a}_1 = \min\{s_0, s_0\} = s_0, \quad \bar{a}_2 = \min\{s_{-2}, s_1\} = s_{-2}$$

$$\bar{a}_3 = \min\{s_{-1}, s_{-1}\} = s_{-1}, \quad \bar{a}_4 = \min\{s_{-2}, s_{-3}\} = s_{-3}$$

Thus,

$$b_1 = s_0, \quad b_2 = s_{-1}, \quad b_3 = s_{-2}, \quad b_4 = s_{-3}$$

Therefore,

$$\begin{aligned} HLWA_{w,\omega}(s_0, s_1, s_{-1}, s_{-2}) &= \max\{\min\{s_{-2}, s_0\}, \min\{s_{-3}, s_{-1}\}, \\ &\quad \min\{s_{-1}, s_{-2}\}, \min\{s_{-4}, s_{-3}\}\} \\ &= s_{-2} \end{aligned}$$

which completes the proof.

Theorem 9.8 [127] The LWM operator is a special case of the HLWA operator.

Proof Let $\omega = (s_L, s_L, \ldots, s_L)$, then

$$\begin{aligned} HLWA_{w,\omega}(a_1, a_2, \ldots, a_n) &= \max_j \min\{\omega_j, b_j\} = \max_j\{b_j\} = \max_i\{\bar{a}_i\} \\ &= \max_i \min\{w_i, a_i\} \end{aligned}$$

which completes the proof.

Theorem 9.9 [127] The LOWA operator is a special case of the HLWA operator.

From Theorems 9.8 and 9.9, we can know that the HLWA operator extends both the LWM and LOWA operators, it reflects not only the importance degrees of the linguistic labels themselves, but also the importance degrees of the positions of these linguistic labels.

9.3.2 Decision Making Method

Now we introduce a MAGDM method based on the LWM and HLWA operators [127]:

Step 1 For a MAGDM problem, let X, U and D be the set of alternatives, the set of attributes and the set of decision makers, and let $w=(w_1,w_2,\ldots,w_n)$ be the weight vector of attributes, $\lambda=(\lambda_1,\lambda_2,\ldots,\lambda_n)$ be the weight vector of the decision makers $d_k(k=1,2,\ldots,t)$, and w_j, $\lambda_k \in S$, $j=1,2,\ldots,n$, $k=1,2,\ldots,t$. Suppose that the decision maker $d_k \in D$ provides the linguistic evaluation information (attribute value) $r_{ij}^{(k)}$ of the alternative $x_i \in X$ with respect to the attribute $u_k \in U$, and constructs the decision matrix $R_k=(r_{ij}^{(k)})_{n\times m}$, and $r_{ij}^{(k)} \in S$.

Step 2 Aggregate the attribute values of the i line in $R_k=(r_{ij}^{(k)})_{n\times m}$ by using the LWM operator, and get the overall attribute value $z_i^{(k)}(w)$ of the alternative x_k:

$$\begin{aligned} z_i^{(k)}(w) &= LWM_w(r_{i1}^{(k)},r_{i2}^{(k)},\ldots,r_{im}^{(k)}) \\ &= \max_j \min\{w_j, r_{ij}^{(k)}\}, \quad i=1,2,\ldots,n,\ k=1,2,\ldots,t \end{aligned}$$

Step 3 Utilize the HLWA operator to derive the overall attribute values $z_i^{(k)}(w)$ of the alternative x_i corresponding to the decision makers $d_k(k=1,2,\ldots,t)$, and get the group's overall attribute value $z_i(w)$ of the alternative x_i:

$$\begin{aligned} z_i(\lambda,\omega) &= HLWA_{\lambda,\omega}\left(z_i^{(1)}(w), z_i^{(2)}(w),\ldots,z_i^{(t)}(w)\right) \\ &= \max_k \min\{\omega_k, b_i^{(k)}\},\ i=1,2,\ldots,n \end{aligned}$$

where $\omega=(\omega_1,\omega_2,\ldots,\omega_t)$ is the associated with the HLWA operator, and $\omega_k \in S$, $k=1,2,\ldots,t$, $b_i^{(k)}$ is the k th largest of a collection of the weighted linguistic arguments $(a_i^{(1)},a_i^{(2)},\ldots,a_i^{(t)})$, where

$$a_i^{(l)} = \min\left\{\lambda_l, z_i^{(l)}(w)\right\},\ l=1,2,\ldots,t$$

Step 4 Rank and select the alternatives $x_i (i = 1, 2, \ldots, n)$ according to $z_i(\lambda, \omega)$ $(i = 1, 2, \ldots, n)$.

9.4 Practical Example

Example 9.5 In order to assess the teachers' quality of a middle school of Nanjing, Jiangsu, China, the following eight indices (attributes) are put forward: (1) u_1: the quality of science and culture; (2) u_2: ideological and moral quality; (3) u_3: body and mind quality; (4) u_4: teaching and guiding learning ability; (5) u_5: scientific research ability; (6) u_6: the ability of understanding students' minds; (7) u_7: teaching management ability; and (8) u_8: independent self-study ability. The weight vector of these indices is given as $w = (s_1, s_0, s_4, s_3, s_3, s_0, s_2, s_1)$, where $s_i \in S$, and

$$S = \{extremely\ poor, very\ poor, poor, slightly\ poor, fair, slightly\ good, good, very\ good, extremely\ good\}$$

Three decision makers $d_k (k = 1, 2, 3)$ (whose weight vector is $\lambda = (s_0, s_4, s_2)$) using the linguistic label set S to evaluate four physical education teachers (alternatives) $x_i (i = 1, 2, 3, 4)$ with respect to the indices $u_j (j = 1, 2, \ldots, 8)$. The evaluation values are listed in Tables 9.2, 9.3, and 9.4.

In what follows, we solve the problem with the method of Sect. 9.4:

Step 1 Aggregate the attribute values of the ith line in the decision matrix R_k using the LWM operator, and obtain the overall attribute value $z_i^{(k)}(w)$:

Table 9.2 Decision matrix R_1

	u_1	u_2	u_3	u_4	u_5	u_6	u_7	u_8
x_1	s_2	s_4	s_4	s_1	s_2	s_3	s_4	s_2
x_2	s_4	s_3	s_1	s_2	s_4	s_3	s_2	s_3
x_3	s_3	s_2	s_4	s_1	s_4	s_4	s_3	s_4
x_4	s_2	s_3	s_0	s_1	s_4	s_1	s_3	s_3

Table 9.3 Decision matrix R_2

	u_1	u_2	u_3	u_4	u_5	u_6	u_7	u_8
x_1	s_0	s_3	s_3	s_0	s_2	s_4	s_1	s_2
x_2	s_2	s_1	s_0	s_0	s_4	s_3	s_4	s_0
x_3	s_0	s_1	s_4	s_3	s_4	s_3	s_4	s_2
x_4	s_1	s_1	s_1	s_1	s_2	s_3	s_1	s_0

Table 9.4 Decision matrix R_3

	u_1	u_2	u_3	u_4	u_5	u_6	u_7	u_8
x_1	s_1	s_3	s_3	s_1	s_4	s_3	s_1	s_2
x_2	s_2	s_1	s_1	s_2	s_2	s_0	s_4	s_3
x_3	s_4	s_3	s_2	s_2	s_4	s_3	s_3	s_4
x_4	s_1	s_1	s_0	s_0	s_1	s_3	s_1	s_4

$$\begin{aligned} z_1^{(1)}(w) &= LWM_w(r_{11}^{(1)}, r_{12}^{(1)}, \ldots, r_{18}^{(1)}) \\ &= \max\{\min\{s_1, s_2\}, \min\{s_0, s_4\}, \min\{s_4, s_4\}, \min\{s_3, s_1\}, \min\{s_3, s_2\}, \\ &\quad \min\{s_0, s_3\}, \min\{s_2, s_4\}, \min\{s_1, s_2\}\} \\ &= \max\{s_1, s_0, s_4, s_1, s_2, s_0, s_2, s_1, s_2\} \\ &= s_4 \end{aligned}$$

Similarly, we have

$$z_2^{(1)}(w) = LWM_w(r_{21}^{(1)}, r_{22}^{(1)}, \ldots, r_{28}^{(1)}) = s_3, \quad z_3^{(1)}(w) = LWM_w(r_{31}^{(1)}, r_{32}^{(1)}, \ldots, r_{38}^{(1)}) = s_4$$

$$z_4^{(1)}(w) = LWM_w(r_{41}^{(1)}, r_{42}^{(1)}, \ldots, r_{48}^{(1)}) = s_3, \quad z_1^{(2)}(w) = LWM_w(r_{11}^{(2)}, r_{12}^{(2)}, \ldots, r_{18}^{(2)}) = s_3$$

$$z_2^{(2)}(w) = LWM_w(r_{21}^{(2)}, r_{22}^{(2)}, \ldots, r_{28}^{(2)}) = s_4, \quad z_3^{(2)}(w) = LWM_w(r_{31}^{(2)}, r_{32}^{(2)}, \ldots, r_{38}^{(2)}) = s_4$$

$$z_4^{(2)}(w) = LWM_w(r_{41}^{(2)}, r_{42}^{(2)}, \ldots, r_{48}^{(2)}) = s_2, \quad z_1^{(3)}(w) = LWM_w(r_{11}^{(3)}, r_{12}^{(3)}, \ldots, r_{18}^{(3)}) = s_3$$

$$z_2^{(3)}(w) = LWM_w(r_{21}^{(3)}, r_{22}^{(3)}, \ldots, r_{28}^{(3)}) = s_2, \quad z_3^{(3)}(w) = LWM_w(r_{31}^{(3)}, r_{32}^{(3)}, \ldots, r_{38}^{(3)}) = s_3$$

$$z_4^{(3)}(w) = LWM_w(r_{41}^{(3)}, r_{42}^{(3)}, \ldots, r_{48}^{(3)}) = s_1$$

Step 2 Suppose that $\omega = (s_4, s_2, s_1)$, then we utilize the HLWA operator to aggregate the overall attribute values $z_i^{(k)}(w)(k = 1,2,3,4)$ of the alternative x_i corresponding to the decision makers $d_k(k = 1,2,3)$, and get the group's overall attribute value $z_i(\lambda, \omega)$ of the alternative x_i:

$$z_1(\lambda, \omega) = HLWA_{\lambda,\omega}\left(z_1^1(w), z_1^2(w), z_1^3(w)\right) = s_3$$

$$z_2(\lambda, \omega) = HLWA_{\lambda,\omega}\left(z_2^1(w), z_2^2(w), z_2^3(w)\right) = s_4$$

$$z_3(\lambda,\omega) = HLWA_{\lambda,\omega}\left(z_3^1(w), z_3^2(w), z_3^3(w)\right) = s_4$$

$$z_4(\lambda,\omega) = HLWA_{\lambda,\omega}\left(z_4^1(w), z_4^2(w), z_4^3(w)\right) = s_2$$

Step 3 Rank the four physical education teachers (alternatives) $x_i (i = 1, 2, 3, 4)$ according to $z_i(\lambda,\omega)(i = 1, 2, 3, 4)$:

$$x_2 \sim x_3 \succ x_1 \succ x_4$$

and thus, x_2 and x_3 are the best ones.

Part IV
Uncertain Linguistic MADM Methods and Their Applications

Chapter 10
Uncertain Linguistic MADM with Unknown Weight Information

With the complexity and uncertainty of objective thing and the fuzziness of human thought, sometimes, a decision maker may provide uncertain linguistic evaluation information because of time pressure, lack of knowledge, or the decision maker's limited attention and information-processing capabilities. Thus, it is necessary to investigate the uncertain linguistic MADM problems, which have received more and more attention recently. In this chapter, we first introduce the operational laws of uncertain linguistic variables, and introduce some uncertain linguistic aggregation operators, such as the uncertain EOWA (UEOWA) operator, the uncertain EWA (UEWA) operator and the uncertain linguistic hybrid aggregation (ULHA) operator, etc. Moreover, we introduce respectively the MADM method based on the UEOWA operator and the MAGDM method based on the ULHA operator, and then give their applications to the partner selection of an enterprise in the field of supply chain management.

10.1 MADM Method Based on UEOWA Operator

10.1.1 UEOWA Operator

Definition 10.1 [123] Let $\tilde{\mu}=[s_a,s_b]$, $s_a,s_b \in \bar{S}$, s_a and s_b are the lower and upper limits, respectively, then $\tilde{\mu}$ is called the uncertain linguistic variable.

Let $\tilde{S}$ be the set of uncertain linguistic variables. Consider any two linguistic variables $\tilde{\mu}=[s_a,s_b]$, $\tilde{v}=[s_c,s_d]\in\tilde{S}$, β, β_1, $\beta_2 \in [0,1]$, and define their operational laws as follows [123, 128]:

1. $\tilde{\mu}\oplus\tilde{v}=[s_a,s_b]\oplus[s_c,s_d]=[s_a\oplus s_c, s_b\oplus s_d]=[s_{a+c},s_{b+d}]$;
2. $\beta\tilde{\mu}=\beta[s_a,s_b]=[\beta s_a,\beta s_b]=[s_{\beta a},s_{\beta b}]$;
3. $\tilde{\mu}\oplus\tilde{v}=\tilde{v}\oplus\tilde{\mu}$;

Z.S. Xu, *Uncertain Multi-Attribute Decision Making*,
DOI 10.1007/978-3-662-45640-8_10

4. $\beta(\tilde{\mu}\oplus\tilde{\nu})=\beta\tilde{\mu}\oplus\beta\tilde{\nu}$;
5. $(\beta_1+\beta_2)\tilde{\mu}=\beta_1\tilde{\mu}\oplus\beta_2\tilde{\mu}$.

Definition 10.2 [128] Let $\tilde{\mu}=[s_a,s_b]$, $\tilde{\nu}=[s_c,s_d]\in\tilde{S}$, and let $l_{ab}=b-a$, $l_{cd}=d-c$, then the possibility degree of $\tilde{\mu}\geq\tilde{\nu}$ is defined as:

$$p(\tilde{\mu}\geq\tilde{\nu})=\max\left\{1-\max\left\{\frac{d-a}{l_{ab}+l_{cd}},0\right\},0\right\} \tag{10.1}$$

Similarly, the possibility degree of $\tilde{\nu}\geq\tilde{\mu}$ is defined as:

$$p(\tilde{\nu}\geq\tilde{\mu})=\max\left\{1-\max\left\{\frac{b-c}{l_{ab}+l_{cd}},0\right\},0\right\}$$

By using Definition 10.2, we can prove the following conclusion:

Theorem 10.1 [128] Let $\tilde{\mu}=[s_a,s_b]$, $\tilde{\nu}=[s_c,s_d]$, $\tilde{\gamma}=[s_e,s_f]\in\tilde{S}$, then

1. $0\leq p(\tilde{\mu}\geq\tilde{\nu})\leq 1$, $0\leq p(\tilde{\nu}\geq\tilde{\mu})\leq 1$.
2. $p(\tilde{\mu}\geq\tilde{\nu})=1$ if and only if $d\leq a$. Similarly, $p(\tilde{\nu}\geq\tilde{\mu})=1$ if and only if $b\leq c$.
3. $p(\tilde{\mu}\geq\tilde{\nu})=0$ if and only if $b\leq c$. Similarly, $p(\tilde{\nu}\geq\tilde{\mu})=0$ if and only if $d\leq a$.
4. $p(\tilde{\mu}\geq\tilde{\nu})+p(\tilde{\nu}\geq\tilde{\mu})=1$. Especially, $p(\tilde{\mu}\geq\tilde{\mu})=\frac{1}{2}$.
5. $p(\tilde{\mu}\geq\tilde{\nu})\geq\frac{1}{2}$ if and only if $a+b\geq c+d$. Especially, $p(\tilde{\mu}\geq\tilde{\nu})=\frac{1}{2}$ if and only if $a+b=c+d$.
6. $p(\tilde{\mu}\geq\tilde{\nu})\geq\frac{1}{2}$ and $p(\tilde{\nu}\geq\tilde{\gamma})\geq\frac{1}{2}$, then $p(\tilde{\mu}\geq\tilde{\gamma})\geq\frac{1}{2}$.

Definition 10.3 [128] Let $UEA:\tilde{S}^n\rightarrow\tilde{S}$, if

$$UEA(\tilde{\mu}_1,\tilde{\mu}_2,\ldots,\tilde{\mu}_n)=\frac{1}{n}(\tilde{\mu}_1\oplus\tilde{\mu}_2\oplus\cdots\oplus\tilde{\mu}_n) \tag{10.2}$$

then the function *UEA* is called the uncertain EA (UEA) operator.

Example 10.1 Given a collection of uncertain linguistic variables:

$$\tilde{\mu}_1=[s_2,s_4],\ \tilde{\mu}_2=[s_3,s_4],\ \tilde{\mu}_3=[s_1,s_3],\ \tilde{\mu}_4=[s_2,s_3]$$

then

$$UEA(\tilde{\mu}_1,\tilde{\mu}_2,\ldots,\tilde{\mu}_n)=\frac{1}{4}([s_2,s_4]\oplus[s_3,s_4]\oplus[s_1,s_3]\oplus[s_2,s_3])$$
$$=[s_2,s_{3.5}]$$

Definition 10.4 [128] Let $UEOWA:\tilde{S}^n\to\tilde{S}$, if

$$UEOWA_\omega(\tilde{\mu}_1,\tilde{\mu}_2,\ldots,\tilde{\mu}_n)=\omega_1\tilde{v}_1\oplus\omega_2\tilde{v}_2\oplus\cdots\oplus\omega_n\tilde{v}_n \tag{10.3}$$

where $\omega=(\omega_1,\omega_2,\ldots,\omega_n)$ is the weighting vector associated with the UEOWA operator, $\omega_j\in[0,1]$, $j=1,2,\ldots,n$, $\sum_{j=1}^n\omega_j=1$, $\tilde{\mu}_i\in\tilde{S}$, and $\tilde{v}_j$ is the j th largest of a collection of uncertain linguistic variables $(\tilde{\mu}_1,\tilde{\mu}_2,\ldots,\tilde{\mu}_n)$, then the function *UEOWA* is the uncertain EOWA (UEOWA) operator.

Especially, if $\omega=\left(\frac{1}{n},\frac{1}{n},\ldots,\frac{1}{n}\right)$, then the UEOWA operator reduces to the UEA operator.

The UEOWA operator generally can be implemented using the following procedure [128]:

Step 1 Determine the weighting vector $\omega=(\omega_1,\omega_2,\ldots,\omega_n)$ by Eqs. (5.13) and (5.14), or the weight determining method introduced in Sect. 1.1 for the UOWA operator.

Step 2 Utilize Eq. (10.1) to compare each pair of a collection of uncertain linguistic variables $(\tilde{\mu}_1,\tilde{\mu}_2,\ldots,\tilde{\mu}_n)$, and construct the possibility degree matrix (fuzzy preference relation) $P=(p_{ij})_{n\times n}$, where $p_{ij}=p(\tilde{\mu}_i\geq\tilde{\mu}_j)$. Then by Eq. (4.6), we get the priority vector $v=(v_1,v_2,\ldots,v_n)$ of P, based on which we rank the uncertain linguistic variables $\tilde{\mu}_i(i=1,2,\ldots,n)$ according to $v_i(i=1,2,\ldots,n)$ in descending order, and obtain $\tilde{v}_j(j=1,2,\ldots,n)$.

Step 3 Aggregate $\omega=(\omega_1,\omega_2,\ldots,\omega_n)$ and $\tilde{v}_j(j=1,2,\ldots,n)$ by using

$$UEOWA_\omega(\tilde{\mu}_1,\tilde{\mu}_2,\ldots,\tilde{\mu}_n)=\omega_1\tilde{v}_1\oplus\omega_2\tilde{v}_2\oplus\cdots\oplus\omega_n\tilde{v}_n$$

Example 10.2 Suppose that $\omega=(0.3,0.2,0.4,0.1)$, and consider a collection of uncertain linguistic variables:

$$\tilde{\mu}_1=[s_2,s_4],\ \tilde{\mu}_2=[s_3,s_4],\ \tilde{\mu}_3=[s_1,s_3],\ \tilde{\mu}_4=[s_2,s_3]$$

Then we utilize Eq. (10.1) to compare each pair of $\tilde{\mu}_i\ (i = 1,2,3,4)$, and establish the possibility degree matrix:

$$P = \begin{pmatrix} 0.5 & 0.333 & 0.750 & 0.667 \\ 0.667 & 0.50 & 1 & 1 \\ 0.250 & 0 & 0.5 & 0.333 \\ 0.333 & 0 & 0.667 & 0.5 \end{pmatrix}$$

whose priority vector can be derived from Eq. (4.6) as follows:

$$v = (0.271, 0.347, 0.174, 0.208)$$

based on which we rank the uncertain linguistic variables $\tilde{\mu}_i\ (i = 1,2,3,4)$ in descending order:

$$\tilde{v}_1 = [s_3, s_4],\quad \tilde{v}_2 = [s_2, s_4],\quad \tilde{v}_3 = [s_2, s_4],\quad \tilde{v}_4 = [s_1, s_3]$$

Since $\omega = (0.3, 0.2, 0.4, 0.1)$, then we aggregate $\tilde{\mu}_i\ (i = 1,2,3,4)$ using the UEOWA operator:

$$\begin{aligned} & UEOWA_{\omega}(\tilde{\mu}_1, \tilde{\mu}_2, \ldots, \tilde{\mu}_4) \\ & = 0.3 \times [s_3, s_4] \oplus 0.2 \times [s_2, s_4] \oplus 0.4 \times [s_2, s_3] \oplus 0.1 \times [s_1, s_3] \\ & = [s_{0.9}, s_{1.2}] \oplus [s_{0.4}, s_{0.8}] \oplus [s_{0.8}, s_{1.2}] \oplus [s_{0.1}, s_{0.3}] \\ & = [s_{2.2}, s_{3.5}] \end{aligned}$$

10.1.2 Decision Making Method

In what follows, we introduce a MADM method based on the UEOWA operator, which has the following steps [128]:

Step 1 For a MADM problem, let X and U be the set of alternatives and the set of attributes. The decision maker provides the linguistic evaluation value $\tilde{r}_{ij}$ of the alternative $x_i \in X$ with respect to the attribute $u_j \in U$, and constructs the uncertain linguistic decision matrix $\tilde{R} = (\tilde{r}_{ij})_{n \times m}$, and $\tilde{r}_{ij} \in \tilde{S}$.

Step 2 Utilize the UEOWA operator to aggregate the linguistic evaluation information of the i th line in $\tilde{R} = (\tilde{r}_{ij})_{n \times m}$, and get the overall attribute value $\tilde{z}_i(\omega)(i = 1,2,\ldots,n)$ of the alternative x_i:

$$\tilde{z}_i(\omega) = UEOWA_{\omega}(\tilde{r}_{i1}, \tilde{r}_{i2}, \ldots, \tilde{r}_{in})$$

Step 3 Calculate the possibility degrees

$$p_{ij} = p(\tilde{z}_i(\omega) \geq \tilde{z}_j(\omega)),\ i, j = 1, 2, \ldots, n$$

using Eq. (10.1) by comparing each pair of $\tilde{z}_i(\omega)(i = 1, 2, \ldots, n)$, and construct the possibility degree matrix $P = (p_{ij})_{n \times n}$.

Step 4 Use Eq. (4.6) to derive the priority vector $v = (v_1, v_2, \ldots, v_n)$ of P, and then rank and select the alternatives $x_i (i = 1, 2, \ldots, n)$.

10.1.3 Practical Example

Example 10.3 Here we take Example 9.2 to illustrate the method above. Suppose that the decision maker evaluate the four potential partners $x_i (i = 1,2,3,4)$ with respect to the factors $u_j (j = 1, 2, \ldots, 8)$, and constructs the uncertain linguistic decision matrix $\tilde{R} = (\tilde{r}_{ij})_{8 \times 8}$ (see Table 10.1) using the linguistic label set:

$$\begin{aligned} S &= \{s_i \mid i = -5, \ldots, 5\} \\ &= \{\textit{extremely poor, very poor, rather poor, poor, slightly poor, fair,} \\ &\quad \textit{slightly good, good, rather good, very good, extremely good}\} \end{aligned}$$

Below we utilize the method of Sect. 10.1.2 to illustrate the solution process of the problem:

Table 10.1 Uncertain linguistic decision matrix $\tilde{R}$

	u_1	u_2	u_3	u_4
x_1	$[s_1, s_2]$	$[s_2, s_4]$	$[s_0, s_1]$	$[s_2, s_3]$
x_2	$[s_0, s_2]$	$[s_0, s_1]$	$[s_3, s_4]$	$[s_1, s_3]$
x_3	$[s_2, s_3]$	$[s_1, s_2]$	$[s_2, s_4]$	$[s_4, s_5]$
x_4	$[s_1, s_2]$	$[s_4, s_5]$	$[s_1, s_3]$	$[s_{-1}, s_1]$
	u_5	u_6	u_7	u_8
x_1	$[s_1, s_3]$	$[s_3, s_4]$	$[s_{-2}, s_0]$	$[s_0, s_2]$
x_2	$[s_{-1}, s_0]$	$[s_{-2}, s_{-1}]$	$[s_2, s_4]$	$[s_1, s_2]$
x_3	$[s_3, s_4]$	$[s_{-1}, s_1]$	$[s_1, s_3]$	$[s_3, s_5]$
x_4	$[s_0, s_2]$	$[s_3, s_4]$	$[s_2, s_4]$	$[s_2, s_3]$

Step 1 Compare each pair of the uncertain linguistic variables of the i th line in the decision matrix $\tilde{R}$ by using Eq. (10.1), and establish the four possibility degree matrices $P^{(l)} = (p_{ij}^{(l)})_{8\times 8}$ $(l = 1,2,3,4)$:

$$P^{(1)} = \begin{pmatrix} 0.5 & 0 & 1 & 0 & 0.333 & 0 & 1 & 0.667 \\ 1 & 0.5 & 1 & 0.667 & 0.750 & 0.333 & 1 & 1 \\ 0 & 0 & 0.5 & 0 & 0 & 0 & 1 & 0.333 \\ 1 & 0.333 & 1 & 0.5 & 0.667 & 0 & 1 & 1 \\ 0.667 & 0.250 & 1 & 0.333 & 0.5 & 0 & 1 & 0.750 \\ 1 & 0.667 & 1 & 1 & 1 & 0.5 & 1 & 1 \\ 0 & 0 & 0 & 0 & 0 & 0 & 0.5 & 0 \\ 0.333 & 0 & 0.667 & 0 & 0.250 & 0 & 1 & 0.5 \end{pmatrix}$$

$$P^{(2)} = \begin{pmatrix} 0.5 & 0.667 & 0 & 0.250 & 1 & 1 & 0 & 0.333 \\ 0.333 & 0.5 & 0 & 0 & 1 & 1 & 0 & 0 \\ 1 & 1 & 0.5 & 1 & 1 & 1 & 0.667 & 1 \\ 0.750 & 1 & 0 & 0.5 & 1 & 1 & 0.250 & 0.667 \\ 0 & 0 & 0 & 0 & 0.5 & 1 & 0 & 0 \\ 0 & 0 & 0 & 0 & 0 & 0.5 & 0 & 0 \\ 1 & 1 & 0.333 & 0.750 & 1 & 1 & 0.5 & 1 \\ 0.667 & 1 & 0 & 0.333 & 1 & 1 & 0 & 0.5 \end{pmatrix}$$

$$P^{(3)} = \begin{pmatrix} 0.5 & 1 & 0.333 & 0 & 0 & 1 & 0.667 & 0 \\ 0 & 0.5 & 0 & 0 & 0 & 1 & 0.333 & 0 \\ 0.667 & 1 & 0.5 & 0 & 0.333 & 1 & 0.750 & 0.250 \\ 1 & 1 & 1 & 0.5 & 1 & 1 & 1 & 0.667 \\ 1 & 1 & 0.667 & 0 & 0.5 & 1 & 1 & 0.333 \\ 0 & 0 & 0 & 0 & 0 & 0.5 & 0 & 0 \\ 0.333 & 0.667 & 0.250 & 0 & 0 & 1 & 0.5 & 0 \\ 1 & 1 & 0.750 & 0.333 & 0.667 & 1 & 1 & 0.5 \end{pmatrix}$$

$$P^{(4)} = \begin{pmatrix} 0.5 & 0 & 0.333 & 1 & 0.667 & 0 & 0 & 0 \\ 1 & 0.5 & 1 & 1 & 1 & 1 & 1 & 1 \\ 0.667 & 0 & 0.5 & 1 & 0.750 & 0 & 0.250 & 0.333 \\ 0 & 0 & 0 & 0.5 & 0.250 & 0 & 0 & 0 \\ 0.333 & 0 & 0.250 & 0.750 & 0.5 & 0 & 0 & 0 \\ 1 & 0 & 1 & 1 & 1 & 0.5 & 0.667 & 1 \\ 1 & 0 & 0.750 & 1 & 1 & 0.333 & 0.5 & 0.667 \\ 1 & 0 & 0.667 & 1 & 1 & 0 & 0.333 & 0.5 \end{pmatrix}$$

According to Eq. (4.6), we get the priority vectors of the possibility degree matrices $P^{(l)}(l=1,2,3,4)$:

$$v^{(1)} = (0.1161, 0.1652, 0.0863, 0.1518, 0.1339, 0.1816, 0.0625, 0.1027)$$

$$v^{(2)} = (0.1205, 0.1042, 0.1816, 0.1458, 0.0804, 0.0625, 0.1711, 0.1339)$$

$$v^{(3)} = (0.1161, 0.0863, 0.1339, 0.1816, 0.1518, 0.0625, 0.1027, 0.1652)$$

$$v^{(4)} = (0.0982, 0.1875, 0.1161, 0.0670, 0.0863, 0.1637, 0.1473, 0.1339)$$

based on which we rank all the uncertain linguistic arguments $\tilde{r}_{ij}(j=1,2,\ldots,8)$ of the i th line in $\tilde{R}$ in descending order, and then use the UEOWA operator (suppose that its associated weighting vector is $\omega=(0.15,0.10,0.12,0.10,0.12,0.13,0.15,0.13)$) to aggregate them, i.e.,

$$\begin{aligned}\tilde{z}_1(\omega) &= UEOWA_{\omega}(\tilde{r}_{11},\tilde{r}_{12},\ldots,\tilde{r}_{18}) \\ &= 0.15\times[s_3,s_4]\oplus 0.10\times[s_2,s_4]\oplus 0.12\times[s_2,s_3]\oplus 0.10\times[s_1,s_3] \\ &\quad \oplus 0.12\times[s_1,s_2]\oplus 0.13\times[s_0,s_2]\oplus 0.15\times[s_0,s_1]\oplus 0.13\times[s_{-2},s_0] \\ &= [s_{0.85},s_{2.31}]\end{aligned}$$

$$\begin{aligned}\tilde{z}_2(\omega) &= UEOWA_{\omega}(\tilde{r}_{21},\tilde{r}_{22},\ldots,\tilde{r}_{28}) \\ &= 0.15\times[s_3,s_4]\oplus 0.10\times[s_2,s_4]\oplus 0.12\times[s_1,s_3]\oplus 0.10\times[s_1,s_2] \\ &\quad \oplus 0.12\times[s_0,s_2]\oplus 0.13\times[s_0,s_1]\oplus 0.15\times[s_{-1},s_0]\oplus 0.13\times[s_{-2},s_{-1}] \\ &= [s_{0.46},s_{1.80}]\end{aligned}$$

$$\begin{aligned}\tilde{z}_3(\omega) &= UEOWA_{\omega}(\tilde{r}_{31}, \tilde{r}_{32}, \ldots, \tilde{r}_{38}) \\ &= 0.15\times[s_4, s_5] \oplus 0.10\times[s_3, s_5] \oplus 0.12\times[s_3, s_4] \oplus 0.10\times[s_2, s_4] \\ &\quad \oplus 0.12\times[s_2, s_3] \oplus 0.13\times[s_1, s_3] \oplus 0.15\times[s_1, s_2] \oplus 0.13\times[s_{-1}, s_1] \\ &= [s_{1.85}, s_{3.31}]\end{aligned}$$

$$\begin{aligned}\tilde{z}_4(\omega) &= UEOWA_{\omega}(\tilde{r}_{41}, \tilde{r}_{42}, \ldots, \tilde{r}_{48}) \\ &= 0.15\times[s_4, s_5] \oplus 0.10\times[s_3, s_4] \oplus 0.12\times[s_2, s_4] \oplus 0.10\times[s_2, s_3] \\ &\quad \oplus 0.12\times[s_1, s_3] \oplus 0.13\times[s_1, s_2] \oplus 0.15\times[s_0, s_2] \oplus 0.13\times[s_{-1}, s_1] \\ &= [s_{1.46}, s_{2.98}]\end{aligned}$$

Step 2 Calculate possibility degrees $p_{ij} = p(\tilde{z}_i(\omega) \geq \tilde{z}_i(\omega))$ $(i, j = 1, 2, 3, 4)$ using Eq. (10.1) by comparing each pair of the overall attribute values $\tilde{z}_i(\omega)(i = 1, 2, 3, 4)$, and establish the possibility degree matrix:

$$P = \begin{pmatrix} 0.5 & 0.6607 & 0.1575 & 0.2852 \\ 0.3393 & 0.5 & 0 & 0.1189 \\ 0.8425 & 1 & 0.5 & 0.6208 \\ 0.7148 & 0.8811 & 0.3792 & 0.5 \end{pmatrix}$$

Step 3 Derive the priority vector of the possibility degree matrix P by using Eq. (4.6):

$$v = (0.2169, 0.1632, 0.3303, 0.2896)$$

based on which we rank the potential partners $x_i (i = 1, 2, 3, 4)$:

$$x_3 \succ x_4 \succ x_1 \succ x_2$$

and thus, x_3 is the best potential partner.

10.2 MAGDM Method Based on UEOWA and ULHA Operators

10.2.1 UEWA Operator

Definition 10.5 [128] Let $UEWA : \tilde{S}^n \to \tilde{S}$, if

$$UEWA_w(\tilde{\mu}_1, \tilde{\mu}_2, \ldots, \tilde{\mu}_n) = w_1\tilde{\mu}_1 \oplus w_2\tilde{\mu}_2 \oplus \cdots \oplus w_n\tilde{\mu}_n$$

where $w = (w_1, w_2, \ldots, w_n)$ is the weight vector of the uncertain linguistic variables $\tilde{\mu}_i (i = 1, 2, \ldots, n)$, $w_j \in [0,1]$, $j = 1, 2, \ldots, n$, and $\sum_{j=1}^{n} w_j = 1$, then the function *UEWA* is called the uncertain EWA (UEWA) operator.

Especially, if $w = \left(\frac{1}{n}, \frac{1}{n}, \ldots, \frac{1}{n}\right)$, then the UEWA operator reduces to the UEA operator.

Example 10.4 Suppose that $w = (0.1, 0.3, 0.2, 0.4)$, and consider a collection of uncertain linguistic variables:

$$\tilde{\mu}_1 = [s_3, s_5],\ \tilde{\mu}_2 = [s_1, s_2],\ \tilde{\mu}_3 = [s_3, s_4],\ \tilde{\mu}_4 = [s_0, s_2]$$

then

$$\begin{aligned} UEWA_w(\tilde{\mu}_1, \tilde{\mu}_2, \tilde{\mu}_3, \tilde{\mu}_4) &= 0.1 \times [s_3, s_5] \oplus 0.3 \times [s_1, s_2] \oplus 0.2 \times [s_3, s_4] \oplus 0.4 \times [s_0, s_2] \\ &= [s_{0.3}, s_{0.5}] \oplus [s_{0.3}, s_{0.6}] \oplus [s_{0.6}, s_{0.8}] \oplus [s_0, s_{0.8}] \\ &= [s_{1.2}, s_{2.7}] \end{aligned}$$

It can be seen from Definitions 10.4 and 10.5 that the UEOWA operator weights only the ordered positions of the linguistic labels, while the UEWA operator weights only the linguistic labels. Thus, both the UEOWA and UEWA operators have one sidedness. To overcome this limitation, in what follows, we introduce an uncertain linguistic hybrid aggregation (ULHA) operator.

10.2.2 ULHA Operator

Definition 10.6 [128] Let $ULHA: \tilde{S} \to \tilde{S}$, if

$$ULHA_{w,\omega}(\tilde{\mu}_1, \tilde{\mu}_2, \ldots, \tilde{\mu}_n) = \omega_1\tilde{v}_1 \oplus \omega_2\tilde{v}_2 \oplus \cdots \oplus \omega_n\tilde{v}_n$$

where $\omega = (\omega_1, \omega_2, \cdots, \omega_n)$ is the weighting vector (position vector) associated with the ULHA operator, $\omega_j \in [0,1]$, $j = 1, 2, \ldots, n$, $\sum_{j=1}^{n} \omega_j = 1$, $\tilde{v}_j$ is the jth largest of a collection of the weighted uncertain linguistic variables $(\tilde{\mu}_1', \tilde{\mu}_2', \ldots, \tilde{\mu}_n')$ $(\tilde{\mu}_i' = n w_i \tilde{\mu}_i,\ i = 1, 2, \ldots, n)$, here, $w = (w_1, w_2, \cdots, w_n)$ is the weight vector of the uncertain linguistic variables $(\bar{\mu}_1, \bar{\mu}_2, \ldots, \bar{\mu}_n)$, $w_j \in [0,1]$, $j = 1, 2, \ldots, n$,

$\sum_{j=1}^{n} w_j = 1$, and n is the balancing coefficient, then the function $ULHA$ is called an uncertain linguistic hybrid aggregation (ULHA) operator.

Example 10.5 Let $\tilde{\mu}_1 = [s_0, s_1]$, $\tilde{\mu}_2 = [s_1, s_2]$, $\tilde{\mu}_3 = [s_{-1}, s_2]$, and $\tilde{\mu}_4 = [s_{-2}, s_0]$ be a collection of uncertain linguistic arguments, $w = (0.2, 0.3, 0.1, 0.4)$ be their weight vector, $\omega = (0.3, 0.2, 0.3, 0.2)$ be the weighting vector associated with the ULHA operator. By Theorem 10.6, we have

$$\tilde{\mu}_1' = 4 \times 0.2 \times [s_0, s_1] = [s_0, s_{0.8}],\ \tilde{\mu}_2' = 4 \times 0.3 \times [s_1, s_2] = [s_{1.2}, s_{2.4}]$$

$$\tilde{\mu}_3' = 4 \times 0.1 \times [s_{-1}, s_2] = [s_{-0.4}, s_{0.8}],\ \tilde{\mu}_4' = 4 \times 0.4 \times [s_{-2}, s_0] = [s_{-3.2}, s_0]$$

Then we utilize Eq. (10.1) to compare each pair of the uncertain linguistic variables $\tilde{\mu}_i' (i = 1, 2, 3, 4)$, and then construct the possibility degree matrix:

$$P = \begin{pmatrix} 0.5 & 0 & 0.6 & 1 \\ 1 & 0.5 & 1 & 1 \\ 0.4 & 0 & 0.5 & 0.909 \\ 0 & 0 & 0.091 & 0.5 \end{pmatrix}$$

whose priority vector can be derived from Eq. (4.6):

$$v = (0.2583, 0.3750, 0.2341, 0.1326)$$

After that, by using $v_i (i = 1, 2, 3, 4)$, we rearrange the uncertain linguistic variables $\tilde{\mu}_i' (i = 1, 2, 3, 4)$ in descending order:

$$\tilde{v}_1 = [s_{1.2}, s_{2.4}],\quad \tilde{v}_2 = [s_0, s_{0.8}],\quad \tilde{v}_3 = [s_{-0.4}, s_{0.8}],\quad \tilde{v}_4 = [s_{-3.2}, s_0]$$

thus,

$$\begin{aligned} ULHA_{w,\omega}(\tilde{\mu}_1, \tilde{\mu}_2, \tilde{\mu}_3, \tilde{\mu}_4) &= 0.3 \times [s_{1.2}, s_{2.4}] \oplus 0.2 \times [s_0, s_{0.8}] \\ &\quad \oplus 0.3 \times [s_{-0.4}, s_{0.8}] \oplus 0.2 \times [s_{-3.2}, s_0] \\ &= [s_{-0.40}, s_{1.12}] \end{aligned}$$

Theorem 10.2 [128] The UEWA operator is a special case of the ULHA operator.

Proof Let $\omega = \left(\frac{1}{n}, \frac{1}{n}, \ldots, \frac{1}{n}\right)$, then

$$
\begin{aligned}
ULHA_{w,\omega}(\tilde{\mu}_1, \tilde{\mu}_2, \ldots, \tilde{\mu}_n) &= \omega_1 \tilde{v}_1 \oplus \omega_2 \tilde{v}_2 \oplus \cdots \oplus \omega_n \tilde{v}_n \\
&= \frac{1}{n}(\tilde{v}_1 \oplus \tilde{v}_2 \oplus \cdots \oplus \tilde{v}_n) \\
&= w_1 \tilde{\mu}_1 \oplus w_2 \tilde{\mu}_2 \oplus \cdots \oplus w_2 \tilde{\mu}_2
\end{aligned}
$$

which completes the proof.

Theorem 10.3 [128] The UEOWA operator is a special case of the ULHA operator.

Proof Let $w = \left(\frac{1}{n}, \frac{1}{n}, \ldots, \frac{1}{n}\right)$, then $\tilde{\mu}_i' = \tilde{\mu}_i, i = 1, 2, \ldots, n$, which completes the proof.

From Theorems 10.2 and 10.3, we can know that the ULHA operator extends both the UEWAA and UEOWA operators, it reflects not only the importance degrees of the linguistic labels themselves, but also the importance degrees of the positions of these linguistic labels.

10.2.3 Decision Making Method

In what follows, we introduce a MADM method based on the UEOWA and ULHA operator [128], whose steps are as below:

Step 1 For a MADM problem, let X, U and D be the set of alternatives, the set of attributes, and the set of decision makers. The information on attribute weights is unknown completely. The weight vector of the decision makers is $\lambda = (\lambda_1, \lambda_2, \ldots, \lambda_t)$, $\lambda_k \geq 0$, $k = 1, 2, \ldots, t$, and $\sum_{k=1}^{t} \lambda_k = 1$. The decision maker $d_k \in D$ provides the linguistic evaluation value $\tilde{r}_{ij}^{(k)}$ of the alternative $x_i \in X$ with respect to the attribute $u_j \in U$, and constructs the uncertain linguistic decision matrix $\tilde{R}_k = (\tilde{r}_{ij}^{(k)})_{n \times m}$, and $\tilde{r}_{ij}^{(k)} \in \tilde{S}$.

Step 2 Utilize the UEOWA operator to aggregate the linguistic evaluation information of the i th line in $\tilde{R}_k$, and get the overall attribute value $\tilde{z}_i^{(k)}(\omega)$ of the alternative x_i corresponding to the decision maker d_k:

$$
\tilde{z}_i^{(k)}(\omega) = UEOWA_{\omega}(\tilde{r}_{i1}^{(k)}, \tilde{r}_{i2}^{(k)}, \ldots, \tilde{r}_{in}^{(k)})
$$

Step 3 Aggregate the overall attribute values $\tilde{z}_i^{(k)}(\omega)$ $(k=1,2,...,t)$ of the alternative x_i corresponding to the decision makers $d_k\,(k=1,2,\ldots,t)$ by using the ULHA operator, and then get the group's overall attribute value $z_i^{(k)}(\lambda,\omega')$ of the alternative x_i:

$$\tilde{z}_i(\lambda,\omega') = ULHA_{\lambda,\omega'}(\tilde{r}_i^{(1)},\tilde{r}_i^{(2)},...,\tilde{r}_i^{(t)}) = \omega_1'\tilde{v}_i^{(1)} \oplus \omega_2'\tilde{v}_i^{(2)} \oplus \cdots \oplus \omega_t'\tilde{v}_i^{(t)}$$

where $\omega' = (\omega_1', \omega_2',..., \omega_t')$ is the weighting vector associated with the ULHA operator, $\omega_k' \in [0,1]$, $k=1,2,...,t$, $\sum_{k=1}^{t}\omega_k' = 1$, $\tilde{v}_i^{(k)}$ is the k th largest of a collection of the weighted uncertain linguistic variables $(t\lambda_1\tilde{z}_i^{(1)}(\omega), t\lambda_2\tilde{z}_i^{(2)}(\omega), \ldots, t\lambda_t\tilde{z}_i^{(t)}(\omega))$, and t is the balancing coefficient.

Step 4 Calculate the possibility degrees

$$p_{ij} = p(\tilde{z}_i(\lambda,\omega') \geq \tilde{z}_j(\lambda,\omega')),\ i,j=1,2,...,n$$

using Eq. (10.1) by comparing each pair of $\tilde{z}_i(\lambda, w')(i=1,2,\ldots,n)$, and construct the possibility degree matrix $P=(p_{ij})_{n\times n}$.

Step 5 Use Eq. (4.6) to derive the priority vector $v=(v_1,v_2,\ldots,v_n)$ of P, and then rank and select the alternatives $x_i(i=1,2,\ldots,n)$.

10.2.4 Practical Example

Example 10.6 Here we use Example 10.3 to illustrate the method of Sect. 10.2.3. Suppose that there are three decision makers $d_k(k=1,2,3)$, whose weight vector is $\lambda=(0.3,0.4,0.3)$. The decision makers express their preference values over the four potential partners $x_i(i=1,2,3,4)$ with respect to the factors $u_j(j=1,2,\ldots,8)$, and construct the uncertain linguistic decision matrices $\tilde{R}_k=(\tilde{r}_{ij}^{(k)})_{8\times 8}(k=1,2,3)$ (see Tables 10.2, 10.3, and 10.4).

Step 1 Aggregate the linguistic evaluation information of the ith line in $\tilde{R}_k$ by using the UEOWA operator (suppose that its associated weighting vector is $\omega=(0.15,0.10,0.12,0.13,0.15,0.13)$), and get the overall attribute value $z_i^{(k)}(\omega)$ of the alternative x_i corresponding to the decision maker d_k, where

$$\begin{aligned}\tilde{z}_1^{(1)}(\omega) &= 0.15\times[s_2,s_4]\oplus 0.10\times[s_2,s_3]\oplus 0.12\times[s_1,s_3]\oplus 0.10\times[s_1,s_3]\\&\oplus 0.12\times[s_0,s_2]\oplus 0.13\times[s_0,s_2]\oplus 0.15\times[s_0,s_1]\oplus 0.13\times[s_{-2},s_0]\\&=[s_{0.46},s_{2.21}]\end{aligned}$$

Table 10.2 Uncertain linguistic decision matrix $\tilde{R}_1$

	u_1	u_2	u_3	u_4
x_1	$[s_0, s_2]$	$[s_2, s_3]$	$[s_0, s_2]$	$[s_1, s_3]$
x_2	$[s_1, s_2]$	$[s_0, s_1]$	$[s_2, s_4]$	$[s_2, s_3]$
x_3	$[s_2, s_4]$	$[s_1, s_2]$	$[s_3, s_4]$	$[s_3, s_4]$
x_4	$[s_1, s_3]$	$[s_3, s_5]$	$[s_1, s_2]$	$[s_{-1}, s_0]$
	u_5	u_6	u_7	u_8
x_1	$[s_1, s_3]$	$[s_2, s_4]$	$[s_{-1}, s_0]$	$[s_0, s_1]$
x_2	$[s_{-1}, s_1]$	$[s_{-2}, s_0]$	$[s_2, s_3]$	$[s_1, s_3]$
x_3	$[s_2, s_4]$	$[s_{-2}, s_1]$	$[s_2, s_3]$	$[s_4, s_5]$
x_4	$[s_0, s_1]$	$[s_2, s_4]$	$[s_2, s_3]$	$[s_2, s_4]$

Table 10.3 Uncertain linguistic decision matrix $\tilde{R}_2$

	u_1	u_2	u_3	u_4
x_1	$[s_1, s_2]$	$[s_0, s_3]$	$[s_1, s_2]$	$[s_1, s_2]$
x_2	$[s_0, s_2]$	$[s_{-1}, s_1]$	$[s_3, s_4]$	$[s_2, s_3]$
x_3	$[s_3, s_4]$	$[s_1, s_3]$	$[s_3, s_5]$	$[s_3, s_4]$
x_4	$[s_1, s_2]$	$[s_3, s_4]$	$[s_1, s_3]$	$[s_{-1}, s_1]$
	u_5	u_6	u_7	u_8
x_1	$[s_1, s_4]$	$[s_3, s_4]$	$[s_{-1}, s_1]$	$[s_0, s_2]$
x_2	$[s_{-2}, s_1]$	$[s_{-2}, s_{-1}]$	$[s_2, s_4]$	$[s_1, s_4]$
x_3	$[s_2, s_3]$	$[s_{-1}, s_1]$	$[s_0, s_1]$	$[s_3, s_5]$
x_4	$[s_0, s_2]$	$[s_2, s_3]$	$[s_2, s_4]$	$[s_2, s_3]$

Table 10.4 Uncertain linguistic decision matrix $\tilde{R}_3$

	u_1	u_2	u_3	u_4
x_1	$[s_1, s_4]$	$[s_1, s_3]$	$[s_0, s_3]$	$[s_0, s_2]$
x_2	$[s_0, s_3]$	$[s_{-1}, s_1]$	$[s_2, s_3]$	$[s_1, s_3]$
x_3	$[s_1, s_3]$	$[s_0, s_3]$	$[s_2, s_4]$	$[s_2, s_4]$
x_4	$[s_0, s_2]$	$[s_3, s_5]$	$[s_0, s_2]$	$[s_{-1}, s_0]$
	u_5	u_6	u_7	u_8
x_1	$[s_1, s_2]$	$[s_2, s_3]$	$[s_0, s_1]$	$[s_0, s_1]$
x_2	$[s_0, s_1]$	$[s_{-3}, s_{-1}]$	$[s_1, s_2]$	$[s_1, s_2]$
x_3	$[s_1, s_4]$	$[s_0, s_2]$	$[s_0, s_2]$	$[s_3, s_4]$
x_4	$[s_{-1}, s_2]$	$[s_2, s_5]$	$[s_0, s_3]$	$[s_1, s_3]$

$$\tilde{z}_2^{(1)}(\omega) = 0.15\times[s_2,s_4]\oplus 0.10\times[s_2,s_3]\oplus 0.12\times[s_2,s_3]\oplus 0.10\times[s_1,s_2]$$
$$\oplus 0.12\times[s_1,s_2]\oplus 0.13\times[s_0,s_1]\oplus 0.15\times[s_{-1},s_1]\oplus 0.13\times[s_{-2},s_0]$$
$$=[s_{0.55},s_{2.08}]$$

$$\tilde{z}_3^{(1)}(\omega) = 0.15\times[s_4,s_5]\oplus 0.10\times[s_3,s_4]\oplus 0.12\times[s_3,s_4]\oplus 0.10\times[s_2,s_4]$$
$$\oplus 0.12\times[s_2,s_4]\oplus 0.13\times[s_2,s_3]\oplus 0.15\times[s_1,s_2]\oplus 0.13\times[s_{-2},s_1]$$
$$=[s_{1.85},s_{2.33}]$$

$$\tilde{z}_4^{(1)}(\omega) = 0.15\times[s_3,s_5]\oplus 0.10\times[s_2,s_4]\oplus 0.12\times[s_2,s_4]\oplus 0.10\times[s_2,s_3]$$
$$\oplus 0.12\times[s_1,s_3]\oplus 0.13\times[s_1,s_2]\oplus 0.15\times[s_0,s_1]\oplus 0.13\times[s_{-1},s_0]$$
$$=[s_{1.21},s_{2.70}]$$

$$\tilde{z}_1^{(2)}(\omega) = 0.15\times[s_3,s_4]\oplus 0.10\times[s_1,s_4]\oplus 0.12\times[s_1,s_2]\oplus 0.10\times[s_1,s_2]$$
$$\oplus 0.12\times[s_1,s_2]\oplus 0.13\times[s_0,s_3]\oplus 0.15\times[s_0,s_2]\oplus 0.13\times[s_{-1},s_1]$$
$$=[s_{0.76},s_{2.50}]$$

$$\tilde{z}_2^{(2)}(\omega) = 0.15\times[s_3,s_4]\oplus 0.10\times[s_2,s_4]\oplus 0.12\times[s_2,s_3]\oplus 0.10\times[s_1,s_4]$$
$$\oplus 0.12\times[s_0,s_2]\oplus 0.13\times[s_{-1},s_1]\oplus 0.15\times[s_{-2},s_1]\oplus 0.13\times[s_{-2},s_{-1}]$$
$$=[s_{0.30},s_{2.15}]$$

$$\tilde{z}_3^{(2)}(\omega) = 0.15\times[s_3,s_5]\oplus 0.10\times[s_3,s_5]\oplus 0.12\times[s_3,s_4]\oplus 0.10\times[s_3,s_4]$$
$$\oplus 0.12\times[s_2,s_3]\oplus 0.13\times[s_1,s_3]\oplus 0.15\times[s_0,s_1]\oplus 0.13\times[s_{-1},s_1]$$
$$=[s_{1.65},s_{3.16}]$$

$$\tilde{z}_4^{(2)}(\omega) = 0.15\times[s_3,s_4]\oplus 0.10\times[s_2,s_4]\oplus 0.12\times[s_2,s_3]\oplus 0.10\times[s_2,s_3]$$
$$\oplus 0.12\times[s_1,s_2]\oplus 0.13\times[s_1,s_2]\oplus 0.15\times[s_0,s_2]\oplus 0.13\times[s_{-1},s_1]$$
$$=[s_{1.21},s_{2.71}]$$

$$\tilde{z}_1^{(3)}(\omega) = 0.15\times[s_2,s_3]\oplus 0.10\times[s_1,s_4]\oplus 0.12\times[s_1,s_3]\oplus 0.10\times[s_1,s_2]$$
$$\oplus 0.12\times[s_0,s_3]\oplus 0.13\times[s_0,s_2]\oplus 0.15\times[s_0,s_1]\oplus 0.13\times[s_0,s_1]$$
$$=[s_{0.62},s_{2.31}]$$

$$\tilde{z}_2^{(3)}(\omega) = 0.15\times[s_2,s_3]\oplus 0.10\times[s_1,s_3]\oplus 0.12\times[s_1,s_2]\oplus 0.10\times[s_1,s_2]$$
$$\oplus 0.12\times[s_0,s_3]\oplus 0.13\times[s_0,s_1]\oplus 0.15\times[s_{-1},s_1]\oplus 0.13\times[s_{-3},s_{-1}]$$
$$=[s_{0.08},s_{1.70}]$$

$$\tilde{z}_3^{(3)}(\omega) = 0.15\times[s_3,s_4]\oplus 0.10\times[s_2,s_4]\oplus 0.12\times[s_2,s_4]\oplus 0.10\times[s_1,s_4]$$
$$\oplus 0.12\times[s_1,s_3]\oplus 0.13\times[s_0,s_3]\oplus 0.15\times[s_0,s_2]\oplus 0.13\times[s_0,s_2]$$
$$=[s_{1.11},s_{3.19}]$$

$$\tilde{z}_4^{(3)}(\omega) = 0.15\times[s_3,s_5]\oplus 0.10\times[s_2,s_5]\oplus 0.12\times[s_1,s_3]\oplus 0.10\times[s_0,s_3]$$
$$\oplus 0.12\times[s_0,s_2]\oplus 0.13\times[s_0,s_2]\oplus 0.15\times[s_{-1},s_2]\oplus 0.13\times[s_{-1},s_0]$$
$$=[s_{0.49},s_{2.71}]$$

Step 2 Aggregate the overall attribute evaluation values $z_i^{(k)}(\omega)(k=1,2,3)$ of the alternative x_i corresponding to the decision makers $d_k(k=1,2,3)$ by using the ULHA operator (suppose that its associated weighting vector is $\omega' = (0.2, 0.6, 0.2)$). We first utilize λ, t and $z_i^{(k)}(\omega)$ to calculate $t\lambda_k z_i^{(k)}(\omega)$:

$$3\lambda_1 z_1^{(1)}(\omega)=[s_{0.414},s_{1.989}],\ 3\lambda_1 z_2^{(1)}(\omega)=[s_{0.495},s_{1.872}]$$

$$3\lambda_1 z_3^{(1)}(\omega)=[s_{1.665},s_{2.097}],\ 3\lambda_1 z_4^{(1)}(\omega)=[s_{1.089},s_{2.430}]$$

$$3\lambda_2 z_1^{(2)}(\omega)=[s_{0.912},s_{3.000}],\ 3\lambda_2 z_4^{(2)}(\omega)=[s_{1.452},s_{3.252}]$$

$$3\lambda_3 z_1^{(3)}(\omega)=[s_{0.558},s_{2.079}],\ 3\lambda_3 z_2^{(3)}(\omega)=[s_{0.072},s_{1.530}]$$

$$3\lambda_3 z_3^{(3)}(\omega)=[s_{0.999},s_{2.871}],\ 3\lambda_3 z_4^{(3)}(\omega)=[s_{0.441},s_{2.439}]$$

by which we get the group's overall attribute evaluation values $\tilde{z}_i(\lambda,\omega')(i=1,2,3,4)$:

$$\tilde{z}_1(\lambda,\omega')=0.2\times[s_{0.912},s_{3.000}]\oplus 0.6\times[s_{0.558},s_{2.079}]\oplus 0.2\times[s_{0.414},s_{1.989}]$$
$$=[s_{0.600},s_{2.245}]$$

$$\tilde{z}_2(\lambda,\omega')=0.2\times[s_{0.360},s_{2.580}]\oplus 0.6\times[s_{0.495},s_{1.872}]\oplus 0.2\times[s_{0.072},s_{1.530}]$$
$$=[s_{0.383},s_{1.945}]$$

$$\tilde{z}_3(\lambda, \omega') = 0.2\times[s_{1.980}, s_{3.792}]\oplus 0.6\times[s_{1.665}, s_{2.097}]\oplus 0.2\times[s_{0.999}, s_{2.871}]$$
$$= [s_{1.595}, s_{2.591}]$$

$$\tilde{z}_4(\lambda, \omega') = 0.2\times[s_{1.452}, s_{3.252}]\oplus 0.6\times[s_{1.089}, s_{2.430}]\oplus 0.2\times[s_{0.441}, s_{2.439}]$$
$$= [s_{1.032}, s_{2.596}]$$

Step 3 Calculate the possibility degrees:

$$p_{ij} = p(\tilde{z}_i(\lambda, \omega') \geq \tilde{z}_j(\lambda, \omega')),\ \ i, j = 1,2,3,4$$

using Eq. (10.1) by comparing each pair of $\tilde{z}_i(\lambda, \omega')(i = 1,2,3,4)$, and construct the possibility degree matrix:

$$P = \begin{pmatrix} 0.5 & 0.5806 & 0.2461 & 0.3780 \\ 0.4194 & 0.5 & 0.1368 & 0.2921 \\ 0.3539 & 0.8632 & 0.5 & 0.6090 \\ 0.6220 & 0.7079 & 0.3910 & 0.5 \end{pmatrix}$$

Step 4 Derive the priority vector of P from Eq. (4.6):

$$v = (0.2254, 0.1957, 0.2772, 0.2684)$$

based on which we rank the alternatives $x_i (i = 1,2,3,4)$:

$$x_3 \succ x_4 \succ x_1 \succ x_2$$

from which we get the best potential partner x_3.

Chapter 11
Uncertain Linguistic MADM Method with Real-Valued Weight Information

For the MADM problems where the attribute weights are real numbers, and the attribute values take the form of uncertain linguistic variables, in this chapter, we introduce the MADM method based on the positive ideal point, the MADM method based on the UEWA operator, the MAGDM method based on the positive ideal point and the LHA operator, and the MAGDM method based on the UEWA and ULHA operators. Moreover, we illustrate the methods above with some practical examples.

11.1 MADM Method Based on Positive Ideal Point

11.1.1 Decision Making Method

Definition 11.1 [115] Let $\tilde{R}=(\tilde{r}_{ij})_{n\times m}$ be an uncertain linguistic decision matrix, then $\tilde{x}^{+}=(\tilde{r}_1^{+},\tilde{r}_2^{+},\dots,\tilde{r}_m^{+})$ is called the positive ideal point of alternatives, which satisfies:

$$\tilde{r}_j^{+}=[r_j^{+L},r_j^{+U}],\ r_j^{+L}=\max_i\{r_{ij}^{L}\},\ r_j^{+U}=\max_i\{r_{ij}^{U}\},\ j=1,2,\dots,m$$

where r_j^{+L} and r_j^{+U} are the lower and upper limits of $\tilde{r}_j^{+}$ respectively.

Definition 11.2 [115] Let $\tilde{\mu}=[s_a,s_b]$ and $\tilde{v}=[s_c,s_d]$ be two uncertain linguistic variables, $c\geq a$, $d\geq b$, then we define

$$D(\tilde{\mu},\tilde{v})=\frac{1}{2}(s_{c-a}\oplus s_{d-b})=s_{\frac{1}{2}(c-a+d-b)} \tag{11.1}$$

as the deviation between $\tilde{\mu}$ and $\tilde{v}$.

Z.S. Xu, *Uncertain Multi-Attribute Decision Making*,
DOI 10.1007/978-3-662-45640-8_11

According to Definition 11.2, we can define the deviation between the alternative x_i and the positive ideal point of alternatives as:

$$D(\tilde{x}^+, \tilde{x}_i) = w_1 D(\tilde{r}_1^+, \tilde{r}_{i1}) \oplus w_2 D(\tilde{r}_2^+, \tilde{r}_{i2}) \oplus \cdots \oplus w_m D(\tilde{r}_m^+, \tilde{r}_{im}), \quad i = 1, 2, \ldots, n \tag{11.2}$$

where $w = (w_1, w_2, \ldots, w_m)$ is the weight vector of attributes, $\tilde{x}_i = (\tilde{r}_{i1}, \tilde{r}_{i2}, \ldots, \tilde{r}_{im})$ is the vector of the attribute values of the alternative x_i.

Clearly, the smaller $D(\tilde{x}^+, \tilde{x}_i)$, the closer the alternative x_i to the positive ideal point $\tilde{x}^+$, and thus, the better the alternative x_i.

In what follows, we introduce a MADM method based on the positive ideal point of alternatives, whose steps are given as below [115]:

Step 1 For a MADM problem, let X and U be the set of alternatives and the set of attributes. $w = (w_1, w_2, \ldots, w_m)$ is the weight vector of the attributes $u_j\,(j = 1, 2, \ldots, m)$, where $w_j \geq 0$, $j = 1, 2, \ldots, m$, and $\sum_{j=1}^{m} w_j = 1$. The decision maker provides the uncertain linguistic evaluation value $\tilde{r}_{ij}$ of the alternative $x_i \in X$ with respect to the attribute $u_j \in U$, and constructs the uncertain linguistic decision matrix $\tilde{R} = (\tilde{r}_{ij})_{n \times m}$, and $\tilde{r}_{ij} \in \tilde{S}$. Let $\tilde{x}_i = (\tilde{r}_{i1}, \tilde{r}_{i2}, \ldots, \tilde{r}_{im})$ be the vector corresponding to the alternative x_i, and $\tilde{x}^+ = (\tilde{r}_1^+, \tilde{r}_2^+, \ldots, \tilde{r}_m^+)$ be the positive ideal point of alternatives.

Step 2 Calculate the deviation $D(\tilde{x}^+, \tilde{x}_i)$ between the alternative x_i and the positive ideal point $\tilde{x}^+$ by using Eq. (11.2).

Step 3 Rank and select the alternatives $x_i\,(i = 1, 2, \ldots, n)$ according to $D(\tilde{x}^+, \tilde{x}_i)\ (i = 1, 2, \ldots, n)$.

11.1.2 Practical Example

Example 11.1 China is vast in territory, and its economic development is extremely unbalanced, which results in the significant differences among regional investment environments. Therefore, foreign investment in China has been facing an investment location selection problem. There are ten main indices (attributes) used to evaluate the regional investment environment competitiveness [86]: (1) u_1: the size of the market; (2) u_2: the open degree of economy; (3) u_3: the degree of marketization of the enterprise; (4) u_4: regional credit degree; (5) u_5: the efficiency for approving foreign-funded enterprises; (6) u_6: traffic density; (7) u_7: the level of communication; (8) u_8: the level of industrial development; (9) u_9: technical level; and (10) u_{10}: the status of human resources. The weight vector of these indices is $w = (0.12, 0.08, 0.10, 0.05, 0.08, 0.11, 0.15, 0.07, 0.11, 0.13)$. The evaluator utilizes the linguistic label set:

$$S = \{s_i \mid i = -5, \ldots, 5\}$$

$$= \{extremely\ poor,\ very\ poor, rather\ poor, poor, slightly\ poor,\ fair,$$

$$slightly\ good, good, rather\ good,\ very\ good, extremely\ good\}$$

to evaluate the investment environment competitiveness of the five regionals $x_i (i = 1, 2, 3, 4, 5)$ with respect to the ten indices $u_j (j = 1, 2, \ldots, 10)$. The evaluation results are contained in the uncertain linguistic decision matrix $\tilde{R}$ (see Table 11.1).

Now we use the method of Sect. 11.1.1 to solve the problem:

Step 1 Derive the vector $\tilde{x}_i$ of attribute values corresponding to the alternative x_i, and the positive ideal point $\tilde{x}^+$ of alternatives from Table 11.1:

$$\tilde{x}_1 = ([s_0, s_1], [s_2, s_5], [s_{-1}, s_1], [s_1, s_3], [s_2, s_3], [s_2, s_3], [s_{-1}, s_1], [s_1, s_2], [s_2, s_3], [s_2, s_4])$$

$$\tilde{x}_2 = ([s_1, s_2], [s_1, s_3], [s_1, s_4], [s_0, s_1], [s_1, s_3], [s_0, s_1], [s_3, s_4], [s_3, s_5], [s_1, s_4], [s_2, s_3])$$

$$\tilde{x}_3 = ([s_2, s_4], [s_0, s_2], [s_1, s_3], [s_2, s_3], [s_2, s_3], [s_0, s_2], [s_2, s_3], [s_3, s_4], [s_1, s_3], [s_2, s_4])$$

$$\tilde{x}_4 = ([s_{-2}, s_0], [s_3, s_5], [s_0, s_3], [s_0, s_2], [s_0, s_1], [s_3, s_4], [s_3, s_4], [s_2, s_4], [s_2, s_3], [s_1, s_3])$$

Table 11.1 Uncertain linguistic decision matrix $\tilde{R}$

	u_1	u_2	u_3	u_4	u_5
x_1	$[s_0, s_1]$	$[s_2, s_5]$	$[s_{-1}, s_1]$	$[s_1, s_3]$	$[s_2, s_3]$
x_2	$[s_1, s_2]$	$[s_1, s_3]$	$[s_1, s_4]$	$[s_0, s_1]$	$[s_1, s_3]$
x_3	$[s_2, s_4]$	$[s_0, s_2]$	$[s_1, s_3]$	$[s_2, s_3]$	$[s_2, s_3]$
x_4	$[s_{-2}, s_0]$	$[s_3, s_5]$	$[s_0, s_3]$	$[s_0, s_2]$	$[s_0, s_1]$
x_5	$[s_{-1}, s_2]$	$[s_1, s_4]$	$[s_0, s_2]$	$[s_1, s_3]$	$[s_1, s_3]$
	u_6	u_7	u_8	u_9	u_{10}
x_1	$[s_2, s_3]$	$[s_{-1}, s_1]$	$[s_1, s_2]$	$[s_2, s_3]$	$[s_2, s_4]$
x_2	$[s_0, s_1]$	$[s_3, s_4]$	$[s_2, s_5]$	$[s_1, s_4]$	$[s_2, s_3]$
x_3	$[s_0, s_2]$	$[s_2, s_3]$	$[s_3, s_4]$	$[s_1, s_3]$	$[s_2, s_4]$
x_4	$[s_3, s_4]$	$[s_3, s_4]$	$[s_2, s_4]$	$[s_2, s_3]$	$[s_1, s_3]$
x_5	$[s_2, s_4]$	$[s_0, s_2]$	$[s_0, s_3]$	$[s_1, s_4]$	$[s_0, s_1]$

$$\tilde{x}_5 = ([s_{-1}, s_2], [s_1, s_4], [s_0, s_2], [s_1, s_3], [s_1, s_3], [s_2, s_4], [s_0, s_2], [s_0, s_3], [s_1, s_4], [s_0, s_1])$$

$$\tilde{x}^+ = ([s_2, s_4], [s_3, s_5], [s_1, s_4], [s_2, s_3], [s_2, s_3], [s_3, s_4], [s_3, s_4], [s_3, s_5], [s_2, s_4], [s_2, s_4])$$

Thus, the deviation elements of the alternative x_i and the positive ideal point $\tilde{x}^+$ are listed in Table 11.2.

Step 2 Calculate the deviation between the alternative x_i and the positive ideal point $\tilde{x}^+$:

$$D(\tilde{x}^+, \tilde{x}_1) = s_{1.480},\ D(\tilde{x}^+, \tilde{x}_2) = s_{0.930},\ D(\tilde{x}^+, \tilde{x}_3) = s_{0.860}$$

$$D(\tilde{x}^+, \tilde{x}_4) = s_{1.070},\ D(\tilde{x}^+, \tilde{x}_5) = s_{1.620}$$

Step 3 Rank the alternatives $x_i (i = 1,2,3,4,5)$ according to $D(\tilde{x}^+, \tilde{x}_i)\ (i = 1,2,3,4,5)$ in ascending order: $x_3 \succ x_2 \succ x_4 \succ x_1 \succ x_5$, which indicates that x_3 is the best one.

Table 11.2 Deviation elements $D(\tilde{r}_j^+, \tilde{r}_{ij}) (i = 1,2,3,4,5, j = 1,2,\ldots,10)$

	u_1	u_2	u_3	u_4	u_5
$D(\tilde{r}_j^+, \tilde{r}_{1j})$	$s_{2.5}$	$s_{0.5}$	$s_{2.5}$	$s_{0.5}$	s_0
$D(\tilde{r}_j^+, \tilde{r}_{2j})$	$s_{1.5}$	s_2	s_0	s_2	$s_{0.5}$
$D(\tilde{r}_j^+, \tilde{r}_{3j})$	s_0	s_3	$s_{0.5}$	s_0	s_0
$D(\tilde{r}_j^+, \tilde{r}_{4j})$	s_4	s_0	s_1	$s_{1.5}$	s_2
$D(\tilde{r}_j^+, \tilde{r}_{5j})$	$s_{2.5}$	$s_{1.5}$	$s_{1.5}$	$s_{0.5}$	$s_{0.5}$
	u_6	u_7	u_8	u_9	u_{10}
$D(\tilde{r}_j^+, \tilde{r}_{1j})$	s_1	$s_{3.5}$	$s_{2.5}$	$s_{0.5}$	s_0
$D(\tilde{r}_j^+, \tilde{r}_{2j})$	s_3	s_0	s_0	$s_{0.5}$	$s_{0.5}$
$D(\tilde{r}_j^+, \tilde{r}_{3j})$	$s_{2.5}$	s_1	$s_{0.5}$	s_1	s_0
$D(\tilde{r}_j^+, \tilde{r}_{4j})$	s_0	s_0	s_1	$s_{0.5}$	s_1
$D(\tilde{r}_j^+, \tilde{r}_{5j})$	$s_{0.5}$	$s_{2.5}$	$s_{2.5}$	$s_{0.5}$	$s_{2.5}$

11.2 MAGDM Method Based on Ideal Point and LHA Operator

11.2.1 Decision Making Method

In the following, we introduce a MAGDM method based on the positive ideal point and the LHA operator:

Step 1 For a MAGDM problem, let X, U and D be the set of alternatives, the set of attributes, and the set of decision makers. The vector of attribute weights is $w=(w_1,w_2,\ldots,w_m)$, $w_j \ge 0$, $j=1,2,\ldots,m$, and $\sum_{j=1}^{m} w_j = 1$. The weight vector of the decision makers is $\lambda=(\lambda_1,\lambda_2,\ldots,\lambda_t)$, $\lambda_k \ge 0$, $k=1,2,\ldots,t$, and $\sum_{k=1}^{t}\lambda_k = 1$. The decision maker $d_k \in D$ provides the linguistic evaluation value $\tilde{r}_{ij}^{(k)}$ of the alternative $x_i \in X$ with respect to the attribute $u_j \in U$, and constructs the uncertain linguistic decision matrix $\tilde{R}_k = (\tilde{r}_{ij}^{(k)})_{n\times m}$, and $\tilde{r}_{ij}^{(k)} \in \tilde{S}$, $\tilde{r}_{ij}^{(k)} = [\tilde{r}_{ij}^{L(k)}, \tilde{r}_{ij}^{U(k)}]$. Let $\tilde{x}_i^{(k)} = (\tilde{r}_{ij}^{(k)}, \tilde{r}_{i2}^{(k)},\ldots,\tilde{r}_{im}^{(k)})$ be the attribute vector of the alternative x_i corresponding to the decision maker d_k, $\tilde{x}^+ = (\tilde{r}_1^+, \tilde{r}_2^+,\ldots,\tilde{r}_m^+)$ is the positive ideal point of alternatives, where

$$\tilde{r}_j^+ = [\tilde{r}_j^{+L}, \tilde{r}_j^{+U}], \quad \tilde{r}_j^{+L} = \max_i \max_k \{\tilde{r}_{ij}^{L(k)}\}$$

$$\tilde{r}_j^{+U} = \max_i \max_k \{\tilde{r}_{ij}^{U(k)}\},\ j=1,2,\ldots,n \tag{11.3}$$

Step 2 By using Eq. (11.2), we calculate the deviation $D(\tilde{x}^+, \tilde{x}_i^{(k)})$ between the alternative x_i and the positive ideal point $\tilde{x}^+$ corresponding to the decision maker d_k.

Step 3 Aggregate the deviations $D(\tilde{x}^+, \tilde{x}_i^{(k)})$ (k=1,2,…,t) corresponding to the decision makers $d_k (k=1,2,\ldots,t)$ by using the LHA operator, and then get the group's deviation $D(\tilde{x}^+, \tilde{x}_i)$ between the alternative x_i and the positive ideal point $\tilde{x}^+$, where

$$D(\tilde{x}^+, \tilde{x}_i) = LHA_{\lambda,\omega}(D(\tilde{x}^+, \tilde{x}_i^{(1)}), D(\tilde{x}^+, \tilde{x}_i^{(2)}),\ldots, D(\tilde{x}^+, \tilde{x}_i^{(t)}))$$

$$= \omega_1 \tilde{v}_i^{(1)} \oplus \omega_2 \tilde{v}_i^{(2)} \oplus \cdots \oplus \omega_t \tilde{v}_i^{(t)}$$

where $\omega = (\omega_1, \omega_2,\ldots,\omega_t)$ is the weighting vector associated with the LHA operator, $\omega_k \in [0,1]$, $k=1,2,\ldots,t$, $\sum_{k=1}^{t}\omega_k = 1$, $\tilde{v}_i^{(k)}$ is the k th largest of a collection of the weighted linguistic variables $(t\lambda_1 D(\tilde{x}^+, \tilde{x}_i^{(1)}), t\lambda_2 D(\tilde{x}^+, \tilde{x}_i^{(2)}), \ldots, t\lambda_t D(\tilde{x}^+, \tilde{x}_i^{(t)}))$, and t is the balancing coefficient.

Step 4 Rank and select the alternatives $x_i (i = 1, 2, \ldots, n)$ according to $D(\tilde{x}^+, \tilde{x}_i)$ $(i = 1, 2, \ldots, n)$.

11.2.2 Practical Example

Example 11.2 Here we take Example 11.1 to illustrate the method of Sect. 11.2.1. Suppose that three evaluators give the uncertain linguistic decision matrices $\tilde{R}_k (k = 1, 2, 3)$ (see Tables 11.3, 11.4, and 11.5):

Table 11.3 Uncertain linguistic decision matrix $\tilde{R}_1$

	u_1	u_2	u_3	u_4	u_5
x_1	$[s_1, s_2]$	$[s_3, s_4]$	$[s_0, s_1]$	$[s_1, s_4]$	$[s_2, s_4]$
x_2	$[s_1, s_3]$	$[s_2, s_3]$	$[s_2, s_4]$	$[s_0, s_2]$	$[s_2, s_3]$
x_3	$[s_3, s_4]$	$[s_1, s_2]$	$[s_2, s_3]$	$[s_2, s_4]$	$[s_1, s_3]$
x_4	$[s_{-1}, s_0]$	$[s_4, s_5]$	$[s_1, s_3]$	$[s_1, s_2]$	$[s_{-1}, s_1]$
x_5	$[s_{-1}, s_1]$	$[s_2, s_4]$	$[s_1, s_2]$	$[s_2, s_3]$	$[s_2, s_3]$
	u_6	u_7	u_8	u_9	u_{10}
x_1	$[s_1, s_3]$	$[s_{-1}, s_2]$	$[s_1, s_3]$	$[s_2, s_4]$	$[s_2, s_3]$
x_2	$[s_{-1}, s_1]$	$[s_3, s_5]$	$[s_4, s_5]$	$[s_1, s_3]$	$[s_2, s_4]$
x_3	$[s_1, s_2]$	$[s_2, s_4]$	$[s_2, s_4]$	$[s_1, s_2]$	$[s_3, s_4]$
x_4	$[s_2, s_4]$	$[s_3, s_5]$	$[s_3, s_4]$	$[s_1, s_3]$	$[s_2, s_3]$
x_5	$[s_1, s_4]$	$[s_0, s_1]$	$[s_1, s_3]$	$[s_2, s_4]$	$[s_{-1}, s_1]$

Table 11.4 Uncertain linguistic decision matrix $\tilde{R}_2$

	u_1	u_2	u_3	u_4	u_5
x_1	$[s_0, s_2]$	$[s_2, s_5]$	$[s_{-1}, s_1]$	$[s_1, s_3]$	$[s_2, s_3]$
x_2	$[s_1, s_3]$	$[s_1, s_2]$	$[s_1, s_3]$	$[s_0, s_3]$	$[s_1, s_4]$
x_3	$[s_2, s_5]$	$[s_0, s_1]$	$[s_1, s_2]$	$[s_2, s_4]$	$[s_2, s_4]$
x_4	$[s_{-2}, s_1]$	$[s_3, s_4]$	$[s_0, s_1]$	$[s_0, s_1]$	$[s_0, s_2]$
x_5	$[s_{-1}, s_3]$	$[s_3, s_4]$	$[s_0, s_1]$	$[s_1, s_4]$	$[s_1, s_4]$
	u_6	u_7	u_8	u_9	u_{10}
x_1	$[s_2, s_3]$	$[s_{-1}, s_1]$	$[s_1, s_2]$	$[s_2, s_3]$	$[s_2, s_4]$
x_2	$[s_0, s_2]$	$[s_3, s_5]$	$[s_3, s_4]$	$[s_1, s_3]$	$[s_2, s_4]$
x_3	$[s_0, s_3]$	$[s_2, s_4]$	$[s_3, s_5]$	$[s_1, s_2]$	$[s_2, s_3]$
x_4	$[s_3, s_5]$	$[s_3, s_5]$	$[s_2, s_5]$	$[s_2, s_4]$	$[s_1, s_2]$
x_5	$[s_2, s_3]$	$[s_0, s_3]$	$[s_0, s_4]$	$[s_1, s_3]$	$[s_0, s_2]$

Table 11.5 Uncertain linguistic decision matrix $\tilde{R}_3$

	u_1	u_2	u_3	u_4	u_5
x_1	$[s_0, s_2]$	$[s_2, s_3]$	$[s_0, s_1]$	$[s_2, s_3]$	$[s_0, s_3]$
x_2	$[s_1, s_3]$	$[s_1, s_4]$	$[s_3, s_4]$	$[s_{-1}, s_1]$	$[s_2, s_3]$
x_3	$[s_3, s_4]$	$[s_1, s_2]$	$[s_2, s_3]$	$[s_0, s_3]$	$[s_1, s_3]$
x_4	$[s_{-1}, s_0]$	$[s_2, s_5]$	$[s_1, s_3]$	$[s_{-1}, s_2]$	$[s_{-1}, s_1]$
x_5	$[s_{-1}, s_1]$	$[s_2, s_4]$	$[s_1, s_2]$	$[s_2, s_3]$	$[s_2, s_3]$
	u_6	u_7	u_8	u_9	u_{10}
x_1	$[s_2, s_4]$	$[s_0, s_1]$	$[s_0, s_2]$	$[s_1, s_3]$	$[s_3, s_4]$
x_2	$[s_0, s_2]$	$[s_1, s_4]$	$[s_4, s_5]$	$[s_3, s_5]$	$[s_1, s_3]$
x_3	$[s_1, s_2]$	$[s_1, s_3]$	$[s_2, s_4]$	$[s_2, s_3]$	$[s_2, s_4]$
x_4	$[s_4, s_5]$	$[s_1, s_4]$	$[s_3, s_4]$	$[s_1, s_3]$	$[s_2, s_3]$
x_5	$[s_3, s_4]$	$[s_{-1}, s_2]$	$[s_2, s_3]$	$[s_3, s_5]$	$[s_{-1}, s_1]$

Step 1 Calculate the positive ideal point by using Eq. (11.3):

$$\tilde{x}^+ = ([s_3, s_5], [s_4, s_5], [s_3, s_4], [s_2, s_4], [s_2, s_4], [s_4, s_5], [s_3, s_5],$$
$$[s_4, s_5], [s_3, s_4], [s_3, s_4])$$

Step 2 Calculate the deviation elements $D(\tilde{r}_j^+, \tilde{r}_{ij}^{(k)})$ $(i = 1,2,3,4,5,\ j = 1,2,\ldots,10)$, shown in Tables 11.6, 11.7, and 11.8.

Then we calculate the deviation between the alternative x_i and the positive ideal point $\tilde{x}^+$ corresponding to the decision maker d_k:

$$D(\tilde{x}^+, \tilde{x}_1^{(1)}) = s_{1.865},\ D(\tilde{x}^+, \tilde{x}_2^{(1)}) = s_{1.315},\ D(\tilde{x}^+, \tilde{x}_3^{(1)}) = s_{1.285}$$

$$D(\tilde{x}^+, \tilde{x}_4^{(1)}) = s_{1.535},\ D(\tilde{x}^+, \tilde{x}_5^{(1)}) = s_{2.295},\ D(\tilde{x}^+, \tilde{x}_1^{(2)}) = s_{2.085}$$

$$D(\tilde{x}^+, \tilde{x}_2^{(2)}) = s_{1.430},\ D(\tilde{x}^+, \tilde{x}_3^{(2)}) = s_{1.445},\ D(\tilde{x}^+, \tilde{x}_4^{(2)}) = s_{1.645}$$

$$D(\tilde{x}^+, \tilde{x}_3^{(3)}) = s_{1.285},\ D(\tilde{x}^+, \tilde{x}_4^{(3)}) = s_{1.535},\ D(\tilde{x}^+, \tilde{x}_5^{(3)}) = s_{2.295}$$

Step 3 Aggregate the deviations $D(\tilde{x}^+, \tilde{x}_i^{(k)})$ $(k = 1,2,3)$ corresponding to the evaluators d_k $(k = 1,2,3)$ by using the LHA operator (suppose that its weighting vector $\omega = (0.3, 0.4, 0.3)$): We first utilize λ, t and $D(\tilde{x}^+, \tilde{x}_i^{(k)})$ to solve $t\lambda_k D(\tilde{x}^+, \tilde{x}_i^{(k)})(k = 1,2,3)$:

Table 11.6 Deviation elements $D(\tilde{r}_j^+, \tilde{r}_{ij}^{(1)})(i=1,2,3,4,5,\ j=1,2,\ldots,10)$

	u_1	u_2	u_3	u_4	u_5
$D(\tilde{r}_j^+, \tilde{r}_{1j}^{(1)})$	$s_{2.5}$	s_1	s_3	$s_{0.5}$	s_0
$D(\tilde{r}_j^+, \tilde{r}_{2j}^{(1)})$	s_2	s_2	$s_{0.5}$	s_2	$s_{0.5}$
$D(\tilde{r}_j^+, \tilde{r}_{3j}^{(1)})$	$s_{0.5}$	s_3	s_1	s_0	s_1
$D(\tilde{r}_j^+, \tilde{r}_{4j}^{(1)})$	$s_{4.5}$	s_0	$s_{1.5}$	$s_{1.5}$	s_3
$D(\tilde{r}_j^+, \tilde{r}_{5j}^{(1)})$	s_4	$s_{1.5}$	s_2	$s_{0.5}$	$s_{0.5}$
	u_6	u_7	u_8	u_9	u_{10}
$D(\tilde{r}_j^+, \tilde{r}_{1j}^{(1)})$	$s_{2.5}$	$s_{3.5}$	$s_{2.5}$	$s_{0.5}$	s_1
$D(\tilde{r}_j^+, \tilde{r}_{2j}^{(1)})$	$s_{4.5}$	s_0	s_0	$s_{1.5}$	$s_{0.5}$
$D(\tilde{r}_j^+, \tilde{r}_{3j}^{(1)})$	s_3	s_1	$s_{0.5}$	s_2	s_0
$D(\tilde{r}_j^+, \tilde{r}_{4j}^{(1)})$	$s_{1.5}$	s_0	s_1	$s_{1.5}$	s_1
$D(\tilde{r}_j^+, \tilde{r}_{5j}^{(1)})$	s_2	$s_{3.5}$	$s_{2.5}$	$s_{0.5}$	$s_{3.5}$

Table 11.7 Deviation elements $D(\tilde{r}_j^+, \tilde{r}_{ij}^{(2)})(i=1,2,3,4,5,\ j=1,2,\ldots,10)$

	u_1	u_2	u_3	u_4	u_5
$D(\tilde{r}_j^+, \tilde{r}_{1j}^{(2)})$	s_3	s_1	$s_{3.5}$	s_1	$s_{0.5}$
$D(\tilde{r}_j^+, \tilde{r}_{2j}^{(2)})$	s_2	s_3	$s_{1.5}$	$s_{1.5}$	$s_{0.5}$
$D(\tilde{r}_j^+, \tilde{r}_{3j}^{(2)})$	$s_{0.5}$	s_4	s_2	s_0	s_0
$D(\tilde{r}_j^+, \tilde{r}_{4j}^{(2)})$	$s_{4.5}$	s_1	s_3	$s_{2.5}$	s_2
$D(\tilde{r}_j^+, \tilde{r}_{5j}^{(2)})$	s_3	s_1	s_3	$s_{0.5}$	$s_{0.5}$
	u_6	u_7	u_8	u_9	u_{10}
$D(\tilde{r}_j^+, \tilde{r}_{1j}^{(2)})$	s_2	s_4	s_3	s_1	$s_{0.5}$
$D(\tilde{r}_j^+, \tilde{r}_{2j}^{(2)})$	$s_{3.5}$	s_0	s_1	$s_{1.5}$	$s_{0.5}$
$D(\tilde{r}_j^+, \tilde{r}_{3j}^{(2)})$	s_3	s_1	$s_{0.5}$	s_2	s_1
$D(\tilde{r}_j^+, \tilde{r}_{4j}^{(2)})$	$s_{0.5}$	s_0	s_1	$s_{0.5}$	s_2
$D(\tilde{r}_j^+, \tilde{r}_{5j}^{(2)})$	s_2	$s_{2.5}$	$s_{2.5}$	$s_{1.5}$	$s_{2.5}$

Table 11.8 Deviation elements $D(\tilde{r}_j^+, \tilde{r}_{ij}^{(3)})(i = 1,2,3,4,5,\ j = 1,2,\ldots,10)$

	u_1	u_2	u_3	u_4	u_5
$D(\tilde{r}_j^+, \tilde{r}_{1j}^{(3)})$	$s_{2.5}$	s_1	s_3	$s_{0.5}$	s_0
$D(\tilde{r}_j^+, \tilde{r}_{2j}^{(3)})$	s_2	s_2	s_1	s_2	$s_{0.5}$
$D(\tilde{r}_j^+, \tilde{r}_{3j}^{(3)})$	$s_{0.5}$	s_3	s_1	s_0	s_1
$D(\tilde{r}_j^+, \tilde{r}_{4j}^{(3)})$	$s_{4.5}$	s_0	$s_{1.5}$	$s_{1.5}$	s_3
$D(\tilde{r}_j^+, \tilde{r}_{5j}^{(3)})$	s_4	$s_{1.5}$	s_2	$s_{0.5}$	$s_{0.5}$
	u_6	u_7	u_8	u_9	u_{10}
$D(\tilde{r}_j^+, \tilde{r}_{1j}^{(3)})$	$s_{2.5}$	$s_{3.5}$	$s_{2.5}$	$s_{0.5}$	s_1
$D(\tilde{r}_j^+, \tilde{r}_{2j}^{(3)})$	$s_{4.5}$	s_0	s_0	$s_{1.5}$	$s_{0.5}$
$D(\tilde{r}_j^+, \tilde{r}_{3j}^{(3)})$	s_3	s_1	$s_{1.5}$	s_2	s_0
$D(\tilde{r}_j^+, \tilde{r}_{4j}^{(3)})$	$s_{1.5}$	s_0	s_1	$s_{1.5}$	s_1
$D(\tilde{r}_j^+, \tilde{r}_{5j}^{(3)})$	s_2	$s_{3.5}$	$s_{2.5}$	$s_{0.5}$	$s_{3.5}$

$$3\lambda_1 D(\tilde{x}^+, \tilde{x}_1^{(1)}) = s_{1.846},\ 3\lambda_1 D(\tilde{x}^+, \tilde{x}_2^{(1)}) = s_{1.302},\ 3\lambda_1 D(\tilde{x}^+, \tilde{x}_3^{(1)}) = s_{1.272}$$

$$3\lambda_1 D(\tilde{x}^+, \tilde{x}_4^{(1)}) = s_{1.520},\ 3\lambda_1 D(\tilde{x}^+, \tilde{x}_5^{(1)}) = s_{2.272},\ 3\lambda_2 D(\tilde{x}^+, \tilde{x}_1^{(2)}) = s_{2.189}$$

$$3\lambda_2 D(\tilde{x}^+, \tilde{x}_2^{(2)}) = s_{1.502},\ 3\lambda_2 D(\tilde{x}^+, \tilde{x}_3^{(2)}) = s_{1.517},\ 3\lambda_2 D(\tilde{x}^+, \tilde{x}_4^{(2)}) = s_{1.727}$$

$$3\lambda_2 D(\tilde{x}^+, \tilde{x}_5^{(2)}) = s_{2.168},\ 3\lambda_3 D(\tilde{x}^+, \tilde{x}_1^{(3)}) = s_{1.790},\ 3\lambda_3 D(\tilde{x}^+, \tilde{x}_2^{(3)}) = s_{1.310}$$

$$3\lambda_3 D(\tilde{x}^+, \tilde{x}_3^{(3)}) = s_{1.234},\ 3\lambda_3 D(\tilde{x}^+, \tilde{x}_4^{(3)}) = s_{1.474},\ 3\lambda_3 D(\tilde{x}^+, \tilde{x}_5^{(3)}) = s_{2.203}$$

Then we calculate the group's deviation $D(\tilde{x}^+, \tilde{x}_i)$ between the alternative x_i and the positive ideal point $\tilde{x}^+$:

$$D(\tilde{x}^+, \tilde{x}_1) = 0.3 \times s_{2.189} \oplus 0.4 \times s_{1.846} \oplus 0.3 \times s_{1.790} = s_{1.932}$$

$$D(\tilde{x}^+, \tilde{x}_2) = 0.3 \times s_{1.502} \oplus 0.4 \times s_{1.310} \oplus 0.3 \times s_{1.302} = s_{1.365}$$

$$D(\tilde{x}^+, \tilde{x}_3) = 0.3 \times s_{1.517} \oplus 0.4 \times s_{1.272} \oplus 0.3 \times s_{1.234} = s_{1.334}$$

$$D(\tilde{x}^+, \tilde{x}_4) = 0.3 \times s_{1.727} \oplus 0.4 \times s_{1.520} \oplus 0.3 \times s_{1.474} = s_{1.568}$$

$$D(\tilde{x}^+, \tilde{x}_5) = 0.3 \times s_{2.272} \oplus 0.4 \times s_{2.203} \oplus 0.3 \times s_{2.168} = s_{2.213}$$

Step 4 Rank the alternatives $x_i (i = 1, 2, 3, 4)$ according to $D(\tilde{x}^+, \tilde{x}_i)$ $(i = 1, 2, 3, 4)$:

$$x_3 \succ x_2 \succ x_4 \succ x_1 \succ x_5$$

and thus, x_3 is the best investment regional.

11.3 MADM Method Based on UEWA Operator

11.3.1 Decision Making Method

In what follows, we introduce a MADM method based on the UEWA operator:

Step 1 For a MADM problem, let X and U be the set of alternatives and the set of attributes. The vector of attribute weights is $w = (w_1, w_2, \ldots, w_m)$, $w_j \geq 0$, $j = 1, 2, \ldots, m$, and $\sum_{j=1}^{m} w_j = 1$. The decision maker $d_k \in D$ provides the linguistic evaluation value $\tilde{r}_{ij}$ of the alternative $x_i \in X$ with respect to the attribute $u_j \in U$, and constructs the evaluation matrix $\tilde{R} = (\tilde{r}_{ij})_{n \times m}$, and $\tilde{r}_{ij} \in \tilde{S}$.

Step 2 Aggregate the linguistic evaluation information of the i th line in $\tilde{R}$ by using the UEWA operator, and get the overall evaluation value $\tilde{z}_i(w)$ of the alternative x_i:

$$\tilde{z}_i(w) = EWA_w(\tilde{r}_{i1}, \tilde{r}_{i2}, \ldots, \tilde{r}_{im}) = w_1 \tilde{r}_{i1} \oplus w_2 \tilde{r}_{i2} \oplus \cdots \oplus w_m \tilde{r}_{im}, \ i = 1, 2, \ldots, n$$

Step 3 Calculate the possibility degrees $p_{ij} = p(\tilde{z}_i(w) \geq \tilde{z}_j(w)) (i, j = 1, 2, \ldots, n)$ using Eq. (10.1) by comparing each pair of $\tilde{z}_i(w)$ $(i, j = 1, 2, \ldots, n)$, and establish the possibility degree matrix $P = (p_{ij})_{n \times n}$.

Step 4 Use Eq. (4.6) to derive the priority vector $v = (v_1, v_2, \ldots, v_n)$ of P, and then rank the alternatives $x_i (i = 1, 2, \ldots, n)$ according to the elements of $v_i (i = 1, 2, \ldots, n)$.

11.3.2 Practical Example

Example 11.3 Repair services are the essential services that the manufacturing enterprises provide for their customers, and are also the support for the specific products due to that these products require repair and maintenance. In order to achieve the management goal of a manufacturing enterprise and ensure that the repair service providers can better complete the repair services, to select and evaluate the repair service providers is a problem that the decision maker(s) of a manufacturing enterprise must face. The factors which effect the selection for repair service providers are as follows: (1) u_1: user satisfaction; (2) u_2: repair service attitude; (3) u_3: repair speed; (4) u_4: repair quality; (5) u_5: technical advisory level; (6) u_6: informatization level; (7) u_7: management level; (8) u_8: charging rationality; and (9) u_9: the scale of the company. Suppose that the weight vector of the factors $u_j (j=1,2,\ldots,9)$ is $w=(0.10,0.08,0.12,0.09,0.11,0.13,0.15,0.10,0.12)$. The decision maker utilizes the linguistic label set:

$$S=\{s_i \mid i=-5,\ldots,5\}$$

$$=\{\textit{extremely poor, very poor, rather poor, poor, slightly poor, fair,}$$

$$\textit{slightly good, good, rather good, very good, extremely good}\}$$

to evaluate the five repair service providers $x_i (i=1,2,3,4,5)$ with respect to the factors $u_j (j=1,2,\ldots,9)$, and constructs the uncertain decision matrix R (see Table 11.9):

Table 11.9 Uncertain decision matrix $\tilde{R}$

	u_1	u_2	u_3	u_4	u_5
x_1	$[s_{-1}, s_1]$	$[s_3, s_4]$	$[s_{-1}, s_0]$	$[s_3, s_4]$	$[s_1, s_3]$
x_2	$[s_0, s_2]$	$[s_0, s_1]$	$[s_3, s_4]$	$[s_1, s_3]$	$[s_3, s_4]$
x_3	$[s_1, s_2]$	$[s_0, s_3]$	$[s_1, s_3]$	$[s_1, s_2]$	$[s_0, s_2]$
x_4	$[s_1, s_2]$	$[s_3, s_5]$	$[s_2, s_3]$	$[s_1, s_3]$	$[s_1, s_2]$
x_5	$[s_0, s_2]$	$[s_2, s_3]$	$[s_1, s_3]$	$[s_2, s_4]$	$[s_1, s_3]$
	u_6	u_7	u_8	u_9	
x_1	$[s_1, s_3]$	$[s_0, s_2]$	$[s_1, s_2]$	$[s_0, s_3]$	
x_2	$[s_1, s_3]$	$[s_3, s_4]$	$[s_2, s_4]$	$[s_2, s_4]$	
x_3	$[s_{-1}, s_1]$	$[s_1, s_3]$	$[s_3, s_4]$	$[s_1, s_4]$	
x_4	$[s_4, s_5]$	$[s_2, s_4]$	$[s_2, s_3]$	$[s_2, s_3]$	
x_5	$[s_2, s_3]$	$[s_0, s_2]$	$[s_1, s_3]$	$[s_2, s_4]$	

Below we give the solution process of the problem by using method of Sect. 11.3.1:

Step 1 Aggregate the linguistic evaluation information of the i th line in R using the UEWA operator, and get the overall attribute evaluation value $\tilde{z}_i(w)$:

$$\begin{aligned} z_1(w) = & 0.10\times[s_{-1},s_1]\oplus 0.08\times[s_3,s_4]\oplus 0.12\times[s_{-1},s_0]\oplus 0.09\times[s_3,s_4] \\ & \oplus 0.11\times[s_1,s_3]\oplus 0.13\times[s_1,s_3]\oplus 0.15\times[s_1,s_2]\oplus 0.10\times[s_1,s_2] \\ & \oplus 0.12\times[s_0,s_3]=[s_{0.78},s_{2.36}] \end{aligned}$$

$$\begin{aligned} z_2(w) = & 0.10\times[s_0,s_2]\oplus 0.08\times[s_0,s_1]\oplus 0.12\times[s_3,s_4]\oplus 0.09\times[s_1,s_3] \\ & \oplus 0.11\times[s_3,s_4]\oplus 0.13\times[s_1,s_3]\oplus 0.15\times[s_3,s_4]\oplus 0.10\times[s_2,s_4] \\ & \oplus 0.12\times[s_2,s_4]=[s_{1.80},s_{3.34}] \end{aligned}$$

$$\begin{aligned} z_3(w) = & 0.10\times[s_1,s_2]\oplus 0.08\times[s_0,s_3]\oplus 0.12\times[s_1,s_3]\oplus 0.09\times[s_1,s_2] \\ & \oplus 0.11\times[s_0,s_2]\oplus 0.13\times[s_{-1},s_1]\oplus 0.15\times[s_1,s_3]\oplus 0.10\times[s_3,s_4] \\ & \oplus 0.12\times[s_1,s_4]=[s_{0.75},s_{2.66}] \end{aligned}$$

$$\begin{aligned} z_4(w) = & 0.10\times[s_1,s_2]\oplus 0.08\times[s_3,s_5]\oplus 0.12\times[s_2,s_3]\oplus 0.09\times[s_1,s_3] \\ & \oplus 0.11\times[s_1,s_2]\oplus 0.13\times[s_4,s_5]\oplus 0.15\times[s_2,s_4]\oplus 0.10\times[s_2,s_3] \\ & \oplus 0.12\times[s_2,s_3]=[s_{2.04},s_{2.36}] \end{aligned}$$

$$\begin{aligned} z_5(w) = & 0.10\times[s_0,s_2]\oplus 0.08\times[s_2,s_3]\oplus 0.12\times[s_1,s_3]\oplus 0.09\times[s_2,s_4] \\ & \oplus 0.11\times[s_1,s_2]\oplus 0.13\times[s_2,s_3]\oplus 0.15\times[s_0,s_2]\oplus 0.10\times[s_1,s_3] \\ & \oplus 0.12\times[s_2,s_4]=[s_{1.17},s_{2.96}] \end{aligned}$$

Step 2 Calculate the possibility degrees $p_{ij} = p(\tilde{z}_i(w)\geq \tilde{z}_j(w))(i,j=1,2,3,4,5)$ using Eq. (10.1), and establish the possibility degree matrix:

$$P=\begin{pmatrix} 0.5 & 0.1795 & 0.4613 & 0.1103 & 0.3531 \\ 0.8205 & 0.5 & 0.7507 & 0.4545 & 0.6517 \\ 0.5387 & 0.2493 & 0.5 & 0.1920 & 0.4027 \\ 0.8897 & 0.5455 & 0.8080 & 0.5 & 0.7042 \\ 0.6469 & 0.3483 & 0.5973 & 0.2958 & 0.5 \end{pmatrix}$$

Step 3 Use Eq. (4.6) to derive the priority vector of P:

$$v = (0.1552, 0.2339, 0.1691, 0.2474, 0.1944)$$

and then rank the alternatives $x_i (i = 1, 2, 3, 4, 5)$ according to the elements of $v_i (i = 1, 2, 3, 4, 5)$:

$$x_4 \succ x_2 \succ x_5 \succ x_3 \succ x_1$$

from which we get the best repair service provider x_4.

11.4 MAGDM Method Based on UEWA and ULHA Operators

11.4.1 Decision Making Method

Below we introduce a MAGDM method based on the UEWA and ULHA operators [122]:

Step 1 For a MADM problem, let X, U and D be the set of alternatives, the set of attributes, and the set of decision makers. The weight vector of attributes is $w = (w_1, w_2, \ldots, w_m)$, $w_j \geq 0$, $j = 1, 2, \ldots, n$, and $\sum_{j=1}^{m} w_j = 1$. The weight vector of the decision makers is $\lambda = (\lambda_1, \lambda_2, \ldots, \lambda_t)$, $\lambda_k \geq 0$, $k = 1, 2, \ldots, t$, and $\sum_{k=1}^{t} \lambda_k = 1$. The decision maker $d_k \in D$ provides the uncertain linguistic evaluation value $\tilde{r}_{ij}^{(k)}$ of the alternative $x_i \in X$ with respect to the attribute $u_j \in U$, and constructs the uncertain linguistic decision matrix $\tilde{R}_k = (\tilde{r}_{ij}^{(k)})_{n \times m}$, and $\tilde{r}_{ij}^{(k)} \in \tilde{S}$.

Step 2 Utilize the UEWA operator to aggregate the uncertain linguistic evaluation information of the i th line in $\tilde{R}_k$, and get the overall attribute value $\tilde{z}_i^{(k)}(w)$ of the alternative x_i corresponding to the decision maker d_k:

$$\tilde{z}_i^{(k)}(w) = UEWA_w(\tilde{r}_{i1}^{(k)}, \tilde{r}_{i2}^{(k)}, \ldots, \tilde{r}_{in}^{(k)}) = w_1 \tilde{r}_{i1}^{(k)} \oplus w_2 \tilde{r}_{i2}^{(k)} \oplus \ldots \oplus w_m \tilde{r}_{im}^{(k)})$$

Step 3 Aggregate the overall attribute values $\tilde{z}_i^{(k)}(w)$ $(k = 1, 2, \ldots, t)$ of the alternative x_i corresponding to the decision makers $d_k (k = 1, 2, \ldots, t)$ by using the ULHA operator, and then get the group's overall attribute value $z_i(\lambda, \omega')$ of the alternative x_i:

$$\tilde{z}_i(\lambda,\omega') = ULHA_{\lambda,\omega'}(\tilde{z}_i^{(1)}(w),\tilde{z}_i^{(2)}(w),\ldots,\tilde{z}_i^{(t)}(w)) = \omega_1'\tilde{v}_i^{(1)} \oplus \omega_2'\tilde{v}_i^{(2)} \oplus \cdots \oplus \omega_t'\tilde{v}_i^{(t)}$$

where $\omega' = (\omega_1', \omega_2', ..., \omega_t')$ is the weighting vector associated with the ULHA operator, $\omega_k' \in [0,1]$, $k = 1,2,...,t$, and $\sum_{k=1}^{t} \omega_k' = 1$, $\tilde{v}_i^{(k)}$ is the kth largest of a collection of the weighted uncertain linguistic variables $(t\lambda_1\tilde{z}_i^{(1)}(w), t\lambda_2\tilde{z}_i^{(2)}(w), \ldots, t\lambda_t\tilde{z}_i^{(t)}(w))$, and t is the balancing coefficient.

Step 4 Calculate the possibility degrees

$$p_{ij} = p(\tilde{z}_i(\lambda,\omega') \geq \tilde{z}_j(\lambda,\omega')),\ i,j = 1,2,\ldots,n$$

using Eq. (10.1) by comparing each pair of $\tilde{z}_i(\lambda,\omega')(i=1,2,\ldots,n)$, and construct the possibility degree matrix $P = (p_{ij})_{n\times n}$.

Step 5 Use Eq. (4.6) to derive the priority vector $v = (v_1, v_2, \ldots, v_n)$ of P, and then rank and select the alternatives $x_i (i = 1,2,\ldots,n)$.

11.4.2 Practical Example

Example 11.4 Here we use Example 11.2 to illustrate the method of Sect. 11.4.1. Suppose that three evaluators $d_k (k = 1,2,3)$ (whose weight vector is $\lambda = (0.35, 0.33, 0.32)$) give the uncertain linguistic decision matrices $\tilde{R}_k (k = 1, 2, 3)$ (see Tables 11.10, 11.11, and 11.12).

Step 1 Aggregate the linguistic evaluation information of the i th line in $\tilde{R}_k$ using the UEWA operator, and get the overall attribute evaluation value $\tilde{z}_i^{(k)}(w)$ of the alternative x_i corresponding to the decision maker d_k:

Table 11.10 Uncertain linguistic decision matrix $\tilde{R}_1$

	u_1	u_2	u_3	u_4	u_5
x_1	$[s_0, s_2]$	$[s_3, s_4]$	$[s_{-2}, s_0]$	$[s_2, s_4]$	$[s_2, s_3]$
x_2	$[s_0, s_3]$	$[s_0, s_2]$	$[s_3, s_5]$	$[s_1, s_4]$	$[s_2, s_4]$
x_3	$[s_1, s_3]$	$[s_2, s_4]$	$[s_2, s_4]$	$[s_1, s_3]$	$[s_0, s_1]$
x_4	$[s_0, s_2]$	$[s_3, s_4]$	$[s_2, s_4]$	$[s_2, s_3]$	$[s_0, s_2]$
x_5	$[s_{-1}, s_2]$	$[s_1, s_3]$	$[s_2, s_3]$	$[s_3, s_4]$	$[s_1, s_2]$
	u_6	u_7	u_8	u_9	
x_1	$[s_2, s_3]$	$[s_0, s_1]$	$[s_1, s_3]$	$[s_0, s_1]$	
x_2	$[s_1, s_2]$	$[s_2, s_3]$	$[s_1, s_4]$	$[s_2, s_3]$	
x_3	$[s_{-1}, s_0]$	$[s_1, s_3]$	$[s_1, s_3]$	$[s_1, s_2]$	
x_4	$[s_3, s_4]$	$[s_2, s_3]$	$[s_1, s_3]$	$[s_2, s_4]$	
x_5	$[s_1, s_2]$	$[s_0, s_3]$	$[s_1, s_2]$	$[s_3, s_5]$	

Table 11.11 Uncertain linguistic decision matrix $\tilde{R}_2$

	u_1	u_2	u_3	u_4	u_5
x_1	$[s_{-1}, s_0]$	$[s_2, s_3]$	$[s_{-1}, s_1]$	$[s_2, s_3]$	$[s_1, s_2]$
x_2	$[s_0, s_1]$	$[s_0, s_2]$	$[s_2, s_3]$	$[s_1, s_2]$	$[s_2, s_3]$
x_3	$[s_0, s_2]$	$[s_0, s_1]$	$[s_1, s_2]$	$[s_1, s_3]$	$[s_0, s_1]$
x_4	$[s_1, s_3]$	$[s_3, s_4]$	$[s_1, s_2]$	$[s_2, s_3]$	$[s_1, s_2]$
x_5	$[s_0, s_1]$	$[s_2, s_4]$	$[s_1, s_2]$	$[s_3, s_4]$	$[s_1, s_4]$
	u_6	u_7	u_8	u_9	
x_1	$[s_2, s_3]$	$[s_0, s_1]$	$[s_1, s_3]$	$[s_0, s_1]$	
x_2	$[s_1, s_2]$	$[s_2, s_3]$	$[s_1, s_4]$	$[s_2, s_3]$	
x_3	$[s_{-1}, s_0]$	$[s_1, s_3]$	$[s_1, s_3]$	$[s_1, s_2]$	
x_4	$[s_3, s_4]$	$[s_2, s_3]$	$[s_1, s_3]$	$[s_2, s_4]$	
x_5	$[s_1, s_2]$	$[s_0, s_3]$	$[s_1, s_2]$	$[s_3, s_5]$	

Table 11.12 Uncertain linguistic decision matrix $\tilde{R}_3$

	u_1	u_2	u_3	u_4	u_5
x_1	$[s_1, s_2]$	$[s_3, s_4]$	$[s_2, s_3]$	$[s_1, s_2]$	$[s_2, s_3]$
x_2	$[s_2, s_4]$	$[s_0, s_1]$	$[s_3, s_4]$	$[s_2, s_4]$	$[s_1, s_2]$
x_3	$[s_{-1}, s_1]$	$[s_2, s_3]$	$[s_{-1}, s_1]$	$[s_3, s_4]$	$[s_1, s_3]$
x_4	$[s_3, s_4]$	$[s_3, s_4]$	$[s_2, s_3]$	$[s_0, s_2]$	$[s_2, s_3]$
x_5	$[s_{-1}, s_1]$	$[s_3, s_4]$	$[s_0, s_1]$	$[s_3, s_5]$	$[s_3, s_4]$
	u_6	u_7	u_8	u_9	
x_1	$[s_2, s_4]$	$[s_0, s_2]$	$[s_1, s_2]$	$[s_2, s_3]$	
x_2	$[s_1, s_3]$	$[s_1, s_2]$	$[s_3, s_4]$	$[s_3, s_4]$	
x_3	$[s_2, s_3]$	$[s_0, s_1]$	$[s_3, s_5]$	$[s_2, s_4]$	
x_4	$[s_2, s_3]$	$[s_3, s_4]$	$[s_2, s_4]$	$[s_0, s_3]$	
x_5	$[s_{-1}, s_0]$	$[s_1, s_2]$	$[s_2, s_3]$	$[s_2, s_4]$	

$$\tilde{z}_1^{(1)}(w) = 0.1\times[s_0,s_2]\oplus 0.08\times[s_3,s_4]\oplus 0.12\times[s_{-2},s_0]\oplus 0.09\times[s_2,s_4]$$

$$\oplus 0.11\times[s_2,s_3]\oplus 0.13\times[s_1,s_2]\oplus 0.15\times[s_0,s_1]\oplus 0.10\times[s_1,s_3]$$

$$\oplus 0.12\times[s_1,s_2] = [s_{0.75}, s_{2.16}]$$

Similarly, we have

$$\tilde{z}_2^{(1)}(w) = [s_{1.64}, s_{2.33}],\ \tilde{z}_3^{(1)}(w) = [s_{1.16}, s_{2.55}],\ \tilde{z}_4^{(1)}(w) = [s_{1.79}, s_{3.34}]$$

$$\tilde{z}_5^{(1)}(w)=[s_{1.07},s_{2.48}],\ \tilde{z}_1^{(2)}(w)=[s_{0.59},s_{1.81}],\ \tilde{z}_2^{(2)}(w)=[s_{1.32},s_{2.60}]$$

$$\tilde{z}_3^{(2)}(w)=[s_{0.45},s_{1.89}],\ \tilde{z}_4^{(2)}(w)=[s_{1.78},s_{3.10}],\ \tilde{z}_5^{(2)}(w)=[s_{1.25},s_{2.97}]$$

$$\tilde{z}_1^{(3)}(w)=[s_{1.49},s_{2.77}],\ \tilde{z}_2^{(3)}(w)=[s_{1.79},s_{3.11}],\ \tilde{z}_3^{(3)}(w)=[s_{1.12},s_{2.67}]$$

$$\tilde{z}_4^{(3)}(w)=[s_{1.91},s_{3.34}],\ \tilde{z}_5^{(3)}(w)=[s_{1.20},s_{2.51}]$$

Step 2 Aggregate the overall attribute evaluation values $\tilde{z}_i^{(k)}(w)(k=1,2,3)$ of the alternative x_i corresponding to the decision makers $d_k(k=1,2,3)$ by using the ULHA operator (suppose that its associated weighting vector is $w=(0.3,0.4,0.3)$). We first utilize λ, t and $\tilde{z}_i^{(k)}(w)$ to calculate $t\lambda_k\tilde{z}_i^{(k)}(w)$:

$$3\lambda_1\tilde{z}_1^{(1)}(w)=[s_{0.788},s_{2.268}],\ 3\lambda_1\tilde{z}_2^{(1)}(w)=[s_{1.722},s_{2.447}],\ 3\lambda_1\tilde{z}_3^{(1)}(w)=[s_{1.218},s_{2.678}]$$

$$3\lambda_1\tilde{z}_4^{(1)}(w)=[s_{1.880},s_{3.507}],\ 3\lambda_1\tilde{z}_5^{(1)}(w)=[s_{1.124},s_{2.604}],\ 3\lambda_2\tilde{z}_1^{(2)}(w)=[s_{0.584},s_{1.792}]$$

$$3\lambda_2\tilde{z}_2^{(2)}(w)=[s_{1.307},s_{2.574}],\ 3\lambda_2\tilde{z}_3^{(2)}(w)=[s_{0.446},s_{1.871}],\ 3\lambda_2\tilde{z}_4^{(2)}(w)=[s_{1.762},s_{3.069}]$$

$$3\lambda_2\tilde{z}_5^{(2)}(w)=[s_{1.238},s_{2.940}],\ 3\lambda_3\tilde{z}_1^{(3)}(w)=[s_{1.401},s_{2.604}],\ 3\lambda_3\tilde{z}_2^{(3)}(w)=[s_{1.683},s_{2.923}]$$

$$3\lambda_3\tilde{z}_3^{(3)}(w)=[s_{1.053},s_{2.510}],\ 3\lambda_3\tilde{z}_4^{(3)}(w)=[s_{1.795},s_{2.510}],\ 3\lambda_3\tilde{z}_5^{(3)}(w)=[s_{1.128},s_{2.360}]$$

by which we get the group's overall attribute evaluation values $\tilde{z}_i(\lambda,\omega)(i=1,2,3,4,5)$:

$$\begin{aligned}\tilde{z}_1(\lambda,\omega)&=0.3\times[s_{1.401},s_{2.604}]\oplus 0.4\times[s_{0.788},s_{2.268}]\\&\oplus 0.3\times[s_{0.584},s_{1.792}]=[s_{0.9107},s_{2.2260}]\end{aligned}$$

$$\begin{aligned}\tilde{z}_2(\lambda,\omega)&=0.3\times[s_{1.683},s_{2.923}]\oplus 0.4\times[s_{1.722},s_{2.447}]\\&\oplus 0.3\times[s_{1.307},s_{2.574}]=[s_{1.5858},s_{2.6279}]\end{aligned}$$

$$\begin{aligned}\tilde{z}_3(\lambda,\omega)&=0.3\times[s_{1.218},s_{2.678}]\oplus 0.4\times[s_{1.053},s_{2.510}]\\&\oplus 0.3\times[s_{0.446},s_{1.871}]=[s_{0.9204},s_{2.3687}]\end{aligned}$$

$$\tilde{z}_3(\lambda,\omega) = 0.3\times[s_{1.880}, s_{3.507}]\oplus 0.4\times[s_{1.762}, s_{3.069}] \oplus 0.3\times[s_{1.795}, s_{2.510}] = [s_{1.8073}, s_{3.0327}]$$

$$\tilde{z}_5(\lambda,\omega) = 0.3\times[s_{1.238}, s_{2.940}]\oplus 0.4\times[s_{1.124}, s_{2.604}] \oplus 0.3\times[s_{1.128}, s_{2.359}] = [s_{1.1594}, s_{2.6313}]$$

Step 3 Calculate the possibility degrees $p_{ij} = p(\tilde{z}_i(\lambda,\omega) \geq \tilde{z}_j(\lambda,\omega))$ $(i, j = 1,2,3,4)$ using Eq. (10.1), and construct the possibility degree matrix:

$$P = \begin{pmatrix} 0.5 & 0.2716 & 0.4724 & 0.1648 & 0.3827 \\ 0.7284 & 0.5 & 0.6856 & 0.3295 & 0.5841 \\ 0.5276 & 0.3144 & 0.5 & 0.2100 & 0.4141 \\ 0.8352 & 0.6705 & 0.7900 & 0.5 & 0.6945 \\ 0.6173 & 0.4159 & 0.5859 & 0.3055 & 0.5 \end{pmatrix}$$

Step 4 Derive the priority vector of P from Eq. (4.6):

$$v = (0.1646, 0.2164, 0.1733, 0.2495, 0.1962)$$

based on which we rank the alternatives $x_i (i = 1,2,3,4,5)$:

$$x_4 \succ x_2 \succ x_5 \succ x_3 \succ x_1$$

and thus, x_3 is the best investment regional.

Chapter 12
Uncertain Linguistic MADM Method with Interval Weight Information

In this chapter, we first introduce the concept of interval aggregation (IA) operator, and then introduce a MADM method based on the IA operator, and a MAGDM method based on the IA and ULHA operators. We also give their application to the evaluation of socio-economic systems.

12.1 MADM Method Based on IA Operator

12.1.1 Decision Making Method

Let $\tilde{\eta}=[\eta^L,\eta^U]$ and $\tilde{\mu}=[s_a,s_b]$ be an interval number and an uncertain linguistic variable. We first define the following operational laws [122]:

$$\tilde{\eta}\otimes\tilde{\mu}=[\eta^L,\eta^U]\otimes[s_a,s_b]=[s_{a'},s_{b'}]$$

where

$$a'=\min\{\eta^L a,\eta^L b,\eta^U a,\eta^U b\},\ b'=\max\{\eta^L a,\eta^L b,\eta^U a,\eta^U b\}$$

Definition 12.1 [122] Let $(\tilde{w}_1,\tilde{w}_2,\ldots,\tilde{w}_n)$ be a collection of interval numbers and $(\tilde{\mu}_1,\tilde{\mu}_2,\ldots,\tilde{\mu}_n)$ be a collection of uncertain linguistic variables, where $\tilde{w}_j=[w_j^L,w_j^U]$, $w_j^L,w_j^U\in R^+$, $\tilde{\mu}_j=[s_{\alpha_j},s_{\beta_j}]$, $s_{\alpha_j},s_{\beta_j}\in\bar{S}$, $j=1,2,\ldots,n$. Then

Z.S. Xu, *Uncertain Multi-Attribute Decision Making*,
DOI 10.1007/978-3-662-45640-8_12

$$IA_{\tilde{w}}(\tilde{\mu}_1, \tilde{\mu}_2, \ldots, \tilde{\mu}_n) = \tilde{w}_1 \otimes \tilde{\mu}_1 \oplus \tilde{w}_2 \otimes \tilde{\mu}_2 \oplus \cdots \oplus \tilde{w}_n \otimes \tilde{\mu}_n$$

is called the interval aggregation (IA) operator.

Below we introduce a MADM method based on the IA operator [122]:

Step 1 For a MADM problem, let X and U be the set of alternatives and the set of attributes. The weight information about attributes is expressed in interval numbers, i.e., $\tilde{w}_j = [w_j^L, w_j^U]$, $w_j^L, w_j^U \in \Re^+$, and let $\tilde{w} = (\tilde{w}_1, \tilde{w}_2, \ldots, \tilde{w}_m)$. The decision maker provides the uncertain linguistic evaluation value $\tilde{r}_{ij}$ of the alternative x_i with respect to the attribute $u_j \in U$, and constructs the uncertain linguistic decision matrix $\tilde{R} = (\tilde{r}_{ij})_{n\times m}$, and $\tilde{r}_{ij} \in \tilde{S}$.

Step 2 Aggregate the linguistic evaluation information of the i th line in $\tilde{R}$ using the IA operator, and get the overall attribute evaluation value $\tilde{z}_i(\tilde{w})$ of the alternative x_i:

$$\tilde{z}_i(\tilde{w}) = IA_{\tilde{w}}(\tilde{r}_{i1}, \tilde{r}_{i2}, \ldots, \tilde{r}_{im}) = \tilde{w}_1\tilde{r}_{i1} \oplus \tilde{w}_2\tilde{r}_{i2} \oplus \cdots \oplus \tilde{w}_m\tilde{r}_{im}$$

Step 3 Calculate the possibility degrees $p_{ij} = p(\tilde{z}_i(\tilde{w}) \geq \tilde{z}_j(\tilde{w}))(i, j = 1, 2, \ldots, n)$ using Eq. (10.1) by comparing each pair of $\tilde{z}_i(\tilde{w})(i = 1, 2, \ldots, n)$, and construct the possibility degree matrix $P = (p_{ij})_{n\times n}$.

Step 4 Use Eq. (4.6) to derive the priority vector $v = (v_1, v_2, \ldots, v_n)$ of P, and then rank and select the alternatives $x_i(i = 1, 2, \ldots, n)$.

12.1.2 Practical Example

Example 12.1 The evaluation of socio-economic systems, such as the evaluation of investment environment, the effectiveness of reform measures and urban planning program, etc., involves the political, economic, technological, ecological and cultural aspects. Considering the complexity of this type of decision making problems, the decision information provided by the decision maker is usually uncertain or fuzzy. Here, we consider an investment decision making problem, in which there are five cities $x_i(i = 1, 2, 3, 4, 5)$, the evaluation indices (attributes) used to evaluate the cities are as follows [57]: (1) u_1: political environment; (2) u_2: economic environment; (3) u_3: financial environment; (4) u_4: administrative environment; (5) u_5: market environment; (6) u_6: technical condition; (7) u_7: material basis; (8) u_8: legal environment; and (9) u_9: natural environment. Suppose that the weight information on the evaluation indices is expressed in interval numbers, i.e.,

$$\tilde{w}_1 = [0.08, 0.10],\ \tilde{w}_2 = [0.05, 0.09],\ \tilde{w}_3 = [0.10, 0.12]$$

Table 12.1 Uncertain linguistic decision matrix $\tilde{R}$

	u_1	u_2	u_3	u_4	u_5
x_1	$[s_1, s_2]$	$[s_2, s_3]$	$[s_2, s_3]$	$[s_2, s_3]$	$[s_0, s_1]$
x_2	$[s_0, s_3]$	$[s_{-1}, s_1]$	$[s_2, s_3]$	$[s_0, s_1]$	$[s_2, s_4]$
x_3	$[s_0, s_1]$	$[s_0, s_2]$	$[s_1, s_2]$	$[s_0, s_1]$	$[s_1, s_3]$
x_4	$[s_0, s_1]$	$[s_2, s_3]$	$[s_1, s_2]$	$[s_2, s_3]$	$[s_0, s_2]$
x_5	$[s_0, s_1]$	$[s_0, s_3]$	$[s_1, s_4]$	$[s_1, s_2]$	$[s_1, s_4]$
	u_6	u_7	u_8	u_9	
x_1	$[s_2, s_3]$	$[s_{-1}, s_2]$	$[s_2, s_3]$	$[s_2, s_3]$	
x_2	$[s_2, s_3]$	$[s_2, s_3]$	$[s_3, s_4]$	$[s_1, s_2]$	
x_3	$[s_0, s_2]$	$[s_2, s_3]$	$[s_2, s_3]$	$[s_1, s_2]$	
x_4	$[s_1, s_2]$	$[s_3, s_4]$	$[s_1, s_3]$	$[s_0, s_2]$	
x_5	$[s_1, s_2]$	$[s_0, s_1]$	$[s_0, s_2]$	$[s_2, s_3]$	

$$\tilde{w}_4 = [0.08, 0.11],\ \tilde{w}_5 = [0.10, 0.13],\ \tilde{w}_6 = [0.12, 0.14]$$

$$\tilde{w}_7 = [0.14, 0.16],\ \tilde{w}_8 = [0.09, 0.11],\ \tilde{w}_{10} = [0.11, 0.15]$$

The decision maker employs the additive linguistic evaluation scale:

$$\begin{aligned} S &= \{s_i \mid i = -5, \ldots, 5\} \\ &= \{\textit{extremely poor}, \textit{very poor}, \textit{rather poor}, \textit{poor}, \textit{slightly poor}, \textit{fair}, \\ &\quad \textit{slightly good}, \textit{good}, \textit{rather good}, \textit{very good}, \textit{extremely good}\} \end{aligned}$$

to evaluate the investment environments of the cities $x_i (i = 1, 2, 3, 4, 5)$ according to the evaluation indices $u_j (j = 1, 2, \ldots, 9)$, and constructs the linguistic decision matrix $\tilde{R}$ (see Table 12.1).

In the following, we solve the problem using the method of Sect. 12.1.1:

Step1 Aggregate the linguistic evaluation information of the i th line in $\tilde{R}$ using the IA operator, and get the overall attribute evaluation value $\tilde{z}_i(\tilde{w})$ of the alternative x_i:

$$\begin{aligned} \tilde{z}_1(\tilde{w}) = {} & [0.08, 0.10] \otimes [s_1, s_2] \oplus [0.05, 0.09] \otimes [s_2, s_3] \\ & \oplus [0.10, 0.12] \otimes [s_1, s_2] \oplus [0.08, 0.11] \otimes [s_2, s_3] \\ & \oplus [0.10, 0.13] \otimes [s_0, s_1] \oplus [0.12, 0.14] \otimes [s_2, s_3] \\ & \oplus [0.14, 0.16] \otimes [s_{-1}, s_2] \oplus [0.09, 0.11] \otimes [s_2, s_3] \\ & \oplus [0.11, 0.15] \otimes [s_2, s_3] = [s_{0.94}, s_{2.69}] \end{aligned}$$

$$\begin{aligned}\tilde{z}_2(\tilde{w}) = & [0.08,0.10]\otimes[s_0,s_3]\oplus[0.05,0.09]\otimes[s_{-1},s_1] \\ & \oplus[0.10,0.12]\otimes[s_2,s_3]\oplus[0.08,0.11]\otimes[s_0,s_1] \\ & \oplus[0.10,0.13]\otimes[s_2,s_4]\oplus[0.12,0.14]\otimes[s_2,s_3] \\ & \oplus[0.14,0.16]\otimes[s_2,s_3]\oplus[0.09,0.11]\otimes[s_3,s_4] \\ & \oplus[0.11,0.15]\otimes[s_1,s_2] = [s_{1.25},s_{2.92}]\end{aligned}$$

$$\begin{aligned}\tilde{z}_3(\tilde{w}) = & [0.08,0.10]\otimes[s_0,s_1]\oplus[0.05,0.09]\otimes[s_0,s_2] \\ & \oplus[0.10,0.12]\otimes[s_1,s_2]\oplus[0.08,0.11]\otimes[s_0,s_1] \\ & \oplus[0.10,0.13]\otimes[s_1,s_3]\oplus[0.12,0.14]\otimes[s_0,s_2] \\ & \oplus[0.14,0.16]\otimes[s_2,s_3]\oplus[0.09,0.11]\otimes[s_2,s_3] \\ & \oplus[0.11,0.15]\otimes[s_1,s_2] = [s_{0.77},s_{2.41}]\end{aligned}$$

$$\begin{aligned}\tilde{z}_4(\tilde{w}) = & [0.08,0.10]\otimes[s_0,s_1]\oplus[0.05,0.09]\otimes[s_2,s_3] \\ & \oplus[0.10,0.12]\otimes[s_1,s_2]\oplus[0.08,0.11]\otimes[s_2,s_3] \\ & \oplus[0.10,0.13]\otimes[s_0,s_2]\oplus[0.12,0.14]\otimes[s_1,s_2] \\ & \oplus[0.14,0.16]\otimes[s_3,s_4]\oplus[0.09,0.11]\otimes[s_1,s_3] \\ & \oplus[0.11,0.15]\otimes[s_0,s_2] = [s_{1.05},s_{2.75}]\end{aligned}$$

Step 2 Calculate the possibility degrees $p_{ij} = p(\tilde{z}_i(\tilde{w}) \geq \tilde{z}_j(\tilde{w}))(i,j=1,2,3,4,5)$ using Eq. (10.1) by comparing each pair of $\tilde{z}_i(\tilde{w})(i=1,2,3,4,5)$, and construct the possibility degree matrix:

$$P = \begin{pmatrix} 0.5 & 0.4211 & 0.5664 & 0.4754 & 0.5405 \\ 0.5789 & 0.5 & 0.6495 & 0.5549 & 0.6133 \\ 0.4336 & 0.3505 & 0.5 & 0.4072 & 0.4812 \\ 0.5246 & 0.4451 & 0.5928 & 0.5 & 0.5635 \\ 0.4595 & 0.3867 & 0.5188 & 0.4365 & 0.5 \end{pmatrix}$$

Step 3 Use Eq. (4.6) to derive the priority vector of P:

$$v = (0.2002, 0.2198, 0.1836, 0.2063, 0.1901)$$

based on which we rank the alternatives $x_i (i=1,2,3,4,5)$:

$$x_2 \succ x_4 \succ x_1 \succ x_5 \succ x_3$$

from which we know that x_2 is the best one.

12.2 MAGDM Method Based on IA and ULHA Operators

12.2.1 Decision Making Method

In what follows, we introduce a MAGDM method based on the IA and ULHA operators [122]:

Step 1 For a MADM problem, let X, U and D be the set of alternatives, the set of attributes, and the set of decision makers. The weights of attributes are interval numbers $\tilde{w}_j = [w_j^L, w_j^U]$, $w_j^L, w_j^U \in \Re^+$, and let $\tilde{w} = (\tilde{w}_1, \tilde{w}_2, \ldots, \tilde{w}_m)$. The weight vector of the decision makers is $\lambda = (\lambda_1, \lambda_2, \ldots, \lambda_t)$, $\lambda_k \geq 0, k = 1, 2, \ldots, t$, and $\sum_{k=1}^{t} \lambda_k = 1$. The decision maker $d_k \in D$ provides the uncertain linguistic evaluation value $\tilde{r}_{ij}^{(k)}$ of the alternative $x_i \in X$ with respect to the attribute $u_j \in U$, and constructs the evaluation matrix $\tilde{R}_k = (\tilde{r}_{ij}^{(k)})_{n \times m}$, and $\tilde{r}_{ij}^{(k)} \in \tilde{S}(i = 1, 2, \ldots, n,\ k = 1, 2, \ldots, t)$.

Step 2 Utilize the IA operator to aggregate the uncertain linguistic evaluation information of the i th line in $\tilde{R}_k$, and get the overall attribute value $\tilde{z}_i^{(k)}(\tilde{w})$ of the alternative x_i corresponding to the decision maker d_k:

$$\tilde{z}_i^{(k)}(\tilde{w}) = IA_{\tilde{w}}(\tilde{r}_{i1}^{(k)}, \tilde{r}_{i2}^{(k)}, \ldots, \tilde{r}_{im}^{(k)}) = \tilde{w}_1 \tilde{r}_{i1}^{(k)} \oplus \tilde{w}_2 \tilde{r}_{i2}^{(k)} \oplus \ldots \oplus \tilde{w}_m \tilde{r}_{im}^{(k)}$$

Step 3 Aggregate the overall attribute values $\tilde{z}_i^{(k)}(\tilde{w})$ $(k = 1, 2, \ldots, t)$ of the alternative x_i corresponding to the decision makers $d_k\ (k = 1, 2, \ldots, t)$ by using the ULHA operator, and then get the group's overall attribute value $z_i(\lambda, \omega)$ of the alternative x_i:

$$\tilde{z}_i(\lambda, \omega) = ULHA_{\lambda,\omega}(\tilde{z}_i^{(1)}(\tilde{w}), \tilde{z}_i^{(2)}(\tilde{w}), \ldots, \tilde{z}_i^{(t)}(\tilde{w})) = \omega_1 \tilde{v}_i^{(1)} \oplus \omega_2 \tilde{v}_i^{(2)} \oplus \cdots \oplus \omega_t \tilde{v}_i^{(t)}$$

where $\omega = (\omega_1, \omega_2, \ldots, \omega_t)$ is the weighting vector associated with the ULHA operator, $\omega_k \in [0,1]$, $k = 1, 2, \ldots, t$, $\sum_{k=1}^{t} \omega_k = 1$, $\tilde{v}_i^{(k)}$ is the k th largest of a collection of the weighted uncertain linguistic variables $(t\lambda_1 \tilde{z}_i^{(1)}(\tilde{w}), t\lambda_2 \tilde{z}_i^{(2)}(\tilde{w}), \ldots, t\lambda_t \tilde{z}_i^{(t)}(\tilde{w}))$, and t is the balancing coefficient.

Step 4 Calculate the possibility degrees $p_{ij} = p(\tilde{z}_i(\lambda,\omega) \geq \tilde{z}_j(\lambda,\omega))\,(i,j=1,2,\ldots,n)$ using Eq. (10.1) by comparing each pair of $\tilde{z}_i(\lambda,\omega)(i=1,2,\ \ldots,n)$, and construct the possibility degree matrix $P=(p_{ij})_{n\times n}$.

Step 5 Use Eq. (4.6) to derive the priority vector $v=(v_1,v_2,\ldots,v_n)$ of P, and then rank and select the alternatives $x_i(i=1,2,\ldots,n)$.

12.2.2 Practical Example

Example 12.2 Here we use Example 12.1 to illustrate the method of Sect. 12.2.1. Suppose that three decision makers $d_k(k=1,2,3)$ (whose weight vector is $\lambda=(0.34,0.33,0.33)$) give the uncertain linguistic decision matrices $\tilde{R}_k(k=1,2,3)$ (see Tables 12.2, 12.3, and 12.4).

Step1 Aggregate the linguistic evaluation information of the i th line in $\tilde{R}_k$ using the IA operator, and get the overall attribute evaluation value $\tilde{z}_i^{(k)}(\tilde{w})$ of the alternative x_i corresponding to the decision maker d_k:

$$\begin{aligned}\tilde{z}_1^{(1)}(\tilde{w}) &= [0.08,0.10]\otimes[s_{-1},s_0]\oplus[0.05,0.09]\otimes[s_0,s_1]\\ &\oplus[0.10,0.12]\otimes[s_3,s_4]\oplus[0.08,0.11]\otimes[s_1,s_2]\\ &\oplus[0.10,0.13]\otimes[s_0,s_2]\oplus[0.12,0.14]\otimes[s_3,s_4]\\ &\oplus[0.14,0.16]\otimes[s_2,s_3]\oplus[0.09,0.11]\otimes[s_3,s_4]\\ &\oplus[0.11,0.15]\otimes[s_1,s_3]=[s_{1.32},s_{2.98}]\end{aligned}$$

Table 12.2 Uncertain linguistic decision matrix $\tilde{R}_1$

	u_1	u_2	u_3	u_4	u_5
x_1	$[s_{-1}, s_0]$	$[s_0, s_1]$	$[s_3, s_4]$	$[s_1, s_2]$	$[s_0, s_2]$
x_2	$[s_2, s_3]$	$[s_2, s_3]$	$[s_4, s_5]$	$[s_2, s_3]$	$[s_1, s_2]$
x_3	$[s_2, s_4]$	$[s_1, s_2]$	$[s_0, s_1]$	$[s_2, s_4]$	$[s_1, s_3]$
x_4	$[s_0, s_1]$	$[s_0, s_1]$	$[s_3, s_5]$	$[s_3, s_4]$	$[s_1, s_2]$
x_5	$[s_0, s_3]$	$[s_2, s_3]$	$[s_0, s_1]$	$[s_3, s_4]$	$[s_0, s_1]$
	u_6	u_7	u_8	u_9	
x_1	$[s_3, s_4]$	$[s_2, s_3]$	$[s_3, s_4]$	$[s_1, s_3]$	
x_2	$[s_{-1}, s_1]$	$[s_3, s_5]$	$[s_3, s_4]$	$[s_1, s_2]$	
x_3	$[s_2, s_3]$	$[s_0, s_3]$	$[s_3, s_5]$	$[s_0, s_1]$	
x_4	$[s_2, s_4]$	$[s_1, s_2]$	$[s_3, s_4]$	$[s_2, s_3]$	
x_5	$[s_2, s_3]$	$[s_2, s_3]$	$[s_3, s_4]$	$[s_1, s_3]$	

Table 12.3 Uncertain linguistic decision matrix $\tilde{R}_2$

	u_1	u_2	u_3	u_4	u_5
x_1	$[s_3, s_4]$	$[s_1, s_3]$	$[s_1, s_4]$	$[s_3, s_4]$	$[s_1, s_3]$
x_2	$[s_{-1}, s_1]$	$[s_0, s_1]$	$[s_1, s_2]$	$[s_0, s_2]$	$[s_1, s_2]$
x_3	$[s_3, s_4]$	$[s_1, s_3]$	$[s_2, s_4]$	$[s_2, s_3]$	$[s_{-1}, s_0]$
x_4	$[s_0, s_3]$	$[s_2, s_3]$	$[s_0, s_2]$	$[s_1, s_3]$	$[s_0, s_2]$
x_5	$[s_1, s_3]$	$[s_3, s_4]$	$[s_2, s_3]$	$[s_3, s_5]$	$[s_{-1}, s_0]$
	u_6	u_7	u_8	u_9	
x_1	$[s_0, s_2]$	$[s_2, s_3]$	$[s_0, s_1]$	$[s_2, s_3]$	
x_2	$[s_0, s_1]$	$[s_3, s_4]$	$[s_3, s_4]$	$[s_2, s_4]$	
x_3	$[s_2, s_3]$	$[s_2, s_3]$	$[s_0, s_1]$	$[s_2, s_3]$	
x_4	$[s_2, s_4]$	$[s_0, s_3]$	$[s_2, s_3]$	$[s_{-1}, s_0]$	
x_5	$[s_0, s_2]$	$[s_1, s_2]$	$[s_2, s_3]$	$[s_3, s_4]$	

Table 12.4 Uncertain linguistic decision matrix $\tilde{R}_3$

	u_1	u_2	u_3	u_4	u_5
x_1	$[s_0, s_1]$	$[s_1, s_2]$	$[s_3, s_4]$	$[s_3, s_5]$	$[s_0, s_1]$
x_2	$[s_3, s_4]$	$[s_3, s_4]$	$[s_2, s_4]$	$[s_3, s_4]$	$[s_2, s_3]$
x_3	$[s_2, s_3]$	$[s_3, s_4]$	$[s_1, s_2]$	$[s_2, s_3]$	$[s_2, s_3]$
x_4	$[s_3, s_4]$	$[s_3, s_5]$	$[s_2, s_4]$	$[s_0, s_1]$	$[s_2, s_3]$
x_5	$[s_0, s_1]$	$[s_2, s_4]$	$[s_{-1}, s_1]$	$[s_3, s_4]$	$[s_1, s_4]$
	u_6	u_7	u_8	u_9	
x_1	$[s_1, s_3]$	$[s_2, s_3]$	$[s_3, s_4]$	$[s_1, s_3]$	
x_2	$[s_2, s_3]$	$[s_0, s_2]$	$[s_3, s_4]$	$[s_2, s_4]$	
x_3	$[s_3, s_4]$	$[s_{-1}, s_1]$	$[s_3, s_4]$	$[s_3, s_4]$	
x_4	$[s_1, s_3]$	$[s_3, s_4]$	$[s_2, s_3]$	$[s_2, s_3]$	
x_5	$[s_1, s_2]$	$[s_0, s_2]$	$[s_1, s_3]$	$[s_3, s_5]$	

Similarly, we have

$$\tilde{z}_2^{(1)}(\tilde{w}) = [s_{1.60}, s_{3.44}],\ \tilde{z}_3^{(1)}(\tilde{w}) = [s_{0.98}, s_{3.13}],\ \tilde{z}_4^{(1)}(\tilde{w}) = [s_{1.51}, s_{3.26}]$$

$$\tilde{z}_5^{(1)}(\tilde{w}) = [s_{1.24}, s_{3.05}],\ \tilde{z}_1^{(2)}(\tilde{w}) = [s_{1.23}, s_{3.30}],\ \tilde{z}_2^{(2)}(\tilde{w}) = [s_{1.03}, s_{2.73}]$$

$$\tilde{z}_3^{(2)}(\tilde{w}) = [s_{1.29}, s_{2.94}],\ \tilde{z}_4^{(2)}(\tilde{w}) = [s_{0.49}, s_{2.77}],\ \tilde{z}_5^{(2)}(\tilde{w}) = [s_{1.22}, s_{3.10}]$$

$$\tilde{z}_1^{(3)}(\tilde{w}) = [s_{1.37}, s_{3.23}],\ \tilde{z}_2^{(3)}(\tilde{w}) = [s_{1.76}, s_{3.85}],\ \tilde{z}_3^{(3)}(\tilde{w}) = [s_{1.59}, s_{3.38}]$$

$$\tilde{z}_4^{(3)}(\tilde{w})=[s_{1.73},s_{3.67}],\ \tilde{z}_5^{(3)}(\tilde{w})=[s_{0.88},s_{3.22}]$$

Step 2 Aggregate the overall attribute values $\tilde{z}_i^{(k)}(\tilde{w})$ (k = 1,2,3) of the alternative x_i corresponding to the decision makers $d_k (k=1,2,3)$ by using the ULHA operator (let its weighting vector be $\omega=(0.3,0.4,0.3)$): i.e., we first use λ, t and $\tilde{z}_i^{(k)}(\tilde{w})$ (k =1,2,3) to calculate $t\lambda_k\tilde{z}_i^{(k)}(\tilde{w})$:

$$3\lambda_1\tilde{z}_1^{(1)}(\tilde{w})=[s_{1.346},s_{3.040}],\ 3\lambda_1\tilde{z}_2^{(1)}(\tilde{w})=[s_{1.632},s_{3.509}]$$

$$3\lambda_1\tilde{z}_3^{(1)}(\tilde{w})=[s_1,s_{3.193}],\ 3\lambda_1\tilde{z}_4^{(1)}(\tilde{w})=[s_{1.540},s_{3.325}]$$

$$3\lambda_1\tilde{z}_5^{(1)}(\tilde{w})=[s_{1.265},s_{3.111}],\ 3\lambda_2\tilde{z}_1^{(2)}(\tilde{w})=[s_{1.218},s_{3.267}]$$

$$3\lambda_2\tilde{z}_2^{(2)}(\tilde{w})=[s_{1.020},s_{2.703}],\ 3\lambda_2\tilde{z}_3^{(2)}(\tilde{w})=[s_{1.277},s_{2.911}]$$

$$3\lambda_2\tilde{z}_4^{(2)}(\tilde{w})=[s_{0.485},s_{2.742}],\ 3\lambda_2\tilde{z}_5^{(2)}(\tilde{w})=[s_{1.208},s_{3.069}]$$

$$3\lambda_3\tilde{z}_1^{(3)}(\tilde{w})=[s_{1.356},s_{3.198}],\ 3\lambda_3\tilde{z}_2^{(3)}(\tilde{w})=[s_{1.742},s_{3.812}]$$

$$3\lambda_3\tilde{z}_3^{(3)}(\tilde{w})=[s_{1.574},s_{3.346}],\ 3\lambda_3\tilde{z}_4^{(3)}(\tilde{w})=[s_{1.713},s_{3.633}]$$

$$3\lambda_3\tilde{z}_5^{(3)}(\tilde{w})=[s_{0.871},s_{3.188}]$$

and then get the group's overall attribute value $\tilde{z}_i\,(\lambda,\omega)$ of the alternative x_i:

$$\begin{aligned}\tilde{z}_1(\lambda,\omega)&=0.3\times[s_{1.356},s_{3.198}]\oplus0.4\times[s_{1.218},s_{3.267}]\oplus0.3\times[s_{1.346},s_{3.040}]\\&=[s_{1.298},s_{3.178}]\end{aligned}$$

$$\begin{aligned}\tilde{z}_2(\lambda,\omega)&=0.3\times[s_{1.742},s_{3.812}]\oplus0.4\times[s_{1.632},s_{3.509}]\oplus0.3\times[s_{1.020},s_{2.703}]\\&=[s_{1.481},s_{3.358}]\end{aligned}$$

$$\begin{aligned}\tilde{z}_3(\lambda,\omega)&=0.3\times[s_{1.574},s_{3.346}]\oplus0.4\times[s_{1.277},s_{2.911}]\oplus0.3\times[s_1,s_{3.193}]\\&=[s_{1.283},s_{3.126}]\end{aligned}$$

$$\begin{aligned}\tilde{z}_4(\lambda,\omega)&=0.3\times[s_{1.713},s_{3.633}]\oplus0.4\times[s_{1.540},s_{3.325}]\oplus0.3\times[s_{0.485},s_{2.742}]\\&=[s_{1.275},s_{3.243}]\end{aligned}$$

$$\tilde{z}_5(\lambda,\omega) = 0.3\times[s_{1.265}, s_{3.111}] \oplus 0.4\times[s_{1.208}, s_{3.069}] \oplus 0.3\times[s_{0.871}, s_{3.188}]$$
$$= [s_{1.124}, s_{3.117}]$$

Step 3 Calculate the possibility degrees $p_{ij} = p(\tilde{z}_i(\lambda,\omega) \geq \tilde{z}_j(\lambda,\omega))$ $(i, j = 1,2,3,4,5)$ using Eq. (10.1) by comparing each pair of $\tilde{z}_i(\lambda,\omega)(i = 1,2,3,4,5)$, and construct the possibility degree matrix:

$$P = \begin{pmatrix} 0.5 & 0.4517 & 0.5090 & 0.4945 & 0.5198 \\ 0.5483 & 0.5 & 0.5578 & 0.5417 & 0.5773 \\ 0.4910 & 0.4422 & 0.5 & 0.4857 & 0.5219 \\ 0.5055 & 0.4583 & 0.5143 & 0.5 & 0.5350 \\ 0.4697 & 0.4227 & 0.4781 & 0.4650 & 0.5 \end{pmatrix}$$

Step 4 Use Eq. (4.6) to derive the priority vector of P:

$$v = (0.1993, 0.2113, 0.1970, 0.2006, 0.1918)$$

and then rank the alternatives $x_i(i = 1,2,3,4,5)$:

$$x_2 \succ x_4 \succ x_1 \succ x_3 \succ x_5$$

Thus, the best alternative is x_2.

References

1. Aczél J, Alsina C (1987) Synthesizing judgements: a functional equation approach. Math Model 9:311–320
2. Barbean E (1986) Perron's result and a decision on admissions tests. Math Mag 59:12–22
3. Beliakov G, Pradera A, Calvo T (2007) Aggregation functions: a guide for practitioners. Springer, Heidelberg
4. Blankmeyer E (1987) Approaches to consistency adjustment. J Optim Theory Appl 54:479–488
5. Bonferroni C (1950) Sulle medie multiple di potenze. Boll Mat Ital 5:267–270
6. Bullen PS (2003) Handbook of mean and their inequalties. Kluwer, Dordrecht
7. Chen SH (1985) Ranking fuzzy numbers with maximizing set and minimizing set. Fuzzy Set Syst 17:113–129
8. Chen DL, Li ZC (2002) The appraisement index insuring of information system investment and method for grey comprehensive appraisement. Syst Eng Theory Pract 22(2):100–103
9. Chen CY, Xu LG (2001) Partner selection model in supply chain management. Chin J Manage Sci 9(Suppl):57–62
10. Chen Y, Luo XM, Gu QP (2003) The application of mathematical programming to the study of space equipment system construction project and planning auxiliary decision system. Proceedings of the fifth Youth scholars Conference on operations research and management. Global-Link Informatics Press, Hongkong, pp 409–415
11. Chiclana F, Herrera F, Herrera-Viedma E (1998) Integrating three representation models in fuzzy multipurpose decision making based on fuzzy preference relations. Fuzzy Set Syst 97:33–48
12. Chiclana F, Herrera F, Herrera-Viedma E (2001) Integrating multiplicative preference relations in a multipurpose decision making model based on fuzzy preference relations. Fuzzy Set Syst 122:277–291
13. Chiclana F, Herrera F, Herrera-Viedma E, Martinez L (2003) A note on the reciprocity in the aggregation of fuzzy preference relations using OWA operators. Fuzzy Set Syst 137:71–83
14. Choquet G (1953) Theory of capacities. Ann Inst Fourier 5:131–296
15. Cogger KO, Yu PL (1985) Eigenweight vector and least-distance approximating for revealized preference in pairwise weight ratios. J Optim Theory Appl 46:483–491
16. Cordón O, Herrera F, Zwir I (2002) Linguistic modeling by hierarchical systems of linguistic rules. IEEE Trans Fuzzy Syst 10:2–20
17. Crawford G, Williams C (1985) A note on the analysis of subjective judgement matrices. J Math Psychol 29:387–405
18. Da QL, Liu XW (1999) Interval number linear programming and its satisfactory solution. Syst Eng Theory Pract 19(4):3–7
19. Da QL, Xu ZS (2002) Singule-objective optimization model in uncertain multi-attribute decision making. J Syst Eng 17(1):50–55

Z.S. Xu, *Uncertain Multi-Attribute Decision Making*,
DOI 10.1007/978-3-662-45640-8

20. Dai YQ, Xu ZS, Li Y, Da QL (2008) New assessment labels based on linguistic information and applications. Chin Manage Sci 16(2):145–149
21. Dantzig GB (1963) Linear programming and extensions. Princeton University Press, Princeton
22. Du D (1996) Mathematical transformation method for consistency of judgement matrix in AHP. Decision science and its application. Ocean press, Beijing
23. Du XM, Yu YL, Hu H (1999) Case-based reasoning for multi-attribute evaluation. Syst Eng Electron 21(9):45–48
24. Dubois D, Prade H (1986) Weighted minimum and maximum operations in fuzzy set theory. Inf Sci 39:205–210
25. Duckstein L, Zionts S (1992) Multiple criteria decision making. Springer, New York
26. Facchinetti G, Ricci RG, Muzzioli S (1998) Note on ranking fuzzy triangular numbers. Int J Intell Syst 13:613–622
27. Fan ZP, Hu GF (2000) A goal programming method for interval multi-attribute decision making. J Ind Eng Eng Manage 14:50–52
28. Fan ZP, Zhang Q (1999) The revision for the uncertain multiple attribute decision making models. Syst Eng Theory Pract 19(12):42–47
29. Fan ZP, Ma J, Zhang Q (2002) An approach to multiple attribute decision making based on fuzzy preference information on alternatives. Fuzzy Set Syst 131:101–106
30. Fernandez E, Leyva JC (2004) A method based on multi-objective optimization for deriving a ranking from a fuzzy preference relation. Eur J Oper Res 154:110–124
31. Gao FJ (2000) Multiple attribute decision making on plans with alternative preference under incomplete information. Syst Eng Theory Pract 22(4):94–97
32. Genc S, Boran FE, Akay D, Xu Z S (2010) Interval multiplicative transitivity for consistency, missing values and priority weights of interval fuzzy preference relations. Inf Sci 180:4877–4891
33. Genst C, Lapointe F (1993) On a proposal of Jensen for the analysis of ordinal pairwise preferences using Saaty's eigenvector scaling method. J Math Psychol 37:575–610
34. Goh CH, Tung YCA, Cheng CH (1996) A revised weighted sum decision model for robot selection. Comput Ind Eng 30:193–199
35. Golden BL, Wasil EA, Harker PT (1989) The analytic hierarchy process: applications and studied. Springer, New York
36. Guo DQ, Wang ZJ (2000) The mathematical model of the comprehensive evaluation on MIS. Oper Res Manage Sci 9(3):74–80
37. Harker PT, Vargas LG (1987) The theory of ratio scale estimation: Saaty's analytic hierarchy process. Manage Sci 33:1383–1403
38. Harsanyi JC (1955) Cardinal welfare, individualistic ethics, and interpersonal comparisons of utility. J Polit Econ 63:309–321
39. Hartley R (1985) Linear and nonlinear programming: an introduction to linear methods in mathematical programming. ELLIS Horwood Limited, England
40. Herrera F, Martínez L (2001) A model based on linguistic 2-tuples for dealing with multigranular hierarchical linguistic contexts in multi-expert decision making. IEEE Trans Syst Man Cybern 31:227–233
41. Herrera F, Herrera-Viedma E, Verdegay JL (1995) A sequential selection process in group decision making with linguistic assessment. Inf Sci 85:223–239
42. Herrera F, Herrera-Viedma E, Martínez L (2000) A fusion approach for managing multigranularity linguistic term sets in decision making. Fuzzy Set Syst 114:43–58
43. Herrera F, Herrera-Viedma E, Chiclana F (2001) Multi-person decision making based on multiplicative preference relations. Eur J Oper Res 129:372–285
44. Herrera-Viedma E, Herrera F, Chiclana F, Luque M (2004) Some issues on consistency of fuzzy preference relations. Eur J Oper Res 154:98–109
45. Herrera-Viedma E, Martínez L, Mata F, Chiclana F (2005) A consensus support systems model for group decision making problems with multigranular linguistic preference relations. IEEE Trans Fuzzy Syst 13:644–658

46. Hu QS, Zheng CY, Wang HQ (1996) A practical optimum decision and application of fuzzy several objective system. Syst Eng Theory Pract 16(3):1–5
47. Huang LJ (2001) The mathematical model of the comprehensive evaluation on enterprise knowledge management. Oper Res Manage Sci 10(4):143–150
48. Hwang CL, Yoon K (1981) Multiple attribute decision making and applications. Springer, New York
49. Jensen RE (1984) An alternative scaling method for priorities in hierarchy structures. J Math Psychol 28:317–332
50. Kacprzyk J (1986) Group decision making with a fuzzy linguistic majority. Fuzzy Set Syst 18:105–118
51. Kim SH, Ahn BS (1997) Group decision making procedure considering preference strength under incomplete information. Comput Oper Res 24:1101–1112
52. Kim SH, Ahn BS (1999) Interactive group decision making procedure under incomplete information. Eur J Oper Res 116:498–507
53. Kim SH, Choi SH, Kim JK (1999) An interactive procedure for multiple attribute group decision making with incomplete information: Rang-based approach. Eur J Oper Res 118:139–152
54. Li ZM, Chen DY (1991) Analysis of training effectiveness for military trainers. Syst Eng Theory Pract 11(4):75–79
55. Li ZG, Zhong Z (2003a) Fuzzy optimal selection model and application of tank unit firepower systems deployment schemes. Proceedings of the fifth Youth scholars Conference on operations research and management. Global-Link Informatics Press, Hongkong, pp 317–321
56. Li ZG, Zhong Z (2003b) Grey cluster analysis on selecting key defensive position. Proceedings of the fifth Youth scholars Conference on operations research and management. Global-Link Informatics Press, Hongkong, pp 401–405
57. Li SC, Chen JD, Zhao HG (2001) Studying on the method of appraising qualitative decision indication system. Syst Eng Theory Pract 21(9):22–32
58. Lipovetsky S, Michael CW (2002) Robust estimation of priorities in the AHP. Eur J Oper Res 137:110–122
59. Liu JX, Huang DC (2000b) The optimal linear assignment method for multiple attribute decision making. Syst Eng Electron 22(7):25–27
60. Liu JX, Liu YW (1999) A multiple attribute decision making with preference information. Syst Eng Electron 21(1):4–7
61. Mu FL, Wu C, Wu DW (2003) Study on the synthetic method of variable weight of effectiveness evaluation of maintenance support system. Syst Eng Electron 25(6):693–696
62. Nurmi H (1981) Approaches to collective decision making with fuzzy preference relations. Fuzzy Set Syst 6:249–259
63. Orlovsky SA (1978) Decision making with a fuzzy preference relation. Fuzzy Set Syst 1:155–167
64. Park KS, Kim SH (1997) Tools for interactive multi-attribute decision making with incompletely indentified information. Eur J Oper Res 98:11–123
65. Park KS, Kim SH, Yoon YC (1996) Establishing strict dominance between alternatives with special type of incomplete information. Eur J Oper Res 96:398–406
66. Qian G, Xu ZS (2003) Tree optimization models based on ideal points for uncertain multi-attribute decision making. Syst Eng Electron 25(5):517–519
67. Roubens M (1989) Some properties of choice functions based on valued binary relations. Eur J Oper Res 40:309–321
68. Roubens M (1996) Choice procedures in fuzzy multicriteria decision analysis based on pairwise comparisons. Fuzzy Set Syst 84:135–142
69. Saaty TL (1980) The analytic hierarchy process. McGraw-Hill, New York
70. Saaty TL (1986) Axiomatic foundations of the analytic hierarchy process. Manage Sci 20:355–360
71. Saaty TL (1990) Multi-criteria decision making: the analytic hierarchy process: planning, priority setting, resource allocation, the analytic hierarchy process series, Vol. I. RMS Publications, Pittsburgh

72. Saaty TL (1994) Fundamentals of decision making and priority theory with the analytic hierarchy process, the analytic hierarchy process series, Vol. VI. RMS Publications, Pittsburgh
73. Saaty TL (1995) Decision making for leaders, the analytic hierarchy process for decisions in a complex world. RWS Publications, Pittsburgh
74. Saaty TL (1996) The hierarchy network process. RWS Publications, Pittsburgh
75. Saaty TL (2001) Decision making with dependence and feedback: the analytic network process. RWS Publications, Pittsburgh
76. Saaty TL (2003) Decision making with the AHP: why is the principal eigenvector necessary. Eur J Oper Res 145:85–91
77. Saaty TL, Alexander JM (1981) Thinking with models. Praeger, New York
78. Saaty TL, Alexander JM (1989) Conflict resolution: the analytic hierarchy approach. Praeger, New York
79. Saaty TL, Hu G (1998) Ranking by the eigenvector versus other methods in the analytic hierarchy process. Appl Math Lett 11:121–125
80. Saaty TL, Kearns KP (1985) Analytic planning—the organization of systems. Pergamon Press, Oxford
81. Saaty TL, Vargas LG (1982) The logic of priorities: applications in business, energy, health, and transportation. Kluwer-Nijhoff, Boston
82. Saaty TL, Vargas LG (1984) Comparison of eigenvalue, logarithmic least squares and least squares methods in estimating ratios. Math Model 5:309–324
83. Saaty TL, Vargas LG (1994) Decision making in economic, political, social and technological environments with the analytic hierarchy process. RMS Publications, Pittsburgh
84. Salo AA (1995) Interactive decision aiding for group decision support. Eur J Oper Res 84:134–149
85. Salo AA, Hämäläinen RP (2001) Preference ratios in multi-attribute evaluation (PRIME)-Elicitation and decision procedures under incomplete information. IEEE Trans Syst Man Cybern A 31:533–545
86. Sheng CF, Xu WX, Xu BG (2003) Study on the evaluation of competitiveness of provincial investment environment in China. Chin J Manage Sci 11(3):76–81
87. Song FM, Chen TT (1999) Study on evaluation index system of high-tech investment project. China Soft Sci 1:90–93
88. Tanino T (1984) Fuzzy preference orderings in group decision making. Fuzzy Set Syst 12:117–131
89. Teng CX, Bi KX, Su WL, Yi DL (2000) Application of attribute synthetic assessment system to finance evaluation of colleges and universities. Syst Eng Theory Pract 20(4):115–119
90. Van Laarhoven PJM Pedrycz W (1983) A fuzzy extension of Saaty's priority theory. Fuzzy Set Syst 11:229–240
91. Wang YM (1995) An overview of priority methods for judgement matrices. Decis Support Syst 5(3):101–114
92. Wang YM (1998) Using the method of maximizing deviations to make decision for multi-indicies. Syst Eng Electron 20(7):24–26
93. Wang LF, Xu SB (1989) An introduction to analytic hierarchy process. China Renmin University Press, Beijing
94. Xia MM, Xu ZS (2011) Some issues on multiplicative consistency of interval fuzzy preference relations. Int J Inf Technol Decis Mak 10:1043–1065
95. Xiong R, Cao KS (1992) Hierarchical analysis of multiple criteria decision making. Syst Eng Theory Pract 12(6):58–62
96. Xu JP (1992) Double-base-points-based optimal selection method for multiple attribute comment. Syst Eng 10(4):39–43
97. Xu ZS (1998) A new scale method in analytic hierarchy process. Syst Eng Theory Pract 18(10):74–77
98. Xu ZS (1999) Study on the relation between two classes of scales in AHP. Syst Eng Theory Pract 19(7):97–101
99. Xu ZS (2000a) A new method for improving the consistency of judgement matrix. Syst Eng Theory Pract 20(4):86–89

100. Xu ZS (2000b) A simulation based evaluat ion of several scales in the analytic hierarchy Process. Syst Eng Theory Pract 20(7):58–62
101. Xu ZS (2000c) Generalized chi square method for the estimation of weights. J Optim Theory Appl 107:183–192
102. Xu ZS (2000d) Study on the priority method of fuzzy comprehensive evaluation. Systems Engineering Systems Science and Complexity Research. Research Information Ltd, United Kingdom, pp 507–511
103. Xu ZS (2001a) Algorithm for priority of fuzzy complementary judgement matrix. J Syst Eng 16(4):311–314
104. Xu ZS (2001b) Maximum deviation method based on deviation degree and possibility degree for uncertain multi-attribute decision making. Control Decis 16(suppl):818–821
105. Xu ZS (2001c) The least variance priority method (LVM) for fuzzy complementary judgement matrix. Syst Eng Theory Pract 21(10):93–96
106. Xu ZS (2002a) Interactive method based on alternative achievement scale and alternative comprehensive scale for multi-attribute decision making problems. Control Decis 17(4):435–438
107. Xu ZS (2002b) New method for uncertain multi-attribute decision making problems. J Syst Eng 17(2):176–181
108. Xu ZS (2002c) On method for multi-objective decision making with partial weight information. Syst Eng Theory Practice 22(1):43–47
109. Xu ZS (2002d) Study on methods for multiple attribute decision making under some situations. Southeast University PhD Dissertation.
110. Xu ZS (2002e) Two approaches to improving the consistency of complementary judgement matrix. Appl Math J Chin Univ Ser B 17:227–235
111. Xu ZS (2002f) Two methods for priorities of complementary judgement matrices—weighted least square method and eigenvector method. Syst Eng Theory Pract 22(1):43–47
112. Xu ZS (2003a) A method for multiple attribute decision making without weight information but with preference information on alternatives. Syst Eng Theory Pract 23(12):100–103
113. Xu ZS (2003b) A practical approach to group decision making with linguistic information. Technical Report
114. Xu ZS (2004a) A method based on linguistic aggregation operators for group decision making with linguistic preference relations. Inf Sci 166:19–30
115. Xu ZS (2004b) An ideal point based approach to multi-criteria decision making with uncertain linguistic information. Proceedings of the 3th International Conference on Machine Learning and Cybernetics, August 26–29, Shanghai, China, pp 2078–2082
116. Xu ZS (2004c) EOWA and EOWG operators for aggregation linguistic labels based on linguistic preference relations. Int J Uncertain Fuzziness Knowl Based Syst 12:791–810
117. Xu ZS (2004d) Goal programming models for obtaining the priority vector of incomplete fuzzy preference relation. Int J Approx Reason 36:261–270
118. Xu ZS (2004e) Incomplete complementary judgement matrix. Syst Eng Theory Pract 24(6):91–97
119. Xu ZS (2004f) Method based on fuzzy linguistic assessments and GIOWA operator in multi- attribute group decision making. J Syst Sci Math Sci 24(2):218–224
120. Xu ZS (2004g) Method for multi-attribute decision making with preference information on alternatives under partial weight information. Control Decis 19(1):85–88
121. Xu ZS (2004h) On compatibility of interval fuzzy preference relations. Fuzzy Optim Decis Mak 3(3):225–233
122. Xu ZS (2004i) Some new operators for aggregating uncertain linguistic information. Technical Report.
123. Xu ZS (2004j) Uncertain linguistic aggregation operators based approach to multiple attribute group decision making under uncertain linguistic environment. Inf Sci 168:171–184
124. Xu ZS (2005a) A procedure based on synthetic projection model for multiple attribute decision making in uncertain setting. Lecture Series Comput Comput Sci 2:141–145

125. Xu ZS (2005b) Deviation measures of linguistic preference relations in group decision making. Omega 33:249–254
126. Xu ZS (2005c) An overview of methods for determining OWA weights. Int J Intell Syst 20(8):843–865
127. Xu ZS (2005d) The hybrid linguistic weighted averaging operator. Inf Int J 8:453–456
128. Xu ZS (2006a) A direct approach to group decision making with uncertain additive linguistic preference relations. Fuzzy Optim Decis Mak 5(1):23–35
129. Xu ZS (2006b) Multiple attribute group decision making with multiplicative preference information. Proceedings of 2006 International Conference on Management Science & Engineering, August 8–10, South-Central University for Nationalities, China, pp 1383–1388
130. Xu ZS (2007a) A survey of preference relations. Int J Gen Syst 36:179–203
131. Xu ZS (2007b) Multiple attribute group decision making with different formats of preference information on attributes. IEEE Trans Syst Man Cybern B 37:1500–1511
132. Xu ZS (2009a) An interactive approach to multiple attribute group decision making with multigranular uncertain linguistic information. Group Decis Negot 18:119–145
133. Xu ZS (2009b) Multi-period multi-attribute group decision-making under linguistic assessments. Int J Gen Syst 38:823–850
134. Xu ZS (2010) Uncertain Bonferroni mean operators. Int J Comput Intell Syst 3:761–769
135. Xu ZS (2011) Consistency of interval fuzzy preference relations in group decision making. Appl Soft Comput 11:3898–3909
136. Xu ZS (2012a) A consensus reaching process under incomplete multiplicative preference relations. Int J Gen Syst 41:333–351
137. Xu ZS (2012b) An error-analysis-based method for the priority of an intuitionistic fuzzy preference relation in decision making. Knowl Based Syst 33:173–179
138. Xu ZS, Cai XQ (2012a) Deriving weights from interval multiplicative preference relations. Group Decis Negot 2012, in press
139. Xu ZS, Cai XQ (2012b) Minimizing group discordance optimization model for deriving expert weights. Group Decis and Negot 2012, in press
140. Xu ZS, Cai XQ (2012c) Uncertain power average operators for aggregating interval fuzzy preference relations. Group Decis Negot 21:381–397
141. Xu ZS, Chen J (2007) An interactive method for fuzzy multiple attribute group decision making. Inf Sci 177:248–263
142. Xu ZS, Chen J (2008) Some models for deriving the priority weights from interval fuzzy preference relations. Eur J Oper Res 184:266–280
143. Xu ZS, Da QL (2002a) Linear objective programming method for priorities of hybrid judgement matrices. J Manage Sci China 5(6):24–28
144. Xu ZS, Da QL (2002b) The ordered weighted geometric averaging operators. Int J Intell Syst 17:709–716
145. Xu ZS, Da QL (2002c) The uncertain OWA operator. Int J Intell Syst 17:569–575
146. Xu ZS, Da QL (2003a) An approach to improving consistency of fuzzy preference matrix. Fuzzy Optim Decis Mak 2:3–12
147. Xu ZS, Da QL (2003b) An overview of operators for aggregating information. Int J Intell Syst 18:953–969
148. Xu ZS, Da QL (2003c) New method for interval multi-attribute decision making. J Southeast Univ (Natural Science Edition) 33(4):498–501
149. Xu ZS, Da QL (2003d) Possibility degree method for ranking interval numbers and its application. J Syst Eng 18(1):67–70
150. Xu ZS, Da QL (2005) A least deviation method to obtain a priority vector of a fuzzy preference relation. Eur J Oper Res 164:206–216
151. Xu ZS, Gu HF (2002) An approach to uncertain multi-attribute decision making with preference information on alternatives. Proceedings of the 9th Bellman Continuum International Workingshop on Uncertain Systems and Soft Computing, Beijing, China, pp 89–95
152. Xu ZS, Sun ZD (2001) A method based on satisfactory degree of alternative for uncertainly multi-attribution decision making. Syst Eng 19(3):76–79

153. Xu ZS, Sun ZD (2002) Priority method for a kind of multi-attribute decision-making problems. J Manage Sci China 5(3):35–39
154. Xu ZS, Wei CP (1999) A consistency improving method in the analytic hierarchy process. Eur J Oper Res 116:443–449
155. Xu ZS, Wei CP (2000) A new method for priorities to the analytic hierarchy process. OR Trans 4(4):47–54
156. Xu RN, Zhai XY (1992) Extensions of the analytic hierarchy process in fuzzy environment. Fuzzy Set Syst 52:251–257
157. Yager RR (1988) On ordered weighted averaging aggregation operators in multicriteria decision making. IEEE Trans Syst Man Cybern 18:183–190
158. Yager RR (1993) Families of OWA operators. Fuzzy Set Syst 59:125–148
159. Yager RR (1999) Induced ordered weighted averaging operators. IEEE Trans Syst Man Cybern 29:141–150
160. Yager RR (2007) Centered OWA operators. Soft Comput 11:631–639
161. Yager RR (2009) On generalized Bonferroni mean operators for multi-criteria aggregation. Int J Approx Reason 50:1279–1286
162. Yager RR, Filev DP (1999) Induced ordered weighted averaging operators. IEEE Trans Syst Man Cybern B 29:141–150
163. Yoon K (1989) The propagation of errors in multiple attribute decision analysis: a practical approach. J Oper Res Soc 40:681–686
164. Yu XH, Xu ZS, Zhang XM (2010) Uniformization of multigranular linguistic labels and their application to group decision making. J Syst Sci Syst Eng 19(3):257–276
165. Yu XH, Xu ZS, Liu SS, Chen Q (2012) Multi-criteria decision making with 2-dimension linguistic aggregation techniques. Int J Intell Syst 27:539–562
166. Zahedi F (1986) The analytic hierarchy process: a survey of the method and its applications. Interfaces 16:96–108
167. Zeleny M (1982) Multiple criteria decision making. McGraw-Hill, New York
168. Zhang FL, Wu JH, Jin ZZ (2000) Evaluation of anti-ship missile weapon system's overall performance. Systems Engineering, Systems Science and Complexity Research, Research Information Ltd, Hemel Hempstead Hp27TD, United Kingdom, pp 573–578.
169. Zhu WD, Zhou GZ, Yang SL (2009) Group decision making with 2-dimension linguistic assessment information. Syst Eng Theory Pract 27:113–118

MIX
Papier aus verantwortungsvollen Quellen
Paper from responsible sources
FSC® C105338

If you have any concerns about our products,
you can contact us on
ProductSafety@springernature.com

In case Publisher is established outside the EU,
the EU authorized representative is:
Springer Nature Customer Service Center GmbH
Europaplatz 3, 69115 Heidelberg, Germany

Printed by Libri Plureos GmbH
in Hamburg, Germany